CONFLICT IN AFRICA
Concepts and Realities

Conflict in Africa

Concepts and Realities

ADDA B. BOZEMAN

Princeton University Press

1976

To Arne Barkhuus

OUTLINE MAP

40° 30° 20° 10° 0° 10°

Azores

Madeira Is.

MOROCCO

R.

A.

TUNISIA

ME

30°

Canary Is.

ALGERIA

LIBYAN

E.A.

SPANISH SAHARA

MAURITANIA

20°

MALI

NIGER

Cape Verde Is.

N.

SENEGAL

D.

B.

GAMBIA

B.

N.

PORT. GUINEA

B.

UPPER VOLTA

O.

NIGERIA

GUINEA

C.

10°

F.

IVORY

GHANA

TOGO

DAHOMEY

L.

SIERRA LEONE

COAST

L.

P.N.

CAMEROON

M.

S.I.

Y.

LIBERIA

A.

A.

EQUATORIAL GUINEA

Príncipe

São Tomé

L.

GABON

0°

ATLANTIC   OCEAN

Annobón

CABINDA

L.

Ascension

10°

St. Helena

20°

AFRICA

United Nations Map no. 1656, January 1972

SINUSOIDAL EQUAL-AREA PROJECTION

30°

0   200   400   600   800 1000

MILES

0   200 400 600 800 1000

KILOMETRES

40° 30° 20° Tristan da Cunha 10° 0° 10°

MAP NO. 1656 REV.1   UNITED NATIONS
JANUARY 1972

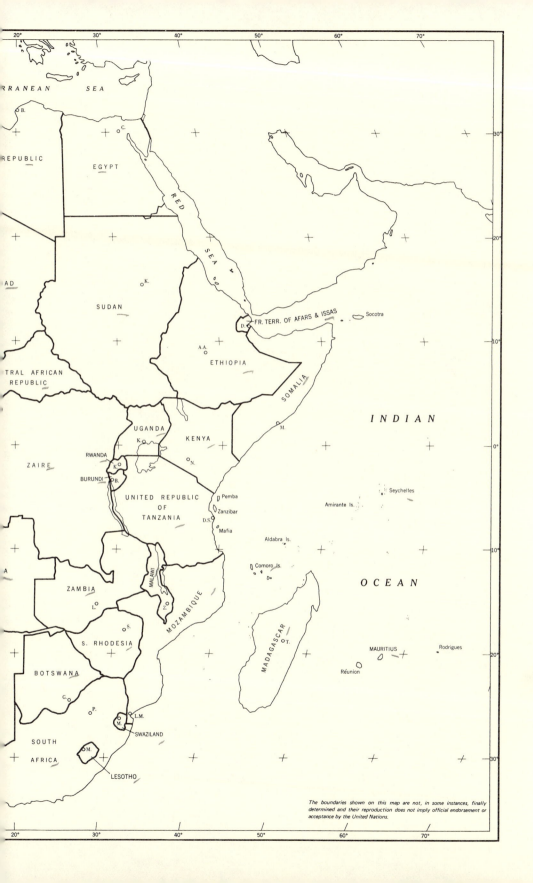

The boundaries shown on this map are not, in some instances, finally determined and their reproduction does not imply official endorsement or acceptance by the United Nations.

PREFACE

As its title indicates, this book pursues certain specific inquiries, among them the following: What are the meanings and functions commonly ascribed to conflict in Africa south of the Sahara, and how are disputes, enmities, and tensions managed in that culture world? Are African patterns of conflict and accord, and of war and peace, sufficiently similar to those recorded in the West to allow for secure accommodation to the theories of conflict fashioned in Europe and North America? Or do comparative studies indicate instead that the African experience of dissension, hostility, and strife cannot be integrated readily in our conceptual schemes because it offers different, perhaps entirely new, perspectives on these perennial human concerns?

The present study of these themes has its general antecedents in my earlier work, which addressed the need to recognize civilizations as morally and intellectually distinct orders by isolating the substructural forces that lend authenticity and continuity to a given realm. *Politics and Culture in International History* (Princeton, 1960) suggests that affinities and differences between various political and cultural systems can be uncovered only after the historic sources of locally significant forms of thought and behavior have been thoroughly explored, and that comparative studies of societies, institutions, processes, and ideas would miss the mark if they were to proceed on the assumption that a word, however common its usage, has unequivocal connotations, the same in all areas of the world. "Law" as we have come to think of it in the Occident, may thus commend itself to us as a unifying, universally acceptable device of political order, but no compound definition exists that would do justice to the diverse associations which this verbal symbol evokes in the societies of Asia, Africa, and the non-democratic states of Europe and Latin America. It is, therefore, not surprising that the rule of law, which had been carefully implanted in non-Western states under the guidance of Europeans and Americans, is being disestablished almost everywhere—a projection that concluded my analysis of the issue in *The Future of Law in a Multicultural World* (Princeton, 1971). Indeed, and as Mr. Justice Douglas remarks in his review of this book, on the planes of international relations and international organization, "the differences are so enormous that theoretically no system except the ancient one of balance of power and of 'war,' 'peace,' diplomacy, and espionage would seem to have any chance of universal acceptance."[1]

The cluster of phenomena included in the term "conflict" presents equally complex problems of understanding and analysis in the frame-

---

[1] *Political Science Quarterly*, 87 (March 1972), 90–92.

work of comparative culture studies. Thus it is one thing to examine the protracted and acrimonious disputes about the historical, diplomatic, legal, and economic implications of certain duty-free and neutralized zones in the region surrounding Geneva,[2] and quite another to study discords between the Portuguese and the Arabs, the Chinese and the Tibetans, or the English and the Kikuyu. In the European arena a great variety of antagonists were pitted against each other in times of peace as well as war, but the conflicts occurred within a historically and legally unified civilization, in which men representing different national, dynastic, or cantonal interests could yet assume a wide-ranging consensus on the meanings carried by all major basic references. The latter disputes, by contrast, usually put in question the primary or core norms, values, assumptions, and modes of reasoning that inform a given people how to think of war and conflict.

Several case studies of the incidence of conflict in non-Western, as well as between culturally diverse, societies led me to write a brief paper on "Approaches to the Study of Conflict in a Multicultural World," presented at the Eighth World Congress of Sociology in August 1974, more particularly its Working Session on "problems of scope and method in the comparative study of civilizations"; an essay on "War and the Clash of Ideas," presented in November 1974 at the Conference on National Frontiers and Humanistic Perspectives,[3] in which different modes of thinking about war are compared; and an article on "Civilizations under Stress: Reflections on Cultural Borrowing and Survival,"[4] in which the effect of war on the survival of civilizations is analyzed. Apart from dealing with their specific assignments, these pieces also suggested that orientations to conflict and its management are important indicators of the structure of a given civilization.

The concentration of the present book on Africa south of the Sahara represents an intense preoccupation with this region that began in the early 1950s, when I prepared myself to write *Politics and Culture in International History*. At that time it was my intention to open the volume with a discussion of several nonliterate cultures, among them the world of Black Africa, in which societies had evolved unique styles of thought, communication, and organization by relying not on writing but on speech. This plan was dropped when it was decided to limit the

[2] Adda Bruemmer Bozeman, *Regional Conflicts around Geneva: An Inquiry into the Origin, Nature, and Implications of the Neutralized Zone of Savoy and the Customs-free Zones of Gex and Upper Savoy* (Stanford: Stanford University Press, 1949. The Hoover Library on War, Revolution, and Peace, Publication No. 22).

[3] This was held under the auspices of the National Endowment for the Humanities and the University Seminars of Columbia University.

[4] *The Virginia Quarterly Review*, 51 (Winter 1975), 1–18.

work to literate civilizations; but it provided, eventually, the nucleus of the present book.

My research, which could be accelerated after the earlier writing had been completed, was greatly furthered by a year's sojourn in Africa in 1961-1962. There I was doubly privileged, for I had a home base at the regional office of the World Health Organization in Brazzaville, Congo, where scientists and scholars with vast experience in African affairs were always ready to help me in my various quests, and, thanks to a travel grant from the Rockefeller Foundation, I was also able to travel extensively in central, southern, eastern, and western Africa, as well as in Madagascar. Wherever I went I was received most hospitably, and received invaluable assistance from the different staffs of universities, research institutes, and libraries, nowhere more so than at Lovanium, Makerere, Ibadan, Salisbury, the Rhodes Livingstone Institute, and the Institut Français d'Afrique Noire at Dakar, Senegal.

Among those to whom I am particularly indebted for advice and guidance are the late Melville J. Herskovits, professor of anthropology and director of the program of African studies at Northwestern University, who helped me plan my contacts and itineraries in Africa; the late Heinz Wieschhoff, advisor on African affairs to the secretary general and senior officer in the Trusteeship Department of the United Nations, who read early drafts of some chapters, making numerous valuable suggestions for improvement; the late Daryll Forde, then director of the International African Institute, who invited me to attend the Seminar on Ethno-History in Dakar in December 1961 that the Institute had organized; Théodore Monod, professor of archaeology and director of the Institut Français d'Afrique Noire at Dakar; L.-V. Thomas, professor of sociology at the University of Dakar, and Raymond Mauny, director of the section on archaeology-prehistory at IFAN-Dakar, who were generous, intellectually inspiring hosts in those December weeks in Senegal; and Madame Radaody-Ralarosy, a prominent jurist in Tananarive who introduced me to many interesting sources of Malagasy thought.

My studies in Europe were greatly aided by the research facilities available in Geneva, Brussels, and Paris, and, above all, by the presence of scholarly friends with whom I could discuss the work as it progressed, among them Dr. Marie-Anne de Franz of the Social Science Division of UNESCO. Acknowledgments of assistance in Europe, the United States, and Africa would be legion if I were to express personalized thanks to each of the authors whose works have helped my own along, and if I could remember all occasions in the last fifteen years at which I was stimulated to develop or correct my findings. This brief preface does not permit such extensive listings, but it is the place to give official thanks to the librarians of Sarah Lawrence College, who never failed to help me in locating needed books; to note the privilege I had each year of discussing African affairs in seminars with talented students; and to record the fact that I was given several opportunities to present selected aspects of my research in writing. Analyses of African orientations to conflict and war, as well as to law and other modes of settling disputes, are thus included in most of the publications already listed. They constitute the sole subject matter of several unpublished commissioned monographs, among them "Basic African Dispositions toward Diplomacy, Negotiation, and Conflict Resolution" and "Notes on African Values that Affect the Conduct of International Relations," both for a committee on "Conflict Resolution and Peaceful Change" which functioned under the general auspices of the United Nations Association of the United States, as well as "Negotiation and the Place of Intermediaries in the Practice of Traditional and Modern African Societies" for the Office of the Legal Adviser at the Department of State.

The process of writing this book, then, occurred under various circumstances. The only unchanging elements outside of my own commitment were my husband's steadying support of the entire undertaking, the rich store of knowledge accumulated in decades of medical work in Africa, which was always at my disposal, and the fine critical spirit in which he received the ideas and the pages I presented to him.

The finishing touches to the manuscript were added by Mr. Douglas Waugh, who supplied the map for the index of tribal and linguistic references; Mr. William Golightly, who assisted with the bibliography; and Mr. Peter Rooney, who composed the topical index. These services are greatly appreciated, as is the permission to quote from Margery Perham, ed., *A Collection of Life Stories, Ten Africans* (London, 1936, repr. Evanston, Ill., 1963) which I received from Faber and Faber Ltd., London, and Northwestern University Press, Evanston, Illinois.

The last lines of this preface carry my profound gratitude to Princeton University Press for having converted the manuscript into a book. In particular I want to thank Mrs. Joanna Hitchcock for the calm, incisive guidance and advice she has given me in the last years; Mrs. Margaret Case, whose editing genius combines an unfailing sense for the logic of language with an equally unfailing capacity to appreciate the author's thought; and Mr. Herbert S. Bailey, Jr. who had encouraged me, long ago, to write a book about Africa.

CONTENTS

CONTENTS

PART VI
CONCILIATION, THE ROLE OF INTERMEDIARIES, AND THE SETTLEMENT OF DISPUTES

PART I

THE PLACE OF CONFLICT
IN OCCIDENTAL THOUGHT
AND HISTORY

· 1 ·

NORMS, VALUES, AND
REALITIES

The word "conflict" has multiple ranges of reference and meaning in the vocabularies of the West. On the plane of biography it usually stands for inner stress and tension, as when the self evolves from childhood and dependency; when choices between rival moral challenges or courses of social action have to be made; or when competitive ideas intrude upon the mental process of seeking certainty and truth. Indeed, it is hardly possible to appreciate the stream of scientific discoveries, artistic inventions, or philosophical theories carried by this culture without realizing that each represents the resolution of conflicting principles, and that most have issued from individual lives that were fraught with numerous kinds of conflict, insecurity, and risk. For the preferred human type that emerges from the records has typically been the striving, suffering individual, pitted against destiny, the gods, or nature, defiant of authority and tradition, at odds with inner daemons, yet determined to bring harmony into life and thought by composing his personality and ordering the environment.

The norms traditionally accepted for the conduct of interpersonal relations and the organization of society reflect this ideal image of human destiny. The theme of the adversary, the counterplayer, or the opposite is thus everywhere affirmed—in the school house, the stadium, and the market place, the court room no less than the parliament. It rules modes of reasoning, discourse, and disputation such as the Platonic dialogue or the legal brief; provides the measure of success and failure in competitive enterprises, bargaining proceedings, and elections, and may thus be recognized as the sine qua non in all collisions of interest, clashes of will, and contests of physical and intellectual skill. In short, the civilization affirms conflict between groups and persons as a corollary of individual liberty, and therefore accommodates it also as an attribute of organized political life. On this level, as on that of biography, however, conflict is valued not so much as an end in itself but rather as a process that serves to clarify issues in dispute and narrow areas of contention so as to induce some measure of ultimate conciliation or accord. Furthermore, while the need for opposition is affirmed, it is yet kept subject to the quest for harmony and balance. This value preference explains why the European imagination has fastened itself, especially from the age of the Renaissance onward, to the twin images of the balanced personality and the

3

balanced state; why the language of politics in this culture is so rich in metaphoric allusions to the notion of an equilibrium; and why, by contrast, imbalance, whether in bookkeeping and trade, in the interrelationship of different governing bodies, or the coexistence of separate states, has so often been viewed as a deviation from the norm.[1]

The records of Occidental theory and history thus relay a cultural consensus to the effect that obdurate hostility or aggressiveness in interpersonal relations is abnormal, and that continued social conflict is incompatible with the purposes of civilized society. Above all, they are found to converge upon a common fear of violence. Overt and covert, verbal and behavioral manifestations of conflict have therefore customarily been kept within definite bounds, set either by generally shared moral precepts, special rules of the game, or prescriptions emanating from governing authorities. And among these latter institutions, again, none has been as important as the law. Each category of conflict in the domains of both private and public affairs is thus found allied with a cluster of controlling norms, rules, and sanctions in terms of which it has been possible, for example, to delimit permissible from impermissible modes of voicing grievances and settling discords; to deter or punish injuries to life and property; to isolate threatening mental dispositions or conspiracies to disrupt society, and to narrow irreconcilable positions to the dimensions of justiciable controversies so as to render them capable of resolution by a court of law. Furthermore, the various legal orders in the jurisdictions of the civil and the common law stress the notion of agreement by providing contractual forms for the approximation of consensus between contending parties, as well as constitutional processes of government (such as representative assemblies) in which regulated debate is expected to transpose factional discord into compromise or unity.

No century comes to mind in which these understandings and arrangements have not been found deficient, or in which the fabric of an Occidental state has not been torn by civil discontent or violent strife. But such occurrences do not seem to have undermined the general belief that the search for harmony is a necessary undertaking, and that conflicts in private and public life can be effectively muted, managed, or resolved by resort to orderly processes of change. Peace within the morally and politically unified society has thus been traditionally experienced not only as a supreme value but also as a distinct, definable, and attainable social condition.

[1] See Alfred Vagts, "The Balance of Power; Growth of an Idea," *World Politics*, 1, No. 1 (October 1948), 82–101. In the course of tracing the history of this political principle, Vagts writes: "The balance with its beams and scales and moderate and circumscribed gyrations may well be declared the most favored esthetico-political figure of the Renaissance" (p. 94).

The norms and expectations with which the conduct of interstate relations was associated before the twentieth century were similar to, but not analogous with, the principles that had shaped the inner order. The history of the culturally unified European world thus instructs us that conflicts of national interest were commonly postulated as inherent in the very notion of political unity and independence, and that violence in the form of war was accepted as a legitimate, morally defensible mode of resolving conflicts that could not be composed by other means. Reflecting on the records of Classical, Jewish, and Christian thought and action as he had assembled them in the seventeenth century, when the outlines of the so-called modern European states system were becoming apparent, Grotius thus concluded that war per se is not condemned either by the voluntary law of nations or by the law of nature;[2] that states, not unlike individuals, can reduce each other to subjection, and by this means acquire a civil, absolute, or mixed dominion; that the boundaries of states and kingdoms, or nations and cities, can often be settled by the laws of war;[3] that wars, for the attainment of their objects, must employ force and terror as their most proper agents;[4] and that the grounds of war are as numerous as those of judicial actions. "For where the power of law ceases, there war begins."[5]

Enduring international peace, by contrast, is presented by this pioneering theorist of international law as a remote condition. The prophesy of Isaiah, who says the time shall come "when nations shall beat their swords into plow-shares, and turn their spears into pruning hooks," and when "nation shall not lift up sword against nation, neither shall they learn war any more," is thus in his opinion inconclusive and irrelevant insofar as the justice of war is concerned, since it alludes to the state of the world that would take place only if all nations would submit to the law of Christ.[6] Pending the consummation of this utopian dream, peace is perforce limited in time and space. A significant passage suggests, in fact, that it may not always be easy to distinguish clearly between war and peace, or to assert that every war must end; for war, Grotius notes, is a name for a situation that can exist even when warlike operations are not being carried on.[7] Belligerent powers may thus agree on still points or truces in the intercourse of war. There is, however, no uniform period

[2] Hugo Grotius (Huig van Groot), *De jure belli ac pacis*, first published in 1625. The following quotations are from Hugo Grotius, *The Law of War and Peace; De jure belli ac pacis*, Louise Ropes Loomis, trans. (New York, 1949). But see also Grotius, *The Rights of War and Peace, Including the Law of Nature and of Nations*, A. C. Campbell, trans. (Washington, D.C. & London, 1901); see Book I, ch. 2, 4.
[3] *Ibid.*, Book III, ch. 8, 1.   [4] *Ibid.*, Book III, ch. 1, 6.
[5] Grotius, Loomis translation, Book II, ch. 1, 2.
[6] Book I, ch. 2, 8.   [7] *Ibid.*, Book III, ch. 21, 1.

fixed for the continuance of such an arrangement, which one of his classical authorities describes as "a transitory peace, in travail with war"; "and I shall add," Grotius writes, "that they [truces] are made too for years, twenty, thirty, forty, even a hundred years."[8] In other words, conflict or belligerency may well be semipermanent or protracted.

These findings and propositions, which were to be fully borne out in the ensuing centuries by the realities of inter-European relations, are presented in close alliance with two other major themes, also destined to remain dominant in the civilization: the reference on the one hand to law, on the other to ethics.

The weight of the argument in *The Rights of War and Peace* is carried by the thesis that law inheres in each mode of conducting international intercourse, whether circumscribed as peace, war, truce, or neutrality, and that states ought to be bound by the rules that go with the situation in which they find themselves. Law should thus inform a government of the circumstances that make war just and necessary; what the privileges and obligations are, alike of the victor, the vanquished, and the neutral; when reprisals and punishments are called for; how prisoners, inoffensive civilians, ambassadors, and other categories of persons are to be treated; and just which formalities are requisite if war is to be properly initiated or brought to a close. Although the provisions under each of these—and numerous other law-related headings—are quite explicit, they are derived almost exclusively from norms established by the Greeks and Romans, notably those embodied in the Roman civil law concerning property and contract. That is to say, this foremost text of the law of nations, upon which all subsequent manuals are based, is in its most significant respects an internationalization of the law governing the conduct of natural persons in certain politically unified European societies.

All European systems of legal norms, ancient and modern, are inseparably linked to prevalent ethical values. It was, therefore, entirely logical for Grotius and his followers to posit a like connection between values and norms for the operation of an inter-European body of law. References to justice, conscience, the Christian "law" of charity, moderation, and above all, good faith thus pervade the work, providing the sinews, as it were, for the integrity and sustenance of the projected jural framework. For example, the text is dominated by the assumption that good faith, being the mortar by which all governments are bound together, will be the keystone also for the unity of the larger society of nations, and this in times of peace as well as in times of war.[9] Taking

---

[8] *Ibid.*

[9] Grotius, Campbell translation, Book III, ch. 25, 1. The Campbell translation is used here rather than that by Loomis because the latter is much less explicit in its selections on this issue than the former.

issue with the views of some of the Ancients, among them Plutarch, who noted that most powers "employ the relative situations of peace and war, as a current specie, for the purchase of whatever they deem expedient,"[10] Grotius also warns against undue resort to feints, deceptions, and dissimulations. Furthermore, he insists that treaties, even between hostile powers, must be founded upon good faith, expressed or tacit, since it is by such pledges alone that peace can be concluded or the rights of war enforced;[11] that peace must be kept on whatever terms it has been made;[12] that states must guard against rashly engaging in war, even when the grounds are just, and that they should practice moderation in acquiring dominion or despoiling the country of the enemy when engaged in combat.

It is in the context of this culturally shared value system, then, that nations are expected to keep alive the hope of peace even in the midst of war;[13] find the "usual and practical topics of negotiation,"[14] and to practice arbitration in strict accordance with the rules of justice[15]—in short, to find pacific means of resolving conflicts that do not justify belligerent action.

Post-Grotian generations up to the middle of the twentieth century have held rather steadfastly to the major themes as they had been summarized in the seventeenth century. That is to say, war continued to be a legitimate instrument of statecraft, but its conduct remained subject to rules, and its place in international politics, strategic doctrine, and value theory was strictly circumscribed. Clausewitz (b. 1780), who laid the basis for the systematic study of war as a field of human knowledge,[16] composed his work *On War* after Europe had been subjected to decades of warfare in the Napoleonic period; he restated Grotius in defining war as a conduct of political intercourse by other means, a form of human enterprise belonging to social existence, and a conflict of great interests that is settled by bloodshed.[17] Although his special concern was quite different from the task Grotius had set for himself, being mainly addressed to the question of whether such a conflict of living elements is subject to general laws, and if so, whether these can serve as a guide to action,[18] he too inveighed against the folly of viewing war as an act of unrestrained violence, a mere passion for daring and winning, or "an in-

---

[10] *Ibid.*, Book III, ch. 22, 4.
[11] *Ibid.*, Book III, ch. 20, 1.
[12] *Ibid.*, Book III, ch. 25, 6.
[13] *Ibid.*, Book III, ch. 25, 1.
[14] *Ibid.*, Book III, ch. 19, 19.
[15] *Ibid.*, Book III, ch. 20, 46–49.
[16] Karl von Clausewitz, *War, Politics, and Power, Selections from "On War" and "I Believe and Profess,"* Col. Edward M. Collins, USAF, trans. and ed. (Chicago, 1962), Editor's Introduction, p. 59.
[17] Karl von Clausewitz, *On War*, O. J. Matthijs Jolles, trans. (New York, 1943), Book I, "On the Nature of War," ch. 1, "What is War?" p. 24; Book II, "The Theory of War," ch. 3, 3.
[18] *Ibid.*, Book II, ch. 3, 4.

dependent thing in itself."[19] To Clausewitz it was quite clear that war is a serious means to a serious end, only a part of political intercourse, and therefore always subject to the political design.[20] And the latter, whether understood as referring to a particular foreign policy or to the realm of politics in general, is here decidedly not viewed as "war by other means" —a theoretical construction in the communist doctrine of conflict that Lenin elaborated several decades later when he stood Clausewitz "on his head." Indeed, the modern histories of diplomacy and the law of nations point persuasively to the conclusion that conflict-related thought and politics in the West continued to favor the rule of law and peace, even though they also bear out Clausewitz' conclusion that "peace seldom reigns over all Europe, and never in all quarters of the world."[21]

These approaches to conflict and war in international relations are organically related to the preferred cultural style on the level of social relations within the state. Common legacies of domestic law and government made for a value system that instructed diplomats and political representatives, as well as their domestic constituencies, to believe, first, that international quarrels, whether acute or lingering, should be settled if at all possible; second, that governments and their agents will do so most successfully when they resort to the methods of discussion and negotiation customary in domestic constitutional processes; and third, that intergovernmental accords are best entrusted to the type of document used for registering interpersonal compacts. In other words, since individuals are presumed capable of making promises and abiding by commitments, states, too, are held to compliance with such norms. The law of treaties, which constitutes the core of modern international law, could therefore evolve logically as an international extension of the Western law of contract.

Next, Occidental understandings of the nature of disputes and their settlement also reflect the dominant moral order; for although law-conscious elites have insisted throughout the ages—successfully on the whole—that law is distinct from morality, it is nevertheless impossible to disassociate either the common law or the civil law—in particular the law of contract and hence also that of treaties—from certain deeply rooted ethical convictions, whose evolution has paralleled that of law and government. To break one's word, betray a trust, violate an agreement, deceive "the other" deliberately, or enter into negotiations under false pretences or for illegal objectives, are activities that have customarily been viewed as immoral, whatever their actual legal connotations and

[19] *Ibid.*, Book I, ch. 1, 27.
[20] *Ibid.*, Book I, ch. 1, 23; Book VIII, ch. 8, "War as an Instrument of Policy."
[21] *Ibid.*, Book I, ch. 8 (p. 57).

consequences may be in personal, corporate, or other kinds of human relations. It was natural, therefore, that these fundamental convictions should also have entered the Occidental systems of international law, diplomacy, negotiation, and conflict resolution. Together with the legal and ethical connotations carried by the idea of peace, they go a long way toward explaining why diplomacy is commonly supposed to serve the cause either of adjustment or of peace. The warrior style of diplomacy, in accordance with which diplomacy is "war by other means," has by contrast not been favored in the West. Indeed, episodes in the diplomatic history of the West during which diplomacy was conducted "cynically" are usually viewed as lapses from the norm.

This association of diplomacy with peace and agreement was solidified early in the history of European trade, when the new and influential class of merchants and townsmen concluded from its involvement in commercial activities that international trade was most profitable when conducted as a peaceful calling in an atmosphere of mutual trust. The members of these social classes thus became particularly ardent proponents of the view that diplomacy should be auxiliary to pacific exchanges between cities and states, and that all negotiations ought to aim at compromise and conciliation rather than victory. In terms of this shopkeeper or mercantile diplomacy,[22] good diplomatic method has therefore usually been likened to good banking: it is to be founded upon the establishment of credit, and it should not lead to "credibility gaps." Legal, moral, and practical reasons have thus combined to establish the general view, first stated methodically by François de la Callières in "De la Manière de negocier avec les souverains" (1716), that the secret of "good" negotiating techniques is to harmonize the real interests of the parties concerned; that menaces, deceptions, or any kind of blackmail are not only immoral but also impractical; that honesty is here and everywhere the best policy. Sound diplomacy, relevant texts keep repeating, should be based on the creation of confidence, and confidence can be inspired only by good faith and sincerity.

The modern European states system, within which most of these beliefs matured, contributed yet another distinct feature to the complex of conflict-related dispositions; in accordance with this regional scheme of organization, there had to be not only states existing as more or less durable political organisms, but also governments reliably representative of these states. The rule stressed by Richelieu that each party to a negotiation should know from the outset that the other party actually speaks for the sovereign of his country, has ever since been a commonplace in the Occidental system of negotiation. It explains, along with the primary

---

[22] The terminology is borrowed from Harold Nicolson, *Diplomacy* (London and New York, 1950), pp. 51–54.

influences already cited, why Western nations tend to expect certainty and precision in their diplomatic dealings. Similarly, the dictates of law, morality, experience, and expediency have combined throughout the centuries to contribute to the expectation that negotiations are meant to result in agreement, and that the wording of an agreement should be so precise and unambiguous as to leave as little scope as possible for misunderstanding or evasion.

In view of these multifarious but interlocking factors, it is not surprising that the treaty should have emerged as the major and most trusted agency in the pacific settlement of disputes; and that the international conference or congress, modeled upon local legislative assemblies, should have become, after the Congress of Constance in 1414, the favorite forum for the settlement, by parliamentary diplomacy, of European disputes. Moreover, all trends toward an interpenetration of diplomacy, law, and ethics were to receive steady support from the evolution of the federating instinct in Europe and America, and from the development of two types of international system, commonly viewed in the United States as antithetical to each other. These are: the "balance of power," conceived in Renaissance Italy and elaborated after the Napoleonic wars as "the Concert of Europe," in terms of which the interplay of sovereign powers was allowed to be fluid even as aspirations for hegemony were to be held in check; and the "collective security organization," first called into being in 1919, when the League of Nations was designated to overcome the principle of diverse but balanced power. The pattern of invoking one system in counterpoint to the other was to continue, as when disillusionment with the working of the League and later the United Nations served to activate the older, rival principle or order. It is important to note for purposes of the present discussion, however, that each of these initiatives was taken in the aftermath of war or in the presence of great upheavals and uncertainties. Each of the recorded designs was meant to prevent the rise of monolithic power, keep conflicts from degenerating into war, and provide time, opportunity, and method for the peaceful settlement of disputes. In fact, as one international organization after another was set up on foundations of constitutionalism and in the service of international peace and cooperation, the notion became prevalent throughout the Occident that conciliation, mediation, and arbitration— each carefully circumscribed in the preferred value language of law— were indeed the primary aims that a rational diplomatic method was called upon to pursue.

On the inner level of the modern democratic state, meanwhile, these aspects of the diplomatic design were being progressively accentuated as European and American governments felt compelled—rightly or wrongly—to please the public or assuage its anxieties by announcing foreign commitments as simply and unambiguously as possible, and as representatives of the increasingly influential media of communication, working within the intellectual and practical limits of their crafts, insisted on pressing governments and negotiators to come out with quotable certainties. Moreover, the popularization of foreign policy concerns that ensued from these practices naturally activated the inclination—always latent in a democracy—to transfer private sentiments from the realm of interpersonal to that of interstate relations. The tendency to treat all nations, regardless of their culture and form of government, as though they were cocitizens in a world-spanning democracy was thus destined to become a widespread trait.

No task in the administration of modern foreign affairs has been more gravely affected by the ensconcement of these orientations than that requiring the analysis of international disputes. As the boundaries between personal, national, and international domains have been permitted to become blurred in the West, interstate conflicts have often been confounded with internal conflicts, and this again has naturally conduced to a disregard of historical perspective and to the disassembling of such comprehensive concepts as the national interest. Indeed, the intensity of personal anxiety in the face of political uncertainty and the insistent assumption that all disputes in foreign affairs—including even that conglomerate of ideological enmities between the Occidental and communist worlds commonly known as "the cold war"—should be capable of resolution, just as personal quarrels are put to rest, has come to obsess vast sectors of public opinion to a degree unparalleled in history. For not only do these modern trends diverge dramatically from those observed and sanctioned in the war-torn but culturally unified Grotian system of states; they are contrary also to assumptions prevalent in much earlier epochs. European history begins, after all, with the stamina displayed by classical Greece during continuous military and psycho-diplomatic encroachments by imperial Persia, and in regard to the later medieval epoch it instructs us firmly that Christians and Muslims coexisted for centuries in the Mediterranean region, notably in the Iberian Peninsula, by absorbing the facts of war and sustaining a political climate dense with ideological tensions and hostilities that were already then summarily described as "guerra fria."[23]

In short, by comparison with other times, present generations in the Occident, especially the United States, may be said to suffer from a

[23] A thirteenth-century Spanish writer, Don Juan Manuel, applied the term "guerra fria" to the situation that prevailed in his native land during the coexistence of Islam and Christendom. For this reference see Luis Garcia Arias, *El Concepto de guerra y la denominada "Guerra fria,"* Vol. III of *La Guerra moderna* (Zaragoza, 1956).

failure of nerve when it comes to facing disorder beyond their national boundaries. Quite at variance with their realistic acceptance of conflict as a persistent motif within their own societies, they seem to have surrendered to the view that all wars are avoidable and that all conflicts can be solved.

· 2 ·

CULTURAL DIVERSITY, THE VARIETIES
OF CONFLICT, AND OCCIDENTAL
DESIGNS OF UNITY

Present Western dispositions to become unnerved by the incidence of war and conflict in the world environment are due to several interlocking causes. Unlike other epochs, as, for example, the medieval age, there are no trusted moral agencies in the Occident comparable to those brought forth by Christendom, which could quell doubt and insecurity by giving authoritative direction to decision making in matters of peace, truce, and war. And, in contrast to such "ages of reason" as those identified with classical Greece, the Renaissance, and ensuing centuries, during which theorists did not suspend their mental skills when it came to analyzing war as an instrument of statecraft, there is a dearth today of this type of objective intellectual exploration. For one thing, modern generations have not brought forth counterparts of Herodotus, Thucydides, Grotius, or Clausewitz; and for another, academic scholarship has not been stimulated by the heavy incidence of violence in all parts of the technically unified world to review the suppositions that had been elaborated in the restricted framework of the Atlantic civilization. Data assembled in the European and American past thus continue to be cited today in support of propositions for which universal relevance is claimed. But in this context of normative thought, little attention has been paid to the histories of Africa and Asia—all well documented now—that are replete with references to culturally different theories and practices of warfare.

The absence of transculturally valid norms provides one explanation of why thought on war has been allowed to escape into realms of ideology or private sentiment. Certain wars are thus condemned as absolutely unjust, others, by contrast, are applauded as entirely justified; but most judgments of this kind are found, upon examination, to derive from value preferences rather than from the application of firm criteria of differentiation. The other major reason for the paucity of rationally convincing approaches to the subject is the pronounced revulsion against war that has pervaded many intellectual circles in the West. Academic literature, as it has accumulated in the United States since the Second World War, thus suggests not only that moral certainties concerning warfare are more firmly fixed in the present secular age of multiple cultures than they have ever been in the integral Occidental systems of the past, but also that

13

pacifism, however selective in its concerns, has had the effect of stilling the very sources of discriminating and steadying thought upon which intellectually and politically progressive Occidental societies have traditionally relied.

These developments in the climate of political opinion have led to a significant blurring of distinctions between wars and conflicts short of war. For example, the continuous use of the term "war" as a metaphor for admittedly acrimonious tensions between the rival moral orders of communist and non-communist states has gradually conditioned people to believe that this cold war of nerves has somehow been "declared," and can therefore just as suddenly be terminated, in much the same way as armies are ordered to withdraw from a battlefield. More importantly, sheer fear that conflict may lead to military engagements, or possibly even to nuclear confrontations, appears to have crowded out the historically indisputable fact that all international relations—even those in culturally unified regions—are by definition adversary relations, and to have installed instead the assumption that all interstate conflict is "a bad thing"[1] and a deviation from the norm.

The further or ultimate question, namely just what the norm is, has not received serious attention. Allusions to world peace abound, but definitions of this condition are, perforce, missing; for no one, least of all the international historian, can point to a single year in the last decades, or for that matter in the millennia of recorded time, during which some provinces of the world have not been caught up in bitter enmities and armed struggles of one kind or another. The very word "peace" is thus an embattled term. It is true that it continues to denote certain concrete situations, as when two or more states are not involved in military combat, or when peace is deliberately instituted after such hostilities have come to a close. Yet these traditional, essentially negative meanings seem to have been superseded under the impact of a world environment in which scores of different but coordinate states are found to coexist. At any rate, the word "peace," as commonly used in the West today, refers to the world at large, and in this new context it has come to signify a cluster of indeterminate yearnings for an entirely new international order —one from which even the specter of war is banned.

---

[1] Paul Bohannan in the "Introduction," p. xi, to Paul Bohannan, ed., *Law and Warfare; Studies in the Anthropology of Conflict* (Garden City, N.Y., 1967). But see *infra*, Ch. 4 for a discussion of research on conflict *within* modern Western societies.

For a lucid and forthright presentation of the inadequacy of traditional categories of war, hostilities short of war, peace, neutrality, diplomacy, and so forth in contemporary international politics see Harold Sprout and Margaret Sprout, *Toward a Politics of the Planet Earth* (New York, Toronto, London, and Melbourne, 1971), pp. 135–140.

The pursuit of this compelling image has occupied many scholarly minds. Most peace studies, like most war studies, however, have been conducted in a culturally closed milieu; inquiries into the meanings carried by "peace" in non-Western nations have seldom if ever been rigorously pursued. More importantly, perhaps, the polarized conception of international relations as either war or peace has made for a rather reductive view of the vast spectrum of variegated conflict situations. The latter, which may range from mere friction or misunderstanding to irreconcilable enmity, are clearly identifiable in the actual world, but they will resist analysis as long as they are rendered in the simplistic language of war and peace.

Limited as these Occidental perspectives may be, they have been rationalized and solidified on the planes, respectively, of sentiment, social science, and political structure. The inauguration of the nuclear age may thus be said to have legislated the belief, notably among Americans, that peoples and governments everywhere—however far apart from each other culturally and politically—must henceforth share the same kind of dread of nuclear war, and therefore be equally apprehensive about conflictual relationships, particularly when these might affect the conduct of nuclear powers. Findings by specialists that levels of fear in some countries are significantly lower than those registered in the United States do not seem to have significantly weakened the wave of pacifist and egalitarian sentiments now sweeping the West. In fact, the inclusion of all the world's nations in the one Occidental web of hopes and anxieties has only served to confirm the tendency to think of conflicts, their causes, and their chances for resolution in the context of prevalent Western susceptibilities rather than in those implied from case to case by the realities of the actual foreign situation.

Analogous leveling trends have long been evident in certain politically crucial academic disciplines. Too many of the norms, models, and social laws for which absolute validity is being claimed in the ranks of sociologists, political scientists, economists, psychologists, and lawyers, are actually abstractions of exclusively Western patterns of thought and life.[2] Far too few of these general truths have been tested in light of greatly divergent data that historians, anthropologists, and linguists have painstakingly assembled in other parts of the world. The presumption of an overall accord on values related to peace and war—largely uncontested in the mid-twentieth century, when the cause of world peace was entrusted to international law under the general auspices of the United Nations Organization—was thus allowed to stand in the ensuing decades, all the more so as it had been voluntarily and officially endorsed by spokesmen for Asian, African, and communist states. Sentiment,

[2] *Infra*, Chs. 4 and 8.

15

thought, and organization thus combined to buttress the supposition that what is experienced as conflict "here" is also perceived and treated as conflict "there"; that levels of toleration for friction and antagonism are essentially the same everywhere, and that governments would be equally prepared, therefore, to abide by the contractual commitments of the Charter, which require member states to refrain from engaging in certain kinds of conflict and to settle disputes peacefully and in good faith by resort to conciliation, mediation, arbitration, or judicial settlement.

The references to modes of coping with conflict as outlined, for example, in articles 1, 2, 33, and 38 of the United Nations Charter, originated as corollaries of classical Western approaches to the maintenance of peace and order in the European world and, as suggested earlier, they therefore carry quite specific connotations in the diplomatic and juridical systems of this civilization. The further question, namely, just how applicable these devices are to culturally different realms, had not been thoroughly explored before the Charter was drafted. It is true that the principle of "regional organization" is officially recognized. The Charter thus invites states to make use of "regional arrangements," urges them to exhaust "other means" of settling disputes before resorting to the United Nations machinery proper, and acknowledges the need for "fact-finding." Each of these references appears to imply that regions are culturally and politically different from one another, and that each is likely, therefore, to have its own preferred approaches to international conflict and accord. No effort was made before 1945, however, to assemble the actual, regionally trusted techniques for muting tensions, or to spell out what might be meant by "other means" of settling disputes. In fact, "regionalism" is nowhere defined conceptually. Even its obvious spatial implications were left indeterminate, with the result that different specialized agencies and United Nations councils could divide the world along geographically different lines. Deference to the concept of regionalism thus turns out to have been not much more than a rather perfunctory admission that any global administration requires some kind of decentralization.

Some of these structural weaknesses were to receive oblique recognition twenty years later, when a study group reviewed the actual operation of the United Nations provisions for the peaceful settlement of international disputes.[3] The authors of the report were persuaded that communist states and new states were openly distrustful of settlement by judicial means, and quite doubtful, furthermore, about the very substance of international law. However, the evidence assembled by the experts had not weakened the rapporteurs' steadfast faith in the timeless

[3] David Davies Memorial Institute of International Studies, *Report of a Study Group on the Peaceful Settlement of International Disputes* (London, 1966).

16

and transcultural validity of Occidental legal systems. In their view "the fundamental principles and the general body of international laws have their roots in the essential nature of inter-state relations and the considerations which led to their formation have a value which is independent of the particular historical conditions in which they were created. Consequently they have as much importance for new as for old states."[4]

No significance seems to have been attached to the fact—also extensively noted in the report—that at least one group of non-Western states, namely the Organization of African Unity, chose not to incorporate recourse to international law and the Permanent Court in its machinery of peaceful settlement, even while borrowing other provisions from the UN Charter, as well as from earlier Occidental texts on the general subject.[5] Moreover, in addressing themselves to what were vaguely termed "other" procedures, the rapporteurs noted that arbitration appeared to be "outmoded," and that mediation had not proved successful.[6] The emphasis—described as "overwhelming" in the case of communist states—was found to be on negotiation. And yet the commentary simply takes note of this, without ascribing reasons for the preference.[7]

The fact that "negotiation" and "diplomacy" are general, elastic, and value-neutral references, capable therefore of covering regionally dominant norms, interests, and dispositions, has not received sufficient attention either in this or in any other comparable comprehensive study. What seems to be trusted now, as it was then, is the written record of a pact—a treaty that assures reconciliation, the cessation of hostilities, and above all peace. And in this connection it is relevant to recall that in Western thought and language there is a close connection between "pact" and "peace." For since the word "peace" is akin to the word "pact" (see Webster's *Standard College Dictionary*), the *idea* of peace is also apt to evoke the complementary notion of a pact to preserve the peace. What is surprising about much modern theory and practice, then, is not the continuation of these deeply rooted traditional modes of thinking, but the rather blithe assumption that culturally different conceptual systems have brought forth equivalent principles of obligation.

The theoretical and practical validity of Occidental orientations to international conflict and its management or resolution has been put in question by several developments in the last decades. Foremost among them is the obstinate actuality of war in all major component regions of the world; the proliferation of types of war, and the spread of war-affirming theories. For whether the war in question is classified as an insurrection, a civil war, a war of national liberation, guerrilla warfare, war by

[4] *Ibid.*, p. 36.
[6] *Ibid.*, pp. 91ff., also pp. 72, 80.
[5] *Ibid.*, pp. 27ff., 110.
[7] *Ibid.*, pp. 36, 56ff., 59.

17

proxy, a United Nations war to preserve peace, or a traditional inter-state war (and the lines of differentiation have certainly become blurred in recent times); whether it is viewed as aggressive or defensive, just or unjust—the fact remains that world politics has been marked by war rather than by peace in the last decades.

Next, the interpenetration of external war, internal war, and such other manifestations of social conflict as coups d'état, assassinations of leading personalities, massive terrorism, conspiracies in behalf of foreign principals and causes, or insurgencies and counterinsurgencies, which has been discernible in each of the numerous regional theaters of war, has rendered inoperative long-accepted categories of contentious and combative behavior, as well as customary Western ways of dealing with the phenomena themselves. And in each of these respects, again, note must be taken of the irrefutable fact that conflict and resort to violence are accepted in most areas outside the Occidental realm as normal inci-dents of life, socially legitimate tools of government and foreign policy making, or morally sanctioned courses of action.

The strong stress on pacifism that is relayed by many modern Western interpretations of Christianity as the politically appropriate stance in international relations, is thus as absent in present-day Hinduism, Bud-dhism, Judaism, Islam, and animism, as it was in earlier eras of orga-nized Christendom. Likewise, one looks in vain for such an affirmation of peace in communist ideology. Here all ruling precepts are corollaries of a dialectical mode of thinking and reasoning—conceived by Marx and Engels and elaborated by Lenin, Stalin, and Mao Tse-tung—that stipu-lates the absolute need for contradictions, and presents conflict develop-ment as the essential form of progress in society. In Marxist-Leninist logic, social and political organization must comply with the dictates of the class struggle; and international relations, being manifestations of irreconcilable principles, are therefore quite naturally cast in terms either of protracted conflict or of "no war–no peace," at least until it can be claimed that the forces of communism have prevailed over those in the noncommunist camp.

Peace, then, is by no means the dominant value in all provinces of the world; war is not acknowledged everywhere as the most calamitous of human conditions, and conflict, far from carrying essentially negative connotations, is widely accepted as a positive, socially structuring force. Furthermore, studies of the world's numerous strife-torn regions show conclusively that moral, intellectual, social, or political conflicts are ex-perienced in greatly varying ways; that levels of conflict tolerance are not convergent; and that allowance must be made, therefore, for culturally or regionally different ways of managing tensions and disputes. In brief, then, it is evident today, three decades after the establishment of the first

18

world-spanning collective security organization, that most of our comprehensive unifying structures—whether built under the auspices of scholarship or of statesmanship—have been assembled much too hastily.

What seems needed in these circumstances are cultural inventories, bearing first on pivotal, conflict-centered concepts, values, attitudes, and institutions; and second on all major customs and dispositions that are favorable to conciliation and the settlement or management of disputes. When the world is mapped and analyzed in this fashion, comparisons of all culturally discrete vocabularies of conflict will become possible; and these comparisons, again, may open up new avenues for mutual adjustments. The present study of Africa south of the Sahara belongs in this general frame of reference. Its two specific purposes are to understand conflict as it is being experienced in Africa, and to contrast the findings with norms and suppositions developed in the thought world of the West.

PART II

THE AFRICAN PRESENCE
IN THE MODERN WORLD:
A SYNOPTIC VIEW

· 3 ·

PATTERNS OF CONFLICT
AND ACCORD

A comparison of the independent black African states in the area bounded in the north by Islamic polities commonly included in the Middle Eastern zone and in the south by the Union of South Africa shows several common traits. Apart from Ethiopia and Liberia, all are "new" states, having been constituted in the second half of this century by European colonial administrations on the model of the democratic Occidental state. None, however, with the possible exception of Somalia, can be convincingly described as a nationally and territorially unified state, for all are also conglomerates of multiple, often hostile, tribal communities. As states, then, they would appear to be precarious structures, if only because they are amalgams of two sets of constitutive principles that cannot be easily fused or reconciled. A few felicitous resolutions of these systemic incongruities may be cited,[1] and others may become recognizable in future times, but a study of actually existing states justifies the conclusion that the interplay of the two culturally disparate elements has so far favored the resurgence of the traditional, and the eclipse of the European. Indeed, it is difficult not to acquiesce in an African scholar's judgment that the modern African state exists under the trusteeship of indigenous forces.[2]

Thus it is the obdurate persistence of ethnicity in politics that explains why the state cannot rely on the public's commitment to nationalism, civic loyalty, or territorial integrity, and why it must contend instead with

[1] See, for example, C. S. Whitaker, Jr., *The Politics of Tradition; Continuity and Change in Northern Nigeria 1946–1966* (Princeton, 1970), for the view that the northern emirates in Nigeria are illustrative of a stable symbiosis of modern and traditional elements. It should be noted, however, that the author is dealing with only one culturally and ethnically rather homogeneous region of the vast Nigerian state. Also I. M. Lewis, *A Pastoral Democracy; A Study of Pastoralism and Politics among the Northern Somali of the Horn of Africa* (London and New York, 1961), p. 266 to the effect that modern party politics and legislative bodies have provided new media for the expression of all-pervasive traditional political forces.

[2] Christian Vieyra, "Structures politiques traditionnelles et structures politiques modernes," in Rencontres internationales de Bouaké, *Tradition et modernisme en Afrique noire* (Paris, 1965), pp. 203, 207. Fear that tribalism will erupt in violence pervades most African states today. On the worsening of these tribal conflicts in Sierra Leone, where the Creoles continue to be hostile to the peoples of the "Protectorate," and where the latter are again sharply divided by conflicts between the northern tribes on the one hand and the dominant Mende group on the other, see John R. Cartwright, *Politics in Sierra Leone 1947–67* (Toronto and Buffalo, 1970).

23

an essentially biological kind of patriotism, and this in a double sense; for there is first the traditional loyalty to the tribe, the kindred, or some other subgroup in the polyethnic state; and there is second the modern pigmentational notion of Africanism or mere Blackness. Both forms of consciousness tend to reduce the concept of the nation state. In these circumstances, it is not surprising that so many African states are plagued today either by secessionist, separatist movements, or by revisionist expansionist designs that aim at the creation, for example, of a Greater Guinea, a Greater Ghana, a Greater Somalia, or, in the case of certain Saharan states, of some greatly enlarged Arab orbit. Yet the very factors that make for this instability also explain why successive regimes in the great majority of African states have been determined to prevent fragmentation and hold fast to the territorial contours bequeathed them by their former European rulers. For as President Nyerere of Tanzania is said to have observed in 1963, African boundaries are so absurd that they must be recognized as sacrosanct.[3]

This widespread conviction did not prevent the gradual dismantling of the original federations that had been set up in East, Central, and West Africa, but it goes a long way toward explaining why most of the core states have succeeded in retaining their original identity; why, for example, only four of forty members of the Organization of African Unity chose to recognize secessionist Biafra when Nigeria was threatened with dissolution, and why major open wars between separate black African states have not been fought. In short, then, the new idea of the state has so far survived the countless conflicts that came in the wake of its concretization.

This success has been registered at the expense of the democratic institutions with which the states were allied at the start. Indeed, the latter have crumbled everywhere, quite contrary to the prognoses submitted by many Western scholars,[4] and contrary also to the fervent hopes of Westernized African elites that the integration of separate tribes into a nation would proceed within the framework of constitutionalism as this term is understood in the Occident.[5] It became clear almost immediately

[3] For this reference see Rupert Emerson, "African States and the Burdens They Bear," *African Studies Bulletin*, 10, No. 1 (April 1967), 2.

[4] See, for example, Michael Crowder, *The Story of Nigeria* (London, 1962), p. 273, to the effect that the foundations for an independent Nigeria have been solidly built, and that peoples of various ethnic heritage have begun to think of themselves as Nigerians rather than as Hausa, Ibo, or Yoruba. Also see David E. Apter, *The Gold Coast in Transition* (Princeton, 1955), p. 273. See Thomas R. Adam, *Government and Politics in Africa South of the Sahara*, rev. ed. (New York, 1967), p. 111, to the effect that by and large the pattern of government in the Republic of Ghana rests on a firm constitutional base. If Ghana remains a one-party state, the author argues, this is because a majority of the electorate so desires.

[5] See, for example, Kofi A. Busia, *Africa in Search of Democracy* (London, 1967), pp. 111ff.

after independence had been gained that the goal of transcending tribal-ism was indeed the most intractable of the many problems faced by all African governments, and that Occidental types of democratic rule and public law, being fundamentally incompatible with long-established native patterns of transacting politics, would not provide favorable auspices for nation building in this continent. Constitutions and bills of rights soon became inoperative or practically irrelevant; parliaments did not evolve into supratribal associations, and multiparty systems foun-dered because European concepts of an "organized opposition" or "al-ternate government," or of an issue-oriented party program could not replace the deeply entrenched meanings that Africans assigned to parti-sanship, conflict, and accord. These complex circumstances, confounded as they have been by continuous racial mistrust and public disorder, ac-count for the fact that the single party state is the norm in Africa today. As the late Kwame Nkrumah explained after taking great pride in having authored the One Party System, no other recourse had been open, for he had had to "combat not only tribalism but the African tradition that man's first duty is to his family."[6]

The word "party" continues to carry different connotations in different African states. In some it is officially identified as synonymous with the state itself; in others it stands for the paramount influence of a dominant tribe. Yet none exists in which the term does not denote a group of men who associate their own political prospects with the power and prestige of a dominant personality in the country. That is to say, government in the single party state is in essence an extension of the ruling man's char-acter. At its worst it may thus be tyrannous, self-seeking, short-sighted, and unresponsive to public needs; and at its best it may exert itself in behalf of internal order, economic development, and national survival. No African state comes to mind, however, in which government is not arbitrary and unpredictable either in terms of compliance with preexist-ing legal or administrative norms, or in terms of personal steadfastness of purpose. W. Arthur Lewis may have been too harsh and pessimistic in his 1965 estimate of West African dictatorships, but his comments on the "incredible power" of decision makers, its corrupting effects on the power wielders, the stultifying social climate of fear born from suppres-sion, the rarity of the charisma complex, and the language of hatred and violence employed by political leaders toward political opponents have most certainly been justified by later developments throughout Africa south of the Sahara.[7] Indeed, studies of the multiple local scenes of vio-

[6] Kwame Nkrumah, *Dark Days in Ghana* (New York, 1968), pp. 66–67.

[7] W. Arthur Lewis, "Beyond African Dictatorship; The Crisis of the One-Party State," *Encounter* 25, No. 2 (August 1965), pp. 3ff. After stating that decision making is quite arbitrary, since most West African ministers consider themselves to

lence and disorder show that relations between rival leaders and their retinues have been marked rather consistently by plot and counterplot, assassination or regicide, abduction, expulsion, or arrest, and that changes of regime have usually been brought about by coups d'état. As one scholar concluded after surveying the evidence in 1968, the coup can be viewed as an institutionalized pattern of African politics on statistical grounds, since in recent years it has become the modal form of government and changes of regime.[8]

Each coup has had its official rationale and should, of course, be evaluated on its own merits. However, a review of this phenomenon in such different countries as Ghana, Nigeria, Dahomey, Mali, Sierra Leone, Chad, Upper Volta, Gabon, Togo, Central African Republic, Sudan, Rwanda, Uganda, Zanzibar (now part of Tanzania), Madagascar, the Congo-Brazzaville, the Congo-Kinshasa (Zaire), and Ethiopia[9] also reveals many common traits. For example, although abortive coups outnumber successful ones, it is possible to say that African governments succumb rather easily to onslaughts from within, and this whether the initiative comes from military or civilian quarters. It appears, next, that the new administration does not effect profound changes in the government's basic structure, and here again it cannot be said, on balance, that military men have been more successful rulers than the civilians they replaced.[10] Such a qualitative difference was widely expected when, to the surprise of many academic observers, the armed forces emerged as a vital factor in internal politics; for on the analogy of modernization processes in certain North African, Asian, and Latin American states, in which "the men on horseback" came to play pivotal roles in processes of modernization and "nation-building," it was assumed that African military elites too would succeed where civilians failed.[11]

---

be above the law, Lewis argues that only a minority of the presidents or premiers have the wide, conciliatory, appeal that is, in his view, the basis of charismatic leadership.

[8] Aristide R. Zolberg, "The Structure of Political Conflict in the New States of Tropical Africa," *American Political Science Review*, 62, No. 1 (March 1968), 77.

[9] The present volume was completed when the royal Ethiopian regime was overthrown in the revolutionary coup of 1974.

[10] Compare, to the same effect, John Michael Lee, *African Armies and Civil Order* (London, 1969), p. 184. But see Zolberg, "Structure of Political Conflict," p. 83, where it is suggested that military men in power are mostly concerned with establishing honesty, the rule of law, and financial responsibility.

[11] As Edward Feit rightly observes in "Military Coups and Political Development: Some Lessons from Ghana and Nigeria," in Marion E. Doro and Newell M. Stultz, eds., *Governing in Black Africa; Perspectives on New States* (Englewood Cliffs, N.J., 1970), pp. 221ff., scholarly authorities did not rate the political potential of African armies very highly before the coups actually began occurring. See, for example, James S. Coleman and Belmont Price, Jr., "The Role of the Military in Sub-Saharan Africa," in John J. Johnson, ed., *The Role of the Military in Under-*

These assumptions have gradually ceased to be persuasive. Several military takeovers, in Ghana and Nigeria in particular, may qualify as "custodial" or "reform" coups, if only because they were at least intended to replace regimes that appeared incapable of assuring the survival of the state.[12] Most have originated, however, in personal power drives and tribal hatreds of the kind that pitted Ibo officers against Hausa rule, or Ashanti and Ewe elements against Nkrumah; and some are best described as gestures of frustrations.[13] In other words, since the African army, including its officers' corps, is now itself lacerated by the very forces from which it was supposed to protect the state, and since its warmaking patterns are marked to an ever-increasing degree by the resurgence of traditional motifs that Western military education was supposed to have excised, it is difficult today to isolate a military coup from the mutiny, rebellion, movement of secession or liberation, civil war, interracial massacre, or other flight into violence with which it was en-

---

developed Countries (Princeton, 1962), p. 359; S. E. Finer, *The Man on Horseback* (London, 1962), p. 228; William F. Gutteridge, *Military Institutions and Power in the New States* (New York, 1965), pp. 141–144.

[12] For this typology see Ernest W. Lefever, *Spear and Scepter; Army, Police, and Politics in Tropical Africa* (Washington, D.C., 1970), pp. 28ff.

[13] Lee, *African Armies*, p. 184, says that "the characteristic African *coups* are gestures of frustration by the employees of the state or 'care-taker' actions to preserve the state apparatus in existence." But see also *ibid.*, pp. 47ff., 57ff., 76, 86.

On the role of national leaders in formerly French Africa, see Guy de Lusignan, *French-Speaking Africa since Independence* (London, 1969), pp. 75ff., 83ff.; see pp. 366ff. on the anatomy of army coups and the fragility of African governing institutions; pp. 268ff. on the incidence of quarrels and shifting alliances in interstate relations. Other treatments of these issues are found in Claude E. Welch, Jr., ed., *Soldier and State in Africa* (Evanston, Ill., 1970); Ronald Mathews, *African Powderkeg; Revolt and Dissent in Six Emergent Nations* (London, 1966) (the study deals with Ghana, Congo-Brazzaville, Gabon, Dahomey, Malawi, and Algeria); Norman J. Miners, *The Nigerian Army, 1956–1966* (New York, 1971) (this study traces the evolution of ethnic consciousness in the originally apolitical Nigerian army); see also Ralph Uwechue, *Reflections on the Nigerian Civil War; Facing the Future*, rev. ed. (New York, 1971); Crawford Young, "The Congo Rebellion," *Africa Report*, 10, No. 4 (April 1965), pp. 6ff. See also Fred Greene, "Toward Understanding Military Coups," *Africa Report*, 11, No. 2 (February 1966), p. 10. See Nkrumah, *Dark Days in Ghana*, pp. 47ff. on the record of the military coups between December 1962 and March 1967; Akwasi A. Afrifa, *The Ghana Coup, 24th February 1966*, London and New York, 1966. See Willard Scott Thompson, *Ghana's Foreign Policy, 1957–1966; Diplomacy, Ideology, and the New State* (Princeton, 1969), for a review of the diplomatic circumstances in which some of the coups occurred.

P. C. Lloyd, *Africa in Social Change; Changing Traditional Societies in the Modern World* (Harmondsworth, Middlesex, 1967), pp. 320ff. points out that the army coups of 1966 in Upper Volta, the Central African Republic, Nigeria, and Ghana proceeded in the same fashion as the coups of 1967 in, for example, Sierra Leone, even though the forms of government were different. On the same general subject see Lee, *African Armies*, ch. 6, "Comparisons in Military Actions." See also Crawford Young, *Politics in the Congo; Decolonization and Independence* (Princeton, 1965), pp. 238ff.

tangled.[14] And this confusion of categories that Western students of politics are accustomed to view as discrete, gains in poignancy when one remembers that changes of regime in numerous traditional African societies habitually occurred in very similar ways.[15] That is to say, the "coup" is a postcolonial phenomenon only in the sense that it had not been taking place under the auspices of the rather short-lived imperial administrations.[16]

Incongruities between Occidental theory and African reality face us also when we insist on juxtaposing military and civilian administrations in a political system that allows, indeed often requires, the fusion of these opposites. The determining factor in either case appears to be the personality of the leading man. In the early 1970s one is thus justified in saying that Gowon's conception of his task in Nigeria is as different from (or similar to) that entertained by Amin in Uganda, or by Mobutu in Zaire, as it is from the role projected by Kaunda upon Zambia, Nyerere upon Tanzania, or Houphouet-Boigny upon the Ivory Coast. The internal policies of African states are pragmatic, therefore, not only because the leadership is subject to sudden changes, but also because each African leader, regardless of the auspices in which he originally gained his preeminent position, has the implicit yet uncertain mandate to modify his programs so that he may stay in power, defy, defeat, or inactivate opponents, and forestall or manage feuds and conflicts as they arise.

The modern culturally syncretic African state, then, does not provide reliable norms and institutions for the governance of political behavior. This vacuum invites capricious conduct on the part of the ambitious and the powerful, makes for apathy, fear, or insecurity in the public, and is generally unfavorable to the sustained execution of long-range social,

[14] Each of the works listed in note 13 contains illustrative material to this effect. See also Lefever, *Spear and Scepter*, pp. 22ff. on the return to pre-Western forms of warfare; Jean Buchmann, *Le Problème des structures politiques en Afrique noire* (Université Lovanium, Institut de Recherches Economiques et Sociales, Notes et documents, No. 20/SP–1, Leopoldville, Congo, July 1961), pp. 63ff.; Kenneth W. Grundy, *Guerrilla Struggle in Africa; An Analysis and Preview* (New York, 1971), pp. 77ff., 113ff., 118ff.; Lee, *African Armies*, pp. 86ff., 98ff., 169ff. On the strength of ethnic ties in the army, security forces, police, and government in general, see Lee, *African Armies*, pp. 65, 78.

On the persistence of these themes, see, for example, the policies of General Amin in Uganda, where the army was purged of men belonging to the Acholi and Langi tribes on the ground that these had been friendly to Milton Obote, Amin's predecessor. Those who did not die in the purge appear to have gone to Tanzania. See the *New York Times*, September 21, 1972.

[15] See Chs. 13 and 14.

[16] Victor T. LeVine, "The Course of Political Violence," in William H. Lewis, ed., *French-Speaking Africa; The Search for Identity* (New York, 1965), ch. 3, p. 67 to the effect that the coup and the attempted coup are postcolonial phenomena.

legal, and political reforms.[17] More importantly for purposes of this discussion, it conduces to the proliferation of all manner of tensions and conflicts. Since each of these is left undiagnosed and unattended, all are allowed to accumulate and to interpenetrate until the sheer momentum of their combined force pushes toward release in explosive action.

African foreign policies cannot be separated from this psychological environment in which they originate and to which they are addressed. However different their national auspices and particularized goals, they therefore share certain important characteristics. Like domestic policies, they are shaped almost exclusively by the head of state; in the absence of an informed public opinion that can unify time-transcendent theories or well-developed concepts of long-range national interest, they, too, are therefore situational, eclectic, and subject to abrupt and frequent shifts in orientation—usually with a view to reenforcing the leader's position at home and in relation to his peers and competitors in the wider arena of interstate affairs. Inter-African relations are thus marked by the kind of uncertainty that ensues when no actor on stage really knows who his counterplayers will be in the next scene, and what they are likely to say or do. The general climate is therefore heavy with suspicion and intrigue, nowhere more so than between neighboring societies, as when national boundaries divide an ethnically unified group, separate traditionally hostile tribes, or enable refugees, rebels, exiled rulers, or other dissident elements to use the adjoining state as a sanctuary or base area in which to plot subversive activities against the enemy "at home."

Multiple versions of international enmity have thus been enacted and reenacted in all parts of black Africa, from the early years of independence onward. On the plane of physical violence they have included bloody border wars, armed incursions, interventions in so-called civil wars, and guerrilla operations. Indeed, the record warrants the conclusion that warfare of one kind or another has been conducted on a prodigious scale, even if one leaves out of account the United Nations war in the Congo-Kinshasa (during which African military contingents and such unconventional units as the Simbas played prominent parts), and the activities of liberation armies and guerrilla bands on or within the borders of Rhodesia, the Union of South Africa, and the originally Portuguese territories of Guinea, Angola, and Mozambique.

[17] For a synoptic view of the role of law in the development of African states, see Adda Bozeman, *The Future of Law in a Multicultural World* (Princeton, 1971), pp. 85–120, and authorities there cited. Compare in particular T. O. Elias, "The Evolution of Law and Government in Modern Africa" in Hilda Kuper and Leo Kuper, eds., *African Law: Adaptation and Development* (Los Angeles, 1966), pp. 184ff.; p. 192 to the effect that "for all the recent judicial and constitutional developments, the task of nation building is yet to be accomplished in Africa."

It has been argued that there is nothing "uniquely new" about African patterns of violence.[18] This conclusion is certainly tenable if the definitions for "coup d'état," "civil war," or "international war," to give but a few illustrations, are sufficiently loose, and if each of these occurrences is viewed in isolation not only from other acts of violence with which it usually is conjoined, but also from the peculiarly African milieu in which it is encountered.[19] For example, there is certainly nothing new about border wars, since adjoining states elsewhere in the world are also inclined to be hostile to each other. Nowhere else, however, is the idea of the territorial state rendered in terms remotely comparable to those characteristic of modern Africa; nowhere is the line between the internal and the external environment as hard to draw, and nowhere, therefore, is it as difficult to extrapolate the actuality of interstate hostilities from the web of internal violence in which they are normally incubated or subsumed. Western definitions of acts of war, aggression, or defence, whether recorded by Grotius, Clausewitz, or twentieth-century theoreticians of the United Nations Charter, can therefore not be said to cover these realities adequately. Furthermore, no culturally distinct subsystem comes to mind in which resort to violence is as tenuously linked to a validating ideology or master plan, as closely controlled by premodern beliefs in magic, and as unaffected by rules of the game as it is here.[20] Reliance on laws of war or upon an all-African body of customs dealing, for example, with the treatment of prisoners or modes of ending military engagements, would thus be out of place here, all the more so as transitions from "war" to "no war," or from "no war" to "war" are made more lightly and informally here than in the civilization in which the "rights of war and peace" originated. Wherever fighting has broken out in modern Africa, it has therefore tended to be uninhibited, ruthless, and protracted—a circumstance that may have persuaded one authority to conclude that the

[18] LeVine, "Course of Political Violence," pp. 59, 63.

[19] See notes 13 and 14, *supra*.

[20] Pan-Africanism and the antiwhite feeling system are generally not viewed as ideologies, since they are not systems of consistent ideas. See Diallo Telli, "The Organization of African Unity in Historical Perspective," *African Forum*, 1, No. 2 (Fall, 1965), 18, that Pan-Africanism has never succeeded in developing a body of identifiable socio-economic and political philosophy. Marxism-Leninism has so far had limited appeal among African elites, and African guerrilla movements do not appear to have been greatly affected by communist doctrine. In analyzing the Congo rebellion of 1964, Crawford Young draws attention to the absence of ideology ("The Congo Rebellion," pp. 6ff.); and Kenneth W. Grundy notes in "Ideology and Insurrection; The Theory of Guerrilla Warfare in Africa" (paper presented to the Annual Convention of the International Studies Association, San Francisco, March 1969), pp. 40ff. that the guerrilla leaders—with the possible exception of Pierre Mulele—lacked ideological armor. But see modern trends in Mozambique.

only unique aspect of African violence is its frequency.[21] In the present analysis, by contrast, this aspect is regarded as the function of several important factors, all resulting from "something inherently systemic"[22] in African life and thought that requires exploration.

Western typologies of violence, then, do not readily accommodate African orientations toward the uses of physical force.[23] Being the work of theorists in a highly literate civilization, they should, perhaps, not be expected to assimilate conceptions, images, and behavioral practices that evolved without the benefit of what we call "theory." As many scholars of modern African warfare, among them Grundy, have pointed out, our taxonomies fail in particular to take into account that complex of pre-European residual beliefs and customs—foremost among them the central operational roles of magic—that are being reactivated so dramatically in modern conflict situations throughout the ancient continent.[24]

[21] LeVine, "The Course of Political Violence," pp. 59, 63, observes rightly in connection with expressing this view that the starting point of any typology of political violence in Africa must be the data itself, and he notes that in the period 1946–1964 there occurred somewhere between three and four hundred instances of political violence in forty states and territories.

[22] This phrase is used by Edward Feit, "Military Coups," pp. 221ff., for purposes of analyzing African coups.

[23] See for example, Samuel P. Huntington, "Patterns of Violence in World Politics," in Samuel P. Huntington, ed., *Changing Patterns of Military Politics* (New York, 1962); and Harry Eckstein, ed., *Internal War* (New York, 1964).

[24] Grundy, *Guerrilla Struggle*, ch. 3, "African Conceptions of Violence" (pp. 27ff.), comments instructively on African guerrilla movements, their relationship to Maoist military writings on the one hand, and indigenous rituals and belief systems on the other. See p. 77 on the practice of oathing; pp. 82ff. on resort to magic and magicians; p. 113 on the choice of terrorism and ritualistic violence; p. 116 on the Simbas' resort to ritualized forms of magic in the Kwilu operations of 1964–1965. Also compare works cited *supra*, notes 11–16.

In his "Thoughts on Assassination in Africa," *Political Science Quarterly*, 83 No. 1 (March 1968), 40–59, Ali A. Mazrui presents the thesis that resort to assassination in the newly independent African states occurs in "situations of inadequate national integration and in situations of weak legitimacy of accepted authority" (p. 45). Since assassination itself as a political solution was rare during the colonial period, he concludes that "assassination comes near to being a post-independence phenomenon in Africa" (p. 46). As some of the following chapters will attempt to demonstrate, this view cannot be supported by African history.

On the general subject of resort to violence and coercion within African states, Mazrui argues that there is a direct relation between "national unity" or its absence, on the one hand, and the degree of compulsion needed to assure it. Thus he writes in 1968: "The Congo is less united than Uganda; therefore the Congo needs more coercion or compulsion in its system than does Uganda." The events of Uganda's history in the few years that have elapsed since 1968 do not sustain this thesis.

On the persistence or resurgence of "political magic" see, for example, the accounts of an attempted military coup against the Ivory Coast's President Felix Houphouet-Boigny in 1973. The main plotter, Captain Sio Koulahou, was arrested on June 20 after he had first abducted five Mauritanian fishermen on Lake Kossou in the Ivory Coast and then sacrificed them to an idol fetish on the advice of a

But the full force of this "almost unresearchable aspect" of the magical qualities surrounding the exercise of power[25] can be appreciated only after one has come close to understanding how Africans think about death and its infliction, and what place they assign to force and power in their value system.[26]

Representative African thinkers and statesmen were intensely aware of the bearing that their conflict-related heritage might have on the new tasks of building nations and developing orderly relations between them when the Organization of African Unity was founded in 1963. They seem to have recognized, in particular, that regicide was bound to have far more serious consequences in African societies than in others because the governmental machinery of the former is so closely identified with the physical person of the head of state. In this context Prime Minister Balewa of Nigeria warned the conference bluntly that "we cannot achieve . . . unity as long as some African countries continue to carry on subversive activities in other African countries," and President Houphouet-Boigny of the Ivory Coast sounded the same theme when he said: "What we consider contrary to the spirit of unity that animates all of us is assassination or murder organized from abroad, or with the tacit complicity of foreign countries, in order to overturn a government or

---

sorcerer, so as to ensure the success of the coup that he planned. Four other captains and seven lieutenants—all commanders of army units—were subsequently arrested in the same affair. See *To The Point*, 2, No. 14 (July 14, 1973), 28.

On the role of magic in some coups directed at Nkrumah, and on the latter's "reliance on supernatural forces" see Henry L. Bretton, *The Rise and Fall of Kwame Nkrumah; A Study of Personal Rule in Africa* (London and New York, 1967), pp. 30–32. Also David Apter, "Nkrumah, Charisma and the Coup," in *Daedalus* (Summer 1968), a volume entitled *Philosophers and Kings; Studies in Leadership*, pp. 780ff. on other aspects of the coup phenomenon.

J. Bowyer Bell concludes his analysis of "Assassination in International Politics: Lord Moyne, Count Bernadotte, and the Lehi," *International Studies Quarterly* 16, No. 1 (March 1972), 82 with the question whether "some international cultures breed assassins and others not," but suggests, rightly (p. 60), that "At the moment, . . . the structure of assassination theory should wait on the manufacture of a few substantive bricks." He also notes (p. 78) that "terror and assassination, however saving of lives, however rational and explicable, have remained anathema through much of the Western world."

On the hold of ideologies upon the minds of Nkrumah, Keita, Sékou Touré, and members of the earlier, Western-trained elites see specialized and biographical works. Also Willard Scott Thompson, *Ghana's Foreign Policy*, p. 263, on "Scientific Socialism"; pp. 290ff. on "Permanent Revolution," "Marxism-Nkrumahism," "Consciencism," etc. I. William Zartman, *International Relations in the New Africa* (Englewood Cliffs, N.J., 1966); Ali A. Mazrui, *Towards a Pax Africana; A Study of Ideology and Ambition* (Chicago, 1967), and by the same author, *On Heroes and Uhuru-Worship; Essays on Independent Africa* (London, 1967). Doudou Thiam, *La Politique étrangère des états africains, ses fondements idéologiques, sa realité présente, ses perspectives d'avenir* (Paris, 1963), and *supra*, n. 29.

[25] To this effect see Lee, *African Armies*, pp. 54, 86ff.
[26] *Infra*, Chs. 9–11.

regime."[27] Article III of the Addis Ababa Charter registers this shared anxiety in stipulating "unreserved condemnation in all its forms of political assassination, as well as of subversive activities on the part of neighbouring States or any other States," and "non-interference in the internal affairs of States." Furthermore, since many of the participants had reason to be uneasy about the safety of the national frontiers and the specter of what President Keita of Mali referred to as "black imperialism," they attached special significance to another clause of Article III—this one borrowed from the United Nations Charter—that requires "respect for the sovereignty and territorial integrity of each Member-State and for its inalienable rights to independent existence."

The records of inter-African relations in the last decade justify the conclusion that these prescriptions command little respect. The response has been altogether different, however, when it comes to compliance with the sixth clause of Article III, which enjoins the members of the OAU to be absolutely dedicated to the total emancipation of the African territories that are still dependent on white regimes. Contrary to the other declarations, which have not been made concrete, as it were, in operational or procedural arrangements, this one elicited immediately a unanimous resolution calling for the acceleration of "liberation" movements by peaceful and nonpeaceful ways. And the latter include not only severance of diplomatic relations between "all African states" and "the governments of Portugal and South Africa," and a total economic boycott of these two countries, but also "unification of the different liberation movements"; "creation of liberation armies and volunteer corps on the territories of different independent African states"; and "establishment of a coordinating committee to organize direct action with a view to liberating dependent African territories." As indicated by the actual formation of a coordinating committee and the training and development of fighting forces, these directives have been, and continue to be, complied with faithfully.

Some of the reasons for this total and insistent reversal of norms are more complex and controversial than others, but all are relevant for an understanding of modern African approaches to conflict and its management.

[27] Boutros Boutros-Ghali, *The Addis Ababa Charter; A Commentary* (International Conciliation, January 1964, No. 546; New York, 1964), pp. 28ff. For statements by different heads of state and representatives, see Présence africaine, *Conférence au sommet des pays indépendants africains, Addis-Abéba, mai 1963* (Paris, 1964). See also Norman J. Padelford, "The Organization of African Unity," *International Organization*, 18, No. 3 (Summer 1964), 521ff.; Telli, "Organization of African Unity," pp. 7ff. For a brief account of the formation of the OAU and the early course of regional relations within this framework, see Zartman, *International Relations in the New Africa*, pp. 35–45.

It thus appears that resentment of the immediate colonial past carries more weight in institutionalizing standards of international behavior than either the hope of overcoming the tribal hatreds of the remoter pre-colonial past, or the wish to be consistent with the Charter of the United Nations, which inveighs against the type of aggression that the Charter of Addis Ababa prescribes. Furthermore, it is interesting to find that the sovereign state is, after all, not accepted here as the ultimate and equalizing referent in international relations that it was meant to be when national independence was desired and acquired. For example, on the plane of continental coexistence with "white" regimes, the Union of South Africa—one of Africa's oldest states—is not differentiated from Portugal's provinces. Indeed, in many respects it is not distinguished from so-called neocolonialist European states, which have no territorial possessions at all in the continent. On the plane of relations between so-called black states—a category that included the nonblack United Arab Republic as signatory of the 1963 Addis Ababa Charter—the concept of the state continues to be embattled because Africa's political elites, having dedicated themselves early to the espousal of Africanism, the realization of one great African commonwealth, and the eradication of tribalism, have so far not been able to develop a system of norms and values for the unification of citizens in a nation state, even as they have failed in realizing either of the two other aims. The uneasy compounding of three sets of references that appear mutually exclusive to a Western mind, and their reduction to the common denominator of ethnicity and race, have had the effect of exploding the meanings inherent in such state-supporting principles as respect for domestic jurisdiction, self-determination, and sovereignty. A whole cluster of inhibitions against intervention, aggression, and war is thus removed, officially only in respect to white regimes, but actually also in relations between black states, especially when it can be argued—as it was in the case of Arab Zanzibar and Tschombe's Congo regime—that the government is not sufficiently conscious or representative of blackness.[28]

[28] On the matter of these incongruities see Boutros-Ghali, *The Addis Ababa Charter*, p. 36: "It is difficult to reconcile the establishment of a cordon sanitaire around Portugal and South Africa with the idea of cooperation within the framework of the United Nations." Telli, "Organization of African Unity," p. 25, on the absence of a domestic jurisdiction clause in the Charter of African Unity and other ambiguities. Ali A. Mazrui, "On the Concept: 'We Are All Africans,'" *American Political Science Review* 57, No. 1 (March 1963), and, by the same author, *Towards a Pax Africana*, where the transformation of the Western vocabulary of politics and law into suitably African terms receives a stimulating treatment. See, for example, pp. 10ff. on "nomadic" and "pigmentational" self-determination; pp. 38ff. on the difference between interstate and interracial interferences. See also Ibrahim Abu-Lughod, "Nationalism in a New Perspective: the African Case," in Herbert J. Spiro, ed., *Patterns of African Development; Five Comparisons* (Englewood Cliffs, N.J., 1967), pp. 35ff. See especially pp. 37, 42, 54, 58ff., to the effect

By way of further comment on the unqualified acceptance of the color factor as the major determinant of the legitimacy of war, it is important to bear in mind that all African administrations—both black and white —are authoritarian in the sense that scant attention is paid to democratic principles of rule, majority representations, civil and individualized liberties, or the supremacy of law over government. In these respects, too, political elites have favored the denaturing of borrowed Occidental concepts. The term "human rights" has thus been made to refer exclusively to the "racial rights" of black Africans against African citizens of European provenance, and, as the records of expropriation and expulsion in some East African states suggest, also against Asians. That is to say, it is quite unrelated here to individual freedom, and it does not appear to have anything to do with the exploitation, oppression, or massacre of one black African group by another—incidents traditionally associated with tribalism.

The break between traditional and modern approaches to violence is more apparent than real, however, and the inconsistencies in the system of norms that one notices in the Addis Ababa Charter, as well as in the actual interstate behavior of African regimes, are less extreme in the psycho-cultural context of Africa than they would be in that of the West. Two motifs in particular unify the apparent opposites and lend logic to what seems illogical to the outsider: the need for an enemy, and the acceptance of fighting as a normal and noble activity.[29] Traditional animosities between tribes or tribal subgroups have thus by no means been transcended or suspended with the aid of the new xenophobia, but they can be and are being played down effectively, particularly in world diplomacy, because the "new" enemies are generally accepted in the forum of world opinion as worthier and more plausible targets of belligerence than the host of old ones. In short, clause 6 of Article III in the Charter of African Unity is a more faithful rendition of African values, norms, and realities than the exhortations against resort to violence that precede it.

The records of diplomacy support the view that African governments are most likely to approximate the goals of inter-African unity and conciliation when they have occasion to plan militant actions against white regimes in the continent. It was an African accord on the functions of the African liberation bureau that persuaded the United Nations Com-

---

that the territorial state is losing its mystique in Africa, and that African states look upon sovereignty as a device for the achievement of higher objectives.

See Bozeman, *The Future of Law in a Multicultural World*, pp. 3ff. for general comments on the relation between words and ideas and on processes of cultural borrowing; pp. 85–120 and authorities there cited for analyses of the place of law in African political organization.

[29] See *infra*, Ch. 14.

mittee on Decolonization, then chaired by the representative of Mali, that it would be legitimate to resort to military force against Portugal—a call to arms by the peace organization that moved President Nyerere of Tanzania to express his "deep faith" in a military solution also of the entire Rhodesian problem.[30]

Episodes like these attest to the priority that African delegations assign to the defense rather of "racial rights" than of the cause of international peace, and to the supremacy, therefore, of Article III, clause 6 of the OAU Charter over UN Charter provisions for the peaceful settlement of disputes. In fact, the record of conflict situations in the world organization and the various specialized agencies suggests strongly that representatives of this culture realm do not view peace as a preferred fundamental value, and do not fear war as the worst of mankind's possible destinies. Furthermore, members of Africa's political elites have been forthright in maintaining that they are more interested in promoting their political causes than in complying with the existing law of nations or with the technical and substantive provisions of international constitutions. Such legal agreements have therefore frequently been bypassed, ignored, distorted, or overturned, often on the ground, well circumscribed by Boutros-Ghali, that "to Africans classical international law has been merely a projection of colonialism."[31]

Diplomatic offensives against states ruled by white minorities could thus be pursued in a great variety of ways. For example, African delegations did not feel inhibited by existing rules of procedure when they tried in 1964 to strike a particular speech by South Africa's delegate from the record of the General Assembly of the United Nations on the ground that they did not agree with its contents,[32] or when they engaged in sustained parliamentary campaigns to suspend the voting rights of South Africa and Portugal, or to expel these states from such mainly technical associations as the International Labor Office, the World Health Organization, UNESCO, or the semiprivate International Conference for Public Education. Each of these international agencies was supposed to aim at universality in membership without regard to a particular member state's form of government so as to do justice to the major purpose of its existence, and each had in fact consistently endeavored to exclude politically

---

[30] See Ali A. Mazrui, "Anti-Militarism and Political Militancy in Tanzania," *Journal of Conflict Resolution*, 12, No. 3 (1968), 269–283. The same author remarks in *Toward a Pax Africana*, p. 136, that Africans are determined to promote the rights of black Angolans, irrespective of the effect that such "reforms" of United Nations principles may have on peace at large.

[31] Boutros-Ghali, *The Addis Ababa Charter*, p. 5. Similar explanations are found in almost every chapter of Mazrui, *Toward a Pax Africana*.

[32] See Thomas Hovet, Jr., *Africa in the United Nations* (Evanston, Ill., 1963), p. 223, for a discussion of this matter.

controversial issues from its deliberations. African arguments in favor of overturning these precedents and constitutional commitments are well illustrated by the records of meetings held by the World Health Organization and its Regional Committee for Africa between 1963 and 1965. The major positions then maintained were that it would be impossible, after Addis Ababa, to participate in meetings with Portugal and the Union of South Africa; that political issues could not be separated from the health factor;[33] that it was futile to rely on legal technicalities;[34] that the constitution of the World Health Organization might just have to be set aside since African nations, being in a state of evolution, regarded it as a means to an end and not as an end in itself;[35] and, finally, that members ignoring the humanitarian principles of the World Health Organization should be suspended or excluded from it.[36] Needless to say, only white Africa-based governments were considered guilty of violating the dictates of humanism.

Urgent pleas made at various meetings by the director general of the World Health Organization, the presiding officer at one of the plenary meetings (Dr. Evang), and other delegations that amendments or resolutions to these ends would be unconstitutional and ruinous not only to the organization but also to the cause of international law,[37] proved unavailing in the face of the steadfast, uncompromising, and solidly unified African presence.[38] Neither of these policy positions or orientations was

[33] See the official précis of the 13th session of the World Health Organization, Regional Office for Africa, 13th Session, held in Geneva, 23–24 September 1963 (Afr/RC/13/Min/15 November 1963).

[34] Official Records WHO, No. 144, 18th Assembly, Geneva, 4–21 May, 1965, Part II, Plenary Meeting, Verbatim Records (November 1965), p. 451.

[35] 13th Session of the Regional Office for Africa, September 1963 (see *supra*, note 33), when this proposition was formulated by Dr. Dolo, Mali's representative.

[36] Amendment proposed by the Ivory Coast, see Official Records WHO, No. 144, Part II, Plenary Meeting, Verbatim Records (November 1965), p. 450. For other African statements to this effect, all later consolidated in the amendment offered by the Ivory Coast, see Part I of the Official Records of these proceedings, No. 143, Annex 14 (proposed amendments to article 7 of the constitution, 9 April 1965), pp. 143ff.

[37] For some of these objections by the director general and the delegates of the United Kingdom and France see Afr/RC/13/Min/15 November 1963. Others, to the same effect, were raised at the 18th Assembly in Geneva; see in particular Official Records WHO, No. 144, Part II, Plenary Meeting, Verbatim Records, (November 1965), pp. 445ff., 452 for statements by the delegates for Australia, the United Kingdom, the Netherlands, and Dr. Evang.

[38] One of the most tumultuous sessions occurred when the International Conference on Public Education convened in Geneva in 1964. This meeting, the twenty-seventh of the International Bureau of Education (a private organization), was cosponsored by UNESCO for the purpose of discussing problems relating to literacy, adult education, and languages in secondary education. However, none of these issues got a hearing, nor could Professor Piaget present his scheduled speech on "the child," because the African delegations were adamant in their refusal to sit in the presence of Portugal, a state declared guilty of inhumanity, despotism,

to undergo significant modification in the subsequent decade.[39]

Reflections on these records suggest not merely that African governments have their own national interests, as do all other states in the world, but also that they perceive and pursue their interests in certain peculiarly African ways.[40] Indeed, the entire complex of "the African Personality," which Occidental scholars are often inclined to belittle, but which Africans take seriously, is commonly understood to be a function precisely of diplomatic behavior in the forum of world affairs—a connection of ideas that Nkrumah had been the first to make explicit. That is to say, it is success in this realm rather than in that of economic development, for example, or of social harmony at home, which is being sought and appreciated with greatest eagerness. The fact that it has also been attained in considerable measure—and this in a relatively short span of time by "new" states that are poor and devoid of material power —adds poignancy to any inquiry into the characteristics exhibited by African diplomacy, specifically as these have become manifest in international disputes and conflict situations.

One of the most notable traits to emerge from such an inquiry is the perseverance that is consistently displayed in handling selected race-related issues—to be exact, the implementation of Article III, clause 6 of the OAU Charter.[41] On other controversial issues, by contrast, Afri-

---

and abhorrent policies. The meeting ended in shambles. A study of the meetings held by other United Nations councils, commissions, and specialized agencies shows no significant deviation from these patterns.

[39] See World Health Organization, *Handbook of Resolutions and Decisions of the World Health Assembly and the Executive Board*, Vol. I: *1948–1972*, 1st to 25th World Health Assemblies; 1st to 50th sessions of the Executive Board (Geneva, 1973), pp. 319ff.; 353ff.

For official pronouncements by the Regional Committee for Africa on the matter of Portugal's presence in Africa, see the committee's resolutions AFR/RC15/R2 adopted on 9 September 1965 and AFR/RC17/R2, which was brought before the Twenty-First World Health Assembly in March 1968. For a report on the Ninth Session of the Economic Commission for Africa (ECA), held in Addis Ababa in February 1969, see UN Press Release ECA/333, 13 February 1969. A resolution adopted on this occasion (document E/CN.14/Res. 194) recommends that the inhabitants of Angola, Mozambique, so-called Portuguese Guinea, and Namibia be represented and that the OAU should nominate these delegates.

[40] For a somewhat different approach see Vernon McKay, "International Conflict Patterns," in Vernon McKay, ed., *African Diplomacy; Studies in the Determinants of Foreign Policy* (New York, 1966), pp. 1ff., particularly p. 3.

[41] The same disposition appears, however, also to have governed the first phase, at least, of the 1961 trade negotiations with the European Economic Community, which originated in the need for economic cooperation and assistance rather than in the desire to further the cause of enmity. For a detailed account of the negotiations that led to the Yaoundé Convention see I. William Zartman, *The Politics of Trade Negotiations between Africa and the European Economic Community: The Weak Confront the Strong* (Princeton, 1971), pp. 24ff., 30; but see pp. 58ff. for some reservations. Compare *infra*, Ch. 19, with several analyses of traditional African approaches to commercial negotiations.

can governments have felt free to waver and change their stands, and this in global as in inter-African relations. In fact, abrupt shifts, even total reversals of position, have been so common on the part of diplomatic establishments representing this particular region as to warrant the conclusion that pragmatism or opportunism rather than principle is the norm.[42]

The mode of thought that allows inconsistencies in action, thought, or verbalization, naturally also sanctions what Occidental minds tend to view negatively, namely disregard for precedent and for the integrity of an abstract proposition, a legal rule, or a constitutional provision.[43] In other words, it explains why that which in our perception appears irresponsible or illogical is often accepted in the African context as perfectly normal, either as an intellectual construction, a practical response to an existing crisis, or simply as a change of mood. Neither the incidence nor the outcome of conflicts involving African parties is therefore readily predictable, all the more so as African governments themselves have so far not appeared to engage in long-range foreign policy programming or contingency planning.[44]

The twin ideas of making commitments ahead of time and of intending to abide by them are greatly discouraged, furthermore, by the predominance of the personality factor in the conduct of all government, notably that of foreign affairs.[45] However different the characters of individual national leaders—for example of Kenyatta, Kaunda, Nyerere, Mobutu, and Amin—all reflect, albeit in varying degrees, the general African

[42] For records that justify these conclusions see the minutes of different international conferences and authoritative news releases. Also see Hovet, *Africa in the United Nations*, pp. 218ff.; Zartman, *International Relations in the New Africa*, pp. 53ff. points out that, for the most part, intra-African foreign policy has little to do with domestic needs or purposes, and that it is usually a struggle for external influence for its own sake—often with no other observable criteria than whim, emotion, or accident. The language of "the national interest" is nonetheless kept alive, although it may have neither reality nor meaning. See pp. 60ff. to the effect that policy papers are little used by West African governments, and that, for example, no serious preparations had taken place for summit conferences except for the holding of a few meetings by the Monrovia-Brazzaville bloc of states; see pp. 111 for charts that show just when and where the stress was placed on personal relations.

[43] Nothing in this discussion is meant to suggest that Occidental governments always abide by the principles they profess.

[44] This point has been established by Zartman's research as far as West Africa is concerned. See *International Relations in the New Africa*, p. 66 and citations given *supra*, note 41. A review of the trade negotiations with Europe, however, seems to justify certain qualitative differences between African states: whereas the Nigerians are said to have understood the rules of the negotiations, the East Africans did not. At any rate, the latter were engaged in trying to change the rules rather than apply them for the attainment of objectives. Zartman, *The Politics of Trade Negotiations*, pp. 64ff.

[45] *Supra*, p. 28.

psycho-cultural order and thought world that has brought them forth; and in this respect it cannot be said that the "new" generation of governors is much different from that which presided over the early years of independence.[46] It bears remembering also that Africa's presidents have broader discretionary powers, and therefore greater options for changing or reversing course, than heads of state in culture regions in which the notion of the national interest is well developed. For the duration of their stewardship—and this again is unpredictable, for reasons cited earlier—they thus personify their states. This important reality, which is clearly recognized in the conception of the OAU as an organization rather of "Heads of African States and Governments" than of states or peoples, explains why treaties can be viewed, officially or unofficially, as interpersonal pacts[47] that do not have to be considered binding on successors. Most importantly for the purposes of this discussion, it explains why approaches to interstate conflicts or disputes are apt to be manifestations of the ruling personality's ever-changing needs—including the need for political and physical survival—and why they usually reflect rather faithfully his shifting personal enmities and suspicions.

African conflict diplomacy, then, is essentially personal, situational, and behavioral. It is also, and for these very reasons, quite combative in tone and thrust, even if not always in intent, as the records of numerous conferences and negotiating sessions show. For example, the Nigerian delegate staged a personalized verbal attack on the representative of the director general of UNESCO during the 1964 meeting of the International Conference on Public Education in Geneva, charging that the latter was personally responsible for leading the meeting into error, since he insisted on the need for legality. Likewise, a torrent of abusive language was showered upon the United States during a 1964 session of the United Nations Security Council, when the rescue of white hostages in the Congo was luridly described by African delegates as "a murderous operation" and "massive cannibalism."[48] The intense resentment of white regimes in Africa and of Western interferences in African affairs

---

[46] See Bozeman, *The Future of Law in a Multicultural World*, pp. 85–120, and 169ff. for the view that the new political elites are less Westernized and more consciously African than the preceding ones.

[47] See *infra*, Ch. 19 B, for a full discussion of traditional pacts.

[48] See text of Statement on the Congo Question, United States Mission to the United Nations, Press Release no. 4479, December 14, 1964. See also the proceedings of a symposium on African diplomacy as summarized in McKay, ed., *African Diplomacy*, p. 194, during which reference was made, first, to a newspaper headline in Ghana that proclaimed: "BRITAIN MURDERS HAMMARSKJOLD," and second, to an episode in which "[the] Somalis declared *persona non grata* a Ghanaian Ambassador to Somalia who denounced an American journalist as 'this pink, cancerous, leperous neocolonialist of a woman' because she had publicized a strain in Ghana-Somalia relations."

was of course a determining factor in both instances. Accusatory or insulting language of the kind here employed has, however, been equally common in exchanges between African governments. In fact, reliance upon militant idioms of discourse is today one of the generally accepted aspects of intra-African communications[49]—and one, it is important to note, that does not necessarily make either for physical aggression or for lasting enmity and conflict. One cannot, therefore, explain its incidence as due exclusively to the internal environment of stress in which African diplomacy operates in modern times, all the more so as less aggressive diplomatic styles are also deployed in such conditions. The real source of this particular dimension of African verbal behavior is to be found in certain very complex cultural traditions that are the subject of investigation in a subsequent chapter.[50]

Modern approaches to conciliation and the lessening of tensions in inter-African relations are as uniquely African as the manifestations of conflict and hostility to which they are addressed. Contrary to preferred Western patterns, they do not and cannot stress the need for enduring bilateral or multilateral accords. The diplomatic records are certainly replete with alliances and counteralliances, but these have proved to be shifting, short-term, and unreliable, partly because of continuous fluctuations in the identities and orientations of governments, but mainly because a body of mutually binding norms of inter-African communications is missing. As Dr. John Karefa-Smart of Sierra Leone pointed out in the course of a discussion on African diplomacy, even "the very notion of 'foreign policy' is of secondary importance in Africa; it is significant primarily in connection with the necessity of U.N. membership, and in the receiving and sending of diplomatic missions as an external evidence of independence and national sovereignty."[51]

In this cultural context it is not surprising, first, that efforts to settle or mitigate disputes are as situational as the occasions that call them forth, and second, that the OAU Charter recommends precisely this approach by providing a system of institutionalized persuasion. That is to

[49] Compare Ali A. Mazrui, "Anti-Militarism and Political Militancy in Tanzania," pp. 269ff. on Tanzania as the vanguard of militancy, the militarization of Tanzanian political rhetoric, and the neomilitaristic rendition of such concepts as self-reliance and economic development that is found in the Arusha Declaration of February 1967. On the general significance of the Arusha Declaration see also Henry Bienen, *Tanzania; Party Transformation and Economic Development* (Princeton, 1970). For other references to mutual vilification, see Zartman, *International Relations in the New Africa*, pp. 57ff., 77.

[50] *Infra*, Ch. 10, 11, 17. Compare in this respect McKay, ed., *African Diplomacy*, pp. 194ff., where such an "investigation of traditional African characteristics of 'verbal violence,' such as the use of shrill exhortations, accusations, slogans, and vindictives" is recommended.

[51] *Ibid.*, p. 201; for a similar view, *ibid.*, p. 180; cf. also Thiam, *Politique étrangère des états africains*, p. 71.

say, in this respect as in others previously mentioned, it was clearly recognized by the architects of the organization that patient palavers under the auspices either of diplomacy, mediation, or the good offices of bureaus and other intermediaries were more in line with African custom and tradition[52] than resort to law and judicial settlement—methods perfected in the West and incorporated in the United Nations Charter.[53]

The OAU peace-making provisions have been invoked on several occasions in the organization's history, most frequently when neighboring states were at odds with each other on the subject either of frontiers or of interference in domestic affairs. And in these situations the mediating mission has usually been entrusted to an impartial head of state, as, for instance, when Houphouet-Boigny acted as middleman between Niger and Dahomey; when Kaunda presided over a meeting between the leaders of Kenya and Somalia in 1968; when Kenyatta mediated one of several disputes between Uganda and Tanzania; and, in regard to the same parties, when Somalia was asked to work out an agreement for the settlement of these hostilities. A dispute over frontiers between Guinea and Senegal was, by contrast, discussed by the two governments at Monrovia in the neutralizing presence of several of their neighbors, and the stubborn border controversy between Ethiopia and Somalia, which had resisted many attempts at conciliation in the past, was referred to a "Good Offices Committee" comprising Tanzania, Sudan, Lesotho, Nigeria, Liberia, and Senegal when the OAU met in Addis Ababa in May 1973.[54] This tenth African summit meeting also provided an occasion for Emperor Haile Selassie to conciliate Presidents Idi Amin and Julius Nyerere. A "peace pact" was duly signed, in accordance with which each party undertook to see to it that its territory was not used as a base of subversion against the other; that Uganda would accept responsibility for the deaths of twenty-four Tanzanian nationals, and would not demand the eviction from Tanzania of Obote, Amin's predecessor; and

[52] *Infra*, Part VI, esp. Ch. 18, for discussions of these modes of conciliation.

[53] See Article III, paragraph 4 and Article XIX of the Charter. Neither of these articles provides for resort to juridical settlement or mentions the International Court of Justice. For a discussion of these discrepancies, see the *Report on the Peaceful Settlement of International Disputes* (as cited *supra*, Ch. 2, note 3), pp. 27ff., 45, 110ff., 185, 224. See also Hovet, *Africa in the United Nations*, ch. 4, on "unity through persuasion"; *ibid.*, p. 88 on a 1960 session of African United Nations delegates on the subject of the Congo, during which one state had it announced that it would abstain in the forthcoming vote. Another thereupon threatened this member by announcing that in response to such a deviant vote all other members of the group would in future oppose the erring state on every possible occasion.

[54] For discussions of the OAU meeting and this agreement, see *To the Point*, 2, No. 12 (June 16, 1973), 25ff.; 2, No. 14 (July 14, 1973), 29 on the effect of the accord upon the East African community. See also the *New York Times*, May 27 and May 31, 1973.

that Ethiopia would continue to use its good offices in the implementation of the accord.

Such efforts to mitigate or resolve tenacious interpersonal or interstate disputes contrasted, at the tenth OAU meeting, with the open acknowledgment of long-smoldering dissensions between black Africa on the one hand, and Arabized North Africa on the other. Representative Africans certainly realize now, as they did in former times, that the interpenetration of Arabs and Negroes, and of Islam and animism or Christianity, is not only an historical fact, but also an ongoing, irreversible process,[55] and that it is not possible, therefore, to isolate the African destiny from developments in the Middle East, or the Organization of African Unity from the Arab League. North African states have thus been members of the African regional organization from its inception onward, and disputes in their midst have at times been handled in the framework of the Charter's conciliation provisions.[56] The view has also been expressed rather freely in non-Islamic African circles, however, that the Arab factor is apt to have adverse effects on the cause of Pan-African unity, if only because the North African states have long been known to give priority to "Arabness" rather than to "Africanness."[57] This awareness—together with the experience of the long civil war in the Sudan (during which hundreds of thousands of southern blacks lost their lives); and with the interventionist roles played by the governments of Algeria and Morocco in the southern areas bordering their ill-defined frontiers, by a Syrian-backed Eritrean Liberation Front in Ethiopia's Red Sea province, and by Libya in Chad—had already contributed to an exacerbation of anti-Arabism, when the Libyan government of Colonel Quaddafi initiated particularly aggressive diplomatic moves with a view toward drawing black African states into the Arab anti-Israel coalition. As the proceedings of the 1973 Addis Ababa conference indicate, all manner of tensions were thus stirred up.[58]

[55] See *infra*, Ch. 7, 14, 19, for discussions of these relationships.

[56] The emperor of Ethiopia and the president of Mali (a Muslim) thus exerted themselves in the 1960s to facilitate a settlement of the border dispute between Algeria and Morocco. See Patricia Berko Wild, "The Organization of African Unity and the Algerian-Moroccan Border Conflict," *International Organization*, 20 (1966), 18–36.

[57] To this effect, see Dr. John Karefa-Smart in the proceedings of a discussion on "external political pressures" in African diplomacy. The Arab presence in Africa, he added, was a relic of colonialism comparable to European colonialism, and there is "no real conviction that we belong together." McKay, ed., *African Diplomacy*, p. 201.

[58] In conjunction with his accusation that General Idi Amin was guilty of genocide in having tens of thousands of Ugandans killed, Dr. Milton Obote (one of the original thirty-one signers of the Charter of the Organization of African Unity and the deposed head of Uganda) also charged that Libya and the Palestine liberation organizations had assisted in these 1971 killings. See the *New York Times*, May 27, 1973.

In the light of present and past realities, it is hardly likely that conflicts in Afro-Arab relations can be eliminated or appreciably affected by resort to the OAU or one of its subsidiary agencies of persuasion. And the same prognosis seems justified when it comes to the incidence of civil wars, rebellions, or wars of secession within African states. In these respects it became clear during the Sudanese war, the abortive Biafran war of self-determination, the bloody upheavals in Rwanda and Burundi, as well as at the occasion of secessionist attempts in Ghana,[59] that the OAU will refrain from mediating between antagonistic groups even when racial hatreds or power struggles contribute to the massacre or persecution of civilian populations and the unredeemable plight of refugees.[60] This disposition to nonfeasance conforms to the OAU Charter, and reflects a shared political concern for the preservation of existing states.[61] However, and in conjunction with the circumstance that human suffering on a vast scale has so far not elicited public sympathy, protest, or demands for ameliorative and preventive action, it also reveals that contemporary generations of Africans are morally and politically composed when faced with violent death and destruction in their midst.

The foregoing survey of modern African patterns of conflict and accord points to the conclusion that conflicts have become intensified in the last decades, both within each state and in relations between states. Specifically, one finds on the domestic scene that bitter ethnic divisions and interpersonal rivalries for power are taken for granted everywhere, and that the cause of social order is served almost exclusively by reliance upon authoritarian rule or military force. In other words, internal accords are in the final analysis functions of conflict-inducing factors.

[59] When members of an Ewe group calling itself the Togolese National Liberation Movement arrived in Addis Ababa in May 1973 in order to seek OAU support for the secession of Ghana's eastern region, they too were ignored, on the same ground. However, the specter of the Biafran case persuaded Colonel Ignatius Akyeampong of Ghana and General Etienne Eyadema of Togo to engage in direct negotiations. These resulted in the freeing of most of the Ewe chiefs and headmen who had been arrested by the Ghanaian government. See *To the Point*, 2, No. 15 (July 29, 1973), p. 73.

[60] See Hugh C. Brooks and Yassin El-Ayouty, eds., *Refugees South of the Sahara; An African Dilemma* (Westport, Conn., 1970), for several revealing accounts of the staggering dimensions of this problem. According to the report of the United Nations High Commission for Refugees, more than one million people had been uprooted from twelve African countries by April 1970. Not included in the count were persons displaced by civil war, nomads leaving impoverished homelands, and aliens expelled from former places of residence.

[61] *Supra*, notes 27 and 28 of this chapter, on the ambivalence of this concern. Reporting on the Monrovia meeting of April 1969, the *New York Times* (April 21, 1969) quoted Sir Louis Mbanefo to the effect that the OAU was ill-equipped to mediate between the opposing Nigerian factions because it was committed to the preservation of Nigeria's territorial integrity. Mentioning the United States, the United Nations, France, and West Germany, he expressed the hope that someone else would try a new peace initiative.

On the plane of relations between black African states, distrust and acrimonious competitions for continental and international leadership predominate. Here covert belligerent interventions across state boundaries are accepted as normal, but open warfare is avoided. Orientations toward nonblack governments within and outside Africa, and toward individual African residents of European and Asian origins, are suffused by xenophobia, and this complex of enmities is allowed ready expression in offensive speech and action, including war. Such behavioral responses are officially sanctioned by the OAU Charter as politically requisite to support modern Africa's uneasy unity. They are also hallowed, however, by precolonial African tradition, as a subsequent discussion is designed to show.[62] The expulsions of Asians, Americans, and Europeans from many African states, and the determined all-African efforts to eliminate the remaining white regimes are thus not only manifestations of modern nationalism or statements of just grievances. They are also present-day variations on the theme of the "carrier" or "scapegoat"—the stranger to the closely knit ethnic group whose very presence is automatically held responsible for whatever evil, failure, or misfortune the community is facing in a given moment. "To run the carrier out" was a morally valid injunction then, as it is now. Conflict, then, whether actual or presumed, violent or nonviolent, carries particular significance in present-day Africa as a constitutive force in political organization, a structuring element of unity, and as the main mode of communication between states and their political elites. Sharp dichotomies between conflict and accord, war and peace, or law and power are not favored in such conditions, whereas inconsistencies in reference, argument, and behavior of the type found troublesome in most Occidental circles are readily accommodated. In fact, the records bearing on these dispositions leave the overwhelming impression that Africans in all walks of life have a pronounced talent for living with different kinds of ambiguity and for tolerating or absorbing all manner of conflicts. Furthermore, they suggest strongly that ways of perceiving critical situations or experiencing tensions are guided by norms and values that are different from those considered dominant in the West.

[62] *Infra*, Parts IV and V.

· 4 ·

THE NORMS OF CONFLICT THEORY
AND THE FACTS OF
CULTURAL CONSCIOUSNESS

The study of conflict, its meanings, causes, and effects has preoccupied modern Western scholarship in many fields of learning, notably in political science, sociology, psychology, economics, and international relations. The recorded findings are quite various, but a review of the literature also points to certain convergent trends.[1]

The focus of inquiry in the last decades has been decidedly on social conflict and on war; and in respect to war, the accent falls heavily on ways of avoiding or ending war. The preferred time dimension is the present, with overtones of futurist concern, and the phenomena or data considered relevant for theory are encountered in the Occident, notably North America. Moreover, and quite in contrast to earlier thinkers,[2] conflict is generally seen negatively, as an unfortunate interruption of the normal flow of social life, a failure in communication, an aberration from patterns of rational behavior, or an unregulated, and hence illegitimate, transaction. It is usually not overtly associated with sentiments, values, or psychic states of being. The stress in most writings is, rather, on concrete struggles or overt episodes in which persons or groups of persons contend for tangible rewards. Only few conflict theorists today will be found ready to accede to Bernard's view that actual conflict may exist in latent form for years before there is a formulation of issues or a showdown or crisis; that it is a mistake, therefore, to limit our thinking about

---

[1] See Clinton F. Fink, "Some Conceptual Difficulties in the Theory of Social Conflict," *Journal of Conflict Resolution*, 12, No. 4 (December 1968), 412–460 for a review of modern theories, definitions, and usages of conflict-related terms; pp. 429ff. on some conceptual and terminological confusions; p. 456 for the definition of social conflict as "any social situation or process in which two or more social entities are linked by at least one form of antagonistic psychological relation or at least one form of antagonistic interaction."

[2] Georg Simmel, *Conflict and the Web of Group Affiliations* (Glencoe, Ill., 1955), and "The Sociology of Conflict," *American Journal of Sociology*, 9 (1903–1904), 490–525, 672–689, 798–811. For other broad contexts of inquiry see Robert M. McIver, *Society; A Textbook of Sociology* (New York, 1937); Lewis A. Coser, *The Functions of Social Conflict* (Glencoe, Ill., 1956), see especially his extensive commentaries on Simmel's work; and by the same author, *Continuities in the Study of Social Conflict* (New York, 1967); and Raymond W. Mack and Richard C. Snyder, "The Analysis of Social Conflict—Toward an Overview and Synthesis," *Journal of Conflict Resolution*, 1, No. 2 (June 1957), 212–248; pp. 227ff. on the functions of conflict.

conflict to its overt phase; and that we should instead accustom ourselves to thinking of latent conflict as going on day in, day out, in varying degrees of intensity, whether or not the issues are clearly formulated.[3] Yet, as the foregoing discussion of conflicts in modern Africa suggests, this approach is capable of accommodating the African phenomena, whereas the other does not.

The further question as to just which patterns, models, and norms form the context from which conflict is treated as a deviation, is seldom explicitly addressed. The texts suggest that we are here in the presence of some universal givens, which need only be alluded to by implication. Thus it appears that the norm of society is the modern industrial society of the West; that the norm of the state is the territorial democratic nation state of the West; and that the typical human being is a man functioning rationally in the economic environment of a twentieth-century Western society. These pervasive assumptions may explain why a recent volume containing no substantive references to non-American or non-European manifestations of "human conflict" could yet be entitled "The Nature of Human Conflict."[4]

Several factors explain the steady narrowing of frames of inquiry and research that has marked the history of conflict literature in the last decades. There is, first, the obvious, widely shared wish to ban uncertainty from scholarly quests and attain the security of theory—a goal that can be realized best if the number of variables is starkly reduced and if only those data are considered which can be readily quantified. Since conflict-related feelings, values, processes, and other intangibles resist quantification and storage in data banks, they have gradually become irrelevant. Primary attention is now directed instead to specific events sufficiently simple to be counted, compared, and unified in categories.

The second major cause of retrenchment and insularity is the preoccupation with the recent incidence of international war, notably as fought by the United States, and the strongly felt commitment to find ways of resolving or controlling conflicts that might lead to war. This particular syndrome of scholarly concerns, social values, and personal sentiments

---

[3] Jessie Bernard, *American Community Behavior; An Analysis of Problems Confronting American Communities Today* (New York, 1949), p. 106; also Kurt Singer as quoted in Fink, "Some Conceptual Difficulties," p. 434.

[4] Elton B. McNeil, ed., *The Nature of Human Conflict* (Englewood Cliffs, N.J., 1965). Conflicts in Africa and Asia are bypassed even in a chapter by two noted anthropologists, both specialists in certain non-Western societies. But see *supra*, Ch. 3, notes 8–18 for works by area specialists that deal with violence; also Robert A. LeVine, "Anthropology and the Study of Conflict; Introduction," *Journal of Conflict Resolution*, 5, No. 1 (March 1961), 3–15; Bohannan, ed., *Law and Warfare*. What is interesting and significant in this regard is the fact that findings by specialists are rarely used by generalists who are intent on building theory in the field of conflict research.

emerges rather forcefully from a searching analysis of the papers published in the *Journal of Conflict Resolution* between 1957 and 1968.[5] The major findings noted by Elizabeth Converse are the following: contributors stressed the issue of conflict control rather than conflict itself; they were nearly unanimous in their assumptions that violence is something to be avoided; the phrase "organized violence" carried the connotation of illegitimacy; and "international war" was the category of central interest. Conspicuously absent were inquiries into the antecedents to military aggression and the causes of war. Historical approaches were neglected, while statistical treatments were stressed.[6] And analogous

[5] Elizabeth Converse, "The War of All against All; A Review of *The Journal of Conflict Resolution*, 1957–1968," *Journal of Conflict Resolution*, 12, No. 4 (December 1968), 471–532.

[6] Compare Philip P. Everts, "Developments and Trends in Peace and Conflict Research, 1965–1971: A Survey of Institutions," *Journal of Conflict Resolution*, 11, No. 4 (December 1972), 477–510; p. 499 to the effect that "peace research itself," "United Nations problems" and "international organization" scored highest as research topics (namely, 67 percent, 66 percent, and 65 percent respectively). Also Berenice A. Carroll, "Peace Research; The Cult of Power," in the same issue of the journal, pp. 585–616; p. 599: "If there is any distinguishing common feature among the highly varied works in the field of peace research, it is an avowed commitment to 'peace' "; see pp. 585ff. on "conceptions of power."

For significantly different approaches to conflict and its management through bargaining, adjudication, or referral to collective security arrangements, see T. C. Schelling, *The Strategy of Conflict* (Cambridge, Mass., 1960), especially pp. 4–6, where the author suggests that viewing conflict behavior as a bargaining process is useful because it keeps us from becoming exclusively preoccupied with either the conflict or the common interest. To characterize the maneuvers and actions of limited war as a bargaining process is to emphasize, he writes, that, in addition to the divergence of interest over the variables in dispute, there is a powerful common interest in reaching an outcome that would not violate the protagonists' value systems.

For related insights into the art of bargaining, see Fred Charles Iklé, *How Nations Negotiate* (New York, Evanston, and London, 1964). However, both Schelling and Iklé seem to assume that every war must end. For the most complete treatment of this entire syndrome of issues, which is also replete with original insights and suggestions for research, see Wesley L. Gould and Michael Barkun, *International Law and the Social Sciences* (Princeton, 1970). See in particular pp. 225ff. on bargaining agents and peaceful settlement; p. 244 to the effect that war and other manifestations of violence have been and continue to be processes integral to both the maintenance and the change of international systems—a fact suggesting, the authors write, that the function not just of conflict but specifically of violence requires systematic investigation. And the same advice is given for the treatment of culturally diverse values (p. 216), particularly insofar as they may have a bearing on the universal applicability of international law, which is viewed here as an emanation of typically Western thoughts and values.

For similar approaches see Myres S. McDougal and Harold D. Lasswell, "The Identification and Appraisal of Diverse Systems of Public Order," *American Journal of International Law*, 53, No. 1 (1959), 1–29; Adda B. Bozeman, "Representative Systems of Public Order Today," *Proceedings*, American Society of International Law (1959), pp. 10–20; Adda B. Bozeman, ed., "Appraising the Impact of International Law upon Contemporary Political and Social Processes; Techniques and Conclusions," *Proceedings*, American Society of International

trends have come to dominate the general field of research in international relations. Commenting on the subtle but profound evolution from concern with the causes of war to the study of peace and the construction of "alternate futures," Alger could thus conclude in 1970 that participants in "peace research" (most of them North Americans and Western Europeans) have high value commitments to the nonviolent solution of international conflicts, endeavor to do work relevant to policy making, and stress "scientific work," including "systematic data-collection techniques and rigorous methods of analysis."[7]

The quest on the one hand for scientific precision and symmetric simplicity, and on the other for the gratification of strong moral impulses—incongruous as these objectives may appear to be—explains two other characteristics in modern conflict research: the reduction of politics to manifestations of economics, and the subordination of historically, politically, and psychologically crucial realities to rigid prefabricated systems of mental abstractions. The first trend is lucidly presented by Morgenthau, who finds that international conflict is visualized in contemporary theories of international relations as a special case of social conflict whose paradigm is economic conflict.[8] In such a theoretical scheme, he

---

Law (September 1972), pp. 32–61, notably papers by Hayward R. Alker, Jr., "Assessing the Impact of the U.N. Collective Security System; An Operational, Multicultural Approach"; and Bernard K. Gordon, "The Uses of International Law for Issue Identification and Conflict Resolution in Southeast Asia."

On the reluctance of new states to use the International Court of Justice and the neglect of judicial proceedings on the part of military and revolutionary governments, see Ibrahim F. I. Shihata, "The Attitude of New States toward the International Court of Justice," *International Organization*, 19 (1965), 203–222; also Robert L. Friedheim, "The 'Satisfied' and 'Dissatisfied' States Negotiate International Law; A Case Study," *World Politics*, 18 (1965), 20–41, where the conclusion is reached that the new, that is, "dissatisfied," states prefer not to rely on lawyers, have a distaste for expertise and detailed regulation, and experience difficulties in communicating with "satisfied," that is, Western states, whose representatives are at ease with legal vocabularies of thought and discourse. Valuable comments on the new states' objections to use of the International Court of Justice and international law in general—at least insofar as its rules were made without their participation—are found in Arthur Lall, *Modern International Negotiation; Principles and Practice* (New York, 1966).

[7] Chadwick F. Alger, "Trends in International Relations Research," in Norman D. Palmer, ed., *A Design for International Relations Research: Scope, Theory, Methods, and Relevance* (Philadelphia, October 1970), pp. 7–28.

[8] Hans J. Morgenthau, "International Relations; Quantitative and Qualitative Approaches," in Palmer, ed., *International Relations Research*, pp. 67ff. Morgenthau's critique of the quantitative approach also points out that since the aspiration for a pervasively rational theory is hemmed in by the insuperable resistance of the subject matter, the theoretician attempts to use the tools of modern economic analysis in a modified form so as to understand international relations. After all, he notes, concepts such as "systems analysis," "feedback," and "output" were first developed by economic theory, and the influence of Marxian economic models is still discernible.

writes, nations confront each other not as living historic entities with all their complexities, but as rational abstractions, after the model of "economic man," playing games of military and diplomatic chess according to a rational calculus that exists nowhere but in the theoretician's mind. Although wealth may be quantifiable (and even this with considerable reservations), power is not—least of all, one might add, the kind of power that continues to be recognized and respected in Africa south of the Sahara.

Retreat into closed systems of trusted norms or values often indicates the same intellectually isolationist stance. For scholars who "rest their hope for a diminution of international war on an increase in supranational institutions within, or even spanning, the international system"[9] are usually also concerned with planning the perfection of existing international systems or building models of new systems so as to prepare the realization of their hopes. Most of these "systems in the mind" are simplified conceptualizations of human nature and the real world environment,[10] and some have been constructed quite arbitrarily by selecting only such data from the records of Occidental civilization as would support the subjective value judgment that war should not be considered an acceptable or proper political instrument.[11]

[9] Converse, "War of All against All," p. 485; *ibid.*, pp. 485ff., for a review of "international systems" and "systems analysis" as treated by *Journal of Conflict Resolution* authors.

[10] For some poignant early warning signals see Harold Sprout and Margaret Sprout, "Environmental Factors in the Study of International Politics," *Journal of Conflict Resolution*, 1, No. 4 (1957), 309–328.

[11] Richard Rosecrance, *Action and Reaction in World Politics* (Boston, 1965), p. 100. This author purports to deal with international history and world politics, but confines himself to European history as the exclusive source of allegedly universal truths. In his chosen narrow framework he singles out certain periods of Europe's diplomatic history—all well documented—during which carefully selected "independent" states are found to have interacted in the context of several "systems." The major lesson of these "systems"—allegedly valid for the world at large —is that states are stable when there is no major war.

A European historian with wider interests must wonder just how classical Greece or Rome can be integrated in such a scheme. And it is, of course, obvious to anyone familiar with the histories of the Middle East, the Near East (including the European Balkans), southern Asia, eastern Asia, or Africa that the correlations between war and stability are different in these regions. Furthermore, in none of these cases would it be technically possible to apply the "Data-Making Procedures," "Master Lists of Events," and "Tables of Independent and Dependent Variables" that were presented by Rosecrance and his associates in several subsequent papers under the auspices of the "Situational Analysis Project" at Cornell University in 1972. In fact, it is doubtful whether the "scale for the measurement of cooperation-conflict in international events" is as valid for the behavior of European powers in the period 1870 to 1881 as the authors of the papers claim it is. (See Ronald Goodman, Jeffrey Hart, and Richard Rosecrance, "Methods and Data in a Situational Analysis of International Politics," and Jeffrey Hart, "Symmetry and Polarization in the European International System: 1870–1879"; being Papers No. 2 and

Where does Africa belong in any of these systems of models, norms, and values? Does it belong at all? Modern conflict theories do not profess to be applicable to Occidental societies only, yet they are obviously not constructed to fit African realities. One may also ask just how valid the theories are. For as scholars in the social and behavioral sciences intensify efforts to simplify their visions of political life so as to produce "theory," not only for each of their several disciplines, but also, perhaps even more emphatically, for the entire field claimed by the social sciences collectively, "stumbling blocks in the discovery of uniformities," long obvious to scholars working in the humanities, cultural history, and anthropology, are becoming increasingly apparent even in their own ranks—as David Easton remarks in a discussion of "the prestige and authority of theory."[12] One of the major impediments conducive to the "illusion of theory," this author suggests, is the deepening bias in favor of patterns deduced from Western political systems; for scholarship in systems analysis, he continues, is motivated by an overriding interest in "democratic systems and the way in which they come about."[13] Non-Western, nondemocratic systems, meanwhile—variously designated as transitional, developing, and by Easton himself as "exotic"—are being perceived and analyzed as political organisms moving ineluctably toward this known, established Western norm. All normative theory, he concludes, thus revolves today around dominant values taken from this concept of democracy. The hope of constructing "a simple over-arching theory" is therefore bound to remain "a remote ideal" as long as efforts are not made to enlarge the sample of political systems so as to include "all types of systems past as well as present."[14]

3, Situational Analysis Project, Cornell University, January 5 and 14, 1972.) This is all the more true as it is admitted in Paper No. 4 (p. 10) that the authors cannot really come to terms with the phenomenon of power. "Of course," they write, "some typical measures of power, such as national morale, or the quality of government, are not amenable to quantitative approximation and have therefore been left out." (Richard Rosecrance, Alan Alexandroff, Brian Healy, and Arthur Stein, "The Balance of Power: Theories in Search of Reality," Paper No. 4, Situational Analysis Project, Cornell University, November 1, 1972.)

For succinct critical analyses of recent "systems theory," see John J. Weltman, "Systems Theory in International Relations; A Critique," *Polity*, 4, No. 3 (Spring 1972), 301–329. Also, by the same author, "The Processes of a Systemicist," *Journal of Politics*, 34, No. 2 (May 1972), 592–611; and "Is There a Paradigm in the House?" *Orbis*, 16, No. 4 (Winter 1973), 1043–1056.

[12] David Easton, *A Systems Analysis of Political Life* (New York, London, and Sydney, 1965), pp. 15ff.

[13] *Ibid*.

[14] *Ibid*., pp. 482ff. Another eloquent critique of the modern use of western perceptions, norms, and models is found in Hugh Tinker, *Ballot Box and Bayonet* (Oxford, 1964), p. 2. At a somewhat higher level of sophistication, Tinker writes, the group known as the Princeton Behaviorists have attempted to analyze "the politics of the developing areas" by abstracting a model of "transitional politics";

The trends in systems analysis noted by Easton dominate much of political science and conflict theory, perhaps because these fields of thought are today heavily influenced by economic, notably Marxian, theory. This is particularly true of the widespread and persistent assumption that "new" states in Africa and elsewhere are fledglings, as it were, whose evolution toward maturity in political organization and behavior is determined more or less exclusively by economic development. Once the economic target has been reached, so the reasoning goes, these states too will fit the molds prepared for them by theory. Observations by specialists in African affairs that economic classes in the Marxian sense do not exist in Africa;[15] that terms carrying very definite meanings in European and American economic history cannot be readily used here,[16] and that our development norms imply deeply rooted concepts of time that have no equivalents in the African milieu,[17] do not seem to have con-

this term is applied to the contemporary situation of Asia and Africa, which are supposed to be in transit from traditional to modern political systems. But the Princeton Behaviorists insist that the essence of a modern political system is the element of competitiveness: that is, the evolution of a party system—or, more precisely, the operation of the two-party system of nineteenth-century Anglo-American political theory. Almost the whole of this debate about democracy in the new states has been conducted in terms of a comparison with the West, which is taken as the norm—the "control," we might say—and the experience of Asia and Africa is measured in terms of this norm. Where governments have assumed the Anglo-American mold, as in the Philippines, democracy is deemed to have succeeded; where there has been a marked variation from the mold, democracy has "failed" or has "failed to take root." If Western scholars can only approach Afro-Asian development in terms of their own shibboleths, then they are proving themselves as rigid and limited in their methodology as the Marxists.

[15] Lloyd, *Africa in Social Change*, p. 234, remarks in the course of discussing African party politics that in the Marxist thinking of many African leaders economic classes can provide no basis for rival political parties because they just do not exist. In the last resort, Lloyd notes, development policies have been determined more by the willingness of expatriate firms to invest and the generosity of international aid agencies than by the ideologies of the politicians. On the absence of evidence for the existence of "economic classes," see also Zartman, *International Relations in the New Africa*, p. 51.

[16] Paul Bohannan, "Land Use, Land Tenure and Land Reform," in Melville J. Herskovits and Mitchell Harwitz, eds., *Economic Transition in Africa* (Evanston, Ill., and London, 1964), p. 133, on the difficulty of using terms with very definite meanings in European economic history. On this general subject see also E. M. Chilver, " 'Feudalism' in the Interlacustrine Kingdoms," in Audrey I. Richards, ed., *East African Chiefs; A Study of Political Development in Some Uganda and Tanganyika Tribes* (London, 1959), pp. 378–393, in which attention is directed to the fact that the state systems of the Interlacustrine area (in the nineteenth century, at least), on the one hand, and those of Western Europe in the early Middle Ages, on the other, are structurally so different as to render improper the use of historical analogies—in this case the institutions of feudalism. On this subject see also *infra*, Ch. 5, n. 65.

[17] This is discussed *infra*, Chs. 5 and 6. Leonard W. Doob, *Becoming More Civilized; A Psychological Exploration* (New Haven, Conn., 1960), refers briefly to notions of time in what he calls "less civilized" societies. The stress here is on the American Indians; for cursory references to Africa and Jamaica see pp. 88, 185, 190ff.

duced to modifications of these normative assumptions. Nor has confidence in such projections been disturbed by reminders on the part of economists with expertise in Africa that "any attempt to apply to rural African societies concepts of underemployment like those of the International Labour Office which are derived from wage employment in the industrial nations, is full of pitfalls and not worth pursuing."[18] For in the African world, in which economic activities are totally enmeshed in religious, artistic, ceremonial, and other concerns, and in which the lines dividing work from leisure are blurred, it is difficult to know just what is "economic."

Predictions as to how groups of people will develop or behave are hard to make in these circumstances, as W. Beckerman explains: "People who believe that economists should be capable, provided they are smart enough and provided they equip themselves with the necessary gadgets, such as input-output tables, demand functions, . . . really to foretell the future are, to my mind, in the same category as members of ancient tribes who attributed similar powers to their witch doctors."[19] Models, too, are difficult to use, we learn from Harbison, since they depend upon the validity of the assumptions that have been made on the basis of empirical facts.[20] To the extent to which such empirical evidence is insufficient or not available, one must continue to rely on experienced judgment alone. And similar reservations are made by this scholar when it comes to comparisons of economic targets; if these are to be realistic, Harbison writes, they must be extended to include comparisons of social and cultural objectives.

Objective comparative evaluations of political developments require the same kind of corrective research. For Africa, this need has been lucidly exposed by Zolberg: "Africa is now uniformly viewed through the best lenses of contemporary comparative politics with a focus on political modernization, development and integration. Unfortunately, it appears that when we rely exclusively on these tools in order to accomplish our task, the aspects of political life which we, as well as non-spe-

[18] Social Science Research Council, *Items*, 22, No. 1 (March 1968). After commenting on the blurred dividing lines between "work" and "leisure," attention is drawn to the fact that leisure, again, is not always easily differentiated from illness. For example, when the Mossi are observed just sitting idly, according to our perception, they may actually be suffering from a debilitating disease. For the proposition that illness in Africa may not necessarily be measurable by our standards, see *infra*, Chs. 5 and 9.

[19] "Long Term Projections of National Income" (a lecture delivered in September 1962, available through OECD, Directorate of Scientific Affairs, Paris), quoted by Frederick Harbison, "Human Resources and Development" in UNESCO, *Economic and Social Aspects of Educational Planning* (Paris, 1964), p. 123.

[20] Harbison, "Human Resources and Development," p. 122, referring in particular to the Tinbergen-Correa model. To like effect see A. H. Hanson, *The Process of Planning; A Study of India's Five-Year Plans 1950–1964* (London, New York, and Bombay, 1966), ch. 13, p. 525.

cialists, see most clearly with the naked eye of informed common sense, remain beyond the range of our scientific vision."[21] And, with special reference to the incidence and structure of political conflict, Zolberg has this to say: "With little regard for the comfort of social scientists, the incidence of conflict and disorder appears unrelated to such variables as type of colonial experience, size, number of parties, absolute level or rate of economic and social development, as well as to the overall characteristics of regimes."[22] With theory and reality thus at odds, the conclusion is irrefutable that "there is little place for countries such as these in the conceptual universe of political science. Yet more often than not, these countries do persist."[23]

Other authors close to the African scene corroborate these judgments. Michael F. Lofchie thus writes that the trust shown by political scientists in "value neutral" theory—whether in the form of structural-functional analysis or modernization theory—is not well founded because, being sustained by models and patterns developed from Occidental experience, it is as alien to Africa as constitutionalism. What is needed today, this scholar suggests, is a set of concepts based on African history

[21] Zolberg, "The Structure of Political Conflict," p. 70.

[22] *Ibid.* To similar effect, see Henry L. Bretton, "Current Political Thought and Practice in Ghana," in *American Political Science Review*, 52, No. 1 (March 1958), pp. 47–48: "the overly zealous application to underdeveloped areas of research methods derived from experience in advanced, highly developed countries leads to the promulgation of wholly unrealistic theories."

See Lloyd, *Africa in Social Change*, pp. 163ff. on two rival models of society, the "functional" or "integrational" model, and the "conflict" model. The use of either, Lloyd writes (p. 165), tends to determine both the choice of data in describing society and the type of change that is discussed. See *ibid.*, p. 169 on the applicability to Africa of games theory. Although this theory provides a useful tool in understanding sociological situations of conflict, its ability to predict outcomes is vitiated by the complexity of these situations and by the number of independent variables involved.

See also Whitaker, Jr., *The Politics of Tradition*, where the validity for Africa of the unilinear model of change propounded by scholars of the Weberian school is seriously questioned. To like effect, see Paul Verhaegen, "Study of the African Personality in the Belgian Congo," in F. R. Wickert, ed., *Readings in African Psychology from French Language Sources* (East Lansing, Mich., 1967), p. 243: "Western peoples often consider their culture as the standard and normal, but is it not rather an exception? Admittedly an important exception, many aspects of which become the common property of humanity." See *ibid.*, p. 242, for Verhaegen's view of the relation between "the basic psychology" of a people on one hand, and the effects of "cultural transition" on the other, and for his definition of "the basic" in African culture: "Those characteristics that are dominant in the bush and remain obvious in even the most Westernized Africans are part of the basic equipment that African culture confers on its members and, as such, are worthy of our attention."

[23] Zolberg, "Structure of Political Conflict," p. 70.

and tradition; and this political scientists have so far failed to produce, with the overall result that we now have, in his view, a "theoretical vacuum."[24] And the same warning is sounded by Otonti Nduka's comment on "the gap between Western and indigeneous moral and legal systems."[25]

The disappointments thus registered in numerous fields of theory and normative thought bring to mind some probing questions that Richard N. Frye raised in the course of his exhaustive analysis of *The Heritage of Persia*:

> But have we not perhaps asked the wrong questions of the Orient in antiquity, as we still do today? One asked why the Orient remained behind the Greeks, as we ask why the Orient today remains underdeveloped. Is it not more appropriate to ask instead why the Greeks developed as they did, or why the Renaissance and the Industrial Revolution made the Occident what it is now? In other words, perhaps we should explain why the West is abnormal while Asia and Africa have developed as expected in the course of history. Then the West today would be over-developed rather than the East underdeveloped. These may appear to be glib words, but if we change our perspective, perhaps we can understand some things better in the present as well as in the past.[26]

At any rate, in regard to the modern West's projections of its major political, economic, legal, and moral norms upon African societies, it is clear in the 1970s that most of these norms have been either rejected or muted beyond recognition. No academic field is as vitally affected by these borrowing processes as psychology, for it is in this discipline that most standards and assumptions of what is "normal" or "abnormal" have been culled from patterns of personality set up in the Occidental culture realm. In fact, all processes of perception and modes of distinguishing between the real and the unreal, or the rational and the irrational, that make up the conceptual core of the sociology of knowledge, are commonly taken for granted as universally valid, even though they have actually been tested only in the life style of the West. African modes of perception, imagination, and thought, by contrast, are either not yet fully known in their authenticity, as concluded by participants in a seminar convened by the Regional Office of the World Health Organization

[24] Michael F. Lofchie, "Political Theory and African Politics," *Journal of Modern African Studies*, 6, No. 1 (May 1968), 3–15. See *infra*, Chs. 6–8 for elaborations on these themes.
[25] Otonti Nduka, *Western Education and the Nigerian Cultural Background* (Ibadan, 1964), pp. 108ff. On the development of law in Africa see Bozeman, *The Future of Law in a Multicultural World*, pp. 85–120 and authorities there cited.
[26] Richard N. Frye, *The Heritage of Persia* (New York, 1966), p. 151.

for Africa South of the Sahara in 1958,[27] or they may not be recognized as being different.

In attempting to understand psychiatric disorder among the Yoruba in present-day Nigeria, Leighton, Lambo, and their associates became convinced that there is a world of difference in the way various kinds of disorder are defined in the two cultures—that covering Europe and America, in which, as the authors put it, the discipline of psychology has its base; and the African system, in which psychiatrists trained in the West were attempting to identify "disorder."[28] The Yoruba, we learn from this particular investigation, do have a conception that corresponds substantially to what is known as "psychiatric disorder" in the West, but descriptions show few correspondences to the diagnostic categories of psychiatry. These findings, together with the realization that depression seems to be an unfamiliar concept, make it appear "possible that we have come upon some genuine cultural difference of some importance,"[29]—a conclusion greatly reenforced by the team's further observation that ideas of cause are radically different in the two worlds. In sharp contrast with psychiatry, all Yoruba, including the professional healers, were thus found to think of malignant influences, both superhuman and human, as the most likely cause of any sickness or disturbance.

These findings on the plane of psychic being, corroborated as they are by other analyses and impressions of modern African patterns of thought and sentiment, are organically related to the perception and experience of disorder on the level of social and intersocietal relations. They go a long way toward explaining why present-day African reactions to the incidence of conflict are significantly different from the norms taken for granted in Europe and America.

What has been suggested here about the precarious nature of officially accepted norms also seems true with respect to contemporary Western interpretations of values. For, even if one should find that processes of perception are everywhere essentially the same as those considered normal in the Occident, value orientations and priorities are almost certainly different. This particular conclusion, which was reached in 1943 by Dr. Erwin H. Ackerknecht when he reviewed the subject of "Psychopa-

---

[27] Bureau régional pour l'Afrique de l'Organisation Mondiale de la Santé, Seminaire sur la santé mentale en Afrique au sud du Sahara, *Rapport Final Novembre-Decembre, 1958* (Brazzaville, 1959), see especially pp. 44 and 70ff. Close collaboration between psychologists and ethnologists is here recommended if greater certainty in the field is desired.

[28] A. H. Leighton, T. Adeoye Lambo, *et al., Psychiatric Disorder among the Yoruba* (Ithaca, N.Y., 1963), pp. 102ff., "The Problem of Cultural Distortion."

[29] *Ibid.*, p. 112. See also Lloyd, *Africa in Social Change*, pp. 250ff. on modern West African modes of coping with tension, disturbance, and aggression.

thulogy, Primitive Medicine and Primitive Culture,"[30] has been argued
by many scholars in a great variety of ways and with reference to diverse
cultures.[31] The thesis does not imply that there is an easy way to reconstruct, establish, or define the vocabularies of basic values by which societies live. Nor does it suggest that comparative studies in this field are
at present amenable to reliable scientific treatment. However, if one accepts Albert's broad definition that a cultural value system represents
what is expected, hoped for, required, or forbidden, and that it may thus
be viewed as a scheme of criteria by which conduct is judged and sanctions applied,[32] it is possible to identify the focal values of a given society
by dwelling on issues such as these:

the prevalent mode of thought and its main concerns;
conceptions of the universe, the supernatural, and the order of man;
attitudes to time;
understandings of the meanings of life and death, and of health and
    disease;
man's relation to nature and the animal world;
factors determining human relations and the idea of "society";
economic activities and dispositions toward work and leisure;
determinants of political organization;
meanings attributed to "order," "power," "justice," "wealth,"
    "prestige";
the rights and responsibilities of man as an individual and as a member
    of society;
approaches to the alien and identification of the enemy.

[30] *Bulletin of the History of Medicine*, 14, No. 1 (June 1943). See *ibid.*, p. 55
for the observation that the very criterion of rationality that is generally assumed
may well be a delusion.
[31] See in particular Clyde Kluckhohn, "Values and Value-Orientations in the
Theory of Action; An Exploration in Definition and Classification," in Talcott
Parsons and Edward A. Shils, eds., *Toward a General Theory of Action* (Cambridge, Mass., 1951); and "Toward A Comparison of Value-Emphases in Different
Cultures," in Leonard D. White, ed., *The State of the Social Sciences* (Chicago,
1956). Melville J. Herskovits, "Cultural Relativism and Cultural Values," in
Melville J. Herskovits, *Cultural Anthropology* (New York, 1955); and Florence
R. Kluckhohn and Fred L. Strodtbeck, *Variations in Value Orientations* (Evanston, Ill., 1961), ch. 1.
[32] Ethel M. Albert, "Value Systems," in David L. Sills, ed., *International Encyclopedia of the Social Sciences* (New York, 1968), Vol. 16, 287ff.; for these definitions see p. 288; p. 290 for the reminder that "few languages have a general term
equivalent to 'value.'" Also see, by this author, "The Classification of Values: A
Method and Illustration," *American Anthropologist*, 58 (1956), 221–248. For
another discussion of the concept of "Values," see Robin M. Williams, Jr., in
David L. Sills, ed., *International Encyclopedia of the Social Sciences* (New York,
1968), Vol. 16, 283ff.

Findings under these titles are likely to indicate how conflict is experienced in thought and emotion, and on the planes, respectively, of social and intersocietal relations; which kinds of conflict are taken for granted, sanctioned, or required, and how they are to be expressed; and which, by contrast, must be muted or resolved. All modalities of fighting, including war, are functions of the understandings inherent in these norms and values, and the same holds for processes of bargaining or negotiating, and for the meanings assigned to such words as conciliation and peace. That is to say, both conflict and conciliation have to be researched and analyzed against the background of the total social system in which they occur.[33] Just as we cannot assume that African orientations to "conflict" are the same as ours, so is it unreasonable to believe that "conciliation" is desired, pursued, and attained in manners customary in the West. Internationally valid models for institutionalizing conflict resolution and general theories of mediation are therefore bound to remain as premature as the conflict models that have called them forth, until the world's diverse "total social systems" have been reliably mapped.[34] This

[33] Compare in this respect Mack and Snyder, "The Analysis of Social Conflict," pp. 225ff. for the view that conflict must be researched and analyzed against the background of the total social system in which it occurs, and for the reminder (Proposition 30) that international conflict has its own social context.

[34] For a critical review of modern conflict theory as it relates to resolution by third-party intervention, see Ronald J. Fisher, "Third Party Consultation: A Method for the Study and Resolution of Conflict," *Journal of Conflict Resolution*, 16, No. 1 (March 1972), 67–94. Most of the approaches here discussed, including Fisher's own model of third-party consultation, are highly theoretical constructions that rest on modern American life experiences and project typically Western hopes for locating techniques of "resolving" conflicts. See, for example, p. 88 to the effect: "It is difficult to see how conflict and conflict resolution can be conceptualized comprehensively without ethical considerations." However, Fisher also notes (p. 93) "that the development of the method would be enhanced by the materialization of eclectic, interdisciplinary theories of conflict. While the history of the study of conflict shows some promising general and descriptive steps in that direction, much contemporary work has tended toward the premature limitation and quantification of variables, with a resultant lack of applicability to the real world. For example, most of the recent models of cooperation and conflict discussed by Patchen (1970) are so oversimplified as to be of little use to an eclectic method of studying and resolving conflict."

For other theories requiring corrective adjustment to multicultural realities, see J. Galtung, "Institutionalized Conflict Resolution: A Theoretical Paradigm," *Journal of Peace Research*, 2, No. 4 (1965b), 348–396; J. W. Burton, *Conflict and Communication; The Use of Controlled Communication in International Relations* (London, Macmillan, 1969), and the same author's article, "Resolution of Conflict," *International Studies Quarterly*, 16, No. 1 (March 1972), 5–29; see, for example, p. 20 to the effect that many aspects of a conflict can be analyzed reliably by those without knowledge of the geographical, historical, institutional, and other structural and environmental features; that such knowledge may, indeed, only attract attention to some superficial differences between conflicts. For critical responses to this view see essays by Jean-Pierre Cot and Laura Nader in the same issue of the journal.

See Leonard W. Doob, ed., *Resolving Conflict in Africa; The Fermeda Work-*

has not been done. Furthermore, peace research, as pursued in the recent past, has been instrumental in obscuring the incontrovertible fact that war is a generally accepted political instrument in all parts of the modern world, including Africa south of Sahara. Also screened from the modern theoretician's field of vision is the related reality that fighting is a highly valued activity in many if not most societies, and that, as Simmel put it, victory is "the simplest and most radical sort of passage from war to peace," whereas conciliation, defined by him as "a removal of the roots of conflict," is difficult to effect and often appears as "a purely subjective method of avoiding a struggle."[35]

Common norms and values, then, are missing when it comes to conflict in the modern world. An appreciation of this phenomenon in any given society therefore presupposes an effort to understand the entire life-style and culture with which it is associated. And "culture" in the

---

shop (New Haven, 1970). This interesting workshop, which was organized by Americans but included eighteen African academics, was assigned the task of producing solutions to the border conflicts dividing Ethiopia, Somalia, and Kenya by applying sensitivity training. Not surprisingly, it appears to have failed to attain the objective.

For some stimulating and promising approaches to this entire set of issues see Michael Barkun, *Law without Sanctions; Order in Primitive Societies and the World Community* (New Haven and London, 1968), especially pp. 36ff. on "Integration and Conflict." The term "conflict resolution," Barkun suggests (p. 39), is often a misnomer, for it implies conflict elimination, and the chimera of conflict elimination has in his view plagued the social sciences far too long. "An underlying thesis of this study," Barkun writes (p. 154), "is that activities that apparently are devoid of function or meaning seem so only because they are viewed in the perspectives of our own culture."

[35] Consult Simmel, "The Sociology of Conflict," p. 500, on conflicts stimulated exclusively by love of fighting; pp. 800ff. to the effect that the question as to just how struggle comes to an end is usually left open in the West. The main source of assumptions in this civilization, he notes, appears to be reliance on the general longing for peace. See p. 802 on the function of "victory," p. 806 on conciliation as a removal of the roots of conflict.

For a brief but apt critique of a modern theoretician's approach to conflict resolution techniques, see Laura Nader, "Some Notes on John Burton's Paper on 'Resolution of Conflict,'" *International Studies Quarterly*, 16, No. 1 (March 1972), 55, where it is pointed out that whereas Burton understands very well the importance of the perceptions of the parties, "he has not adequately considered culture as a variable to be considered in working out any set of universal components of conflict resolution techniques."

For affirmations of the need to study "culture" in the context of research in African diplomacy, see Robert A. Lystad, "Basic African Values" in William H. Lewis, ed., *New Forces in Africa* (Washington, D.C., 1962), pp. 10–24; and, by the same author, "Cultural and Psychological Factors" in McKay, ed., *African Diplomacy*, pp. 91–118; on research needs in this field, *ibid.*, 191ff. And in this respect see also Eugene Victor Walter, *Terror and Resistance; A Study of Political Violence, with Case Studies of Some Primitive African Communities* (London and New York, 1969), for several significant typologies of violence and of African social systems using violence. The main case study here is Shaka's use of terror for the purpose of expanding and consolidating the Zulu domain.

context of such an inquiry is best defined as a people's total equipment of ideas, institutions, and conventionalized activities, and as that which is most enduring about the ways of a society persisting in history.[36] Above all, it refers to those fundamental ways of thought that suggest just how conflict is to be perceived and managed.

Now, it goes without saying that all civilizations and conceptual systems undergo transformations in the course of history, usually in response to willed or unwilled encounters with other, culturally different, great ensembles. These processes of intercultural relations, too, must remain subject to watchful scrutiny if one is to ascertain just what has actually been borrowed; what, by contrast, rejected; and how the grafts have taken. Indeed, despite the fact that civilizations change more slowly than political systems, such comparative studies should be undertaken as often as one has reason to believe that the phenomena have changed.[37]

The revolutionary resurgence of cultural consciousness that marks developments in all "New States" that also qualify as "Old Societies"[38] is best understood in the framework of the aforementioned perspectives. With special regard to Africa, it cannot be denied that the essence of the contemporary condition is flux; for not only are the borrowing processes linking African to Euro-American and Asian culture worlds by no means over, but the much more complex quest for identity, through which present generations try to reach the authentic, essentially pre-European, African past has been steadily gaining in intensity since the attainment of independence. What is being sought, consciously and unconsciously, is the constant that resists the flux of time, proves resilient in the face of intrusions from without, and thus merits the appellation of being "African," on the plane of politics as well as on that of literature or religion.

[36] Robert Redfield, *The Primitive World and Its Transformations* (1953, repr. Ithaca, N.Y., 1958), pp. 61 and 85 for some of these definitions.

[37] J. J. Bachhofen, *Myth, Religion, and Mother Right, Selected Writings*, Ralph Mannheim, trans. (Princeton, 1967), p. 245 to the effect that different types of tradition arise in the course of the centuries, each according to a definite formative law; that, since transformations in habits of thought occur, the work of truly objective explanation must be done not once but as often as the phenomena change. Throughout his work Bachhofen stresses the importance of "Grundgedanken," or elementary ideas in each distinct civilization.

For stimulating modern approaches to this entire subject see Nelson, "Civilizational Complexes and Intercivilizational Encounters," pp. 79–105. For my own understanding of the concept of "culture" or "civilization" and of processes of intercultural relations, including cultural borrowing, see Bozeman, "Civilizations under Stress, Reflections on Cultural Borrowing and Survival," *Virginia Quarterly Review*, 51, No. 1 (Winter 1975), 1–18; "Do Educational and Cultural Exchanges Have Political Relevance?" *International Educational and Cultural Exchange*, 5, No. 2 (Fall 1969), 7–21; *The Future of Law in a Multicultural World*, pp. 3–33, and several case studies of cultural borrowing in *Politics and Culture in International History* (Princeton, 1960).

[38] Compare Clifford Geertz, ed., *Old Societies and New States* (New York, 1963).

Members of the educated Westernized elites were the first to express this urge to return to sources. When a wise and well-known African member of Parliament in the French Union was questioned about the supposed disappearance of Negro customs, he replied, "Custom may hide, it may bury itself beneath the feet of the newcomers, but it is all the more alive for that." Marcel Griaule, who told this story in the early 1950s, added the following comment

> This remark gives food for thought. In the first place it shows what a thin veneer the imported culture is. In military parlance, it is like a screen put up to deceive the enemy. In the large majority of cases it remains a debased culture, merely satisfying the vanity of an elite. In the second place, custom is obliged to hide because of an inferiority complex saddled on its devotees by the teacher. . . . But the fact that custom . . . buries itself in order to keep alive, means that it is holding itself in reserve, fully prepared, complete in its salient features and slightest details, ultimate body of an unconscious which, meanwhile, thrusts as best it can through the borrowed cultural crust.[39]

And a very similar explanation for the resurrection of the ancient orders was given several years later by Emily Radaody, a noted jurist in Madagascar: "Man cannot deny his past, he can only push it back into his unconscious: One day or another, however, it will return with a ven-

---

[39] "The Problem of Negro Culture" in UNESCO, *Interrelations of Cultures; Their Contribution to International Understanding* (Paris, 1953), pp. 357–358. Griaule's own prediction of the ultimate outcome of this process was pessimistic: this tactical position to which the harried society falls back in order to launch later counterattacks is, when all is said, a sign of decadence. Compare also UNESCO, *Asie, Etats Arabes, Afrique—Education et progrès*, Paris, 1960, p. 51, to the effect that African intellectuals proclaim with fervor the need for a return to sources. This will no doubt take place, whatever the great administrative reforms now in progress. The deepest African traditions are thus likely to maintain themselves even as they change form or appearance. For other early speculations on these themes, see Davidson Nicol (then principal of the University College of Sierra Leone), who remarked in 1961 that "the shift of intellectual life in West Africa is now becoming more and more provincial." Davidson Nicol, "The Formation of a West African Intellectual Community" (Ibadan, 1962), p. 13. This volume contains the records of a seminar sponsored by the Congress for Cultural Freedom and held in Freetown in December 1961.
Also see Report and Recommendations contained in Scientific Council for Africa South of the Sahara, *Mental Disorders and Mental Health in Africa South of the Sahara* (CCTA/CSA-WFMH-WHO Meeting of Specialists on Mental Health) (Bukavu, 1958), p. 89: "The emerging and educated African goes through a phase in which he is rather contemptuous of his original tribal background, but . . . in countries which have become free and autonomous such as the Sudan and Ghana, this tendency is declining." See also Michael Crowder, *Senegal; A Study in French Assimilation Policy* (London, 1962), who points out that the very Africans who had achieved the greatest distinction within the French cultural framework were the first to champion a return to the African past in search of their own personality.

geance. Man can get used to a new language, he may change his habits, he may even transform his substance. But his psychical instinctual substratum is beyond the field of applicability of law, and no will however determined can change this."[40]

Outsiders who follow, through observation and research, African quests for authenticity, and who are interested in gauging the likely outcome of these processes, cannot help but take note that the African culture world has come to terms with numerous alien systems of thought without surrendering its essence. One of the first Occidental scholars to develop this theme was Leo Frobenius, who concluded after tracing the influences of, for example, Byzantium on the political organization of Nupe, and Islamic forces on the indigenous Sudanic culture world, that the most striking psychical traits of Negro Africa include a truly remarkable capacity for absorbing foreign cultures and assimilating and transforming them into something definitely "African."[41] And the same overall impression was relayed in 1949 by Diederich Westermann:

African cultures have always manifested an extraordinary stability and power of assimilation. Neither the migrations of the Hamites and the political upheavals caused by them, nor the settlements of the Arabs and their devastating slave-raids; neither the Indian and Persian immigrants on the east coast, nor even the slave and alcohol trade of Europe have been able fundamentally to change the face of Africa. The Negro has remained and his civilizations have remained; the foreign elements which they adopted have been so completely absorbed and adapted that to-day they appear indigenous.[42]

[40] Quoted in L. Marx, "Notes de psychologie Merina," in Scientific Council for Africa South of the Sahara, *Mental Disorders and Mental Health in Africa South of the Sahara*, pp. 141–142. For a discussion of the relationship between Madagascar and the Merina on the one hand, and Africa and Pacific realms on the other, see Raymond K. Kent, *Early Kingdoms in Madagascar 1500–1700* (New York, 1970), especially chs. 1 and 2.
[41] Leo Frobenius, "Early African Culture as an Indication of Present Negro Potentialities," in *Annals of the American Academy of Political and Social Science*, 3 (November 1928), p. 163. But see in particular his monumental study *Und Afrika Sprach. . . . Wissenschaftlich erweiterte Ausgabe des Berichts ueber den Verlauf der dritten Reiseperiode der Deutschen Inner-Afrikanischen Forschungs-Expedition in den Jahren 1910 bis 1912*, 4 vols. (Berlin-Charlottenburg, 1912); Vol. II, *An der Schwelle des verehrungswuerdigen Byzanz*, 2, 192ff., 303ff., 324, for some interesting comments.
S. F. Nadel restates some of Frobenius' findings in *A Black Byzantium; The Kingdom of Nupe in Nigeria* (London, New York, Toronto, 1942), and *The Nuba, An Anthropological Study of the Hill Tribes in Kordofan* (London, New York, Toronto, 1947). See *infra*, Ch. 7, n. 32.
[42] Diedrich Westermann, *The African To-Day and To-Morrow* (London, 1949), p. 131. For numerous astute observations of interactions between Negro and Muslim systems of thought, behavior, and organization in the nineteenth century, see

On the level of present-day politics, meanwhile, two contrary yet interrelated trends can be delineated. Since each separate state is now being guided by its governing regime to seek the lost "authenticity" of its precolonial past, and since this precolonial past was marked by ethnic and linguistic divisions as well as by enmity and violence in intergroup relations, instability and conflict have to be accepted as part of the communal legacy. That is to say, the return to Africanism on such local scenes as Zaire, Uganda, Chad, or Nigeria brings in its stride not only the rehabilitation of traditional religious practices, social rites, leadership roles, and modes of speech or of naming persons, but also the reassertion of old antagonisms that are not susceptible to control by agencies of the "modern state."[43] Culture consciousness in the context of statehood would thus be an entirely negative, frustrating, and ultimately inconclusive sentiment if it could not be integrated, sublimated, or neutralized in the form of a higher cultural consciousness. And such manifestations of an Africanism transcending space and state, whether rendered in the language of Pan-Africanism, negritude, the African Personality, African

---

Henry Barth, *Travels and Discoveries in North and Central Africa*, 3 vols. (New York, 1857–1859).

Scholarly acknowledgments of the survival of African traditions are too numerous for extensive listing. See, for example, Kenneth Little, "African Culture and the Western Intrusion," *Journal of World History* 3, No. 4 (1957), 941–964, who says that even a cursory examination of the facts of Western contact is sufficient to show that there is no such thing as the complete disintegration of African culture. On the contrary, Little writes, it is evident that a number of indigenous institutions, particularly kinship, are extremely viable, even in the most unfavorable circumstances. To the same effect see Lloyd, *Social Change in Africa*, p. 314, who adds that townsmen, too, find security and recreation in the ethnic associations. On this subject also Hortense Powdermaker, *Copper Town: Changing Africa; The Human Situation on the Rhodesian Copperbelt* (New York, 1962). Thomas Hodgkin, *African Political Parties; An Introductory Guide* (London, 1961), observes that modern political parties in Africa can be understood only if preparty forms of organization—from which they usually arose—are understood. See also Apter, "Nkrumah, Charisma and the Coup," p. 790. Commenting on conditions in Ashanti (Ghana) he refers to the resilience of an earlier generation of Ashanti and the continued strength of traditional loyalties. See, to like effect, the analyses by William Tordoff, *Ashanti under the Prempehs 1888–1935* (London, 1965), p. 361; Dennis Austin, *Politics in Ghana 1946–1960* (London, 1964); and Richard Wright, *Black Power; A Record of Reactions in a Land of Pathos* (New York, 1954), Part III, "The Brooding Ashanti." For another treatment of the "identity crisis," see Aristide R. Zolberg, "In Search of Seraphima," *Africa Report*, 12, No. 7 (October 1967), 62–66; and by the same author, "The Structure of Political Conflict in the New States of Tropical Africa," pp. 70–71, where the view is expressed that values, norms, and structures have survived to a significant extent everywhere, even where their existence was not legally recognized during the colonial era.

[43] On the reassertion of old antagonisms as a source of violence in new states, see Clifford Geertz, "The Integrative Revolution; Primordial Sentiments and Civil Politics in the New States," in Geertz, ed., *Old Societies and New States* pp. 109, 111, 125.

Socialism, or the Organization of African Unity, have certainly not been lacking. Indeed, one of the three topics that came up most frequently in the planning sessions for the OAU was the cultural base of African solidarity and its relation to the precolonial past and to prehistory.[44] Wars and disputes may thus pit state against state, contribute to the fragmentation of a nation, or threaten it with extinction, yet leading spokesmen of all factions and representatives of greatly various linguistic and ethnic communities continue to be in ready agreement on propositions such as these:

> The great majority of our masses has remained African, original and authentic, without the varnish of French, English, or any other alien culture. . . . To speak of African unity is to speak also of the restitution of all our moral and cultural values.
>
> (M. François Tombalbaye [former President of Chad] at the Summit Conference of Independent African States in Addis Ababa, 1963)

> The African Personality is primarily the resultant of a community of history, traditions and values, which throughout the centuries has gradually established itself in our lives. This heritage does exist, and its existence constitutes its primary virtue. We have become conscious of it, and this consciousness constitutes its second virtue. A certain language of culture (different from any the West has taught us) has emerged from our common historical experience. We are now discovering it, and this discovery constitutes its third claim to virtue. The dangers and imperatives of modern society compel us to accept joint responsibilities, like the all-important obligation of organizing for unity. This constitutes the fourth virtue of the African Personality. We have devoted our activities to developing and harnessing the drive behind this personality.
>
> (Alioune Diop, "The Spirit of *Présence africane*")[45]

The viewpoints and attitudes which people adopt towards their political, economic, or social questions are influenced by their historical experiences and judgments [and these are] based ultimately on their

[44] Boutros-Ghali, *The Addis Ababa Charter*, p. 14.
[45] In Lalage Bown and Michael Crowder, eds., *The Proceedings of the First International Congress of Africanists* (London, 1964), p. 48. The term "African Personality" was first used by Edward W. Blyden in a lecture in Freetown in 1893; see Hollis R. Lynch, "Edward W. Blyden: Pioneer West African Nationalist," *Journal of African History*, 6, No. 3 (1965), 373–388, to the effect that Blyden wanted to create a consciousness of a West African community by fostering pride in the culture and history of the race. On modern African definitions and discussions of "The African Personality" see in particular the writings and pronouncements of Kwame Nkrumah; also Alex Quaison-Sackey, *Africa Unbound; Reflections of an African Statesman* (London, 1963), ch. 2; and cf. *supra*, Chs. 3 and 4.

world outlook which, conscious or unconscious, derives from their cultural heritage. The contemporary problems of Africa must be seen in the context of Africa's own cultural heritage. . . .

From such studies as have already been done on the religious beliefs and rites of different communities, it is possible to discern common religious ideas, and assumptions about the universe held throughout Africa, and which provide a world-view that may be described as African.

(K. A. Busia, *Africa in Search of Democracy*)[46]

The reality of traditional structures has survived intact in almost all modern African states.

(Christian Vieyra, "Structures politiques traditionnelles et structures politiques modernes")[47]

Africa's cultural consciousness is an undisputed fact today,[48] but the task of comprehending it in its uniqueness is difficult for reasons not encountered in the study of other civilizations. For one thing, this is a traditionally nonliterate world in which thought patterns, not having been reduced to writing by the Africans themselves, cannot be reconstructed by relying on any one of the many tools made available by the humanities and the social and behavioral sciences. For another, the unity of African culture projects the sum total of values, beliefs, and institutions that have been shared by countless generations representing a socially complex mosaic of heterogeneous elements in a spatially immense area —an area, furthermore, where present lines of political organization are fluid, and where neither anthropologists nor political scientists have as yet been able to agree upon generally applicable categories or classificatory schemes. These conditions explain why there is no single pathway to the psychological and intellectual substratum of African society, and why multidisciplinary approaches must be taken if one is to gain the necessary insights.[49] Indeed, as Young suggested after an exhaustive

---

[46] (London, 1967), pp. 1, 4.

[47] In Rencontres internationales de Bouaké, *Tradition et modernisme en Afrique noire* (Paris, 1965), p. 211.

[48] The "cultural revolutions" in behalf of "Africanization" and "authenticity," and against modern, notably Western, education, Christianity, and laws and customs of European origin, which have swept over some African nations—notably Chad, Zaire, and, in significant respects, also Kenya, Ethiopia, and Uganda, occurred in the 1970's, after the present book had been completed. These movements, which include the restoration of precolonial tribal rites and institutions, confirm some of the theses presented in the foregoing pages.

[49] Compare Marcel Griaule for the view that priority in research is at this time rightly assigned to an examination of African thought. "One obstacle (to a meaningful appreciation of Negro culture) is the diversity of the various groups in Negro Africa, which form as it were a mosaic of heterogeneous elements, each demanding lengthy study. But the greatest difficulty is still the inscrutability of the

analysis of modern Congo politics, there may be no escape from the requirement of an adequate application of political intuition.[50] And the same cautioning advice was given in the nineteenth century by Dr. Henry Barth, one of the greatest African explorers: "Any writer who attempts to recall from obscurity and oblivion the past ages of an illiterate nation, and to lay before the public even the most elementary sketch of its history, will probably have to contend against the strong prejudices of numerous critics, who are accustomed to refuse belief to whatever is incapable of bearing the strictest inquiry."[51]

The following, then, is an attempt to isolate the major structuring principles in African life and thought that justify references to the region as a politically and culturally distinct zone, in order to locate the constant themes in African approaches to conflict and its resolution or control. The discussion is structured so as to bring into play two general assumptions already announced in the preceding outline of the Western design, namely, that present modes of politically relevant behavior are understood best if past patterns are known, even if the latter are explicitly repudiated by the living. Second, that there is an organic relation between the inner normative order of a given society and that society's approach to its external environment; or, to put it differently, that the conduct of international relations is, in the final analysis, a derivative of values, dispositions, and institutions that control domestic life. This means that the latter have to be comprehended before the former can come into view.

Negro world which, while willing to reveal the outward aspects of its institutions and techniques, is at pains to conceal its philosophy and metaphysics, i.e. its inner thought, the only factor that is of any ultimate significance for the organization of the world today." "The Problem of Negro Culture," UNESCO, *Interrelations of Cultures*, p. 359.

[50] Young, *Politics in the Congo*, Appendix, "Note on Methodological Assumptions," pp. 602ff. This author also suggests that some of the tools made available by the behavioral mood of American political science have not absorbed or come to terms with change and flux, which he views as the main vectors in African politics today.

[51] Barth, *Travels*, II, 15. And see the works of another outstanding explorer of the African mind, Leo Frobenius, in particular *Das Sterbende Afrika, Die Seele eines Erdteils* (being Vol. v of *Erlebte Erdteile*) (Frankfurt-am-Main, 1928), pp. 19ff. for a brief outline of his approach.

PART III

AFRICA SOUTH OF THE SAHARA: SHARED CULTURAL REALITIES

· 5 ·

NONLITERATE THOUGHT AND
COMMUNICATION

African modes of thought about everything, including conflict and its control, have been shaped decisively by three separate but interlocking factors: nonliteracy, a concept of undifferentiated time, and tribalism.

Nonliteracy refers to a cultural condition in which language, not being reduced to some form of writing, is used exclusively for purposes of speech. Africa's approximately eight hundred separate communities[1] had existed for millennia in such a context, remaining resistant to literacy as represented by Egyptian, Arabic, and Coptic influences, until their destinies became indissolubly linked to the world of writing through European interventions. Today most of Africa's languages are alphabetized and the domain of orality is steadily being constricted. Indeed, the tendency is widespread to associate the diffusion of writing with the modern complex of development, and to identify nonliteracy with preliteracy by regarding it as a phase in the evolution toward the acceptance of the norms of literacy. This approach is justified if speaking and writing are viewed as mere techniques, or as purely technical aspects of a given language; if the stress is placed on the essential uniformity of human destiny and experience, and if attention is focussed upon the present and the future as the time in which the desired development toward conformity is expected to take place. It is insufficient, however, for those who distinguish between different cultures in the contemporary world, even as they may acknowledge certain trends toward uniformity; who regard language as an organic component of the culture and mode of thought with which it is associated, and who do not believe that the past can ever be completely overcome or superseded. From this point of view, the distinction between literacy and nonliteracy is not obliterated by the recent dif-

[1] For ways of classifying tribally and linguistically distinct communities in Africa see George Peter Murdock, *Africa, Its Peoples and Their Culture History* (London, New York, and Toronto, 1959), especially the "Tribal Map" at the back of the book; pp. 425ff., "Index of Tribal Names"; and pp. 12ff. for major linguistic divisions. See Joseph H. Greenberg, *The Languages of Africa* (Bloomington, Ind., 1963), "Index of Languages," pp. 163–171, maps pp. 172–178, and summaries of classifications; also, by the same author, *Studies in African Linguistic Classification* (reprinted from the *Southwestern Journal of Anthropology*, 5, Nos. 2–4; 6, Nos. 1–4; 10, No. 4) (Branford, Conn., 1955). Compare also Hugo Adolph Bernatzik, ed., *Afrika; Handbuch der angewandten Voelkerkunde*, 2 vols. (Innsbruck, 1947). See index of tribal and linguistic groupings for usages followed in the present work.

fusion of reading and writing skills, especially not in Africa south of the Sahara, where thought patterns, values, norms and institutions had been fashioned by exclusive reliance on the spoken, not the written word, and where a civilization continues to exist that African as well as Occidental authorities on Africa recognize as uniquely African. In short, and before discussing specifically African manifestations of thought and communication, it is important to suggest that nonliteracy or orality is not inferior to literacy. It makes, rather, for cultures that are totally different from, indeed antithetical to, those established on the base of literacy, as Maurice Houis points out in his stimulating essay on this subject.[2]

Literacy renders possible mental processes and human relations that cannot evolve in nonliterate societies; and the latter, conversely, are identified with conceptual orders and social institutions not found among the literate. What is to be noted most particularly is that all forms of writing and reading, whether of ideographic, syllabic, or alphabetic scripts, and whether associated with predominantly utilitarian or aesthetic, political or artistic, purposes, involve an abstract, highly intellectual activity that is unknown to speaking and listening under conditions of orality alone. Writing fixes meanings that in speech tend to remain fluid, and reading then requires a full and instantaneous comprehension of the fixed sign. Literacy thus invites the mind to a special kind of analytical observation: to be continuously conscious of the multiple relationships between signs and sounds on the one hand, and the ideas and objects they represent, on the other; to weigh every word, and to verify the particular functions of the word in terms of the idea it is supposed to represent. In brief, writing stimulates precision and differentiation in both thought and expression; stresses coherence and consistency in the thinking process; guards against drifting from one plane of reflection, or one frame of reference, to another; and promotes detachment and objectivity by disengaging the mind from the immediate experience and directing it, instead, to the level of conceptualization.

These implications of literacy make the interval between the inception of an idea and its expression in writing not only much longer but also infinitely more challenging for the thinking person than that which separates the idea from its embodiment in the spoken word. Furthermore, the actual activity of writing yields a record; and the individual's confrontation with this record tends not only to prevent forgetting, but also to induce additional forms of reflection, such as reviews, revisions, cancellations, and extensions of the ideas already written down: activities altogether beyond the reach or sphere of interest of nonliterate minds. Hence, literate thinking favors—although it does not ensure—the genesis

[2] Maurice Houis, *Préalables à un humanisme nègre* (reprinted from *Esprit*, November 1958; Dakar, Senegal, n.d.), pp. 8, 12, 18.

of well-delineated images, clearly distinct from each other, and it promotes, furthermore, an interest in the correlation, comparison, juxtaposition, classification, and unification of these distinct abstractions. Clusters or systems of ideas, theories, doctrines, and conceptual schemes, such as Kant's "categorical imperative," Confucius' "rule by benevolence," the Buddha's "fivefold path," Trotsky's "permanent revolution," "the quantum theory," "manifest destiny," or the "law of nations," are therefore possible only in literate civilizations. And in this vast category of cultures, some word systems—notably those derived from Greek and Latin—are, again, more favorable than others to the formation of compounds of ideas.[3]

The tendency to conceptualization, latent in all literate thought styles, is everywhere associated with certain risks that do not attend the thinking process in nonliterate societies. Its accent upon abstraction and analysis may smother faculties for mythical thinking, and arrest emotion; thought may crystallize too early or too rigidly in a definition or a concept; images may become too tenuous, brittle, or specious as a result of excessive differentiation and refinement; theories may degenerate into dogmas that impede the inception or flow of critical and creative thought. Other associated casualties may touch spontaneity, the sense of immediacy, and that ability to understand the whole of an occasion which often issues from an intuition uninhibited by the desire to dissolve a given whole into its separate components. Furthermore, certain arts of reaching other minds by speech—whether as developed in the subtle innuendo, the intonation proper to the moment, or the ringing phrase of oratory—may be neglected by minds attuned exclusively to literacy, so that few if any functions may remain to gestures and those other wordless languages that men perfect where writing cannot tempt them.

Writing, then, affects fundamentally the nature and quality of thought and its expression. Furthermore, it provides options for the fashioning of individual life and human relations that are not open to men in cultures governed by the spoken word. Through literate thinking and by recourse to wisdom stored in books, the individual may emancipate himself from actuality and proximity. He may lessen his dependence on society and increase his self-reliance by cultivating privacy, developing his

[3] Compare Redfield, *The Primitive World and Its Transformation*, pp. 82ff. See also Benjamin Lee Whorf, *Collected Papers on Metalinguistics* (Washington, D.C., 1952), pp. 6ff. Commenting on the subject of "natural logic," the relativity of all conceptual systems, and their dependence upon language, Whorf writes that if only Indo-European languages are considered, one finds a common culture, derived from the common Greek and Latin. (Whorf is obviously referring here exclusively to Western civilization.) The fact that modern Chinese or Turkish scientists describe the world in the same terms as Western scientists thus means only that they have taken over the entire Western system of rationalizations, not that they have corroborated that system from their native posts of observation.

imagination, and acquiring knowledge. And since writing assures the transmission of experience, he may immeasurably expand his intellectual horizon; for anyone knowing how to read and write can relate to the thoughts of men he has not known, just as he may project his own ideas to others he has never seen. A simple letter or a complex contract can thus transcend the limits to communication set by the spoken word. Reaching beyond the narrow bounds of physical association of the village or kinship group, it can link human destinies in different continents and cultures. And in the domain of public life, much the same is true of a decree, a law, a covenant, or a constitution. Whether in the ancient Near Eastern city state of the third millennium B.C., where kings addressed letters to their gods, even as they themselves were being petitioned by their subjects, or in the vast transterritorial and transnational commonwealths of the second millennium A.D., writing has everywhere decisively affected the style and pattern of all social and political organization, by supplying the conceptual and practical equipment for the creation and administration of cities, corporations, states, empires, and societies of nations, as well as for the conduct of all manner of social, political, and cultural relations. In brief, writing spans space. It is the great symbol of the distant and the far away, as Spengler has put it in a memorable passage.[4] Furthermore, writing suggests an orientation toward time that is unknown to nonliterate folk societies. For with the aid of script and the allied art of making accurate notations, men are able to chronicle adventures and events, each accurately placed and fixed in the flux of time. They thus acquire the power to distinguish clearly between the actual and all that once occurred, what yesterday was valid and what is new today; and so, also, to envision a future that need not be merely a repetition of either the past or the present. In such modes of thought "eternity" may become a concept apart from "time," and "history" may be disengaged as a particularized perspective upon time.

The spoken word, by contrast, relates directly to the moment in which it is uttered and to the immediate physical environment in which it is heard. Actuality and proximity, then, are the principal references here. Within these limits of effectiveness in time and space, speaking can faithfully convey not only the speaker's ideas and experiences, but also his actual state of being, his sense of the occasion, and his understanding of those to whom he speaks. Success or failure to communicate thus depends greatly upon performance in a given moment. And performance here is not necessarily measured solely by the quality of the thoughts expressed, since it impresses itself upon the listener together with the speaker's personality, gestures, facial expressions, tone of voice, method

---

[4] Spengler, *Decline of the West*, Vol. II (German ed., pp. 180, 184); (English ed., p. 151). Also Julian Huxley, *Africa View*, London and New York, 1931, p. 113.

of delivery, and other factors quite extraneous to the actual content of the communication. In fact, the speaker himself may upon occasion be more interested in creating a general social mood than in conveying a set of particular ideas. What comes across is thus not necessarily a particular thought or set of thoughts, but a syncretic comprehensive understanding of a situation replete with different kinds of meaning.

Viewed as a means of expression and communication, the spoken word is also fragile and vulnerable for certain other reasons. Not only can it be forgotten or ignored more readily than the written word, but in the normal course of events it is apt to be remembered differently by different listeners. And additional distortions of an original statement are apt to occur in the further stage of communication—that of relaying the spoken word with its accumulated associations to those who were not there to hear it. Nothing short of an exceptionally well-trained memory can thus guard a thought from complete oblivion or mutilation; a circumstance that explains why the twin arts of listening and remembering have usually been assiduously cultivated in nonliterate societies. Even there, however, where an official memory keeper is in charge of "storing" episodes and statements, records are bound to be unreliable from the Occidental point of view. The memory keeper is, after all, not the person who conceived the thoughts or spoke the words in the first place; and his span of remembrance, however extensive, is also severely limited, being subject, albeit in reduced measure, to the same impediments that are generally implicit in orality. All expressions of ideas or opinions are therefore, in the nature of this situation, so heavily encumbered with matter extraneous to the original message that the ideas themselves are apt to become casualties in the complex process of social interaction. Or, to put it differently, the authenticity of an orally communicated thought cannot be reliably secured. Indeed, it is doubtful whether concern for this type of authenticity can be generated at all in conditions of nonliteracy, since thought, speech, and society are inextricably intertwined in any given moment.

Two other general conclusions are suggested by this syndrome of oral communication—both to be elaborated in subsequent chapters. The time dimension stressed here is the present, whether in terms of the moment in which the word is first uttered and heard, or in those of the moment in which it is remembered, reexperienced, rephrased, and heard. For in this latter context, too, the past is experienced as the present. That is to say, clear lines of demarcation between past and present are not favored in these conditions.

Next, orality also suggests definite directives for the conduct of human relations in space. Since speech requires proximity, the distant and the far-away begin where the impact of the spoken word ends, whether in the experience of "actuality" or of remembrance. The socially and politically effective speech community is therefore bound to be small—a fact persuasively demonstrated by ethnographic and linguistic maps of sub-Saharan Africa—and the radius of intersocietal contacts is restricted as a matter of course.

The limitations implicit in nonliterate modes of expression have been offset by many ingenious compensatory devices. The flow of language may not be captured and retained, but such apt condensations of communally accepted wisdom as proverbs can easily be remembered and repeated in their authentic spoken forms, thus assuring some continuity of meaning in space and time. And similar purposes are served when ideas are rendered through allegory and allusion, symbols, rite, or gestures. Furthermore, most nonliterate peoples have developed music, rhythm, dance, sculpture, or design as languages of sound or vision that are capable of carrying a social consensus and allowing discourse around shared values and convictions. Indeed everything that is decorated, whether it is a basket or a face, is in this sense a kind of "writing" that transmits some socially meaningful message. Yet each of these modes of communication, whether used singly or in combination with another, is truly effective only in spatially limited contexts, and this holds even for drum languages—highly developed in several African regions[5]—that convey knowledge of significant events. In their essentials, then, most of these nonverbal means of expression can be viewed as variations on the elementary themes associated with speech: their signals are comprehensible only to the initiated; they usually convey clusters of interdependent ideas that cannot be disengaged from each other easily, and they transmit socially fixed truths, thus leaving only small margins for differentiated use and understanding.

The interaction between nonliteracy on the one hand, and modes of communication and expression on the other, can be observed and ascertained with reasonable certainty because it manifests itself overtly, and because it can be isolated from the general cultural environment in which the communication takes place, as well as from the particular persons who express themselves in this environment. The relation between nonliteracy and modes of thinking resists a similar treatment. This is so because thinking, whether in literate or nonliterate contexts, is not an overt process unless it finds some kind of expression. Linguists, physiologists, logicians, philosophers, psychologists, and other professional students of the subject have developed their various understandings of the phenomena involved in thinking, but they do not agree on just what "thought" is, how man thinks, or which different levels of thinking are

[5] See J. F. Carrington, *Talking Drums of Africa* (London, 1949), pp. 8ff.; see p. 30 for the reminder that there is no inter-African drum language.

to be distinguished. Furthermore, the reciprocal relations between thought and language are far from clear. No one seems to doubt that language has a formative impact on both the thinking individual mind and the culture and society associated with a given speech community. But we also know that the mind and the environment in which it functions are affected by factors other than language.

It is, therefore, probably impossible, even for literate thinkers in literate societies, to be absolutely sure in which ways their knowledge of writing has shaped their thinking processes. They may distinguish between verbal and pictorial or visual thinking, between thinking on the levels of consciousness or waking, and those of unconsciousness or dreaming. But each of these processes occurs, after all, in an environment that has been literate for millennia, and is, therefore, in the final analysis inseparable from literate modes of experiencing all of life.

This circumstance has a natural bearing on all research aimed at uncovering the sources and modes of thought in nonliterate speech communities, if only because most pioneering scholars in this field were tutored by the literate civilization of the West.[6] The following discussion has issued from their discoveries—tentative as many of them may be—even as it incorporates the written testimony of modern Africans.

The major aspect of the nonliterate African way of experiencing life that has intrigued all sympathetic students of the present and the past is the dominance of a comprehensive bent of mind and of a mythical or magical mode of thought. Here, as in other societies in which reading and writing were unknown arts, men could not engage in prolonged individualized reflections or develop commitments to purely intellectual pursuits. They were, therefore, in no position to abstract principles and formulate theories in juxtaposition to the actual concrete environment in which they lived, in the manner taken for granted by the highly literate Europeans. What the nonliterate African excelled in was the art of creating intricate forms and institutions that effectively subsumed their systems of belief. Theory and fact thus fused in this culture world, and mental dispositions and values were encased in social structures, rites, and nonverbal symbols—an interpenetration that explains why the latter had to be maintained in their full complexity if the former were to be sustained by succeeding generations. For example, unlike an American who can contrast in his mind a presiding principle of law with its particular realization in the context of government, the African *lives* his law, as

---

[6] As Wilfred H. Whiteley remarks in "Political Concepts and Connotations; Observations on the Use of Some Political Terms in Swahili," in Kenneth Kirkwood, ed., *African Affairs; Number One* (St. Antony's Papers, No. 10) (London, 1961), p. 10, there is a singular lack of data concerning the way in which concepts are built up in local African languages.

he also lives his social commitments and his faith, without thinking of either of them as a subject fit for conceptualization, elaboration, or critical review. Thought and action are thus equally constrained by established patterns of behavior. With conformity thus assured on each of the two levels, an individual—if this concept is applicable at all—cannot possibly gain distance from established truths, any more than he can emancipate himself from the group to which he belongs.[7]

This identification of what the Western mind usually distinguishes as opposites is also implicit in the very nature of speech. Whereas writing and reading are removed from the immediacy of interpersonal or group relations, speaking is, after all, an organic aspect of social conduct. Present-oriented, conditioned by the occasion, linked with appropriate gestures or tone of voice, it is also a part of a person's physical actuality. Thought in nonliterate cultures is thus not only institutionalized but also behavioral in its very nature. In such circumstances, it is easy to see why spoken words are apt to be regarded as of the same order of reality as the matters and events to which they refer,[8] and why selected words are often assumed to carry powers not readily fathomed in a literate civilization. These aspects of activist thought and word magic are well illustrated by Jomo Kenyatta's explanations of the nature of love magic and the use of the curse as these practices were known among the Kikuyu: "It is very important to acquire the correct use of magical words and their proper intonations, for the progress in applying magic effectively depends on uttering these words in their ritual order. . . . In performing these acts of love magic the performer has to recite a magical formula. . . . After this recitation he calls the name of the girl loudly and starts to address her *as though she were listening.*"[9] Commenting on the power of a curse, Jomo Kenyatta has this to say after describing the tribal execution of a Kikuyu witch doctor: "He was asked to declare that he had not, and would not, at the time of his death, utter, *silently* or loudly, curses on anyone."[10]

The potency of spoken words, especially when they are institutionalized as formulae of the type just illustrated, is of course offset by their general vulnerability as carriers of thought. Remembrance in nonliterate conditions has of necessity a shorter span; temperament and general instinctual faculties are given greater play. Indeed, human communication comes to depend, almost of necessity, upon the display of emotion, as

[7] See subsequent pages, this chapter.
[8] J. C. Carothers, "Culture, Psychiatry, and the Written Word," in *Psychiatry*, 22, No. 4 (1959), 312.
[9] *Facing Mount Kenya* (London, 1938, repr. 1959), pp. 287ff. (italics mine).
[10] *Ibid.*, p. 302 (italics mine). K. A. Busia explained to Richard Wright that oath taking, libation pouring, and related ritual activities were common practice at the rallies of the Convention People's party in Nkrumah's Ghana. See *Black Power*, p. 228.

76

Richard Wright observed in the course of exploring modern African culture and society: "Unless you exhibit strong, almost passionate emotion, the African is never quite sure that you are honest. Consequently, he possesses an inordinate faith in the force of mere words to dispel or hide facts. With many Africans words assume an omnipotent power."[11] Other related aspects of this style of thought have been stressed by Léopold Senghor. In outlining what he calls the physiopsychology of the negro, Senghor wrote in 1956:

> He is a sensualist. . . . He is first of all sounds, odors, rhythms, forms, and colors. I mean that he is touch before he is sight, unlike the white European. He feels more than he sees. . . . This is not to say that the Negro is traditionally devoid of reason. . . . But his reason is not discursive; it is synthetic. . . . Negro reason does not impoverish things. It does not mold them into rigid categories, eliminating the juices and the sap. . . . White reason is analytical through use. Negro reason is intuitive through participation.[12]

These qualities of speech-related thought and oral communication, together with the narrowing of distance between thought and conduct, are apt to make for what scholars from literate civilizations call unpredictable or explosive behavior, particularly in encounters that occur under "new" auspices. And on such occasions anxieties are often vented—and temporarily dispelled—by sudden outbursts of violence.[13] However, such

[11] Wright, *Black Power*, p. 290.

[12] Léopold Sédar Senghor, "African-Negro Aesthetics," *Diogenes*, No. 16 (Winter 1956), pp. 23–38; compare *infra*, pp. 78ff., 82, notably with the analysis by Father P. Tempels.

Leo Frobenius' analysis of traditional African thought patterns anticipated most of these findings: "The bearers of such a culture are schooled in piety, receptive to the irrational, capable of deep enthusiasm, joyously expressive and at one with fate, whatever it may have in store for them. . . . They are naive, never intellectual even though intelligent." This African ("Ethiopian" in Frobenius' classification) culture does not "move toward some goal or purpose determined intellectually but, on the contrary, is guided under the aegis of the emotional life." See "Early African Culture," p. 165.

[13] Writing about nonliterate peoples in general, Marvin K. Opler observes that psychotics in these societies more typically direct hostility outward, and express it with greater freedom and directness than European patients, who tend to disguise and internalize basic hostility and anxiety. *Psychiatry and Human Values* (Springfield, Ill., 1956), p. 135. Compare *supra*, pp. 61ff. for references to Scientific Council for Africa South of the Sahara, *Mental Disorders and Mental Health in Africa South of the Sahara*, pp. 87, 127ff., 135ff. Although participants at this symposium agreed that there are "mental syndromes which seem specific to Africa and which present difficulties as regards diagnosis," they took note of a special kind of anxiety, variously described as "frenzied anxiety," "non-specific frenzy," "twilight or confusional state," "pseudo-running amok." Confusion and the dominance of action by emotion is said to mark this condition. The emotion is one of acute anxiety, and it is followed by generalized hostility, fear, or even panic. Such epi-

conflict situations as the disquieting present dichotomy between two in-compatible value references—the African and the Occidental—also make for widespread and deeply felt tensions that cannot find an easy outlet. In analyzing this modern problem, Dr. T. Adeoye Lambo first explained "that one is justified in speaking of an all-African mentality, psychology, or soul ["une seule âme africaine"] since the social and cultural institutions of one tribe are not significantly different from those of other tribes." "All values as well as all categories of thought emanate from the group," Lambo continues, "and this explains why intellect and emotion are indissolubly intertwined, even though the affective principle is everywhere predominant."[14] An intense consciousness of supernatural forces and a blind, almost fanatical, trust in the magical powers of certain symbols have been fostered by this way of thought—one that Lambo finds persistent everywhere, in both literate and traditional circles. In-deed, his research in Nigeria convinced him that Westernized students, in particular, were apt to seek refuge in traditional beliefs when they felt isolated or bewildered as a result of their contacts with the alien world of thought. To Lambo it seems clear, therefore, that newly acquired so-cial values and ideologies are so vulnerable in the conflict situation with which modern Africans are confronted as to make it likely that old be-liefs in magic and the power of the ancestors will continue to reassert themselves in all mental lives,[15] at least until a satisfying symbiosis be-tween the two cultures has been attained. In the interim or transitional period—which is of uncertain duration—thought is likely to be con-trolled by fear and the pervasive influence of the awe-inspiring mystical principle.[16]

The absence of premeditation and planning, however, and the often overwhelming presence of passion, emotion, and spontaneity to which expert opinion attests, are apt to find wholly different expressions in non-threatening situations. Here they may make for sensitivities to the de-mands of the moment, such as are not commonly cultivated in highly

---

sodes are attended by various degrees of violence, as a rule externally directed, but they tend to resolve spontaneously within a limited time. To similar effect Carothers, "Culture, Psychiatry, and the Written Word"; M. F. Field, *Search for Security; An Ethno-psychiatric Study of Rural Ghana* (Evanston, Ill., 1962); and Lloyd, *Africa in Social Change*, pp. 251ff., where several violent popular outbursts —none showing clear social aims—are described.

[14] T. Adeoye Lambo, M.D., "Ame africaine et conflit contemporain—Par quoi remplacer la magie?" *Journal de Genève*, No. 173 (July 26, 1972), p. 1.

[15] *Ibid.*, No. 175 (July 28, 1972), pp. 1, 12. And see *infra*, p. 215.

[16] All authorities appear to be in agreement with L. Marx, "Psychologie Merina," p. 144, even though Madagascar is in many respects quite unlike continental sub-Saharan Africa; the infrastructure of Hova mentality, Marx notes, is marked by the dominance of fear and the pervasive influence of "the mystical principle." Thought here is not sequential, and notions of space, time, object, and reality are apt to be imprecise.

literate civilizations of the Occidental type. This dimension of the African mode of thinking—which has obvious bearings on the conduct of diplomacy in general and the approach to conflict situations in particular[17]—has found implicit recognition in the following statement by Bouah Niangoran: "We can make use of arguments that a European cannot invoke because he is so thoroughly conditioned by writing."[18]

One of the consequences of writing as developed in the West is the disposition to systematize knowledge and distinguish between different types of arguments. Such tendencies are absent from the African context of reflection and discourse, in which references to a great variety of subjects are allowed to mix and mingle freely. It is in this sense that Léopold Senghor can refer to African thinking as comprehensive and totalitarian, and that another distinguished West African scholar, M. Hampaté Ba, could warn his Occidental colleagues at a symposium on the continuity of tradition in his native world that they must get accustomed to a spiritual stance that thrives on what appears to be intellectual chaos. All African discourse, he explains, is round about, without any obvious semblance of a systematic ordering of thoughts, or of causal relationships between separate statements: "If you systematize in Africa, you are bound to lose"[19]—a suggestion also implicit in the following remark by Richard Wright: "System is the enemy of the tribal mind; action proceeds on the basis of associations of images: if feeling is absent, the tribal African mind is in doubt."[20]

The merger of thought with emotion, behavior, and social structure, and the synthetic approach to all knowledge and experience have combined to foster a metaphysical world view that requires the confounding of all phenomena: the natural world is thus not perceived as separate from supernatural realms; animals and men exist in symbioses unimaginable in literate thought contexts; masks are treated as persons; shadows are real; the dead are presumed alive, and the living can interchange identities and destinies.[21] As L. Lévy-Bruhl was the first to note in his pathmaking studies of the nonliterate mind, a mutual interpenetration

[17] See *infra*, Part VI.

[18] Rencontres internationales de Bouaké, *Les Religions africaines traditionnelles* (Paris, 1965), p. 31.

[19] *Ibid.*, p. 28; see also pp. 33–42 for Ba's essay, "Animisme en savane africaine."

[20] *Black Power*, p. 265. There are obvious affinities between these African orientations, on the one hand, and the American Negro's stress on "soul" and emotion, on the other.

[21] See also Marcel Griaule, "The Problem of Negro Culture," p. 360, that religions and legal structures, symbols and actions, technical skills and gestures, are equally emanations from a single rigid system of thought that is ideally suited to assure the undisturbed continuity of the tribe by providing a closed metaphysical interpretation of the universe. See R. E. Dennett, *At the Back of the Black Man's Mind, or Notes on the Kingly Office in West Africa* (1st ed. 1906, repr. London, 1968), for some sensitive renditions of this theme.

and mystic participation links all that is and all that is being imagined in a universal order in which separations of the internal and the external, subject and object, the psychical and the physical, dreaming and waking, past and present would be nonsensical.[22]

The nature of this magical circle in which all opposites are cancelled, as it were, by the creative force of the nonliterate imagination, has been illustrated by many thoughtful observers, African and European. Reminiscing on his youth in southeast Nigeria, Victor Uchendu recalls that his father's mother "was my mother in my previous life," and that his "actual" widowed mother—being a trader and needing help—"married" one wife after another, quite in accord with Igbo custom, so that one could then play the social role of the missing father. The latter was dead, of course, but his periodic appearances in the mother's dreams had such upsetting effects that the children implored "him" to stay away.[23] And similar realities are conveyed by Noni Jabavu's recollections of family life in South Africa. She remembered that her father's "mother" was a whitehaired maternal uncle, whom the children were taught to call "grandmother," and that a chief who had been dead for a couple of hundred years could be spoken of quite convincingly by a woman as her son.[24] These ways of confounding time dimensions and generations, forms and substances, as well as such faculties as seeing, hearing, speaking, and acting, made a deep impression upon Mary Kingsley when she explored West Africa in the nineteenth century. "When I was with the Fans," she writes, "they frequently said: 'We will go to the fire, so we can see what they say' when any question had to be decided after dark."[25] And many of the same themes have been captured vividly by some of modern Africa's most gifted writers. "Immediately I died in our town I went to several towns . . . to establish the Christianity works . . ." is one

---

[22] Lucien Lévy-Bruhl's works are set out in the bibliography. Other scholars who have been preoccupied with these contrasts in modes of thinking include Jean Cazeneuve, *La Mentalité archaique* (Paris, 1961); Vincent Monteil, *L'Islam noir* (Paris, 1964), ch. 2, "La Pensée sauvage"; Claude Levi-Strauss, *La Pensée sauvage* (Paris, 1962) (translated as *The Savage Mind*, London, 1966); James W. C. Dougal, "Characteristics of African Thought" in *Africa*, 5, No. 3 (July 1932); Raoul Allier, *Le Non-civilisé et nous* (Paris, 1927); also Bureau régional pour l'Afrique de l'Organisation Mondiale de la Santé, *Seminaire sur la santé mentale en Afrique au sud du Sahara, Rapport final* (November-December 1958; Brazzaville, 1959), see especially pp. 70ff. and 44ff.

[23] Victor C. Uchendu, *The Igbo of Southeast Nigeria* (New York, 1965), pp. 6ff.

[24] Noni Jabavu, *Drawn in Colour; African Contrasts* (London, 1961), pp. 1–53, for this and numerous other classificatory references to family relationships.

[25] Mary H. Kingsley, *Travels in West Africa* (London, 1897), p. 504; *West African Studies* (London and New York, 1899; 2nd ed., 1901), p. 201. Mary Kingsley remarks in this connection that "at least one third of African language consists in gesture, and the gesture part is fairly common to all Tribes. The African's intelligence is far ahead of his language."

of numerous such episodes in Tutuola's phantasy, *My Life in the Bush of Ghosts*.[26] Mazrui's poetic analysis of the major issues involved in the recent Biafran war of secession, which is cast in the form of a trial in "After Africa," begins with the recognition that the ancestors were deeply disturbed by the turn of events in Nigeria, and that those who fought this war had to account for their motives as well as their actions after death. The living, too, could be called as witnesses, but only in their subconscious or sleeping state of being; for the simple and obvious principle of simultaneity must be invoked as the arbiter of any and all contradictions, as these may occur in the relationships between the living, the dead, and those who are to be born.[27]

Equally poignant illustrations of this order of mystic participation are encountered in the interdependence of animate and inanimate, human and animal categories. A crocodile may thus leave the water, hang up his skin on a tree, and take part in a game as a man (Kpelle), and a buffalo can trade as a human being as other men do, and then change on his way home once more into a buffalo (Ewe).[28] Likewise, fear of a dead leopard may be banished effectively when the eyes of the shot animal are bound so that it cannot see the hunter who killed it and take vengeance.[29] Countless myths and folk tales render this mode of understanding life, as for example, a Somali story that begins with the statement that "once a Lion, a Snake, a Thorny Fence, Fire, Flood, Deceit, and Honesty owned a she-camel together." But the most eloquent records of these culturally distinct thoughtways are probably the plastic arts of certain peoples in West and Central Africa. Sculpted figures combining the stylized generic essences of totemic animal and human forms can here be made to concretize all that is enduring in the social covenant with nature and the invisible world beyond. Masks made of many separate parts, each fully intelligible to the beholder, may thus be persuasive abstractions of the major cosmic and spiritual forces by which existence is controled. Rooted in the cult of death and the ancestors, dedicated to the remembrance of the constant in the past, these objects are nonetheless

[26] Amos Tutuola, *My Life in the Bush of Ghosts* (London, 1954), p. 145; other thematically similar novels by this Yoruba author include *Simbi and the Satyr of the Dark Jungle* (London, 1955); and *The Palm-Wine Drinkard and His Dead Palm-Wine Tapster in the Dead's Town* (New York, 1953).

[27] Ali A. Mazrui, *The Trial of Christopher Okigbo* (New York, 1971), pp. 72ff., 79.

[28] Diedrich Westermann, *The African To-day and To-morrow*, ch. 8, "The Supernatural World," pp. 83ff.; see note 1 on p. 85 for a curious example of this "law of participation," as given by M. J. Herskovits and Frances Herskovits in *Suriname Folklore* (New York, 1936), p. 485. See the following chapters on "intermediaries" and "sacred sanctions" for other references to this matter.

[29] Westermann, *The African To-day and To-morrow*, p. 84.

dynamic and presumed to be alive—active agents of social control that are trusted to ensure fertility, initiate the young into the mysteries of the fearful life, or exorcise and unify the group.

The ruling principle that assures the flux of forms, permits mystic participation or enmeshment, and thus controls all human thought is what F. Plastide Tempels has called "la force vitale."[30] This concept, widely used today by African scholars and writers of both poetry and prose, covers the belief that all relations, especially those between the living and his dead ancestors, and between the visible and invisible worlds, are kept going by a magical life force. To share in this vital energy, conserve, and if possible increase it, is the supreme challenge in tribal existence; for as Ki-Zerbo explained it some years ago,[31] the "good" life consists in having these powers working for oneself, one's ancestral spirits, and one's kith and kin. Any diminution of the life force, as announced in sickness, sterility, or other untoward events and failures is, by contrast, tantamount to "evil."[32] Invariably viewed as a calamity or a portent of worse to come, it requires the intervention of countermanding occult agencies, since spirit is everywhere supposed to work on spirit.

The conception of the universe as essentially malevolent, always capable of releasing mystic aggressions on the realm of man, thus demands a moral value system in terms of which men are enjoined to admire power and success in the human sphere and to scorn weakness and failure, without asking how a person gained his goods, or why he is in his plight. Such questions are irrelevant here, for the assumption rules that he who has misfortunes merits them; otherwise the ancestors would not have assigned them to his earthly lot. The major existential task is therefore to assuage the ancestors, who are the ever-watchful, jealous carriers of the all-encompassing life-sustaining force.

All reasoning processes, activities, and human associations are thus dominated by powers over which men do not presume to have any real control. Fear, distrust, and insecurity are the ruling principles, and these cannot be overcome by thought, for the free-floating human imagination

[30] *La Philosophie bantoue* (first published by Lovania, Elizabethville, Belgian Congo, 1945); trans. as *Bantu Philosophy* (Paris, 1959). See *infra*, p. 85 for flurther references to this principle; also see Benjamin Akiga, *Akiga's Story: The Tiv Tribe as Seen by One of Its Members*, Rupert East, trans., 2nd ed. (London, 1965), on the common belief in "tsav," which is the Tiv version of "vital energy."

[31] "La Crise actuelle de la civilisation africaine" in *Tradition et modernisme*, pp. 118ff.

[32] L.-V. Thomas, "The Study of Death in Negro Africa," in Lalage Bown and Michael Crowder, eds., *Proceedings of the First International Congress of Africanists* (London, 1964), 146ff. To the same effect, Richard Wright, *Black Power*, p. 196: failure in Africa is a sign of badness, winning a sign of goodness. See also Simon Biesheuvel, *Race, Culture and Personality* (Johannesburg, 1959), pp. 36ff. Paul Verhaegen, "Study of the African Personality in the Belgian Congo," pp. 247–248.

is absent here, as Mary Kingsley already noted during her exploratory travels in West Africa. The rules of logic and causality that Africans (and other nonliterate peoples) have brought forth in the context of their essentially metaphysical world view are therefore naturally diametrically opposed to those with which the West has identified for centuries. Conceptions of death and disease—particularly relevant for a discussion of conflict and its possible physical effects—illustrate vividly what the issues are in such a situation: "For most nonliterate peoples," Jack Goody writes,

> the causes that contemporary Europeans would regard as natural do not by themselves provide a sufficient explanation of the death of a human being. I do not mean to imply that they are not aware that the bite of a snake can "cause" a man to die. But factors of this sort are seen not as final but rather as intermediary agents. What has to be ascertained is the person or shrine that was associated with the snake at the moment it struck. In the end this resolves itself into an inquiry as to who or what had grounds for hostility against the dead man, and so the cause of death is seen as a function of the individual's network of spiritual and human relationships. Death is treated as a social phenomenon and attributed to some conflict in the social system, either with living persons (witches, workers of curses, and sorcerers), or with past members of the society (ancestors), or with non-human agencies (shrines).[33]

And the same mystical explanations attend the incidence of disease: "Even where the disease is of plainly organic origin," we learn from F. B. Welbourn, "the first question to be answered is, often enough, 'Who sent the illness?' It is unlikely that what scientific medicine would call the necessary psychological predisposition for organic cure can be achieved, unless the question is taken at its most unscientific face value and the necessary ritual fulfilled."[34] After analyzing contemporary evi-

---

[33] *Death, Property and the Ancestors; A Study of the Mortuary Customs of the LoDagaa of West Africa* (London, 1959), pp. 208ff. Goody distinguishes three levels of causation in this analysis: the immediate, namely the technique used to kill the deceased, such as disease, snake bites, or other natural causes, as well as forms of mystical aggression; the efficient causes, that is, those found among the members of the community itself—namely, the person who was behind the act of killing; and thirdly, the final cause, which is an ancestor, the earth shrine, or a medicine shrine.

[34] "An Empirical Approach to Ghosts" in Lalage Bown and Michael Crowder, eds., *Proceedings*, pp. 124ff. See also M. J. Field, M.D. "Mental Illness in Rural Ghana" in Scientific Council for Africa South of the Sahara, *Mental Disorders and Mental Health in Africa South of the Sahara*, pp. 158–163; by the same author, *Search for Security*; and the works of Michael Gelfand, M.D., notably *The African Witch, with Particular Reference to Witchcraft Beliefs and Practice among the Shona of Rhodesia* (London, 1967); *The Sick African; A Clinical Study*, 3rd. rev.

dence gathered in East and West Africa, this scholar concludes that "there is an appreciable—possibly even an increasing—incidence of disease, which fails to yield to the techniques of scientific medicine, but is nevertheless cured—and apparently permanently cured—by priests and mediums and diviners who treat it on the assumption that witchcraft and ghosts have a real existence. For since belief in these things has real existence in the minds of men in this culture, it must also be taken seriously in therapy." As Welbourn suggests, this means that our experience in Africa makes it necessary for the time being to accept both the scientific and the mystical hypothesis, however apparently incompatible, as each covering, for its own particular culture, the same fundamental phenomenon of the ill-adjusted personality.[35]

Scientific thinking and objectivity in the Western sense, then, could not be accommodated by the traditional African mentality, for as Hoernlé put it in a discussion of magic and medicine in Bantu thought, "thinking in such an emotion-charged atmosphere fails to discriminate, in the welter of simultaneous happenings, the events which belong together and are, as scientists say, 'causally connected,' from those which are merely associated by the same emotional reaction to them." Bantu thought thus "perceives identities of essence where we can see only difference and disconnection. It assumes relevancies of power, where for science there is no relation of cause and effect at all."[36] This order of thought, which is sentimental and mystical rather than rational and empirical, explains —we learn from a modern Malgasy scholar—why inconsistent ideas can be held by his countrymen with the greatest of ease in the realm not just

---

ed. (Cape Town, 1957; 1st ed., 1943); *Medicine and Custom in Africa* (London, 1964). For valuable insights see also Albert Schweitzer, *A L'Orée de la forêt vierge, récits et réflexions d'un médécin en Afrique équatoriale française,* new ed. (Paris, 1962). Compare Westermann, *The African,* p. 85, to the effect that illness is not viewed as a process but rather as a thing: it may be a stone or a piece of wood that must be removed from the body, or it may be a being that is wandering about in the body. The notion that illness is a being that has a life and volition of its own is also well explained in Leighton, Lambo, *et al., Psychiatric Disorder,* pp. 113ff.

For mythical renditions of this conviction see also Hans Abrahamsson, *The Origin of Death; Studies in African Mythology* (Upsala, 1951). On the continuity of these understandings of illness and health see Margaret Read, *Education and Social Change in Tropical Areas* (London and New York, 1955), notably p. 11, where Read points out that by far the greatest range of illness is attributed to some supernatural or occult influence, and pp. 20ff. on the business of the doctor in the context of divination.

[35] "An Empirical Approach to Ghosts."

[36] A. Winifred Hoernlé, "Magic and Medicine," in I. Schapera, ed., *The Bantu-Speaking Tribes of South Africa; An Ethnographic Survey* (London, 1946; first pub. 1937), p. 225.

of religion but also of health.[37] What matters is the unassailable certainty that facts and images, hopes and fears, desires and aversions, however disparate and contradictory in terms of Western normative reason, are indissolubly linked in one universal web of participation. No allowance can here be made for the inexplicable or the accidental, for doubts and misunderstandings; nor, indeed, for the possibility of not knowing or the urge to probe the reaches beyond the known. Participation is, therefore, perforce mystical, not willed or calculated. It is also a category more of action than of thought, for it stipulates that one must "live strongly" by manipulating phenomena in support of "vital energy,"[38] or, if one is weak, by sharing in the strength of someone stronger than oneself—a

[37] Richard Andiamanjato, *Le Tsiny et le Tody dans la pensée malgache* (Paris, 1957). Compare Max Gluckman, *Custom and Conflict in Africa* (Oxford, 1960), p. 122, that Africans have not worked out elaborate dogmas to explain the nature of the universe.

[38] Placide Tempels, *La Philosophie bantoue* (Paris, 1959), on the principles of "vital forces" (p. 45) and Bantu psychology (pp. 68ff.). Whether this set of understandings is properly called "philosophy" is, of course, debatable. As Franz Crahay points out in "Conceptual Take-Off; Conditions for a Bantu Philosophy" (Victor A. Velen, trans.), *Diogenes*, No. 52 (Winter 1965), pp. 55–78, philosophical reflection requires the recognition and exploitation of a certain distinction between subject and object; it cannot be "implicit," or "irrational," and it is not a language *of* experience but a language *on* experience. What Tempels sets forth is, in this scholar's view, "a vision of the world," a code of morals, or a tradition of wisdom, but not philosophy.

See Lévy-Bruhl's first works on the "loi de participation" as listed in the bibliography, notably *Les Fonctions mentales dans les sociétés inférieures* (Paris, 1910), and Roger Bastide, "Contribution à l'étude de la participation," *Cahiers internationaux de sociologie*, 14 (1953), 32–39; and by the same author, *Le Candomblé de Bahia (rite magô)* (Paris, 1958), pp. 236–237, for a stimulating elaboration of the "law of participation."

Many of Lévy-Bruhl's original ideas about primitive or mystical mentality are critically discussed and developed by Jean Cazeneuve, *La Mentalité archaique*; and compare earlier references to this set of issues, and *supra*, note 22 for related references. The question of whether this culturally distinct mind system is properly called primitive, archaic, or savage is irrelevant to the present analysis. It is, of course, quite true that some of the mental qualities singled out as characteristic of African thought are also present in Occidental patterns of reflection. The crux of the matter, however, is that they have been and are absolutely dominant in Africa, whereas they are only partial or secondary aspects of thinking elsewhere. The thesis presented by Levi-Strauss, for example, that "savage thought" is the normal form of human intelligence everywhere before this intelligence becomes disciplined and domesticated, is obviously not tenable for those who do not regard African culture as undeveloped, or African thought as a phase in the evolution toward mature thought. It should be mentioned that Levi-Strauss has not made Africa the laboratory of his explorations.

See Maurice Houis, "Préalables" in *Esprit*, p. 18, for the conclusion that "l'oralité . . . n'est pas une insuffisance foncière, ni l'absence d'écriture, c'est positivement un type de communication qui a ses constantes psychologiques et sociologiques." (Orality . . . should not be understood negatively as some basic insufficiency or as the absence of writing; rather, it should be viewed positively as an altogether different mode of communication which has its own psychological and sociological constants.)

tendency that may well have facilitated the conquests and colonial developments in the periods both of Islamization and Europeanization.

It goes without saying that individuation cannot be recognized in this structure of thought. Considered a link in the chain of vital forces rather than an independent entity, each man must engage himself inexorably to maintain the primacy of his community. Any disturbance of this closed and established order of things—whether actual or felt—has therefore consistently been viewed as a clear, incontrovertible indication that inexorable laws have been transgressed, and that someone has erred. This somebody must then be ferreted out if the community is to return to harmony, and no one doubted that he could be located by setting in motion the proper magical processes and by relying on the services of multiple types of intermediaries[39]—all trusted for their expertise in matters of dreams, omens, rituals, divinations, witchcraft, or sorcery. Witchcraft, then, is not a simple superstition here. As the supreme manifestation of the "force vitale," it is the ultimate arbiter, the cause of causes, the kingpin of the African system of logic. Without it, the world would disintegrate and life become incomprehensible, as Mary Kingsley explains after her pioneering exploration of the African "mind forest":

> The more you know the African, the more you study his laws and institutions, the more you recognise that the main characteristic of his intellect is logical, and you see how in all things he uses this sound but narrow thought-form. He is not a dreamer nor a doubter; everything is real, very real, horribly real to him . . . the quality of the African mind is strangely uniform. . . . It is this power of being able logically to account for everything that is, I believe, at the back of the tremendous permanency of Fetish in Africa.[40]

This sensitive appraisal of prevalent African modes of thinking has been echoed by many twentieth-century scholars and artists, both African and Occidental, even as it had been prefigured, as it were, by numerous earlier observers of the scene.[41] Significant testimony through the ages thus converges on the impression that we are here in the presence of a mental, psychological, and moral order that has successfully resisted

[39] See Ch. 18 on the role of intermediaries in conflict situations.

[40] Olwen Campbell, *Mary Kingsley; A Victorian in the Jungle* (London, 1957), p. 124. Frobenius develops very similar understandings of African thoughtways; see, for example, *Kulturgeschichte Afrikas, Prolegomena zu einer Historischen Gestaltlehre* (Frankfurt-am-Main, 1933), Part 3, pp. 247ff. on "Das Afrikanische als Eigensinn," the primacy of myth and sentiment and the strong trend to accept all facts as expressions of a metaphysical reality. And see Isak Dinesen (pseud.), *Out of Africa* (New York, 1938), p. 101, on the African "gift for myth," which allows the mind to move naturally and easily upon the deep and shadowy paths of mythological or theological thinking.

[41] See preceding references to explorers and travelers; also notes 42 and 43, *infra*.

the introduction of culturally contrary trends, notably those elsewhere associated with the written word. The conclusion is tenable, in fact, that literacy, whether associated with the intrusion of Islam and Arabic or of the West and its written languages, has been effectively absorbed by the receiving indigenous system of orality, magic, and myth. Mungo Park noted, in the course of his exploratory travels in West Africa, that the horns of sheep were highly valued in certain pagan communities because they served as containers for saphies, namely "prayers or rather sentences, from the Koran, which the Mahomedan priests write on scraps of paper, and sell to the simple natives, who consider them to possess very extraordinary virtues." For example, they might guard the bearer against snake bites, or, in time of war, against hostile weapons. Careful observations of these practices convinced this eighteenth-century explorer that it is impossible

> not to admire the wonderful contagion of superstition; for, notwithstanding that the majority of the Negroes are Pagans, and absolutely reject the doctrines of Mahomet, I did not meet with a man . . . who was not fully persuaded of the powerful efficacy of these amulets. The truth is, that all the natives of this part of Africa consider the art of writing as bordering on magic; and it is not in the doctrines of the Prophet, but in the arts of the magician, that their confidence is placed.[42]

The demand for "book magic" remained constant in the nineteenth and twentieth centuries, and this in the Islamic as well as the European context. René Caillié thus notes in the account of his journey to Timbuktu in 1827 that the pagan Bambara had plenty of respect for Mohammed's writing, and that he himself was begged to write a charm that would make the particular pleader as rich as the whites.[43] The same association of literacy with superior juju is relayed a century later by Dinesen, as when she describes the reassuring effects that a little piece of writing had on her East African friends;[44] and in 1968, by Peter Lienhardt in his introduction to a modern Swahili ballad that tells of the disappearance and death of a young woman and of the ensuing criminal in-

[42] Mungo Park, *Travels in the Interior Districts of Africa; Performed in the Years 1795, 1796, and 1797. With an Account of a Subsequent Mission to that Country in 1805*, new ed., 2 vols. (London, 1816), pp. 37–38.

[43] *Travels through Central Africa to Timbuctoo; and across the Great Desert, to Morocco; Performed in the Years 1824–1828*, 2 vols. (London, 1830, repr. 1968), 1, 259. Observations such as these abound in the memoirs of all explorers. See also P. Marty, *Etudes sur l'Islam en Côte d'Ivoire* (Paris, 1922), p. 52.

[44] *Out of Africa*, pp. 121ff. For similar episodes see Joyce Cary's novel, *The African Witch* (New York and Evanston, 1963; 1st pub. 1936), pp. 297ff. on Tom wanting to "learn book" so as to rival the power of the white man, and on the tragic degeneration of this effort.

vestigation into sorcery. After commenting on the evolution of numerous syncretisms between native and Islamic customs and religious practices, and on the powerful role of Muslim holy men, Lienhardt writes:

> Learning is thought to hold secret powers of influencing other people's lives and attitudes. This gives rise to "Book magic," the Book being the Koran. Possessed of this magic, the erudite write charms appropriate to various occasions and control spirits which, though of junior rank in the spirit creation, are nevertheless powerful enough to make formidable interventions in politics and private quarrels. . . . Such learned men as are willing to engage in the business can charge heavy fees for charms intended to make people more tractable in their dealings with those who acquire them and wear them as amulets, or carry them under their caps in court cases. . . . Those conscious of wrongs can, if they choose, read or have read for them a prayer invoking all those who were present with the Prophet in the famous Battle of Badr, the first great military victory of Islam, and turn the prayer upon their oppressor, so long as they are sure they are in the right. The prayer can be used against known people or against unknown ones such as undetected thieves. In one case I heard of the mere threat to use it caused (causing) stolen goods to be returned.[45]

In this region, as in others, book magic is one of the Islamic antidotes to evil. That is to say, it has not liberated the individual mind from subservience to superstition, custom, or other forms of authority. Here, as elsewhere where many people cannot read or write at all, and where most of those who can are unaccustomed to reading books, the scholarly idea of learning cannot have much appeal. Indeed, a survey of the mental environment convinced Davidson Nicol in the early 1960s that literacy has not brought happiness to Africa.[46] Even its political benefits are said to have been scant. Scribes at the Imerina (Merina) court in Madagascar seem to have contributed greatly to the success of holding the kingdom together[47]—and Goody's evidence from modern northern Ghana is to the effect that writing enabled chiefs and Muslims to deal with one another at a distance. By and large, however, it appears that "the slender literate strand" has everywhere been heavily affected by the structure of

[45] Hasani bin Ismail, *The Medicine Man; 'Swifa Ya Nguvumali*, Peter Lienhardt, ed., and trans. (Oxford and London, 1968), pp. 49–50. Compare *infra*, n. 49, this chapter.

[46] Davidson Nicol, *Africa, A Subjective View* (London and Accra, 1964), p. 65.

[47] M. Bloch, "Astrology and Writing in Madagascar," in Goody, ed., *Literacy in Traditional Societies*, p. 286. The scribes, who carried out government business in Arabic script, had dual roles as diviner-astrologers and secretaries. Compare *supra*, pp. 72ff. for the thesis, eloquently presented by Oswald Spengler and Julian Huxley, that writing makes for spatial cohesion.

the illiterate society.[48] Valued as a different kind of speech, a magic new means of communicating with ancient supernatural forces, an integral part of the "conceptual system of sorcery"[49] or as the dominant power symbol, literacy has been effectively integrated into nonliterate modes of thought and communication—a metamorphosis subtly rendered by Chinua Achebe in *No Longer at Ease*:

Once before he went to England, Obi heard his father talk with deep feeling about the mystery of the written word to an illiterate kinsman:

"Our women made black patterns on their bodies with the juice of the *uli* tree. It was beautiful, but it soon faded, although no one had ever seen it. We see it today in the writing of the white man. If you go to the native court and look at the books which clerks wrote twenty years ago or more, they are still as they wrote them. They do not say one thing today and another tomorrow, or one thing this year and another next year. Okoye in the book today cannot become Okonkwo tomorrow. . . . It is *uli* that never fades."[50]

Contemporary testimony, as found in the African press as well as in scholarly studies of the social and political situation, justifies the conclusion that beliefs in magic have, so far, survived the collision with the totally different Western system of reasoning. In fact, recent research suggests strongly that witchcraft has tightened its hold on minds left troubled and disconcerted by the strains of modernization and change, and that relief from psychological tensions is being widely sought by immersion in new religious cults; trust in antiwitchcraft shrines, both old and new; use of power pills; and recourse to other forms of magic.[51] For example, a 1957 study of unemployment in Brazzaville revealed that 79

[48] This formulation is taken from I. M. Lewis, "Literacy in a Nomadic Society," in Goody, ed., *Literacy in Traditional Societies*, p. 266.

[49] Lienhardt, trans., Hasani bin Ismail, *The Medicine Man*, p. 79.

[50] *No Longer at Ease* (New York, 1961), pp. 126–127.

[51] See, in particular, John Middleton and E. H. Winter, eds., *Witchcraft and Sorcery in East Africa* (London, 1963), p. 25: "Most Africans see the situation as having deteriorated; their defences against witches have been weakened and the practice of sorcery is on the rise"—a psychological and social condition that conduces to imbalance and invites manipulation from within and without. Also Max Gluckman, *Order and Rebellion in Tribal Africa; Collected Essays* (London and New York, 1963), ch. 4, pp. 137ff., "The Magic of Despair," especially p. 143: "Throughout Africa, while ancient religious rituals have faded, fears of witchcraft have burgeoned and magic has blossomed." Another movement, Gluckman writes, has been the emergence of nativistic cults—religious movements of return to old rituals. To similar effect, see Dr. C.G.F. Smartt, "An African Witch-Hunt," in Scientific Council for Africa South of the Sahara, *Mental Disorders and Mental Health*, pp. 183–190; and M. Leiris, "La Possession par le zâr chez les Chrétiens du nord de l'Ethiopie" in the same volume, pp. 168–175; this particular possession cult, while outlawed by the government, is firmly rooted as an institution in Christian as well as in Muslim, Jewish, and pagan communities of the state.

percent of the young, literate, and unemployed did not deny the existence of witchcraft; in fact all feared it and had experienced it either personally or in the context of their immediate families. Recourse to fetishists was thus had whenever success was wanted, as in competitions, job applications, or love affairs, with lack of money the only inhibition[52]—findings that Dr. Lambo took occasion to confirm in 1972.[53] Nor has the modern political scene been exempt from the recrudescence of traditional practices and cults. An official inquiry in Basutoland to discover the underlying causes of the outbreak in 1947 and 1948 of "medicine murders" yielded the conclusion that these murders had been due in large measure to chiefs or headmen who were anxious to recover, by resort to magic, the positions they had lost or feared to lose as modern reforms were instituted.[54] And rather similar motivations must have impelled modern literate incumbents in power positions, as well as their various rivals, to seek refuge in the traditional world of pagan or Islamic magic.[55]

The general question as to whether an end is in sight for witchcraft as a social institution and causal system has so far received ambiguous answers. A close survey of conditions in Bunyoro (East Africa) persuaded John Beatty that reliance on magical means of defense and aggression would decline only as general standards of education and social and economic well-being advanced to a stage where causal explanations in other than magical terms became acceptable.[56] And similar views have been advanced by N. G. Otieno in a critique of projects designed to educate

[52] Gerard Althabe, "Etude du chômage à Brazzaville en 1957," in Wickert, ed., *Readings in African Psychology from French Language Sources*, pp. 211ff.; see also P. C. Lloyd, *Africa in Social Change*, pp. 244ff., 250, 262; Ulli Beier, *Art in Nigeria, 1960* (Cambridge, 1960), p. 16, finds that posters in Nigeria are uniform in the sense that all seem to promise "power," whether they aim at selling medicine or drink or petrol. Here, as elsewhere, authorities report that literate Africans are more susceptible to anxiety than illiterates.

Authorities on the general subject of African witchcraft are too numerous to be listed here. But see Jean Rouch, *La Religion et la magie songhay* (Paris, 1960); C. W. Hobley, *Bantu Beliefs and Magic, with particular reference to the Kikuyu and Kamba Tribes of Kenya Colony* (London, 1922; repr. 1938); S. F. Nadel, "Witchcraft in Four African Societies; An Essay in Comparison," *American Anthropologist*, 54 (1952), 18–29; E. E. Evans-Pritchard, *Witches, Oracles, and Magic among the Azande* (Oxford, 1937, repr. 1950); Rev. Robert Hamill Nassau, M.D., *Fetishism in West Africa; 40 Years' Observation of Native Customs and Superstitions* (New York, 1904).

[53] See note 14, this chapter.

[54] William Malcolm, Lord Hailey, *An African Survey; A Study of Problems Arising in Africa South of the Sahara*, rev. ed. (London, New York, and Toronto, 1957), p. 507.

[55] Afrifa, *The Ghana Coup, 24 February 1966*, p. 123; and Lucy C. Behrman, *Muslim Brotherhoods and Politics in Senegal* (Cambridge, Mass., 1970), both on the late Kwame Nkrumah's recourse to magical resources. See also *infra*, Chs. 10, 11, and 18.

[56] Middleton and Winter, eds., *Witchcraft and Sorcery*, p. 55.

African scientists. What is missing today, this observer noted in 1962, is the inculcation of a creative critical spirit, a view beyond the village, and objectivity. So far, however, the programs have produced "scientists . . . who hold views and beliefs that are at variance with their scientific knowledge and who have, in fact, allowed such views to invade the field proper to science and led them to adopt a distorted approach to purely scientific questions. It is a matter of marvel," Otieno writes, "that we have not produced many scientists in Africa with split personalities."[57]

Just as it was impossible to extrapolate something called "science" from the sum total of knowledge in which nonliterate man was immersed, so was it impossible in his thought world to think of "politics" or "government" as separate objects of concern, outside the comprehensive vital order of mutually dependent perceptions and activities. The same metaphysical world view that Africans created and maintained by their exclusive reliance upon the power of mythical thinking reached a climax here, as it did there, in the absolute primacy of what we in the West call "religion." That is to say, contrary to Durkheim's well-known thesis, it is not possible here to separate the sacred from the profane.[58] "The most important thing to bear in mind," we learn from A. A. Nwafor Orizu, "is that in Nigeria as a whole and in Ibo particularly politics was synonymous with ethics and religion. If there is anything common in our political system, that is it."[59] And what is true of Nigeria, with its many separate component communities, is equally true of all other sub-Saharan regions and societies: the message upon which thoughtful African observers appear to agree is that no intruding Asian or European factor has materially modified the sense of total dependence upon supernatural powers and ancestors, and that modern, that is, European, political systems are functioning at present under the close tutelage, as it were, of traditional systems of thought.[60]

[57] Bown and Crowder, eds., *Proceedings of the First Congress of Africanists*, p. 310. See also Field, *Search of Security*, and authorities cited earlier.

[58] Emile Durkheim, *The Elementary Forms of the Religious Life*, Joseph Ward Swain, trans. (London, 1915), p. 415, conclusion and *passim*. Compare Busia, *Africa in Search of Democracy*, p. 9: "life is not comparted into sacred and secular."

[59] *Without Bitterness: Western Nations in Post-War Africa* (New York, 1944), pp. 113ff.

[60] Busia, *Africa in Search of Democracy*, especially the chapters "The Religious Heritage" and "The Political Heritage"; Busia, *The African Consciousness; Continuity and Change in Africa* (New York, 1968), p. 15: "A very experienced President of an African State, one who has weathered many political storms, said calmly when asked about this [the relationship between traditional and modern forms of government]: No President or Prime Minister in Africa today can keep his place for long without the backing of large tribes." Compare *supra*, Ch. 3 and Vieyra, "Structures politiques traditionnelles," pp. 201ff.; see also Fernand Lafargue in the same volume, pp. 49ff. To the same effect, Buchmann, *Le Problème des structures politiques en Afrique noire indépendante*, pp. 40ff., 90ff., 111ff., 130.

Several of the foregoing comments and illustrations have already indicated that the concept of time in nonliterate African thought is radically different from that which has ruled life in the West. Not only are speaking and listening present-oriented activities, but the actually functioning social and cosmological order with all of its interpenetrating forms, models, and norms, is perceived as perfect and unchangeable. The awesome dynamic that keeps it going may cause contractions here, expansions there, but its movement is essentially circular, not linear. To distinguish past, present, and future dimensions in such a closed universe would be nonsensical; for just as the ancestors are presumed to be living, so must the present reproduce what in our perspective is called the past. Ideas such as aspiration, progress, development, reform—all futuristic in tone, content, and purport—could thus not have been generated; as M. Hampaté Ba explains: "the African is like a hunter; he foresees nothing. His decisions are made in the moment. Content to live in actuality he is completely thrown off balance when asked what tomorrow will bring. The question which concerns us [in the symposium] namely what Africa's language should be in the future, simply would not occur to him."[61] And similar observations are relayed by Richard Wright: "it bothered me that I couldn't find among educated Africans any presentiment of what the future of their continent was to be. . . . The African did not strain to feel that which was not yet in existence: he exerted his will to make what happened happen again. His was a circular kind of time: the present had to be made up like the past. Dissatisfaction was not the mainspring of his emotional life, enjoyment of that which he had once enjoyed was the compulsion."[62]

[61] *Les Religions africaines traditionnelles*, p. 52.

[62] *Black Power*, pp. 175, 222. Wright adds that the more highly educated Africans were, the more unfit they seemed to him to weigh the forces that were shaping the modern world. As a preceding discussion has suggested, long-range foreign policies are not favored by the African concept of time, nor is consistency in points of view. For valuable comments on this particular aspect of nonliteracy, see Daniel F. McCall, *Africa in Time Perspective* (Boston, 1964), pp. 21, 26.

One of the most concise and comprehensive commentaries on the causes and effects of the peculiarly African disposition toward time is found in the following excerpt from John Goody and Ian Watt, "The Consequences of Literacy," *Comparative Studies in Society and History*, 5 (October 1962–July 1963), 311: "The Tiv have their genealogies, others their sacred tales about the origin of the world and the way in which man acquired his culture. But all their conceptualisations of the past cannot help being governed by the concerns of the present, merely because there is no body of chronologically ordered statements to which reference can be made. The Tiv do not recognise any contradiction between what they say now and what they said fifty years ago, since no enduring records exist for them to set beside their present views. Myth and history merge into one; the elements in the cultural heritage which cease to have a contemporary relevance tend to be soon forgotten or transformed; and as the individuals of each generation acquire their

The norms and values engendered by this approach to time have made for what an African observer calls "anti-economic" motivations and attitudes that continue to impede the cause of modern political and economic development.[63] For example, the idea of saving cannot be substantiated easily in African economies, because no value attaches to work per se in the traditional social order. One worked to satisfy immediate needs, not in anticipation of distant goals. Continuous labor thus formed little or no part of tribal training, and leisure rather than effort emerged on the value scale as the mark of the prestigious man.[64]

The third all-African theme that is here regarded as a major determinant of the inner normative order is the complex of tribalism and kinship-related patterns of organization. It, too, may be viewed in the final analysis as a function of nonliteracy; for just as orality sets limits to

---

vocabulary, their genealogies, and their myths, they are unaware that various words, proper-names and stories have dropped out, or that others have changed their meanings or been replaced." For further references see Laura Bohannan, "A Genealogical Charter," *Africa* 22 (1952), 301–315.

[63] See reports and discussions of "La Notion de temps" and "Valeurs africaines traditionnelles et economie moderne" in *Tradition et Modernisme*; compare Etienne Dumont, *L'Afrique noire est mal partie* (Paris, 1962), and consult recent reports and surveys of economic conditions in African regions and nations. The latter, as accumulated in the 1970s, bear out many of the analyses and prognoses made by Dumont and others—for example, authorities listed in note 64, *infra*.

[64] Kenneth Kaunda, *Zambia Shall Be Free* (London, Toronto, and Ibadan, 1962), Appendix I, p. 163. After explaining that all Bantu tribes in Northern Rhodesia (i.e., Zambia) have the same approach to land problems, hold similar religious beliefs, are nonliterate, and have a firm belief in magic and witchcraft, the author of the appendix writes: "Where perhaps the conditions under which they have lived are most likely to produce conflict with the Europeans . . . is in their attitude to continuous labour, which forms little or no part of their tribal training." Compare Audrey I. Richards, *Land, Labour, and Diet in Northern Rhodesia; An Economic Study of the Bemba Tribe* (Oxford, 1939, repr. 1951), pp. 381ff.; also 161ff., for the view that under tribal conditions amongst the Bemba the necessary labor required to maintain the community only occupies its members for about seven months in any year. See Lloyd, *Africa in Social Change*, p. 45, that the successful West African today tends to symbolize his achievement by conspicuous leisure; and *ibid.*, p. 250, that anxiety produced by striving is often mitigated by resort to bribery and magic. See also *supra*, n. 52.

To similar effect, Denise Paulme, "Structures sociales traditionnelles en Afrique noire," in *Cahiers d'études africaines*, 1 (January 1960), p. 17 for the explanation that wealth is viewed and evaluated in Africa not by the living standard or other obvious, external symptoms, but rather by the gift exchanges that seem so utterly superfluous to Europeans; by what foreigners are apt to regard as conspicuous ways of wasting time; and above all by the number of dependents or parasites an influential man is able to maintain.

For an interesting discussion of "economic illiteracy" in Uganda, see Cyril Ehrlich, "Implications of Paternalism in Uganda," *Journal of African History*, 4, No. 2 (1963), 275–285. What continues to be lacking, Ehrlich writes, are entrepreneurial skills. The "paucity of economic sense" and "initial apathy" that are built into the people is here said to be enhanced by tribal custom, extended family obligation, and narrow horizons of expectations. Compare Ch. 19 A.

man's conception of time, so does it prescribe his orientation toward space.

Contrary to the situation in literate civilizations, where it is possible, with the aid of writing and adjunct intellectual skills and methods of communication, to extend the boundaries of the politically unified or unifiable group to control vast, even separate, terrains, and to develop such space-transcendent ideas as "humanity," "collective security," "world peace," or "world war," nonliterate societies have to be small and self-sufficient if they are to be effective and enduring. Furthermore, each must be composed exclusively of people who speak the same language, actually and figuratively; for cohesion and order cannot be assured in conditions of orality unless all people think in terms of the same symbols, identify with the same ancestral spirits, obey the same taboos—in short, communicate with each other in the firm and tacit understanding that every nuance of meaning, whether conveyed through word or through gesture, is instantly and accurately understood.

The order of the folk society, expressed in tribal and village formations, has ensured this type of closely knit, kinship-centered solidarity and conformity for millennia. The particular inflections that this general principle of organization has received in African societies have been greatly various, and the same can be said of the classificatory schemes that Africanists in different disciplines of the Occidental world of scholarship have devised.[65] And yet political scientists, historians, and law-

[65] Anthropological definitions of social structures and distinctions between different groupings are greatly various. The attributes that one scholar singles out as essential aspects of, for example, a tribe may not be the same as those stressed by his colleagues. Furthermore, different scholars are interested in different aspects of the same problem, and usually they have greatly varied opportunities for pursuing their quests. In short, what is known of a particular African community is often a function of the particular focus chosen by a particular scholar. Neither the communities themselves nor the scholarly approaches to the communities, as they emerge from the profusion of ethnographic researches in Africa, are easily comparable along reliable lines. Generalists in the field of comparative culture history and comparative political systems, being dependent upon the work of specialists, can neither overlook nor level these discrepancies. Rather, they must respect the terminology that is used in each given case.

Another range of terminological difficulties intrudes itself when vocabularies developed in the context of one culture area for the description of political organization are used to carry the meanings of government as it functions in another culture world. In discouraging the tendency to see close analogies between feudal states in Europe and the Interlacustrine states in Africa, E. M. Chilver rightly notes that the imprudent use of historical analogies may have some heuristic value, but that analogies often do as much violence to the example as to the parallel: feudalism as it existed in Europe for half a millennium has to be caricatured to be contrasted with other ways of ordering political relations; and Interlacustrine Bantu institutions must be deprived of their personality if they are to be presented divorced from the sentiments that surround them. See Richards, ed., *East African Chiefs*, pp. 378–393.

See to like effect Leroi-Gourhan and Poirier, *Ethnologie de l'Union Française,*

yers, concerned with crosscultural comparisons of literate and nonliterate, or of Asian, European, and African societies, can find significant concordances in the welter of African forms that justify references to a common core of African approaches to government.[66]

Vol. I, 340ff., who point out that it would be quite illusory to see parallelisms between political organizations in Africa on one hand, and the Occident on the other.

[66] See, among modern authorities: Murdock, *Africa*, pp. 24–39; Meyer Fortes and E. E. Evans-Pritchard, eds., *African Political Systems* (London, 1940); and J. J. Maquet, "Sub-Saharan Africa" in *International Encyclopedia of the Social Sciences*, Vol. I, 137ff. Specialized studies include Jan Vansina, *Kingdoms of the Savanna; A History of Central African States until European Occupation* (Madison, Milwaukee, and London, 1966, repr. 1968, 1970); see especially pp. 24ff. on common traits of social organization and pp. 28ff. on political structures. The cornerstone almost everywhere, Vansina writes, is the village; beyond the village level, nearly all societies are organized in kingdoms or chiefdoms; belief in witchcraft or sorcery is universal.

On common traits in the political organization of West Africa, see Daryll Forde and P. M. Kaberry, eds., *West African Kingdoms in the Nineteenth Century* (London, 1967). Lloyd, *Africa in Social Change*, p. 314, writes: "Throughout West Africa, primordial loyalties to the ethnic group remain powerful. Most men have not moved away from the villages of their ancestors in which the traditional social structure is strongly maintained. Those in the towns find security and recreation in the ethnic associations." Compare also Busia, *Africa in Search of Democracy*; and Maquet, "Sub-Saharan Africa." Paulme, "Structures sociales traditionnelles en Afrique noire," pp. 16 and 19, remarks that life everywhere in black Africa is controlled by certain attitudes toward persons and property that are not shared by contemporary Western societies. Among these special traits, none is more distinctly African than the complex of family relations that have absolute priority. What Evans-Pritchard writes about the Nuer of the Sudan, she finds applicable everywhere, namely that all rights, privileges, obligations, and so forth, are determined in kinship terms. Every individual must be either a real or a fictitious relative; unless he is capable of filling such a status, he is a stranger toward whom one is not linked by any reciprocal relations and whom one must treat as a virtual enemy.

See David Apter, *Ghana in Transition* (New York, 1963), p. 365, to the effect that the concept of chieftaincy is the essence of the African Personality; that the modern Ghanaian state may be viewed as an ensemble of clans; and that Nkrumah's position as head of state was really that of a chief. Leonard W. Doob, *Communication in Africa; A Search for Boundaries* (New Haven, 1961, repr. 1966), p. 288, for the view that the meaningful unit is the small community or tribe, and that in general there is no awareness in Africa of what is going on beyond the boundaries of the group.

A search for what is authentically African led J. Richard-Molard, *Problèmes humains en Afrique occidentale*, 2nd ed. (Paris, 1958), and *Afrique occidentale française* (Paris, 1949), to the conclusion that all African societies are, in the final analysis, reducible to peasant societies. To similar effect, Little, "African Culture and the Western Intrusion," p. 955, that kinship is the major shared culture trait. And see L.S.B. Leakey, *Mau Mau and the Kikuyu* (London, 1952, repr. 1953), pp. 31ff. for the following illustration of this principle: the term "brother" is extended to all of a man's brothers and half-brothers, and also to his male first cousins on his father's side. All of these men ranked as "father" to the males of the next generation. The fundamental basis of the Kikuyu classificatory system is to be found in three equations, Leakey explains: 1) I and my grandfather are one; 2) I and my brother and my sister are one; 3) I and my wife are one. The "father" of an extended family is plural. All brothers, half-brothers, and male cousins on the patrilineal side are one person, and it is this one person (who is yet many people) who is the head or "father" of the family.

The major feature of such a composite profile of society is the comprehensiveness of the organizational view. True to the nonliterate conceptual system of which it is an intrinsic part, the tribal order encompasses material and incorporeal, human and animal worlds. Surrealist in its ultimate reference, sustained by a human genius for creative symbolism, it allows men to ignore or supersede what the literate Western mind perceives and respects as empirical facts. The origins of a community may thus be traced securely to the fabled feats of nameless hunters or strangers from afar; confidence in existing patterns of authority can be assured by believing in the exploits of a legendary sorcerer-king, and communal identity may be derived from fictions of biological exclusiveness or of special alliances with a serpent, a crocodile, or some other creature. The social system must render the world view or ideology peculiar to each small group if it is to support the consciousness of unity; and it has done so everywhere in nonliterate Africa by relying on rites and festivals that transcend time and space, and on legends, proverbs, and taboos, masks, drums, stools, and other symbolic forms and conventions. A tribal "constitution" is thus imbedded in the sum total of myths by which the entire metaphysical community is maintained; credentials of rule are mystical, and tribal "laws" are not just to regulate human behavior, but also—indeed primarily—to assure the proper workings of superior powers, to keep evil away, and to prevent untoward things from happening. What counts on the strictly human level is the continued existence of the group in conditions of strict conformity with all traditional arrangements and beliefs, for the core of the indigenous culture is kinship, real or imaginary.

The individual alone, endowed with rights and duties by virtue of being a member of the human race, cannot be conceived of in such a set-up. Viewed, above all, as a representation of superior energies and a rather insignificant aspect of the family and clan into which he is born, he is expected to play the roles assigned to him in the cosmic and social hierarchies. It is in this context that Jomo Kenyatta identifies the Kikuyu as "first and foremost several people's relative and several people's contemporary," a man expected to speak as a member of a particular group rather than in the first person singular;[67] and that Noni Jabavu describes relations between her Xhosa "umbilicals" in South Africa: "you represent others or others represent you so that you are ever conscious even of relative status, classification and interdependent relationships in terms of which your conduct is being judged."[68] What society requires are

---

[67] *Facing Mount Kenya*, p. 309; also pp. 119 and 195; see p. 179 for a Kikuyu saying: "It is witch-doctors who live and eat alone."

[68] *Drawn in Colour*, p. 51. At the occasion of consulting with her relatives on the subject of her father's remarriage, all other interested parties expressed them-

"transparent lives," Victor Uchendu remembers.[69] Solitude is therefore regarded by the Igbo (southeast Nigeria) as "a mark of wickedness," and secretive persons are held in contempt. When things go wrong and scapegoats are being sought, the secretive are impugned as a matter of course, often to become victims of aggression or accusations of witchcraft.

Rules, taboos, and rituals are the principal devices by which a person's mental development is shaped in childhood and adolescence, so that compliance with communal expectations could become the norm.[70] Self-awareness, initiative, and ambition, which can be furthered when individuals are guided by a few broad principles requiring personal decisions for their application, obviously cannot be developed in the hypercollectivized circumstances of tribal life, except in the context of duties that a person must perform for the benefit of the group.[71] And the same conditioning explains why we cannot expect a system of feeling here, capable of generating love or hatred, compassion or insult, innocence or guilt, in an individualized way.[72]

---

selves to her through the proper "mouths" or intermediaries; and she herself was spoken to collectively because she stood for her absent sister and brother. *Ibid.*, p. 33.

[69] *The Igbo of Southeast Nigeria*, pp. 14–18.

[70] Compare Akiga, *Akiga's Story;* Stephen I. O. Anaibe, *The Wisdom of My People*; L. Bouckaert, "The Intellectual Development of the Ngwaka Child," *Tropical and Geographical Medicine*, 13, No. 1 (March 1961), 8ff.; Camara Laye, *L'Enfant noir* (Paris, 1953); Lorene K. Fox, ed., *East African Childhood; Three Versions* (Nairobi and New York, 1967); Kenyatta, *Facing Mount Kenya*; Busia, *Africa in Search of Democracy*; Margery Perham, ed., *Ten Africans* (London, 1936; repr. Evanston, Ill., 1963).

[71] Compare Carothers, "Culture, Psychiatry and the Written Word"; J. Faublée, "Madagascar au XIXᵉ siècle; Esquisse d'histoire economique et sociale," *Journal of World History*, 5, No. 2 (1959), 466: "The individual does not exist in this society. There are only personages, and their roles are determined by the family and by each man's place in the family." For a sensitive and detailed account of the making of "social man" in Senufo society (West Africa), and the role of the secret (Poro) society in this process, spanning twenty-seven years, see B. Holas, *Les Senoufu, y compris les Minianka* (Paris, 1957), especially pp. 95, 150, 167.

[72] Kenyatta, *Facing Mount Kenya*, p. 118, remarks in this connection that if one member is insulted, the whole group must seek satisfaction. And Wright, *Black Power*, p. 265, notes: "The tribal African does not really love, he worships; he does not hate, he curses." Many modern African writers focus on precisely these motifs when they treat of the culture conflict between African and European life patterns. When the Ibo hero in Chinua Achebe's novel *Things Fall Apart* adopts the Western ideal of individualism, things *do* fall apart. Indeed, as James Olney explains it in "The African Novel in Transition: Chinua Achebe," *South Atlantic Quarterly*, 70, No. 3 (Summer 1971), pp. 299–316, individualism, if it is conceived of at all in the world informing this novel, is clearly seen as a positive evil. To like effect, the South African novelist Peter Abrahams writes that "tribal man is not an individual in the Western sense. Psychologically and emotionally he is the present living personification of a number of forces, among the most important of which are the ancestral dead." Also Léopold Senghor, who remarked in one of

The interpenetration of these themes and their combined effects upon a particular tribal man, upon his norm-dispensing community, and upon the Occidental observer, have been rendered poignantly by Paul Bohannan's study of "A Man Apart" in Tiv land.[73] This man was literally nobody because he had nobody: nobody he could rely on, no mediating forces or human agents in the extreme circumstances in which he had to live and eventually die. Degraded and unclassified because genealogical irregularities prevented him from claiming either his father's or his mother's lineage, seized by terror, mentally deranged and physically sick, he was reduced to a freak, and left unaided so that he would hurry into death. No funeral rites were necessary, for even his spirit was expendable.

In the absence of a moral order enjoining pity for the weak and unfortunate, and in the overwhelming presence of a social system in which human identities and relationships are perceived and regulated in exclusive kinship contexts, the category of outcasts and outsiders is of course immense. The man who does not "belong" can have no standing here, unless he has a special protector in the community he enters, or unless he becomes a fictitious relative through adoption or blood brotherhood.[74] Outside of such exceptional circumstances, the stranger is a calamity, an object of extreme suspicion—indeed, an enemy; and as such he is liable to be robbed, maltreated, or murdered with impunity.[75] But such is the

---

his essays on African writing that none of the actors is in the European sense an individual confronting society. Every figure represents in the first instance a type; it is paradigmatic, like an African mask. See Olney, "The African Novel," pp. 307–308.

[73] *Natural History*, 77, No. 8 (October 1968); see also Paul Bohannan, *Justice and Judgment among the Tiv* (London and New York, 1957); Laura Bohannan, "Political Aspects of Tiv Social Organization," in J. Middleton and D. Tait, eds., *Tribes without Rulers; Studies in African Segmentary Systems* (London, 1958), pp. 33–66.

[74] The institution is well described by Nadel, *The Nuba*, pp. 108ff.: blood brothership in Nuba practice is a form of adoption into another clan. Two men, usually in young age groups, become "brothers" (with all that this relationship implies in regard to marriage rules) by eating together the heart of a goat killed especially for the purpose. Blood brothers must attend one another's feasts and are expected to help one another. Psychologically, Nadel writes, blood brotherhood represents a permanent form of friendship; sociologically, it is an extension of kinship bonds. And the same effects attend adoption as this occurs in certain Nuba societies, as when captured slaves or strangers are allowed to become full members of the tribe. See also E. E. Evans-Pritchard, "Zande Blood Brotherhood," in *Africa*, 6 (1933), 369ff. See *infra*, pp. 107, n. 16; 158, n. 13; 269ff.; 280; 362ff. for the significance of this institution in intertribal and international relations.

[75] See Westermann, *The African To-day and To-morrow*, p. 93; also p. 119, but see p. 26 for the incidence of hospitality and of assigned quarters for groups of "strangers." Certain exceptional categories of people who do not "belong" enjoy a favored status in many areas of Africa—for example, the foreign trader, and the member of a special casted group, notably that of the smiths. The latter are

intricacy of the traditional world view that the very abjectness of a particular human condition may be made to serve the moral and social interests of the group: the stranger can thus become part of "the system" by being cast in the ritual role of scapegoat or "carrier"—a special kind of "intermediary" between the erring living and the vengeful dead, who is saddled with all the evil that has accumulated in the community. Reduced to a symbol or an object, he must then be driven out or killed if the in-group is to survive in harmony with its ancestral spirits.[76]

---

respected in terms of their professional or ritual callings even though they are usually despised socially. Kenneth Little, in *Journal of World History*, p. 951: the kinship system "is inclined to be very exclusive and parochial, and its treatment of persons as human beings with human wants tends to be limited to its own members. The person outside is a stranger. He is to be regarded with suspicion and even with hostility." Compare also Paulme, "Structures sociales traditionnelles," p. 19; see Perham, ed., *Ten Africans*, p. 153 for the story of Amini bin Saidi, of the Yao tribe (Nyasaland, now Malawi): "I left [a European service] because the cook was always picking quarrels. He was jealous because I was put in charge of the store and everything. Mr. M. said that it would be a good thing to get rid of the cook and I should find another who did not make quarrels. But I said that as the cook lived in Mikindani it was better that I should go, as my home was far off and I feared that if he lost his job he would kill me, I being a stranger."

[76] This motif is widespread in the cultures of the world. But as Sir James George Frazer reports in his monumental study, *The Golden Bough: A Study in Magic and Religion*, 1 vol. abridged ed. (New York, 1922), it is particularly highly developed and brutally implemented in Nigeria. See pp. 538ff. on the theme as encountered in African societies, 569ff. on its incidence in Nigeria. Wole Soyinka, one of Nigeria's most gifted modern writers, has dramatized this motif in *The Strong Breed*. See Soyinka, *The Swamp-Dwellers* (Ibadan, 1963). The hero of this play is a Westernized Nigerian who returns to his native village as a teacher and reformer. Determined to pursue his goal, he is stymied at every step, harassed, and persecuted until he is eventually killed as the carrier of antagonistic forces that require this kind of exorcism. And the same destiny is treated by another Nigerian author, Chinua Achebe, in "Death of a Boy"; see Ellis Ayitey Komey and Ezekiel Mphahlele, eds., *Modern African Stories* (London, 1964), pp. 28–33. Compare also Paul Bohannan, "A Man Apart."

On widespread modern movements to exorcise Western education and religion from social life, so as to return African nations to the authenticity of ethnicity and tribalism, see *supra*, pp. 23ff., 62ff., as well as reports on developments in, among others, Chad, Zaire, Kenya, Uganda, and Ethiopia during the 1970s.

· 6 ·

MYTHICAL VISION, HISTORY,
AND SOCIETY

In the nonliterate African culture world, the individual was cancelled by society, and the human dimension was overwhelmed by that of nature. Here man was not the measure, in the sense traditionally taken for granted in the post-Hellenic West. His shape was dwarfed by the immensity of deserts, rivers, steppes, and forests; the artifacts, abodes, and other works he fashioned could not endure, and the narrow paths he found or carved were quickly lost. In such vast reaches of uncharted space and unknown time the small community preserved its identity by contracting its field of perception, severely limiting relationships with other groups, and insisting on self-sufficiency and exclusiveness. Mythical thinking assured the continuity of this type of self-awareness and discouraged kinship-transcendent notions of a collective destiny. But in response to certain kinds of challenges and experiences, it could also soar beyond the narrow confines of "the here and now," and extend the frontiers of perception and remembrance to accommodate the destinies of other groups—those that had made their marks on the environment in previous times, as well as those found to coexist in nearby but alien quarters.

Such mythical visions of "a greater society" have had a particularly strong hold on the imagination of generations in the western Sudan, where, as we now know, empires comprising different groups of Negroes, Berbers, and Arabs, did in fact arise in pre-Islamic times, and where animists, Christians, and Mohammedans were to coexist thereafter. Here myths and memories mingled in a rich epic folklore that in the nineteenth and early twentieth centuries was still part of the living tradition—fully audible to a few literate European scholars with an ear for oral poetry. And among these enduring legends there is one that symbolizes most vividly the nature of the greater vision: a cycle of Soninke stories telling of the loss and rediscovery of the mythical city of Wagadu. The overture to one version of this cycle of tales, "Gassire's Lute," opens with the following theme:

> Four times Wagadu stood there in all her splendor. Four times Wagadu disappeared and was lost to human sight—once through vanity, once through falsehood, once through greed and once through dissension. Four times Wagadu changed her name—first she was

100

called Dierra, then Agada, then Ganna, then Silla. Four times she turned her face—once to the north, once to the west, once to the east and once to the south. For Wagadu, whatever men have seen has always had four gates—one to the north, one to the west, one to the east, and one to the south. Those are the directions whence the strength of Wagadu comes, the strength in which she endures no matter whether she be built of stone, wood and earth, or lives but as a shadow in the mind and longing of her children. In reality, Wagadu is the strength which lives in the hearts of men and is sometimes visible because eyes see her and ears hear the clash of swords and ring of shields, and is sometimes invisible because the indomitability of men has overtired her, so that she sleeps. Sleep came to Wagadu for the first time through vanity, for the second time through falsehood, for the third time through greed and for the fourth time through dissension. . . .

Every time that the guilt of man caused Wagadu to disappear she won a new beauty which made the splendor of her next appearance still more glorious. Vanity brought the song of bards which all peoples imitate and value today. Falsehood brought a rain of gold and pearls. Greed brought writing as the Burdama still practice it today and which in Wagadu was the business of women. Dissension will enable the fifth Wagadu to be as enduring as the rain of the south and the rocks of the Sahara, for every man will then have Wagadu in his heart.[1]

One of the surviving fragments of the epic song declares that Wagadu lost its strength and went to sleep when it was Dierra (identified by Frobenius with a present day ruin in Fezzan) because Gassire, the princely heir and martial hero, had determined to seek power and glory in his own right. Tired of longing for his ruling father's death, heedless of the destiny of Wagadu, he collected his sons and followers and moved away, beyond the reach of loyalties to kith and kin, entrusting the cause of his renown to a lute that a magician-smith had made for him after a partridge in the steppe had asked him to believe that whereas kings and heroes are born to die and cities built to perish, the songs of great exploits endure forever, outlasting every Wagadu.

Perishable but floating, as it moved from place to place with migrating folk and conquering heroes, Wagadu, in its later incarnations, may well have been identical at one time with what is Agades today, at another,

---

[1] Recorded and reconstructed by Leo Frobenius, who heard it from a bard in Togo in 1909; see *Monumenta Africana* (being Vol. 6 of *Erlebte Erdteile*), pp. 41ff.; for an English translation see Frobenius and Fox, *African Genesis* (New York, 1937), pp. 97ff., 109–110. For a different treatment see Charles Monteil, *La Légende du Ouagadou et l'origine des Soninké, Mémoire*, IFAN, No. 23, Etude 6, 359–408. (Dakar, 1953), and see authorities cited *ibid.*, p. 367.

with ancient Ghana (to the west of Timbuktu, in Mauretania), then with Silla, to be subsumed, thereafter, by the next contender for supremacy over the region, the empire of Mali.[2] But its historicity is finally irrelevant; for in the African consciousness Wagadu is primarily a city of the mind: a potent word or name, capable of evoking differing but related memories of glory; an image summarizing centuries of human movement and encounter; a symbol of the flux of power and shift of cultural strength from one center of gravity to the next.[3]

These ways of visualizing the great comprehensive society find eloquent confirmation in Charles Monteil's masterful presentation of the Wagadu theme.[4] As heard by him in 1898 from a Soninke "geseru" (bard) in Medina, the tale revolved around the origins of the Soninke and the founding of Kumbi-Wagadu as the capital of the old Ghana empire in Mauretania.[5] Although Islamized in many of its references and assumptions, this version of the story, too, abounds in narratives of

[2] Frobenius, *Monumenta Africana*, pp. 59ff. A second version of the legend includes Tirka as the fifth Wagadu.

[3] Ezra Pound, a great admirer of Frobenius' quality of mind and method of reconstructing history and tracing the metamorphoses of culture, borrowed the image of Wagadu in *The Pisan Cantos* (Canto LXXIX). Here Wagadu, "Now in the mind indestructible," stands for one of Pound's paradisical visions. See Guy Davenport, "Pound and Frobenius," in Lewis Leary, ed., *Motive and Method in the Cantos of Ezra Pound* (New York, 1954), pp. 52ff.

Leo Frobenius has been greatly neglected by English and French writers on Africa. Yet he is one of very few Europeans who recognized early that the African realm was a distinct and unified culture zone, marked by thoughtways and a sense for the past that required careful reconstruction by multidisciplinary methods. It is interesting to note that Frobenius' contributions have recently been recognized explicitly in African intellectual circles. See, for example, Dualla Misipo, "Léo Frobenius, le Tacite de l'Afrique," in *Présence africaine*, No. 37 (2ème trimestre 1961), pp. 151–156. Furthermore, a "Frobenius exposition" (supported by German academic institutions and UNESCO) was presented in 1973 in twenty African states. At one of these occasions Senghor summarized Frobenius' work by saying: "il nous a rendu notre dignité." (He has given us back our dignity, or, he has returned us to our dignity.)

[4] See "La Légende de Ouagadou."

[5] *Ibid.*, p. 377, for a map of the legendary Wagadu; p. 385 for a map tracing the dispersals of the Soninke; compare Raymond Mauny, *Tableau géographique de l'Ouest africain au moyen age d'après les sources écrites, la tradition et l'archéologie* (*Mémoire*, IFAN, No. 61) (Dakar, 1961), p. 72 on the site of Kumbi-Saleh-Ghana in Mauretania; pp. 54ff. on the relevance of legends and other oral traditions in the work of archeologists and historians, pp. 67ff. on the difficulties of locating towns securely in time and place, especially in pre-Islamic times. Ouagadougou is today the capital of Upper Volta. For a close study of Ouagadougou in the 1960s see Elliott P. Skinner, *African Urban Life, The Transformation of Ouagadougou* (Princeton, 1974). The aim of the work, as stated on p. 10, is to view this particular town as a framework in which to analyze the human activities characteristic of African urbanism. See Leo Frobenius, *Spielmannsgeschichten der Sahel*, Vol. VI of *Atlantis, Volksmaerchen und Volksdichtungen Afrikas* (Jena, 1921), pp. 50ff., for a tentative mapping of the different incorporations of the idea of Wagadu.

flights and migrations.[6] Here, as in all other Wagadus, the ordinary mortal was expected to yield to the power of magic, whether vested in a special type of man or in certain special animals—in the present case, an old hyena and a mighty serpent. The end of Wagadu-Kumbi came to pass when a young man killed the serpent to whom his beloved was about to be sacrificed in accordance with an age-old custom. The monster's severed head announced that, as a consequence of the impious act, no drop of water would henceforth fall and no morsel of gold ever again be found. Wagadu was ruined and its people dispersed, but the magic of the image captured in the name remains, ever ready to be rediscovered, reshaped, and revivified by other peoples consumed by dreams of an enduring power.[7]

For example, the legend of this city, capable of rising phoenix-like from all manner of havoc and destruction, seems to have possessed the Sudanese Tuareg[8] and to have been echoed also in Yoruba land.[9] Indeed,

[6] See Monteil, "La Légende du Ouagadou," for the rather typically Islamic love motif and for the fusion of the "geseru" with the Islamic "marabout" (p. 376). See Mauny, *Tableau géographique*, pp. 72ff. to the effect that the image of Kumbi-Saleh-Ghana was conveyed intact in the Tarikh el-Fettach (probably composed between A.D. 1519 and 1665), about three hundred years after the town had been totally destroyed by Sundiata, king of Mali.

[7] Mauny writes in *Tableau géographique*, pp. 72ff., that the indigenous animist population of Kumbi was, in fact, displaced, probably in the direction of Walata and neighboring sites, when Islamic rulers razed the quarter of the town to which the original inhabitants had been assigned. See *ibid.*, p. 74, that the Ghana of the animist kings is still to be rediscovered.

[8] The Tuareg, who represent a vital but generally destructive force in the records of West Africa, are said to have conquered, occupied, enlarged, and embellished a town originally built by the blacks. This town, we learn from the myth, was then destroyed three times: the first time through jealousy; the second time because men could not find a place wherein to pray to God, the land being overcome by thicket; and the third time through devastation by an enemy. See Henri Lhote, "Contribution à l'étude des Touaregs soudanais" in *Bulletin de l'IFAN*, 17, ser. B., Nos. 3–4 (1955), 334–370; 18, Nos. 3–4 (1956), pp. 391–408. Historical research relating to the destiny of Tadmekka in the desert region of the Niger bend supports the general purport of the legend; a town once crucial for trade relations between the Mediterranean region and "the country of the Blacks" was dismembered by Islamic forces coming from the northwest. Brutally pillaged by Sonni Ali in the fifteenth century, abandoned by neighboring tribes whose mutual relationships were rent by strife, the town disappeared because it had no reason to exist. For another interesting discussion of the place of the Tuareg in the vicissitudes of Wagadu see Frobenius, *Monumenta Africana*, p. 80. Also *infra*, pp. 117; 197, n. 76; 278–80.

[9] A Yoruba king is said to have consolidated his realm by burying charms in several places of his capital so that it might never be destroyed by war. In further support of this desire, he is said to have offered his newborn child to his medicine man so that it might be pulverized for medicinal purposes. This act, Johnson writes in *The History of the Yorubas from the Earliest Times to the Beginnings of the British Protectorate* (London, first pub. 1921, repr. 1969), p. 167, is to this day highly regarded by the people. Oyo was deserted and lay in ruins, but it was

103

in the light of this strong African tradition entrusting the twin causes of collective identity and aspiration to a name that has proven its magical potency—albeit in different places and at different times—it is not too farfetched to view the recent transfer of the name "Ghana" from the past of the Sudanese steppes to the present of the Gold Coast as the latest rediscovery of Wagadu, incarnated this time in the city of Accra, which modern Ghanaian leaders have presented to the world as the locus of Africa's future power and destiny.

Now and then, here as there, myth overrides reality. Regions remote from each other on a modern map are allowed to interpenetrate; generations separated by centuries, perhaps millennia, coalesce; conquerors and conquered, slavers and enslaved, the light and the dark complexioned, intermingle in the imagination, in defiance of historical facts that establish them as pairs of opposites. Here personalities are not delineated, names need not be verified, events can be accepted without dates, and relationships between tribes, lineages, and other groupings, fathomed or remembered as significant without inquiry into the actuality of incidents; empires can be admired or feared without knowledge of just how vast they are or were, or what inequities they perpetrated. What counts in the West African understanding of the past is the reputation of success and greatness as relayed by the magic of the spoken word. No personage, therefore, is more respected than the mythmaking lutist (usually a member of a casted group), who is committed to remember and propagate the honor and glory of the hero-chief or the ruling lineage to which he is attached. Whether described in ethnographic literature as "bard," "griot," or "geseru," he is "le magicien du verbe"[10]—a master in the art of fashioning indestructible cities of the mind and images of greater societies, which are trusted by the living even though floating in time and space.

---

never destroyed by war. Compare Meek, *A Sudanese Kingdom*, p. 36, on the wide currency of the legend of Wagadu and on the general role of the Mande as a major unifying factor in the region. Compare *infra*, Ch. 7.

[10] Monteil, "La Légende du Ougadou," p. 365. For a masterful treatment of the African bard in different parts of West Africa, see Frobenius, *Spielmannsge-schichten der Sahel*, p. 35; see p. 41 on his greatly various roles: for example, whereas bards were important primarily as advisors at the courts of the Fulani, concerned mainly with the military expeditions of their patrons, they were esteemed at Mali courts mostly for their eloquence, shrewdness, and diplomatic skills. In this region, every nobleman had one or more of these "Dialli," who were then used as royal messengers, negotiators, or "public relations experts," in addition to being honored as custodians of mythical and epical truths.

It is thus no accident that one of the most successful modern African novels treats of West African history in just this bardic manner. In writing *Le Devoir de violence* (Paris, 1968), Yambo Ouologuem merges oral tradition, Arab chroniclers, and other forms of the remembered past much in the manner of a griot. See Ch. 18 for other references to this interesting profession.

History, then, is not a meaningful reference in African culture and politics. In the Sudan, as well as in parts of the continent in which the tradition of the griot was not developed, political identity is an outgrowth of nonliterate ways of experiencing the past.[11] These, it must be stressed, are antithetical to the Occidental historical approach to self-understanding, which is grounded in literate modes of thought and in the commitment, honored from the days of Herodotus onward, to remember the individual, the specific, and the episodic as precisely as possible.

The distinction made here between these two culturally different styles of collective self-awareness does not imply, however, that African history, as it is now being reconstructed with the aid of literate skills, is going to be significantly different in conception and in kind from the histories of other peoples. Rather, it is designed to draw attention to the fact that Africans can accept as "real" images or models of a unified society that Europeans would dismiss out of hand either as remnants of folklore or as utopian dreams. As Ian Cunnison has explained the case in a sensitive analysis of historical notions among tribes on the Luapula (Congo),[12] Africans have no difficulty in accepting at face value occurrences from a remembered time transmitted by their elders, which a Western mind would regard as inconceivable or highly unlikely. The meanings carried by African history for Africans themselves are therefore as closed to logical analysis of the type developed in the Occident as are the meanings held for them by witchcraft. In short, history in this culture is caught up in a wider mythical cycle, in the context of which it is sociologically and intellectually irrelevant whether the events named might be possible, improbable, or downright mythical. Cunnison's Luapula informants went so far as to rationalize the mythical renditions of their past by saying that the strangest of things could and did in fact take place until the Europeans tried to stop indigenous medical practices.

Anyone attempting to unify the past records of different but neighboring communities so as to prepare a common political destiny has to contend in Africa with yet another difficulty, one to which allusion has already been made. For not only is time as such undifferentiated and irrelevant unless associated with episodes to which significance has been attached, but each clan, subclan, immigrant group, or other unit, has its own notion of a significant time to which it must cling, if only in order to perpetuate knowledge of its own origins and of its arrival in the place

[11] *Supra*, Ch. 5.

[12] Ian Cunnison, *History on the Luapula; An Essay on the Historical Notions of a Central African Tribe* (London and Cape Town, 1951), pp. 21ff. Cunnison notes (p. 22) that the presence of writing today has not dispelled the tradition of mythical thought. See also the same author's *The Luapula Peoples of Northern Rhodesia; Custom and History in Tribal Politics* (Manchester, 1959).

now shared with others. The outsider-historian may view the Luapula Valley as an entity; he may correlate and juxtapose the peregrinations of its groups, compare the constructs of their imagination, and arrive at a "unity" in space as well as time; the human objects of these unifying sets of conceptualization are, however, likely to remain unmoved and unconvinced. Up to the present, at any rate, they will have relied on other, traditionally tested manners of relating to their common environment, while at the same time preserving their respective identities.

A quasi-organic unity between ethnically or linguistically different groups may thus be assured in some regions by invoking the sanction of such a special unifying legend as, for example, that of Wagadu; in others by simply assuming that the first and crucial encounter between two groups will have remained perpetually valid in all particulars. And this second device will have had the effect of screening from consciousness any changes that might have occurred in the actual identities either of the human representatives or in the conditions of their de facto coexistence; for it will have presented the relationship as linking, not two concrete human communities, but the two names signifying the original forebears.

For example, descendants of the Shila and the Lunda in the Luapula Valley continue, in midtwentieth century, to think of themselves and their reciprocal relations in terms of the original historical situation in which the Lunda had been victorious over the Shila. This meant that the latter were to be forever connected with the swamp, the land, and the water—and therefore privileged in respect to fishing rights—whereas the Lunda were to be forever associated with the tasks of government. Later immigrant groups to the valley, by contrast, Cunnison reports, have tended to view the two communities as one; and another constitutive myth has it, in effect, that the chief of the defeated Shila became a Lunda, duly invested with a Lunda cloth and endowed with a Lunda slogan that could be played on the Lunda Talking Drum. In this respect the descriptive formula or proverb reads: "We are Lunda-Shila," or, "We married each other."

By viewing tribal members as mere agents of a name or of the role suggested by the name, a change-resistant, tribe-transcendent, regional order can evolve. All generations from the first to the latest are then telescoped into one, the past is made to coincide with the present, and time is, as it were, annulled. The device of perpetuation thus affects not only names and roles but also the total social and natural context in which the relation between the names originated. Indeed, the crucial aspect in this type of situation is probably the land that accommodates the different groups.

According to mythical charters in force almost everywhere in Africa, land is closely associated with the spirit world. Any group installed in a given territory is believed to live there in symbiosis with tutelary spirits in whom the real ownership of the soil, the river, or the forest is supposed to vest. In order to be accepted by these powers, immigrant and conquering groups usually invoke the mediating services of those who first settled there; for it is this original community that is presumed to have set up the compact with the spirit world in the first place. Recognized from one generation to the next as "chiefs of the earth" ("maitres du sol," "chefs de terre"), "chiefs of water," and so on, these representatives are traditionally associated by all other inhabitants with certain exclusive ritual functions that must be properly complied with, if nature is to yield its boons to any of the separate communities. Under the terms of such a legendary pact—found to be still in force in 1957—the first immigrant chief of the Bariba (Northern Dahomey) is said to have assured those whom he defeated that he would respect their religious practices, and that the burial of his own descendents would be entrusted to them as chiefs of the earth. Other understandings seem to have included, besides an exchange of women, a division of administrative functions such that, while the Bariba prince should have the right to name the chief of the earth, the latter should be entitled to officiate in the designation of the royal successor.[13] Here, as in a number of similar arrangements, the victor was associated permanently with ultimate political power and the vanquished with the representation of the land's spirit world.[14] In other words, the two groups were kept distinct, but their coexistence was hallowed by a shared myth.

Mystic participation in a common destiny is also recognized in joking-pacts that link communities in a system of privileged verbal insult on the analogy of similar intracommunity practices,[15] taboo-fellowships, blood pacts,[16] and numerous categories of quasi-professional guilds and secret societies whose jurisdictions reach beyond the boundaries of official or overtly functioning local governments. Some of these may quite openly promote essentially practical interests. For example, the Sukuma in East Africa accommodate dance societies, working parties for mutual aid in field cultivation, and fraternities for the hunting of snakes, elephants, and

[13] J. Lombard, "Un Système politique traditionnel de type féodal: les Bariba du Nord-Dahomey," *Bulletin de l'IFAN*, 19, ser. B, Nos. 3–4 (1957), 487ff.
[14] See also Rouch, *Les Songhay*, pp. 35ff.; Cunnison, *History on the Luapula*, p. 15; and *The Luapula Peoples*, pp. 212ff., 228. J. Cuvelier, ed. and trans., *Relations sur le Congo du Père Laurent de Lucques (1700–1717)* (Brussels, 1953), p. 146; J. C. Froehlich, *Cameroun-Togo* (Paris, 1956), p. 32; Westermann, *Geschichte Afrikas*, p. 405, where the institution of "Erdherren" is discussed in the context of the Bantu states of Central Africa.
[15] *Supra*, Ch. 5 and *infra*, Ch. 11, "Verbal Aggression and the Muting of Tensions."
[16] *Supra*, Ch. 5, n. 74, and *infra*, pp. 158, 173, 269, 280, 362 on blood pacts between members of the same society and between different communities.

alligators that are responsive to the needs of outsiders of the community.[17] And much the same was true in the context of commerce as conducted in southern Nigeria, where effective authority was long exercised not by the kings of the major trading towns, but by the all-pervading Egbo Society and its component "houses." Each of these was at once a cooperative trading unit and a local government institution controlled by wealthy merchants with a membership of hundreds or thousands of slaves, bound together by a common loyalty and a common system of rewards and punishments.[18]

The vast majority of the societies here selected for consideration emanate from religious convictions, however, and serve the intangible purposes of a dominant cult. Based on the belief that the dead continue to live and take an active interest in the affairs of the living, and that nature is peopled by spirits and ghosts, they are there to control human behavior and maintain the existing order by the exercise of ultimate sacred sanctions. Their statecraft is thus magical par excellence, for it relies on the monopolistic administration of a body of esoteric knowledge, communicated in conditions of secrecy through the medium of masks, occult words, signs, and rites; and on institutions and disciplines —usually including oathing—that are designed to rally the membership into absolute obedience to the purposes of the society as interpreted by a hidden government.[19] Furthermore, the cause of dissimulation and covert organization is enhanced in many instances by the belief that the human realm is related inextricably to that of the animal world, and by the common incidence, in widely separated parts of the continent, of certain animal species. To imitate the habits, particularly the modes of killing, peculiar to a locally paramount beast—as, for example, the leopard, the panther, the lion, the crocodile, or the python—and in so doing increase the sense of awe and mystery by disguising the human will or

[17] Hans Cory, *The Indigenous Political System of the Sukuma and Proposals for Political Reform* (Nairobi, 1954), pp. 72ff., 87ff.

[18] K. O. Dike, *Trade and Politics in the Niger Delta, 1830–1885* (Oxford, 1956), pp. 37–41. On markets as aspects of intertribal cooperation see *infra*, Ch. 19 A.

[19] On secret societies among the Ibo, see Meek, *Law and Authority in a Nigerian Tribe*, pp. 53ff., especially pp. 66ff., where the Mmo, ancestral spirits personated by maskers, are discussed. The Ogboni lodges in the southern and western Yoruba kingdoms represent similar principles and practices.
On the role of secret societies among the Ewe and related tribes, see Froehlich, *Cameroun-Togo*, pp. 168ff. For general analyses of the subject see F. W. Butt-Thompson, *Secret Societies in West Africa* (London, 1929); P. E. Joset, *Les Sociétés secrètes des hommes-léopards en Afrique noire* (Paris, 1955), pp. 153ff. on the reasons for the stubborn survival of some of the ritual practices in the twentieth century. Also Ch. Béart, "D'Une Sociologie des peuples africains à partier de leurs jeux," *Bulletin de l'IFAN*, 21 Nos. 3–4 (July-October, 1959), p. 293, on the spread of secret societies in modern times; what the modern African fails to find today in his traditonal organization, this author argues, he now seeks and finds in the secret society.

action, could thus become the constitutional source, as it were, for such secret societies as the leopard men.[20] This does not mean, of course, that the human leopards of, for example, the Congo, have actually been known to be affiliated with the leopard men in Sierra Leone and Liberia. The parallelisms have rather been coincidental, being functions primarily of the same basic belief system, and secondarily of the presence in the two places of the same animal species.

Another major common motif needs to be mentioned in this connection if the record of Africa's great covert societies is to be appreciated in its full complexity. Most, if not all of them, including those that rely on the mediating or representational roles of animals, are linked directly or obliquely with overt governments and social institutions. However, whereas some may be said to support or otherwise implement the operation of established authorities, others are commonly dreaded as antisocial forces, serving the ends of witchcraft and black, rather than white, magic. To give but one illustration: when the Leopard Society of the Mende had fallen into disrepute toward the end of the nineteenth century as a result of having engaged in wanton acts of terrorism and ritual murder, a counterforce, known as the Tonga Players, swiftly arose to combat these excesses. But this secret grouping, too, was destined to degenerate into a lawless band, defiant of traditional restraints.

One of the most complex, influential, and enduring of Africa's numerous mystical guilds is the West African Poro. Among the Senufo in the region of the Ivory Coast, this organization was recognized as the main training and proving ground for initiates from all autonomous and economically self-sufficient villages, the depositary of common religious values and social customs, and the sole custodian of ultimate hermetic wisdom by which the realms of humans and spirits were held together. Poro members, gathered into age groups regardless of their local origins, and initiated into the magic fraternity by rigid disciplines distributed over a life cycle of twenty-one years (divided into three phases of seven years each), received continuous instruction in this occult knowledge and the secret language that went with it, until they shed their individualities and family allegiances to become obedient, socially perfect units of the supreme collective. A Senufo Poro (the particulars of the organizational set-up varied from place to place) was thus primarily a mystical brotherhood. But it was also the most trusted agency for the maintenance of order. For since men were Poro members first, and family or village representatives second, and since all acts performed in the Poro's name were

[20] The concept underlying this type of society is not to be confused with totemism. See Frederick William Hugh Migeod, *A View of Sierra Leone* (New York, 1927), pp. 222ff. on this point and on the significance of masking, voice impersonation, and other disguises. See also *infra*, p. 112, 155ff., 166ff.

presumed to relay the superior power of ancestral spirits, the corporation was naturally capable of exerting decisive pressure in all fields of practical politics. Indeed, a survey of its astonishing vitality in the face of invasions by the neighboring Diula and continuous Islamic and French inroads convinced Holas that the Poro is the most effective shield for the preservation of the original Senufo culture.[21]

But it is among the Mende and peoples influenced by the Mende or otherwise related to them, that the Poro has registered its impact most consistently, for it seems to have been as important in these regions between the sixteenth and nineteenth centuries, when several travellers and explorers noted its existence, as it proved to be in the 1890s at the occasion of the Mende Rising (initiated by a protest against the imposition of a hut tax in the newly established British Protectorate), and again in 1955–1956, when the Poro, discontent with certain aspects of chiefly rule, succeeded by dint of secret preparations in staging riots and battles that took the governing authorities completely by surprise.[22]

The Mende of Sierra Leone and Liberia, estimated in mid-twentieth century as numbering close to one million, live in small towns and villages that are distributed among politically independent, mutually antagonistic chiefdoms. They are, nonetheless, described by Little as "a nation," first because they inhabit a fairly well defined territory; and second because their love of war, pride in the records of belligerent exploits left by their ancestors, and disdain for non-Mende peoples had combined, from early times onward, to imbue them with a strong conscious-

[21] Holas, *Les Sénoufo*, pp. 49–167. For a brief discussion of the Poro and other secret societies in some parts of West Africa see also Denise Paulme, *Sculptures de l'Afrique noire* (Paris, 1956), pp. 45ff., 90ff., and cf. *supra*, pp. 105ff.; *infra*, pp. 155ff., pp. 166ff., p. 347.

[22] For excerpts from the observations left by Valentin Fernandes between 1506–1510 and other early travellers, see Christopher Fyfe, *Sierra Leone Inheritance* (London, 1964), pp. 27, 32. Informative reports were recorded by Olfert Dapper, the Dutch geographer, in 1670; Lieutenant John Matthews, *A Voyage to the River Sierra Leone* (London, 1788; 2nd ed., 1791); this work was read in the German edition: Johann Matthews, Lieutenant bei der Grosbrittanischen Flotte, *Reise nach Sierra Leone auf der Westlichen Kueste von Afrika* (Leipzig, 1789). Page references in following text refer to this German edition. Major A. G. Laing, whose work was published in 1825, and Caillié, *Travels through Central Africa to Timbuctoo*, Vol. I, 153ff. on the function of the society among the tribes on the banks of the Rio Nuñez.

The Poro was indicated by the geographer Ptolemy under the name of *Purrus campus*, a term translated by Migeod, *A View of Sierra Leone*, p. 210, as "Poro bush." See M. McCulloch, *Peoples of Sierra Leone* (London, 1950), p. 30, to the effect that Poro means "no end, far behind." D. Westermann, *The African To-day and To-morrow*, 3rd ed., pp. 94ff. expresses the view that the influence of the Poro and other secret societies on Kpelle communities in Liberia was declining in the 1940s.

ness of being a single people.[23] And since the Poro is generally acknowledged to subsume these determinants effectively, it is rightly regarded as the third and probably most important connecting link between the separate political units.[24]

The supremacy of the Poro in Mende affairs was assured by interlocking systems of initiation, communication, and administration. Introduced to the unifying spirits of the secret bush by the same harsh disciplines, potent medicines, and rituals, novices in different localities were made to think, feel, and act in total concert with their fellow initiates, both near and far.[25] This tutelage, analogous in major respects to that in force among the Senufo, was deemed indispensable for anyone hoping to occupy a position of authority in a chiefdom, apart from being valued as the most important experience in the life of the ordinary Mende. All emerge from the process of psychological conditioning as Poro men, committed to keep Poro secrets, acknowledging Poro law as the supreme directive of their lives, and obeying the orders of the elders in the different Poro chapters. Furthermore, anyone initiated in one area of the land was allowed to participate in Poro gatherings outside his own locality, always, of course, according to the status he enjoyed in his own lodge. Next, all could recognize each other instantly as Poro members by virtue of common secret watchwords, symbols, and scarification marks. No specific instructions were thus required in this system of communication if the society wanted to mobilize its manhood in a common cause. For example, war against the Sierra Leone government simply became a fact in 1898 after half a burnt leaf had been sent through the land as a symbolic token of the Poro's decision.[26]

These arrangements help to explain why the society was able to function without a permanent central government. The initiative for action was invariably taken by a high chief in one of the autonomous local lodges. He would convene his inner circle, place the subordinate chiefs under the Poro oath, and they in turn would call up and bind their people in similar fashion. The oath, secret in its nature, then became the password signaling to all concerned that the person knowing the name of the oath was indeed a Poro member. A web of oaths could in this way be made to cover the country at very short notice and before the actual

[23] Kenneth Little, *The Mende of Sierra Leone; A West African People in Transition*, rev. ed. (London, 1967), pp. 72ff.; *ibid.*, p. 52, that war is the major industry of the Mende and that their estimation of another people's worth is based largely on the latter's prowess in conducting war. For a detailed analysis of the Poro see Little, "The Political Function of the Poro," *Africa*, 35, No. 4 (October 1965), 349ff. and 36, No. 1 (January 1966), 62ff.

[24] Migeod, *A View of Sierra Leone*, p. 234.

[25] Little, "Political Function of the Poro," Vol. 35, 362.

[26] Migeod, *A View of Sierra Leone*, p. 235.

object of the oath had become generally known, as lodge after lodge responded to the call that had originated in "the birthplace of the oath."[27]

It was in the assurance of this kind of solidarity that Poro authorities were invariably successful in calling up the far-flung membership in behalf of embargos on trade or farm work,[28] military operations, or programs of pacification. Indeed, native informants and foreign observers have repeatedly noted that Poro power was absolute in internal as well as external affairs. What Caillié found on the banks of the Rio Nuñez at the beginning of the nineteenth century—namely that the Poro government, while invisible to the uninitiated, was nevertheless the major, if not the only, effective agency for making laws, supervising their execution, administering ordeals, and adjudicating disputes and crimes[29]—was confirmed by scholars in the present century. Migeod thus notes that Poro medicine continued to be used for swearing in new chiefs, and that decisions reached by the highest Poro authorities were accepted as binding in all Mende-speaking chiefdoms, since they issued from what was commonly accepted as "a council of delegates of the manhood of the nation."[30] In deference to this authority, Little writes, all matters of serious concern to a chiefdom, notably offences involving sorcery, murder, and other capital crimes, quarrels between men of consequence, disputes between rival towns, and feuds with other chiefdoms were submitted to moots of Poro elders, usually disguised to impersonate the spirit world they represent. Each decision was reached and summarily executed in strict secrecy, contrary to non-Poro Mende custom, which stipulated public hearings for most cases. No serious fighting was allowed while the Poro was in session or in the process of settling conflicts. Poro tribunals and councils, by contrast, could decree fierce punishments, inflict death without ever accounting for it, initiate war internally and against foreigners, and end hostilities either by edict and arbitration or by means of punitive expeditions. The latter were usually composed of bands of armed and masked agents who were empowered to kill anyone in sight.[31]

The interaction of overt and covert governments and the interpenetration of violence and law, or war and peace, that marked the Poro's constitution and patterns of action has been relayed by Matthews in the fol-

[27] Little, "Political Function of the Poro," Vol. 35, 363; and *The Mende of Sierra Leone*, pp. 183ff.

[28] See Christopher Fyfe, *A History of Sierra Leone* (London, 1962), for numerous references to such episodes in modern Sierra Leone politics.

[29] *Travels*, Vol. I, 157; also p. 227. Little, *The Mende of Sierra Leone*, pp. 40ff. for a Mende's account.

[30] *A View of Sierra Leone*, p. 234.

[31] *The Mende of Sierra Leone*, pp. 183, 248, 251; also Migeod, *A View of Sierra Leone*, pp. 246ff. on the interpenetration of Poro and other secret societies, notably the ancient Wondi War Society.

lowing way.[32] When two warring tribes or ethnic groups wished to conclude their hostilities, but were too proud to send out peace feelers directly, they would first ask the ruler of a neighboring country to send mediators. That chief would usually agree to do so, but only on condition that the decision of his agents would be uncontested by the parties. When compliance was not forthcoming, the chief, being also a Poro man, would mobilize the secret society against the party he considered aggressive. Groups of about fifty armed and masked men would then descend on the land, striking terror wherever they appeared, putting to death whomever they encountered, and erasing all the evidence of their various activities. Law and order has thus long been maintained in the Mende region by a combination of armed force and supernatural power, both transcendent of local political jurisdictions.

In view of this historical record, it is not surprising that Western scholars of African affairs have spoken of the Poro as a type of African freemasonry,[33] an institutional structure bearing resemblance to the medieval Christian church, or as an agent of a kind of League of Nations applying what Europeans call international law.[34] But, as Lord Hailey warns, it is always dangerous to attempt to illustrate the character of African institutions by European analogies.[35] The African concept of the regionally unified or intertribal "great society," of which the Poro is perhaps the most impressive manifestation, is unique, since it is fathomable only in the context of the all-African belief in the relevance of vital magical forces for the governance of men. And the same principles are substantiated by another nontypical but singularly interesting "union" found in certain parts of southern Africa, where comprehensive hierarchically structured spirit-realms are known to have had considerable social and political influence as late as the end of the last century.

As conceived and realized in the Zambezi region by the Korekore and other Shona-speaking peoples, among whom spirit possession and confidence in the mediating powers of ancestral and other spirits is particularly highly developed, this design emerges as a network of tightly struc-

[32] See his Fifth Letter in Matthews, *Reise nach Sierra Leone*.

[33] To this effect see Matthews' Fifth Letter and Caillié, *Travels*, Vol. I, 157; cf. also Westermann, *The African To-day and To-morrow*, p. 95 where taboo-fellowships are so characterized following suggestions left by M. Delafosse in *Haut-Sénégal-Niger*, 3 vols. (Paris, 1912), Vol. III, 105. The parallel to the medieval church is made, among others, by Little, *The Mende of Sierra Leone*, pp. 240ff., 246.

[34] Compare Frobenius, *Menschenjagden und Zweikaempfe* (Jena, no date), p. 200. For a general description and analysis of secret societies in different parts of Africa, see Frobenius, *Monumenta Africana*, ch. 6, "Der Geheimbund," pp. 213–273; also *Vom Voelkerstudium zur Philosophie, der neue Blick* (Frankfurt, 1925, being Vol. IV of *Erlebte Erdteile*), pp. 130ff.

[35] William Malcolm, Lord Hailey, *Native Administration in the British African Territories*, 5 vols. (London, 1950–1953), Part III (1951), pp. 297ff.

tured links between the parallel worlds of the dead and the living, as well as between the rival references to the principles, respectively, of kinship and territoriality.[36] It seems to have arisen in "the remote past" (probably the fifteenth century) after Mutota (identified by several modern scholars with Monomotapa, founder of the Monomotapa kingdom,[37] had led the group of original invaders into the land they eventually came to occupy. This Mutota, from whom many present-day Korekore chiefs claim patrilineal descent, and several of his deceased descendants continue to be represented by "spirit mediums," that is to say, by certain men and women deemed qualified, when spiritually possessed, to mediate between the transient living and the eternal spirits of the original owners of the earth. Viewed by the people as guardians of the moral, as distinct from the purely social, system, these mediums are expected to intervene whenever a crisis is felt to exist in the relationship between the natural and the human orders, as, for example, when the rain does not fall, or when doubts arise about the fertility of the soil.

According to the mythical charter here in force, all land—whether now occupied or not—is divided into what Garbett calls "spirit provinces," each named after, and associated with, the spirit of a man who is thought to have been one of the original Karanga invaders, a descendant of an invader, or, less commonly, an autochthon. Each spirit and its representative living medium function within known territorial boundaries that may not be transgressed by other spirits or their respective mediums dominant in different districts. What is important here is the fact that one "spirit province" often cuts across boundaries of two or more chiefdoms; that is to say, spirit provinces and chiefdoms do not coincide. Furthermore, each spiritual district is part of a greater, quasi-federal "spirit realm," the latter held together by means of a long genealogy that shows the kinship relations between functioning spirit-guardians. The entire scheme has in this way made possible vast unified domains: Mutota's "spirit realm" is said to cover more than three thousand square miles, including much of the Zambezi Valley east of the Angwa River, parts of the plateau to the south of the Zambezi escarpment, and sections even of (formerly) Portuguese Africa. And this realm, again, is linked with others of its kind by the understanding that a perpetual kinship exists between the persons occupying the mediumships in the different hierarchies, and the assumption, furthermore, that the presiding "senior medium" (that is, the representative of "the found-

[36] For a detailed discussion see G. Kingsley Garbett, "Spirit Mediums as Mediators in Korekore Society," in John Beattie and John Middleton, eds., *Spirit Mediumship and Society in Africa* (New York, 1969); the terminology used here is part of Garbett's original analysis. See also Michael Gelfand, M.D., *Shona Ritual, with Special Reference to the Chaminuka Cult* (Cape Town, 1959).

[37] *Infra*, Ch. 7, note 4.

er" of a given "spirit realm,") being biologically linked to the same type of functionary in the other great spirit realms, is entitled to seek and consummate concerted action in behalf of common interests. In short, a wider, socially effective, Shona polity comprising different Shona chiefdoms, peoples, and tribes had actually been called forth by concretizing potent aspects of the shadow world.

However, what needs to be stressed by way of general comment upon Africa's magical commonwealths is the fact that these associations have been exceptional and tenuous in nature. Some of them have proved to be culturally enduring in a variety of metamorphoses; but few, if any, can be said to have provided politically suggestive models, blueprints, or designs for the *voluntary* fusion or confederation of separate societies. In fact, none of the images or arrangements has ever been actually intended to supersede the norms of the small, kinship-oriented group. A so-called ritual "pact," such as the one linking the Lunda and the Shila, is thus not comparable, for example, to the Gruetli Oath, through which the founders of what was to become Switzerland committed themselves to both a common long-range destiny and a plan for immediate action. Traditional African conceptions of an essential community of interest between neighboring peoples, by contrast, have not originated in ascertainable human wills, nor been furthered deliberately to achieve some defined or definable purpose. They are perhaps best understood as either mythical rationalizations of existing conditions, or poetic explanations of the circumstances through which unrelated peoples have come to coexist or depend upon each other. And among the factors that have been allowed to shape the explanations, few have been quite as important as the natural environment. Unifying mythical formulae of this kind have been of common occurrence throughout nonliterate Africa, serving to substantiate symbolically and ritually what is suggested by features of the landscape, notably by the presences of such overwhelming rivers as the Niger and the Congo.

Openness at once to the implications or requirements of ecological factors, and to certain properties inherent in mythical thought and in nonliterate modes of communication, has tended to favor yet another involuntary process of unification, namely, the diffusion of certain languages across the boundaries of socially, ethnically, and even linguistically separate groups.

Such a syndrome is exemplified by the Songhai, whose historical destiny was dominated by the Niger,[38] and whose speech form became

---

[38] See Jean Rouch, *Les Songhay* (Monographies ethnologiques africaines, publiés sous patronage de l'Institut international africain, Londres, P.U.F.), (Paris, 1954), to the effect that the history of Songhai is above all the history of the Niger, which lent unity to disparate groups and territories. See pp. 3–9, 35ff. for the different

a lingua franca in the western Sudan. For it was the magnetic power of the arterial waterway that persuaded lesser groups in the basin to acknowledge the ritual supremacy of the leading Songhai lineages and families in the administration of the river's life; and it was the usefulness and attractiveness of the language that drew people irresistibly into the Songhai sphere of influence. By virtue of this dual source of moral prestige, the Songhai came to represent what a noted French Africanist has called "une ligne de force"[39] that made for a considerable measure of cultural assimilation and consensus in the ethnically varied Sudanese world.

The peoples of the great Mande-speaking group—who have been singled out by one authority as the originators of the Sudanic complex[40]—were even more successful than their Songhai rivals in shaping an orbit for themselves. Recognized in the nuclear Mande domain as "masters of the land," they ranged far into adjoining territories, developing commercial contacts, dominating regional trade, and even establishing colonies as early as about 200 B.C.[41] However, neither here nor in the Songhai realm did reliable forms of multitribal unity ever evolve freely and spontaneously. In response to powerful influences emanating from the culturally dominant centers, dependent communities underwent changes in their ethnic composition, territorial limits, customs, and manners of speech; yet even the most passive or receptive subgroup remained committed to the cause of the small self-possessed community, and was therefore willing to imitate and to borrow only what it could securely make its own. Its factual incorporation into a superior political system

linguistic divisions in the Songhai group and for the estimate that there were 652,500 Songhai and Songhai "assimilates" in West Africa in 1950.

Commenting on the role of the "routes transversales saheliennes" and the Niger in lending a measure of unity to certain states, Mauny remarks that these routes were nonetheless insufficient in gathering together outlying provinces. Mauny, *Tableau géographique*, pp. 437ff. The formation, in March 1968, of "The Organization of States Bordering the Senegal River" is a faint echo of the theme here presented. The new regional grouping joined Senegal, Mali, Guinea, and Mauritania. See the *New York Times*, April 3, 1968.

[39] Maurice Houis, "Problèmes linguistiques de l'Ouest africain," *Guides bleus, Afrique occidentale française Togo* (Paris, 1958), pp. ccv ff. Houis uses the term "ligne de force" in speaking of certain ethnic groups that have maintained themselves through long periods of time, and that succeeded in imposing some measure of control over their neighbors. On the coast this had been true of the Wolof, the Susu (Soso), the Temne, the Ashanti, and the Fon.

[40] Murdock, *Africa*, p. 75.

[41] J. D. Fage, *An Introduction to the History of West Africa* (Cambridge, 1962), p. 6. Frobenius expressed the view that the Mande might well have succeeded in unifying the entire area had rival imperialisms, extraneous to Africa, not appeared upon the scene, because they—notably their Soninke branch—combined a genius for warfare and colonization with talents in peaceful callings such as commerce. *Erlebte Erdteile*, Vol. IV, 85–110.

was accomplished in almost every instance rather by the military force of a politically talented and expansionist people than by the persuasive attractions of a shared mythical vision, a unifying language, or any mutual commercial advantages.

Ancient Ghana, the earliest of the Sudanese empires, emerges from the records as a notable exception to the rule. Probably founded by an immigrant group of Berber pastoralists from North Africa,[42] it brought forth dynasties that did not rely exclusively upon armed might in establishing and securing what their conquests had gained. Moreover, it was served by merchants who knew how to become consummate masters in the art of regulating and exploiting the trans-Saharan exchange of gold and slaves from the south, for salt, copper, cowries, and so on, from the Maghreb.[43] The realm was continuously harassed, particularly in its outlying vassal territories, by the nomadic Tuareg, whose separate tribes joined in a "confederation"[44] for the purpose of raiding, waylaying and ransoming caravans in passage through the desert. In the eleventh century it was smashed by the Almoravids;[45] and yet it succeeded in recovering its independence when its conquerors fell out—only to lose it again, however, in A.D. 1203, this time as a result of intertribal disputes in its own midst. When Kumbi's rich Arab and Soninke traders marched out into the Sahara to build themselves another city, the town disappeared, and all that remained of triumph in the annals of this most illustrious of African empires was the mythical vision of Wagadu.

[42] This is the theory proposed by Fage, *History of West Africa*, p. 18.

[43] See E. W. Bovill, *The Golden Trade of the Moors* (London, 1958), pp. 83ff., for analyses and descriptions of trading patterns in this region, including the silent trade between indigenous peoples and North Africans. The largest market in the Sudan was Kumbi, and the major articles of trade were gold and slaves, the latter procured by raids on the primitive bush tribes on the empire's southern frontiers. See also an earlier volume by the same author, *Caravans of the Old Sahara* (London, 1933), in which the general question of trade and trade routes between North and West Africa is fully discussed.

[44] Bovill, *The Golden Trade of the Moors*, p. 69; Lhote, "Contributions à l'étude des Touaregs soudanais," pp. 400ff. to the effect that the Tuareg knew how to profit from the state of regional anarchy and rivalry, and that they might have become the masters of Timbuktu, Gao, and the region of the middle Niger had they been able to unite politically. Also by Henri Lhote, *Les Touaregs du Hoggar* (Paris, 1944).

[45] Commenting on the political impact left by the Almoravids in the eleventh century A.D., Bovill writes: "The chief weakness of the Almoravids was their inability to control their adherents. They have no state, but an empire consisting of a loosely knit confederation of nomadic tribes held tenuously together by a common creed and a common fear of the consequences of secession." The creed as well as the fear diminished in proportion to the distance from the ruling center. Intertribal jealousies continued unabated. *Golden Trade of the Moors*, p. 73.

STATES, EMPIRES, AND THE
FOLK SOCIETY

Great societies comprising multiple kinship-oriented communities have arisen in all parts of Negro Africa. Variously described in scholarly literature as states, empires, hegemonies, federations, confederations, and tributary systems, they were initiated by conquest and held together by reliance on armed might and the prestige of a dominant king or chief.[1] But in the absence of other bonds between their component units, all have proved readily susceptible to dissolution under pressure of belligerent aggressions from within and from without—the same forces that accounted originally for their creation and existence.[2]

Among the most impressive of these indigenous comprehensive systems were the Kuba kingdom, which at one time gathered eighteen different tribes in a complex arrangement under the aegis of the Bushongo, allowing each unit a wide range of autonomy that included the right to

[1] I. D. Fage explains the origin of states and empires in the Sudan in the following way: the original impulse for the change from small descent-groups to territorial states came from North Africa. The North Africans possessed horses and camels before the Negroes did, and were therefore able to penetrate the northern Negro lands with comparative ease. Territorial states emerged because the invaders tended to appoint rulers for specific areas of the conquered territory rather than for the different groups of people already inhabiting the land. The conquerors were usually fewer in numbers than the conquered, and in the course of time became absorbed by them, so that the Negroes acquired the techniques of the conquerors and were enabled to undertake further conquests, establishing territorial empires of their own. *Introduction to the History of West Africa*, p. 9; but see *infra*, this chapter, note 38 for the view that territoriality was not a major aspect of African states.

[2] Ethiopia presents an exceptional case, having had a continuous history as a state for almost two thousands years. See *infra*, p. 127, for brief comments on the uniqueness of this realm.

Another atypical case is the Malagasy state of Madagascar, where Indonesian antecedents can be dated from the first century onward, and where social and political organization derives from the fusion of ancient Egyptian, Bantu, and Malay components and from the effects of diverse trading patterns with Asian peoples, including the Arabs. See H. J. Deschamps, *Les Antaisaka* (Tananarive, 1936); also *Histoire de Madagascar* (Paris, 1960); J. Faublée, *La Cohésion des sociétés bara* (Paris, 1953), and *Ethnographie de Madagascar* (Paris, 1946); J. Sibrée, *The Great African Island* (London, 1880); Murdock, *Africa, Its Peoples and Their Culture History*, pp. 212ff. and pp. 204ff. on "Ancient Azanians" and their likely links with Madagascar. But see Raymond K. Kent, *Early Kingdoms in Madagascar 1500–1700* (New York, 1970), for other interpretations.

wage war upon other members;[3] the empires in Central and South Africa of Muata Jamwo and Monomotapa,[4] each of which comprised several subsidiary kingdoms; the immense Zulu hegemony, composed of the remnants of more than one hundred tribes that Shaka forged together at the end of the last century, after ruthlessly obliterating every vestige of tribal unity among those he conquered; also the intricate confederacy of the Ashanti, within the framework of which villages were grouped in divisions, and these divisions in political entities that the British recognized in the nineteenth century as "states"; further, the Fante association of semi-independent communities along the coast of present-day Ghana;[5] the pre-Islamic Jukun empire; and the great orbits of the Oyo and Dahomey despotisms. All of these realms had intricately fashioned hierarchical governments, each a tribute to the plastic talents of its Negro founders. And yet a review of their governmental schemes and operations shows that most, if not all, of the conglomerates were in reality loose confederations of diverse folk groups and villages, not unified "empires" or "nations"; for their regimes had neither the moral authority nor the technical power to control the destinies of the separate entities, nor even the ability to instill among them a consciousness of membership in a superior society. In almost every case it was the clan, the village, the canton, or some other small subservient unit, that rallied the people effectively around their shared interests and commitments.[6]

[3] For detailed discussions of different Congolese empires see J. Cuvelier and L. Jadin, *L'Ancien Congo d'après les archives romaines (1518–1640)* (Brussels, 1954). Also J. Cuvelier, *L'Ancien royaume du Congo* (Brussels, 1941). It would appear that the Portuguese exaggerated the power of the king of Kongo as well as the expanse of the kingdom. Cuvelier describes the realm not as a unitary kingdom but as a loose federation of semiautonomous tribes that shared certain customs and accepted a common focus in the institution of kingship.

[4] See Frobenius, *Erytraea, Laender und Zeiten des Heiligen Koenigsmordes* (Berlin-Zurich, 1931), on the two empires. At the time of the arrival of the Portuguese, the present area of Southern Rhodesia and Portuguese East Africa was under the rule of a king or chief, referred to by the title of Monomotapa. The first Monomotapa was mentioned about A.D. 1500. For an analysis of Portuguese and other sources, and for a discussion of this empire, its relation to Zimbabwe, and to the present Mashona, see H. A. Wieschhoff, *The Zimbabwe-Monomotapa Culture in Southeast Africa* (Menasha, Wisc., 1941), particularly pp. 8ff., 106ff. for the view that the probable origins of the empire are to be sought in invasions of the same type of Hamitic groups that was also responsible for the creation of states in Uganda, Ruanda, and other parts of East Africa. See also P. P. Schebesta, "Die Zimbabwe-Kultur in Afrika," *Anthropos*, 21 (1926), 484–522; several comments in Guenther Spannaus, *Zuege aus der Politischen Organisation Afrikanischer Voelker und Staaten* (Leipzig, 1929); and, for a recent discussion of this matter, P. S. Garlake, *Great Zimbabwe* (New York, 1973).

[5] This confederation originated in 1868 in an alliance against the Ashanti and the Dutch that favored the British position. See William E. F. Ward, *A History of the Gold Coast* (London, 1948), pp. 225–260.

[6] Specialists on West Africa who have stressed this character of the ancient

And this traditional communal pattern was not significantly altered through successive generations of Islamic conquerors and organizers. The new Mohammedan designs for the shaping of African society soon forfeited the qualities that had seemed, at first, to make them distinct, either because they proved to be inferior to indigenous forms,[7] or because the newcomers did not really differ very much culturally from the people over whom they took control.[8] In the eastern or Nilotic Sudan, and in East Africa, the Muslim faith was either absorbed by the existing tribal traditions of those it won over—notably the Somali—or accepted as the regal cult by dominant lineages. Apart from stimulating the evolution of coastal trading towns and of the state of Zanzibar, it thus had few discernible effects upon native political organization.

The situation was different in the west, where the new jural and religious sanction for the exercise and expansion of authority was attractive to native political and commercial elites, and where several outstanding—albeit shortlived—achievements in the area of political unification were in fact recorded. Even here, however, the Fulani, "the strongest Muslims in the Sudan"[9] and probably the most active and talented of the new state-makers, failed when they tried to transform their far-flung conquests into theocracies based upon the ideals of Islam. They attained a considerable measure of success, on the other hand, in the central Sudan, when they fell back upon the systems of the Hausa, whom they had dispossessed.[10]

---

empires include Leroi-Gourhan and Poirier, *Ethnologie de l'Union française*, Vol. I, 347ff.; Virginia Thompson and Richard Adloff, *French West Africa* (London, 1958), p. 19; and Richard-Molard, *Problèmes humains en Afrique occidentale*. This author suggests that the "peasant" aspect of African society will continue to characterize the continent's political destiny in modern times. And see C. K. Meek, *A Sudanese Kingdom*, p. 342.

[7] This was Frobenius' view, see *infra*, notes 28, 29, and 30, this chapter. See also J. C. Froelich, "Essai sur les causes et méthodes de l'islamisation de l'Afrique de l'Ouest du XIᵉ siècle au XXᵉ siècle," in I. M. Lewis, ed., *Islam in Tropical Africa* (London, 1966), p. 162, to the effect that the Mohammedan Mali empire compares unfavorably with the earlier pagan Mali empire because the former was more heterogeneous and superficially organized than the latter, and because it was too dependent upon military force and not sufficiently respectful of the kinship principle.

[8] Little, "African Culture and the Western Intrusion," p. 951.

[9] J. Spencer Trimingham, *A History of Islam in West Africa* (London, Glasgow, and New York, 1963), p. 160.

[10] *Ibid.*, pp. 203ff. and maps, particularly map No. 7, for vivid descriptions of Islamic and native governments and their interpenetrations; see accounts by European explorers of the eighteenth and nineteenth centuries as previously cited, notably H. Clapperton, Major Dixon Denham, Réné Caillié, and Dr. Henry Barth. For excerpts from their journals see C. Howard and J. H. Plumb, eds., *West African Explorers* (London, 1955); Thomas Hodgkin, *Nigerian Perspectives; An Historical Anthology* (London, 1960); A. H. M. Kirk-Greene, ed., *Travels*

A close analysis of the complex interaction between native and Islamic norms in West and East Africa convinced J. Spencer Trimingham that the revolutionary religion and ideology of the invading literate civilization had become thoroughly Africanized, and that the so-called Islamic states that had flourished in the western and central Sudan before the nineteenth century had actually been organized on the pattern of advanced Negro societies. Indeed, this scholar suggests, the compelling force of such societies remained evident even during the nineteenth century, when many of the new states foundered, not primarily because they could not withstand the rival organizing activities of the incoming Europeans, but because they could not transcend the basic African organization of society.[11]

---

in Nigeria; Extracts from the Journal of Heinrich Barth's Travels in Nigeria, 1850–1855 (London, 1962); Margery Perham and J. Simmons, African Discovery: An Anthology of Explorations (London, 1942). Also The Kano Chronicle, probably composed about 1890, but based upon earlier, pre-Fulani, records; this text in H. R. Palmer, Sudanese Memoirs. Being Mainly Translations of a Number of Arabic Manuscripts Relating to the Central and Western Sudan, 3 vols. (Lagos, 1928).

For a specialized study of government in this part of Central Sudan, see M. G. Smith, Government in Zazzau, 1800–1950 (London, 1960), particularly pp. 73ff. On the Almoravids, see Bovill, The Golden Trade of the Moors, pp. 73ff. For a discussion of strong and stimulating Islamic influences upon the Fulani empire of Macina in the western Sudan, see A. H. Ba and J. Daget, L'Empire Peul du Macine, Vol. I: 1818–1853 (Dakar, 1955).

[11] Trimingham, History of Islam in West Africa, pp. 232ff; also Islam in East Africa. Report of a Survey Undertaken in 1961 (London, 1962), pp. 31ff. and 43ff. Speaking of the resilience of Bantu culture, Trimingham points out that whereas in the Near East peasant beliefs were thoroughly Islamized, in Africa the parallel elements bear the mark of their African origin. Here the traditional world remains real and its emotional hold vivid. Religious life thus rests on a double structure, namely the animistic substratum and the Islamic superstructure. Nowhere does Islam seem to have erased tribal or racial differences, nor to have weakened family and clan bonds. On the same subject, and to like effect, see Raymond Leslie Buell, The Native Problem in Africa, 2 vols. (New York, 1928), Vol. I, 242ff.; and Melville J. Herskovits, The Human Factor in Changing Africa (New York, 1962), pp. 418ff., 427ff. This scholar concludes that the retention of the ancestral cult, which began to reappear openly in Christian sects and had never been given up by Islamized Africans, demonstrates persuasively the power of traditional beliefs. For a special case study of this interaction see Mary F. Smith, Baba of Karo, A Woman of the Muslim Hausa (New York, 1954), p. 222. See Murdock, Africa, pp. 144–147 on the priority and endurance of African features of government as represented in "the African despotisms" and on the negligible influence exerted by the Arabs, who arrived too late to influence the political structure of the Sudan fringe peoples.

Westermann, Geschichte Afrikas, pp. 390, 399, observes, speaking of the old Kongo empires, that four hundred years of Portuguese influence and rule were simply absorbed without leaving significant modifications in the culture and institutions of the peoples that had experienced this close contact with the European world. See infra, Part VI, and supra, Part II.

Several parallels between the ancient African and later Mohammedan hegemonies must be briefly noted if the resilience of the kinship order is to be fully appreciated.

In both contexts, empires and kingdoms were dynamic in their inception, expansionist in their growth, shortlived in time, and undelimited in space.[12] Territorial consolidation was nowhere a major concern, the two traditions converging in certain attitudes toward land and toward physical mobility in space. In Negro Africa the order of the tribal community did not require a secure land base. Land was traditionally viewed as the spatial expression of social relations rather than of strategic, material, or ideological functions, and wherever geographic factors favored the evolution of numerous pastoral and nomadic societies, migrations were continuously taking place.[13] Indeed, the great majority of the peoples arrived in their present locations only after long peregrinations. Some moved voluntarily and spontaneously; others, on command of absolutist governments, in fear of persecution, under the pressure of incoming foreigners, or in response to insoluble quarrels within their own communities.[14] What is significant is that the small kinship group was actually capable of retaining its identity while in motion. For example, the pattern of organization in the society of the Fort Jameson Ngoni remained the same despite all movements of the tribe from region to region, and despite the absence of any definite boundaries between territorial segments. The constant elements in this case, as we learn from J. A. Barnes,[15] were the residential villages; but even these were like ships pre-

[12] Compare Westermann, *Geschichte Afrikas*, pp. 31ff., who writes in connection particularly with the Kongo empire: "As in all African states, the frontiers were undetermined and fluctuating." Also *ibid.*, p. 390. Speaking of the Mvata Jumvo, this scholar observes that his residence was actually a camp that changed its location at each enthronement; *ibid.*, p. 388. Robert Cornevin, *Histoire des peuples de l'Afrique noire* (Paris, 1960), ch. 21, pp. 381ff., 667ff.; Henri Labouret, *L'Afrique précoloniale* (Paris, 1959), pp. 65ff.

[13] Jean Rouch, "Problèmes rélatifs à l'étude des migrations traditionnelles et des migrations actuelles en Afrique occidentale," *Bulletin de l'IFAN*, 22, ser. B., Nos. 3–4 (July-October 1960), 372ff. This essay deals mainly with the migration of the Malinke people and its effect on other communities. For another intensive study of migrations and population transfers see J. Lombard, "Le Problème des migrations locales; Leur rôle dans les changements d'une société en transition (Dahomey)," *Bulletin de l'IFAN*, 22, Nos. 3–4 (1960), pp. 455ff.

J. F. Holleman, *Shona Customary Law, with Reference to Kinship, Marriage, the Family and the Estate* (Cape Town, London, and New York, 1952), p. 322, explains that the kind of shifting cultivation practiced by the Shona in southern Africa was not conducive to permanent land rights. Here land, whether cultivated or uncultivated, was never regarded as "wealth" or even as "property" in the ordinary sense. As his informants told him: "Land is not property; it is something you use for a time and then abandon."

[14] See Part v.

[15] J. A. Barnes, "The Fort Jameson Ngoni," in Elizabeth Colson and Max Gluckman, eds., *Seven Tribes of British Central Africa* (London, 1951), pp. 196ff., 208.

serving identity in motion, for no village was likely to stay in one place more than about twelve years.

Another variation on the theme of motion in political organization is the so-called band—usually a small, autonomous group whose members coalesce for the purpose of charting a common itinerary and exploiting the local resources of the areas traversed—activities that might involve them either in fights or in alliances with other like-minded bands. Refugees, uprooted by slave raids or invading armies, are thus known to have roved the countryside in East Africa in particular, often incorporating droves of captives as they moved along. Likewise, there were groups of traders and caravans, initially organized for reasons of security, that degenerated into marauding bands intent on terrorizing the countryside or usurping political power in regions in which effective local authorities were missing. As Colson points out in a discussion of these various "forming processes," the membership of all such bands was heterogeneous and fleeting, authority resided in a leader, and collective identity derived from this man's name or connections.[16] Yao bands from eastern Tanzania thus controlled much of northern Mozambique and eastern Malawi by the mid-nineteenth century. And at about the same period, Swahili and Arab traders established themselves as rulers in Ugogo and around the shores of Lake Nyasa.[17] The bands, as well as many of the states they founded, however, proved to be short-lived improvisations as a rule, since they could not rely on the sanctioning effects of established offices and of legitimate succession. What these polities illustrate well is the African capacity to fuse diverse human elements by compromising or fictionalizing the ruling kinship principle. The Lozi, who controlled much of the Zambezi region in mid-nineteenth century, contended with sizeable refugee groups by allowing intermarriage or by acquiescing in incomplete assimilation;[18] and the Lunda, who ruled an impressive empire, bestowed "Lundahood" upon all sorts of folk who could not claim Lunda ancestry officially, by resorting to the hallowing effects of myth, custom, and symbolic actions.[19]

In short, and as the foregoing references were designed to illustrate, it is hardly surprising that throughout Negro Africa collective identities should be rooted in origin myths in which themes of wandering and dis-

---

[16] Elizabeth Colson, "African Society at the Time of the Scramble," in L. H. Gann and Peter Duignan, eds., *Colonialism in Africa 1870–1960*, Vol. I; *The History and Politics of Colonialism 1870–1914* (Cambridge, 1969), pp. 27ff.

[17] *Ibid.*, p. 34.

[18] *Ibid.*, p. 30, to the effect that Lozi captives or descendants of captives usually merged with the free population in the course of one or two generations. Colson argues that the word "tribe" is a misnomer, since political and tribal boundaries rarely coincided in precolonial Africa.

[19] Cunnison, *The Luapula Peoples of Northern Rhodesia*, pp. 174ff.

persal are paramount. The accent in all mythical charters—whether they relay the miraculous founding of a community by a hunter from afar, the ruthlessness of acts of spoliation, the panic of an escape, or the vagaries of seeking asylum—is upon the continuance of the family tree or at least the ideology of kinship, not upon the homes and settlements that were found and lost.

Turning now to the West Asian homeland of the Arabs, we note that there, too, ecology made for a tribal existence marked by relentless and boundless wanderings; and that this could be readily sublimated by the missionary zeal imparted by Islam. Committed to a life style symbolized by the caravan, the pilgrimage, and the *jihad*, the Muslim Arabs were most sure of themselves when on the move, least adept when called upon to stabilize their gains—an orientation that explains why even the most formidable of their khalifates and sultanates are best characterized as empires-in-motion.[20] The innate pattern in Africa's indigenous Negro culture was thus repeatedly reconfirmed in the period between the seventh and the nineteenth centuries A.D., during which northern, western, central, and eastern Africa were submitted to continuous intrusions and invasions first by a variety of Berbers and pagan Arabs, and, after the seventh century, by Muslim forces. These circumstances greatly favored territorial indeterminacy and formlessness in the evolution of African and Afro-Islamic states, nowhere more so than in the western Sudan.

But fundamentally it was endemic war, waged for millennia in all parts of the continent, that set the norm of the territorially fluid state. For Hamites, Semites, and Negroes, war itself and preparation for war summed up the social purpose of the masculine life. Legitimized and sanctified by pagan creeds no less than by Islam, it became the mainstay of kingdoms and empires, and the principal commitment of the ruling elites. Most, if not all, of the great societies known to African history may thus be said to have originated in conquest and to have made military expansion into adjoining domains their primary cause.[21]

Nonbelligerent orientations to relations between ethnically and politically distinct entities had, by contrast, negligible effects upon the forma-

[20] For a discussion of the cultural and political constants in the Muslim realm of the Middle East, see Bozeman, *Politics and Culture in International History*, Part III, pp. 215–389, and Part IV, pp. 389–438.

[21] Spannaus, *Zuege aus der Politischen Organisation Afrikanischer Voelker und Staaten*, p. 195, to the effect that most states in Africa originated in the actions of conquerors and that few, if any, had firm frontiers; also *ibid.*, pp. 39ff. For the relevance of this common theme to that of social and political fragmentation, see *infra*, Part V. Compare also Charles Monteil, *Les Bambara du Segou et du Kaarta* (Paris, 1924), for the view that the concept of "boundary," as it is understood in the West, is unknown or incomprehensible to the blacks. And cf. Westermann, *Geschichte Afrikas*, p. 390; also p. 388.

tion of comprehensive organizational schemes. For reasons set out earlier,[22] pagan religions did not instruct the small groups to seek greater intertribal unities by peaceful means, and the revolutionary Islamic spirit of fraternity, which rallied so many ethnically and politically separate Asian nations into voluntary unions, was ineffective in this regard on the African political scene, even while imparting here, as elsewhere, a strong sense of social solidarity to such human ventures as the pilgrimage. In every case—whether native African or Islamic—one can say that the religious impulse came to serve, not to mitigate, the cause of war.

Trade, too, was turned into channels favored by war. Berbers and Arabs, Tuaregs and Negroes, were equally avid traders, successful in varying degrees in establishing regional markets and in organizing trade routes transcending deserts and linking far-flung, separate societies. But few of the participants seem to have been persuaded that trading is best conducted when supported by continuous political cooperation or by reliable regional arrangements. Nothing is recorded for Africa that might be compared to any of the numerous joint efforts registered in the Mediterranean area by such concerts as the Rhodian federation of merchants and the Rhodian sea law in ancient times, or the Consulato del Mare of Barcelona in the medieval age, or again—in the Baltic region—by the Hanseatic League. It is possible, of course, to infer from the records of the past, notably those relating to West Africa, that a certain type of "state" sometimes evolved in the context of regional trading patterns; but it is dubious—to say the least—that any such evolution was *intended*, or that in the field of state making, long-range decisions were ever actually made in terms of such a design. As in other spheres of administration, so also here: governments seem to have hoped for quick returns and to have pursued essentially short-range goals—perspectives encouraging the waylaying of caravans, the raiding of neighboring communities, and the forcible seizure and despoliation of market towns.

Commerce, then, was very much a matter of large and petty forays that had the effect of reducing to waste what had been prosperous and promising in neighboring societies. Most importantly, the chief articles of African trade as conducted from the seventh to the nineteenth century were human beings, and these were customarily acquired either by razzias or by full-fledged military campaigns. Here again, it is important to note certain consonances or complementarities matching Negro and Arab customs and dispositions. For although the objects of the trade were usually Negroes, slavery itself was a recognized institution in both cultures, and the trade in slaves could thus be conducted as a cooperative

[22] *Supra*, Chs. 6 and 7.

or competitive enterprise by pagans and Mohammedans, Arabs and Negroes.[23] It is, therefore, not surprising to find that some unions or composites of states were held together more or less exclusively by shared understandings of the importance of war and slaving. This aspect emerges forcefully from the *Chronicle of Abuja*,[24] in which two brothers of the ruling emir of Abuja explain that it was the traditional function of Zassau, the southernmost of the seven Hausa states of which Abuja had once been a part, to provide slaves for each of the other six, whereas it was the duty of Gobir in the north to defend the rest of the common-wealth from invasion. In short, slave raiding, taken for granted every-where in Africa, became an absolute economic and political necessity for many of the indigenous kingdoms and empires, especially after the ini-tiation of the Atlantic slave trade; and in some regions, notably West Africa, it had the effect of radically altering the demographic composi-tion of states and other settlements. More than half of the population of Kano (northern Nigeria) were slaves when this traditional market town was visited by Captain Hugh Clapperton, the noted explorer, in the early nineteenth century,[25] while in the western Sudan, where war was a permanent condition, slaves came to constitute the great majority of the

[23] Islamic law as embodied in the Koran and other sources, and as interpreted before the twentieth century, makes full allowance for slavery. It was commonly invoked in Africa to justify slave raids as well as *jihad*.

[24] Frank Heath, trans., *A Chronicle of Abuja* (Lagos, 1962), p. 3.

[25] See "Journal of an Excursion" in Major Dixon Denham, Captain Hugh Clapperton, and Doctor Oudney, *Narrative of Travels and Discoveries in North-ern and Central Africa in the Years 1822, 1823 and 1824* (London, 1826), p. 49; also pp. 54ff. for a description of the slave market in Kano and other comments on the subject.

But see Hugh Clapperton, *Journal of a Second Expedition into the Interior of Africa from the Bight of Benin to Soccatoo* (London, 1829), p. 171, to the ef-fect that Hadje Salah, the chief of the Arabs, and "the principal Arabs" told him when they called on him, that the proportion of slaves to free men in Kano was thirty to one.

See Kirk-Greene ed., *Travels in Nigeria*, pp. 132ff. on the role and effect of slavery in Fulani-dominated regions. Describing the rule of Bokhari in Katsena, Barth writes of the state of misery in which he found the people and the land, for "this warlike chieftain instead of founding a strong kingdom and showing himself a great prince, chose rather, like most of his countrymen, to base his power on the destruction and devastation of the country around him, and to make himself a slave-dealer on a grand scale. Tens of thousands of unfortunate people, pagans as well as Mohammedans, unprotected in their well-being by their lazy and effeminate rulers, have from the hands of Bokhari passed into those of the slave-dealer."

Eyewitness reports on the slave trade and its effects have been left by almost all explorers of the continent. See also Trimingham, *History of Islam in West Africa*, and numerous other references; C. K. Meek, *The Northern Tribes of Ni-geria; An Ethnographical Account of the Northern Provinces of Nigeria together with a Report on the 1921 Decennial Census*, 2 vols. (London, 1925), Vol. I, 257ff.; Vol. II, 10. On the paramountcy of slavery in Mendeland, see Little, *The Mende*, in particular pp. 37ff.

population, as we learn from Charles Monteil.[26] Reviewing the ethnic and social components of the Kaniaga, Mali, and Songhai empires, this scholar reports on the authority of primary Arab sources that all three rested on the same base, namely a bloc of twenty-four "slave" tribes that belonged successively to each of them.

The connotations of being a slave differed from state to state and from ruler to ruler, and so did the methods of government-sponsored enslavement. Few were as ferocious as those associated with the Fulani empires, yet even the most benign were more akin to war than to what is commonly known as commerce. Whatever definition one chooses to apply, the slave trade, like endemic war, had certain irreversible effects upon the nature of the African state: it accentuated the territorially inchoate nature of the kinship-transcendent society, and it made for an ever-shifting human base.

The Islamic thrust from the northwest and the northeast, to which Negro governments in the Sudanic belt were subjected relentlessly for almost fifteen hundred years, could certainly be pronounced successful in mid-nineteenth century, when modern European notions of political organization were slowly introduced. However, and as preceding comments have suggested, the resilience of certain preexisting patterns of rule is an equally noteworthy historical phenomenon—nowhere more so, it appears, than in the land of the Mossi, who withstood Muslim impacts until recent times; in Nubia, whose independence was respected by powerful and prestigious Near Eastern and Mediterranean khalifates for six hundred years, namely until the Egyptian Fatimids annexed the region; and in Ethiopia, which had been officially excluded from the *dar al-ḥārb* (domain of war) on the Prophet's personal order. Whereas the status of Ethiopia in Islamic international law may be likened to "neutralization," that of Nubia appears to have been much more complex, if only because the rulers of the latter, having originally forced the new aggressors to respect their country's independence, were subsequently allowed to treat with their northern neighbors on the basis of reciprocity.[27]

A thorough exploration of the question of why these particular African societies proved to be so remarkably resistant in the face of overwhelming odds against them convinced Frobenius that Islam was here countered by traditional orders that had been politically consolidated

---

[26] *La Légende de Ouagadou*, p. 403; the author notes that slavery is one of the least-known subjects in Sudanese sociology. On the slave trade in West Africa and on Ghana's supply source in particular, see Bovill, *The Golden Trade of the Moors*, pp. 54–110; also subsequent chapters. Compare Mauny, *Tableau géographique*, p. 399, on the circumstances in which parents could sell their children, and so on. See *infra*, Part v, on the slave trade as a species of conflict.

[27] Majid Khadduri, *War and Peace in the Law of Islam* (Baltimore and London, 1955; repr. 1969), pp. 251ff., 259ff.

in pre-Islamic times by effective grafts of Byzantine and Persian practices unifying rite and rule.

Nubia, the land of "Old Egypt" (also known at times as Napata or Nupata), which had been Christianized directly by Byzantium rather than by Egypt, was, according to this thesis, thus saturated with Byzantine influences even as it remained the scene of rivalries between the eastern Christian empire and Persia until the advent of Islam.[28] As a result of this close and continuous connection with Constantinople, Nubia evolved a royal establishment that came to correspond closely to patterns found at the Byzantine court. The cause of political unity could therefore be served not only by the principles of the Greek Orthodox— and in the case of Ethiopia, the Coptic—faith, but also by the assiduous cultivation of dynastic principles, the meticulous ordering of role assignments, respect for titles, ranks, and symbols, and the maintenance of an elaborate ongoing bureaucratic machinery. What particularly impressed Frobenius in his research was the fact that Nubia was a replica of the Palatinate ("Pfalz"), complete with well-structured electoral offices ("Erzaemter")—a rather unusual structural order that had also been introduced to western Europe after Otto the Great's marriage to a Byzantine princess. Indeed, Frobenius claims that we find here in Nubia, in A.D. 641, "a fully developed Palatinate, an electoral order of Palatine offices just as this was cultivated everywhere else in the orbit of Byzantine influence."

Next, the cause of independence in Nubia and the westward realms— notably Nupe and Mossi, into which these ideas were diffused in that east-west movement to which Frobenius attached such historical significance—was greatly served, according to this scholar, by a peculiar brand of possession cult or shamanism that is said to be of Persian origin. Informants in Kordofan—here identified as the principal locus and distribution center of the remnants of Persian motifs—thus seem to have asserted categorically that this so-called Beri religion, also found along the Nile; in Ethiopia, where it appears under the name "zâr";[29] as well as in Nupe, Mossi, Hausa, and Yoruba domains, was being carried by ghosts that were "winds from Persia." In Kordofan and among the Nubians, the belief was widespread at the beginning of the twentieth century that the daemons of possession come with the winds, just as it was taken for granted by the Mossi (whose realm is also described by Frobenius as the replica of an Imperial Palatinate) that their emperors had many magical

---

[28] Leo Frobenius, *Und Africa Sprach*, Vol. II, *An der Schwelle des verehrungswuerdigen Byzanz* (Berlin-Charlottenburg, 1912), pp. 303ff., 332, 338, 340ff. Since the issues here analyzed have not received any attention in the English-speaking scholarly world, it has seemed useful to point to this analysis of some rather baffling matters in cultural history, at least in summary fashion.

[29] *Ibid.*, pp. 247ff.; and cf. *supra*, Ch. 5, n. 51.

powers, among them the capacity to conjure winds.[30] Here as elsewhere in the East, it is noteworthy, furthermore, that the cult was closely associated with music, notably the sound of the lute.[31]

Pre-Fulani Nupe—described by Nadel in mid-twentieth century as "A Black Byzantium"—was held together by analogous or closely similar principles.[32] Here, as in the Mossi realm, Frobenius had noted strong

[30] Frobenius, *Und Africa Sprach*, Vol. II, 268ff.

[31] Compare *supra*, Ch. 6 for several versions of "Gassire's Lute" and the powerful myth of Wagadu in the area.

[32] Nadel, *A Black Byzantium*, writes on p. 87: "We know little about the system of kingship in pre-Fulani times. I have mentioned one piece of information already which I obtained from various sources, namely, the ancient rule of succession which made the eldest son 'born in the purple,' that is, the son first born during the father's reign, the heir to the throne of Nupe. A few other facts concerning the person of the king I was able to ascertain from the *Etsu* of Patigi. Certain ritual rules obtained at the king's court—and some of these rules are still observed in Patigi. Thus the *Etsu* may only wear white; he can travel and go out whenever he likes, but may not eat any food save that prepared by his wives; nor may any stranger watch him eat. Finally, no one may be killed in the presence of the king or in the town in which he is residing. (This helps us to understand the organization of the 'King's Hangmen,' the crucial fact of which was that the royal executioners killed their victims in places far away from the king's capital.)" In subsequent chapters Nadel explains that Nupe society qualifies as a state because it is kept together by attachment to the principle of kingship, acceptance of the brotherhood of Islam, and common participation in a uniform system of law and justice. In other words, Nupe is a state, in Nadel's view, because Islam has effectively transcended the kinship principle. Apart from the reference to princes "born in the purple," no case is made in this work for "A Black Byzantium." In fact, even the index has no entry under "Byzantium." Frobenius' work, which anteceded Nadel's by several decades, is nowhere mentioned, even though the information listed on p. 87 of *A Black Byzantium* had first been presented in greatly amplified form by Frobenius, and must have been accessible to Nadel, a German-speaking scholar from Vienna writing in the 1940s.

Westermann, *Geschichte Afrikas*, p. 198, refers to both scholars and concludes that Nupe kingship is quite evidently impregnated by what Frobenius had identified as the neo-Sudanic Eritraean culture. See Murdock, *Africa*, pp. 158ff. for an anthropological and historical overview of Nubia, aptly circumscribed as "The Nile Valley south of ancient and modern Egypt, from the second cataract near Wadi Halfa to the junction of the Blue and White Niles at Khartoum"; pp. 159ff. on extensive borrowings from Pharaonic Egypt, Nubia's independence after 1050 B.C. as a strong state centered first at Napata and after 550 B.C. at Meroe, the introduction of Christianity in A.D. 543, and the subsequent establishment of a kingdom with institutions modeled on those of Byzantium, which proved strong enough to withstand attacks first by Arabs from Egypt and half a millennium later by Bedouin Arabs. These continuous invasions and pressures toward Islamization, however, greatly weakened the realm. In 1315 the last Christian king was succeeded by a Moslem. Farther south, in the domain of the indigenous Nubians, the Christian kingdom of Alwa proved capable of resisting Arab penetration until 1504, when it succumbed to the Moslem Fung state of Sennar. This removed the last barrier to Bedouin expansion from eastern and central Sudan into this part of Africa. Groups of Nubians, resisting absorption, sought refuge in the hills of Kordofan and Darfur, where remnants survive to the present day. On these peoples see Nadel, *The Nuba*. He claims on p. 4 that little is known about the ancient history of the Nuba tribes, and that "it often seems as if historical traditions had

echoes of the eastern Christian empire, notably the accent on imperial rule; the insignia of office, which included sceptre, crown, and orb; elaborate ceremonious make-believe; a bureaucratic establishment in which each of numerous functionaries was assigned his special role, with eunuchs and court jesters singled out for particularly prestigious positions; and, above all, the four-fold division of the imperial domain.[33] The virtual autonomy of each of these districts made for continuous internecine conflicts and wars—a condition that greatly favored Mohammedan bids for power in times to come.

The ultimate victory of Islam in this vast Sudanic region naturally implied the eclipse of older rival principles of rule—those associated by Frobenius with Persia and Byzantium. Only Nubia and Ethiopia were able to withstand the thrust, perhaps because the tradition of Meroe or Napata was firmly imbedded here, perhaps because Byzantinism supplied the necessary armor.[34] In the course of this prolonged encounter between rival systems and cultures, however, some elements of the recessive or defeated order were destined to survive in Islamized areas, either because they could be assimilated and adapted by the victor, or because they could not be dislodged from social life and consciousness. The symbol of the cross thus retained wide currency in the entire region stretching from the Nile and Nubia westward to the Senegal; "devil dancing" at Bori gatherings "has been known in Abuja since the days of the first

---

been cut short by the overpowering experience of the Mahdist regime (1881–1898), which must have severed all links with a more distant—and possibly less disturbed—past." See pp. 357ff., 440ff. for discussions of the shamanistic conception of spirit possession as the main unifying principle among three different Nuba groups. Compare Frobenius, *Und Africa Sprach*, Vol. II, 340, for the suggestion that the Mahdist phenomenon may be a remnant of the early Christian belief system.

[33] On the Mossi realm as vanguard of the horizontal east-west culture movement, and as a bastion standing guard against the vertical Islamic thrust from the north, see Frobenius, *Und Africa Sprach*, Vol. II, 155ff., 273ff., 303ff.; see pp. 320ff. for parallelisms between Nupe and Mossi institutions; pp. 328 and 349 to the effect that the king of Nupe had the same regalia as the Byzantine emperor, and that the functions of the court jester in the two states were exactly alike; on the role of this intermediary in Africa, see *infra*, Ch. 18. Frobenius, *Und Africa Sprach*, Vol. II, ch. 14, 334ff. is a brilliant exposition of cultural relations between Byzantium and Islam. See *ibid.*, pp. 620ff. on the diffusion of the cross and other motifs. E. F. Gautier, *L'Afrique noire occidentale* (Paris, 1935), reports on pp. 124ff., that the Byzantine coat of mail ("Cataphract") has survived in the padded armor that continues to be the parade uniform of the Life Guards in the Sultanates of Chad and Northern Cameroon.

[34] See preceding notes 32 and 33 on the evidence for these conclusions and on Murdock's confirmation of most of Frobenius' speculations regarding Nubia. Additional comments on some of the issues here involved can be found in Basil Davidson, *Africa in History; Themes and Outlines* (London, 1968; New York, 1969), pp. 21–44 and 99ff.

Emir . . . and long before that in Zaria and the rest of the Hausa lands";[35] and legends linking the inception of kingly rule to Persian origins are widespread, even as "Persian" may stand in one place for "Muslim," in another for "Coptic" or for "Napata." The Abuja Chronicle thus has it that the Habe of Abuja, one of "three small islands of resistance . . . against the flood of the (Fulani) conquest," had come from Zazzau, and that "the origins of the rulers of Zazzau are the same as those of the Habe rulers of Biram, Daura, Kano, Katsina, Gobir and Rano; indeed they all spring from the same man, one Bayajida dan Abdullahi, who reigned in Baghdad long ago."[36] And in respect of Gobir, again, folklore teaches that the dynastic founders were Persians, who represented Christ.[37]

The records of Africa's responses to foreign creeds, cultures, and political systems are certainly multifarious, lacking in precision, and subject, therefore, to greatly various interpretations. And yet, obscure and controversial as they may be, they allow for the conclusion that African societies have always been talented borrowers in the sense that they were able to Africanize and thus absorb themes or episodes with which they were compelled to come to terms. Identities of foreign peoples or their individual representatives could thus be either confounded or reduced to myths. Alien creeds and ideas were allowed to interpenetrate and forfeit that original uniqueness that could not be accommodated. Uncongenial political institutions were either dismantled into separate elements and recomposed, or abstracted into some appealing symbols. Indeed, the whole complex of foreign relations has often been portrayed as a wandering personage who founds kingdoms, marries, begets descendants, and then moves on to establish other realms and other families. That is to say, it too is caught securely in the local kinship net by virtue of the power of nonliterate thought.

The great African societies, then, were neither territorial states nor nation states in the Occidental senses of these terms. The normative principle that presided over their inception, survival, and decline was the personality of the king or paramount chief, who might or might not represent a dynasty or lineage. In fact, most of the states did not even have names until outsiders, notably Arabs, began identifying them by their rulers' titles or places of residence. Ghana thus seems originally to have been a title borne by Soninke kings, only later extended to the empire

---

[35] Heath, trans., *A Chronicle of Abuja*, p. 65.
[36] *Ibid.*, p. 1.
[37] Frobenius, *Und Africa Sprach*, Vol. II, 342. *Ibid.*, pp. 334, 341, on the widespread diffusion of the Persian Kisra legend, which seems to have had its inception in Chosroes' conquest of Egypt in the early seventh century A.D.

and its capital. Mali meant "where the king lives," and is thus, as Fage reminds us, properly the name for any capital of a Mandingo empire.[38] Muato Jamvo and Kazembe were titles, respectively, of the paramount ruler and a quasi-independent subking in the Lunda empire of Central Africa,[39] and the like was true of the Monomotapa, whose appellation became the name of a southeast African empire.

In all parts of Africa states are thus best understood as extensions of particular biographies. They were by their very nature as unstable and unpredictable as they were dynamic. For since the ruling men were first and foremost conquering men, their creations were necessarily military monarchies and conquest states. This meant, from the statemaker's point of view, that each newly acquired territory was readily regarded as the forward base for further expansion. And since consolidation of what had been gained was seldom undertaken, existing settlements were readily left to wither or to perish as new ones were established.

In these circumstances, marked as they were by the absence either of regionally shared conceptions about the territorial and national configuration of political entities, or of traditionally fixed or reliable rules for the conduct of statecraft and intertribal relations, states could follow each other in time—often in rapid succession—even while coexisting, superimposed upon each other, in space. This pattern is illustrated in West Africa by the empires of Ghana, Mali, and Gao;[40] in southern

[38] *West Africa*, p. 24.

[39] Westermann, *Geschichte Afrikas*, p. 387. See also Trimingham, *A History of Islam in West Africa*, p. 50; I. Schapera, "Political Institutions" in Schapera, ed., *The Bantu-Speaking Tribes of South Africa; An Ethnographic Survey* (London, 1937), p. 173, writes that it is primarily through their allegiance to the same chief that members of a tribe are conscious of their unity; and indeed, the author continues, the tribe is most often named after the chief himself or one of his ancestors. See Vansina, *Kingdoms of the Savanna*, pp. 78ff., on "The Birth of the Lunda Empire" and the extension of Lunda rule over wide parts of Central Africa. From the nucleus of small groups of Lunda, villages would break off whenever this was warranted by the population increase, and would settle on the plains to the west under their leaders, the "chiefs of the land." The relations between the villages were maintained by the notion of perpetual kinship between the leaders, and in this way, Vansina explains, Lunda land was already a loose but single political unit in the sixteenth century. On the king, the *mvaant yaav* ("the lord of the viper"), the "perpetual kinship" links that tied him to important titleholders, and on tribute paying as the outstanding characteristic of this successful empire, *ibid.*, pp. 80–83.

On the organization of the Luapula peoples see Cunnison, *History on the Luapula*, and *The Luapula Peoples of Northern Rhodesia*.

[40] For this analysis see Houis, "Problèmes linguistiques de l'Ouest africain," ccvff. Cf. also Rouch, *Les Songhay*, p. 9, for the conditions in which the Songhai, after transferring the capital to Gao, became known as "pays de Gao" or, more pompously, "empire de Gao," and how this empire then passed under the authority of the Mali empire.

Africa by extensive multitribal combinations;[41] and in Central Africa by a series of Congolese kingdoms.[42] Neither systematic long-range planning nor economic and strategic calculation seems to have been invested in the development of these states or conglomerates.[43] Most of the realms depended upon the levying of tribute, many were slave states, and all were held together by the same military power that had assembled the separate parts in the first place. Empires and multitribal combinations were thus bound to disintegrate when the armies slackened the discharge of their functions—namely collecting tribute, holding vassals in check, enforcing the subservience of the conquered, and above all, supporting those individual quests for grandeur, wealth, and pleasure, with which the paramount ruler identified the cause of the state.

This type of personalism, nowhere more pronounced than in the great Muslim hegemonies so aptly described by Jacques Richard-Molard as "les empires hâtifs des aventuriers musulmans"[44] (the hastily assembled empires of Muslim adventurers), was buttressed everywhere by endemic dispositions toward magic and religion. In fact, the most successful state-makers in the ranks of both Islamic and pagan politicians were generally fervent exponents of the dominant systems of folk belief: men recognized as saints, priest-kings, gods, god-kings, or magicians, because they knew how to mobilize the latent religious sentiments of the masses they controlled or sought to subjugate, and knew, also, how to invoke mystical

[41] From time to time there have arisen in southern Africa large Bantu states, in which many different tribes were amalgamated into a single political unit. The Zulu under Shaka, the Rhodesian Ndebele under Mzilikazi, the Shangana under Soshangane, the South Sotho under Moshesh, the Swazi under Sobhuza, and others, were all powerful combinations in which one chief had brought under his rule many of his neighbors. However, the composition of most of these units was constantly shifting. See I. Schapera, "Political Institutions," pp. 173ff. Henri A. Junod, *Moeurs et coutumes des Bantous, la vie d'une tribu sud-africaine*, Vol. I, *Vie sociale* (Paris, 1936), 341ff. on the evolution, in the first half of the twentieth century, of several indigenous kingdoms that amalgamated numerous tribes. This trend began in what is today called Zululand around the turn of the nineteenth century, when Shaka launched his conquering armies into adjoining regions. The precedent was followed by two of Shaka's generals; and a very similar development led to the creation of Basutoland. Junod believes that the original idea of transforming the clan into a conquering army was not contributed by Shaka, however, but was introduced into Zululand by another chief who, in turn, was influenced by observing the parade of an English regiment in Cape Town.

[42] See David Livingstone, *Missionary Travels and Researches in South Africa* (New York, 1858), pp. 290ff., 303ff., on the Lunda and related realms. Westermann, *Geschichte Afrikas*, pp. 42, 386ff., and *supra*, Ch. 6, note 13 and Ch. 7, note 39, on the Lunda and other Central African states; also the works of E. Torday and T. Joyce; Cuvelier, *L'Ancien Royaume de Congo*; Vansina, *Kingdoms of the Savanna*. For East Africa, see Richards, ed., *East African Chiefs*.

[43] *Supra*, Ch. 5, on the time concept that controlled African thought.

[44] *Afrique occidentale francaise*, p. 63.

133

credentials for their conquests. Among the Islamic masters of this type of magic statecraft, none rivaled the Fulani leaders of the late eighteenth and the nineteenth centuries, whose priestly vanguards had infiltrated vast regions in West Africa, exhorting pagans and fellow Muslims alike to embrace the cause of a reformed Islam, before Dan Fodio, the greatest of their fighting divines, unleashed the full fury of his armies for the total and pitiless conquest of the Hausa states, Nupeland, and a part of the Yoruba country.[45]

In pagan Africa, meanwhile, where absolutist personal rule was institutionalized and hence more predictable in its various manifestations than in the regions dominated by Islam, the principles of ancestor worship, divine kingship, shamanism, and magic often combined to lend a measure of stability to the political unions of otherwise disparate entities. This was so in the Mossi-Dagomba states of the west; the Hima states of East Africa, whose kings were vested with unlimited powers; the Bantu states of southern Africa, where Shaka was allowed to assume "God-like eminence"[46] notwithstanding the lurid excesses of his regime, and where

[45] On the empire of Uthman Dan Fodio see Trimingham, *History of Islam in West Africa*, pp. 195ff. A full description of the state as it existed about 1851 is given by Barth, *Travels and Discoveries in North and Central Africa*, Vol. II, 503ff.

See Nadel, *A Black Byzantium*, pp. 77, 85, on the Fulani infiltration of Nupe, which was effected by an eloquent priest, Mallam Dendo, who went about the country creating a "fifth column" of followers as the nucleus of future conquests. The Fulani also infiltrated Adamawa in similar ways before subjugating it in the early nineteenth century. See Barth's observation in 1851 on the "loose connections" that marked the organization of the Fulani empires. See Kirk-Greene, ed., *Travels in Nigeria*, pp. 132ff. and pp. 181–182 to the effect that continuous efforts to subjugate the Adamawa region had not been successful: "they have still a great deal to do before they can regard themselves as the undisturbed possessors of the soil. Even here, an independent tribe called Gille still maintains itself."

According to Hodgkin, *Nigerian Perspectives*, introduction, p. 41, the Fulani empire was "discernibly a state," even though ridden by revolts, territorially overstretched, and not always capable of maintaining its political identity. The Fulani state of Masina had been heralded by prophesies and dreams announcing the imminence of such an empire. Its actual evolution was marked by intrigues between rival marabouts and conflicts with pagan fetichists. See Ba and Daget, *L'Empire Peul du Macine*, pp. 1ff., 25ff., 73ff.

Other successful conquerors who gained widespread reputations as zealots or saints were Mansa Musa of Mali (1312–1337), renowned especially in the Arab world for his fantastic pilgrimage through Cairo to Mecca; Sonni Ali of Gao (1464–1492), who was said to have been endowed with great magical powers, even as he conscripted his subjects into an irregular army that engaged in plunder and pillage so that the king's personal needs for affluence might be satisfied; and in the ensuing century, Askia Muhammed I, who created an orderly regional government in the western Sudan by relying on Islamic principles as well as on frequent military expeditions. See Trimingham, *History of Islam in West Africa*, pp. 70–103 for the formation, administration, and disintegration of these realms. On the history of Bornu in this period see Y. Urvoy, *Histoire de l'empire du Bornou* (Paris, 1949).

[46] I. Schapera, "Political Institutions," p. 176.

the ruler of Luongo was endowed with superhuman qualities and rights;[47] the Lunda empire in which Muata Jamvo and his coregent were commonly viewed by the people as sorcerers;[48] also in Oyo, Benin, Dahomey, and Ashanti, the great states of the Guinea forest, where all manner of war and despotism was absorbed because it was in fact an organic aspect of the religious system.

The potency as well as the limitations of mystical and sacred sanctions for the creation and maintenance of great power realms are well illustrated by the Ashanti union, one of the most complex and successful of the continent's political systems, and one also that has received particularly sensitive and scholarly attention from European students of the African scene.

The consummation of this union of Akan communities in the late seventeenth century A.D. was certainly aided by a common language, shared customs, the presence of common enemies, and a firm resolve to conquer neighboring peoples. In the last resort, however, unification was clearly due to the close cooperation of the Ashanti king, Osai Tutu, with his priestly advisor, Okomfo-Anotchi, who had earned a widespread reputation for being the greatest fetish man the Ashanti ever had.[49] It may be that the latter's life and work have been obscured by myth; but in the understanding of the Ashanti, both then and now, it was this priest— referred to by some English commentators as the "Ashanti Cardinal Wolsey" and by others as the "Ashanti Christ"—who united what had seemed to be hopelessly divided groups by exercising the same magical powers that enabled him—it is said—to drain rivers, make good laws, heal people, predict events, and find a medicine against death. When the assembled chiefs drank the magic potion he had brewed, they were ready to constitute a league for the purpose of waging war against common foes. Just where magic stopped and diplomacy began is today difficult

[47] Westermann, *Geschichte Afrikas*, p. 403.

[48] Spannaus, *Zuege aus der Politischen Organisation Afrikanischer Voelker und Staaten*, pp. 39ff.; also Vansina, *Kingdoms of the Savanna*, on mystical powers imputed to rulers and other officials.

[49] R. S. Rattray, *Ashanti* (Oxford, 1923), p. 288; also p. 224; Rattray, *Ashanti Law and Constitution* (London, 1929, repr. 1956), ch. 24. See also W. W. Claridge, *A History of the Gold Coast and Ashanti*, 2 vols. (London, 1915), and Ward, *A History of the Gold Coast*. On the origins, historical and legendary, of the Akan of Ghana, consult Eva R. Meyerowitz, *The Divine Kingship in Ghana and Ancient Egypt* (London, 1960), p. 55, to the effect that the cult of the divine king and the principles of social organization derive largely from ancient Egypt. See also three previous works by the same author on this subject, and William Tordoff, "The Ashanti Confederacy," *Journal of African History*, 3, No. 3 (1962), 414, on the effectiveness of the administrative system, pp. 415ff. on the supremacy of the sacred stool over its occupant, and on such reasons for destoolment as repeatedly rejecting the advice of his elders, breaking a taboo, or acting with excessive cruelty.

to say, especially in the context of Occidental historiography, in which the force of magic is not recognized. It is clear from the records, however, that Anotchi—not unlike his Muslim Fulani counterparts[50]—spent years travelling through the land and many months negotiating patiently with each individual chief in order to arouse a desire for concerted action.[51] Only after these preparations did he counsel Osai Tutu that the moment for union had come, and this event was then sealed by appropriate ceremonies and magical activities. Moreover, once victory over the enemy had been achieved, Anotchi saw to it that the league survived by anchoring it to a regional administrative structure that reasserted, in the new enlarged dimension, the fundamental, locally shared symbols and principles of rule. For example, since the divisional seat of sovereignty had been symbolized in a "stool," the highest was to be so symbolized also. In the presence of all the chiefs and a great multitude of folk, the master of magical diplomacy is said to have brought down from the sky, in a black cloud, amid rumblings, and in air thick with white dust, a wooden stool with three supports and partly covered with gold. And this "golden stool," which alighted slowly upon Osai Tutu's knees, has been commonly believed to incorporate the soul of the Ashanti nation. Entrusted to the guardianship of the Asantehene as the successor of Osai Tutu, it is supposed to have assured the kingdom's welfare, power, and bravery in war.

True to the spirit of its mythical and symbolic charter, the Ashanti union survived only so long as it was engaged in successful war, which included slave raiding on a massive scale. This conclusion is developed persuasively by K. A. Busia, who points out that the Ashanti state, having been "primarily a military council," was engaged in continuous warfare throughout its existence from the latter part of the seventeenth to the beginning of the twentieth century.[52] As an administrative machinery, Busia continues, the union was merely incipient; each of the segments, joined in a loose confederation, had had a previous existence as a distinct community and was endowed with a government that functioned reliably on the levels of the lineage, the village, and the subdivision. Conquered states owed allegiance and military service, yet were left to manage their own internal affairs.[53] And in the absence of rail and road transport or

[50] *Supra*, note 45 of this chapter.

[51] The record of these negotiations is unfortunately lost; see Ward, *A History of the Gold Coast*, pp. 107ff., 133ff. For other aspects of the union's evolution, see Claridge, *A History of the Gold Coast and Ashanti*, Vol. I, 186, 195, and the works of Rattray and others cited previously.

[52] K. A. Busia, *The Position of the Chief in the Modern Political System of Ashanti; A Study of the Influence of Contemporary Social Changes on Ashanti Political Institutions* (London and New York, 1951), p. 101. The Ashanti were defeated by English forces at the beginning of the twentieth century.

[53] *Ibid.*, p. 60, contests Rattray's view (see *Ashanti*, pp. 224ff.) that the Ashanti

any other means of communication, no economic or social bonds ever evolved. Each substate developed its own regional consciousness, and separatist tendencies were vented frequently in revolts and interregional wars.

The supreme achievement of the kings of Kumasi, Busia finds, was "the building up of this loose political system into a strong military power."[54] This was accomplished by making Kumasi's military organization the basis also of its civil administration, and by propagating the ruling notions of power and supremacy in appropriate, generally meaningful, myths, symbols, and ceremonies, among which the stool was pivotal. Other aspects of the symbolic order that rallied people to the support of constitutionally significant understandings were the famous "yam" customs, designed in particular to propitiate the ancestors; the ceremonies purporting to banish the devil; the "ntoro" washing rites;[55] and the great periodic pageants at the palace of the Asantehene, which summed up and restated the hierarchical representative system of the entire union. Vividly described by T. E. Bowdich,[56] who visited Kumasi in 1817, such a spectacle assembled, in the presence of the king, a multitude of common people, tens of thousands of warriors, tributary vassals, chiefs, lieutenants, and the principal royal office holders, among whom were the soul washer, the chamberlain, the gold horn blower, the captain of the messengers, the captain for the royal executions, the captain of the market, the king's eunuch, and the king's four linguists. The particular functions of these personages were made known by their behavior, their attire, their ornaments, and, in certain cases, by special musical themes. Furthermore, their mutual relations in the comprehensive mythical community were symbolized in this dramatization of politics by a vast array of ritually important objects, which included hundreds of immense umbrellas, innumerable small canopies, wolves' and rams' heads, long leopard tails, immense plumes of eagle feathers, quivers of poisoned arrows, jawbones of defeated enemies, a confusion of flags that accommodated, at the beginning of the nineteenth century, those of the new

---

land tenure system and feudalism are analogous to early English forms of land tenure and feudalism. In this respect see *supra*, Ch. 5, note 65 for a discussion of some of the difficulties inherent in transcultural comparisons and for the view, developed at length by Chilver in Richards, ed., *East African Chiefs*, that "feudalism" is not the appropriate term in African contexts.

[54] Busia, *The Position of the Chief*, pp. 87ff., 91. For somewhat different interpretations, see Tordoff, "The Ashanti Confederacy," pp. 415ff.

[55] See Rattray, *Ashanti*, pp. 52ff.

[56] *Mission from Cape Coast Castle to Ashantee, with a Statistical Account of that Kingdom, and Geographical Notices of Other Parts of the Interior of Africa* (London, 1819). See Freda Wolfson, *Pageant of Ghana* (London, New York, Toronto, 1958, repr. 1959), pp. 98ff. for excerpts from journals by Bowdich and others.

European intruders; also strings of fetishes and amulets, among which Bowdich noted "Moorish" charms and "bits of Moorish writing." A deafening tumult of assorted noises, produced by drums, horns, rattles, gong-gongs and the incessant discharge of musketry, enveloped the entire procession as it moved forward slowly but inexorably toward the golden stool, the supreme embodiment of royal rule and of Ashanti power.

In neighboring Dahomey, which is culturally closely related to Ashanti, Richard F. Burton noted greatly similar customs, and what impressed this observer as he watched the dances, the chorus, and, above all, the pageant of amazons with their bullet bags, was the presence throughout of what he termed "the pronounced ceremonial faculty." On all of these occasions, he remarked, "the pageantry of African Courts is to be compared with that of Europe, proportionately with the national state of progress. But it is evidently the result of long and studious practice. Everything goes by clockwork, the most intricate etiquette proceeds without halt or mistake; and it ever superadds the element Terror whose absence in civilized countries often converts ceremonial to a something silly."[57]

What the records of the most effective "greater societies" in pagan Africa illustrate is a marked ingenuity for rendering the principles of power, unity, and hierarchy by nonliterate means. An intricate order of superior and inferior stools can here take the place of a written federal constitution,[58] even as each of these assembled objects, in its own right, communicates shared religious convictions and family traditions. And similar sacred and governmental functions are entrusted to drums, many of which are personalized, as it were, and endowed with intrinsic powers of their own.[59] Whole families of drums, of all sizes and ranks, were thus recognized in some of the Congolese kingdoms, the biggest and most important among them destined for signaling the beginning of war. Each had a special mandate, and people near and far knew by the sound and the rhythm what cause had determined the beating of which drum. Elsewhere special chords, beats, or pieces of music were recognized as representing attributes of sovereignty. For example, by repeating the same phrase: "We are all slaves of the king, our sovereign," trumpets or drums told all those present at a royal procession in Ijebu country (Nigeria)

[57] *A Mission to Gelele, King of Dahome*, Isabel Burton, ed., 2 vols. (London, 1893), Vol. I, 183; see also pp. 154ff.

[58] On the Ashanti federation, *supra*, pp. 135ff.

[59] See Rattray, *Ashanti*, ch. 22, "The Drum Language"; Dennett, *At the Back of the Black Man's Mind*, pp. 76–78, for the role of drums in Kongo; J. Cuvelier, ed. and trans., *Relations sur le Congo*, pp. 83, 121. Westermann, *Geschichte Afrikas*, p. 336, also p. 42, refers to Ankole and other Hima states in East Africa as the domain of the sacred drum. See Junod, *Moeurs et coutumes*, Vol. I, 400, 430ff. on the role of the Great Royal Drum in Thonga society.

that homage was due.[60] Among other insignia of occult or mundane authority that served simultaneously as media of communication, one finds constitutionally important praise songs, common throughout Africa as modes of acknowledging the position and prestige of a chief or king; likewise, heraldically significant pieces of cloth, different types of umbrellas and fly whisks, a variety of physical markings, and specific sacred objects.[61] Each symbol, it is true, has its own frame of reference, but it also serves one overriding purpose; namely, to represent the political community as a continuous rite and to invest it with sacred and magical powers.

These modes of imaging the comprehensive mythical society were capable, in many instances, of accommodating new, essentially alien, forces entering from Asia's and Europe's literate culture worlds. They explain, for example, why persons professing connection with Islam continue to play important roles today in the religious and magical life of the Mende in Sierra Leone, as well as why Mende warrior chiefs used in earlier times to have Muslim priests as advisors.[62] The Ashanti, likewise, knew how to come to terms with the Mohammedans in their midst, and even how to mold the Islamic faith until it had assumed some of the aspects of the native system of beliefs.[63] The British thus found, upon their arrival in Kumasi, that Muslims held important positions, not only in commerce and in the social organization, but also in the realm of magic, without, however, exercising any real influence on Akan traditions. And the same synthesizing spirit has survived in modern Ghana, where Kwame Nkrumah, a nominal Christian and avowed Marxist, is said to have sought reassurance for the continuity of his life and power

[60] P. C. Lloyd, "Osifekunde of Ijebu," in Philip D. Curtin, ed., *Africa Remembered; Narratives by West Africans from the Era of the Slave Trade* (Madison, Milwaukee, and London, 1967), pp. 277ff.

[61] The tenacious hold that such tangible objects continue to exercise upon a people's consciousness was poignantly illustrated in 1973, when the affairs of the small kingdom of the Kom nation—one of seventeen independent kingdoms in the United Republic of Cameroon—were brought into disarray as a result of the disappearance of a particular statue. This object, the Afo-A-Kom, was described by Cameroon's diplomatic representative in Washington as "the heart of the Kom, what unifies the tribe, the spirit of the nation, what holds us together." These circumstances explain why its removal was held directly responsible for the general unrest that descended upon society and the quarrelling that marked human relations. In fact, the Kom firmly believe that it was this incident that "psychologically killed" Law-Aw, ruler of the kingdom, when the statue was taken out. The carving of a duplicate, ordered by the new Fon in response to the disorder, quite failed to assuage the populace. The object, which had been bought by outsiders, was subsequently returned. See the *New York Times*, October 25, 1973; also October 26, 1973.

[62] Little, *The Mende of Sierra Leone*, Appendix I, pp. 273ff. on "The Part of Islam in Mende Life."

[63] See also *supra*, pp. 130ff., but cf. *supra*, pp. 120ff. on the adaptability of Islam to local conditions, and *infra*, Ch. 18 on the prestige and influence of Islamic "intermediaries."

from both pagan soothsayers and Islamic preachers and shrines, notably from Kankan, the major "fetish" in Guinea.[64] Although neither of these moral guides was able to prevent his overthrow in February 1966, Islamic advisors helped to secure his exile in Guinea. The poignancy of the coup, viewed by some Ghanaians as "one of the Ashanti invasions,"[65] resides rather in the fact that the Ashanti, seemingly broken in spirit and alienated from their ancestral stools, were able to return to their traditional institutions and, by virtue of this return, to take over leadership and power in the multitribal society of modern Ghana. Indeed, this swift reversal of political fortunes brought in its wake an open revival of several premodern customs, among them those attending the induction of the new Asantehene. J. Matthew Peku—a British-educated lawyer, Anglican, and Ghana's appointee for the ambassadorial post in Rome—was thus selected by the Ashanti queen mother and the Tribal Chiefs' Council to succeed his uncle, who had died in 1969, and the enthronement of the nephew as Nana Opeku Ware II in 1970 included anointment ceremonies that had not been conducted in thirty-five years. When the new ruler first learned of his selection, he is quoted as having said: "I had my tickets, my traveler's checks, everything . . . But when I was caught by the net, I had no choice."[66]

A review of the relationship between traditional political organizations and belief systems—whether pagan, Islamic, or Christian—permits several conclusions. It appears, first, that in Africa religion and magic are not normally invoked with a view either to limiting the sphere of war or to curbing the fighting instincts of men. Indeed, their effect would usually appear to have been the contrary: incorporeal and spiritual references were conjured up mainly in order to promote belligerence—a fact that

[64] See Afrifa, *The Ghana Coup*, p. 123 and note 2, which quotes the following report from *West Africa*, June 18, 1966: "Mr. Tawiah Adamano, who was consigned to protective custody after the quashing of his conviction for conspiring against the life of Dr. Nkrumah, is one of the latest to give evidence before the Apaloo Commission, enquiring into the private possessions of his former chief. He said that he and Dr. Nkrumah had sought the protection of the Akonodi fetish at Larteh after hearing that some people had asked the chief priestess there, Madam Akuah Oparebea, to kill them. Although she had refused to give the names of these people, the president had said that it did not matter, since he was well protected by his Moslem seer, Kankan; he had asked Mr. Adamano to buy a car for Madam Oparebea." Compare *supra*, Ch. 3, n. 24 and *infra*, Ch. 15, n. 4.

[65] Afrifa, *The Ghana Coup*, p. 33; it should be remarked, however, that some of the revolutionary leaders were Ewe.

[66] *Time*, August 10, 1970, p. 26. The Kumasi correspondent also reports that the ceremony of the enthronement had been preceded, after the demise of the old king, by the enactment of the so-called "customs." Although villagers are said to have formed vigilante groups to guard against the royal executioners, it is generally believed in the country that despite the precautions several dozen lost their lives. However, the reporter continues, nobody in Ashanti will discuss the affair, any more than he would talk about the tribe's mysteries, rituals, or especially the whereabouts, between coronations, of the golden stool.

helps to explain why particular religious enthusiasms have been as short-lived as the causes in behalf of which they have been kindled. The alliance between ritual, religion, and martial force is thus essentially fragile, being dependent in the final analysis upon continuous success in warfare. Unions born of conquest—most if not all of the great societies having issued from this source—have been, therefore, in their very nature as instable as any purely military undertaking.

Furthermore, as adept as some African governments have been in stimulating feelings of unity among ethnically nonrelated peoples by relying upon appropriate mythical and symbolic references, they have not been able to overcome the limitations inherent in all nonliterate modes of political communication. After all, people have to be physically present if a pageant, a rite, a song, or a story is to elicit the desired response. Here, as in other circumstances of life, to which attention has previously been drawn, the appeal is directed to the senses, and the emphasis is on the moment of experience. In short, myth and ritual cannot easily be extended. Furthermore, in Africa most if not all of the religious and mythical schemes have been able to control the minds of men only so long as, and to the extent to which, they have been clearly discernible as functions of the kinship principle. When new peoples, beholden to other customs and traditions, are added to the political body, structural weaknesses in the administrative order are quick to appear, and the unions are apt to dissolve into their component parts.

This process was almost automatic in the Islamic empires. Many of these were saturated, in their formative period at least, by monotheistic religious fervor; and most were immensely successful in military affairs. Yet they were not rooted in the kinship system in the manner of indigenous African states, and they lacked the highly developed sense for synthesizing imagery that was typical of the people over whom they ruled. In such cultural conditions the conquered retained their distinctive institutions and beliefs under the surface of the nominal power exercised by Islam, with the result that political organization was actually dominated by the demands of the tribe and the village, both being representative of the "inferior" or subject groups. As Trimingham reminds us in his comments on what he calls the Sudan State System, the real rulers were not kings and emperors, but patriarchs of families, councils of elders, and chiefs of villages on the one hand, and on the other, the heads of superimposed clans.[67] The state of Mali was such a superimposed

[67] *History of Islam in West Africa*, pp. 34–35. "The Sudan concept of dominium is difficult to define," this scholar continues. "It was the reverse of an imperium if by that is meant a dominium which seeks to extend its form of civilization over diverse types of societies. It was not a political unity, nor based on territorial sovereignty. . . . It is impossible to demarcate these spheres upon a map for the frontier did not exist. Nor was there any capital city. . . . 'Empires'

lineage, according to this analysis, whether it consisted of the primitive community from which it had originated and in which it ended, or whether it represented itself as that amorphous political sphere called the Mali empire in which thousands of groups at all stages of development coexisted without having much in common.

In non-Islamic Africa, several "composite nations," among them those of Basutoland, Swaziland, North Bechuanaland, Ashanti, and the Mossi states, had been able to escape the cycle of swift expansion and retrenchment mainly because their administrative systems were all cast in the same basic molds as that of the "small" community.[68] But here, as in the regions dominated by Islam, most of the great power constellations were brittle, ephemeral, and inconsequential as political organizations. Their central or imperial governments were not interested in building "nations" out of the disparate groups they had assembled, in retaining full and effective jurisdiction over the territory they had acquired, or in developing the economies of their provinces beyond the plane of short-term exploitation. Based on conquest, personified in individuals or families, these imperial regimes were incapable of finding cultural and psychological sustenance in the traditions of the conquered, and unable also to generate any state-supporting culture of their own. Being fundamentally alien rulers, they soon exhausted their tangible and intangible resources and departed from the scene, leaving intact the skeletal frames of the folk societies they had despoiled.[69]

---

were spheres of influence, defined not by territorial or boundary lines but by social strata, independent families, free castes, or servile groups of fixed status regarded as royal serfs."

[68] This explanation is offered by I. Schapera, "Political Institutions," in connection with his analysis of the relative stability of three Bantu "composite nations" listed above. But it appears valid also for Ashanti and the other states in the Guinea forest, and for the Mossi states in which people were unified by the kinship ties of their rulers.

[69] Compare Westermann, *Geschichte Afrikas*, p. 402, who views the imperial establishment of all Luba-Lunda realms as "Fremdherrschaft" (alien rule). *Ibid.*, pp. 31ff., that the purpose of the state (as distinguished from the tribe) was war and exploitation. To the same effect see Monteil, *Les Bambara du Segou et du Kaarta*, who finds no evidence in the Bambara area that the different empires were ever interested in actually controlling regions through government; their main purpose was the exploitation of the greatest possible number of individuals.

See Richard-Molard, *Problèmes humains en Afrique occidentale*, for a study of that which is most authentically "African" about the hierarchical kingdoms of West Africa that succumbed to Islamic governance. Diverse as these societies are, Richard-Molard yet finds that all are reducible to the norm of the conservative peasant society, and this, he believes, will continue to remain the dominant trait in times to come. Compare Lloyd, *Africa in Social Change*, p. 13, on the insufficiency of theoretical models, including those derived from Marxist analyses, and the remarkable persistence of precolonial patterns in modern African societies.

· 8 ·

DESIGN AND DEFINITION

The traditional states of Africa south of the Sahara are not comparable to those of the literate, notably the Western, civilizations. And since they were mature, fully developed associational forms in the context of their own culture, they cannot be forced into a comparative design by being viewed as early or transitional models of the land-based state, the nation state, or the multinational commonwealth, as these political constellations are understood in non-African worlds. In other words, Africa's greater societies cannot be integrated securely into the normative schemes developed by Occidental historiography and political science without misrepresenting the qualities that made the African organisms what they were. The conclusion reached by many psychologists and psychiatrists specializing in Africa, namely, that the discipline of psychiatry has its base in the cultural system covering Europe and America, and that "cultural distortion" may result if one uses Western definitions for the recognition of psychiatric disorders in another culture,[1] is suggestive also in other academic fields. In the social sciences, in particular, evidence has been accumulating steadily that available conceptual tools are inadequate for the analysis of African institutions, or, to put it differently, that African facts elude Occidental theory.

Next, it appears from the records of Africa's "greater societies" that one cannot speak convincingly of an African system of states on the analogy of, for example, the modern European states system, or the city states systems of ancient Mesopotamia and classical Greece, because Africans have not brought forth a shared norm of political organization. The general conclusion is tenable that all African states were fluid and ad hoc creations that did not require a fixed human or territorial base, and that each is best understood as a system of more or less autonomous parts, held together by a dominant personality, family, or lineage.[2] More precise definitions are, however, resisted by the subject matter. Intricate and imaginative classifications of African regimes have been proposed,

[1] See "The Problem of Cultural Distortion" in Leighton, Lambo, *et al., Psychiatric Disorder among the Yoruba*; also W. E. Abraham, *The Mind of Africa* (Chicago, 1962), p. 59, for doubts as to whether findings by psychologists with a European academic background might "stand in Africa without being further checked," and the query: "might the psyche of Africans turn out to be quite distinct and not really support the findings?" The following summation of traditional themes will be found to relate closely to certain discussions of modern African politics in Part II.

[2] *Supra*, Ch. 7.

it is true, but as Murdock remarks in connection with his own scheme of arrangement,[3] none is sufficiently comprehensive and exact to do justice to the great variety of recorded associations.

The major stumbling block in the path toward a more satisfactory recognition and coordination of these African phenomena may well be the fact that the traditional states in this culture world were fleeting representations of an invisible but stable mythical substructure (remnants of myth, as Leo Frobenius suggested), and that all governing institutions, including the most despotic among them, were, in the final analysis, prisoners of a system of sacred rites. Now these are aspects of political organization that contemporary political science, with its stress on what the modern West regards as the real and the rational, is ill-equipped to analyze. Their overwhelming presence in Africa strongly suggests, indeed, that our state-related vocabulary of concepts, values, and words may actually screen more of African society than it can ever reveal.

Both propositions—the absence of an all-African model for "the greater society," and the inadequacy of unifying academic classifications brought in from without—must be appreciated in light of the fact that African thought does not permit the kind of conceptualization and systematization that has elsewhere made not only for the recognition of actually shared norms, but also for philosophical speculation about generally applicable principles or generally valid goals evolving from the maze of different local interests, commitments, and life experiences.[4] And the same indigenous intellectual tradition explains, of course, why the different political entities could not relate to each other through the medium of a shared time scale and common conception of the past,[5] and why they could not fashion technical connections and means of intercommunication. The various species of trade and warfare were willed linkages, it is true, but—as a preceding discussion has suggested—they cannot be viewed as expressions either of a comprehensive vision of regional affairs, or of a long-range concern with mutuality, unity, or interdependence in intersocietal relations. African states were fundamentally self-sufficient and disinterested in each other, and this disposition, together with factors mentioned previously, made for the nearly total

[3] *Africa*, p. 33. Compare also Bretton, "Current Political Thought and Practice in Ghana," especially pp. 47–49.

[4] Compare preceding chapters of Part III; also Redfield, *The Primitive World and Its Transformations*, pp. 82ff. on the impossibility of evolving "general ideas" in the context of nonliterate societies. For some pertinent suggestions see also Crahay, "Conceptual Take-Off," pp. 55–78.

[5] See *supra*, pp. 72ff. and 100ff. on the absence of a concept of history; also *infra*, pp. 223ff.

absence of what is elsewhere called "foreign policy."[6] In default of this dimension of political existence, it is illusory to speak of a "state system."[7]

In short, unifying orders were missing on all planes of actuality and theory, with the result that Africa's greater societies could neither define themselves nor recognize each other in the mirror of shared forms and values. Their interactions—to the extent to which they existed at all—were therefore as pragmatic and unstructured as the acts that had called each of the states and empires into being. Conflicts between them cannot be understood and appraised as long as one holds fast to norms imported from without, or as long as it is assumed that one is dealing with what in other civilizations is called "interstate or international relations." Any inquiry into the role of conflict in politics and society, therefore, requires a shift of focus to the small folk community—the nuclear cell of each comprehensive political organism, and the form of group life that Africans themselves have regarded as enduringly meaningful throughout the centuries.

Even on this reduced scene of social relations, however, one must remember that patterns of conflict can only be extrapolated from the records; for the mode of mythical nonliterate thinking that accounts for the absence in Africa of conceptualization in the context of the "great societies" also explains why "the village," "the clan," "the lineage," or "the tribe" was experienced in each case rather as a concrete and unique community than as the manifestation of a generic norm. Here, as there, men were not enabled by their culture to perceive affinities in social organization or to seek intercommunal accords. The contrary had to be true: since each group treasured its separate identity, it was apt to impute totally different customs to a neighboring community, even in cases in which an outsider would find greatly similar if not identical structures. What Nadel observed in his analysis of the Nupe realm, namely, that the social group as well as the tribe was more likely than not to be sustained by an ideology that ignored and overrode empirical facts,[8] holds generally throughout Africa, as preceding notes and comments have sug-

[6] For exceptions see *supra*, pp. 113 and 116, and *infra*, p. 210.

[7] Westermann points to Leopold von Ranke as he reminds us that it was the overwhelming presence of this dimension that lent special poignancy to Europe's history. The writing of Africa's history is, by contrast, greatly impeded by the absence of the "interaction" motif; *Geschichte Afrikas*, p. 2.

[8] *A Black Byzantium*, p. 39. But see *supra*, Ch. 7, note 32 for Nadel's belief, explained *ibid.*, p. 69, that the Nupe kingdom was "a state," and that it was experienced as such by the inhabitants. Compare Froehlich, *Cameroun-Togo*, p. 28, to the effect that the inhabitants of one Cameroon chiefdom do not recognize any links with their immediate neighbors in another chiefdom.

gested. On all planes of social or political existence one finds that self-definition or self-awareness has traditionally been a function of "biological patriotism,"[9] and as such, has everywhere required not only isolationism but also opposition and hostility to "the other."

[9] Richard-Molard, *Afrique occidentale française*, pp. 88, 104. And see Westermann, *Geschichte Afrikas*, pp. 2–3 for a particularly sensitive and comprehensive rendition of this entire matter: "Im ganzen aber waren die Eigenstaendigkeit jedes Volkes oder Stammes, die Neigung, sich abzuschliessen, die Furcht vor dem Fremden, die Eifersucht oder ueberkommene Abneigung gegen den Nachbarn viel zu gross, um ein Gefuehl der Gemeinsamkeit, ein Verlangen nach engen Beziehungen aufkommen zu lassen. Man lebte fuer sich. Bei staerkeren Staaten aeusserte sich das Beduerfnis nach auswaertigen Beziehungen in Raubzuegen und Unterjochung. Verband man sich mit einem Zweiten, so geschah das zur Beraubung eines Dritten. . . . Das Leben der afrikanischen Staatsvoelker und erst recht das der Staemme erweckt den Eindruck eines stillen Kommens und Gehens, wo jeder durch seine eigene Tuer eintritt, von den anderen Anwesenden im Hause keine Notiz nimmt und wieder fortgeht, ohne sich zu verabschieden." (On the whole, however, it appears that each people or tribe was so self-sufficient and introverted, so fearful of the unknown and the strange, and so deeply imbued with jealousy or antipathy in regard to its neighbors that it could not develop desires for close relations with others. Each community lived for itself. The need for external relations was experienced only by strong states, and here it found expression in raids of conquest and subjugation. Any alliance between two groups had the sole purpose of bringing spoliation to a third. . . . The life not only of Africa's tribes but also of its state-forming peoples thus leaves the impression of a quiet coming and going: it is as if everyone enters through his own door, remains oblivious of the presence of others in the house, and then departs again without saying good-bye.)

PART IV
THE ROLE OF CONFLICT
IN AFRICAN THOUGHT
AND SOCIETY

· 9 ·

ORDER AND DISORDER AS
FUNCTIONS OF MAGIC,
POWER, AND DEATH

The omnipresence of conflict in traditional African thought patterns, value systems, and forms of political and social organization is a function of the fact that power is the major reference in this culture's inner normative order. As previously suggested, power is always and everywhere, in the final analysis, associated with magic. It is usually presumed to be aggressive and malevolent, whether emanating from spirits, from objects incarnating spirits, or from witches or other human beings. In a system of mystical participation in which power is pitted against counterpower, opposition and antagonism become the ruling dynamic. All relationships between tangible and intangible, human and nonhuman entities are thus by definition conflict relations.

The dominant human dispositions that keep the system going, even as they brought it forth, are insecurity and fear. Since all human beings are organic aspects of a superior magical order in which witchcraft is accepted as the ultimate causal principle, all men are suspect as potential carriers of antagonistic or evil forces. Distrust, being "the essence of life,"[1] is thus the rule also in human relations; confidence between man and man is, by contrast, the exception. Interpersonal conflicts are therefore apt to be cast in terms of witchcraft and sorcery whenever men have to contend with death, illness, misfortune, or other inexplicable events. And since such untoward occurrences are usually experienced in the closed circle of people who know each other well, it is here, in the context of relations between neighbors and kinsmen, that frictions, jealousies, and hatreds are most pronounced. For example, accusations of sorcery in Bunyoro society are commonest between relatives and neighbors who are in frequent contact with one another. Here people, eager to forestall misfortune and ward off evil volitions, can plot "counter evil" by choosing from a wide variety of means, all designed to bring illness or some other calamity to the one believed to be the enemy.[2] And much the same patterns marked social and family relations among the Azande, who are described as ridden with malice, hatred, and envy,

[1] This is one of Richard Wright's comments on the Akan personality; see *Black Power*, p. 293.
[2] John Beattie, "Sorcery in Bunyoro," in John Middleton and E. H. Winter, eds., *Witchcraft and Sorcery in East Africa* (London, 1963), pp. 30, 41.

and especially with jealousy among close relatives;[3] the Dan,[4] the Tiv, in whose communities death-causing evil volitions are commonly ascribed to kinsmen,[5] and the Bemba. In the course of reminiscing upon his life, a Bemba tribesman reports that people openly ascribed a certain chief's illness to bewitchment by a scheming brother, and that the afflicted chief himself was terrified when he heard his brother was coming, exclaiming: "my brother is killing me. He is waiting for me to die."[6]

Fear of witchcraft, aptly viewed by one authority as a constantly operative "fifth column" and as "the enemy within,"[7] thus pervades the moral order of the small, closely knit community, generating often unbearable tensions that then find temporary relief in mental and physical aggressiveness.

The touchstone in this system of human associations is death.[8] Commonly ascribed to someone's evil volition, that is to say, to social conflict, it is, in fact, usually identified as homicide. So conceptualized, violence becomes a paramount norm: the wish to kill is accepted as a normal human inclination, and the act of killing is absorbed as long as it occurs in strict accordance with the beliefs by which the community lives. And

[3] E. E. Evans-Pritchard, *Witches, Oracles, and Magic among the Azande* (Oxford, 1937, repr. 1950), pp. 63–119, 176.

[4] Hans Himmelheber, "Le Système de la religion des Dan," in *Les Religions africaines traditionnelles*, pp. 91ff.; also the contributions by Luc de Heusch, Bouah Niangoran, and William Bascom to the same symposium.

[5] Bohannan, "A Man Apart," p. 16; also Bohannan's study of the Tiv in Paul Bohannan, ed., *African Homicide and Suicide* (Princeton, 1960), pp. 46ff.

[6] Margery Perham, ed., *Ten Africans: A Collection of Life Stories* (London, 1936; repr. Evanston, Ill., 1963), pp. 36ff.

[7] E. H. Winter, "The Enemy Within: Amba Witchcraft and Sociological Theory," in Middleton and Winter, eds., *Witchcraft and Sorcery in East Africa*, pp. 277ff. On the continued existence of these traditional mental states of being, see *supra*, pp. 77ff., 89ff. Paul Verhaegen, "Study of the African Personality in the Belgian Congo" in Wickert, ed., *Readings in African Psychology*, pp. 245ff., reports that interpersonal relations in this region are undermined by aggressiveness, jealousy, and the desire to make someone feel inferior. To similar effect, an essay in the same volume on "The Meaning and Values Surrounding Persecution in African Cultures," pp. 362ff.; Perham, ed., *Ten Africans*, notably the first six autobiographical accounts.

See also Lloyd, *Africa in Social Change*, p. 45, who says that tensions between closely related individuals are difficult to manage today, and that witchcraft accusations are one method of coping with the situation. The man who fails to achieve his aspirations attributes his lack of success to the hostility, overt or covert, of his near kin. Young men who do not pass examinations, for example, rather commonly ascribe their failure to the plots of jealous relatives rather than to their own lack of ability.

[8] *Supra*, Ch. 5, n. 33 for analyses by Goody and other scholars. After noting that modern African poetry is consciously and intensively resuscitating traditional themes, Gerald Moore singles out death as the major motif in the work of French and English-speaking African poets, and remarks that death is usually represented in relation to the paramount principle of "vital energy." See Gerald Moore, "The Imagery of Death in African Poetry." *Africa*, 38, No. 1 (January 1968), 57–70.

the same reasoning applies to other metaphysically sanctioned ways of interfering with a person's life. In the quest for supernatural powers, a body may be mutilated or dismembered, and some of its parts eaten or transformed into magically potent devices. In short, in a world in which human life and death are significant primarily as symbols of mystical powers, vital energies, and their multifarious representations, no compelling reason exists to respect a particular individual's physical or spiritual integrity. Force and violence can thus be tolerated as logical dimensions of power and conflict without provoking shock or revulsion. What they affect, and are meant to affect and activate, is the latent disposition toward fear.

As a replica of the mystical universe, society reenacts on numerous levels the magical syndrome of power and conflict, violence and death. Its value system requires human beings to live in awe; its institutions insist that boys shall become men by submitting to the infliction of injury and pain, and that men shall prove their manhood by killing others; and its jural and governmental orders sanction ritual homicide, witch killing, and cannibalism in circumstances that appear arbitrary to the Western mind.[9]

The entire complex of customary patterns of thought, emotion, belief, and expectation in which great and small societies, the rulers and the

[9] See Bohannan, ed., *African Homicide and Suicide*, pp. 231ff. for "ritual killing" and "witch killing" as "non-culpable homicide" or "jural act," fully sanctioned by customary moral and legal systems, and therefore not easily susceptible to prosecution in terms of Western systems of law. Also *ibid.*, p. 188.

On the incompatibility of Western and African legal concepts, especially in the field of homicide, see also J. D. Hargreaves, *A Life of Sir Samuel Lewis* (London, 1958), p. 75, where the distinguished Sierra Leonean jurist is quoted as having made the following "curious" comment: "These murders [judicial massacres inflicted by the Leopard Society] were not connected with any religious rite, or with *bona fide* cases of cannibalism." See also *ibid.*, pp. 91ff. on the role of the Poro Society in the Mende rising during the 1890s, which apparently originated in hostility to Western cultural influences, but resulted in the murder of about three hundred Sierra Leoneans. On the activities of leopard, alligator, and other secret societies in Mende country, as related by young native informants, and on legal cases resulting from these activities, see also Migeod, *A View of Sierra Leone*, pp. 222ff. For comparable incidents in Basutoland during 1947 and 1948, see G. I. Jones, *Basutoland Medicine Murders; A Report on the Recent Outbreak of "Liretlo" Murders in Basutoland* (London, 1951). For Lord Hailey's comments on this case see *An African Survey*, p. 507.

On the socially unifying effects of death and human sacrifices, see Robert S. Rattray, *Religion and Art in Ashanti* (Oxford, 1927), p. 132, to the effect that it was at "customs" that the many loosely bound and often hostile factions came to think themselves part of a nation rather than branches of a family or clan. On funeral customs, *ibid.*, pp. 143ff. On the Atopere Dance of Death, *ibid.*, pp. 88ff. See also Jacob U. Egharevba, *A Short History of Benin*, 4th ed. (Ibadan, 1968), pp. 47ff. on the human sacrifices to which the Oba of Benin resorted in the last years of the nineteenth century so as to ward off certain dangers that had been prophesied.

ruled, were equally caught up, emerges forcefully from the following account of a Bemba tribesman, headman of a small village (proud also of his membership in the royal family of the Babemba and the Crocodile clan), who was about fifty or sixty years old when interviewed by Audrey I. Richards:

And so there was always trouble, for Mubanga Chipoya was a very jealous man, after the fashion of great chiefs. Once Kanyanta, the nephew of Mwamba, seduced one of his wives. Seeing she was pregnant, the chief asked her the name of her lover. First she sat silent for a long time. Then she said, "Sir, it was your sister's son." Without a word the chief sent and razed the village to the ground! Of course he could not kill the adulterer for it was his sister's son.

But sometimes his anger was worse than this. It was bhang that made Mubanga Chipoya so violent. He was a great chief, and he gave good judgments, but sometimes when he had sat smoking all the evening with his big pipe it was as though he was drunk—as though he were mad. . . . Then we of the court would creep about and whisper to each other, "Look out now! Do not make him angry! He is like a madman tonight." We were all afraid. For we knew that if anyone offended him in such a mood he might order that their hands be struck off or their ears slit.

And so one day when this temper was on him, he became suddenly furious because he found out that one of his young wives had been unfaithful. So he cried out that the whole company of this girl's fellows should be burnt alive. They were all to be burnt, about twelve of them, on a great platform, with all the young men of the quarter of the village to which the adulterer belonged.

No! the girls never tried to beg for mercy, they were afraid. They just sat silent on the ground holding on to each other. Only when they had dragged them outside the enclosure, they began to shriek, "Alai! Alai! It was not I who deceived the chief. Let me go! Let me go!" But who knows? Perhaps they were all guilty all the same. . . .

Did the fathers and brothers of these girls try to help them? Why do you ask me that? Of course they had run away a long while ago. . . . They said, "The chief is killing our children, do not let him kill us too." They were afraid of such a powerful chief. After it was over, Mwamba made them come and do obeisance to him. . . . And always after that these people took care to bring Mwamba presents, . . . for they were always afraid that he might remember how their daughters had done him wrong.

Did I try to help the young men, my fellows, who were about to be burnt? You ask if I pleaded for them. No indeed, I was running to fetch the firewood. I went with the others. The whole village was running to and fro bringing in great logs and piling up the fire. . . . You see they were afraid they might be burnt too. . . . And the fire they built! My word! The big fires they make when the Government officials go on tour, they are nothing to this fire. . . . When the fire was lit, we caught hold of the girls and boys and hoisted them up, and thrust them on to the platform. They were all crying out, "Let go! Let go! I never did wrong." But of course, it was too late to cry out then, for the chief had already given the order that they should be burnt. They did not scream for long, either, because the fire was so big. We boys were all standing watching. For a moment they all shouted like madmen, "Ai! Ai! I am dying! Take me out!" But then they stopped crying quickly. It was the smoke in their nostrils that stopped them crying out.

After it was over we went to tell the chief. He sat silent then. He said nothing for the ferocity in his heart had spent itself. There was quiet in the court for many months after that, for the madness had worn itself out.[10]

Traditional structures of social and political organization, whether associated with empires, kingdoms, chiefdoms, or so-called anarchies;

[10] Perham, ed., *Ten Africans*, pp. 29–31. *Ibid.*, pp. 20ff. for an account by the same informant of why a man fled: "it was the custom that when a great chief died, many of his followers were killed. Some of his favourites they slew because they said: 'You, you people who received food every day from the hands of the chief, and beer and meat and clothes and every good thing, now you can follow your chief where he goes.' Others whom they killed were just slaves. They hit them on the forehead with a pole, and those who carried the chief's body stepped over the dead slaves as they bore the corpse out of the royal enclosure. Others were his wives and body servants whom they killed so that they should hold the body of the chief in his grave."

Ibid., p. 41 for "The Story of Udo Akpabio of the Anang Tribe, Southern Nigeria," in which the hero describes certain ritual sacrifices common in his father's chiefdom: "My father then made a great feast in which all the villages joined. A sacrifice was made that the drum should be set apart for its special work. Two men were killed and their heads placed one at each end of the drum. . . . Every harvest, after the seed-yams have been selected and stored, the drum was beaten and there would be much feasting. There would be thousands of yams in one enclosure. They are put together in rows of twenty upright and fifty rows horizontal. Two men were always killed and their bodies were hung at each end of the enclosure. No one ever went near the place until the flesh was gone from their bones. This was done to warn thieves. When the next planting season came round three men were caught and killed and the drum was beaten. Two of these men were for Lkorok [the drum] and the other for the seed-yams. His body was cut to pieces and the blood sprinkled on the yams before they were planted" (pp. 51ff.).

with villages, kinship orders, secret societies, or sub-rosa governments supported by fetishism, derive much of their dynamic and stability from a successful concretization of the themes announced in this and similar accounts. All are grounded firmly in the view that death is an aspect of society rather than of biography, and that fears of violent death are socially positive forces. Furthermore, all accommodate a broad spectrum of conflicts on the planes of thought and action, ranging from latent and covert hostility to open feuding, and from mental assaults—as in parental or ancestral curses, bewitchment and accusations of witchcraft or sorcery—to physical aggression, as in homicide and war. In short, it appears, first, that different forms of conflict are essential for the maintenance of the mythical charter by which a community is ruled; and it appears, second, that modes of managing, muting, or resolving different species of conflict are themselves very often derivatives of conflict rather than of references to some opposite principle. That is to say, Africa's normative order does not require the kinds of polarization that are generally taken for granted in the Occident, where it is assumed that fear and suspicion should give way to confidence and security; that power ought to be challenged by morality; that strife must be countered by law; and that war is to end in peace. There, by contrast, where conflict-inducing forces, whether of a spiritual or a social nature, have to be kept operational even as they are being manipulated or kept under wraps, disputes may be solved by activating feuds, warfare may serve the ends of law, and judges may be required to deal in poison. In other words, conflict and conflict control are not necessarily juxtaposed in Africa as they are in the West. What the records show, instead, is that the two principles interact and reenforce each other in an eternal round.

· 10 ·

FEAR AND THE KILLING POWER
OF THE SPOKEN WORD

No context illustrates the logic of this duality-exploding design as vividly as the use of the potent verb.

Words have the power to wound and to heal in all language communities, literate and nonliterate.[1] But in Africa's oral culture, in which mythical thinking prevails, and in which speech is essentially behavioral,[2] words have the power to kill, even as they have the power to placate forces of aggression or set aside disputes. In either case they are viewed as tantamount to actions—at times even to things—provided they are uttered in conjunction with symbols and rituals that have been evolved in the service of the same purposes.

In the category of specially weighted, magically aggressive verbal formulations, none is as feared and as trusted as are the oath and the curse. Both of these are ritual spells whose ultimate powers emanate from the African faith in the creative force of the proper word or name. Viewed as direct representations of the all-powerful spirit world, these formulae may, in fact, induce death or injury by virtue either of the sheer fear they instill or of the human actions they are designed to set in motion.[3] Oathing and cursing, then, being intrinsic aspects of participatory

---

[1] Some of the traditional motifs treated in the following sections have retained their dominance in modern African approaches to conflict and its management, including diplomacy. Compare Part II, "The African Presence in the Modern World."

[2] *Supra*, Ch. 5.

[3] For interesting comments upon the psychological origins and effects of these practices, as well as upon the relation between witchcraft and oathing, see, among others, Middleton and Winter, eds., *Witchcraft and Sorcery*, especially G.W.B. Huntingford, "Nandi Witchcraft," pp. 175–186; John Middleton, "Witchcraft and Sorcery in Lugbara," pp. 270ff.; and Robert A. LeVine, "Witchcraft and Sorcery in a Gusii Community," pp. 250ff. See Leakey, *Mau Mau and the Kikuyu*, p. 50, to the effect that fear of witchcraft (that is, "black magic," as distinct from "white magic," in Leakey's terminology) is sometimes so great that death actually results. Also Carothers, "Culture, Psychiatry, and the Written Word," p. 316. In John Middleton's analysis of Lugbara belief systems, cursing is an action in which words are actually spoken and which is regarded as distinct from witchcraft and sorcery. "Witchcraft and Sorcery," p. 270.

For some general discussions of this aspect of archaic thought, see Georges Granai, "Problèmes de la sociologie du langage," in G. Gurvitch, ed., *Traité de sociologie*, 2 vols., 2nd ed. (Paris, 1962–1963), Vol. II, 255–277. Also Louis-Vincent Thomas, "Pour un Programme d'études théoriques des religions et d'un humanisme africain," in *Présence africaine*, No. 37 (2ème trimestre 1961), pp. 64, 72.

magic, may be said to provide ultimate sanctions by means of which human behavior is being controlled, whether in the context of the family, the age group, the tribe, or the secret society; of judicial proceedings, religious shrines, witchcraft practices, or war. Whole families of oaths and curses, each intricately structured, have thus been evolved in all parts of Africa, most of them paralleled by equally intricate hierarchies of the various human agents responsible for the impersonation of the magic words.

The following accounts exemplify the range and effectiveness of the potent malevolent word.

In Iboland (southern Nigeria) where each of the multiple spirits and deities has its separate jurisdiction, and where law and order have traditionally been functions of the operation of secret lodges, shrines, and, above all, certain well-known oracles that are accepted as high courts of appeal, oaths and curses have long been indispensable for the consolidation of a given group, the determination of guilt and innocence, and the due execution of a given verdict. One such formulation, traditionally administered by the officers of a secret society to a novice, after he had been subjected to a series of ordeals at the hands of masked agents, reads as follows in C. K. Meek's rendition: "If you go about gossiping, or in any way divulge our secrets, even to your own mother, may this oath bring about your death. And may this oath bind you to obey the instructions of the society, under all circumstances. Otherwise may your life become forfeit to the Mmo."[4] Another oath, "May Mmo eat me," is regarded as the major guarantee of truth-speaking, whereas the incantation "May Mmo eat you (if you do not do as I direct)" is said to have the infallible effect of forcing nonmembers of a secret society to obey members, and the same words are effectively used to stop quarreling among women, or to bully wives into silence.[5]

The Kikuyu and the Kamba, both widely renowned in Kenya for the variety and potency of their ceremonial verbal spells, as well as for the general intricacy of their judicial systems,[6] were similarly concerned with regulating the conduct of their womenfolk. The Kikuyu reserved a series of special oaths for them—a woman might swear an oath against herself in evidence that she was telling the truth, or that some claim of hers was just, or as a contingent curse to prevent a certain course of action, or

---

[4] *Law and Authority in a Nigerian Tribe, A Study in Indirect Rule* (London and New York, 1937, repr. 1950), p. 69.

[5] *Ibid.*, p. 70.

[6] H. E. Lambert, *Kikuyu Social and Political Institutions* (London and New York, 1956, repr. 1965), pp. 107–118; Leakey, *Mau Mau*, pp. 28ff.; D. J. Penwill, *Kamba Customary Law* (London, 1951).

simply as a curse against a gross offender.[7] In one particular case in which the requirement of truth-speaking conflicted with that of keeping silence, the facts seem to have been the following. After a man had seduced a woman, he persuaded her to take the Oath of Muma so that she would not tell her husband of the episode. After a while, however, she did just that, whereupon she died. The husband then sued for blood money, but the elders refused his demand on the ground that if the woman had held her tongue, the Muma would not have killed her. The husband then demanded that the man should jump over the corpse seven times; this the latter refused to do, and the elders would not insist, as they held that the woman had, in fact, committed suicide.[8]

In these societies in which the binding powers of an oath were more feared than regulations of temporal laws, the spirits were commonly invoked in judicial as well as nonjudicial contexts, as, for example, when disputes required settlement, a guilty person had to be unearthed, or an evil-doer needed to be destroyed. However, oath-taking ceremonies were nowhere undertaken lightly in traditional Africa, for fear in its most absolute form made the expectation irrebuttable that an oath, once solemnly sworn, would have inexorable effects upon the taker and his family. Furthermore, in all oathing systems, including those of the Kikuyu and the neighboring Kamba, each oath had its own proper sphere and purpose; its own ceremonies and reputation for potency; and its own operating period, in terms of which the efficacy of the sacred spoken challenge was being judged. For example, the Kikuyu "Oath of the Sheep" (one of three main types of legal oath),[9] which was resorted to when the local authority was unsatisfied as to the facts in a suit for the payment of all alleged debt, was deemed to have given judgment if one of the parties died within one year. Similar expectations were attached by the Kamba to the "kithitu" and the "ndundu" oaths. If, for example, it was not possible to see clearly which of two Kamba parties was in the right, one of them would be made to swear to the truth of his story upon the "kithitu," and he was deemed to have lied if he or his nearest relatives, or both, died. This particular oath, widely known for its fierceness

[7] Lambert, *Kikuyu Social and Political Institutions*, pp. 98ff.; this authority points out that oathing practices among Kikuyu women were highly effective during the period 1934 to 1939 in mobilizing politically significant actions.

[8] Hobley, *Bantu Beliefs and Magic*, p. 243.

[9] See Lambert, *Kikuyu Social and Political Institutions*, pp. 123ff.; 138ff. on Kikuyu practices; p. 126 to the effect that there is a good deal of variation between tribes as to the period that must elapse before an oath can be deemed to be inoperative; in Meru it is a year, in Kikuyu seven seasons approximately three and a half years). In general, however, the view seems to prevail that if the oath is going to operate at all, it will do so quickly. See also C. W. Hobley, *Bantu Beliefs and Magic*, pp. 241ff. and other references *supra*, Ch. 4, note 48; Ch. 5, notes 8–10, 15, 66, 67, 72; Ch. 6, notes 25–28.

by the Kamba, was also legally recognized by the British authorities in the colonial period. Indeed, in 1912 the district commissioner, "with a view to identifying the Native Administration of the Councils . . . more closely with the Government," entered into a solemn compact with the Council of each location, which was ratified by the muma (which was the same as the kithitu) oath.[10] Its time limit, irrevocably set by the elders, varied according to the reputed strength of the oath, but usually did not exceed one year. The oath was believed to have begun when the swearer, or his wife, or his eldest son died within the period so fixed.[11] By contrast, if the "ndundu oath" had been sworn falsely, only the swearer would be affected, with the rest of the family remaining exempt. This particular oath was therefore used when disputes occurred within the same family or clan. It was also taken by newcomers entering a clan settlement, and by warriors before embarking on warfare and raiding.

Intercommunity conflicts, too, were at times susceptible to settlement by reference to the right form of institutionalized oath or curse. Fighting within a Lugbara tribe (who live in the area of the high watershed of the Nile-Congo divide in Uganda, Zaire, and the Sudan) could be stopped by the joint curses of the elders of groups directly concerned, by rainmakers, and by "men whose names are known." There was, however, no institutionalized way of stopping fighting between units of different tribes.[12] The vanquished and the victors of two Kamba groups might be reconciled in a peace ceremony during which the captain of each group of fighters swore by the "kithitu" that he would never again fight the opposite party, and that if any of the latter should come to the villages of his group, they should be received as friends. In the presence of the assembled elders, the companies of warriors would then assent to this by saying: "If you break this oath, may the kithitu slay you."[13] And a very

[10] Penwill, *Kamba Customary Law*, p. 64.

[11] *Ibid.*, pp. 56ff. But see p. 59 for a dramatic case, recorded in the 1920s, where, within some three months, a spate of deaths—eleven to be exact—occurred within a family. See also Hobley, *Bantu Beliefs and Magic*, pp. 239ff.

[12] John Middleton, "The Lugbara," in Richards, ed., *East African Chiefs*, p. 328. Middleton suggests that the term "feud" be used when fighting occurs between major sections of the same tribe, and that the term "warfare" is appropriate when units of different tribes are involved.

[13] Hobley, *Bantu Beliefs and Magic*, pp. 248ff. The ceremony here proceeded as follows: "They kill the ox, skin it, and cut the meat off the goat and also cut out a few of the vertebrae of the neck . . . and place them on the kithitu. An iron head is then produced and tied on to a shaft; it must be tied with the fibre from the lilambia bush, and a few thorns of the mulaa tree are also fastened to the arrow. A small bag is made from a piece of the small intestine of the ox and is filled with blood. The officiating elder then picks up the arrow and slits open this bag and allows the blood to drip on the neck-vertebrae and meat, which are placed on the kithitu, and calls out to the assembly: 'If anyone breaks this peace may he be slit as the mwethi wa kitutu.'" The most sacred and lasting bloodbrotherhood between two Kamba parties was concluded by the same type of ritual.

similar oath is said to have muted, occasionally, the traditional enmity between the Kikuyu and the Masai, we learn from Leakey,[14] for it provided that the two tribes would refrain from certain types of warfare for a period of seven planting seasons (or even for multiples of seven seasons). Even the Nandi, by tradition a seminomadic warrior and pastoral tribe of Nilo-Hamitic origin, generally known for its insular, self-sufficient outlook and strong fighting sense, resorted to a special "Oath of Peace" when seeking a temporary truce with a non-Nandi tribe, as, for instance, in times of famine, when they would want to ensure the safe passage of women to barter food supplies.[15]

The records of intercommunity relations in Ibo country contain several interesting referrals to the ritually perfect verbal thrust when serious disturbances had to be faced. One such case had arisen in the 1930s, when the people of Ugueme accused those of Awgu of murdering one of their members. After the matter had been submitted to Igwe, the ruling spirit, the suspected murderer was made to sit on a mat in front of the deity, and there he swore the following oath: "Igwe-Ke-Ala, if I know how the dead man met his death may you take my life, that I may accompany him to the land of the dead. But if I am wholly ignorant of what befell him, then do you pronounce my innocence."[16] Immediately, it is said, there was a sound of thunder, and the whole place was enveloped in smoke. The sonorous voice of Igwe was then heard to say: "Hold up your right hand. I declare you to be innocent."

Other troublesome occasions requiring oathing as the mediating force arose when the precise cause of a sickness or a death had to be ascertained. Armstrong's record of a West African inquest is here to the point;[17] for it illustrates not only the lethal effect of a certain oath ("If

[14] *Mau Mau*, p. 55.

[15] G. S. Snell, *Nandi Customary Law* (London, 1954), p. 83.

[16] Meek, *Law and Authority in a Nigerian Tribe*, p. 47.

[17] See Robert G. Armstrong, "A West African Inquest," *American Anthropologist*, 56, No. 6 (December, 1954), 1054ff.; also, by the same author, "The Idoma Court-of-Lineages in Law and Political Structure," in Anthony F. C. Wallace, ed., *Selected Papers of the Fifth International Congress of Anthropological and Ethnological Sciences* (Philadelphia, 1956), pp. 380ff. These two accounts are of great interest because they illumine the African use of dream evidence in litigation, and because they show how difficult it is for a Western observer to find out just what had actually happened *physically*, and what, by contrast, had been experienced by the unconscious. Compare *supra*, p. 79 on the absence of distinctions between waking and dreaming. See A.H.M. Kirk-Greene, "On Swearing; An Account of Some Judicial Oaths in Northern Nigeria," *Africa*, 25, No. 1 (January, 1955), 43–53, for other illustrations of oathing in this region of the continent.

But see Meek, *Law and Authority*, p. 48, to the effect that many occult agencies have lent themselves to great abuse as means of committing murder, levying blackmail, dealing in slaves, and fomenting enmities. The abolition of some particularly notorious oracles at the hands of the English colonial administration met, nonetheless, with public outrage.

any one of the Sons of Achumedo begins to play tricks on his brother, may the ancestors kill him"), but also, and more importantly, the subtle distinctions commonly made by native authorities between "judicious" and "malicious" ways of using killing words. The proceedings in this instance thus turned on the question of whether a certain death had been caused by an elder's oath or by witchcraft; more particularly, whether the lineage head had acted in justice, that is, "by day" when administering the oath to the deceased, or in malice, that is, "by night."

Among the multiple conditioning factors in terms of which verbal aggressions were adjudged legitimate supports of the sacred sanction, two in particular need to be stressed. As most of the preceding illustrations have already suggested, oaths and curses had to be materialized, as it were, in definite objects, and they had to be precise and specific with respect to the names invoked.

Traditional Ibo authorities thus insisted that the medium for an oath should be a specially sanctioned object, and that anyone swearing an oath should know the name of the deity immanent in the object. Litigants might swear by some cult, or by a yam, a kola, or the skull of an animal offered to the proper deity; or they might resort to special "drink and confess drugs" and "touch and confess shrines"—techniques singled out by Stephen U. O. Anaibe as among those habitually used by his people for the discovery of a culprit who refuses to turn himself in.[18]

The great ceremonial oaths of the Kikuyu and the Kamba were likewise lodged in selected mediums. Indeed, such a fatal utterance as the "kithitu oath" (the Kikuyu counterpart is the "kithathi oath") depended for its validity upon a highly complex conglomeration of materials. Different "kithitus" existed in the Machakos district of Kenya Colony, but typical ingredients were the teeth of a hyena, the teeth of a dead man, pieces of porcupine quill, special roots and plants, earth from the hearth in the hut of a dead woman, a piece of an earthen food-pot, certain special small stones, and so on. These ingredients were wrapped up in a long binding and carried in a basket-like covering. Formerly, a "kithitu" would never be touched by hand, and very few touch it in modern times,

[18] *Wisdom of My People*, pp. 173ff.; Meek, *Law and Authority*, pp. 235–242 for full accounts of several types of proceedings. Compare R. E. Bradbury, *The Benin Kingdom and the Edo-Speaking Peoples of South-Western Nigeria, together with a Section on the Itsekiri by P. C. Lloyd* (London, 1957), pp. 56ff. for practices among other Nigerian societies. For the role of the oath in Ashanti see Robert S. Rattray, *Religion and Art in Ashanti* (Oxford, 1927), ch. 22; and *Ashanti Law and Constitution*, p. 379; p. 384 to the effect that "the sanctity and nature of the oaths taken and the deadly sanctions behind them seemed to the Ashanti mind to rule out most of the possibilities of bias or lying" on the part of litigants and witnesses. See also pp. 101ff. on oaths of allegiance, and pp. 392ff. on "ordeals."

Penwill reports.[19] The entire apparatus, kept in a hiding place when not required for use, had to be produced and properly used by the officiating agents if the desired processes were to be set in motion by the spoken words, whether as an oath or as a curse.

A case famous in East African customary law illustrates the use of the "kithitu" curse as a mode of guarding boundaries, in this instance those of a certain grazing ground. The occasion arose shortly before the First World War, when a certain Muasya wa Kakonde was fearful lest the land he claimed should be taken by an adversary, whose argument had, in fact, prevailed in an earlier discussion between the two contending parties. Muasya thereupon brought out his "kithitu" and walked the boundaries of the disputed plot, proclaiming that the area was his and that should anyone cultivate and live there without his permission, he should be stricken by this "kithitu." The rival's father did come to live on the land, however, and within six months he, his wife, and three of his sons had all died. Muasya and his contender were still alive in 1950, and a nephew of the former was at that time found to have no other work than to guard the "kithitu" and to bring it out when needed. Reputed as particularly potent, it was frequently used for cases brought before the Machakos Tribunal.[20]

The common assumption that to curse anyone is a very serious matter, and that the person cursed will be very ill at ease, explains why this type of oral attack has been trusted throughout Africa as a remedy for wrongdoing and a means of protecting the community from the hostility of ancestral spirits. Since the curse, whether pronounced by parents, elders, ancestors, or others, is usually an ambivalent utterance (in the sense that the reference to an impending catastrophe may simultaneously be a prayer, a blessing, a prophecy, or, in the case of a dying man's curse, even a mode of settling an inheritance),[21] it is rightly regarded as a major and comprehensive mode of assuring social solidarity and avoiding or resolving conflicts. Furthermore, since fear of the curse, as also of the oath, is naturally great, the mere threat of cursing or oathing often suffices to inhibit a crime or to extract a confession of guilt. And the same psychic condition explains, of course, why cursed men, their families, and descendents, will make the utmost exertions in order to persuade the proper agencies to remove the curse or liberate those afflicted from the obligations of an oath, as, for example, after a confession has been made.

[19] *Kamba Customary Law*, pp. 56ff.; also Hobley, *Bantu Beliefs and Magic*, p. 239; and see Leakey, *Mau Mau*, pp. 54ff. for an analysis of the "oath-stone," especially of the symbolic seven holes in the stone.
[20] Penwill, *Kamba Customary Law*, p. 60. See Hobley, *Bantu Beliefs and Magic*, ch. 7, "The Curse and its Manifestations."
[21] *Ibid.*, p. 145.

Both acts, the infliction as well as the withdrawal of the malevolent or fatal pronouncements, must emanate from the prescribed sources in the proper manner. That is to say, they have to be legitimate if they are to be effective. And since it is often difficult in this shadow-land of "right" and "wrong" to know just what is legitimate and what not, resort has to be had to personages who are renowned for their magico-political competence in matters of casting and removing spells. The ranks of these skilled intermediaries between the spheres of the concretely human and the spiritual include not only the elders and other appointed native authorities, but also, and most importantly in extreme situations, rainmakers, medicine men, prophets, guardians of oathing materials, and other ritual experts; as, for example, the laibons of the Nandi, whose pronouncements carry special weight because they are also known for such powers as foretelling the result of a planned military venture, or preventing sickness;[22] the Lugbara diviners, who "know the words" of spirit in all its forms; or the Ibo masters of the oracle, whose rendition of ancestral words is accepted as absolute truth.

Above all, however, we find the smith, whose magical interventions in the realm of the occult are unrivaled in most parts of Africa. The legendary esteem in which he has been held here, as in other cultures decisively shaped by mystical thinking, is probably a corollary, first, of the awe with which men have long viewed the arts of extracting, smelting, and forging metal, and second, of the air of mystery and secrecy in which generations of smiths have pursued their calling—partly by choice, but partly, no doubt, because they lived beyond the pale of the community proper in conditions of social ostracism. This ambivalent position of the smith as an outsider explains why disputes in the community have often been submitted to him for settlement, and why he has played such a prominent role in the system of occult adjudication.

In Kikuyu society, for example, where the cult of the smith is particularly highly developed, a smith is reputedly capable of making a forest patch immune to any form of destruction by casting a special kind of spell. Tradition recorded in this century has it, furthermore, that if sugar cane was stolen from a garden, or goats were removed from a village by night, an owner was commonly expected to enlist the aid of a smith, taking with him the iron necklet or bracelet of a deceased person. If the smith agreed to intervene, he would then heat this object in his smithy fire and sever it with a chisel, saying: "may the thief be cut as I cut this iron." Or he might take a sword or an axe-head that he was fashioning, heat it in his fire, then quench it in water, saying: "may the body of the thief cool as this iron does," that is, "may he die." Even Masai invasions

[22] Snell, *Nandi Customary Law*, p. 15. And see *infra*, Ch. 18, on "Intermediaries."

162

are supposed to have been checked with the aid of a small piece of iron duly obtained from a smith. If, by contrast, warfare was the order of the day, a smith was called upon to bless the weapons. And this he did by telling the weapon: "if your owner meets with an enemy, may you go straight and kill your adversary; but if you are launched at one who has no evil in his heart, may you miss him."[23] Here, as also in Kamba society,[24] the conviction was absolute and unassailable that the curses and blessings of a smith could not be lifted, and that an oath on a piece of iron used for beating and hammering other pieces of iron, was irrevocable. If a Kamba swore such an oath falsely, nothing could stop the deaths that would follow.

In the nonliterate normative systems of these and other African societies, in which evil-willing is the most fearful type of behavior, the oath and the curse could be generally trusted as ultimate mainstays of social order and solidarity. However, as some of the reported cases illustrate, it was by no means always easy even for native authorities to know just when these sanctions were invoked in behalf of the cause of law and order, and when, by contrast, they served that of sorcery and other forms of social disorder. Abuses could, nonetheless, be minimized or held in check as long as the validity of the entire comprehensive life style was not questioned, and, in particular, as long as individuals continued to be tutored from early childhood onward to comply with established forms of belief and refrain from developing thoughts and aspirations of their own.

These balances and controls, intricate and precarious as they were, have naturally been upset in the last decades by the sudden and intense impact of Western literate thoughtways, laws, and institutions; for as inner tensions multiplied and deepened in response to conflicts between different value systems, the lines of distinction between "right" and "wrong," too, were bound to become blurred in all domains, including that of magic. Societies with well-developed oathing methodologies, such as the Kikuyu, were therefore destined to fall prey to moral chaos when their modern elites chose to exploit oath taking for the new cause of political power, independence, and statehood. The Mau Mau movement, which began in the latter part of 1948 or early 1949 with oath taking by prominent Kikuyu,[25] thus degenerated swiftly into an assault upon age-old social customs and family traditions as rank-and-file Kikuyu were forced, by a modified form of the customary oath, to do things that were totally contrary to native law, even as they were shocking by Western

[23] Hobley, *Bantu Beliefs and Magic*, pp. 171, 186, 169, for foregoing references.
[24] Penwill, *Kamba Customary Law*, p. 61; Lambert, *Kikuyu Institutions*, p. 122, for Kikuyu practices.
[25] Leakey, *Mau Mau*, pp. 95ff.

standards. For not only were people, including women and children, forced to take the oath against their will and in conditions proscribed by custom, for instance at night, inside huts, and so forth, but they were persuaded to resort to the killing form of the oath even in regard to close relatives. Bound by one clause of the Mau Mau oath: "If I do anything to give away this organization to the enemy, may I be killed by the oath,"[26] no ordinary Kikuyu could be expected to go and make a report to the police or to his employer; for were he to do so, Leakey explains, he would be breaking the oath, and thus call down dreaded supernatural penalties upon himself or members of his family. Furthermore, no cleansing ceremony was open to him in these "modern" circumstances, since the Mau Mau organizers—contrary to the ritual experts of an earlier age—felt free to reenforce the fear of supernatural reprisals by threats of physical violence, including arson and murder. Indeed, as Carothers explains the psychology of this movement, the complex of oaths, rituals, and behavior had been devised by the leaders to produce precisely this kind of shock and confusion; and it could have the desired effect upon the Kikuyu because it conformed officially with their traditional ways, even as it reversed or mocked the ancient meaning. "They shocked something deep in these people—so deep that many felt that they were forever outside the pale of their society on these grounds alone, for if they recanted they would die instantly from the power of the oaths. Much of the success of Mau Mau and much of the subsequent difficulty in rehabilitating its exponents—or its victims—has been due to this."[27]

Today, twenty years later, as the Kikuyu dominance in the modern state of Kenya is being put to test by tribal opposition, interpersonal jealousies, and other internecine conflicts, oathings have again begun to terrorize the citizenry with threats of lawless killings. At this juncture in the country's history, the ceremonies are designed to rally the Mau Mau group that had won Kenya's independence, so as to assure the continuation of Kikuyu rule. In their official formulations, the oaths, whether imposed on volunteers or on unwilling victims, appear to proclaim loyalty to the Kano party regardless of tribal association. But behind the modern apparatus of a constitutional multiparty state, the tribal normative order has obviously retained its hold on the minds of literate and nonliterate men alike. For the oathings invoke Kikuyu traditions, are administered by Kikuyu, and aim at the revitalization of Kikuyu dominance, albeit often by perverting custom.

The present moral and political crisis in Kenya illustrates well the find-

[26] *Ibid.*, p. 98, also pp. 80ff.; and Lambert, *Kikuyu Institutions*, p. 126.

[27] Carothers, *The Psychology of Mau Mau* (Nairobi, 1954); also Carothers, "Culture, Psychiatry, and the Written Word," pp. 315ff.

ings recorded by many authorities on traditional and modern African belief systems,[28] namely, that faith in the powers of black magic and witchcraft is being constantly reenforced as tensions and uncertainties multiply, evoking in their turn chain reactions of accusation and counter-accusation, the search for scapegoats,[29] and flights from verbal into physical violence. More importantly—and regardless of whether these trends are properly viewed as symptomatic of decadence or of regeneration—the actualities support Vieyra's observation—cited earlier in the context of a discussion of modern political administrations—that African governments today are functioning under the trusteeship of ancient traditional orders.[30]

[28] See the works of Middleton, Winter, Lloyd, Joset, Leakey, Bohannan, and others, as cited in preceding chapters; also Georges Balandier, *Sociologie actuelle de l'Afrique noire; dynamique sociale en Afrique centrale*, 2nd ed. (Paris, 1963), p. 378, to the effect that sorcery in Congolese society continues to express jealousy, fear, insecurity, and other emotions activated by the stress of modern times.

[29] On this subject see *supra*, Ch. 3 and Ch. 5, n. 76. Compare with news reports from the Kenya scene (1969), where the oathing dilemma was deflected, as it were, by the expulsion of three white editors (of the *East African Standard* and the rival *Daily Nation*), who had published news of the oathings.

[30] *Supra*, pp. 23 and 65; cf. also, and to the same effect, remarks by Busia, *supra*, Ch. 5, n. 60, and John S. Mbiti, *African Religions and Philosophies* (New York, 1969), p. 359, for the confirmation that most if not all Africans continue to fear witchcraft and magic.

· 11 ·

VERBAL AGGRESSION AND THE
MUTING OF TENSIONS

The oath and the curse exemplify the ultimate power of the malevolent word. Other forms of oral combat and abusive speech, also recognized as effective sacred sanctions in the normative orders of most traditional African societies, were insult, ridicule, and certain types of joking. The sharp-edged weapon of derision often seemed, indeed, the only power behind the law, as Rattray observes in his study of Ashanti society: "If I were asked to name the strongest of the sanctions operating in Ashanti to enforce the traditional rule of the community, I think I would place the power of ridicule at the head of these forces of law and order." In this society, he continues, fear of ridicule was so great that "it is doubtful if the worst of humanly inflicted punishments was more dreaded than this subtle weapon which came in laughing guise to rob a man of his own self-respect and the respect of his associates."[1]

Here, as elsewhere in Africa south of the Sahara, where an individual was perceived primarily as an extension or representation of the group to which he belonged, personal identity was of necessity a brittle, vulnerable thing. For not only was a human being unable to think of himself as an integral person capable of building inner defences against social assaults, he also became the prisoner, as it were, of his name. In fact, as Anaibe and Meek explain in their reflections on Ibo society, a person's *physical* integrity was presumed to be imbedded in the name he carried; hence the supreme importance commonly attached to the naming system.[2] And equally significant acts of identification ensued in initiation ceremonies, as, for example, in the context of Senufo secret societies, when the assignment of a ritual name was instrumental in endowing the initiate with what Holas terms "a new and parallel personality," from whose psychologically binding qualities the bearer of the name could not disengage himself.[3]

---

[1] *Ashanti Law and Constitution*, pp. 372, 373.

[2] It should be noted in this connection that the name of the victim had to be correct if a curse was to be effective. Among the Jukun-speaking peoples of Nigeria, the mere mention of the name of a royal ancestor had the immediate effect of bringing an unjust ruler to his senses, since the king or chief was deemed to be at the absolute mercy of his own ancestors. See Meek, *A Sudanese Kingdom*, pp. 334ff.

[3] *Les Senoufo*, pp. 150, 153. L.-V. Thomas writes in an essay on the creative

166

Since the human being in all his aspects was comprehended in his name, he was presumed to be truly alive only as long as he preserved his good name. This meant that verbal attacks upon the name had to be viewed as tantamount to physical assaults, capable in extreme situations of extinguishing life.[4] It goes without saying, then, that *wanton* defamation, ridicule, and insult—socially reprehensible in all cultures—were particularly serious violations of the customary code in Africa's non-literate societies, to which harsh penalties had to be attached.[5] It follows, furthermore and most importantly, that each linguistically unified community had to insist upon a clear differentiation between the positive and negative qualities of abusive speech if these categories of verbal comportment were to retain their functions as reliable means of ensuring conformity and social order.

This vital distinction was, in fact, assured by a set of subtle understandings as to just what was permissible as a joke or insult, and what, by contrast, not; which words were taboo in which circumstances; when, by contrast, ordinarily secret words could be used; and who in the social hierarchy was entitled to resort to which types of insult or ridicule. That is to say, the intricate hierarchical order of critical utterances was organically tied up with the equally intricate system of social relationships. For example, two young Ibo might revile each other in the strongest language for several minutes, then burst into laughter as they walked away, without registering rancor or offence, whereas the same words, if addressed by one of them to an old man or a chief, would in all probability have been interpreted as a deadly insult.[6]

One further aspect of oral belligerence must be noted if the full complexity of this system of conflict control is to be appreciated on its merits: the wide margin commonly allowed to euphemisms, allusive speech, and indirect verbal attacks. Total contempt might thus be delivered in the form of a joke, a curse could be inflicted in the garb of excessive praise, and a blessing might actually function as a curse. Resort to this type of circumlocution or inversion, which commended itself when the employment of the actual offensive words appeared to be inoppor-

---

power of "the word" that African education and initiation procedures aim mainly at inculcating knowledge of secret names and ritually potent words. "Pour un Programme d'études théoriques des religions," pp. 72ff.

[4] Rattray, *Ashanti Law and Constitution*, p. 373, explains why no escape was open for one who had incurred the penalty of ridicule in Ashanti society.

[5] The great percentage of quarrels and lawsuits in Ashanti arose from personal abuse and slander; see *ibid.*, p. 309. Meek reports that anyone in Iboland consistently engaging in such practices risked being sold into slavery; *Law and Authority in a Nigerian Tribe*, p. 231.

[6] Meek, *Law and Authority in a Nigerian Tribe*, p. 230.

tune for one reason or another, was not without grave risks, however. For example, since the Kikuyu assumed that natural evil powers might inadvertently be invoked by undue praise, no one would ever highly praise someone else's favorite bull or child for fear that by doing so he might bring disaster upon it.[7] Similarly, the well-known Ashanti ceremony of "blessing the king" was actually the very antithesis of the idiom employed—namely, one of the most terrible sins of which an Ashanti could be guilty, perpetration of which was certain to result in death.[8]

These essentially African approaches to the use of speech also mark communications in Kiswahili, a relatively modern language that has most of its words in common with vocabularies of the Bantu group of languages, is entirely Bantu in grammatical form, but includes many Arabic words and words that have come from India, as well as modern importations from English and German.[9] As Lienhardt points out in his introduction to a modern Swahili ballad,[10] Swahili is particularly rich and subtle in referring to human qualities, characteristics, and circumstances. "The subtleties of the language," he notes, "are much cultivated in everyday speech. Wit and irony are notable social assets. They can serve as tools of contentiousness, but the people of the coast are not more contentious than others. What matters is the use of language as a weapon of rivalry and emulation, with which the coastal people constantly amuse and occupy themselves." Since the knowing and understanding of Swahili is here assumed to cover the subtleties of the language, an "internal Swahili" has evolved, which consists of the inner meanings of words and phrases. These parts of verbal play, Lienhardt explains, are the ones that serve the purposes of irony; for words a simpleton may take as a literal statement are recognized by others to be a metaphor implying something quite different.

In a thought world in which spoken words had the power to invoke as well as banish dreaded supernatural forces, the freedom of abusive speech could easily get out of hand, as some of the preceding illustrations

[7] Leakey, *Mau Mau*, p. 51; see pp. 346, 396ff. Junod, *Moeurs et coutumes des Bantous*, Vol. I, pp. 346, 396ff., for different inverted forms of praise and praise songs among the southern Bantus, notably the Tonga.

[8] Rattray, *Ashanti Law and Constitution*, p. 311. On the airing of grievances in song and jest and the supposedly mystical effect of these practices, see also Edward Norbeck, "African Rituals of Conflict," in John Middleton, ed., *Gods and Rituals; Readings in Religious Beliefs and Practices* (New York, 1967), pp. 197ff., particularly p. 214.

[9] There are a number of dialectical variations in the Swahili spoken in different parts of the East African coast. "Standard Swahili" as taught in schools and used in most newspapers is a standardization of dialect and orthography in Roman script worked out during the British colonial period. It was based on the type of Swahili spoken in Zanzibar. See Hasani Bin Ismail, *The Medicine Man 'Swifa Ya Nguvumali*, Peter Lienhardt, ed. and trans., p. 2.

[10] *Ibid.*, pp. 2–3.

suggest. However, transgressions of the norm did not detract from the social benefits commonly ascribed to institutionalized, ritually controlled contempt and ridicule, whether these were delivered frontally and directly, or through approved reversals and transpositions of meaning. The major purport here seems to have been the achievement of punitive and cathartic effects. Secret societies in Iboland thus relied on insults, secret words, and abusive songs, often presented in the frame of pantomine, if it was deemed necessary to point out defects in the characters of members of the kindred that threatened the maintenance of the inner social order. Under the terms of one such practice, a specially qualified man was selected so that he might go at night to hurl abuse in a ghostly voice at those whose behavior had given offence.[11] Here and elsewhere, dissimulation was frequently of the essence.[12] Men and animals, the living and the dead, the sick, the angry, and the proud could be impersonated, usually through the medium of disguised voices, so as to strike terror among those requiring intimidation, or simply to vent cooped-up anger, jealousy, or lesser irritations that had accumulated in the community. Nor were foreigners always immune from such attacks. In the period of colonialism, indeed, when material means of expressing opposition to aliens and their administrations were lacking, Africans, being denizens of a culture zone in which the word itself is trusted as an instrument of aggression, were often highly successful in activating this weapon of the indirect, verbally ambiguous attack. The Yoruba are thus said to have delighted in insulting Europeans without fear of reprisal by employing a complimentary form of address in spoken tones showing disrespect and contempt that the Europeans failed to recognize as insolence.[13] And very similar behavior patterns are reported from the Congo, where the thrust of resistance, both verbal and physical, was commonly launched in the 1920s and 1940s in circuitous but highly effective forms.[14]

The major targets of verbal abuse at all times were, however, social and political superiors in the ranks of the native hierarchy, and here, too, circumlocution of one kind or another was common. In some situations public criticism might have to be kept in a low key so as to evoke

[11] Meek, *Law and Authority in a Nigerian Tribe*, pp. 70ff.

[12] Béart, "D'une Sociologie des peuples africains," pp. 308ff.

[13] William R. Bascom, "The Principle of Seniority in the Social Structure of the Yoruba," *American Anthropologist*, New Series 44 (1942), 37–46; see also Leonard W. Doob, *Communication in Africa; A Search for Boundaries* (New Haven, 1961, repr. 1966), pp. 228ff. for comments on this matter.

[14] Balandier, *Sociologie de l'Afrique noire*, pp. 408ff., also pp. 396ff. The actual victims of aggression here were usually not the representatives of the colonial regime, but rather members of indigenous elites and village communities who had been found to collaborate with the administration or to refrain from practicing passive resistance. Compare, to similar effect, the strategy of the Mau Mau organizers in Kenya.

laughter even as it unfailingly hit the mark;[15] in others it was channeled through intermediaries known for their wit and eloquence. One of the most popular of these "magicians of the word" in West Africa was the "griot."[16] Famed as a bard, chronicler, flatterer, praise singer, marriage broker, and so on, he was also called upon at several courts to function as the "official insultor."[17] Similar roles were entrusted by the Tonga and other southern Bantu societies to the "official mad man" ("fou de cour," "Hofnarr"), a kind of court jester who was entitled to pronounce the gravest of insults with total impunity; and to a special type of herald, admired for his tireless eloquence, whose abuse—often dissimulated as praise—the chief had to absorb without becoming annoyed.[18]

Other variations on the dual theme of voicing criticism and resentment, also widely distributed over Africa south of the Sahara, were ceremonious chants of hatred and rejection, customarily directed against chiefs and royal personages.[19] These events, which were often staged as aspects of institutionalized rituals of rebellion,[20] seem to have been remarkably effective in solidifying traditional principles of government, even as they were designed to control the actual conduct of those in ruling positions. And the same purposes were accomplished in Ashanti, where grievances were aired by ridiculing the king in the course of sessions devoted to "tales told after dark." On these occasions subjects ordinarily viewed as sacred were allowed to be treated as profane, and deepseated aggressive instincts could be vented by disguising voices, using animal names, or pretending in some other way that all was make-believe.[21] In the records of this West African society, too, we find accounts of the annual APO Custom, with its attendant "lampooning liberty," during which morals were generally relaxed, and people could curse and insult each other freely. The purpose behind this ceremony, as relayed to Rattray by an old high priest, was the following:

[15] Béart, "D'une Sociologie des peuples africains."

[16] Compare *supra*, pp. 100, 104, and *infra*, pp. 282ff.

[17] B. Holas, "Arts et artisanat en A.O.F.," *Les Guides bleus, Afrique occidentale française Togo* (Paris, 1958), p. clxxix.

[18] Junod, *Moeurs et Coutumes des Bantous*, Vol. I, 399, 428 on "The Public Vituperator." *Ibid.*, pp. 346, 396ff. on praise words, praise chants, and related ceremonies that the author witnessed in 1900, and regards as characteristic of Bantu literature.

[19] Johnson, *The History of the Yorubas*, pp. 40ff., 48, 70; also pp. 212ff., explains the circumstances in which the Alafin could be rejected by being told publicly "we reject you." But the implication here was that a king whose "enormities provoke an open rebuke" had to die. Compare also *infra*, p. 184. For Swazi songs of hatred of the king, chanted at the occasion of the first fruits' ceremony, see Hilda Kuper, *An African Aristocracy; Rank among the Swazi* (London and New York, 1947); chs. 6, 7, and 8; and preceding references to Junod.

[20] See Gluckman, *Order and Rebellion in Tribal Africa*, pp. 18ff. for a discussion of scholarly thought on this subject, and *infra*, pp. 188ff.

[21] Robert S. Rattray, *Akan-Ashanti Folktales* (Oxford, 1930), pp. x–xii.

You know that every one has a sunsum [soul] that may get hurt or knocked about or become sick, and so make the body ill. Very often, although there may be other causes, e.g. witchcraft, ill health is caused by the evil and the hate that another has in his head against you. Again, you too may have hatred in your head against another, because of something that person has done to you, and that, too, causes your sunsum to fret and become sick. Our forbears knew this to be the case, and so they ordained a time, once every year, when every man and woman, free man and slave, should have freedom to speak out just what was in their head, to tell their neighbours just what they thought of them, and of their actions, and not only their neighbours, but also the king or chief. When a man has spoken freely thus, he will feel his sunsum cool and quieted, and the sunsum of the other person against whom he has now openly spoken will be quieted also. The King of Ashanti may have killed your children, and you hate him. This has made him ill, and you ill, too; when you are allowed to say before his face what you think, you both benefit. That was why the King of Ashanti in ancient times, when he fell sick, would send for the Queen of Nkoranza to insult him, even though the time for the ceremony had not yet come around. It made him live longer and did him good.[22]

During this period, too, "the various gods were taking the air and greeting each other," as were all the priests and priestesses with their respective followers, shrines, jujus and sacred implements. But on the following day, Rattray continues his report, no parades took place. All the people sat outside their houses and conversed, waiting for the time that was specially set aside for verbal attacks upon the chief. "Wait until Friday," the officiating chief told Rattray, "when the people really begin to abuse me, and if you will come and do so too it will please me."[23]

The various forms of verbal aggression, including those connected with oathing and cursing, that traditional African societies had perfected into behavioral modes of conflict control, could, in their very nature, be fully operational only within the narrow radius of each linguistically unified community. In this, as in other senses,[24] then, the principle remained supreme that a stranger unable to speak the local language was by definition an enemy,[25] immune therefore to the weapons of derision and the

[22] Rattray, *Ashanti*, p. 153; and see *ibid.* for an analysis of "APO" as meaning "to speak roughly or harshly," "to abuse, to insult," and of a related term as meaning "to wash, to cleanse."

[23] *Ibid.*, p. 155; for some of the songs, pp. 156ff.

[24] Compare *supra*, Ch. 5.

[25] Compare B. Malinowski, "The Problem of Meaning in Primitive Languages," in C. K. Ogden and I. A. Richards, *The Meaning of Meaning; A Study of the Influence of Language upon Thought and of the Science of Symbolism* (New York, 1955).

killing word. A notable exception to this rule was the so-called "joking relationship," for this institution, widespread throughout the continent as a conjunct of the kinship system, was allowed, in some regions, to develop into an intergroup pact that provided for the suspension or mitigation of enmity and isolation.

No generally valid explanation for the evolution of this practice seems to exist;[26] but in line with the premise that dispositions in foreign affairs are everywhere organically related to locally valid systems of belief and organization, it is likely that intergroup "joking" is an extension or an outgrowth of institutionalized in-group "joking." This local arrangement, which anthropologists have noted in many parts of the primitive world,[27] stipulates a preferred relationship, under the terms of which certain kin sets are linked with each other in an order of privileged familiarity that allows, indeed at times insists upon, teasing, criticism, verbal abuse, and such other liberties as the physical exploitation of the joking partner's property—freedoms from which other family members are rigorously excluded. In some societies such a relationship exists between cross cousins (that is, children of the mother's brothers and the father's sisters),[28] in others between a woman and her father's brother, or between an uncle and his nephew. In the course of his analysis of Tonga society, Junod[29] relates the case of an uncle's anger at finding the food upon which he had relied all eaten up. As soon as someone explained to him that it had been eaten by his sister's son, however, he smiled and acquiesced in the loss. For the most important rule in his relationship to his nephew, as in all joking pacts, was the provision that joking partners might not become angry, no matter what the one might say or do to the other.

The records of interclan relations among the Tonga repeat some of

[26] For a review of theories see Gladys Reichard, "Social Life," in Franz Boas, ed., *General Anthropology* (New York, 1938), pp. 446ff., especially p. 448 for a reference to R. H. Lowie's view that the custom should be studied in each case with close attention to the entire social setting: what is plausible as a cause in one region may be quite implausible in another.

[27] For example, among the American Indians, in Hawaii, and in parts of Melanesia. See Reichard, "Social Life," for relevant descriptions and analyses. Also M. Herskovits, *Man and His Works; The Science of Cultural Anthropology*, pp. 289ff. See *supra*, Ch. 6 for references to "the joking pact" as a manifestation of "the greater society."

[28] Reichard reports a typical example of joking among cross cousins in Navajo society in the following way: they may tease each other about shortcomings, and the teasing may go to great length of criticism or even censorship. Joking relatives may make public exhibitions of fondness for each other that are denied other individuals, and they may joke about sex matters, often in ways regarded as obscene even in the native sense of the word. But whatever the exaggeration, a Navajo informant told her that he would never get angry if one of his cousins teased him in that fashion. See Reichard, "Social Life," p. 446.

[29] *Moeurs et Coutumes des Bantous*, p. 219; for the English version of this work, which was published first, see *The Life of a South African Tribe* (London, 1927), Vol. I, 46, 267ff.

these motifs,[30] and the same is true of the Bemba and the Luapula peoples of the former Belgian Congo and Northern Rhodesia (Zambia).[31] Here joking pacts link clans whose totems are either complementary or antipathetic to one another. For instance, two groups identified with the leopard and the goat are affiliated because the leopard kills the goat; the iron and the elephant have a relation because elephants are hunted with iron spears; the mushroom and the anthill are associated, since mushrooms thrive on anthills. In each case the pact obliges clan members to give mutual hospitality, regardless of tribal membership.

Yet another variation on the joking-pact theme is registered among the Lobi peoples, whose roughly hundred fifty thousand members are spread from the Guinea coast to the lake region of Tanganyika, and are divided into six tribes that speak different languages. The tribes belong to four clans, and the clans, divided into twosomes, are joined in joking relationships. No precise reason for this arrangement has been advanced, but some native informants suggested to Montserrat Palau Marti[32] that it might have originated in a blood pact[33] between two chiefs, who promised to never make war on each other, to bury the dead of each other's community, and to settle disputes amicably (in at least one case the latter commitment seems to have been entrusted to a smith).[34] Lobi residents in the Sudan and Guinea, on the other hand, explained the linkage as due either to a common origin of the two clans, or to the wish to simulate a marriage; to a treaty of peace between the two founders of the two clans; or to a mix-up of the clans' ancestors shortly after their birth, which had made it impossible ever since to know just who had founded which clan.[35]

One is on surer ground in a survey of joking alliances between different Dogon groups in the formerly French Sudan, perhaps because the subject has received particular attention from several French scholars. Here people are said to be so keenly aware of the range of linguistic diversity among the constituent communities of the region, and so highly conscious of all possible nuances in the use of vocabulary, grammar, accent, and pronunciation, that they can hear in the instant of an encounter from which village or village section a person originates. Activated by this special aural sensitivity, as well as by an innate critical spirit, the teasing impulse is directed first at the dialect or other linguis-

[30] Ibid. (French ed.), pp. 344ff.

[31] W. Whiteley, "Bemba and Related Peoples of Northern Rhodesia," pp. 37ff., 60 on joking pacts; pp. 5, 25 on the use of blessings and curses; and J. Slaski, "Peoples of the Lower Luapula Valley," both in Ethnographic Survey of Africa, Part II: East Central Africa (London, 1951).

[32] "Conduites abusives permises en Afrique," Bulletin de l'IFAN, Dakar, 22, ser. B., Nos. 1–2 (1960), 299–327.

[33] Compare supra, p. 98, n. 74 and infra, pp. 320 and 362.

[34] Compare supra, p. 162 and infra, pp. 277ff.

[35] Palau Marti, "Conduites abusives permises en Afrique."

tic peculiarity of the opposing conversationalist. But the major, albeit covert, objectives of the verbal thrust are the real or assumed character defects of the partner to the altercation, and this target, again, serves as a conduit pipe through which the critique is channelled so as to hit the "other" village community and its authorities.[36] Dogon lampooning, then, is indirect in its intent, but it proceeds, nonetheless, in systematic ways; for each group in the Bandiagara area has its own repertory of mockeries, usually laid down in fixed formulations. Some leeway for improvisation is allowed, it is true, and this opportunity for the individualized joke in conjunction with general and traditional expertise in this type of linguistic transaction explains why even total strangers—that is, men whose languages are not known—may, on occasion, be drawn into the circle of privileged familiarity.

One of the most far-reaching of recorded intergroup pacts is the joking arrangement between the Dogon and the Bozo, to which Marcel Griaule refers as an "alliance cathartique."[37] The major overt or behavioral aspect here, as in similar pacts, is the requirement to exchange ritually fixed insults and the commitment not to regard them as conflict-inducing defamations. This common provision coexists in this case, however, with certain other rather explicit understandings: the Dogon and the Bozo may not resort to violence in their mutual relations; quarrels in the ranks of the Dogon must stop upon the arrival of a Bozo (and vice versa); marriage and sex taboos are rigidly observed; and, most importantly in the context of regional order or pacification, members of the two societies are obligated to render each other unlimited hospitality and assistance in case of need.

The origins of this friendship are shrouded in legend, but the Bozo and Dogon appear to believe that at some remote time, perhaps when one group first entered the territory occupied by the other,[38] a portion of the Bozo person became lodged, as it were, in the Dogon person. A spiritual, but quasi-physical and therefore indissoluble union had thus come into being, in the context of which it would be fratricidal, even suicidal, for a Dogon to kill a Bozo or a Bozo to kill a Dogon. And the same law of mystic participation[39] explains, of course, why it would be illogical to resent an insult that is directed against oneself.

[36] G. Calame-Griaule, "Les Moqueries de villages au Soudan français," in *Notes africaines; Bulletin de l'information et de correspondences*, IFAN, No. 61 (Dakar, January 1954).

[37] L'Alliance Cathartique," *Africa*, 18, No. 4 (October 1948), 242–258; also Gourhan et Poirier, *Ethnologie de l'union française*, pp. 350, 355.

[38] Compare with greatly similar pacts between immigrant and autochtonous groups, *supra*, pp. 106ff.

[39] Compare *supra*, Ch. 5.

PART V

THE WEB OF WAR AND THE MAINTENANCE OF SOCIETY

· 12 ·

OCCULT GAMES

Since nonliterate thought is essentially behavioral, it is usually difficult to say just when feelings and intentions become operational from the indigenous point of view, or, more particularly, when a scheme to inflict violence is actually translated into deed. Furthermore, since words are often tantamount to acts in this culture, lines of distinction between verbal and physical bellicosity tend to be blurred. Within the hazy contours of these states of being, it is not always easy, therefore, to distinguish the playful from the deadly serious disposition. Thus, what is usually experienced in the Occident as a sport or an athletic event, may be transposed in Africa into a struggle for existence, during which magic is pitted against countermagic.

The following episodes are illustrative of this mode of play. In the coastal society of modern Tanzania, where football has become very popular, two groups of football clubs were spread along the coast in 1959, when Lienhardt had occasion to observe their mutual relations.[1] He found that the making of magic based on secret information was an important part of the game, and that Tanzanian footballers regularly used medicine against their opponents. Every effort was made to conceal from the opposing side who was going to play in which position in any particular match. If the opponents found out, they were better able to take magical precautions, so as to put their rivals out of action. For example, in Dar-es-Salaam a team went out with a medicine-man to the pitch at night. The players undressed while the medicine-man set out eleven lime fruits in the positions of the opposing team. He took a needle and stuck it into the limes one by one, calling each lime by the name of one of the members of the opposing team, according to the team order revealed by a spy. Then he killed a hen over the limes, wrapped the whole lot in a cloth, and buried this "medicine" on the football pitch. The opposing team had not taken such good precautions, and when they came to play the match they lacked the energy and spirit to hold their own.[2]

At a match Lienhardt attended, in which Kilwa Kisiwani played Kilwa Kivinje, both teams were quite naturally suspicious over each other's footballs.

[1] Introduction to Hasani Bin Ismail, *The Medicine Man.*
[2] *Ibid.,* pp. 16ff.

When Kivinje's ball became unlaced in the middle of the game, the Kivinje team almost stopped playing rather than use the ball that Kisiwani had ready. This was because the Kivinje team thought their opponents had taken the ball and slept the night with it in the bush at a holy place on their island called "the graves of the forty sharifs." The Kivinje ball had also been tampered with by being prepared with various medicines helped on by a secret dance performed on the pitch in the middle of the night by the team manager and his wife dressed in skirts of octopus tentacles. Each village asserted itself by its local magic, calling spirits to its aid, though there was a difference in that in the smaller but much more ancient village of Kilwa Kisiwani the appeal was to something in the place—the ancient graves—whereas in the more metropolitan little town of Kivinje it was to a magic that could be acquired and bought.[3]

As the reference to the "forty sharifs" indicates, the competition here was particularly sharp because the Kisiwani team could rely on these reputed descendants of the Prophet, who are commonly believed to have superior supernatural powers by virtue of their control over the "book magic" of the Koran. A special courage to best the opponents also communicated itself to the members of this team during the match in question, when one of the renowned manipulators of written charms, who also happened to be a genuine fan of their sportly cause, was wheeled in his bath-chair to the edge of the pitch.

Here, as elsewhere in Islamized Africa, book magic is accepted as a potent antidote to evil. But whenever people face serious trouble—and this may well include competition in a football field—it is definitely outclassed, as it were, by the magic of plants, if only because this kind of magic, whether wielded by sorcerers or medicine men engaged in detecting or outwitting sorcerers, is believed capable of occasioning injury or death.[4] In either case play is securely integrated into the locally accepted system of conflict-related norms, values, and modes of reasoning.

A similarly tight order of logic subsumes the playing of "rain hockey" in Timbuctoo.[5] This game (*alkura*) was brought from North Africa, where it was played either to bring the rain or to stop overabundant rains. These sacred functions were dropped when it was introduced to Timbuctoo, but a vestige of the old magic remained. When the city was

---

[3] *Ibid.*, p. 17.

[4] *Ibid.*, pp. 48–51. On the distinct but often overlapping functions of these two occult agents, and on the juridical and medical difficulties of coping with the manifestations of this "local system of thought," see in particular pp. 74–80; cf. also *supra*, Ch. 5 and *infra*, Ch. 18.

[5] See Horace Miner, *The Primitive City of Timbuctoo* (Princeton, 1953), pp. 240ff., "Patterns of Conflict."

waiting for its overdue rains in 1940, the emir announced by crier that if any children were caught playing *alkura* before the rains came, both they and their parents would be thrown in prison. The main standing purpose of the Timbuctoo game is, however, that it serves as an outlet for fierce rivalries between the culturally different quarters into which the city is divided. In studying the basis of these interquarter rivalries, Miner found "that the Arab-dominated quarters fight it out with the quarters where most of the Songhai live."[6] Furthermore, *alkura* is popular because it provides opportunities for the expression of other kinds of hostility: it allows slaves to hit nobles with impunity, invites all players to vent accumulated personal enmities and grudges by engaging in rough stick work, and lets nonplayers in the rival quarters indulge in the freedom of taunting and insulting enemies and losing players with impunity. In other words, competitive play is enjoyed because it is an exercise in enmity. As such it is apt to be violent, or activate other latent dispositions toward strife and aggression in social life.[7]

[6] *Ibid.*, pp. 241.

[7] *Ibid.*, pp. 252ff. on the incidence of armed robbery, brigandage, kidnapping of children, and mass resort to violence in Timbuctoo. Modern interstate relations, too, have at times been gravely disturbed by sport events. A football match between teams from Gabon and Congo-Brazzaville in the 1960s thus occasioned grave discords between these adjoining states.

· 13 ·

RITUAL VIOLENCE AND THE
CAUSE OF GOVERNMENT

The records of traditionally prevalent modes of thought, patterns of social relations, and forms of administration as discussed in several earlier chapters indicate that physical violence in human relations has been and continues to be accommodated on a prodigious scale in Africa without offending customary values and norms, and that one or another kind of warfare is generally accepted as a mere variant of conflict, and therefore also as an essential aspect of the community's jural and moral order. This interpenetration of functions goes a long way toward explaining why war has been endemic in the continent. Together with the merging of thought and act, and of categories of conflict and accord, it also explains why it is often difficult to isolate war from other species of hostile and violent behavior.

In the immediate context of war, again, precision and uniformity in the use of such terms as "internal war" and "external war" prove to be elusive goals for three reasons to which attention was drawn earlier, namely, the absence of an all-African norm of political organization, the fluidity of territorial boundaries, and continuous shifts in political identity—themes as constant today as in the annals of traditional Africa. Zones of hostility, as well as degrees of martial violence in the transaction of belligerent relations or the infliction of military force have perforce been greatly various, with the result that unqualified normative distinctions between "internal" and "external" war, or between different species of internal war, are tenuous, to say the least. It is not surprising, then, that no accord exists among Africanists in the West on just how to define and classify the different forays, feuds, revolts, and military expeditions of which the multifarious records tell. Very similar episodes may thus be labeled spontaneous raids by a scholar who specializes in the affairs of one particular community, and as programmed martial campaigns by another expert, who is presenting the institutions of a different ethnic grouping.

Despite these verbal incongruities, certain general conclusions on the place of war in African society appear tenable. It may be affirmed, for instance, that the meanings carried by war and other institutionalized acts of physical violence are everywhere derivatives of culturally dominant understandings of the purposes of life and of the relationship be-

180

tween life and death. As such, they cannot be isolated from prevalent dispositions to other forms of physical injury, oppression, and homicide. In all these respects the records show conclusively that African societies are ready to accommodate the most extreme manifestations of coercive power on the part of their governing authorities without becoming either disorganized or demoralized, as long as it appears that these incidents of rule are sanctioned by the general belief system.

In traditional kingdoms known for orderly sustained governance, such as those of Dahomey, Ashanti, and Benin, men and women, both free and enslaved, could as a matter of course be killed after random choice, irrespective of considerations of culpability, without provoking revulsion or revolt, because the rulers and the ruled were unified in the belief that the living need the dead if communication with the spirit world, and therewith the survival of society, was to be maintained.[1] As Burton explains in his sympathetic account of Dahomean practices, filial piety required intermediaries who would report the king's actions to the ancestors on specified occasions, just as it stipulated at the king's death that the sovereign "must enter Deadworld with royal state, accompanied by a ghostly court of leopard wives, head wives, birthday wives, Afa wives, eunuchs—especially the chief eunuch—singers and drummers, . . . bards and soldiers."[2] In terms of this mythical charter, then, Burton's conclusion is irreproachable, namely, that "to abolish human sacrifices here is to abolish Dahome."[3] Similarly, even such patently arbitrary killings as those perpetrated by a Bemba chief in an apparent outburst of passion were tolerated as aspects of the public order, a twentieth-century informant reports,[4] evidently because the officiating chief was respected for the quality of his judgment in other significant respects. What needs to be borne in mind, then, in a discussion of internal violence and war is the fact that all African governments, including the most despotic among them, were constitutionally limited in the sense that they were prisoners of sacred rites and magical beliefs.

A leading comparative study of several political systems is prefaced by the remark that "Acts of violence, oppression, revolt, civil war, and so forth, chequer the history of every African State."[5] These motifs have found different local expressions, as preceding chapters have shown, but in certain fields of government, notably those having to do

[1] Compare *supra*, Chs. 3, 5, and 9.
[2] *Mission to Gelele*, Vol. II, 13.
[3] *Ibid.*, Vol. II, 17; see also pp. 117, 140ff. for Adahoonzou's speech, and p. 300.
[4] *Supra*, pp. 151ff.
[5] Fortes and Evans-Pritchard, eds., *African Political Systems*, "Introduction," p. 16.

with succession to positions of authority and allocation of power, the separate records converge upon a common pattern of institutionalized tensions, hostilities, intrigues, and feuds.[6]

This is so in the case of succession, a prominent Africanist observes, because "rarely in Africa do we find rules which indicate clearly and definitely a single heir. . . . The result was that almost every succession could raise rival claimants, and after the king's death . . . a unifying war for the kingship between claimants and their supporters . . . might follow."[7] In most types of succession, whether to the name and spirit of a dead man or to his office, the political system of the Bemba tribe allowed for two or three potential heirs.[8] Among the Ngoni, different leaders were always struggling for power within the boundaries of a particular state by manipulating groups and associations.[9] Societies in Southern Rhodesia usually had to contend with an interregnum between one chieftainship and another, and this was invariably marked by great disorder, including civil war.[10] Each accession in the Kingdom of Kongo was preceded by an interregnum, during which intrigue and violence held sway, until one of the late king's relatives succeeded to the office. Indeed, the interregnum here was made to last as long as possible by dignitaries who stood to profit from the situation.[11] In East African chiefdoms, as, for example, in Ankole, it was expected that the succession would be decided by a war to the death between the king's sons, with sorcery, poison, and arms part of the available and permissible weaponry. Nor does any feeling seem to have existed here that states ruled by the same dynasties were bound together as a political family. In fact, specialists in the traditions of this area view dynastic and fratricidal warfare as one of several "common characteristics" in the tribal systems later encompassed by Uganda and Tanganyika.[12] Islamic societies in East Africa,

[6] For modern enactments of these motifs, see *supra*, Chs. 3 and 4.

[7] Gluckman, *Custom and Conflict in Africa*, p. 46. Lucy Mair, *Primitive Government* (Harmondsworth, Middlesex, 1962), makes the same observation in her analysis of East African societies when she writes that "there is no rule that establishes unequivocally how the succession is to go" (pp. 205–206), and that it was therefore never taken for granted that the accession would be peaceful (p. 208).

[8] Audrey I. Richards, "The Political System of the Bemba Tribe," in Fortes and Evans-Pritchard, eds., *African Political Systems*, p. 100.

[9] J. A. Barnes, *Politics in a Changing Society; A Political History of the Fort Jameson Ngoni* (Cape Town and New York, 1954).

[10] Roger Howman, "Chiefs and Councils in Southern Rhodesia," in Raymond Apthorpe, ed., *From Tribal Rule to Modern Government* (Lusaka, 1959), pp. 40ff.

[11] See J. Cuvelier, *Documents sur une mission française au Kakongo 1766–1776* (Brussels, 1953), p. 40; also pp. 37ff., and Cuvelier and Jadin, *L'Ancien Congo d'après les archives romaines (1518–1640)*. Vansina, too, makes it clear in *Kingdoms of the Savanna* that full allowance was made in this region for civil strife and armed conflict between different challengers to ruling positions.

[12] Richards, ed., *East African Chiefs*, preface, p. 33; also pp. 148, 197, 237; to like effect see Mair, *Primitive Government*, p. 209.

too, were rent by endemic feuds, disunity, and open war. Of all traditional Arab customs, none appears to have been more tenaciously kept up than that sanctioning strife over the succession to the rulership of each little "city state," as well as strife between state and state for political and commercial supremacy.[13] And the same patterns were reenacted in Islamized western Africa. Commenting on the primacy of interpersonal enmities among the Fulani as he observed them in the nineteenth century, Barth reports that one brother often cherished the most inveterate hatred against another, and that fratricide was therefore a common occurrence—a trait also noted by a twentieth-century researcher, who observes that rebellions and attempts to capture the throne by force were the greatest weakness in the Fulani system of government.[14] Among the Bamoum in Cameroon, to whom belligerence and intrigue were the spice of life, a king—who was always surrounded by rivals—could survive only by wielding absolute power, resorting to all manner of ruses, or by enlisting the aid of the neighboring Fulani. And very similar patterns of incessant fratricidal conflicts marked relations among Songhai dignitaries, as well as between the princely contenders to power in the domain that Askya Mohammed had created in the western Sudan.[15] Royal branches of the Bariba in northern Dahomey and Niger, too, were perennially engaged in such wars, even though custom had it that succession to authority should alternate between them. This was not followed, Lombard explains,[16] because each prince had one exclusive purpose in life, namely, to capture power and deny it to his rivals. Evasions of what appear, at least in retrospect, to have been customary procedures have also been noted in Central Togo (once a German possession), where the chieftainship of "Tschaudjo" was supposed to rotate between the heads of several villages, but rarely did because pretenders were so numerous that the question of succession was usually decided by war;[17] likewise in Anuak society (in the former Anglo-Egyptian Sudan), where civil war for the possession of a circulating kingship was constant. Mossi country,

[13] R. Coupland, *East Africa and Its Invaders, from the Earliest Times to the Death of Seyyid Said in 1856* (Oxford, 1938; repr. 1956), especially ch. 2, pp. 26ff., 34, and chs. 5, 9, 10, and 11.

[14] See Barth, *Travels and Discoveries in North and Central Africa, 1849–1855*, Vol. I, 544. For other accounts of raids, succession struggles, and internal warfare in this area see H. R. Palmer, *Sudanese Memoirs*, Vol. I, on the Kanem wars of Mai Idris Alooma. Also M. G. Smith, *Government in Zazzau*, pp. 100ff., on the weaknesses in the Fulani system of government. On the prevalence of such disturbances in Bornu (northern Nigeria), see Urvoy, *Histoire de l'empire du Bornou*, pp. 51ff.

[15] Compare Jean Rouch, *Contribution à l'histoire des Songhay* (*Mémoire*, IFAN, No. 29), (Dakar, 1953), pp. 197ff. and 201ff.

[16] Lombard, "Un Système politique traditionnel de type féodal," pp. 464ff.

[17] See report by Dr. Kersting, district officer of Sokode, in O. F. Metzger, *Unsere Alte Kolonie Togo* (Neudamm, 1941).

meanwhile, was commonly plunged into an interregnum marked by ritual and actual anarchy when the Mogho Naba's death was announced. Looting and pillaging were then the order of the day, while aspirant princes fought for possession of the throne, and satellite rulers contested powers at lesser courts.[18]

To summarize: whether in the tribal societies of southern Africa, the conquest states of the Interlacustrine Bantus, the imperial domains of pagan and Islamic peoples in the Sudan, the Arab colonies on the coast of East Africa, or the kingdoms of the savanna and West Africa, ruling circles were rent by quarrels, jealousies, and intrigues that were expected to erupt in dynastic, fratricidal, or civil wars, and to lead to prolonged periods of anarchy, until the contest for power had been temporarily resolved.[19]

These violent occurrences were preceded in many societies by institutionalized regicide and related acts of homicide. In fact, scholarly conclusions are on record that "king killing was almost a universal custom among African peoples."[20] In most of the East African states, rulers had to be poisoned, strangled, or otherwise disposed of when their physical powers were failing.[21] The divine king of the Jukun-speaking peoples (Nigeria) was strangled after the allowed seven years' span of rule;[22] paramount chiefs in the lower Luapula Valley were strangled when they were on the point of death in order then to be buried in the company of their wives,[23] and Congolese sovereigns faced death on dates appointed

[18] Elliott P. Skinner, *The Mossi of the Upper Volta; The Political Development of a Sudanese People* (Stanford, Calif., 1964), pp. 50ff., 70ff. See also *ibid.*, pp. 92–106 on "warfare."

[19] Compare Gluckman, *Order and Rebellion in Tribal Africa*, p. 32: "every analysis of African states show[s] that they all have recurrent 'civil war,'" and p. 36 on the "rebellious structure" of African politics, and on rebellion as an ever-present, persistent, repetitive process. Also I. Schapera, *Government and Politics in Tribal Societies* (London, 1956), who comments extensively upon different types of factionalism in the chiefly and royal families of several southern African societies, as well as upon the revolts that then ensued.

[20] P. Hadfield, *Traits of Divine Kingship in Africa* (London, 1949), ch. 5, pp. 41ff. on "The Killing of the Divine King," and p. 52 for his conclusion. For the geographic distribution of the motifs of the ritual murder of the king, isolation of the king, anarchy after the king's death, and related phenomena, see Leo Frobenius, *Atlas Africanus; Belege zur Morphologie der Afrikanischen Kulturen* (Berlin, 1921), pp. 183ff. By the same author, also *Erythraea, Laender und Zeiten des Heiligen Koenigsmordes*, pp. 41ff. Cf. also E. A. Wallis Budge, *Osiris and the Egyptian Resurrection*, 2 vols. (London, 1911), especially the chapter on "The African Doctrine of Last Things" in Vol. II, and authorities there cited.

[21] Richards, ed., *East African Chiefs*, pp. 38, 148, 237ff.; also Mair, *Primitive Government*, especially p. 232.

[22] Meek, *A Sudanese Kingdom*, pp. 120ff. on "The Divine King," pp. 164ff. on relevant aspects of his death.

[23] Whitely, "Bemba and Related Peoples of Northern Rhodesia," and Slaski, "Peoples of the Lower Luapula Valley," pp. 24ff.; also Cunnison, *The Luapula*

by the courts. In most cases the demise was kept secret for some time. A Yoruba king had to die by his own hand after he had been openly rebuked or "rejected"—a prerequisite for suicide that gradually disappeared, Samuel Johnson explains in his classical *History of the Yorubas*, as the feeling gained ground that no king should die a natural death.[24] Mossi custom required that all rulers, including village chiefs, be done away with after they had been deposed because of misadministration or rebellion.

Nor was internal peace expected once the issue of succession had been decided. Since dissension and hostility were de rigueur, as it were, revolts by subordinate princes and chiefs were always expected. For example, in East Africa many so-called princes were put to death by each new king who wished to rid himself of possible rivals as he ascended the throne.[25] In the West African Sudan it was customary to render princely brothers harmless by blinding them, cutting their vocal chords, or mutilating them in other ways.[26] Elsewhere precautions against rebellions took the form of banishment. To avoid palace revolts, Malagasy rulers often exiled from their capitals royal sons who were not favored.[27] Obsessed by fear lest their sons murder them, Shilluk kings did not allow princes to be in the capital at night, and appointed special officials for the sole purpose of guarding all potential rivals. In Ethiopia the entire male line of the royal house was kept in seclusion save the reigning king, his sons, and grandsons: "As each king was crowned all his brothers were relegated to an impregnable amba and there they lived and died with their families, completely cut off from all communication with the kingdom." Amply provided with revenues, they were yet strictly imprisoned by a select body of guards, so that no one might enter the amba on pain of frightful penalties.[28]

It goes without saying that in the logic of traditional African politics

---

Peoples, pp. 167ff. on regicide in Luapula communities. On the ritual murder of the Monomotapa, see Wieschhoff, *The Zimbabwe-Monomotapa Culture in Southeast Africa*, pp. 95ff.

[24] See p. 177. Compare Fyfe, *A History of Sierra Leone*, p. 162 to the effect that King George of Kafu Bulom, crowned by Governor Day, is said to have been the first monarch to die naturally (in 1826); normally the people slew their kings when they grew old.

[25] Richards, ed., *East African Chiefs*, p. 35; pp. 46ff. on mass murders of members of lineage groups and the slaughter of Buganda princes of the blood. But see *ibid*. on the gradual eclipse of royalty and the ascendence of a bureaucracy.

[26] Guenther Spannaus, *Zuege aus der Politischen Organisation Afrikanischer Voelker und Staaten* (Leipzig, 1929), pp. 156ff.; also Labouret, *L'Afrique précoloniale*, pp. 77ff. On Mossi practices of banishing contenders, see Frobenius, *Und Afrika Sprach*, Vol. II, 164ff. and Skinner, *The Mossi*, p. 76.

[27] Kent, *Early Kingdoms in Madagascar*, p. 41.

[28] A.H.M. Jones and Elizabeth Monroe, *A History of Ethiopia* (London, 1955, repr. 1960), p. 71.

and religion, no one could escape the net of fear and death-inducing conflicts by which government was held together. Many systems of administration, notably those found in the well-consolidated great societies of West Africa, thus suggest the prevalence of unrelieved despotism, at least when viewed in traditional Western perspectives. Different perceptions impose themselves, however, when the same phenomena are considered in the local context; for here orderly government is more often than not a precarious process of administering the chronic interplay of diverse, interlocking patterns of conflict.

Some episodes from the history of the Yorubas—peoples as renowned before 1892 for their addiction to human sacrifices as for their superior skills in government[29]—are illustrative of this proposition. Indeed, the connection between these two aspects of rule was so close in premodern times that when attempts were made in the nineteenth century to persuade the Oni of Ife to abolish human sacrifices, he objected, saying that the sacrifices were for the benefit of the whole human race, the white man not excepted, and that if the sacrifices made on his behalf were to be discontinued, his superior knowledge and the arts derived therefrom would depart from him.[30]

An appreciation of these concepts of government requires understanding that kings in this region were trusted to hold their realms together because they were great magicians. Most of them were given, upon installation, potent medicine to guard them against envy and the magic of malevolent subjects, rivals, or foreign potentates,[31] and all were expected to deal out death on a massive scale in deference to the enterprise they represented. A nineteenth-century Oba of Benin was thus obligated to place a curse on the Olu of Jekri and his family by way of punishing an insult, and no one was surprised when the malefactor died in agony about a year later, and when even those who should have been made Olu after him died in quick succession—events that moved a prince of the Itsekiri royal family to come to Benin City and beg for the curse to be removed.[32] Likewise, the Oba was as entitled to force a dreaded juju man to commit suicide, since the oracle had charged him with having caused the illness of the Oba's eldest son, as he was to schedule human massacres toward the end of the nineteenth century, when the oracle of the Oni of Ife predicted that some great calamity was coming to Benin City

[29] Johnson, *History of the Yorubas*, p. 19.

[30] Budge, *Osiris and the Egyptian Resurrection*, Vol. I, 225ff.

[31] Colson, "African Society at the Time of the Scramble," p. 44.

[32] Jacob U. Egharevba, *A Short History of Benin*, 4th ed. (Ibadan, 1968), pp. 43ff. On Benin see in particular the accounts of Portuguese, Dutch, and English explorers, the work of the seventeenth-century Dutch geographer, Olfert Dapper, and Dr. Henry Ling Roth. *Great Benin* (Halifax, England, 1903). Also J. W. Blake, *Europeans in West Africa, 1450–1560*, 2 vols. (London, 1942). Compare *supra*, Ch. 10.

in connection with the presence of the British. As Egharevba explains the ensuing catastrophe, the British experienced difficulty in dealing with the king because the latter was himself a big juju in which the natives had unbounded confidence. They were thus absolutely certain that he would never be captured, and that, if the British did succeed in arriving at the city, he would turn into a bird or some animal, and so escape.[33]

As the supreme head of all Yoruba kings,[34] the Alafin, too, was by definition the administrative agent of all occult affairs. This explains, Johnson writes,[35] why one Alafin attempted to consolidate the kingdom and protect it from the ravages of war by burying charms in the city and offering his newborn child to his medicine-men so that it might be pulverized and used for their purposes—an act, the Yoruba chronicler notes, which "is to this day highly regarded by the people." Likewise, his office required him to arrange for sacrifices, even as it made it incumbent upon him or his eldest son to commit suicide or accept poison when royal councillors and their magicians decided, for one reason or another, that the elimination of one or both incumbents would benefit the cause of state. Resort to ritual and magic thus had horrendous effects upon life throughout Oyo history, but it also served as the major check on one man's or one group's tendencies to despotism. As a modern analyst of Oyo's "constitutional troubles" explains,[36] the Alafin's absolutism was controlled by the Oyo Mesi, a council of seven nonroyal chiefs, as well as by the latter's chief officer, the Basorun. The reigns of nine Alafins had thus been terminated by assassination, others were cut short by rejection and, in 1774 and 1796, by coups d'état that prefigured many traits also encountered in twentieth-century upheavals of this kind. Quarrels, intrigues, and dissensions rent the ruling circles, notably the relationships between the Alafin on one hand, and his crown prince or the Basorun on the other. Plot and counterplot, murder and revenge, rebellion and punishment for rebellion, army mutinies, wars of succession and

[33] Egharevba, *A Short History of Benin*, pp. 47–59.

[34] Johnson, *History of the Yorubas*, p. 41.

[35] *Ibid.*, pp. 166–167; also *supra*, Ch. 6, n. 9.

[36] R.C.C. Law, "The Constitutional Troubles of Oyo in the Eighteenth Century," *Journal of African History*, 12, No. 1 (1971), 25–44. This scholar concludes from his study that the eighteenth-century coups originated in competition for control of new sources of wealth that became available when the kingdom expanded. But see also Johnson, *History of the Yorubas*, ch. 14, pp. 269ff., 289ff. on the incidence of civil wars, fratricidal wars, and the place of "the interregnum" in Yoruba politics; also Egharevba, *A Short History of Benin*, pp. 34, 38, 40, 43, 46 for numerous accounts of rebellions within the royal families of Benin; also for other types of uprising, systems of massacre, and the connection of many of these episodes with magic and sorcery. On traditional town rivalries and civil wars in the south of present-day Nigeria, see S. O. Biobaku, "An Historical Account of the Evolution of Nigeria as a Political Unit," in Lionel Brett, ed., *Constitutional Problems of Federalism in Nigeria* (Lagos, 1961).

civil wars made up the system of conflict within which the mythical charter was imbedded. The realm gradually weakened, it is true, and little resistance could therefore be offered in the 1820s, when the Fulani were bent to ravage and conquer.[37] Yet the magic of political mythology continued to rally people in mid-twentieth century, as Ulli Beier tells us:

> According to an ancient custom, the death of the Alafin or king had to be followed by a number of suicides by people who had to accompany the king to the next world. Particularly important was the commander of the cavalry, who celebrated the day of his death with great ceremony, dancing through the town all day, in his "robe of death" until he returned home in the evening to die. This custom should have been celebrated for the last time in 1946, but on that occasion the British district officer interfered. The commander of the cavalry was arrested in the middle of the ceremonial dance and charged with attempted suicide. He was let off lightly, but in any case the spell was broken and he remained alive. However, his son, who was trading in the Gold Coast, hurried home to bury his father when he read of the death of the king. But when he entered the house and met his father alive he was so shocked and ashamed that he killed himself on the spot.[38]

A survey of different traditional ways of staging, managing, or preventing wars of succession, or of merely dramatizing political conflict and hostility to the ruler in dances, chants of hatred and rejection, and other rites and ceremonies, suggests that rebellion against the established authority is widely accepted in Africa as an integral aspect of administration.[39] Just why this should be so is a question to which unequivocal answers cannot be given. The evidence leads one to believe that these contests are regarded as reliable modes of assuring succession and continuity; that they have cathartic effects upon the community by providing outlets for cooped-up angers, frustrations, and suspicions; and that they serve to reaffirm existing political structures. Indeed, the most interesting aspect of this type of internal war is surely the fact that substantive changes in the political structure are neither intended nor effected. Indi-

[37] See authorities cited in notes 29–36, in particular Johnson, *History of the Yorubas*, ch. 9, p. 217; ch. 10, pp. 223ff.; ch. 12 on wars for the consolidation of the realm and power clashes between Ibadans, Egbas, and Ijebus; ch. 14 on the "interregnum," fratricidal wars, and the Fulani campaigns.
[38] Ulli Beier, *Contemporary Art in Africa* (New York and London, 1968), p. 6.
[39] Compare also Max Gluckman, *Rituals of Rebellion in South-east Africa* (Manchester, 1954), and *Order and Rebellion in Tribal Africa*; and see *supra* for references to other discussions of rituals in politics. See Mair, *Primitive Government*, p. 209 to the effect that the political structure as a whole does not collapse in the aftermath of such disorders.

vidual kings, chiefs, or pretenders to power may thus be allowed to perish, but the idea of kingship emerges triumphantly intact from power-play and murder.

Other categories of intracommunity feuds and competitions for power confirm the impression left by the record of wars of succession, namely, that African government, whether pagan, Christianized, or Islamic, thrives on conflict, both acute and lingering, overt and covert, violent and nonviolent. To give but a few illustrations. Fights between two kindreds or two local factions of the same village group, between two separate village groups, or between a section of one village group and a section of another were constant occurrences throughout Iboland in pre-British days.[40] Chronic belligerence marked life in Tivland;[41] reduced relations between individual Yoruba states, as well as between descent groups composing Yoruba towns, to conditions of perpetual military feuding,[42] and pitted different sections of the Nupe,[43] the Mossi, and the Zande empire against each other. And the same pattern emerges from the record of interactions between the dynastic segments of the Fulani emirates and different divisions of Hausa societies.[44] In this part of West Africa, where pagan and Islamic traditions of rule have been intermingling for centuries, local intrigues, fights, and raids combined to form a web of war from which no generation could escape.

Violent internecine conflict was also the norm in southern Africa, where it produced permanent states of hostility between the different territorial units of the Zulu, the Swazi, the Barotse, and other major groups. And the same was true in the East African areas of the Kamba, where people on one hillside regularly fought those on the adjoining hill; of the Nandi; and the Masai, who viewed the Kwavi (Kwafi) as their mortal enemies.[45] Among the Nuer, war was endless because opposition not

[40] Meek, *Law and Authority*, pp. 242ff.

[41] See authorities listed *supra*, Ch. 5, n. 73. Relationships between the Tiv, who are not divided into discrete political units by recognized boundaries, are defined solely in terms of genealogical distance: against those more closely related one fights with sticks and stones; against the distantly related, with bow and arrow, intending to kill rather than wound. See P. C. Lloyd, *Africa in Social Change*, pp. 34ff.

[42] Johnson, *History of the Yorubas*, pp. 131, 247ff., 289ff.; Jacob Egharevba, *The Benin Laws and Customs* (Lagos, 1947), pp. 32ff.; also J. F. Ade Ajayi and Robert Smith, *Yoruba Warfare in the Nineteenth Century* (Ibadan, 1964).

[43] Nadel, *A Black Byzantium*, pp. 108ff. Nupe raids, rebellions, and military expeditions were conducted with considerable regard for appropriate etiquette, but they had a ruinous effect on Nupe fortunes, as Frobenius shows in *Und Afrika Sprach*, Vol. II, 272ff., 286ff., 300ff.

[44] See Heath, trans., *A Chronicle of Abuja*; S. J. Hogben and A.H.M. Kirk-Greene, *The Emirates of Northern Nigeria* (London, 1966); Forde and Kaberry, eds., *West African Kingdoms in the Nineteenth Century*.

[45] See Johann Ludwig Krapf, *Reisen in Ost-Afrika, ausgefuehrt in den Jahren 1837–1855* (Stuttgart, 1858; reissue, 1964), Part I, p. 233, Part II, p. 288. Also

only between territorial segments, but also between the lineages composing each segment was supposed to find expression either in open fighting or in the acceptance of the fact that a dispute ought not to be settled in any but a belligerent way.[46] And similar dispositions prevailed among the Amba of Uganda, who recognized the village as the war-making group. In this area warfare was conducted according to the rules of the feud. If a man of village A killed a man living in village B, the members of village B felt themselves bound to avenge his death by killing someone in village A. That is to say, a village party seeking to avenge the death of one of its members did not make an effort to seek out the killer himself. Instead, it was satisfied if it could kill any member of his village. The practice of this type of feud was officially superseded by the imposition of English principles of law and order, but the values underlying it have been found to continue to play an important part in intervillage relations today.[47]

Struggle was omnipresent also in interlineage relations among the pastoral northern Somali (at the Horn of Africa). In this Muslim community, rancor and enmity persisted even after compensation had been offered and accepted by way of settling cases arising from serious injury or homicide. Unprepared to accept any settlement as final, individuals and groups were ever ready to resort to violence. Somali destinies were thus caught in a perpetual vicious circle of dispute, negotiation, conciliation, and further feuding and dissension—a traditional pattern that modern Somali nationalism has not yet superseded or replaced.[48] Organized attacks on life or property were also a normal thing between Nuba hill communities, even of the same tribe; and once intergroup hostility had become settled or permanent, every man in one community was automatically a sworn enemy of every individual in the other group, free to fight and kill without observing restraints. Not even the rainmaker could assure tribal unity or prevent communal attempts at secession. Despite his powers as the major representative of superior occult forces, who was presumed to be capable of divining events, inflicting supernatural punishments, giving or withholding victory, and, most importantly, stopping the rain, he remained passive when it came to assuring internal

Coupland, *East Africa and Its Invaders*, pp. 343ff.; Roland Oliver and Gervase Mathew, eds., *History of East Africa*, Vol. I (Oxford, 1963), 303ff., on the Kamba; H. E. Lambert, *Kikuyu Social and Political Institutions* (London and New York, 1956); G.W.B. Huntingford, *The Nandi of Kenya; Tribal Control in a Pastoral Society* (London, 1953).

[46] E. E. Evans-Pritchard, *The Nuer; A Description of the Modes of Livelihood and Political Institutions of a Nilotic People* (Oxford, 1940, repr. 1950), especially the chapter on "The Political System."

[47] E. H. Winter, "The Enemy Within; Amba Witchcraft and Sociological Theory," in John Middleton and E. H. Winter, eds., *Witchcraft and Sorcery in East Africa* (London, 1963), p. 279.

[48] I. M. Lewis, *A Pastoral Democracy*, pp. 242–266.

peace. Furthermore, his jurisdiction seemed deliberately ambiguous because it coexisted and often conflicted with that of the war leader, who was charged with leadership in actual war situations and who claimed superior magic. Other sets of conflict were apt to arise, since the rainmaker as well as the war chief were frequently challenged by rivals; and in such cases the entire community was delivered up to the reign of chaos, as interpersonal enmities hardened into chronic social feuds, with successive generations caught up in a net of clashing prophesies and contradictory advice.[49]

In the great composite societies or tributary systems, meanwhile, where unifying administrative structures were usually tenuous and ambiguous, belligerence on the part of rulers and ruled was naturally taken for granted, as earlier discussions have shown.[50] Its major manifestation was the revolt, with vassals and other subordinate chieftains forever eager to test the limits of their dependence, and with central authorities equally determined to maintain their uneasy control over the realm. War was thus waged more or less regularly by the kings or paramount chiefs in the imperial domains of West Africa and the Sudan when unruly behavior on the part of subject peoples required this type of administrative action, and when rebellious vassals had to be reconquered or warded off.[51] Here, as in other regions—as, for example, those dominated by the Ngoni, Zulu, and Swazi—established regimes could last only as long as the martial tradition of government was maintained.

Other types of institutionalized conflict within societies relate to slavery. Indeed, the prodigious incidence of this phenomenon, upon which observers have commented from early times onward, convinced Leo Frobenius that Africa was "the classical land of slavery."[52] This conclusion was reached after the continent had been subjected for centuries to the slave trade of both the Arabs and the Europeans. It is important to remember, however, that slavery and slave raiding were not only wellestablished practices in Negro Africa before they were activated in new and virulent forms, first by the onslaught of Islam and later the Atlantic slave trade; they were also generally sanctioned by the inner normative

[49] Nadel, *The Nuba*, pp. 147ff., 452ff.

[50] *Supra*, Ch. 7.

[51] Compare, for example, R. E. Bradbury, *The Benin Kingdom and the Edo-Speaking Peoples of South-Western Nigeria* (London, 1957), pp. 44ff.; Johnson, *History of the Yorubas*, ch. 12 and ch. 14; Y. Urvoy, *Histoire de l'empire du Bornou*, pp. 51ff., 62ff., 75ff.; and M. G. Smith, *Government in Zazzau*, on the inherent instability in the hierarchical relations between Zaria and its vassal states on the one hand, and Sokoto, its suzerain, on the other.

[52] *Menschenjagden und Zweikaempfe*, p. 202; also p. 212 on the alliance for slave dealing between the kingdoms of Kongo and Portugal. Compare Murdock, *Africa*, p. 297, to the effect that slavery is universal among the southern Bantu, and p. 37, that slavery is an aspect of "African Despotism."

orders of societies great and small, whose strength and cohesion derived not from concepts of individual liberty and egalitarianism, but rather from respect for nonhuman vital forces and intricate gradations of social status. All forms of African enslavement, whether or not they are viewed as expressions of social conflict, are therefore best discussed in this general context of permissible discrimination.

Domestic slavery, widespread in the continent, might ensue in full conformity with custom when a man pawned or sold his child or wife in deference to debt, "the great enslaver";[53] when a tribunal decreed it as legal punishment, for adultery, for example; or when society had to rid itself of undesirable elements. Commenting on conditions in Sierra Leone and the Sherbro at the end of the eighteenth century, Matthews observes that slavery or death were, after all, the major punishments for nearly every crime, just as they were the only options for the treatment of prisoners of war.[54] And the same conclusion is related in 1847 by a Portuguese traveller in Central Africa, who was told by Muata ya Mvo that "it is customary for us to sell as slaves those who commit murder or robbery, and those who are guilty of adultery, insubordination, and sorcery," and in 1863 by Burton, who heard the chiefs of Bonny in southern Nigeria begging openly for a relaxation of the rules against slavery "in order that they might get rid of their criminals."[55]

Other specific purposes served by slavery were dictated by prevalent considerations of political power and prestige. Many royal and chiefly establishments were so dependent upon slaves as working forces, symbols of authority, or members of retinues in military campaigns, court ceremonies, and funeral rites that slaves had to be acquired from without.[56] To raid neighboring realms for slaves, enslave the captured and de-

---

[53] See Wolfson, *Pageant of Ghana*, pp. 144–147, for excerpts from a memorandum by Sir Benjamin Pine (1857) bearing on "the universal prevalence of domestic slavery throughout the Gold Coast." After explaining that slaves may be generally divided into three classes—those born in their masters' families, those purchased, and those "pawns or persons who have been pledged by their relatives, masters or themselves, for repayment of a debt with fifty per cent interest," and that enslavement takes many forms, Pine writes: "For debt is the great enslaver; and all the customs, institutions and habits of the people tend to produce it and supply it with victims." *Ibid.*, p. 145.

[54] Matthews, *Reise nach Sierra Leone*, discusses at considerable length in his Seventh Letter the various incidents of slavery and the slave trade as he observed them in the Sierra Leone region. Here, too, parents often pawn their children, he reports. Appalled by his findings, Matthews expressed the thought that slavery could never be abolished in Africa. See also Barth, *Travels*, Vol. I, 439, 527, on "the quiet course of domestic slavery."

[55] Sir Richard F. Burton, *Mission to Gelele, King of Dahome* (London, 1893), Vol. II, 184, note 1. See Meek, *Law and Authority*, pp. 6–9, for a summary account of such testimonies in this part of Africa.

[56] Compare *supra*, Ch. 7, where the subject is treated in connection with the organization of greater societies.

192

feated, or insist on tribute in the form of slaves were, in considerable measure, adjunct activities of administration, as it were, even as they were often corollaries of the customary martial style of life.[57]

All of these practices have, no doubt, always lent themselves to abuse, even in the strict context of indigenous African value systems. But they were bound to degenerate in ways offensive and unsettling to the native Negro orders under the influence first, of Egyptian and Arab notions of slavery, and next, of Islamic forms of war, religious fervor, imperialism, and trade.

This confluence of African and Asian dispositions[58] toward the use of human beings was already recorded about A.D. 80 in *The Periplus of the Erythraaen Sea*,[59] which relays the information that slaves of the better sort were at that time brought to Egypt from East Africa in increasing numbers. But its exploitation on a massive scale came with the establishment of Arab colonies on the East African coast, where Negroes were enslaved for export to Egypt, other Mediterranean lands, Arabia, Persia, India, and even China, or consigned to slave labor in such Arab states as Zanzibar, where they accounted in the nineteenth century for 150,000 out of 200,000 inhabitants.[60] And very similar developments shaped the destinies of societies in West and Central Africa. Here, as in East Africa, Muslims espoused the twin causes of war and enslavement in a more determined manner than they did elsewhere in the world of unbelievers. The major reason for this discriminating approach may well have been the color prejudice and sense of ethnic and intellectual superiority toward "the blacks" that appears to have possessed the Arabs as well as other Islamized peoples in their actual dealings with Negroes, in counter-

---

[57] See, for example, contemporary accounts (written in 1889) from the Kingdom of Buganda, where it is pointed out that slaves were drawn from the surrounding countries, chiefly Bunyoro and Busoga, and that they were acquired by warlike excursions. If acquired in excess of the master's requirements, slaves were bartered for cattle, or, after the advent of the Arabs, sold for cowrie shells. John Roscoe, *The Baganda; An Account of Their Native Customs and Beliefs* (London, 1911), p. 14; cf. also Edwin S. Haydon, *Law and Justice in Buganda* (London, 1960), pp. 64–66.

[58] Compare *supra*, Ch. 7.

[59] Wilfred H. Schoff, trans. and ed. (New York, 1912). On the antiquity of the slave trade see Diedrich Westermann, *Geschichte Afrikas* (Cologne, 1952), pp. 62, 64.

[60] Coupland, *East Africa and Its Invaders*, pp. 30ff., 183. See J. L. Krapf, *Reisen in Ost-Afrika* (Stuttgart 1858; reissue, Stuttgart 1964), Part I, pp. 182, 223, 318, 337, and Part II, pp. 279ff. for descriptions of the incidents of slavery as observed by this explorer. Also Joseph E. Harris, *The African Presence in Asia; Consequences of the East African Slave Trade* (Evanston, Ill., 1971), 27ff. on the slave traffic to Arabia and the Persian Gulf region, the role of Zanzibar and other slave marts, and maps on the scope of the trade. See pp. 38ff. on the technicalities of the trade; p. 44 to the effect that the Bahr el Ghazal, southwest of Ethiopia, appears to have been the major source of slaves, with between 80,000 and 100,000 slaves exported from this area between 1875 and 1879.

point to the official Koranic precepts stipulating egalitarianism. This thesis has been carefully documented by Bernard Lewis in rebuttal of the myth that Muslims are free of racial prejudices.[61] It explains why Ethiopians, Egyptians, and other North African peoples were held in considerable esteem—with Nubians occupying an intermediate position[62]—whereas pagan Negroes, described by a Persian author of the tenth century as "people distant from the standards of humanity," and by Ibn Khaldun as the only people who accept slavery "owing to their low degree of humanity and their proximity to the animal stage,"[63] were hunted relentlessly in their native lands, even as they were converted to the faith, and why black slaves were singled out for rough labor in domestic and administrative employment from which "white slaves" were exempt.

The major West African agents of this dual mandate of enslavement and benefaction through conversion were the Fulani, who viewed themselves proudly as "white" and superior to the blacks when Mungo Park observed them toward the end of the eighteenth century.[64] Following "their instinctive principle of perpetually extending their dominion and sway,"[65] and indulging continuously in their "passion for slave raiding,"[66] these adventurous tribes denuded the countryside and degraded native societies, as they built new types of states and initiated new patterns of regional relations by activating significant parallelisms and convergences between Islamic and pagan styles of life.[67]

The symbiotic political systems that evolved from this interplay are exemplified by the slave states of northern and central Nigeria. In describing Adamawa in mid-nineteenth century as a "Mohammedan Kingdom ingrafted upon a mixed stock of pagan tribes"[68] in the heart of Central Africa, Barth has this to say:

[61] "Race and Colour in Islam," *Encounter*, 35, No. 2 (August, 1970), pp. 18ff. See p. 35, n. 20 to the effect that "slavery in the Islamic world still awaits a comprehensive study." On its massive and persistent incidence, and for a discussion of the distinction between white and black slaves, see Gabriel Baer, "Slavery in Nineteenth Century Egypt," *Journal of African History*, 8, No. 3 (1967), 417–441.

[62] Compare in this connection Frobenius' theory of the special cultural and historic position occupied in African by the Nubians; *supra*, pp. 127–130.

[63] Charles Issawi, *An Arab Philosophy of History* (London, 1950), p. 98, for this translation: Ibn Khaldûn, *The Muqaddimah; An Introduction to History*, F. Rosenthal, trans. 3 vols. (New York, 1958), Vol. I, 301, renders the passage somewhat differently. See Lewis, "Race and Colour," p. 36, note 41, on this subject.

[64] *Travels*, Vol. I, 57.

[65] Barth, *Travels*, Vol. II, 554; on tribute in slaves, *ibid.*, p. 552.

[66] F. D. Lugard, *Colonial Report* (London, 1903), p. 21. But see *ibid.*, p. 26, to the following effect: "I believe myself that the future of the virile races of this Protectorate lies largely in the regeneration of the Fulani. Their ceremonial, their coloured skins, their mode of life and habits of thought, appeal more to the native population than the prosaic businesslike habits of the Anglo-Saxon can ever do."

[67] Compare *supra*, n. 58.   [68] Barth, *Travels*, Vol. II, 127.

Slavery exists on an immense scale in this country, and there are many private individuals who have more than a thousand slaves. In this respect the governor of the whole province is not the most powerful man, being outstripped by the governors of Chámba and Kóncha—for this reason, that Mohammed Lowel has all his slaves settled in rumdé or slave-villages, where they cultivate grain for his use or profit, while the above-mentioned officers, who obtain all their provision in corn from subjected pagan tribes, have their whole host of slaves constantly at their disposal; and I have been assured that some of the head slaves of these men have as many as a thousand slaves each under their command, with whom they undertake occasional expeditions for their masters. I have been assured, also, that Mohammed Lowel receives every year in tribute, besides horses and cattle, about five thousand slaves, though this seems a large number.[69]

At that time, Barth remarks, the Islamic conquerors were in possession only of detached settlements, with the intermediate country still in the hands of the pagans. But fear of attack and enslavement, and revenge in response to injury, combined with the general contagion carried by slave hunts and military exploits to trigger an unending course of war and lawlessness. The ruler of Bagirmi, attacked by Bornu, was thus induced to subdue a great many pagan countries to the south and then levy upon them fixed tribute, consisting almost entirely of slaves. This tribute, Barth continues, the pagan chiefs could produce only by waging war with their neighbors, or by staging predatory expeditions upon caravans.[70]

The same chain of war eventually destroyed the once-impressive kingdom of Nupe. Weakened by internecine princely rivalries, divided by local pretenders and Fulani usurpers, yet mustering the strength, at times, to stage rebellions or cope with internal revolts, it had been reduced to a petty emirate by the deployment of Fulani intrigue and aggression when the British conquered it in 1900. And a similar trans-

---

[69] *Ibid.*, pp. 191–192. Before the Fulani occupied the region, slave-hunting expeditions by the people of Bornu had often extended to the very core of Adamawa. See *ibid.*, Vol. II, 128–130. For Clapperton's report on the ratio of slaves to freemen in a Nigerian city, see *supra*, Ch. 7, n. 25. Elsewhere, too, slaves often outnumbered masters. Matthews estimated during his sojourn in eighteenth-century Sierra Leone that three-fourths of the inhabitants among the tribes he was familiar with were slaves. In this area a major chief ordinarily possessed about 200 slaves; among the Mandingoes, by contrast, he was more likely to have between 700 and 1000. See Matthews', *Reise nach Sierra Leone*, Seventh Letter.

[70] *Travels*, Vol. II, 556, 557 to the effect that the caravan road from Fezzan to Bornu was constantly under attack. For other comments on the subject of slave hunts and slavery, *ibid.*, Vol. I, 311, 515, Vol. II, 98, 179, 314, 326, 361, 394, 396; Vol. III, 606. For earlier testimonies see in particular the journals of the European explorers, for example, Park, *Travels in the Interior Districts of Africa*, Vol. I, 55, 75, 133, 185ff., and 315–320 on the coffles of slaves with which he traveled.

formation affected Abuja, to the east of Nupe; for its fortunes, too, were tossed about in ceaseless internal and external wars, with slavery the mutual focus of contending forces. This nineteenth-century emirate, its modern spokesmen tell us,[71] had been founded by Abu Ja, whose praise song was:

> Light of skin, lord and master
> Of the walled town
> And in the open field
> First to draw blood.[72]

Populated "in olden times" by several pagan tribes, all part of the vast reservoir of potential slaves upon which northern invaders preyed at will, Abuja had originally been the southwestern part of the Kingdom of Zassau, the southernmost of the seven Hausa states, whose traditional function it was to provide slaves for the other six by virtue of a quasi-confederate arrangement that made it incumbent upon Gobir in the north to defend the other states from invasion by outside forces.[73] The relentless and successful aggressions of the Fulani, notably those connected with the nineteenth-century *jihad*, put an end to the independent exploits of most of these Nigerian states, but they are said to have been largely ineffectual in respect to Abuja. This was so, the native chroniclers proudly maintain, because the rulers of Abuja allowed themselves no respite from fighting, just as they never ceased raiding neighboring peoples so as to secure the needed slaves and bolster the emirate's waning strength.[74]

A review of the general pattern thus imprinted upon the region shows that no exit from the round of war was really open either to the victorious or to the defeated. For the continuous interaction of pagan and Islamic traditions had produced parasitic political systems that were inextricably linked to slavery; rulers were slave dealers on a grand scale, slaves often vastly outnumbered masters, and the economy was greatly— sometimes totally—dependent upon slaves as laborers, artisans, and soldiers. In each of these domains, then, unrest, instability, and lawlessness had to be taken for granted. And the same was true of the massive incidence of institutionalized abuse and suffering that issued as a matter of course from the merger of pagan and Islamic forces of social discrimination, exploitation, and oppression, as well as from the brutal, albeit shortlived and geographically limited, impact of the American slave

---

[71] Heath, trans., *A Chronicle of Abuja*, pp. 4ff. For scholarly accounts of the tangled relations between the various Hausa states on the one hand, and those societies and the Fulani on the other, see authorities cited earlier.

[72] *Ibid.*, p. 8.　　　　　　　　　　　　　[73] Compare *supra*, p. 126.

[74] *A Chronicle of Abuja*, pp. 18–26.

trade.[75] In sum, African conditions of enslavement spawned very distinct varieties of conflict. However, and not surprisingly, they also suggested many ingenious, socially constructive ways of turning bondage into mutual security, using an immutable conflict as the cornerstone for a new modus vivendi between superior and inferior human groupings, or of absorbing the adversary and, at times, even the cause of the adversity, by exerting will, instinct, or imagination.

For example, enslavement is known to have provided moral incentives as well as organizational models for the formation of politically effective slave bands, the staging of successful rebellions, or the usurpation of power on the part of individual slave leaders, who might then become chiefs and slaveowners in their turn—a process often conducive to a reversal of the roles of master and slave.[76] That is to say, the traditional

[75] The major work on this subject is Philip D. Curtin, *The Atlantic Slave Trade: A Census* (Madison, Wisc., 1969). Fage, *Introduction to the History of West Africa*, pp. 97ff. concludes that the Ashanti Union, which had begun as a movement of national resistance to encroaching neighboring peoples, developed into a vast organization for slave raiding and trading in response to the advantages offered by the Atlantic slave trade. But see the same author's "Slavery and the Slave Trade in the Context of West African History," *Journal of African History*, 10, No. 3 (1969), 393–404, where the view is expressed that slavery and the making, buying, and selling of slaves were means by which certain privileged individuals in West African society sought to mobilize the wealth inherent in the land and the people on it, and that this process had already gone some distance before the Europeans arrived. Compare Westermann, *The African To-day and To-morrow*, p. 93, for the reminder that the softening or abolition of war, slavery, and the slave trade, all recognized institutions in pre-European Africa that did not suggest either moral revulsion or its opposite, was due entirely to Europe's various colonial administrations.

[76] For instances of the spirit of combination among slaves in West Africa see Hodgkin, *Nigerian Perspectives*, p. 287. This excerpt is from Hope Masterton Waddell, *Twenty-Nine Years in the West Indies and Central Africa* (London, 1863), pp. 377–379 and 476–478, and bears on the formation of a covenant of blood for mutual protection on the part of slaves in Calabar, and on the native king's way of coping with this movement. On the same subject and on slave revolts in Old Calabar, see Dike, *Trade and Politics in the Niger Delta*, pp. 152–159. See also J. F. Ade Ajayi, "Samuel Ajayi Crowther of Oyo," in Philip D. Curtin, ed., *Africa Remembered; Narratives by West Africans from the Era of the Slave Trade* (Madison, Wisc., 1967), pp. 299ff. Matthews, *Reise nach Sierra Leone*, Seventh Letter, on the great slave revolt against the ruling Mandingoes in 1785, which was staged when the warriors of the master race had gone to war. The slaves killed those who were left, burned the rice that had ripened, then withdrew into their slave towns and barred all roads from which the Mandingoes might have expected help.

Writing about "War Towns in Sierra Leone; A Study in Social Change," *Africa*, 38, No. 1 (January 1968), D. J. Siddle describes how each of more than one thousand defensive villages was supported by a variable number of satellite villages, often manned by slaves. The need to staff these villages promoted a considerable increase in slavery in an area already saturated by war and slavery.

On the careers of some of the presumptive usurpers and slave chiefs in the western Sudan, see Monteil, *La Légende du Ouagadou*, pp. 403ff. These men, who had their own titles, prerogatives, and notions of mythical origin, were able

normative order within a given African society validated and subsumed not only slavery, but also certain modes of opposing slavery, perhaps because neither had ever been conceptualized in the form of ideology or principle. Furthermore, where slavery was linked to total residential segregation, as when slave populations were confined to slave towns, slave villages, or slave quarters, it often had long-range effects comparable to those induced by normal processes of fission and segmentation, in the sense that it could make for the gradual emergence of a new small, morally unified community—traditional Africa's base unit of social and political organization. In some of these situations slave populations buttressed their collective identities by imitating the patterns of conflict of the master race. In Timbuctoo, for instance, which Tuareg nobles were in the habit of looting almost at will—where banditry, robbery, and murder were established institutions, and where even the semblance of civic unity was missing—the enslaved, too, had organized themselves and their intergroup relations in accordance with locally prevalent practice. Visiting the city in the last decade of French rule, Miner found that Tuareg slaves (the Bela) and Arab slaves coexisted in a state of chronic enmity, taking every opportunity to lord it over each other and often indulging in vicious, uninhibited fighting.[77] In some of the great societies of the western Sudan, by contrast, where few inhabitants can actually claim descent from nonslave origins, but where ruling elites nonetheless continue to this day to hold fast to the myth of a clear distinction between slavery and nonslavery, whole empires had, in fact, been kept going by a bloc of twenty-four so-called slave tribes.[78]

Whether in empires, cities, or small folk communities, slavery was indeed "interwoven with the whole framework of society."[79] This meant that the destinies of slaves and nonslaves were forever intermingling, either in response to coexistence in close quarters, when intermarriage took its course even in the face of an originally strict interdiction; or imperceptibly and ex post facto, as it were, when mergers of formerly disparate entities were sanctioned by the structuring force of mythical thought or clearly perceived advantage. For example, the Portuguese "prazo system," which was based on the granting of crown land, could

to lead slave peoples into freedom by means of revolt. For an excellent review and analysis of the role of slavery and the slave trade in the organization of West Africa's Islamic states and empires, see Mauny, *Tableau géographique*, pp. 336–343, 377ff., 422ff.

[77] Miner, *The Primitive City of Timbuctoo*, pp. 252ff. Compare *supra*, Ch. 12, "Occult Games."

[78] Compare *supra*, p. 127.

[79] See Wolfson, *Pageant of Ghana*, pp. 144–145, for Sir Benjamin Pine's discussion of Brodie Cruickshank, *Eighteen Years on the Gold Coast*, 2 vols. (London, 1853).

thus spawn a rather traditional type of African chieftaincy in the Zambezi region; for not only did the prazo holder often stand in the place of chief to the indigenous inhabitants, who remained on their land as free "colonos," but the resulting clientship was also capable of further evolution, as slaves sought protection from war or famine by voluntary attachment to the prazo holder. These retinues tended to desert, however, when the situation appeared secure, in order then to regroup around a stronger man or one of the independent chiefs. In other words, the slave was by no means the passive partner in this "marriage of Europe and Africa."[80] Livingstone tells of meeting an African on the Zambezi who had recently sold himself to a Portuguese master because he was "all alone in the world," but who then proceeded to use his own purchase price for setting himself up in the world.[81] And Lugard illustrates the same proposition—namely, that freedom and enslavement are not necessarily experienced as irreconcilable opposites in Africa—by noting that "the slaves freed by Mackenzie with such a big flourish of trumpets value their freedom so little that two that he knows well named Ferunzi and Abechizi went back of their own accord to their master Mbaruk bin Rāchid."[82] Ferunzi's wife, meanwhile, also a freed slave, cared so little for the freedom paper for which $25 had been paid, that she left it unclaimed when she joined her husband in slavery again. By way of further comment on some of these disconcerting dispositions, Lugard notes that other liberated slaves may sell their papers, spend the proceeds, and then either go voluntarily into slavery to their old masters, or join the nearest village of runaways.[83]

Traditional African patterns of rebellion, civil war, war of succession and enslavement—to name only the dominant forms of internal warfare —are as various as the social and political systems in which they have been recorded, and it would be misleading, therefore, to subsume them in simple generic norms or categories. Several general conclusions are inescapable, however. It appears clear that peace, as this condition is understood in the West, is not a prerequisite for the maintenance of the inner public order; that conflict is allowed to express itself in violence; that enslavement, whether muted, condoned, or enforced by war, does

[80] For this analysis see M.D.D. Newitt, "The Portuguese on the Zambezi: An Historical Interpretation of the Prazo System," *Journal of African History*, 10, No. 1 (1969), 67–85.

[81] David Livingstone and Charles Livingstone, *Narrative of an Expedition to the Zambezi and Its Tributaries* (New York, 1866), pp. 49–50.

[82] Margery Perham, ed., *The Diaries of Lord Lugard*, Vols. I, II, and III (Evanston, Ill., 1959); Vol. IV (Evanston, Ill., 1963); see Vol. I, *East Africa*, November 1889 to December 1890, pp. 56, 57 for some of his prognoses, including the view that "the time for the total abolition of domestic slavery has hardly come yet, but it is fast approaching."

[83] *Ibid.*, p. 56.

not invalidate the inner social order; and that warfare between component units of the community, far from being a breach of the norm, is accepted as an organic part of the conflict-resolving machinery—provided, of course, that it is used for purposes considered permissible in a given society. But whether the allowed objective is cattle, slaves, or women; the exercise of vengeance, or of punishment; the acquisition of grazing or water rights; the realization of a desire for aggrandizement, the allocation of power, or the reshuffling of available power, the fact remains that violence in the rendering of tension and hostility carries no opprobrium. Sanctioned by the prevalent systems of values and beliefs,[84] it provides in one form or another the structuring principles for the education of men as well as for the administration of society. Indeed, internal war and organization for war, as well as other forms of violence and conflict, are more likely to sustain than to disrupt existing schemes of government, whether in the village, the tribe, the subtribe, the clan, the kingdom, the multikingdom, or the empire.

[84] *Supra*, Part III.

· 14 ·

WAR AND POLITICAL IDENTITY
IN INTER-AFRICAN
RELATIONS

When one shifts the focus from the plane of government to that of the political society within which central and subsidiary administrations function, the conclusion is somewhat different. In this context war and other forms of physical violence, both organized and unorganized, usually had disruptive effects. That is to say, they contributed greatly to the instability and indeterminacy of Africa's political entities, even as they provided the major impetus for the joining of ethnically and spatially separate communities.

This was so for several reasons. Internal feuds, rebellions, wars of succession, and civil wars were, after all, often successful in the sense that they conduced to cleavages and group secessions. As sons, brothers, nephews, rebels, subordinate chiefs, or satellite rulers set up their own independent governments, established political societies were broken up or otherwise altered from their original identity. New polities arose, and these, again, might either segment further, attract accretions in their turn, or coalesce with different groups, unless they disappeared altogether among the surrounding segmentary societies. Local patterns of fission, or fission with fusion, differed, of course. Some were innate, as in Nuer society, where central power was often frittered away by permanent feuds between sections, and where what looked like a tribe one day would appear as two tribes the next day. Others were institutionalized, as in the Azande system, where "fission with addition" was a recognized mode of enlarging the empire, and where it was taken for granted that the defeated party in a civil war would secede.[1] In the realms of the Mossi, Yoruba, Zulu, and those of the Interlacustrine Bantus, by contrast, the process was usually spontaneous, for here a nuclear society was apt to spawn offshoots that would, in turn, become founding cells for new societies.[2] Fission and fusion, then, were complementary aspects of one

[1] For an analysis of this system, see P.T.W. Baxter and Audrey Butt, *The Azande, and Related Peoples of the Anglo-Egyptian Sudan and Belgian Congo* (London, 1953).

[2] See Gluckman, *Custom and Conflict in Africa*, pp. 32ff., 44ff., especially his comments on the formation of the Matabele nation. Compare Skinner, *The Mossi*, for the conclusion that Mossi kingdoms remained essentially segmentary, despite centralizing forms of rule; Richards, ed., *East African Chiefs*, pp. 34, 178, for similar tendencies among the Interlacustrine Bantus.

another in many instances,[3] but everywhere the accent was persistently on fragmentation, thus justifying the conclusion that "most African states are more likely to have constant secessions than they are to remain united."[4]

It should also be noted that political identities were floating and unstable because they were being shaped and reshaped by belligerent actions from without. Bands of intruding strangers or conquering armies—the former often invested with heroic qualities in mythological accounts of the founding societies—were thus accepted throughout Africa as natural agents of political change. These might sweep over adjacent territories, triggering flights, migrations, and segmentations among the peoples they displaced; or they might settle among the conquered as ruling elites; or, again, they might merge with them in new symbiotic arrangements.[5] Whether the foreign aggressor came from near or afar, however; whether the military activity emanated from settled or nomadic, pagan or Muslim Africans; and whether it took the form of sustained raids or full-fledged campaigns, the effect of each intervention was a modification of the political identity not only of the victimized, but also of the victorious community. Conquest states, snowball states, multikingdom conglomerates, and other political systems arose in this fashion, yet few could maintain themselves in their newly acquired identity for any length of time. Caught in the rhythm of war and counterwar, raid and counterraid; precariously held together by military rule, slave raiding or the levying of tribute, political entities were thus forever expanding and contracting, rising and dissolving. These circumstances fully justify the following conclusion that "if we look widely enough at the history of Africa, we are looking at a picture in which states like the Zulu rose to temporary power over neighbours, persisted for a time with the dominance of the cycle of rebellions, and then broke up, either under external attack or under the

[3] On the relationship between political identity and social structure in Tale society, see Meyer Fortes, *The Dynamics of Clanship among the Tallensi; Being the First Part of an Analysis of the Social Structure of a Trans-Volta Tribe* (London and New York, 1945), and *The Web of Kinship among the Tallensi; The Second Part of an Analysis of the Social Structure of a Trans-Volta Tribe* (London, 1949). This scholar concludes that Tale society is best defined as a sociogeographic region, since the people are spread across the land, wedged between other communities. Although the Tallensi think of themselves as a common polity, they cannot be marked off as a distinct group. Lacking government as well as history, they are held together only by cults of the earth and of lineage ancestry. Even enmity toward neighboring communities has not induced a sense of internal unity among them. Fortes describes the Tale social structure as the product of tensions between corporate units in a system of balanced ties and cleavages. These are so ordered that there are both regions of high tension, where groups are coupled in polar opposition, and regions of low tension, where the units of structure are articulated in complementary relations to one another.
[4] Gluckman, *Order and Rebellion in Tribal Africa*, p. 33, also p. 40.
[5] Compare *supra*, Chs. 6 and 7 on the creation of "Greater Societies."

pressure of civil wars aggravated by increasing pressures on land through increase of population, or because they grew in size beyond the limits their technology and economic system would carry."[6]

In view of these facts, then, it is hardly possible to circumscribe Africa's political communities in terms that do justice to the actualities as experienced by African contemporaries. Since territorial boundaries, ethnic components, and centers of power were shifting everywhere, political identities, too, were always fluid, and phenomena that are in constant flux naturally elude precise definition by fiat of theory coming from without.[7] Only one common criterion of self-definition emerges from the multifarious records, namely, hostility to "the other." And, among the various species of hostile behavior, again, it is war and the readiness to resort to war that endows a given grouping of peoples at a given moment with the consciousness of being politically unified, even as it suggests the configuration of the enemy.

In deference to these controlling dispositions, intersocietal, intertribal, or regional relations were inevitably conceived as bellicose relations. A Bemba tribesman thus recollects that "people honoured us more because they were afraid of us," because "we are fiercer than other tribes," and because "we had wonderful war magic."[8] And the same general norms of perceiving the self and the other are relayed by Little's study of Mendeland (Sierra Leone and Liberia): "War was the major industry of the Mende, and their estimation of another people's worth was based largely on the latter's prowess in conducting it."[9] Rattray's portrayal of the Ashanti is to like effect: this people's remarkable persistence as a clearly identified, politically successful nation was due in large measure to the continuous cultivation by martial means of their self-image as the bravest and most warlike of all peoples in the region.[10] Here, as elsewhere—for example, in Dahomey and Benin—the cause of regional reputation was buttressed assiduously by the staging of regular military campaigns and the maintenance at all times of a fully credible, generally

[6] Gluckman, *Order and Rebellion in Tribal Africa*, p. 40. Very similar conclusions have been reached by Westermann, *Geschichte Afrikas*, pp. 29ff., and Robert Cornevin, *Histoire de l'Afrique des origines à nos jours* (Paris, 1956). Shaka's military achievements and the creation of a Zulu nation are also analyzed by E. A. Ritter, *Shaka Zulu* (London, 1955), where it is pointed out that an original domain, consisting of 100 square miles and 500 men, grew to comprise 200,000 square miles and 50,000 men at the time of the great conqueror's death. After this event, it is interesting to note, the old hierarchical Zulu mode of life reasserted itself, with almost no visible evidence of Shaka's twelve-year rule.

[7] Compare *supra*, Parts I and II on these and other obstacles in the path of scholarly efforts to find the typical that comprehends the particular and the diverse, and the constant that resists all flux.

[8] Perham, ed., *Ten Africans*, pp. 24, 29, 54.

[9] *The Mende of Sierra Leone*, p. 52.

[10] *Ashanti Law and Constitution*, p. 120.

known threat of impending invasions into neighboring lands.[11] Military exploits of this kind, then, must be understood not only as the ineluctable consequences of an inner social order that was dependent upon organization for war, but also as the indispensable condition for sustaining prestige in what, for lack of a better word, may still be called foreign relations. This aspect of political identity in traditional Africa appears to have been clearly understood by the British, as when they recognized in their dealings with Sudanese tribes that military strength was a necessary condition for all negotiations.[12]

Not all African peoples were either equally aggressive or equally successful in offensive action. In fact, some seem to have been chronically on the defensive, as previous references have suggested. Furthermore, the linkage between endemic war and political identity was relaxed in some cases by the customary recognition of intricate gradations of aloofness and enmity as indicators of the alien group's identity. In Iboland, for instance, these would find expression in the choice of weapons used, the treatment of the defeated, or in patterns of ending military engagements.[13] It cannot be said, however, that such locally prevalent discriminations or qualifications had the characteristics of a reliable, systematic law of war. For just as political entities were fluid in their war-deduced identities, so also were zones of militant hostility, types of warfare, and purposes of armed involvement.

Viewed in these perspectives, then, war cannot be said to have functioned as a stabilizing or regulating mechanism capable of assuring either the optimum size of the viable community or the optimum radius of predictable regional relations. That is to say, its effect in this context—at least as observed from without—has been altogether different from that registered on the plane of local administration, where resort to physical combat often served to reaffirm the local mythical charter by reestablishing the permissible distance between centers of control, on the one hand, and subject peoples and localities, on the other.

The overwhelming impression left by records of physically violent contacts between politically unified communities is, rather, that in this sphere war reverted to its primary function, namely, as a major value or amalgam of trusted values. As such, it had its own logic and momentum —one apt to defy utilitarian restraints of the kind that can be isolated when, for example, a war of secession is reviewed on its own merits. Once initiated either as a sacred operation, a display of power, an exer-

---

[11] The Dahomeans and the Yoruba staged such expeditions either once a year or every second year. Egharevba, *Benin Laws and Customs*, p. 33, to the effect that the king would declare war about three years after his accession to the throne.

[12] Robert Collins and Richard Herzog, "Early British Administration in the Southern Sudan," *Journal of African History*, 2, No. 1 (1961), 119–135.

[13] Meek, *Law and Authority*, pp. 242–243.

cise in the dynamics of movement, a test of manhood, a quest for chiefly glory, an economic activity, a form of punishment, or a legal sanction designed to keep neighbors in awe and at bay, war was apt to run its contagious course, activating all manner of latent tensions and serving as the needed outlet for such dominant emotions as fear, pride, suspicion, and revenge. Fine distinctions between interpersonal feuds, internal or little wars, and external or big wars were thus easily transgressed or nullified by those actually involved in a belligerent activity, as the following instances illustrate.[14]

An immediate state of regional warfare usually arose in Iboland if a member of one autonomous village group slew a member of another. The fact of the local homicide was made known by the wailing of the murdered man's kin, and by the whistler, who went through the community summoning all warriors. At daybreak these would then set out for the enemy village in a disorganized mass, proceeding to kill anyone they saw. And a similarly inexorable extension of hostilities was commonly expected when the parents of a wife who had abandoned her husband failed to refund the bride price, or when indebtedness and impermissible adultery pitted families in different localities against each other.[15]

A more complex chain reaction in the domain of war is reported from Sierra Leone. Here, Matthews writes, a vast region was plunged into prolonged warfare just because two Sherbro chiefs were unable to settle a personal quarrel.[16] As their respective communities closed ranks behind their leaders, an internecine war was set in motion, which, in turn, became enmeshed first with a war in adjoining foreign communities that had originated when a Bago was killed by a man from a Suzee (Susu) town; and next, with a massive revolt that Mandingo slaves had staged against their masters. And, similarly, we learn from Mungo Park how a war between Kaarta and Bambara was instrumental in desolating the Kaarta region and spreading terror into neighboring states after a few bullocks belonging to a frontier village of Bambara had been stolen by a party of Moors, in order then to be sold to the chief man of a town in Kaarta.[17] As one act of retaliation led to another in an alternation of brief victories and defeats, this particular dispute became entangled with hostilities of a totally different kind in an adjoining foreign place: here,

[14] Compare also *supra*, Chs. 6 and 7 on the formation of conquest states, and Ch. 13 on the relation between government, enslavement, and war.

[15] Meek, *Law and Authority*, pp. 242ff. After stating that wars, being in fact reprisals for injuries received, were an integral part of the legal system, Meek points out that in spite of all the barbarities of Negro warfare, there were certain rules—as, for example, a recognized system of compensation at the close of the war, and accords on which types of weapons were permissible in which circumstances. See *infra*, Chs. 16, 17, and 18 on modes of resolving or settling conflicts.

[16] *Reise nach Sierra Leone*, Fifth Letter.

[17] *Travels*, Vol. I, 83ff., 106ff., 211ff., 223.

where the ruling king lay dying, a fierce succession struggle raged between two sons. With the common people deserting town after town as
each was threatened by total ruin, and changing their allegiance at each
show of advantage, the entire countryside was being despoiled without
restraint. Furthermore, Mungo Park relates, transterritorial slave raids
followed in the wake of these belligerent activities; for while King Daisy
of Kaarta carried off the inhabitants of the towns he had won, the ruler
of Bambara, forced to sue for peace, had to commit himself to the delivery of sizable contingents of slaves in each ensuing year. In yet another
dispute, also described by the noted explorer, similar enmities between
"the King of Foota Torra and Damel King of the Jaloffs" were exacer-
bated by violent modes of propagating the Islamic faith.[18] In this particular instance, "gruesome slaughter" followed, first in obedience to the
motto: "Convert or have your throat cut," and later, when the tides of
fortune changed again, in deference to the dictates of revenge.

Divisive and devastating as the actual effects of these encounters were
upon the region, they were yet absorbed by the imagination not only as
evidence of long-standing intercommunal hostility, but also as unifying
lore; for "the singing men" of the protagonists in battle glorified the general cause of war as they spread their accounts of heroic deed and trick-
ery in all the kingdoms bordering upon the Senegal and Gambia.[19]

The paramountcy of war in the designation of political identity and
the conduct of inter-African affairs,[20] as the records testify, is a faithful
expression of the inner normative order, as this has been discussed earlier. It epitomizes, in particular, the three major determinants of African
conceptions of existence, in terms of which traditional Africa is here being viewed as a culturally unified realm—namely, a nonliterate mythical
mode of thinking in which thought, word, and act are apt to merge, and
in which magic is accepted as the supreme logic in causal relationships;
a sense of time that subsumes past, present, and future in the experience
of the moment; and an absolute commitment to the kinship or tribal
group as a metaphysical community of the living and the dead, in which
the supremacy of ancestral rule is assured by ritual, and from which individuals cannot disengage themselves as autonomous persons.

As the preceding chapter has suggested, these factors are present also
when the function of war is reviewed in the context of internal organization. However, and for reasons cited earlier, their pervasive presence and
continuous interaction are best observed on the plane of intertribal poli-

[18] *Ibid.*, pp. 328, 332ff.

[19] *Ibid.*, p. 332. Bards and minstrels, also known as "griots," are major figures
in many African realms, nowhere more so than in West Africa and the Sudan.
See *infra* Ch. 18 on this subject.

[20] See Ch. 13, note 41 on this subject; also appendix at the end of this chapter.

tics. Here it is clear without reservation that death—the supreme fact of war—is neither conceived as a personal destiny nor presumed to obliterate identities. Since it is linked to life in a system of mystical participation and accepted as a magical phenomenon, capable in its turn of releasing energies vital to the group, it can, in fact, be celebrated even by the losers, as the following moving account from Livingstone's last journals indicates:

> Six men slaves were singing as if they did not feel the weight and degradation of the slave-sticks. I asked the cause of their mirth, and was told that they rejoiced at the idea of "coming back after death and haunting and killing those who had sold them." Some of the words I had to inquire about; for instance the meaning of the words "to haunt and kill by spirit power"; then it was, "Oh, you sent me off to Manga (sea coast), but the yoke is off when I die, and back I shall come to haunt and to kill you."[21]

And the same set of understandings explains why death is inflicted without regard either for human suffering or for such demographic effects as depopulation. Practices of war that are condemned elsewhere as needless atrocities, such as the razing of villages, the killing or mutilation of prisoners, and the slaughter of women and children, are condoned here as natural sequential corollaries of an original military thrust, and as integral aspects of a sacerdotal code in which the shedding and use of human blood have profound symbolic importance. This aspect of intercommunal warfare emerges from the following passage:

> Every warrior endeavoured to obtain the head of an enemy. Having killed his man he cut off his head with a matchet, and then licked from the blade a little of the dead man's blood. It was said that the slayer thereby became identified with the slain, and so was made safe from pursuit by the dead man's ghost. If, on the conclusion of peace, he attended a feast at the dead man's village, he could drink wine, with impunity, which had been made from the dead man's palm-trees! It was even asserted that, by licking the dead enemy's blood, the enemy would become incarnated as the slayer's son, and would thus become an ally instead of an avenger.[22]

[21] Horace Waller, ed., *The Last Journals of David Livingstone in Central Africa. From Eighteen Hundred and Sixty-Five to His Death* (Chicago, 1875), p. 245 (this entry is dated June 24, 1868).

[22] Meek, *Law and Authority*, pp. 243–244. These rites were observed by separate Ibo communities, whose mutually hostile relations are comparable to intertribal relations in other regions. Meek's account continues as follows: "On returning home the head-getter took the head to the grove of Ekwesu (the war-god), where the priest boiled the head and buried the flesh. He poured a libation on the skull, saying: 'Let not your ghost (nkporobia) worry the man who killed you.' Then,

Trust in occult forces also governed the preparation, conduct, and conclusion of military engagements, attitudes to weaponry, and choices of objectives. Whether in Benin, Kikuyu country, or Nuba society, war chiefs were supposed to take counsel with diviners, rainmakers, sorcerers, or priests before embarking on their military expeditions. Fighting men believed themselves invincible as long as they were protected by the appropriate fetishes, amulets, and war medicines. Conversely, the wounded were inclined to believe that they were doomed because their protective charms had failed them.[23] Oaths and curses, being ultimate sacred sanctions in the inner normative order, were also trusted as effective armor and means of maintaining military discipline in actions against foreign foes—a conviction vividly illustrated in recent times by the Mau Mau uprising in Kenya. Indeed, the categories of corporeal and incorporeal weapons, and of military and magical-ritual planning were scarcely distinguished from each other. Strategic thinking might imply the careful selection of war objectives, war camps, or lines of attack, but it could also cover the custom of burying the warriors' knives at the foot of special trees, on the ground that such an action was bound to give the invaders sore and swollen feet.[24] And the same mode of thought condoned the poisoning of spears and arrows, for this practice assured the hallowing, and therewith the potency, of the actual instruments of death.

cutting a yam in two, he waved the pieces over the skull, and threw them on the ground, saying, 'Take this yam and eat it.' Or the priest might perform this rite with a chicken, and then fix the chicken in a cleft bamboo, where it was left to die. The head-getter shaved his head and smeared himself with camwood. He then went to the market and danced round, holding the skull in his left hand and his matchet in his right. After the dance he hung the skull in the roof of his house."

[23] John Goody, "Restricted Literacy in Northern Ghana," in Goody, ed., *Literacy in Traditional Societies* (Cambridge, 1968), pp. 202ff. on the prevalence of Ashanti belief that the Great War Coats, on which written charms were sewn, could ward off all evil, including an enemy's bullets. As Bowdich observed in 1819, it was this confidence that enabled the Ashanti to undertake their daring military enterprises. The Mossi, who often fought with poisoned spears or arrows, believed that most wounded men were doomed because their protective amulets had failed them. This was also the reason, Skinner writes, why a defeated army fleeing the battlefield made no attempt to retrieve the dead and dying. *The Mossi of the Upper Volta*, pp. 104–125. Commenting on the development of the war spirit in Tonga society, Junod writes in *Moeurs et Coutumes des Bantous*, Vol. I, 417–436, that war chants, war dances, and war medicine—notably a special hate medicine—were necessary to inspire the warriors with certainty of victory; and that once war medicine had been administered, a warrior was convinced of his invulnerability, provided he did not turn his back on the enemy. Regarding the custom of mutilating the dead enemy, Junod points out that this was done mainly in order to exploit the corpse for charms and war medicine; and in regard to cannibalism, this author explains that people were convinced that the eating of enemy flesh implied absorption of enemy strength, and thus a diminution or liquidation of enemy power. See *ibid.*, pp. 441ff.

[24] Hobley, *Bantu Beliefs and Magic*, pp. 244ff.; ch. 4, "War and Peace," for this and other customs of war between the Kikuyu, the Kamba, and the Masai.

Informants on nineteenth-century Abuja thus relate that there was found among the late Abu Ja's symbols of office a quiver in which were kept two hundred arrows poisoned at the tip "so that any they might strike would die." The poison was called "the tribe-slayer," for not only the man who was struck by it would die, but everyone who set eyes on the corpse would likewise perish.[25] No difference seems to have been perceived between this stratagem and that of striking terror in the minds of the enemy by actually killing three hundred prisoners, cutting off their heads and putting them on poles. After reporting this particular incident (it relates to the Battle of White Water in 1893) from the annals of interminable war with the Fulani, the chroniclers continue:

> Then our men heard that a certain robe was being brought to the Emir of Nasarawa. Now had they done nothing to prevent it reaching him, they would have been lost, for this was a magic robe, and if he had put it on and gone out to fight wearing it, he must have destroyed them. So the Madawaki chose some of the boldest of his warriors, . . . and other horse and foot, telling them to block the road from Nasarawa and to seize the charm before it could reach the Emir. So they went and hid on the road between Barno and Buga. Then the Nasarawans came, at their head was the Dallatu, but the warriors fell upon them, killing the Dallatu and seizing all the loads together with the magic robe which they brought to the Madawaki.

> Now when the Emir of Nasarawa heard this and learned that his charm had been captured, he was mad with fury. He collected all his men and rushed out to battle, and on that day the Barden Zuba, one of the Abuja warriors, was killed. After this the Emir conceived a stratagem. He found some white gunpowder and sent certain evil men of his company by night to the Abuja camp. At dawn the camp was fired, and the fire spread over the whole camp so that it was utterly destroyed and not a hut remained standing. Then when the Nasarawans saw that the fire had taken hold, they fell upon the men of Abuja to slaughter them. But when our men saw this, they left the fire to burn itself out and rushed to battle, driving the enemy right back to the gate of Toto. And this day we beheld a wonder, for we had taken a Pagan of the Gade tribe prisoner and had tied him fast. We took him out to an open space and threw him to the ground to slit his throat like a sheep, but he disappeared from the sight of all men and was never seen again.[26]

[25] Heath, trans., *The Chronicle of Abuja*, p. 10.
[26] *Ibid.*, pp. 23–24. Thereafter, we are told, the quarrel was settled: "and there was no more fighting between them, only peace and friendship. After this there were no more wars before the coming of the British."

Several major themes in the long annals of traditional inter-African warfare are accentuated by episodes such as these. It appears, first, that military power, even when wielded by formidable armies, has always been closely associated with magical power and the principle of vital energy as these are understood within a unified society. The records show, second, that intertribal wars were fought primarily in order to best the enemy in a given battle. Although concrete rewards, such as the capture of cattle or slaves, were prized in this extended martial context—as they were also in small raids or other limited engagements—it was the sensation of success left by the investment of superior power that mattered most. And success, again, was savored as the enjoyment of a situation in which the enemy of the day was slain or routed and his habitat reduced to ruin. That is to say, victory here was not controlled by the expectation of permanent aggrandizement, the redemption of territories lost in the past, the extension of a way of life, or—excepting some *jihads*—the installation of a moral system. To those who fought the end of war was war itself.

This was so in strict accordance with the logic of nonliterate, essentially behavioral, thought and present-centered conceptions of time, as well as with the spatial characteristics of African societies. Shrewd calculations of advantage are certainly not missing from the records, and particular campaigns—as, for example, the Ashanti wars of the last century that culminated in the siege of Kumasi—are known to have been prepared methodically.[27] Comprehensive long-range planning was not the rule, however, if only because the future was not fathomed as potentially different from actuality, and because political identity did not depend upon the territoriality of boundaries. Strategic thinking, if the term is applicable at all, thus did not aim at consolidating victory by rehabilitating devastated areas, integrating conquered peoples, or establishing reliable frontiers. And the same thoughtways naturally ruled defeat, since the vanquished were culturally at one with the victorious in their basic understandings of the purport of war in life. Generals might be expected to commit suicide when they lost a battle, as they were in Oyo, and warriors might have to be "instantly despatched" if they returned home without their spears or shields, as was the custom among the Matabele,[28] but the governments in whose behalf they had gone forth to fight were rarely moved by the calamities of battle to refashion their defensive posture or

[27] To this effect see Rattray, *Ashanti Law and Constitution*, pp. 120, 125 on "War and the Army"; also Westermann, *Geschichte Afrikas*, pp. 211–223; Lady Hodgson, *The Siege of Kumassi* (New York, 1901), and Alan Lloyd, *The Drums of Kumassi; The Story of the Ashanti Wars* (London, 1964).

[28] Robert Moffat reports that a Matabele must conquer: if one returns without his spear or shield, he is instantly despatched. Eric Victor Axelson, ed., *South African Explorers* (London, New York, and Cape Town, 1954), pp. 218ff.

redesign their fundamental orientations. Not every society shared the total trust, for example, of the Sukuma in Tanganyika (now Tanzania) that the victorious enemy could not defeat the spirits of the conquered group and their enduring influence in the affairs of the land, however great the devastation or the loss. Yet all accepted with equanimity the ebb and flow of endless war.

BIBLIOGRAPHICAL APPENDIX
TO CHAPTER 14

On the general incidence of war in intertribal or intersocietal relations, and the particular proposition that war was the main factor in preserving political identity, see Thompson and Adloff, *French West Africa*, pp. 19ff. Tribes living in what became French West Africa were isolated from and hostile to each other. Three centuries of almost incessant strife had ravaged the most accessible and fertile regions and driven the weaker peoples to mountains and deep forests. By the mid-nineteenth century, Yatenga, Ouagadougou, Abomey, Porto Novo, and other societies were undergoing periodic attacks by African conquistadors or desert nomads, whose tactics of terror made the French appear as saviors.

Skinner, *The Mossi of the Upper Volta*, pp. 60, 70, 93, 104, says that hostility and war marked relations between separate units within and beyond the vassalage system, and that the Mossi, proud of their warrior tradition, usually pursued their enemies by burning villages, killing all infants as well as the infirm, and, when fighting non-Mossi, capturing young people who would then be sold as slaves. L.-V. Thomas, "Acculturation et déplacements de populations en Afrique de l'Ouest" in *Revue de psychologie des peuples*, 16ème année, No. 1, 1er trimestre (1961), pp. 49ff., 52, comments that Africa, despite its massive appearance of impenetrability, has been the theater of mostly warlike displacements of peoples, and that intercommunity contacts were more often belligerent than amicable, usually occurring under the aegis of conquest. Westermann, *Geschichte Afrikas*, p. 30, writes that war was not experienced as an emergency or otherwise exceptional condition, but rather as an integral part of the normative institutional order. Intertribal war was thus relentless, whether initiated by injury to prestige or some violation of a customary order, or the due execution of the need for regular war expeditions. See Hodgkin, *Nigeria in Perspective*, pp. 47, 96, 100, 110, 167, 272ff., for reports by contemporaries on the constancy of war between various kingdoms and provinces in West Africa—as, for example, between the Ibadan and Egba states, the Oyo Empire and Dahomey, and the invasions by the Kingdom of Bornu. Also Burton, *Mission to Gelele*, for numerous accounts of warfare as conducted by Dahomey, the Egbas, and others, and Urvoy, *Histoire de l'empire du Bornou*, pp. 75–79. See Ayaji and Smith, *Yoruba Warfare in the Nineteenth Century*, pp. 47ff. to the effect that armies were sent out every second year for purposes of military exercise and the acquisition of spoils; that war was conceived as a game of chance and deceit, and conducted with only limited regard for strategy. Meyer Fortes, "The Political System of the Tallensi of the Northern Territories of the Gold Coast" in Fortes and Evans-Pritchard, eds., *African Political Systems*, pp. 241, 245 on the place of war in this society. E. W. Smith and A. M. Dale, *The Ila-Speaking Peoples of Northern Rhodesia*, 2 vols. (London, 1920), Vol. I, 35, say that these peoples were rent by internecine wars, and despoiled and almost extinguished by continuous aggressions from without. Godfrey Wilson, *The Constitution of Ngonde* (Livingstone, Northern Rhodesia, 1939), pp. 59–64, writes that peaceful contacts between the Ngonde and other tribes were very slight indeed. I. Schapera, "Political Institutions," pp. 191ff., says that hostile relations among the Bantu developed out of boundary questions, cattle thefts, and refusals to hand over fugitives; that wars were frequent; and that attacks usually began by surrounding a village by stealth during the night, rush it at dawn, kill as many men as possible, capture cattle, women, and children, burn huts, and then beat a hasty retreat.

Shaka and his imitators carried on more ruthless wars on a vaster scale. In this regard, see Robert Moffat's reports, notably his impressions of Matabele warfare, in Axelson, ed., *South African Explorers*, pp. 218ff. William F. Lye, "The Ndebele Kingdom South of the Limpopo River," *Journal of African History*, 10, No. 1 (1969), 87–104, that Ndebele society, as founded by Mzilikazi, was a permanently mobilized society in which the military system was the core. Mzilikazi, who had started as a regimental commander under Shaka, was continuously on the move with his soldiers, raiding the veld to replenish power, enslaving those he conquered, notably the Sotho, and undertaking wholesale massacres as acts of policy.

See Margaret Read, *The Ngoni of Nyasaland* (London and New York, 1956), pp. 29–44, 116ff., to the effect that these people were deeply attached to warlike activities, and that organization for war was integral to the entire Ngoni structure, as it was to the Swazi military kingdom. On different manifestations of war, including guerrilla warfare and the administrative role of armies in the Congo and various kingdoms of the Savanna, see Jan Vansina, *Kingdoms of the Savanna*. On war in East Africa see Richards, ed., *East African Chiefs*, pp. 234ff. in particular; Lambert, *Kikuyu Social and Political Institutions*, pp. 70ff.; Hobley, *Bantu Beliefs and Magic,* pp. 244ff. on fighting between Kikuyu, Masai, and Kamba; G. M. Wilson, "Homicide and Suicide Among the Joluo of Kenya," in Paul Bohannan, ed., *African Homicide and Suicide* (Princeton, 1960), pp. 179–213, notably p. 181; David Tait, "The Territorial Pattern and Lineage System of Konkomba" in John Middleton and David Tait, eds., *Tribes without Rulers, Studies in African Segmentary Systems* (London, 1958), pp. 167ff. And see earlier references. Authorities and records on the incidence of war in Africa are too numerous to be listed here.

· 15 ·

ANALYSIS VERSUS EXISTENCE

Reflections on such records of traditional African thought and society as those discussed in Parts III, IV, and V, support the conclusion that the inner normative order of this culture world is best understood when seen in relation to conflict. Accepted as the crucible of the causal system, it is also the arbiter of communal relations; institutionalized in patterns of behavior and organization, it is, in fact, a positive focal value and the major structuring principle in African societies. In contrast to inclinations long prevalent in the West, in terms of which it is deemed morally, intellectually, and politically desirable to resolve conflict in order to achieve states of harmony and unity on the various planes of human existence, there is no compelling impulse in African culture to do away with conflict or deny its operations. The requirement is, rather, to maintain the dynamic interplay between rival forces, while insisting that all of its incidents occur in a closed, familiar circuit, along strictly predictable lines.

So conceived, conflict control stands for working *with* rather than *against* the principle of power. On the psychological level this is assured by suppressing conflicts before they reach the fields of consciousness. Converted into states of inward anxiety, muted in outward passivity, they are not likely to provoke socially negative reactions so long as the entire complex system remains intact. In social relations that are normally dominated by fear and suspicion, men are expected to defer to superior power, notably magic, if they cannot cope with forces and occurrences they regard as nefarious. On the plane of local politics, conflict is managed either by simply reshuffling power between contenders, or, as in crises of dynastic succession, by automatically renewing the customary game of intrigue or physical violence that is traditionally associated with a given society's government. In the extended circle of regional or inter-tribal relations, meanwhile, where hostility must be the norm if the small community is to survive intact, conflict is regulated, as it were, by being cast in the form of martial forays or other forms of war. In other words, the instincts, ideas, and devices trusted to control conflict are in every case derivatives of the same mythical thoughtways that allow conflict to exist in the first place. No exit from the round is anticipated or desired.

These patterns are not significantly different from those enacted in modern Africa. For, as the testimony gathered in Part II suggests, the new intellectual and political elites freely affirm the continued validity of Africa's cultural heritage as the inescapable and most invigorating source of reference in the search for personal and national identity, as well as in the furtherance of an all-African unity. This means that conflict, being an integral part of traditionalism, is readily accommodated also in neotraditionalism. Indeed, Africans could scarcely have managed the tensions implicit in the encounter with Western norms and values had they not been able to fall back on customary ways of coping with stressful situations, both acute and lingering.

This modern adjustment has been achieved, however, at the cost of distorting certain customary ways of managing mental anxieties, social conflicts, and intergroup hostilities, including war. Dr. T. Adeoye Lambo thus points out in his study of "The African Mind in Contemporary Conflict"[1] that, whereas in ancient times it was the custom of the African peoples to respond to tribal distress by offering an expiatory sacrifice to a tutelary animal, detribalized Africans today, being cut off from this form of ritual, have, under stress, reverted to certain "malignant forms of ritualistic observance," for which Lambo coined the clinical term "malignant anxiety." In such mental states—diagnosed after close studies of the Leopard Society in Nigeria, the Poro Society in Sierra Leone, the Mau Mau in Kenya, and several instances of "epidemics of mass hysteria" in East Africa between 1962 and 1964—when adaptation to new and stressful life situations becomes difficult, anxiety is apt to be joined with aggressive behavior and to lead at times to crimes "akin to ritual murder."

Departures from traditional norms are also on record in the administration of government. The future of Kenya, for example, was deliberately entrusted in 1969 to new, custom-defying oathing practices, which obligated the Kikuyu to take up arms if necessary in order to keep their tribe absolutely dominant in the multitribal nation.[2] In Lunda politics, where succession to kingship had always been subject to armed struggle and rebellion, modern conflict was expressed in terms of sorcery, since princes could no longer raise the requisite military force. As Cunnison wrote in 1967, aspirants to power now try to bewitch the ruler himself or, alternately, the Lunda aristocracy, which has the traditional mandate to choose the king.[3] The mainspring in each of these situations, we learn from this historian, is jealousy: the son is jealous of the father-king, or the people are jealous of the privileged position that a king may be abus-

[1] The Jacques Parisot Foundation Lecture, 1971; published in *WHO Chronicle*, 25, No. 8 (August 1971), 348.

[2] For a detailed report on these practices, which are said to have involved 90 percent of the Kikuyu, see the *New York Times*, October 13, 1969. Compare also *supra*, Part II.

[3] Cunnison, *The Luapula Peoples of Northern Rhodesia*, pp. 166–169.

ing. In either case, it is believed that the kingship can be acquired and defended by bewitchment.

Analogous or similar instances of transposing "normal" internal war into "abnormal" forms of sorcery have been recorded in numerous African states, among them the Ivory Coast. Here a plot was hatched in the early 1960s by a high-ranking minister who was consumed with ambition to replace President Felix Houphouet-Boigny. Born a Catholic, recruited into the Communist party while a student in Grenoble in 1951–1952, and surreptitiously active in supporting the local communist cause while in office, this man (M. Ernest Boka) was advised by one of the marabouts he consulted that he was indeed destined to be first in the land. An elaborate conspiracy, replete with magical, death-causing practices, was then set in motion—with the aid of communist advisers—to make the prophecy come true. The plot was uncovered in 1964, however, and Boka committed suicide. In explaining the complex issues of the case at a public gathering, Houphouet-Boigny reminded his audience that Africa is unified by fetichism, since Islam and Christianity, being alien creeds and late arrivals, cannot be presumed to have canceled past beliefs. Furthermore, the president insisted that there is nothing wrong with fetichism per se; what is wrong, he emphasized, is its usage in modern times. For in stimulating an uncontrolled trust in occult forces, it is now responsible, in alliance with atheistic communism, for the transmutation of fetichism into total evil.[4]

On the many modern stages of open warfare, meanwhile, the minds of fighting men are also confused by the simultaneous operation of conflicting sets of instructions. In addition to numerous studies already cited, the following may serve to accent the theme of this review. After examining the belief system of Congo guerrillas in the 1960s, Grundy concluded that the men had been methodically subjected to intellectual indoctrination in accordance with Maoist and other modern theories of war and insurrection.[5] Congo guerrillas thus persisted in trusting their own war charms and rites, and in obeying those specialists in occult practices who

---

[4] The facts, including Boka's confession and the president's address, are set out in "Fraternité, Supplément au Numéro du vendredi 17 Avril 1964" (this is a local news sheet).

Compare an earlier case in Gonja as reported by Goody, "Restricted Literacy," pp. 234–235, where this scholar points to a crucial moment in the events leading to the Salaga Civil War of 1892, when the leader of the rebellious party discovered that the chief was consulting the same mallam as he himself in order to try and kill him. When the rebel leader began his revolt, he obtained the assistance of another mallam, who provided him with the magical support necessary to defeat his enemies and enter Salaga. Goody adds that similar services continue to be rendered at the present day to the new generation of political leaders, noting in particular that Nkrumah was assisted in his magical affairs by an important Muslim. Compare *supra*, Ch. 3, n. 64.

[5] Grundy, "Ideology and Insurrection," p. 30.

were attached more or less officially to various armed units, dispensing strength and invulnerability in ways that "would make a calculating Maoist guerrilla fighter shudder." As recorded in the eastern part of the country, where Pierre Mulele and other rural organizers had set up the Armée populaire de libération (APL) by recruiting young activists into the formation of simbas (lions), such methods of control by magic included the following:

> Each APL recruit went through an initiation ceremony, including shallow incisions in his chest and forehead, and baptism with "Mulele water" (later "Lumumba water"), which was held to confer invulnerability upon the initiate. The *Dawa* (Swahili for medicine) lost its protective properties if a certain number of taboos were not observed. Physical contact with an impure person was prohibited. This harsh injunction, which in fact prescribed celibacy, was tempered by the possibility of purchasing dispensations from the unit witchdoctor to restore invulnerability lost through dereliction. In battle, a *simba* was to march straight to the front; turning the head left or right undermined invulnerability, and parenthetically provided an explanation for any casualties which ensued.[6]

Manipulation of magic in the service of political rebellion proved most successful in this instance, at least temporarily; for the conviction of the simbas' invulnerability pervaded not only the local population, in whose midst the bands were operating, but also the armed forces of the Congolese government itself.

The resilience of the indigenous trust in the supremacy of occult power is also illustrated by Mulele's role in the revolt. Observers of the scene report that this leader was greatly revered by his followers, not so much as a well-trained tactician and representative of Maoist ideology, but rather as a messianic savior of the kind brought forth in the 1930s by such movements as the sect of "the talking serpent" or "the snake man," which prophesied the collective rising of the dead, an eclipse of the sun, and the arrival of a man part white, part black. Mulele, too, his constituents believed, was omnipresent, capable of transforming himself into a snake or other animal, of travelling long distances like a spirit or a bird,

---

[6] Young, "The Congo Rebellion," *Africa Report*, 10, No. 4 (April 1965), 10. Apart from stressing the role of magic—"a familiar theme in African revolts"—this scholar also points to the ethnic content of the revolt. In Kwilu the exploited community tended to view itself as Bapende-Bambundu, with Mulele as the armed prophet, and imprisoned Mupende Antoine Gizenga as the martyr. In southern Maniema, the Batetela-Bakusu believed they had been systematically victimized by "Leopoldville," beginning with the assassination of their favorite son, Lumumba. Assassinations and purges were ethnically selective, and the composition of witch-doctor corps and officer corps was likewise ethnically determined.

and of withstanding the onslaught of bullets and other mechanical devices.[7]

Spokesmen for modern African societies appear quite at ease in Westernized strata of academe in which conflict is analyzed in essentially Occidental ways. The most knowledgeable and sensitive among them also realize, however, that traditional conflict-inducing forces and emotions persist in their native lands, and that these are apt to come to the fore when the customary social situation is disturbed, either by an unforeseen event or by confrontation with entirely foreign forms of human action and reaction. In such circumstances—and they have been variously recorded in recent years—familiar controls usually cease to be operative, and individuals not conditioned to think independently and pragmatically in response to the particular requirements of situations, are apt to resolve their internal stress by striking out explosively, without reflection.[8]

The question that suggests itself, then, is whether Occidental theories of conflict can accommodate these traditional and neotraditional African realities.

The comprehensive survey of conflict-related literature in the behavioral sciences that was used as the main indicator of the state of theory in Part II of this work[9] bears impressive testimony to the quality of the research that has been undertaken in this field. Many approaches to the subject have been developed; numerous definitions and typologies are on record, and arguments about the respective merits of each of the

[7] Renée C. Fox, Willy de Craemer, and Jean-Marie Ribeaucourt, " 'The Second Independence:' A Case Study of the Kwilu Rebellion in the Congo," *Comparative Studies in History and Society*, 8 (October 1965–July 1966), 78–110, especially pp. 92–104. The young people involved in the "Brigades de Vigilance" during the 1963 revolution in Brazzaville (Congo) are said to have enjoyed stopping cars and harassing their occupants because they felt imbued with magical qualities while exercising this type of power over the rest of the population. See Lee, *African Armies and Civil Order*, p. 87, for this reference. For the impact of similar religious movements upon political and military affairs in East Africa, see F. B. Welbourn and B. A. Ogot, *A Place to Feel at Home: A Study of Two Independent Churches in Western Kenya* (London and Nairobi, 1966). See Efraim Andersson, *Messianic Popular Movements in the Lower Congo* (Uppsala, 1958), on the close connection between modern messianic movements, racism and armed conflict; and cf. earlier references to Buell, *The Native Problem in Africa*.

[8] Compare *supra*, pp. 76ff. and 82, notably reference to Simon Biesheuvel, *Race, Culture and Personality*, where it is suggested that traditional African culture did not require an inner-directed personality structure, and that Africans today are not likely to develop it.

[9] *Supra*, Ch. 4 for a discussion of Fink, "Some Conceptual Difficulties in the Theory of Social Conflict," pp. 412ff., and bibliography there listed. For certain problems of classification and definition in political science, see *supra*, Ch. 8, "Design and Definition"; on the complex relation between mythical and historical thought, *supra*, Ch. 6.

The present summation, which concludes the exposition of African varieties of conflict, will repeat some references that were made before the subject was fully opened up.

existing theories abound. And yet, various and intricate as these findings are, they appear to have issued in almost every instance from an exclusive concern with such phenomena of social conflict as are known from the inner normative order of Occidental society.[10] It is all the more interesting, therefore, to note that efforts to identify sufficient common ground to support a few generally acceptable concepts have so far failed[11]—a realization that has led one authority to suggest that the very word or notion of "conflict" is now so embattled as to be outmoded, and that other terms should perhaps be substituted.[12]

Since it is difficult to generalize about the incidence of social conflict even in the West, and to reduce Occident-centered schemes of analysis to a few common denominators, it must obviously be questionable whether any of the available theories could interpret such conflict-related phenomena as are encountered in Africa south of the Sahara, without either straining the integrity of its own conceptual design or distorting the African realities. A number of considerations suggest the propriety of a cautious attitude.

Broad in scope and value-neutral as most sociological frames of reference purport to be, they derive from a mode of perception and a system of rationality in terms of which it is thought necessary to distinguish reality from myth, prevent the confusion of tangible and intangible concerns, and, above all, isolate the human dimension from natural and supernatural categories. And, indeed, there would be no "behavioral sciences" at all if life had not been intellectualized in just this way. Every species of conflict, irrespective of the criteria employed for its definition, is thus viewed, quite logically, as a contention between two or more parties of individuals or groups of persons. Furthermore, such contentions—whether analyzed as conflicts or as competitions (and the juxtaposition of these two concepts in one form or another accounts for much of the fireworks in scholarly disputations)[13]—are conceived by most authorities in the polarized terms of antagonistic opposites representing two or more irreconcilable, mutually incompatible, wills, values, or positions. The object of the rivalry is usually perceived as something tangible, and the actual struggle or competitive striving for possession or control of the

---

[10] A notable exception is LeVine, "Anthropology and the Study of Conflict; Introduction."

[11] The conclusion reached by Kenneth Boulding almost twenty years ago, namely that "There is not a single concept of conflict, and therefore there cannot be a single theory of conflict" (*Journal of Conflict Resolution*, 1, No. 2, June 1957), continues to hold, as Fink points out in "Some Conceptual Difficulties in the Theory of Social Conflict," pp. 424, 430ff., 440.

[12] Jessie Bernard, "Parties and Issues in Conflict," *Journal of Conflict Resolution*, 1, No. 2 (June 1957), 111–121.

[13] See Fink, "Some Conceptual Difficulties in the Theory of Social Conflict," pp. 217ff.; 442–452 for a review of positions on this point.

thing desired is generally understood as an overt and episodic action springing from some kind of disagreement or misunderstanding, and interrupting the normal flow of social life. Humanized, personalized, and concretized, conflict is also suspect in respect to its origin and effects (unless it can be identified as, for example, "regulated competition"). In fact, it emerges from most scholarly treatments as a violation of existing social norms and psychological patterns.[14] For even those behaviorists who distinguish carefully between "actual" and "latent" conflict[15]—or who recognize the importance, for any analysis of conflict, of psychic states in which men harbor opposed or hostile sentiments, ideas, and strivings[16]—appear to accede to the view that conflict situations are aberrations on the planes of both society and the psyche. Just what the actual patterns, models, and norms may be, in relation to which feelings, motives, and actions are to be judged normal or abnormal is usually not explicitly set out.

The purpose of the present discussion is not to correct existing theories, but rather to make two sets of suggestions. The first aims at stimulating interdisciplinary approaches to the problem on the ground that "conflict" is, after all, a mobile term carrying multiple but interlocking meanings in whichever civilization it is being observed. Unlike "dispute," for example, which suggests the existence of specific adversaries and objects of contention, "conflict" is a broad and comprehensive concept. As indicated earlier, it may refer to psychic and mental states of being, or to social and political conditions; to open contests, as well as to covert plots; to rivalries between personalities, clashes of interests, collisions of groups, or encounters with alien systems of thought. Furthermore, "conflict" may put in issue relationships between man and nature, or tradition and modernism; it may assume the form of lingering enmity, militant speech, or physical aggressiveness, and, most important-

[14] But see George Simmel, who makes allowance for the positive role of conflict in "The Sociology of Conflict" in *American Journal of Sociology*, 9 (1903–1904), pp. 490–525; 672–89; 798–811. However, the "personality norm" in this work is distinctly Occidental. See also by the same author, *Conflict and the Web of Group Affiliations*. For a modern critique of prevalent conflict theory, see Norman A. Bailey, "Toward a Praxeological Theory of Conflict" in *Orbis*, 11, No. 4 (Winter 1968), 1096: "As with psychological conflict theory, most sociological examinations of conflict see it as an aberration that should and must be reduced, transformed or eliminated. Conflict is seen as situational rather than instrumental, as pathological rather than normal." Bailey refers to incompatibility of perceptions as "dissonance," and points out that such dissonance is often implicitly seen as synonymous with conflict.

[15] Compare *supra*, pp. 46ff. for a reference to Jessie Bernard, *American Community Behavior*, p. 106.

[16] For a discussion of "motive-centered" definitions of conflict and the work of Kurt Singer, Raymond W. Mack, and Richard C. Snyder, see Fink, "Some Conceptual Difficulties in the Theory of Social Conflict," especially p. 434.

ly, perhaps, its incidence may be viewed in one society as a threat to order and security, in another, by contrast, as a vital and constructive force. In short, conflict as a subject-matter transcends particular academic disciplines and methodologies.[17]

The second group of suggestions issues from the recognition that conflict-related thought in the West—whether in psychology, political science, history, sociology, or law—has issued from conceptions of the individual and society that have matured in the inner normative order of the West alone,[18] and for which no ready equivalents can be found in the African order. Conflict may be a form of "social interaction," but "social" in Africa includes all that is mystical and magical. It may be a "match between opponents," but the "opponent" is more often than not invisible—at least to Western eyes, which are not supposed to see ghosts, shadows, or the souls of the dead. Similarly, if conflict is defined as the "overt manifestation of antagonism," the word "overt" requires another reading in African contexts. For, as Lambo explains:

There is still in African civilization an intensely realized perception of supernatural presence, but it is accompanied by a kind of adolescent impetuousness and a fatuous, almost fanatical, faith in the magic power of certain symbols to produce certain results. In parts of Africa where traditional tribal customs still flourish in considerable strength, the style of life and modes of thought have become a great archetype, a centre around which congenial beliefs are formed, a first principle or measure of probability guiding the cultural susceptibility or predispositions of men in all their inquiries and dealings.[19]

Above all, and as preceding remarks have stressed, conflict is not a norm violation in Africa. In that culture world it is more properly viewed as a focal positive value, and as a major structuring principle in society.

[17] For a similar view, see Ronald J. Fisher, "Third Party Consultation," p. 93: "It is suggested that the development of the method would be enhanced by the materialization of eclectic, interdisciplinary theories of conflict. While the history of the study of conflict shows some promising general and descriptive steps in that direction, much contemporary work has tended toward the premature limitation and quantification of variables with a resultant lack of applicability to the real world. For example, most of the recent models of cooperation and conflict discussed by Patchen (1970) are so oversimplified as to be of little use to an eclectic method of studying and resolving conflict."

[18] See *supra*, Parts I and II.

[19] "The African Mind in Contemporary Conflict," p. 344. Lambo identifies the modern mental crises as due almost entirely to the Western impact. His main concerns are: what can be done to minimize transitional stress, render less harmful and less traumatic the impact of social change, and make people accept new standards, new norms—social, economic, political—in the difficult phases of transition from tribal and traditional family controls to modern urban and industrial life and relations?

The inner normative systems of both cultures converge, indeed, upon the desirability of order in society. However, unlike the West—where peace and harmony are posited as primary values, thus dictating, as it were, the definitions of their opposites, and where "order" is viewed as a function of peace—Africa reverses the argument. There, order is understood, symbolized, and institutionalized unequivocally in terms of controlled conflict. Personal and social "peace," as this concept is understood in the different value languages of the Occident, has no counterpart there. Throughout the continent, and irrespective of local differences in the natural environment, men have been content with small pockets of security in "The Forest of a Thousand Daemons" that has enveloped them relentlessly for centuries.[20] And yet, even in these small pockets of peace, "this stillness of life did not resemble a peace. It was the stillness of an implacable force brooding over an inscrutable intention."[21] It is difficult for social scientists to match Joseph Conrad's definition, because our categories and schemes of analysis simply do not accommodate the facts of conflict as these are experienced in Africa. This nonconformity is accentuated when our attention shifts to war.

As a preceding survey of the state of the theory has demonstrated, it is customary in the Occident to distinguish war from social conflict. African understandings of the functions and values associated with war are, by contrast, inextricably mixed up with other types of conflict, both violent and nonviolent. Furthermore, while war carries morally and socially positive meanings there,[22] it is generally viewed in the modern Occident as absolutely calamitous in moral, legal, and political respects. Here, where it is common to think of peace as the polar opposite to war, and as an internationally preferred and attainable condition, even research has moved from war to peace,[23]—a shift toward cultural parochialism in the social sciences that is quite opposite to their original universalist thrust. Typically, African realities of war and violence are thus necessarily being bypassed or avoided. To be sure, the particular incidence of

[20] Wole Soyinka and D. O. Fagunwa, *The Forest of a Thousand Daemons* (London and Camden, N.J., 1968). The same imagery is found in much of contemporary African fiction, for example in the novels of Amos Tutuola.

[21] Joseph Conrad, *Heart of Darkness* and *The Secret Sharer* (New York, 1950), p. 103.

[22] *Supra*, Chs. 13 and 14. For an early and sensitive appraisal of the profound difference between modern African and Occidental values see Elspeth Huxley, "Freedom in Africa: The Next Stage," *Virginia Quarterly Review*, 36, No. 3 (Summer 1960), 350–371. The West has projected its values—peace and democracy—upon the African scene, she writes, but Africans do not desire them with equal passion. Condemnations of violence in which Europeans so often indulge thus strike many Africans as both hypocritical and silly. Few Africans will therefore take seriously the view that a riot is the worst of disasters and law and order the greatest of goods.

[23] Compare *supra*, Part I.

civil wars, struggles of secession, wars of succession, guerrilla wars, or intertribal wars has frequently been subjected to exhaustive scholarly analysis, but the findings thus recorded have not and cannot be integrated into the narrow context of war or conflict theory as it now exists. Perhaps more importantly, they have not been investigated with a view to enlarging or otherwise correcting the general frame of reference within which war and peace are being studied today in academic circles.

The great and constant issues of why men fight and die have thus, perforce, receded from the screen of social science consciousness. And with respect to Africa, this means that some of the most poignant realities of life are simply being overlooked. Here, as in the matter of conflict generally, it has so far been left to artists to create comprehensive designs for the analysis and integration of greatly diverse episodes. Knowledge by indwelling thus enabled Ouologuem[24] to envision the African destiny in terms of a commitment to violence that spans millennia and transcends conflicts between Negroes, Arabs, and Europeans; to render his understanding of shared African values and institutions in the compressed style of the West African "griot"—the only style capable of relaying African conceptions of the flux of time—and to present in this way what has rightly been called "the symbolic autobiography of a continent."[25] The same kind of knowledge informs Mazrui's *The Trial of Christopher Okigbo*,[26] a symbolic novel that deals with the conflict of ideas that made for the Biafran war of secession, and therewith the death of the well-known Ibo poet. The organizing literary device here is an allegorical trial of the dead poet and of the collective states of mind responsible for the succession of violent upheavals that began with the assassination of the president of Togo and led to numerous bloody conflagrations, including those in the Congo and Uganda, before reaching a climax in the Nigerian civil war. Held in the Grand Stadium of "After-Africa," where "all the centuries and generations" are unified by virtue of fighting with each other in continuous soccer matches, the trial comes to depend on witnesses who are called from the ranks of the not-yet-born, the dead, and the living, the latter usually summoned while asleep. For is not simultaneity the obvious and proper measure of relations between the past, the present, and the future? and must one not defer to the ruling African conviction that death is one more ceremonial transition,

---

[24] Yambo Ouologuem, *Le Devoir de violence*, English ed., *Bound to Violence*, Ralph Mannheim, trans. (New York, 1971). For earlier references to this work, *supra*, Ch. 6, n. 10.

[25] James Olney, *Tell Me Africa, An Approach to African Literature* (Princeton, 1973), p. 242. Olney's comprehensive, learned, and remarkably perceptive work had not been published when the bulk of the present book was written.

[26] Mazrui, *The Trial of Christopher Okigbo*; see *supra*, Ch. 5, n. 27 for earlier references to this book.

"no more fundamental than the transition from pre-adulthood to the full status of the adult"? Millions of men have died "in the dignity of kinship," the Court of the Here-After hears, and the Grand Stadium had been the stage of great debates before. But the Congo, Nigeria, and Uganda were simply fragments of an African mirror. In between the cracks of the mirror the pattern of a continent emerged. "Yes," said the prosecuting Counsel for Damnation, "death is indeed an exercise in pan-Africanism. We have been known to kill each other partly because we belong to each other. We kill each other because we are neighbours."[27]

[27] *Ibid.*, p. 107.

PART VI

CONCILIATION,
THE ROLE OF INTERMEDIARIES,
AND THE SETTLEMENT
OF DISPUTES

· 16 ·

THE LEGAL VOCABULARY AND
THE SOCIAL REALITY

The limited relevance of Occidental theories for an appreciation of African varieties of conflict is matched by the uneasy relationship between Western norms of conflict resolution, on the one hand, and African approaches to the problem, on the other. As preceding sections have suggested, order and disorder are not mutually exclusive phenomena in the African world, and war and peace, or conflict and accord, are not necessarily perceived as pairs of opposites. Quite in line with prevalent modes of thought,[1] these categories are interpenetrating, with each present also in the other. Within the unified society war, although a species of conflict, may simultaneously serve as the only legitimate mode of resolving or mitigating a conflict, as when a succession struggle is undertaken to assure the continuance of orderly government, when the feud is practiced to establish peace, or when the utterance of a curse is instrumental in healing social rifts.

In short, there are many types of conflict that require resort to violence, verbal aggression, or other forms of hostile conduct if the basic order is to be preserved. In such instances it is often difficult for a Western mind to distinguish clearly between conflict, on the one hand, and modes of mitigating or controlling conflict, on the other. And similar impediments to perception from without may arise with respect to what one scholar terms "mystical disturbances,"[2] for these require adjustment by resort to rituals that are designed to cloak fundamental disharmonies between rival principles. The issues are less blurred in the case of human tensions that are left dormant even as they are being controlled, or that have been rendered socially harmless by mutation and simulation into ritualized or playful forms of strife. And they are quite clear when it comes to groups of quarrels and disputes that may neither be kept going nor be allowed to erupt, but rather must be settled deliberately and peaceably if the community is to survive.[3]

This last class of actual or potential conflict situations—and it is vast indeed, in view of the fragility of social ties between members of an Afri-

[1] See *supra*, Chs. 5, 9, 10, 11, 13, and 14.

[2] Max Gluckman, *Politics, Law and Ritual in Tribal Society* (London, 1965), ch. 6, and cf. *supra*, Parts IV and V.

[3] See the following chapters of Part VI for the management of conflict in intertribal or interstate relations.

can community—has consistently engaged the traditional genius for maintaining the closely-knit folk society. Each speech community, however small, has thus brought forth its own code of customs and system of referrals for the abatement of antagonisms, the conciliation of disputants and, ultimately, the reestablishment of communal accord. But when these various local institutions are surveyed in the unifying perspective of shared cultural patterns, certain common features readily emerge, and most of these are as different from Western approaches to the problem of settling or mitigating disputes as the situations that have called them forth.

It should be recalled, first, that all African norms in the field of conflict resolution diverge from those perfected in the Occident by virtue of the fact that they are projections of traditional nonliterate ways of thought and communication. Fashioned without the aid of writing, they depend primarily upon the medium of the spoken word, and are respected as aspects of a mythical charter that enjoins trust in surrealist and magical forces; acknowledges the dead as living presences; allows for the interchangeability of humans, animals, and inanimate substances; and often cancels distinctions between processes and things, appearance and reality, or dream and consciousness. Furthermore, and in accordance with these patterns of belief and reasoning, African systems of conflict control emanate from established social practice, rather than from abstract arrangements of ideas, legislative enactments, or innovative empirical agreements reached in response to unprecedented conflict situations. All are, therefore, comprehensive references, virtually synonymous with the entirety of social life. As such, they are not easily amenable to distinctions either between values, behavioral regularities, and institutions; or between ethics, law, and other categories of norms and normative thought that are regarded as discrete in the West.[4] This dis-

[4] Compare in this respect the conclusions reached by Redfield, *The Primitive World and Its Transformations*, pp. 14–15, that the principles of rightness are largely tacit, and thus not the subject of much explicit criticism or even much reflective thought; that each precivilized society was held together by largely undeclared, but continually realized, ethical principles; that institutions are not planned out or modified as a result of deliberate choice and action, and that legislation, though it may occur, is not the characteristic form of legal action. To like effect, Jan Vansina, "A Traditional Legal System: The Kuba," in Hilda Kuper and Leo Kuper, eds., *African Law; Adaptation and Development* (Berkeley and Los Angeles, 1965), esp. pp. 109, 111, 116ff., where it is pointed out that the norms sanctioned by the Kuba are social, not legal, norms. Since the Kuba do not know writing and have no lawyers, they have not defined any institution in legal terms, as distinct from common opinion about what an institution is about. In our society law has duplicated and permeated society, but in Kuba society the social norms have taken the place of the field of law. That is to say, they *function* as legal norms, but they *are* social norms. In accordance with this reasoning, it becomes understandable, Vansina concludes, that the content of substantive law is no less than the totality of the institutions of the society.

crepancy between two cultural traditions that have been interacting on the African scene in the last hundred years continues to present scholars and administrators with acute problems of definition and policy-making, nowhere more so than in the field of law.

The particular concern to isolate law from the sum total of socially informing principles—to which the proceedings of recent conferences, the records of publications, and a stream of reformist local legislation attest[5]—originates in the fact that law has been methodically elaborated by generations of Europeans as the mainstay of their own societies, and that it has been traditionally recognized by them as the most trusted reference in well nigh all disputes. Although Occidental theorists in common law and civil law have never been at one in defining the substance of law, the recorded formulations, disparate as they are, converge upon the view that law, whether viewed as a concept or a structure, is not identical with socially sanctioned behavior or custom, and that it has connotations not shared by other principles of social control. Colonial administrations, being carriers of this tradition, naturally introduced their favorite legacy to the African communities they ruled, even as they also recognized, in practical as well as conceptual contexts, the proven worth of a complex body of established native rules, and, in areas vitally affected by Islam, that of the established *shari'a* law.

The major problem implicit in the coexistence of these dual or plural frames of reference was to understand the native local order on its own merits, and render it in terms that would do justice to its meanings. For since Africans themselves had not been consciously aware before the twentieth century of what was law, what religion, what taboo, and what government,[6] and since juristic thinking of the kind common in the West was unknown here,[7] they had not defined any institutions in specific

---

[5] See, for example, Max Gluckman, ed., *Ideas and Procedures in African Customary Law* (London, 1969); Hilda Kuper and Leo Kuper, eds., *African Law; Adaptation and Development* (Berkeley and Los Angeles, 1965); Hans W. Baade and Robinson O. Everett, eds., *African Law; New Law for New Nations* (Dobbs Ferry, N.Y., 1963); Thomas W. Hutchison, ed., *Africa and Law; Developing Legal Systems in African Commonwealth Nations* (Madison, Milwaukee, and London, 1968); Robert B. Seidman, *Research in African Law and the Processes of Change* (Los Angeles, 1967); and works cited separately in different sections of the present discussion.

[6] Compare Snell, *Nandi Customary Law*, p. 1: "It would, of course, be both impossible and misleading to abstract into explicit categories the cosmological, religious and ethical notions of the Nandi as though they were expressly thought-out dogmas; as with primitive tribes in general, their 'philosophy' and religion were an indistinct combination of attitudes, ideas and beliefs, and they drew no sharp distinction between the moral law and the law of the tribe such as has long been familiar in Western societies."

[7] Antony Allott, *Essays in African Law, with Special Reference to the Law of Ghana* (London, 1960), p. 67. A. Arthur Schiller, "Law," in Robert A. Lystad, ed., *The African World; A Survey of Social Research* (New York, London, and

terms before encountering the literate civilization of the Europeans. In default of native vocabularies, in response to the dictates of practical necessity, and under the compelling influence of ideals of unity and unification, it was natural, then, that Western concepts were often used to illuminate the meanings carried by the folk system, and that the language of Occidental jurisprudence was used to circumscribe the principles most resembling law.[8] Furthermore, since these principles or norms were rightly viewed as "customs," the habit settled of referring to them as "customary law." This meant not only that the distinction between custom and law was at times allowed to become blurred,[9] but also that African customary law was often equated with European customary law, which carries rather different connotations—as an African student of the matter recently observed.[10]

The process of Europeanizing African norms was as beset by semantic and conceptual confusions as other processes of cultural borrowing had been in international history. Among the latter, none is as relevant to the

---

Washington, D.C., 1965), pp. 166–198, to the effect that the body of rules composing indigenous customary law stems from philosophic concepts wholly foreign to our view of life. Robert Redfield, "Primitive Law," in Paul Bohannan, ed., *Law and Warfare; Studies in the Anthropology of Conflict* (Garden City, N.Y., 1967), p. 21: the most obvious general conclusion about primitive law is that there is not much of it, if only because socially disapproved conduct is effectively restrained by supernatural sanctions.

[8] See Bohannan's critique of Malinowski's broad interpretation of law as including all norms of conduct with which people are induced to conform, in Bohannan, ed., *Law and Warfare*, p. 4. Also, A. St. J. Hannigan, "The Imposition of Western Law Forms upon Primitive Societies," in *Comparative Studies in Society and History*, 4 (1961–1962), 1. For a particularly stimulating discourse on the applicability of Occidental theories of law to African realities, and on the relation between "law" and "custom," see T. Olawale Elias, *The Nature of African Customary Law* (Manchester, 1956), notably pp. 37ff.

[9] See H.L.A. Hart, *The Concept of Law* (Oxford, 1961), ch. 5, for the description of law as the union of primary and secondary rules: the former derive from the structure of society and its particular sense of obligation; the secondary rules are concerned exclusively with decisions on how primary rules should be interpreted. Lee, *African Armies and Civil Order*, p. 11, suggests that it is possible in the context of this theory to treat African customary law as "primary rules."

After stressing the difference between primitive law and civilized law, and the need to adhere to the idea of law as we know it in civilized societies, Bohannan notes in "The Differing Realms of the Law," in Bohannan, ed., *Law and Warfare*, pp. 44–47: Customs are norms or rules about the ways in which people must behave if social institutions are to perform their tasks and society is to endure. All institutions, including legal institutions, develop customs, but they are not analogous with customs. A legal institution is one by means of which the people of a society settle disputes and counteract many gross abuses of the rules in at least some of the nonlegal institutions. See also Bozeman, *The Future of Law in a Multicultural World*, pp. 35ff., for the normative legal system of the West; pp. 85ff. for law in sub-Saharan Africa.

[10] Gabriel d'Arboussier, "L'Evolution de la législation dans les pays africains d'expression française et à Madagascar," in Kuper and Kuper, eds., *African Law*, pp. 165ff.

Afro-European dialogue as the impact of Islamic law upon Negro societies on the continent. For just as the unwritten native customs emerged more vigorous and authentic from this long and continuous encounter than the written *shari'a* precepts of the politically victorious literate civilization,[11] they also proved resilient in the face of the European intrusion. When the brief colonial phase of deliberate modernization drew to a close, in fact, it was clear not only that the core of African customary law had remained intact, but also that many significant European ideas and institutions had been effectively Africanized—often, it is true, by deliberate policy-making on the part of the colonial administrations. This is not to suggest, of course, that the panorama of African law had not been greatly altered in the nineteenth and twentieth centuries by the introduction of European laws; the reformulation in written form of native customs; the establishment of separate, clearly differentiated court systems; and the principled distribution of judicial matter among the jurisdictions of indigenous African, Islamic, Indian, Roman-Dutch, and different modern Western systems of law. But local tribunals, variously termed African Courts, Customary Courts, or Native Courts in formerly British areas, were able to maintain the character of native tribunals, even though they derived their powers from statutes rather than traditional authority. Not only were they directed to apply native law and custom, both substantive and procedural—except when it was deemed inconsistent with local legislation or contrary to "natural justice, equity and good conscience," or some such formula—but British magistrates and judges were also extremely cautious in the exercise of their revisionary and appellate powers. In fact, in such socially crucial fields as family law and land law, customary courts retained almost unrestricted jurisdiction.[12]

[11] See *supra*, Chs. 7 and 13 for analyses of this interaction by Goody, Wilks, and Trimingham. See J.N.D. Anderson, *Islamic Law in Africa* (London, 1954) to the effect that native law and custom regarding land tenure won out even in northern Nigeria, where Muslim law is otherwise firmly entrenched. On the recessive nature of the latter in certain parts of West Africa, see also the same author's "The Adaptation of Muslim Law in Sub-Saharan Africa," in Kuper and Kuper, eds., *African Law*, pp. 149ff., 152. But see S. S. Richardson, "Whither Lay Justice in Africa?" in Max Gluckman, ed., *Ideas and Procedures in African Customary Law* (London, 1969), p. 133, on the resilience of Islamic law and *shari'a* courts in predominantly Muslim areas of Nigeria, where the population will not readily accept any adulteration of their personal law and religion by the introduction of Western proceedings.

[12] See, for example, Lloyd Fallers, "Customary Law in the New African States," in Hans W. Baade and Robinson O. Everett, eds., *African Law; New Law for New Nations* (Dobbs Ferry, N.Y., 1963), pp. 78–79. The general conclusions reached in this essay with respect to Busoga District in the Eastern province of Uganda are said to be broadly representative of the position of customary law and customary courts in most African countries formerly under British administration. *Ibid.*, p. 73. Compare Snell, *Nandi Customary Law*, pp. 89ff., 108, on pat-

The convergence of culture, history, and colonial policy upon the recognition of multiple legal systems and the primacy of customary law in local life has presented modern African governments with complex problems not faced by their predecessors. Foremost among these is the fact that the outer order of the new nation state, being modeled upon precedents set in Europe, is a derivative of European law and legal history, whereas much of the inner order is validated today by a plurality of native norms that differ not only from the received law, but also from each other. This standing ambiguity informs the process of nation-building today; for whereas the immediate demands for nationhood and independence could be served only by opting for the foreign frame of reference, the long-range prospects for national unity are everywhere dependent upon the solidity of the inner order. Modernization now requires a considerable measure of Africanization, even though the latter implies a reactivation of the past, and therewith plural, rather than uniform, traditions of legal control. Apart from having to determine priorities in the relation between Occidental and indigenous legal references, African governments thus have the additional task of isolating those principles of native law upon which the ethnically various elements of their culture appear to converge.

The responses that administrators and scholars have so far given to these two challenges point to some conclusions that may be pertinent to a discussion of African approaches to the settlement of disputes.[13] It appears clear, for instance, that indigenous law still displays specific quali-

---

terns of synchronization as they were apparent in the 1950s, and on trends in land law that suggested to this observer the eclipse of the tribe and clan and the emergence of the family as the primary unit in land tenure.

See F. D. Lugard, *The Rise of Our East African Empire*, 2 vols. (Edinburgh and London, 1893), Vol. I, 289, for a description of negotiations with some Kamba elders that pitted very different notions of rights to land against each other; since there was a honey-pot in a tree on a particular site, the land in question could not be acquired for any other use. For an analysis of these complex conflicts of law, see D. J. Penwill, *Kamba Customary Law*, ch. 4. For other observations on the interaction between differing jurisdictions, see N. A. Ollennu, "The Structure of African Judicial Authority and Problems of Evidence and Proof in Traditional Courts," in Gluckman, ed., *Ideas and Procedures in African Customary Law*, pp. 110ff. The major reference on colonial administration in areas formerly under British control is Lord Hailey, *An African Survey*, esp. ch. 6, "Systems of Government," and ch. 9, "Law and Justice." See also Lord Hailey, *Native Administration*. For a critical review of the British legacy and its use, see L.C.B. Gower, *Independent Africa; The Challenge to the Legal Profession* (Cambridge, Mass., 1967), pp. 26ff.

[13] An analysis of African legal systems, in particular African constitutional and administrative law, is outside the scope of the present work, which is concerned with conflict and various—not exclusively legal—ways of mitigating conflict. For a discussion of public law and organization, see Bozeman, *The Future of Law in a Multicultural World*, section on "Africa South of Sahara."

ties differentiating it from European law; that modern African citizens continue to feel morally and legally bound by it, especially in matters of family law, property, and land tenure; and that traditional tribunals are not only endowed with wide jurisdiction, but are more widely trusted and firmly established today than most of the new institutions set up to safeguard public justice in behalf of the modern state.[14] In Nigeria, for example, where the African bar is more strongly developed as a profession than anywhere else on the continent, it is estimated that over 90 percent of the judicial work at first instance is handled by over fifteen hundred customary courts.[15] With special reference to Western Nigeria it has been noted also that the judges of the customary courts are hardly ever conversant with the decisions of the so-called English courts of the region.[16] And with respect to East Africa, a specialist concludes not only that what we see in operation today is a system of courts and a body of law that has deep roots in traditional society and culture, but also that contemporary judges in local courts are usually unwilling or unable to discuss abstract rules of law.[17] Analogous conditions prevail in French-speaking nations,

[14] Compare Vansina, "A Traditional Legal System: The Kuba," p. 117. Bohannan, *Justice and Judgment among the Tiv*, to the effect that the Tiv of northern Nigeria resolve disputes without the use of formal courts or agencies to enforce decisions. Bohannan concludes, therefore, that attempts to translate the Tiv folk system into Western categories are not conducive to an understanding of Tiv law. A.M.R. Ramolefe states in "Lesotho Marriage, Guardianship, and the Customary-Law Heir," in Gluckman, ed., *Ideas and Procedures in African Customary Law*, p. 197, that in Lesotho "Custom is very much still *the* law and no amount of contempt for it by others can alter this fact." I. J. Poirier, "L'Analyse des espèces juridiques et l'étude des droits coutumiers africains," in Gluckman, ed., *Ideas and Procedures in African Customary Law*, p. 99, concludes that "C'est la solution traditionnelle qui est préferée" (the traditional solution is preferred); see also *ibid.*, pp. 97, 107. Pagans in areas of northern Nigeria who are subject to Muslim judges are likely to accept a decision only if the principles of pagan, rather than Islamic, law are enforced. And with regard to an Ethiopian society, it is reported that "no Gurage can live outside the kinship network in Gurageland; and therefore no Gurage can live outside tribal law." For these references see A. N. Allott, A. L. Epstein and M. Gluckman, "Introduction" to Gluckman, ed., *Ideas and Procedures in African Customary Law*, p. 30. Compare also Lee, *African Armies*, pp. 11–12.

[15] Richardson, "Whither Lay Justice in Africa?", p. 128. To like effect see J. Keuning, "The Study of Law in African Countries," in *Higher Education and Research in the Netherlands*, 7, No. 1 (1963), 3–6. Writing in 1968, Thierry Verheist stated with regard to Congo Kinshasa (Zaire) that "at this time nine-tenths of the population of the country still cling to their customary status, and the customary courts remain numerous and active. They render 300,000 to 400,000 judgments per year, and many of the most interesting of these decisions are recorded." *Safeguarding African Customary Law; Judicial and Legislative Processes for its Adaptation and Integration* (Los Angeles, 1968), p. 10.

[16] Keuning, "The Study of Law in African Countries," p. 4.

[17] Fallers, "Customary Law in the New African States," pp. 80, 82. J. Van Velsen, "Procedural Informality, Reconciliation, and False Comparisons," in Gluckman, ed., *Ideas and Procedures in African Customary Law*, pp. 138ff. notes that subordinate courts appear to be more important as forums of dispute settle-

including Madagascar, for here, too, people prefer traditional courts, particularly when it comes to matters affecting their personal status, and view resort to official justice as abnormal and exceptional.[18]

These realities, in conjunction with national pride in the African past, make it unlikely that ancient notions and structures will be swept away altogether. Some trends to that effect certainly existed in the early years of independence as, for example, in Senegal, where it was widely expected "in the frenzy of unification by legislation" that the very foundations of custom would crumble, even though it was also realized that the great mass of the population was continuing to follow the trusted guidelines of the past.[19] And there are dispositions toward that end even today, for many lawyers eager to accelerate modernization, and not content with the eclipse of indigenous norms in such fields as criminal and commercial law, continue to hope for the speedy disappearance of all customary laws and to be suspicious, therefore, of anything that might give them a new lease of life.[20] By and large, however, it appears that African scholars are now intensifying research into the customary law of their respective countries, that judges and law officers are increasingly conscious of the social advantages offered by flexible native traditions of litigation, and that governments are determined to create national legal systems with a decidedly African character.[21] In short, utilitarian and ideological considerations have persuaded most African nations to plan,

---

ment than superior courts, since the bulk of litigation starts and ends there. In this author's view it is only in the urban context, where society tends to be heterogeneous, that the Anglo-Saxon common law really makes sense.

[18] Poirier, "L'Analyse des espèces juridiques," pp. 99ff. H. Deschamps, "La Première Codification africaine: Madagascar 1828–81," in Gluckman, ed., *Ideas and Procedures in African Customary Law*, p. 172.

[19] D'Arboussier, "L'Evolution de la législation," pp. 165ff.

[20] Gower, *Independent Africa*, p. 93; on the problems and crises confronting the African legal profession, *ibid.*, pp. 102ff. See also A. Arthur Schiller, "Introduction," in Thomas W. Hutchison, ed., *Africa and Law* (New York, 1968), for a review of trends and developments in the field of law reform. See *ibid.*, pp. viii–ix for Schiller's own view: "I believe, however, that it is proper and might be fruitful to call attention to one area of African law that deserves more space than is given in the studies in this volume. I refer to customary law, or more properly, indigenous law, generally dismissed as of minor importance by the lawyer immersed in the legal problems of economic development, characterized as antiquarian by the policy-maker, and surrendered to the anthropologist, who normally attempts to reconstitute the pristine, primitive law untainted by contact with Western ways and modern life. . . . This is an area of African law deserving of attention and, to my mind, crucial to the successful development of these legal systems of the future."

[21] Richardson, "Whither Lay Justice in Africa," pp. 123ff. The African Conference on Local Courts and Customary Law, held in Dar-es-Salaam in 1963, was broadly in agreement that professional lawyers should be trained in customary law. However, the experts tended to view the central government as the directing force in the evolution of customary law.

on the one hand, for the Africanization of received systems of law and, on the other, for the coordination, integration, or unification of the multiple local orders within their national frontiers.

Diverse national programs to reform or restate the law have been announced or initiated in recent years, but none can as yet be said to constitute an adequate response to the great challenge of legal unification. As one prominent student of the matter recently observed, after allowing for the fact that, officially at least, all law is African today, nowhere is there as yet a single national system of common law applying equally to all persons within the territory.[22]

Success in the search for a shared body of juridical norms around which ethnically and socially distinct communities might coalesce continues to be impeded by many methodological, terminological, and conceptual difficulties. Not only are scholars by no means in accord as to just what law—either in its Western or in its universal sense—is all about, but they differ also when it comes to circumscribing the general nature of customary law. Furthermore, anthropologists, without whose aid lawyers cannot make much headway in Africa, are apt to be so acutely aware of the uniqueness of the particular folk societies within the immediate purview of their investigations, that they are reluctant to look for convergences and analogies in the various communal systems that lawyers want to unify. On the technical level, meanwhile, obstacles are encountered by virtue of the fact that the records of legally significant processes are not fully available for analysis and comparison, either because they have not been reduced to writing and cannot be recaptured in written form, or because they cannot be isolated from the general social context in which disputes and decisions are traditionally ensconced.

[22] Antony N. Allott, "The Future of African Law," in Kuper and Kuper, eds., *African Law*, p. 223. *Ibid.*, pp. 224–227 for a critical, essentially pessimistic, prognosis of present developments and those likely in the future. Ollennu, "The Structure of African Judicial Authority," p. 118 says that resort to customary law is to be encouraged; *ibid.*, p. 14, for Ollennu's statement that the colonial distinction between introduced and customary law is now felt to be undesirable, and that there is a movement for integration of all types of law.

For a review of achievements and projects in the field of codification and restatement of laws, see the "Introduction" to Gluckman, ed., *Ideas and Procedures in African Customary Law*, notably pp. 28, 32. Not surprisingly, codification has gone farthest in African countries with a civil law tradition.

Poirier, "L'Analyse des espèces juridiques," p. 97, believes that a new kind of customary law is about to evolve in many countries as authorities try to bridge the gaps between modern legislated law, on the one hand, and old customary law, on the other. Keuning, "The Study of Law in African Countries," p. 4, believes that customary law will continue to play a major role in the years to come. See also Lloyd Fallers, "Customary Law in the New African States," p. 72. Writing in 1954, Snell envisioned "some future problems," not only in the relation between Nandi customary law and English law, but also between the customary laws of the Nandi and other tribes. See *Nandi Customary Law*, p. 121.

The search for unifying typologies and categories is difficult today for another set of reasons. As Poirier and other scholars have pointed out, the official customary law has by no means displaced the old secret or esoteric law which, being contrary to the "public order," is not easily documented. Indeed, recourse to supernatural mediating agencies, whether on the level of beneficial or of black magic, has in many regions decidedly increased since decolonization.[23] Three kinds of situations, in particular, are said to invite occult referrals today:

(1) Where central executive and judicial power is not strong enough to enforce its wishes upon the whole population involved, it is likely that the central power will be seen as supported by occult powers, and this support will extend to its judicial functions, in determining guilt and innocence; further dependence on occult support will apply particularly in cases where the contending parties before the judges are too strong for the judges to give a decision against one of them. These may then leave the test to occult powers, through oaths.

(2) Where, in any African society, the offence complained of is itself occult, as in a charge of witchcraft or sorcery.

(3) Where there is strong suspicion, but not definite proof.[24]

Another manifestation of the felt inadequacy of customary law and its modern administration in the nation state is the persistence of so-called "parallel law,"[25] notably that of arbitral justice. Surveys of this trend, which appears to gain rather than lose momentum in many different African regions, have convinced authorities that suspicion of central power, tribalism, trust in supernatural sanctions, and a general preference for elastic modes of conciliating disputants are the major factors making for this renascence of the native style in conflict resolution.[26]

[23] Poirier, "L'Analyse des espèces juridiques," pp. 102ff., and see *supra*, Part IV, where the place of magic and witchcraft in African life and thought is discussed. Compare in particular Meek, *A Sudanese Kingdom*, pp. 347ff. on the importance of the diviner, trials by ordeal, and oaths as agencies of magical power that give expression to the legal conceptions of the Jukun peoples. This system, which has close analogues in all pagan tribes of Nigeria, cannot easily be reduced to terms of "native courts" and modern codes of law. To like effect see Meek, *Law and Authority*, pp. 84, 154ff., 238ff.; Penwill, *Kamba Customary Law*, p. 89, on the secret tribunals of Kamba elders; Huntingford, *The Nandi of Kenya*, pp. 25ff., to the effect that obedience is based on the firm knowledge that behind the judgment of the Council of Elders lies the ancestral spirit, the *oiik*.
[24] Allott, Epstein, and Gluckman, "Introduction," in Gluckman, ed., *Ideas and Procedures in African Customary Law*, pp. 35–36.
[25] Poirier, "L'Analyse des espèces juridiques," p. 101.
[26] *Ibid.*, pp. 100ff., 107, on the situation in Dahomey, Cameroon, Niger, and Madagascar; Ollennu, "The Structure of African Judicial Authority," pp. 112, 117; Allott, *Essays in African Law*, pp. 68ff., 120ff.

Arbitration is, of course, an established legal device also in the West, where it is carefully distinguished, on the one hand, from adjudication and, on the other, from mediation, conciliation, and negotiation. But arbitration in, for example, English law, and "arbitration" in African customary law are not two incidents of a single legal species, but rather two entirely different institutions, with different purposes and different methods—as Allott concludes after a full review of African arbitral proceedings as they "were and are."[27] The latter are rooted in the demands of intrafamily relations, in the context of which it is taken for granted that the family head knows the parties as well as the issue in contention and can be expected, if necessary—with the assistance of the elders or other members of the household—to settle quarrels, discipline those who misbehave, and restore harmony in the group by exerting persuasion rather than by imposing a verdict in strict accordance with customary law. Intrafamily arbitrations of this sort appear to be universal occurrences throughout Africa, as important to societies with chiefs, like those of the Tswana or Ashanti, as to the Bushmen and acephalous societies like the Nuer, Ibo, and Kikuyu. Disputes between more remote relatives, two families, or nonrelated groups give rise to very similar efforts of restoring peace and harmony, either by negotiating a settlement acceptable to both sides, or by arranging a hearing before an impartial arbiter. The latter, who is often asked to intercede after direct negotiations have broken down, may be a village headman, village elders, a council of neighbors, (as, for example, among the Bunyoro in East Africa), a panel allowing for the representation of stool-holders (as in Ashanti), or a priest or some other personality (such as, for example, the Leopard-Skin Chief among the Nuer, who has arbitral power because he is deemed capable of controlling supernatural and psychic forces). And a very similar range of dispositions toward the resolution of disputes is recorded in areas of "restricted literacy" as, for example, those of the nomadic Somalis. Here, where the spread of Islamic literate law has facilitated judicial settlements on a national basis, but where pre-Islamic culture traits—including a strong preference for oral communication—steadfastly persist, sheikhs are expected above all to mediate and arbitrate among contending factions.[28]

Varied as the local arrangements are, all are different from English practices in the sense that they aim at conciliation rather than at rendering justice in compliance with objective norms. Contrary to the usual Western practice, in terms of which the parties agree beforehand to accept an arbitral award, African disputants may, therefore, reject a deci-

---

[27] Allott, *Essays in African Law*, pp. 117–145; cf. also Rattray, *Ashanti Law and Constitution*, pp. 388ff., also pp. 4–5.
[28] See Lewis, "Literacy in a Nomadic Society," pp. 266–270.

sion that does not effect the desired reconciliation. And in such an eventuality, things revert to the status quo ante, the implication being that other attempts at arbitration, perhaps by more powerful authorities, will be forthcoming in due course.

Arbitral proceedings in Africa, then, are more in the nature of informal processes of negotiation and conciliation than of "arbitration" as understood in the West. This conclusion, which is fully developed by Allott,[29] justifies the same author's advice that no purpose is served by forcing African approaches to arbitral settlement into the straightjacket of English law (or, for that matter, any European legal order). The opposite is indicated: they ought to be accepted by scholars and practitioners on their own merits—all the more so, one may add, since they represent the African genius for reaching compromise and accommodation. For whereas native institutions of "adjudication" appear to attract and retain essentially Western meanings, arbitration and conciliation, being culturally congenial and resilient systems of ideas, continue to reflect the force of trusted indigenous "law." In this perspective they are, therefore, rightly viewed as the most promising mainstays of public order in Africa's new states.[30]

[29] *Essays in African Law*, ch. 6, "Arbitral Proceedings in Customary Law," pp. 117–141, upon which this brief explanation is based. See also *ibid.*, pp. 141ff., "Suggestions for a Model Ordinance Regulating Arbitral Proceedings." For different interpretations, see Ollennu's essay, "The Structure of African Judicial Authority," and Elias, *The Nature of African Customary Law*, pp. 212–215, the latter to the effect that "arbitration" is a much misused word in nearly all the contexts in which it is usually applied to African legal procedures. The Nigerian jurist admits, however, that an African judge is primarily a peacemaker, anxious to effect a reconciliation so as to attain the primary objective of the African legal system, namely, the maintenance of the social equilibrium. See *ibid.*, pp. 271ff.

[30] Ollennu, "The Structure of African Judicial Authority, p. 118. Whether this promise is justified appears to be a matter of doubt. Writing in 1965, Allott found that some modern legislatures have tried to repress extrajudicial arbitrations as "usurpations of judicial powers" that threaten the work of the established courts; others have tolerated them; but none appears to have welcomed them as a foundation on which to build a new judicial system. See "The Future of African Law," p. 233. On the relevance of this arbitral tradition in the field of modern inter-African relations, see *supra*, Part II, and *infra*, Ch. 19.

· 17 ·

THE HEALING POWER OF
THE WORD

The foregoing discussion suggests that the situation is not auspicious for the search of unity in African law, as long as one holds exclusively to the exacting norms set by comparative studies in the West. But, when the focus of interest and inquiry is shifted from the plurality of existing ethnic and national legal orders to the general spirit of the law that pervades each African society, uniformities readily appear—in much the same way, one may add, as they do when different Occidental legal systems are drawn together under such presiding concepts as "the spirit of the Roman law," or "the spirit of the common law."

The first Pan-African theme to be stressed in such a frame of inquiry is the obvious fact that all customary laws are different from each of the Western systems in the sense that their validity is not determined by writing. Custom, memory, judgment, and other forms of decision-making are not committed to written records. Also missing are such emanations of literate thought as juridical abstractions, theories of law, and critical philosophical comment upon the function or worth of existing legal institutions. The question as to just what customary law is cannot be settled, therefore, by consulting documents. Rather, it is properly answered by the admonition of a modern Nigerian writer: "Watch how we live."[1] And, indeed, social realities everywhere are found to converge upon the proposition that law is tantamount to the totality of communal life. This means that well nigh every occurrence, however trivial or irrelevant it may appear to the outsider, is apt to be legally significant from the native point of view. It also means that strict divisions into, for example, public and private law, or civil and criminal law, are not always tenable.

It should be recalled, next, that mythical nonliterate thought fathoms the magical universe in which human society is firmly imbedded. Conflicts relating to such overtly secular matters as land tenure, succession to property, crimes, and other fields of law now regarded as distinct from one another, are thus everywhere experienced also as aspects of the general religio-magical superstructure. That is to say, the African spirit of law or "juridical dynamic"[2] envelops mundane as well as surrealist jurisdictions. Since power or vital energy is accepted as the ruling principle in the spirit realm, nature, and society alike, traditional law may be said

---

[1] Anaibe, "The Wisdom of My People."
[2] This term is employed by Poirier, "L'Analyse des espèces juridiques," p. 98.

to have the supreme function of manipulating power in all of its greatly various disguises so that the community may survive intact. Floating, comprehensive, and ever present, it induces a firm collective consciousness of what is wrong and what is right, thus assuring almost as a matter of course the maintenance of order[3] and that sense for social justice that has impressed foreign observers from Ibn Battūta onward.

The paramount juridical subject of all customary law, then, is the community. The individual, by contrast, finds recognition only in his role-playing capacity as a member of the family, lineage, clan, village, or other grouping. In this context he is expected, above all, to comply with traditional obligations. The Occidental legal idea of the autonomous person, endowed with legal rights and responsibilities, has not had an equivalent in traditional African law. It is questionable, indeed, whether it can be rendered in legally and socially meaningful ways even today; for modern developments, revolutionary as they are in many respects, do not appear to detract substantially from the accent on commitments to the social organism.[4] Furthermore, since the community is marked by hierarchically staggered social relationships, law, too, stipulates for intricate gradations of responsibilities. Inequality, not equality, is therefore a basic principle of all African customary law.[5]

On the subject of legal identity, it must be recognized, moreover, that the traditional jural community is peopled not only by natural, but also by a host of supernatural, invisible personalities. Quite in accordance with mythical understandings of the interpenetration of life and death, in terms of which, for example, it is not at all unusual for a person to talk

[3] As previously suggested, the public order accommodates a great variety of conflict situations. See *supra*, Parts II, IV, V.

[4] Compare S. F. Nadel, "Reason and Unreason in African Law," *Africa*, 26, No. 2 (April 1956), pp. 170ff. on "the more or less fixed sum total of roles which societies as it were load upon their individuals." William B. Harvey, *Law and Social Change in Ghana* (Princeton, 1966), pp. 357ff.; also, by the same author, "Post-Nkrumah Ghana," in Thomas W. Hutchison, ed., *Africa and Law* (Madison, Milwaukee, and London, 1968), p. 109. S.K.B. Asante, "Law and Society in Ghana," in Hutchison, ed., *Africa and Law*, p. 130, to the effect that in the traditional order the accent was on the group as the basic juridical unit. *Ibid.*, pp. 131–132, points out that modern presuppositions of the individual as the basic juridical unit—implied, for example, in all colonial regulatory laws as well as in the steady growth of private economic enterprise—have not substantially detracted from the Ghanaian commitment to philosophical or social collectivism. "Neither Oxford nor Harvard," Asante concludes, "has succeeded in extricating the educated Ghanaian from the intricate web of obligations implicit in the traditional family system." On the difficulty of using the Roman *persona* and the English "personality" in the context of African customary law, see also Max Gluckman, ed., *Ideas and Procedures in African Customary Law*, "Introduction," p. 47.

[5] Compare in this respect Etienne Possoz, *Elements de droit coutumier nègre* (Paris, 1944), as cited by Schiller, "Law," pp. 167–168.

with her dead mother as eagerly as if she were alive,[6] the law recognizes ghosts, souls, deities, stools, and ancestors as living, legally active, units. Nuer law thus allows for "Ghost Marriages";[7] Ashanti law accepts the spirits of the departed forbears of the clan as the real landowners; and Ibo law accords legal personality to certain psychological forces in the sense that these can acquire, enjoy, and transfer property rights and interests as freely and fully as natural persons.[8] Similarly, complex identities have long been respected in the case of wrongs or crimes. Reminiscing on his sojourn in West Africa, Dennett recalls that it was considered a crime for a person to trample on, or even to cross, the shadow of another, since the shadow was commonly associated with the very breath of a man. Moreover, since shadows had lives of their own, they could escape or be robbed, thus giving rise to calamitous situations that could be righted only by the prompt institution of elaborate quasi-legal processes and sacred sanctions.[9]

The logic of these understandings of "the legal personality" explains not only why many adversary situations are not readily reducible to legal categories known in the West, but also why African communities have brought forth intricate laws pertaining to status, family relations, succession, and inheritance, while they have not produced equally concise norms for the treatment of, for example, private wrongs and contractual transactions. The chief measure of this differentiated development is to be found in the social and legal neglect of the individualized natural person. For, as Sir Henry Maine explained it so lucidly, contract presupposes the individual's capacity to disengage himself from the group, make up his mind independently, and assume binding obligations voluntarily. In Africa, by contrast, nonliteracy, a rigid attachment to the kinship group, communal isolation, and scant commercial contacts with outside groups had frustrated that movement from status to contract which Maine associates with the evolution of "progressive societies"— all the more so as the concept of time prevalent in the culture is traditionally inhospitable to long-range promises, which presuppose confidence not only in the individual will, but also in the future.[10] And the

---

[6] This particular animated conversation was overheard by Mary Kingsley, the noted explorer; see her *West African Studies*, p. 54.

[7] P. P. Howell, *A Manual of Nuer Law* (London, and New York, 1954), p. 74. On this issue, see also Gluckman, ed., *Ideas and Procedures in African Customary Law*, p. 44.

[8] For these and other illustrations see A. N. Allott, "Legal Personality in African Law," in Gluckman, ed., *Ideas and Procedures in African Customary Law*, pp. 179ff.

[9] Dennett, *At the Back of the Black Man's Mind*, pp. 79ff.

[10] See Y. P. Ghai, "Customary Contracts and Transactions in Kenya," in Gluckman, ed., *Ideas and Procedures in African Customary Law*, p. 334, that a mere

same cluster of factors had, of course, impeded the abstraction and refinement of such ideas as individual motive, intent, adequacy of consideration, mistake, negligence, and duress, that constitute the core of Occidental laws of tort and contract.

The absence or near absence of a contract law comparable to that of the civil or common law in no way implies that African customary law ignores the notion of commitment. On the contrary, as noted previously, each individual is not only born into a network of standing obligations toward his kinsmen and the forces they represent, but becomes readily bound in new collective accords between component groups of his community. What needs to be stressed about customary contracts is the fact that they involve multiple parties within a linguistically and ethnically unified community. Furthermore, each accord, whether concerned with marriage arrangements, land, or credit transactions, constitutes a particular social compact that aims at ordering a particular set of concrete circumstances rather than complying with consistent legal norms. Concluded orally—at least until recently—usually in the presence of witnesses, and often with the aid of tangible objects designed to materialize the spoken words,[11] contracts seem to be generally observed in good faith. This is because they bind people who know each other well, and who are unified in their respect for such ultimate sacred sanctions as the oath and the curse. However, and despite all expectations of compliance, it cannot be said that contracts are commonly regarded as absolutely binding. Commenting on the essential "informality" of customary contract law in Kenya, a noted scholar remarks that "there is no great legal deterrent

---

exchange of promises has no legal validity, and that there exists no generalized concept of an executory contract in customary African law. See *ibid.*, "Introduction," p. 77, to the effect that very few African legal systems had developed a clear conception or general model of contract.

[11] As literacy spreads, contracts today are often written and proved with the aid of written documents. For observations on the issue, see Snell, *Nandi Customary Law*, chs. 3 and 5; I. Schapera, "Contract in Tswana Law," in Gluckman, ed., *Ideas and Procedures in African Customary Law*, pp. 318ff., 327. Even in certain Muslim societies bargaining processes are usually communicated orally, and agreements are rarely, if ever, recorded in writing. Reporting on the Gonja community in northern Ghana, Goody found that they were sworn verbally, but on the Koran. See his essay on "Restricted Literacy in Northern Ghana," p. 211. In Somali society, by contrast, certain collective commitments, notably those made in connection with "insurance associations" that help the payment of blood compensation, have been recorded in writing since colonial times. *Ibid.*, pp. 270ff. On "the concrete element" see Holleman, *Shona Customary Law*, pp. 134ff.; the usage of materializing tokens, Holleman explains, is essentially due to the particular disposition of the Shona mind to express itself in terms of a concrete action or by means of a tangible token, rather than by abstract words or formulae. *Ibid.*, p. 136, n. 1: "I have often witnessed at formal court sessions that court assessors or members of the public insisted: 'we have heard you saying that you are wrong . . . but we must see it too.'"

against committing breach of contract"; that "most contracts, other than the 'once and for all' transactions, are broken wherever any party feels like it"; and that "specific performance in the sense of ordering the carrying out of the agreement is unusual."[12] Here, as elsewhere in Africa, courts are found not to insist on enforcing contractual obligations, but aim instead at settling the underlying dispute; and this they do more often than not by canceling the arrangement and putting the parties back into their original positions.

What is true with regard to violations of customary contract also holds for thefts, killings, intrigues, disputes over debts or boundaries, drunken brawls, or disturbances in family relations; namely, African courts are concerned above all with the restoration of order, social equilibrium, and the status quo. For, just as African law is coterminous with existing social mores and customs, nonformalized except in action, popular, and springing from the people and their practices,[13] so is the African judicial system comprehensive and all-pervasive in its purport, design, and operation. Although local frames of reference differ from each other in particulars, all converge upon the existence of a profusion of assemblies, councils, courts, moots, arbitration boards, oracles, ritual experts, and special intermediaries. Each forum has its special competence, but all are intertwined, often in staggered arrangements that reflect existing hierarchies in the political system. In so-called complex societies—as, for example, those of the Luba and the Kuba—it is possible, therefore, to distinguish clearly between moots that have no fixed membership and are called upon to arbitrate rather than to judge conflicts arising within a lineage, clan, or village, on the one hand, and formal courts, staffed by specially competent judges, on the other.[14] Very similar lines of differentiation mark the realm of legal administration in Ngoni country (Nyasaland, now Malawi), where conflicts not settled by the village headman may be brought first to the chief's court and, if this recourse fails, to the court of the paramount;[15] in Sukuma society, where the chiefly court

[12] Ghai, "Customary Contracts," p. 343; also "Introduction" in Gluckman, ed., *Ideas and Procedures in African Customary Law*, p. 76. Haydon, *Law and Justice in Buganda*, pp. 231ff., begins his discussion of "contracts" by explaining that "prior to the introduction of cowry shells by the Arabs in the reign of the Kabaka Suna (1810–1852), barter was the only type of contract for acquiring interest in property." Among the nobility, ivory, too, was a medium of exchange. It is said that Kabaka Mwanga first sold villages to chiefs for ivory. See p. 232 to the effect that the verbal agreements of the nineteenth century gave way to the written agreements of the twentieth, particularly with respect to cattle and land. Nevertheless, verbal contracts on proof are said to be still valid today with respect to all property. On the relevance of traditional approaches to contract for modern constitutionalism, see *supra*, Part II and *infra*, Ch. 20 B.

[13] Allott, *Essays in African Law*, p. 67.

[14] Vansina, "A Traditional Legal System," pp. 99ff., 111.

[15] Read, *The Ngoni of Nyasaland*, p. 92.

functions in criminal matters, whereas the court of headmen, assisted by assessors chosen from among village elders, is called upon to hear minor cases;[16] and among the Kpelle of Liberia, who rely heavily not only on official courts, but also upon a galaxy of inofficial tribunals set up by town chiefs, church groups, cooperatives of all kinds, the Poro, and so-called house palavers or moots, in which kinsmen of the litigants and neighbors air an existing dispute, but defer the actual settlement to a mediator, who then pronounces the consensus of the group.[17]

Elsewhere, as among the Kikuyu, Kamba, and Nandi in Kenya, in whose ranks the patriarchal principle is strongly developed, social conflicts are frequently subjected to unofficial, often secret, hearings; these are conducted by the head of the senior branch of the extended family, a conclave of elders, or a court that operates as a commission of arbitration, whose decision is then enforced by the respective kinship group.[18] In other politically less complex communities as, for example, those of the Tiv, great reliance is placed on "asking sessions," during which all disturbing issues are expected to be put to rest authoritatively—including, for instance, the question as to just why the kinsmen of a sick or dying man have allowed the particular calamity to happen.[19] In short, this limited survey suggests that the spectrum of judicial or quasi-judicial agencies has always been remarkably broad in an African community—a fact that made a deep impression upon Alvares d'Almada when he visited Sierra Leone toward the end of the sixteenth century:

> Each village possesses its court of justice. This is a large house with an adjoining circular porch; . . . on a raised platform is seated the chief with his councillors on either side and a little below him. Under the porch, whose ceiling and floor are covered with finely woven coloured mats, is a sort of tribunal for the audience. The plaintiffs come forward, each accompanied by an advocate. . . . These lawyers, when they appear in court, deck themselves ingeniously with plumes and bells, and have their faces covered with grotesque masks, for they say that thus disguised they feel more at ease to speak boldly in front of their chief. They also carry lances on which they lean as they talk. Each one speaks in turn, until the arguments of one outweigh those of the other. The case is discussed in secret by the chief and his coun-

[16] Cory, *The Indigenous Political System of the Sukuma*, pp. 8ff., 56ff., 67ff.

[17] James L. Gibbs, Jr., "The Kpelle Moot," in Bohannan, ed., *Law and Warfare* (Garden City, N.Y., 1967), pp. 277ff.; see also *supra*, p. 109 with reference to the Poro; on the role of intermediaries, see *infra*, Ch. 18.

[18] Compare Lambert, *Kikuyu Social and Political Institutions*, pp. 107–118; Penwill, *Kamba Customary Law*, p. 89; Huntingford, *The Nandi of Kenya*, pp. 31ff.

[19] Compare *supra*, p. 98 on the Tiv, and Lloyd, *Africa in Social Change*, pp. 35ff. on arbitral settlements.

cillors, . . . and when the verdict is rendered, the sentence, whatever it be, must be carried out on the spot; thus fines must be paid in full before the court adjourns. Sorcerers are condemned to death, beheaded and their bodies thrown outside the village to be eaten by wild animals. Those condemned to death for other reasons are offered for sale.[20]

The actual judicial processes as they unfold themselves before the customary courts and enclaves, whether sitting officially or informally, openly or in secret, are naturally as diverse as the boards themselves and the cases that come before them. But certain norms emerge as typically African, if only because they are everywhere functions of nonliteracy. As one scholar remarks, since there is no writing, there can be no written memory, no "refurbishing of old precedents," no private pondering over legal principles, no juristic analysis[21]—intellectual activities that depend on the existence of written texts. In default of such activities, indeed, there can be no professional lawyers. The major indispensable requirements in any traditional proceedings are therefore twofold: the parties must be present, and speech must be given free rein, even as it is subjected to regulations.

In connection with the first requirement, it is important to recall that the legal identity of each disputant is usually represented plurally. That is to say, multiple parties, often inclusive of invisible agents, must participate in a given case if the foremost purpose of the proceedings is to be achieved. For just as any particular relationship is just one aspect of all interactions within the unified group—and these are normally permanent in nature—so is each dispute incomprehensible and insoluble outside this total social context. It follows, as Van Velsen notes in his analysis of "multiplex" relationships, that "judges and litigants, and the litigants among themselves, interact in relations whose significance ranges beyond the transitoriness of the court or a particular dispute. Today they are disputing in court, tomorrow they may be collaborating in the same work party."[22] In such circumstances, the supreme purpose of a hearing is usually not the vindication or indictment of an individual,[23] but the

[20] A. P. Kup, *A History of Sierra Leone, 1400–1787* (Cambridge, 1961), p. 9.
[21] Allott, *Essays in African Law*, pp. 62ff.
[22] Van Velsen, "Procedural Informality, Reconciliation, and False Comparisons," p. 138; also Max Gluckman, *The Judicial Process among the Barotse of Northern Rhodesia* (Manchester, 1955), ch. 2. Compare Bohannan, *Justice and Judgment among the Tiv*, pp. 19, 61–65, to the effect that a Tiv court aims at determining a mutually acceptable settlement, not at applying "laws"; also Van Velsen, "Procedural Informality, Reconciliation, and False Comparisons," pp. 143ff., who says that Shona chiefs in Rhodesia would settle rather than decide, appease and reconcile rather than enforce.
[23] Except in accusations of witchcraft; see *supra*, Ch. 5, n. 73. For accounts of highly individualized trials in Iboland, see Meek, *Law and Authority*, ch. 10, pp.

rectification of troubled social relations so that all concerned may continue to live together amicably. This means that African judges are either presumed to know all the relevant facts beforehand, or that they must broaden their inquiries so as to discover not only how the litigants are descendant, but also, and most importantly, just what the total history of the relations between the parties is. In deference to this kind of search for truth and justice, any evidence, including information gathered by divination, ritual imprecations, application of killing oaths, and, in certain communities, dream evidence,[24] is thus considered relevant. Questions may therefore be put to the parties or to witnesses in manners not considered suitable under, for example, English rules of evidence and procedure, and witnesses may identify themselves in ways not recognized in Western courts. In reporting on an action involving a stool or other traditional office in West Africa, Ollennu explains that the incumbent of the office gives evidence in the first person of events that happened in the times of a predecessor as if they occurred in his own time, since in African belief there is social identification of each holder with his ancestors and predecessors[25]—an approach, incidentally, that conforms quite logically with the principle of collective identity and with the undifferentiating sense of time to which attention was drawn earlier.[26]

With these qualifications—if that is what they are—the rule obtains in all African societies, politically centralized as well as uncentralized, that human witnesses are the primary sources of information at a trial in which vital points are in dispute between the parties. Verbal argument thus abounds. Chaos is avoided in some chiefly courts by the intervention of judges, court remembrancers, or court criers, who tirelessly appeal to the audience to keep calm as witnesses testify; in other tribal communities by intricate methods of recording the various points made by the parties and their witnesses. In a vivid account of such procedures, Elias thus explains that the Kikuyu elders require each witness to produce a

---

206ff.; especially pp. 213ff. and 238ff. for the trial of a man accused of having stolen one yam. When the crowded marketplace was seized by general anger and confusion, the elders rose and, clapping their hands, said: "Keep quiet—we do not yet know whether he is guilty or innocent. We shall know when we have heard him." *Ibid.*, p. 240.

[24] See Meek, *Law and Authority*, pp. 342ff. on the close knowledge that Ibo judges had of the personal characters of the parties to a case; also Elias, *The Nature of African Customary Law*, p. 243. See *supra*, Ch. 10 on oathing, and cf. Kirk-Greene, "On Swearing," pp. 43–53, where the author reports on the recent and current use of certain judicial oaths, suggesting that these are valuable sources of customary law in Adamawa Province. *Ibid.*, p. 45, on the "material components" of some of the oaths.

[25] Ollennu, "The Structure of African Judicial Authority," p. 110.

[26] Compare *supra*, Ch. 5.

bundle of sticks. Used like an abacus, these act as tallies to count scores made by either side of relevant points in the course of often windy speeches. The issue of the case may often depend on the final number of sticks piled up before each of the two parties to the dispute.[27]

All inquiries into the circumstances of a dispute are, therefore, in their very nature free ranging. Indeed, no one appears disconcerted in proceedings under customary law if, perchance, the very issue under consideration or the identity of the accused is changed midstream in the deliberation of a given case—all the more so as there is general agreement that the hearing relates not so much to the primary cause of the conflict or disturbance as to the appearances after the fact. Conversely, and in full accord with the behavioral or situational nature of the proceedings, parties are often allowed to try and correct the views of the court while the case is being heard. This is so, for example, in the Ga State (Ghana), where those present and listening are deemed entitled to know just how the councillors are thinking about the testimony—perhaps because no opportunity exists in a nonliterate society to review the reasoning process of a judge in all of its phases and register particularized objections once the proceedings have been closed.[28]

Oral communication, the second major requirement in traditional African trials, hearings, and judicial or quasi-judicial negotiations, is obviously a concomitant of the need for the physical participatory presence of disputants, witnesses, judges, and assorted segments of the public. In fact, the intricate correlation and interaction of these two factors vividly illustrates that affirmative African approach to conflict in its socially and psychically vital functions. For what is being joined and syncretized on these occasions is first, the shared perception of conflict as a structuring or constitutive force in communal affairs; and second, the equally clear recognition that actual, well-regulated adversary confrontations provide the most auspicious circumstances for the blunting or abatement of socially threatening tensions. Whether viewed as an art, a rite, a drama, or a sport, litigation of one sort or another thus conduces to a cleansing of emotions, the relief of accumulated tensions, and therewith, to a renewal of unity around time-tested norms and beliefs. The same conditions combine to explain, of course, why such proceedings are experienced as a source of great enjoyment; why Africans, whether schooled in customary law or not, impress outsiders as born

[27] Elias, *The Nature of African Customary Law*, pp. 243–246.
[28] Ollennu, "The Structure of African Judicial Authority," p. 111. Elias, *The Nature of African Customary Law*, p. 244, to the effect that any member of the audience who has something to say touching the case may ask to be permitted to say it.

advocates and judges; and why traditional societies are generally viewed as markedly litigious in character.[29]

The same logic that allows conflict to discharge its two evidently contradictory functions without detriment to the group, also explains the dual powers that reside in speech: the magic of the wounding or the killing word[30] has its counterpart in the trusted magic of the palliating or the healing word. In fact, no reconciliation or negotiated settlement is fathomable in a nonliterate society without reliance upon the proper use of talk.

There are stages in the proceedings of palavers and trials during which speech must be allowed to be free flowing, voluminous, and roundabout if the purpose of the meeting and the requirements of evidence are to be satisfied. Whatever the auspices in which African deliberations are conducted—and these are usually formalized in one way or another —speakers should not be interrupted, for conflicts and grievances must be talked out and therefore heard out if they are to be dissolved. The Ashanti have thus long honored the customary arrangement for "lampooning liberties," when the people in the federation could sing for eight days of all the faults, villainies, and frauds of their superiors or inferiors with impunity and without interruption. In this case words carrying rebuke, ridicule, and combativeness were entrusted, in the final analysis, with the pacifying mission.[31] At Ewe meetings, too, debates were apt to be long winded, even though quasi-parliamentary rules were strictly observed when Westermann visited Togoland:

> Order rules the meetings. Nobody speaks except at the invitation of the chairman or the speaker or after receiving permission to speak at his own request. The person speaking begins with [an Ewe phrase], after which there is general silence. Interruptions are prohibited, and are censured or are penalized on the spot with a fine. At the conclusion of a speech or at a pause, however, approval or disapproval can be expressed. The address of an important person is acknowledged at the end by a flourish of the court band that is present. Speaking time is not limited, and abundant use is made of this privilege. Addresses of from two to three hours duration are not rare. . . . If the chairman suspects that a speaker in his defense has departed too much from the truth, he suddenly has the band interrupt the address with a vigorous flourish; if after this interruption the speaker immediately finds the

[29] Compare, for example, Redfield, "Primitive Law," p. 20, who says that to go into law is one of the most exquisite enjoyments for the Akamba. Junod, *Moeurs et coutumes*, p. 405; and Henri Philippe Junod, *Bantu Heritage* (Johannesburg, 1938), p. 39. On the African's love of forensic weapons in thrashing out a dispute, see also Rattray, *Ashanti Law and Constitution*, p. 286.

[30] See *supra*, Ch. 10.   [31] Compare *supra*, Chs. 6 and 11.

thread of his argument, then that is a favorable indication of his trust-worthiness.[32]

What matters here and elsewhere in traditional Africa is the understanding that time must be experienced as leisure if the dramatic moment is to be rightly assessed.[33]

The poignancy of these dispositions has received masterful treatment from Isak Dinesen, who was often drawn into native legal affairs during her life on a Kenya coffee farm:

> My relations with the Natives in the legal affairs of the farm were altogether of a queer nature. Since, before anything, I wanted peace on the land, I could not keep out of them, for a dispute between the Squatters, which has not been solemnly settled, was like those sores that you get in Africa, and which they there call veldt sores: they heal on the surface if you let them, and go on festering and running underneath until you dig them up to the bottom and have them cleaned all through. The Natives themselves were aware of this, and if they really wanted a matter settled they would ask me to give judgment.[34]

One such case involved a shooting accident and pitted different ethnic groups against each other:

> Over this matter representatives of the two tribes met at the farm to sit upon the floor of Farah's house and talk, night after night. Old lean men came, who had been to Mekka and wore a green turban, arrogant young Somalis who, when they were not attending to really serious matters, were gunbearers to the great European travellers and hunters, and dark-eyed, round-faced boys, who were shyly representing their family and who did not say a word, but were devoutly listening and learning.[35]

Now the Somali, Dinesen writes, have a very different mentality from the Kikuyu and a deep contempt for them; yet they will sit down in identical manner to weigh up murder, rape, or fraud against their stock at home in Somaliland—"dearly beloved she-camels, and horses, the names and pedigree of which are written in their hearts."[36] To them, as to the African in general, she continues, there is but one way of counterbalancing the catastrophes of existence; it shall be done by replacement. And on behalf of this supreme purpose, endless speculations may have to be in-

[32] D. Westermann, *Die Glidyi-Ewe* (Berlin, 1932). The translation of this passage from the 1935 edition, pp. 221–222, is found in Doob, *Communication in Africa*, p. 139.
[33] *Supra*, Chs. 5 and 6 for discussions of the African conceptions of time.
[34] Dinesen, *Out of Africa*, pp. 99–100.
[35] *Ibid.*, p. 101; see also p. 113.   [36] *Ibid.*, p. 101.

vested if the public sense for justice is to be satisfied, as Dinesen discovered in the following circumstances: "At times, when the problems became difficult, I had to retire and take time to think them over, covering my head with a mental cloak so that nobody should come and talk to me about them. This was always an effective move with the people of the farm, and I heard them, a long time afterwards, talk with respect of the case that had been so deep that no one could look through it in less than a week."[37]

Several other aspects of the relation between speech and time need to be stressed if African negotiations, judicial or other, are to be appreciated in their own setting. In the absence of stenographers, minutes, and other aids to memory, a case or an argument has to be set forth and explained several times, often phrase by phrase and by different agents, if it is to be communicated properly and precisely. Describing one of the numerous palavers he witnessed—this one in Lunda territory—Livingstone writes as follows:

The talker was then called, and I was asked who was my spokesman. Having pointed to Kolimbota, who knew their dialect best, the palaver began in due form. I explained the real objects I had in view, without any attempt to mystify or appear in any other character than my own. . . . Kolimbota repeated to Nyamoana's talker what I had said to him. He delivered it all verbatim to her husband, who repeated it again to her. It was thus all rehearsed four times over, in a tone loud enough to be heard by the whole party of auditors. The response came back by the same roundabout route, beginning at the lady to her husband, etc.[38]

Repetition and circumlocution, then, are not necessarily wasteful of time in customary proceedings. And the same holds true for the use of indirect, allusive, or symbolic language and other popular modes of verbalizing thought that are meant to extend rather than contract the discourse, and therewith also the pleasure of actual and vicarious participation in a public meeting. For the purpose of illustrating the reasoning process or adding persuasive force to a decision, speeches are commonly interspersed with parables, allegories, similes, riddles, whole folk tales, and, most importantly, with proverbs. Indeed, citations of proverbs are seldom missing in verbal communications; for "when the word is lost, the proverb often finds it," and "when conversation slackens, the proverb

---

[37] *Ibid.*, p. 104.
[38] Livingstone, *Missionary Travels and Researches in South Africa*, p. 296; see also *ibid.*, p. 293, for Livingstone's account of an oration that was attended by prescribed gestures. Compare Junod, *Moeurs et coutumes*, Vol. I, 403ff. and B. Akiga, *Akiga's Story*, p. 376.

may revive it." Conversely, proverbs are often esteemed because they serve to control the flow of speech and compress the argument. As a Yoruba saying has it, the proverb is a horse that can carry you swiftly to the discovery of ideas sought. No wonder, then, that we learn from Chief Isaac O. Delano[39] that this horse is constantly being pressed into the services of elders when they deliberate on ways of settling a dispute.

The supreme significance of proverbs in Africa's practices of non-literate communication derives from the fact that these sayings are respected as the wisdom of the ancestors, the distilled record of knowledge and experience within which successive generations may find guidelines for thought and conduct, and beyond which they ought not to venture in their speculations. Some are truisms, others represent philosophical truths, relay customs to be observed in child rearing, state moral norms appropriate in interclan relations, carry definitions of fundamental institutions, outline rules of evidence, warn against wrongdoing, or indicate impending sanctions. Rendered in prose or verse, and in some communities through drumming,[40] proverbs are everywhere aspects of traditional communal lore; that is to say, the messages they carry are not innovational or individualistic in tone and intent.[41] Time-transcendent in their didactic purport, they constitute, together, a code of values that helps to unify society and assure its moral survival.

[39] Òwe l'ẹṣin ọrọ; Yoruba Proverbs, their Meaning and Usage (Ibadan, 1966). On the Idoma (Nigeria) talent for reasoning with proverbs and allusions during verbal battles—as, for example, at an inquest that had been expertly stage-managed by the elders—see Armstrong, "A West African Inquest," p. 1055. Compare Perham, ed., "The Story of Udo Akpabio of the Anang Tribe in Southern Nigeria," in Ten Africans, p. 61, for the statement that "Europeans are different from us in speech; they do not all speak together and do not use parables to illustrate their judgment." For other discussions see H. P. Junod, Bantu Heritage, pp. 45, 57ff., who remarks that proverbs are one of the most interesting sources of information on the Bantu mind. Robert S. Rattray, Ashanti Proverbs (Oxford, 1916), and Hausa Folk-Lore, Customs, Proverbs, etc., 2 vols. (Oxford, 1913, repr. 1969), Vol. ii, 251ff.; in this region the proverbs naturally reflect strong Muslim influences.

[40] See James Boyd Christensen, "The Role of Proverbs in Fante Culture," Africa, 28, No. 3 (July 1958), p. 241, to the effect that some sayings in Fante society (Ghana) have become well known or standardized by the drummers through decades, perhaps even centuries, of drumming. For an exhaustive study of drum proverbs in Ashanti, see Rattray, Religion and Art in Ashanti, pp. 285ff.; see pp. 286–294 for the repertoire of seventy-seven sayings associated with the fontomfrom drums, that is, talking drums that have the special function of drumming sayings.

[41] See on this subject G. P. Lestrade, "Traditional Literature" in Schapera, ed., The Bantu-Speaking Tribes of South Africa (London, 1946), pp. 291–308. In Ashanti, where anyone engaged in trade had his own weights, such gold weights often had proverbs attached to them; see Rattray, Ashanti, pp. 302–319; such sayings include: "A chief's weights are not the same as a poor man's weights"; "No one takes his talking drums and goes and beats them in the war camp to which he has fled"; "The bird caught in a trap is the one to sing sweetly."

The stress of modern developments and the diffusion of literate skills has by no means obliterated the persuasiveness of this kind of wisdom. Proverbs, along with other aspects of nonliterate communication, survived the intrusion of writing that came with Islam. For example, when Goody, an authority on "restricted literacy" in Islamized parts of northern Ghana, visited a diviner in Kumasi in the early 1950s, he found him officiating with the aid not only of such traditional tools of the trade as stones, sticks, pieces of bark, and so on, but also of a school exercise book filled with sums of pounds, shillings, and pence, over which his inspired pencil darted as he conducted the occult interrogation. "And then," Goody relates, "to sum the situation up, he comes out with a succession of proverbs and witty sayings, while those sitting round mutter their approval of the rightness of these appeals to traditional wisdom."[42] And the old verbal art remained intact when the Ashanti encountered other strangers, notably the Europeans. In fact, the need to come to terms with unprecedented types of human relations has stimulated rather than weakened this mode of rendering insights, as the following sayings illustrate:

A stranger is like unto the water running over the ground after a rain storm (which soon dries up and leaves little trace behind).

By virtue of wisdom the white men mount the sea.

It is the native who knows English who directs the white man whom to praise (and whom to blame). (Lit.: this saying shrewdly sums up the position, in the native mind, of the official or other European who has to rely on an interpreter in his dealings with them.)

When your mother lives in Africa and your father in Europe, and when there is a thing you want, you do not have to wait for it.[43]

Furthermore, proverbs today often serve to cushion the shock experienced by the influx of new ideas from abroad, and to conciliate the disaffected "marginal men" with traditional realities. At any rate, it is in this sense that they are recognized and celebrated today by some of Africa's most gifted writers. The young heroes in Chinua Achebe's novels, portrayed as carriers of Western notions that are inimical to their native culture, are frequently invited by their elders to heed the message of a trusted proverb. For example, in *No Longer at Ease* we find Obi (who

---

[42] "Restricted Literacy in Northern Ghana," p. 205. On the popularity of proverbs in the Islamic culture of North Africa, see Edward Westermarck, *Wit and Wisdom in Morocco; A Study of Native Proverbs* (New York, 1931), pp. 54ff. Proverbs here are often used as curses. See p. 131 to the effect that Negroes are treated negatively, with many proverbs openly directed against their blackness.

[43] Rattray, *Ashanti Proverbs*, pp. 142ff.; the comments in parentheses are Rattray's.

had just returned from England) musing: "Our fathers also have a saying about the dangers of living apart. They say it is the curse of the snake. If all snakes lived together in one place, who would approach them? But they live every one unto himself and so fall easy prey to man."[44] And when the young man tries to marry a girl whose status as an unmarriageable outcast is socially established, his old friend tells him, "What you are going to do concerns not only yourself but your whole family and future generations. If one finger brings oil it soils the others."[45] "A man may go to England, become a lawyer or a doctor, but it does not change his blood," for as another proverb warns: "It is like a bird that flies off the earth and lands on an anthill. It is still on the ground."[46]

The fact that "ancient things remain in the ears"[47] explains why proverbs are customarily cited in judicial proceedings by litigants, witnesses, and judges, and why many of them have the force of legal maxims. Some stand for constitutional principles:

There are no bad chiefs, only bad messengers.[48]

One of the royal blood does not place a chief on a stool.[49]

The chief's word is law.

A Kraal is built around the chief's word.[50]

Others may state the axiom of collective responsibility, as, for example, the Tswana saying: "The mother is killed by the calf," or indicate presumptions governing the rights and wrongs of homicide: "When you have a just reason for seizing a man and killing him, you do not hurt him [by doing so]."[51] Accepted as unambiguous verbalizations of norms around which the community is rallied, proverbs may be said to sum up the law and prescribe rules of evidence and procedure; in other words, they are found to govern the entire judicial process, as the following illustrations suggest:

A wrong never decays.

[44] Achebe, *No Longer at Ease*, p. 81.
[45] *Ibid.*, p. 75.
[46] *Ibid.*, p. 160. The selection of these references was greatly aided by Linda Meredith and her unpublished paper, "Africa as Seen through Four Novels by Chinua Achebe" (Sarah Lawrence College, 1970).
[47] Rattray, *Ashanti Proverbs*, p. 190.
[48] Christensen, "The Role of Proverbs," p. 234.
[49] Rattray, *Ashanti Law and Constitution*, p. 85.
[50] I. Schapera, "Tswana Legal Proverbs," in *Africa*, 36, No. 2 (April 1966), pp. 121ff.; see also, by the same author, *A Handbook of Tswana Law and Custom*, 2nd ed. (London, New York, and Cape Town, 1955).
[51] Rattray, *Ashanti Proverbs*, p. 185.

Roosters must crow face to face (that is, both parties must be present).[52]

Wicked and iniquitous is he who decides a case upon the testimony of only one party to it.[53]

A stranger does not break laws. (This Ashanti saying states the native custom that ignorance of the laws *does* excuse.)[54]

When you speak falsehoods in stating a case, you become weary.

One falsehood spoils a thousand truths.

The Smooth-tongued one says: "My witness is in Europe."

He who has won his case never yet carried the sheep. (A fine and so many sheep is a usual judgment in native courts.)

He who is guilty is the one who has much to say.

Who is in the wrong, he who spreads a mat on the path, or he who trod upon it?

A good case is not difficult to state.[55]

The spirit generated by this form of capsuled oral wisdom emerges eloquently from the following passage: " 'Listen,' the speaker exhorts his audience, 'we need not quarrel in today's assembly. If we calmly discuss one point after the other, we shall discover who is to blame and shall know what to do in the case. If little birds are swarming together and a stone is cast among them, usually none is struck; but if a particular one is aimed at, it is sure to be hit.' "[56]

Regulated or ritualized modes of speech are by no means the only verbal forms of dissolving communal conflicts. In a nonliterate culture in which the word is often the equivalent of the act, and in which speech is prized not only for its utilitarian but also for its aesthetic properties, talking invites artistry, just as writing does in literate civilizations. Since few human traits evoke as much public admiration in Africa as eloquence—and that even when the speaker is carried away either by his subject or by the mood of the audience—verbal virtuosity has been traditionally cultivated in all societies, whether for purposes of telling stories or of making formal speeches. On occasions that demand precision in argumentation and memory, apt phrasing, and persuasive deliv-

---

[52] Schapera, "Tswana Legal Proverbs," for this and other pertinent proverbs.
[53] For this Yoruba saying, see Elias, *The Nature of African Customary Law*, p. 243.
[54] Rattray, *Ashanti Proverbs*, p. 142.   [55] *Ibid.*, pp. 156, 186, 187.
[56] R. H. Lowie, *Primitive Society* (London, 1921), pp. 407–408; and see Elias, *The Nature of African Customary Law*, p. 248, for further comments.

ery, however, the cause is commonly entrusted to individuals who are established experts in the art of oral representation.

Variously known as linguists, spokesmen, griots, or bards, these magicians of the word[57] have traditionally been mainstays of the public order, nowhere more so than in West Africa, where they are greatly respected as depositaries of group history, specialists in the etiquette of chiefly courts, poets singing praises of their titled masters, official reciters or insultors, and, above all, as agents speaking for their principals in public conclaves. Trained in the rhetoric of combat as well as of conciliation, such a spokesman was often renowned for his personal power, influence, and wealth. In the Gold Coast he functioned at the turn of the century as "a sort of confidential officer, who is always about the person of the king or chief, and is his mouthpiece in every public function, as well as in judicial proceedings. He is, generally speaking, an intelligent, bright and witty individual, skilled in the use of language, smoothing down an angry word of his master, or putting a keen edge to a retort, when the occasion demands it."[58] In this part of the continent all ceremonial conversations, even between kings or chiefs speaking the same language, were carried on through the medium of such professionals. Reporting on the system of communication as he observed it in Ashanti at the end of the last century, R. A. Freeman has this to say:

At the public palavers each linguist stands up in turn and pours forth a flood of speech, the readiness and exuberance of which strikes the stranger with amazement, and accompanies his words with gestures so various, graceful and appropriate that it is a pleasure to look on, though the matter of the oration cannot be understood. These oratorical displays appear to afford great enjoyment to the audience, for every African native is a born orator and a connoisseur of oratory, a fact that becomes very manifest in the Courts of Justice in the Protectorate, where the witnesses often address the juries in the most able and unembarrassed manner; I have even seen little boys of eight or ten hold forth to the court with complete self-possession and with an ease of diction and a grace of gesture that would have struck envy into the heart of an English member of Parliament.[59]

[57] See *supra*, p. 104 and *infra*, Ch. 18, where the role of intermediaries is discussed.

[58] Hayford, *Gold Coast Native Institutions*, as excerpted in Wolfson, *Pageant of Ghana*, p. 208.

[59] *Travels and Life in Ashanti and Jaman*, as abstracted in Wolfson, *Pageant of Ghana*, p. 193. Freeman observes that the spokesman in this land is commonly a hunchback; for hunchbacks—he was told by native informants—are known for voices of "exceptional sweetness." "And certainly I noticed," he continues, "that the voices of these deformed persons were easily distinguishable from those of the other natives by a clear, high-pitched ringing quality apparently very grateful to the African ear, and which rendered their utterances unusually distinct." *Ibid*.

And a similar impression is relayed by Casely Hayford, who visited Ashanti at the turn of this century:

> When the linguist rises up to speak in public, he leans upon the king's gold cane, or a subordinate linguist holds it in front of him. He is going to make a speech now, and it is sure to be a happy effort. It will sparkle with wit and humour. He will make use freely of parables to illustrate points in his speech. He will indulge in epigrams, and all the while he will seem not to possess any nerves—so cool, so collected, so self-complacent! He comes of a stock used to public speaking and public function.[60]

East African peoples, whose social and political organizations differ greatly from those, for example, of the Ashanti in the west, have traditionally been known to be equally adept in modes of controlled speech, even when dealing with Europeans whom they had not met before. Eloquence, commonly viewed as a test of leadership by the Somali and Masai, here combined with intricate ritual movements, stylized chants of salutation, and ceremonious martial demeanor when Joseph Thomson had occasion in the 1880s to negotiate terms of passage through Masai territory:

> After a few words among themselves in a low tone, a spokesman arose, leisurely took a spear in his left hand to lean upon, and then using his knobkerry as an orator's baton, he proceeded to deliver his message with all the ease of a practised speaker. With profound astonishment, I watched this son of the desert, as he stood before me, speaking with a natural fluency and grace, a certain sense of the gravity and importance of his position, and a dignity of attitude beyond all praise. With much circumlocution, he sketched the story of Fischer's arrival, of the fight, its causes and results, more especially laying stress upon the fact that a woman had been killed, an unheard-of-event in the annals of their quarrels with the Lajombe (Wa-swahili). He then went on to tell how the news of our arrival reached them, and to describe the excitement produced thereby; how a meeting of the married men and the El-moran or warriors was called to discuss the way in which we were to be received; and how, finally, they came to the conclusion, not without blows among themselves, to allow us to pass peaceably; in consequence of which decision, he with his companions were sent to bid us welcome and conduct us to their kraals. During

[60] Hayford in Wolfson, *Pageant of Ghana*, p. 209. On the importance of praise poets and reciters among Bantu-speaking peoples, see C. P. Lestrade, "Traditional Literature," pp. 295ff. For an interesting discussion of the role of "griots" in French-speaking West Africa, see Holas, "Arts et Artisanat en A.O.F.," p. CLXXIX.

this harangue the knobkerry was not idle, but employed with much oratorical effect to emphasize his remarks.

Sadi, on our part, taking also a knobkerry, and with hand resting on his gun, proceeded to reply, and as he has an unrivalled knowledge of the Masai language and modes of speech, besides a natural "gift of the gab," he—inspired by me—told our story. Two or three others of the Masai then spoke to the same effect as their leading orator—no two, however, rising at once, or if they did so, a few words between themselves settled who was to have the ear of the meeting, while not a word was said by the others beyond inarticulate expressions of assent or dissent.

Till the formal speech-making was over each one had sat with unmoved countenance, betraying by neither word nor sign a consciousness that the second white man they had ever seen in their lives was sitting before them.[61]

Decades later, after the world of the written word had been opened to these and other peoples of the region, and the English scheme of law and government had officially set the terms of tribal coexistence, as well as the conditions for the administration of local justice, divisive matters of deep concern to the community were still best settled when full allowance was made for the negotiating style peculiar to each group. The Kikuyu on Isak Dinesen's farm had found their own relationship to written documents, judgments, and accords that they could not read, just as they had absorbed Dinesen's personality and gifts for conciliating disputants into their own traditional frame of reference. When it was clear to all concerned that the Kikuyu elders, having assembled time and time again in endless, but fruitless discussions, were unable to dispose of the social disturbances that had ensued from the shooting accident in their midst, a final meeting was arranged by the cooperative efforts of the European farmer and the big chief, whose rule over more than 100,000 tribesmen was unquestioned, even though he had been appointed by the British.

This Kinanjui, Dinesen tells us, had a manner of his own in meetings. "When he thought the discussions were dragging out too long, he leant back in his chair, and, while still keeping the fire in his cigar alive, he closed his eyes and drew his breath deeply and slowly, in a low regular snore, a sort of official, *pro forma* sleep, which he may have cultivated for use in his own Council of State."[62] His entrances were made with an

---

[61] For this excerpt from Joseph Thomson, *Through Masäi Land* (London, 1885), see Charles Richards and James Place, eds., *East African Explorers* (London, 1960), p. 203. For Livingstone's account of a palaver in Lunda Land, see *supra*, p. 250.

[62] *Out of Africa*, p. 142.

unfailing sense of customary ceremony, even though he usually came in his own car. When he descended and collected his big cloak round him in a majestic gesture, he stepped back, in that one movement, two thousand years into Kikuyu justice. This he did on the occasion in question. Taking his seat with Isak Dinesen at the millstone table that had come to symbolize important palavers for both the European and the African, he heard her tell the squatters that the matter between the parties had been settled and that Kinanjui had come to certify the accord as put on paper, namely, that a cow with a heifer calf at foot was to be handed over to the aggrieved, and that the affair should now be viewed as ended, since nobody could stand it any longer. Wails, shrieks, and deadly remarks then went up in the ranks of the divided clans, until, "in two or three minutes the open place was boiling over like a witch's caldron."[63] Kinanjui sat immovable.

> He turned his side to the screaming crowd, and I realized how much the profile is the true face of a king. It is a Native faculty thus to transform yourself, in a single movement, into lifeless matter. I do not think that Kinanjui could have spoken or moved without fanning the flames of passion, as it was he kept sitting on them to quell them. Not everybody could have done it.
>
> Little by little the fury died down, the people stopped shrieking and began to talk in an everyday manner, in the end they became silent one by one.[64]

When everything was quiet, the cow and heifer were handed over; the document of the agreement received first the thumb marks of the parties, then that of the chief, and, lastly, Dinesen's signature.

[63] *Ibid.*, p. 152.   [64] *Ibid.*, p. 153.

· 18 ·

THE ROLE OF INTERMEDIARIES

The thought world that permitted confidence in direct oral encounters between disputants and negotiators has also produced a myriad of ways to transpose conflict situations indirectly into conditions of acquiescence, conciliation, or accord. No clear lines of demarcation separate these two approaches, either in the general communal life style or in the specific realm of what is generally circumscribed today as customary law. For example, unlike the West, where adjudication has connotations not shared by arbitration or mediation, these processes are often intertwined in Africa.[1] Here, where law is imbedded in custom and religion, the judge himself is more often than not a mediator concerned rather with pacifying the contending parties than with determining who is right or who is wrong; and this conception of his function allows him considerable leeway in the choice among available modes of communication. Nonetheless, and subject to qualifications such as these, it is possible as well as necessary to isolate the roles customarily ascribed to special intermediaries if African dispositions toward the abatement of internal and external tensions are to be appreciated in their full complexity. Since few of the designations here selected can be presented without reference to primary institutions or customs, and since many of these basic structures have already been discussed in other contexts, repetitiveness cannot easily be avoided.

A. Invisible Mediators and Ritual Agents

As preceding chapters have suggested, African thought assumes that life is ruled by invisible but vital, usually malevolent, powers, and that men must assuage this spirit world as they participate in the never-ending mystic conflict. The primary mediating agencies that make these occult exchanges endurable to the living are magical beliefs, ritual practices, and symbolic representations; and, most of these, again, require the services of specialists—that is to say, the interposition of secondary mediators—if communication with the dead and other ruling supernatural forces is to be kept open and effective. Unlike, for example, theology in Occidental religions, which renders all major references in generally valid abstract propositions, even as it supplies selected concrete symbols to elucidate the general concepts, African belief systems require concretiza-

---

[1] Compare *supra*, Ch. 17.

tion on each of the two interlocking levels. Furthermore, since the logic of magic does not require uniformity in reasoning, insisting instead that each conflict-inducing occurrence be resolved in terms of the forces peculiar to its particular incidence, traditional African thought must accommodate a vast plurality of separate intermediaries, visible and invisible, animate as well as inanimate.

Communication with forces dispensing vital energy thus requires everywhere the good offices of the ancestors. In many societies it has called for the sacrifice of human beings, so that these might report to deceased authorities on happenings among the living.[2] Secure correspondence is assured, moreover, by the mediation of selected animal species, such as fish, serpents, crocodiles, hyenas, antelopes, turtles, or—as in the river region of the Niger, Volta, and Zambezi—by a particular family of hippopotami.[3] Elsewhere, leopards are entrusted with quasi-ambassadorial functions, or a special guardian serpent is expected to relay the swearing of an oath.[4] Creatures of this kind are not worshipped for their own sake. They are sacred either as totemic symbols of mystical associations, as models for disguises, or as carriers capable of transmitting messages and receiving orders from on high. And very similar human dispositions attach to certain inanimate agencies, also charged with directing the flow of occult power and information. These include fetishes; magically useful substances and medicines; objects such as shrines, ritual images, idols, effigies, and metaphoric sculptures; and above all, masks.

[2] *Supra,* Chs. 5, 9, 13. For one of the most lucid discussions of the entire matter, see Amadou Hampaté Ba, "Animisme en savane africaine," in Rencontres internationales de Bouaké, *Les Religions africaines traditionnelles* (Paris, 1965), p. 38.

[3] See B. Holas, "L'Imagerie rituelle en Afrique noire," *African Arts,* 1, No. 2 (Winter 1968), 50ff., for a vivid and informative discussion of mythologically conditioned thought in general, and the mediating role of beasts in particular. Compare Wilfrid D. Hambly, *Serpent Worship in Africa* (Chicago, 1931); *The Ovimbundu of Angola* (Chicago, 1934); and *Culture Areas in Nigeria* (Chicago, 1935; all 3 vols. repr. New York, 1968). Among the Ngoni, ancestral spirits could only be approached through cattle. Such intermediaries were required because the remotest ancestors, whose names, praise names, and genealogy were unknown, were not amenable to direct address. In Nuer society, too, cattle had paramount mediating roles.

Even in the animal world men respected hierarchies of intermediaries. Dennett, *At the Back of the Black Man's Mind,* p. 155, writes that "The wild ox in the stories of the Bavili is generally found acting as the servant or ambassador of either the Leopard or some princely animal."

[4] See Kirk-Greene, "On Swearing," p. 45, for the role of such a serpent in northern Nigeria; *ibid.,* on the significance of meeting a red baboon. On pythons as incarnations of ancestral spirits and trusted mediums in modern Tanzania, see R. C. Willis, "Kamcape: An Anti-Sorcery Movement in South-West Tanzania," *Africa,* 38, No. 1 (January, 1968), 1–15; see p. 3. Camara Laye, *L'Enfant noir,* tells of the veneration with which a crocodile was treated in a modern Guinean household. For another literary treatment of the allegoric and mediating significance of crocodiles, see Joyce Cary, *African Witch,* pp. 286–290 in particular.

Masks have qualities and meanings in Africa and other nonliterate cultures that have long intrigued artists and scholars in literate societies, and numerous, greatly various appreciations of their aesthetic and utilitarian attributes are on record.[5] Even in the limited context of the present discussion, masks emerge in manifold roles. As permanent agents of social control, they may be there to initiate and educate the young, mold the individual so that he may fit the social station he is to occupy, celebrate the great causes of fertility and death, exorcise communal troubles, provoke the emotions deemed proper on particular occasions, arbitrate disputes,[6] or inflict punishment upon the guilty. As allegorical representations of ruling cosmogonic concepts, tutelary guardian spirits, or of symbiotic arrangements with, for example, the mediating bestiary world, masks often summarize the entire moral code by which a given people lives. African masks, then, are liaison agents par excellence, functioning not only independently and directly, but also indirectly, as when they materialize a spirit living in the bush, or otherwise subsume the inter-

[5] For some of the most suggestive discussions of the role of masks, see Holas, "L'Imagerie rituelle"; by the same author, *Les Masques Kono* (Paris, 1952), especially pp. 147ff. Holas identifies the mask as "the personified moral code," "the permanent agent charged with maintaining non-written customary law," and "the great initiator who transforms the human embryo into a socially valid unit, guides man through the vicissitudes of life, protects him, and punishes him when this is necessary."

Commenting on the impact of Islam upon the validity of the mask and its role, Trimingham concludes: "It is obvious why the mask must lose its authority when people step over the dividing line. Islam seeks to be the ruling factor in life and although the mask may continue to operate in islamized societies it has lost its former socio-religious function, and may even degenerate into a form of clowning. More commonly the material symbols of the dying cult are not destroyed but simply neglected. Ancestor houses gradually disintegrate under wind and rain and are not renewed, whilst masks are sold to visiting anthropologists." *Islam in West Africa*, pp. 37–38. Paulme, *Les Sculptures de l'Afrique noire*, remarks p. 2, note 2, that Leo Frobenius was the first to study African masks seriously, in his work *Die Masken und Geheimbuende Afrikas* (Halle, 1898). See Paulme, *Les Sculptures de l'Afrique noire*, p. 50, to the effect that masks often intervene in the villages of the Atlantic forest area in order to stop a quarrel, denounce an affront to public order, or punish a guilty person. Also *ibid.*, p. 90, for comments on the role of masks as agents of the Mungala secret society. Here, as also in the Sudan and the Ivory Coast, a mask is responsible for the village peace, the defense of plantations, and the fixing of punishment for infractions of the rule.

Ba, "Animisme en Savane Africaine," pp. 34ff.; see also in this volume the commentaries on the role of masks by Hans Himmelheber, which relate primarily to the Dan. Luitfruid Marfurt, "Les Masques africains," *African Arts*, 1, No. 2 (Winter 1968), 54–60. G. W. Harley, *Masks as Agents of Social Control in Northeast Liberia* (Cambridge, Mass., 1950). See also works on secret societies, including the Poro, cited earlier; and cf. Georges Balandier, *Afrique ambiguë* (Paris, 1957), pp. 114–131; Georges Buraud, *Les Masques* (Paris, 1961), pp. 85ff. Buraud suggests that the blacks took to masks and masking because they felt the need, on the one hand, to avoid all individuation, on the other, to increase the feeling of power.

[6] See *infra*, this chapter.

mediaries of the first resort. Some perform their task by terrorizing, others by amusing mortals. One may refer to evil; the other, by contrast, to benign principles. There are masks charged with disguising those who wear them, and there are others capable of effecting a total transformation. Furthermore, one may be treated as if he were a person, the other as if he were a deity. In either case a mask is often attended by singers, drummers, and servants of all sorts, whose task it is to mediate, as it were, between the ruling object and the public. Immobile and unchanging in their concrete appearances, all masks are nevertheless presumed ever active and dynamic, whether stationed in secret groves and open gatherings, or participating in circumcision rites, ceremonial processions, pantomimes, dances, court rituals, or peace-making.

The masks of the Dan, a farming and hunting people in the forest of Liberia and the savanna of the Ivory Coast, illustrate these various spiritual and social functions in a particularly vivid way. The biggest and most important in the category of so-called profane masks are the "peacemakers." Their major duty, as explained by Himmelheber,[7] is to command peace when some bad fighting is going on in town, and also, on a higher level, if war between different towns or chiefdoms is becoming destructive. The mask appears, sits down on the battlefield, and raises its hand to order peace. Nobody would dare to brandish his sword after that. Furthermore, the mask settles quarrels between important people before serious trouble has sprung from them. On such an occasion it arrives in great ceremony and sits on a rice mortar, its fibre gown being so heavy that it cannot stand upright for a long time. "Experienced Dan readily explain the existence of these masks: 'Our chiefs,' they say, 'never had any soldiers or policemen to enforce obedience. So the elders decided that the masks should be given final respect above men. Otherwise, how could law and order be maintained in our country?' Very strange for us is the fact," Himmelheber continues, "that these almighty masks are always owned by only one quarter in one town of the chiefdom. A Dan town is usually composed of three to five quarters, meaning families. This one quarter has acquired the mask from another such family in another chiefdom along with certain fetishes which guarantee its strength and lend it security from witches." All the other quarters and towns of the chiefdom accept the decision of the mask voluntarily, but on condition that the members of the mask quarter refrain from fighting among themselves.

The complexity of this arrangement has been confounded in the last century by a connection with a particular leopard society, the Gor. Like

[7] Hans Himmelheber, "Sculptors and Sculptures of the Dan," in Lalage Bown and Michael Crowder, eds., *Proceedings of the First International Congress of Africanists, Accra, December 11–18, 1962* (London, 1964), p. 247.

the great mask, the Gor, too, is always the property of one quarter, which has acquired it from the leopard quarter of another chiefdom—usually the quarter that has already specialized in peace-making. "If the Gor-Society comes to a town where there was no peace-making mask before, a mask of lower rank there may rise to be the mask of the Leopard society. Thus, a mask may change its significance altogether."[8]

> The Gor and his mask are respected by the Dan not only as peace-makers, but also as legislators. A town rent by strife between an old aristocratic family and a low one which was ruled by these nobles, thus received the following law: "If ever a fight occurs between two members of these families, the culprits shall pay two cows. But before this fine is imposed, they shall be asked right on the spot what they are doing there. If they reply that they had just been playing, they shall be ordered to walk away with arms on each other's shoulders. If they comply, they shall be free of the penalty."

Disobedience evokes no punishment by the masks, but persistent opposition calls forth death, which the leopard society inflicts by smuggling a deadly poison, the gall of the crocodile, into the recalcitrant man's food. And when a war lasts too long, the guardian of the Gor appears on the battlefield, raising his ceremonial stick. In such a case, we are told, no warrior would dare continue the fight.

The Dan way of rendering thought and experience in matters of strife and conciliation is unique in its symbolic comprehensiveness. In its essentials, however, it illustrates the general African need for intermediaries on the plane of mental construction, as well as on that of personal life and traditional social relations. As an earlier discussion has suggested,[9] the individual African is, after all, not supposed to strive for independence and self-reliance. Tutored to view himself as an integral part of the natural and supernatural environment, he can accept the proposition that persons, animals, plants, things, and spirits are interchangeable for certain purposes, or that one may impersonate, or act as agent for the other. This conscious confusion of identities and roles, which is made possible by the avoidance of individuation, may explain the ease with which Africans can enter trances and other states of possession.[10] It may be the source, also, of that gift for mimicry and imita-

---

[8] *Ibid.*, pp. 248–249; and see Hans Himmelheber, "Le Système de la religion des Dan," in Rencontres internationales de Bouaké, *Les Religions africaines traditionnelles* (Paris, 1965), pp. 80–82, on the Gor society, and pp. 83ff. on Dan masks. On the role of masks in the context of the Poro society, *supra*, p. 109.

[9] *Supra*, Ch. 5.

[10] Compare Rouch, *La Religion et la magie songhay*, for numerous comments on the subject; Pierre Verger, "Les Religions traditionnelles africaines: sont-elles compatibles avec les formes actuelles de l'existence?" in Rencontres internationales

tion upon which so many foreign observers comment with admiration. In short, "the self" emerges as fluid rather than fixed from these manifestations of mystic participation of all in one and one in all. Capable of casting himself and others in multiple roles that change socially and mythically, the African has thus created a cultural universe in which everyone is primarily an intermediary for someone or something else. And in such a conception of life, all important communication is apt to be indirect and round-about.[11]

A noted West African scholar elucidates this syndrome in social relations as follows:

> Everywhere and in all circumstances the Negro tends, by virtue of his very nature, to posit an intermediary between himself and his interlocutor, whoever the latter may be. The polygamous husband will thus address himself to his first wife so that she may convey the orders he wants to give the other wives, to his first-born son if the occasion calls for orders to the other children. Likewise, he who is charged with a commission, will turn to the third person whom he finds in the company of the one for whom the message is intended, rather than transmit it directly. The only exception to this general rule related to personal secrets. It is therefore neither surprising nor unnatural that the Negro in Africa south of Sahara, conditioned to have recourse to an intermediary when dealing with his like, has also created for himself intermediaries in order to conjure *Masa Dambali* (the major Bambara deity).[12]

An authority on Shona customary law illustrates the same principle in the context of marriage preliminaries in this South African society. Here, where the two kin groups negotiating a marriage are separated by a pronounced "distance," both in social and mystical respects, and where the first rapprochement between two independent and totally different structural entities is usually marked by mutual distrust and even animosity, a marriage proposal is a risky undertaking. If the parties are to be drawn

---

de Bouaké, *Les Religions africaines traditionnelles* (Paris, 1965), pp. 97ff. and the comments on patterns of possession among Yoruba, Ibo, Dan, Tonga, and Baule, as well as in Mali, Ethiopia, Haiti, Brazil, and Negro communities in the United States, by Luc de Heusch, Bouah Niangoran, Rev. E.C.O. Ilogu, William Bascom, Philippe de Salverte, Denise Paulme, and A. Hampaté Ba, *ibid.*, pp. 106–118; authorities cited *supra*, pp. 108ff.

[11] Compare *supra*, Chs. 3 and 4 for comments on this subject by representative modern African spokesmen.

[12] Ba, "Animisme en savane africaine," p. 34. It is only this necessity, Ba insists, that has given rise to fetishism and totemism; that is to say, "African fetishes are nothing more and nothing less than sacred instruments for the reception or propulsion of thoughts and words. They are merely intermediate agents, devoid of intrinsic power." For his definition of totemism, *ibid.*, pp. 35ff.

together into a close, enduring, and procreative relationship, the existing gap must be bridged. For this purpose, Holleman explains, the services of a disinterested third party, acting as intermediary, are indispensable:

> This person is employed by the proposing family and acts in the first place as their mouthpiece. But he is also accepted as an essential vehicle of the other party. Often the respective family heads do not even deal directly with the intermediary, but through a subordinate member of the family who serves as a link [i.e., as the secondary go between] between the head of the family and the intermediary, with the result that the distance between the parties is further accentuated.

> Only at an advanced stage of the marriage preliminaries is direct formal contact established between the family heads themselves. Even for the purpose of selecting and accepting the marriage cattle, . . . the bride's party is represented by a responsible but junior member of the *vatezwara* (wife-receiving family). Only just before the conclusion of the marriage (and sometimes not until later) do the father of the bride and the father of the groom meet. The distance which has separated them is then sufficiently narrowed to enable the two families to celebrate their new relationship at a common party.[13]

Next, tradition requires that every formal action, gift or payment, question or answer, with respect to the marriage transaction, can only be expressed or conveyed by one party to the other through the intermediary. Any proposal bypassing the intermediary would not be considered serious from a legal point of view. As the court argued in one instance: "If you had seriously meant to marry her, you would have sent your *munyai* (intermediary) to your father-in-law."[14] Furthermore, if conflicts arise during the subsistence of marriage relations between the two families, the intermediary may be called upon to give evidence; and if conflicting evidence exists, the testimony of the intermediary is usually regarded as conclusive. In Shona law and life, then, the go-between occu-

---

[13] Holleman, *Shona Customary Law*, pp. 131–132.

[14] *Ibid.*, p. 133. Mungo Park observed during his exploratory travels in West Africa that family quarrels sometimes rise to such a height that the authority of the husband can no longer preserve peace in the household. "In such cases, the interposition of Mumbo Jumbo is called in, and is always decisive." "This is a strange bugbear, common to all the Mandingo towns" who is supposed to be either the husband himself, or some person instructed by him. Disguised in a masquerade made of the bark of trees and armed with the rod of public authority, he begins the pantomime at the approach of night and then enters the town where all inhabitants immediately assemble. Every female immediately suspects that the visit may possibly be intended for herself. Yet each appears and participates in the ceremony of song and dance which culminates around midnight with Mumbo fixing on the offender. This unfortunate victim is thereupon immediately seized, stripped naked, tied to a post, and severely scourged with the rod, amidst shouts of derision of the whole assembly. Park, *Travels*, Vol. I, 38–39.

pies a most important position, and great care is taken to select a person who is well disposed toward both families, and whose integrity cannot be doubted.

Other instances of the general African trust in the indirect approach to settling intracommunal quarrels are provided by Tswana society (Botswana), where it is a boy's sisters who are supposed to act as mediators between their brother and their father; the Galla (Ethiopia), whose institutions include the office of a "chief arbiter" within the Gada age-grade system, and that of another mediating magistrate, who intervenes in the interests of the community at large when a conflict erupts between leaders of the Gada system, on the one hand, and some wealthy land-owner, on the other;[15] the Amhara (Ethiopia), who entrust arbitration over, for example, land rights to a "danya" acceptable to both parties, while also allowing for rather formal arbitral proceedings in public village hearings;[16] the Lugbara, who recognize the authority of rainmakers and "men whose names are known" to stop fights and feuds within their tribe by cursing the combatants;[17] the Arusha (Tanzania), who have developed a plurality of mediating practices to correspond to the plurality of social structures within which conflicts are apt to occur;[18] and the Tiv (Nigeria), who counter the latent threat of anarchy in their egalitarian society by insisting upon the peaceful settlement of controversies, at least between closely related groups. When a dispute breaks out between two Tiv men over a rivalry for women, trespass on farm land, or the theft of a goat, each will call to his assistance the men of his own segment. Other conflict situations in this tribal community may require the services either of elders, who are fully familiar with the customs of their group, or of "men of influence" and "prestige persons," who lead the arguments of each faction through their expertise in manipulating rituals, and who can influence others because they are wealthy, generous, and astute, as well as adept in matters of witchcraft and magic. Since the Tiv believe that occult power may be built up on one side by draining the corresponding resources of others, these functionaries are often feared. Their authority is thus frequently ambiguous, as Lloyd points out;[19] for

[15] Herbert S. Lewis, *A Galla Monarchy, Jimma Abba Jifar, Ethiopia 1830–1932* (Madison, Wisc., 1965), p. 32.

[16] Edward Ullendorff, *The Ethiopians; An Introduction to Country and People* (London and New York, 1960), p. 187.

[17] Richards, ed., *East African Chiefs*, p. 328; and cf. *supra*, Ch. 10.

[18] Kenneth S. Carlston, *Social Theory and African Tribal Organization; The Development of Socio-Legal Theory* (Urbana, Chicago, and London, 1968), pp. 321ff., 333ff.

[19] Lloyd, *Africa in Social Change*, pp. 34ff.; Laura Bohannan, "Political Aspects of Tiv Social Organization," pp. 52ff., 58ff., 65; this author also notes that elders are called in to mediate between a suspected witch and the bewitched; also that a "prestige person" is allowed to purchase slaves and form a gang that can furnish safe conduct to strangers in return for tribute, and has the power to rob those who do not reciprocate.

while one is pleased to have the support of such a person in one's own disputes, it is not unreasonable to expect that he will side with one's opponent on another occasion.

Not all African societies are as strongly ruled by beliefs in magic and witchcraft as the Tiv. But few exist in which ultimate authority is not firmly lodged in occult forces. As Hoernlé notes in a provocative comparison of Western and African modes of thinking, "just as we have our experts in scientific thinking and in the practical application of such thinking, there will develop (in the African context) experts, men of special skill and training and endowment, in the methods of this type of thought and of the technique of its practical uses."[20]

The need for divination is a case in point. While most deaths are viewed as cases of homicide—that is to say, as functions of social conflict[21]—it is yet imperative in each case that people know whether the particular conflict had disturbed relations with ancestors, living persons such as witches, workers of curses or sorcerers, or with nonhuman agencies such as shrines. In either case, the truth can be ascertained only by delegating the inquiry to the proper mediating agency. Some of the complexities implicit in the designation of the intermediary in such instances emerge from Goody's discussion of the role of diviners among the LoDagaa in West Africa:

> It is sometimes said that the ancestors, the Earth, and the medicine shrines do not themselves have the power to kill a human being unless the person's tutelary (*sigra*) allows it: "How can you harm a cow unless you have the herdsman's . . . consent?" I was asked. A tutelary is not a special sort of spirit or shrine; the word refers either to a clan shrine, which is theoretically the same for all members, or to the specific shrine or ancestor indicated by a diviner as being a man's own guardian spirit. Each individual has such a tutelary, but will not be aware of its name unless a diviner has been consulted. Although an approach to the tutelary is a necessary step in the chain of events leading to a death, people do not usually say "the *sigra* killed him"; however this name does sometimes occur in the possible causes suggested in the course of funeral divination.
>
> Many attempts are made during the funeral ceremonies to determine why a man died. Broadly speaking, diviners are used to ascertain the final cause, whereas methods such as carrying the corpse indicate the human agent.

[20] Hoernlé, "Magic and Medicine," p. 226; and see *ibid.* for the discussion of one such class of specialist, the *inyanga* in Bantu societies; in some tribes he is a great tribal officer, in others a practitioner at large, putting his skill at the disposal of those prepared to pay for it.

[21] Compare *supra*, Chs. 5 and 9.

Divination is very common among the LoDagaa. Most men are qualified to divine; but there is a great difference in reputation among them, and good diviners are of course most frequently consulted.[22]

In this case, as in others relating, for example, to disease, bad dreams, or failing crops, it is not knowledge of the future that is expected. True to African orientations toward time,[23] the LoDagaa diviner is there rather to diagnose present troubles and formulate the appropriate course of action, as when he guides mortals in finding the right shrine at which to make their offerings. And the same holds for the Sudanese Kingdom of the Jukun (Nigeria), where diviners, respected as spokesmen of the people's legal conceptions and as experts in oathing and ordeals, are commonly entrusted with the task of clearing up thefts;[24] among the Tallensi (Ghana), who depend upon diviners when they want to bring a simmering conflict in the lineage out into the open; and in the Nuba hill tribes of Kordofan, where the mediating power of shamans (*kujurs*) and other trusted third parties appears to have greatly increased in response to the stress of modern times. Nadel, who reported on this state of affairs in the late 1940s, thus found that "*Kujurs* spring up in new surroundings—barracks and soldier camps; young Dilling and Nyima soldiers in El Obeid, for the first time in their lives long separated from family and country, are always consulting their *kujur* comrades to learn about the people at home; a policeman in Dilling, having shot and killed an escaped prisoner who was a fellow tribesman, ran to a *kujur* to learn from him the expiation duties involved in that tangled case."[25]

A major mediating service performed by African magicians, then, is the obvious one of allaying states of acute and unpredictable anxiety, even if only temporarily. Another function with which diviners and other ritual specialists are associated is that of relaying traditional law. In pronouncing a particular verdict, a LoDagaa diviner or Nuba shaman is thus likely to do what regular judges do; that is to say, he will select proverbs, pithy sayings, and other standardized forms of speech that carry common social values and beliefs. Furthermore, since each is also

[22] Goody, *Death, Property and the Ancestors*, p. 210. On the Ifa system of divination among the Yoruba, see William Bascom, *Ifa Divination; Communication between Gods and Men in West Africa* (Bloomington, Ind., 1969). Appeal to Ifa, god of divination, is here made through a corpus of prophetic verses uttered by the diviner as he manipulates sixteen palm nuts in prescribed ways. The verses—from which the client chooses an apt reply—are parables, explanatory of phenomena and of ritual. This practice is by no means dormant today.

[23] Compare *supra*, Ch. 5.

[24] Meek, *A Sudanese Kingdom*, pp. 347ff.

[25] Nadel, *The Nuba*, p. 446; for a related discussion of Nuba institutions, *supra*, Ch. 7, n. 32. See Lucien Lévy-Bruhl, *Primitive Mentality* (London and New York, 1923, repr. Boston, 1966), pp. 159–218 for some stimulating general analyses of "The Practices of Divination."

oonnectcd, directly or indirectly, with permanent or regular institutions of government, he often helps to buttress respect for existing ways of structuring human relations. For example, a Nuba rainmaker is feared and respected not only because he is credited with the omniscient power of controlling rain, sending death through lightning, and giving or withholding victory in battle. The authority he holds in certain communities also devolves from his position as a chief. In this capacity he is viewed not as an agent, but as a principal who is himself dependent both upon scores of secular and priestly messengers and intermediaries (which include, in one locality, the official secular chief) and upon mediating ritual paraphernalia. The latter, again, may become quasi-independent functionaries in periods of interregnum when the rainmaker's agents call them into action as replacements for the missing priest.[26]

All-pervasive in its influence and power, this magic office emerges from Nuba records (more particularly those relating to Nyama and Koalib) as the major focus of tribal unity. A survey of the geographic multicommunal field in which its varied agencies have penetrated suggests, indeed, that we are here in the presence of a rather effective regional organization, all the more so as it is closely linked to blood pacts and related intergroup arrangements to which reference has already been made in connection with the formation of "greater societies."[27]

Such extensions of the rule of interlocking magical agencies were made possible, Nadel explains, because the office of rainmaker, as it was known in Dere,

> implied a spiritual authority which transcended the bounds of the single community. For his seasonal rites were believed to benefit the tribe at large, and in time of drought people from everywhere would appeal to him. His ordeals and powers of divination would equally be invoked by other communities. . . . This wider scope of the . . . office is expressed strikingly in the ceremony of consecration, in the course of which the newly appointed rainmaker would tour the whole country, visiting each community, friend and enemy alike.[28]

Matters of peace and war received only selective attention from this third party; he would order or forbid attacks on other tribes, but ignore internal violence and dissension.[29] But his office, in conjunction with that of the Nyama shaman, is credited with having spawned a separate, diplomatically rather effective type of intermediary, the so-called Chiefs of the Path. These ambassadorial representatives of antagonistic hill districts,

---

[26] Nadel, *The Nuba*, p. 450.   [27] Compare *supra*, Chs. 6 and 7.
[28] Nadel, *The Nuba*, pp. 450–451.
[29] Compare *supra*, Chs. 11 and 13 to the effect that certain internal feuds are part of the constitutive inner order.

who were chosen from the ranks of *kujurs, kujur* families, or simply of men known for their courage and honesty—and who were often linked to each other in blood brotherhoods that also covered their respective families and descendants—could pursue their spirit-sponsored missions by travelling unmolested between specified communities. One hill community did not necessarily maintain such diplomatic relations with every other enemy group. It might reach some through pacts that "hill priests" concluded with the chief or a particularly powerful man in the foreign community; and it might affect others obliquely through the medium of "Men of a Common Clan," who were as inviolable as consecrated *kujurs* or Chiefs of the Path, and are said to have been, in at least one instance, indirect negotiators with third groups.[30]

Here, as elsewhere—for example, among the Plateau Tonga (Zambia), where rain-shrine communities make for cooperation among small groups of villages[31]—magico-political authorities may interpose themselves so as to induce amity or prevent overt discord between different human groups. This purpose is, however, usually incidental or subsidiary to the major mediating task incumbent upon them, namely, that of mitigating doubts in the minds of men by assuring power and success or, conversely, by instilling fearful expectations.

Diviners, rainmakers, medicine men, witch doctors, and other third parties with connections to the domain of the occult, are thus not presumed to operate on the side of order, peace, goodwill, and understanding. The contrary is more likely to be true; they occupy their positions of trust precisely because they are capable of operating beyond good and evil, as it were. Some of Africa's many functionaries who illustrate the ambivalent or amoral nature of this kind of mediating mission are the following: the Masai *Laibon*, who combines divination with witchcraft and the skill of making medicines that vouchsafe profitable cattle raids (with the *Laibon* entitled to part of the spoils); the Kikuyu medicine man and seer, renowned for his cures, accurate prophecies, and capacity to check Masai invasions, as well as for his talent to set propitious dates for the staging of raids, initiation ceremonies, and other group activities;[32] and the Nandi *Orkoiyot*, who wields immense power over tribal

[30] Nadel, *The Nuba*, pp. 454ff.

[31] Elizabeth Colson and Max Gluckman, eds., *Seven Tribes of British Central Africa* (London, 1951), pp. 153–161.

[32] Leakey, *Mau Mau*, pp. 48ff.; Hobley, *Bantu Beliefs and Magic*, pp. 186ff.; pp. 187–191 on Kamiri, a renowned Kikuyu magician, whose power and reputation remained intact in spite of European influences. "Missionaries designate Kamiri as the 'official poisoner'; yet one missionary, who knows him better than any other European, tells me that if Kamiri is hired to poison a man, he will first call that man and tell him so and then he will inquire into the case and endeavour to settle the quarrel, in which respect he is usually successful." *Ibid.*, pp. 326ff. on the *Laibon*.

affairs, even though he has no formal executive or judicial authority. Probably of Masai origin,[33] this rainmaker, prophet, witch, and witch detector is looked upon as something of an interloper. Feared, hated, yet respected as a sacred person, his advice must be obtained through intermediaries before the people can venture forth on such major undertakings as an offensive raid, the sowing of crops, or the opening of a male circumcision festival. A master of secret law and magic ritual, whose curse rates among the most potent, he can predict the results of a planned military campaign, prevent sickness and, by thus forestalling possible calamities, greatly reduce the incidence of conflict in the midst of the folk society he serves.

Prophetism, which subsumes the skill of divination, but refers beyond that to general trances or conditions of possession in which certain human beings are inspired to speak spiritually potent words, is another significant source of arbitral authority.

Widespread in its incidence and multifarious in its institutional forms, it is highly developed, especially among the Valley Korekore, a northern Shona people whose elaborate organization into spirit realms was noted earlier.[34] Here, where spirit possession is a common phenomenon, mediums are not only go-betweens assuring reliable links between the secular and the spirit worlds. They are also charged officially with the task of composing certain types of conflicts at the hamlet and neighborhood levels; and, beyond that, to mediate in succession disputes for a chiefdom and in disputes among neighboring chiefs. "Mediums are peculiarly suited for this role of mediators," Garbett reports, "for, when 'possessed,' they speak as long-dead spirits. Thus, in a sense, they are translated to a level 'outside' the contemporary social system and so can be called upon to act as unbiased intermediaries."[35] Certain intricate devices to separate the two roles of "normal person" and "possessed medium" lend further credence to the objectivity of such "third parties": a medium usually denies awareness of what takes place during seances, and is reluctant to discuss either his esoteric knowledge or decisions reached by "the spirit" outside of the seance situation. Personal blame for unpopular decisions may thus often be avoided. In fact, Garbett notes that the actual decision in some mediations is arrived at by the people through discussions among themselves and at seances, though they will

[33] When the refugee Masai *Laibons* were given shelter by the Nandi in about 1860, they were accepted into a clan called Talai, and soon thereafter they usurped the position and much of the status of the Nandi *Orkoiyot*. See Huntingford, "Nandi Witchcraft," pp. 181ff.; by the same author, *The Nandi of Kenya*, pp. 38–49; Snell, *Nandi Customary Law*, pp. 15ff.

[34] *Supra*, pp. 113ff.

[35] "Spirit Mediums as Mediators in Korekore Society," p. 106; see also pp. 112, 125.

always say that it was the decision of the spirit. What often happens in such situations is that the medium waits for public opinion to crystallize before he makes a decision. Here, as among the Gwembe Tonga, who expect their prophets to be a conduit of public opinion rather than introduce a new course contrary to the general sentiment,[36] communication is preferably indirect and responsibility deflected.

Prophetism has a somewhat different bearing on conflict situations among the pastoral, cattle-loving Nuer of the Nilotic Sudan.[37] Bellicose and predatory by nature, but living in "ordered anarchy" without the support of set governmental organs, codes of customary law, or established tribunals, these tribes have traditionally entrusted the settlement of disputes to leaders or other mediating experts who could lay claim to supernatural authority. Minor specialists devoid of political significance include totemic experts, whose ritual authority derives from their connection with lions, crocodiles, weaverbirds, and certain other animals; "Men of the Cattle," who may be consulted as arbiters in disputes relating to cattle; and "Fetish Owners," whose prestige positions, while considerable, yet do not entitle them to exercise any real control over relations between villagers. The only important functionaries in Nuer society are the Leopard-Skin Chief and the Prophet. The powers of the former, which derive from his sacred association with the earth and include rainmaking as well as the right to curse or bless, may be invoked for the settlement of blood feuds. As soon as a man slays another, he hastens to the home of a Leopard-Skin Chief to cleanse himself from the blood he has spilt, and to seek sanctuary from the retaliation he has incurred. Elaborate rituals follow, while the avengers keep watch on the slayer to see if he leaves his sanctuary (an eventuality that would give them the chance to spear him), before the chief is able to open and then conduct leisurely negotiations between the feuding parties. The arbitration usually concludes with atonement ceremonies and the settlement of compensation in cattle. (The actual payment of the debt may continue for years.) Overt hostility then ceases; yet the offense is never forgiven, for Nuer know that "a feud never ends."[38]

[36] For these references, see *ibid.*, p. 119.

[37] The account of Nuer traditions is based largely on Evans-Pritchard, *The Nuer*, pp. 6, 152, 161ff., 172, 174, 185–191. For other discussions of African prophetism, see B. Skundler, *Bantu Prophets in South Africa* (London, 1948), and specialized works treating, for example, of the Kimbangu movement in the Congo.

[38] Evans-Pritchard, *The Nuer*, p. 155; cf. *supra*, Ch. 13 on "the feud" as a constitutive principle in matters of government and public order. This aspect of Nuer "mediation" suggests parallels for the ordering of modern international relations; see to this effect Michael Barkun, "Conflict Resolution through Implicit Mediation," *Journal of Conflict Resolution*, 8, No. 2 (1964), 121–130. For a

Disputes other than those about homicides—as, for example, thefts—may also be submitted to the Leopard-Skin Chief as mediator, but in this case a settlement is reached only when the opponents and their kinsmen themselves actually reach agreement during the discussion. No one can compel either party to accept a decision, and, indeed, a decision cannot be reached unless there is unanimity.

This Nuer chief, then, has neither executive nor judicial authority. As Evans-Pritchard summarizes his analysis of the office, "He is simply a mediator in a specific social situation and his mediation is only successful because community ties are acknowledged by both parties and because they wish to avoid, for the time being at any rate, further hostilities."[39] In fact, since the equilibrium of the Nuer political system is maintained through the institution of the feud, the chief is rightly viewed here as an intermediate mechanism that helps groups perpetuate the groups' structural distance from each other.

The Nuer prophet—a man possessed by the sky-god—adds certain new, politically significant, dimensions to the principles represented by the earlier native intermediaries. There is some evidence, Evans-Pritchard writes, that the rise of these spokesmen, or "ants of God," as the Nuer called them, was related to the spread of Mahdism from the northern Sudan; and there is no doubt, he continues, that "powerful prophets arose about the time when Arab intrusion into Nuerland was at its height and that after the reconquest of the Sudan they were more respected and had more influence than any other persons in Nuerland."[40] The first of these divine spokesmen to gain social significance in tribal, not just petty local affairs (he died in 1906), appears to have been an immigrant who had practiced as a Leopard-Skin Chief before he acquired his reputation as a prophet by prolonged fasts and other erratic behavior, his skill in curing barrenness and sickness, his prophecies, and his leadership in expeditions against the Dinka, a people culturally closely allied to the

---

richly suggestive discussion of mediation in segmentary lineage systems, see the same author's *Law without Sanctions*, pp. 107ff.; pp. 128ff. on the actual conflict-management situations in which the Nuer Leopard-Skin Chief applied his mediative expertise. On this point see also P. P. Howell, *A Manual of Nuer Law*, p. 28. Barkun, *Law without Sanctions*, p. 132, for comments on the nexus between the mediator and the disputing parties and the law making that ensues.

[39] *Ibid.*, p. 174.

[40] Evans-Pritchard, *The Nuer*, p. 187. Compare Nadel, *The Nuba*, p. 447, also pp. 166ff., on the connection between the beginnings of Koalib chieftainship and the invasion of the country by the Arabs during or shortly before the Mahdist regime: "In the face of the constant slave-raids of the Arabs, the Koalib communities rallied round powerful leaders. The situation seems to have demanded less a military leadership than the creation of the office of a tribal ambassador who could treat with the enemy, arrange about ransom for captives, and conclude alliances and pacts of friendship."

Nuer, but traditionally cast in the role of enemy.[41] Others into whom the spirit entered included his son, and somewhat later a captured Dinka. All achieved regional fame and power, not so much by virtue of their capacity to settle local disputes as by their successful military campaigns against the Dinka and Arab slavers, and, somewhat later, by rallying opposition to European intrusions. Indeed, no extensive raids were undertaken without the permission and guidance of prophets, who received instructions from the sky-gods in dreams and trances, as to just when and what they were to attack.

Cast by their conflict-ridden society into the role of military leaders, and capable of mediating local strife by channeling the warring instinct into successful opposition to the Arabs and the Europeans—new enemies found outside tribal ranks—the prophets emerge as the first Nuer leaders to stand for tribal unity. Moreover, as the influence of the sky-gods and their representatives has spread across tribal boundaries, and as neighboring communities have been induced to join in raiding parties and other aggressive alliances, the prophets have actually come to stand for an entirely new cause in Nuer history, that of intertribal solidarity.

Nuer prophethood is, of course, a unique institution. But it has several aspects that reenforce impressions also left by other African records. For one thing, it confirms the absolute supremacy in Africa of supernatural references as rallying points for action in local and external relations; it also confirms the identification of ultimate arbitral authority with successful use of verbal or physical force. In other words, it presents the figure of the prophet-mediator as essentially unconcerned or neutral with regard to peace, whether the latter be understood as a norm-setting concept or as a factual condition. For another, it may be viewed as yet another persuasive rendition of the general proposition that there is an organic connection between the principles, respectively, of internal and external affairs. For, just as the structural relations between segments of the same tribe are kept going by one variant of physical strife—namely, the feud—so are the structural relations between Nuer tribes and other peoples maintained by the institution of warfare. In either case, one may speak of "balanced hostility"[42] as the divinely ordained condition of existence. Here, as elsewhere in Africa where the same auspices prevail, the mediating guardian-magicians must manage conflict by practicing warrior diplomacy if they are to maintain the norm.[43]

---

[41] Evans-Pritchard, *The Nuer*, p. 186, says that the cult of the sky-god was of Dinka origin.

[42] *Ibid.*, p. 130; also p. 190, and see *supra*, Chs. 13 and 14.

[43] In an interesting attempt "to lay the groundwork for a general theory of mediation," Oran R. Young makes two assumptions that may require elaboration in the context of the African environment. First, he writes, there is the presupposition "that both original players and intermediaries behave for the most part,

B. The Stranger as Third Party

The marked respect in which divine seers and speakers are held in Africa reflects, in many instances, the pervasive influence of foreign, notably biblical, religions. Just as West African records on the subject are permeated by borrowings from Islam, so have such East African phenomena as Sudanese Mahdism and Nuer prophetism deep roots in the corresponding Islamic traditions of Western Asia—especially the image of Mohammed as an invincible warrior, called upon by God to fight the forces of evil. And a very similar case of receptivity to the Islamic prototype is reported from the heavily Islamized coastal peoples. Here, where the fusion of Islam and animism, and of literate and nonliterate traditions, has found expression in numerous social institutions, Muslim "holy men" continue to enjoy extraordinary prestige, even though many now appear well integrated in the ranks of traditional medicine men. As Lienhardt explains in his introduction to Hasani Bin Ismail's modern Swahili ballad of *The Medicine Man 'Swifa Ya Nguvumali*, numerous sharifs are readily believed to have religious powers superior to those of others by virtue of the fact that they continue to be reputed descendants of the Prophet. In fact, many inhabitants attribute the economic decline of Kilwa to the execution of two sharifs, who were mistaken for spies of the British and Germans during the scramble for Africa; their families, so the story goes, cursed the town and so brought about both the decline of its trade and the disagreements that so frequently happen between its people.[1] In parts of Ethiopia, meanwhile, it is the steady remembrance of Jewish kings and prophets that activates the latent trust in the capacity of chosen personages to perform supernatural deeds. And in all regions in which Christianity has made deep inroads, it is the figure of Christ the savior and miracle-maker, and the language of messianism and redemp-

---

rationally. For purposes of this analysis rationality can be defined in terms of the following conditions: (1) The individual evaluates alternatives in his environment on the basis of his preferences among them; (2) His preference ordering is consistent and transitive; and (3) He always chooses the preferred alternative." Second, Young assumes—after stating, quite rightly, that the "power" or "influence" of an intermediary is not necessarily a function of instruments of physical coercion—that "the intermediary's power increases as a function of the extent to which the outcome is closer to the social welfare frontier than it would have been in the absence of mediation." See "Intermediaries; Additional Thoughts on Third Parties," *Journal of Conflict Resolution*, 16, No. 1 (March 1972), 51–65, see p. 52, n. 3; p. 60, note 12. See also pp. 55–56. Unless the concept of "social welfare" is given a very broad meaning—one that includes, for example, the need to assuage nonsocial forces in the realms of magic and religion—it is not a relevant factor in the estimation of the worth of intermediaries in Africa south of the Sahara.

[1] Hasani Bin Ismail, *The Medicine Man*, p. 48.

tion, that are found to exalt the indigenous imagination in its constant quest for the wondrous and the irresistible in religious as well as political life.[2]

This recognition of foreign saints as transcendental mediators of native destinies is, in large measure, a function of the African gift for selective borrowing; only those aspects of the alien creed or culture are accepted that can actually be integrated in the existing scheme.[3] And in this respect it bears remembering that native ritual experts, too, are usually extraordinary rather than ordinary people—foreign in this sense to those who make up the vast majority of a given society. This was as true of the eighteenth-century Ashanti magician-priest Okomfo Anokye, whose inspired ministrations are credited with arousing the desire for unity,[4] as it is of the Ngoni diviners who are accepted as absolutely necessary experts when it comes to sacrificing and addressing ancestors. Described as the most powerful and respected of men, they live as recluses—that is to say, in counterpoint to the norm. In fact, the most highly esteemed members in this hierarchy of diviners are those who dream and then speak on their own initiative. Furthermore, they are accredited only after "fits and other pathological symptoms" have singled them out as qualified for their important roles[5]—a requirement also encountered in Korekore mediumship, where the possessed is trusted as a third party precisely because he speaks as an outsider when transformed in a seance.[6] Witches exhibit similar qualities when viewed as ritual agents, as do most witch-finders; for they, too, are in essence strangers to society. Trained to believe in themselves and never to contemplate failure, they are "individualists," and thus sufficiently different from others in the community to elicit that strange mixture of dread and confidence upon which successful communication with antagonistic men and spirits is commonly believed to depend.[7]

[2] Compare the heavy use of messianic terminology in identifying the political qualifications of Nkrumah, modern Ghana's former "redeemer."

[3] See in this respect Oswald Spengler's theory of cultural borrowing in *The Decline of the West*, Vol. II, *Perspectives of World History*, 57; German ed., Vol. II, pp. 64ff.

[4] Compare *supra*, p. 135, and see Ward, *A History of the Gold Coast*, pp. 95ff. As this scholar points out, the record of the patient negotiations and preparations for war has not been retained. See also Rattray, *Ashanti Law and Constitution*, pp. 273ff. for accounts of the priest's practices.

[5] Read, *The Ngoni*, pp. 178, 188.

[6] For a similar phenomenon in Ethiopia, see Henry A. Stern's description of "Bouda" possession, the "Bouda" being a conjurer who takes possession of people and then speaks through the medium of the possessed. *Wanderings among the Falashas in Abyssinia together with a Description of the Country and its Various Inhabitants* (1st ed., London, 1862; 2nd ed., London, 1968), pp. 152–156.

[7] Compare the essays in Middleton and Winter, eds., *Witchcraft and Sorcery in East Africa*, especially Robert F. Gray, "Some Structural Aspects of Mbugwe Witchcraft," p. 161; and Huntingford, "Nandi Witchcraft," p. 184. See also *supra*, Part IV.

The ambivalent relationship to which strangers are often assigned bears some relation to the ambiguity of meaning generally attached to issues affecting conflict and conciliation. In principle, the foreigner is viewed with extreme suspicion, usually bordering on enmity, and "the man apart" emerges from the records as something of an outcast, as previous discussions have suggested.[8] Both run the risk of being treated as scapegoats upon whom a community can unload the evils by which it is afflicted. The question as to just when and why the outsider becomes a savior or hero rather than a scapegoat or villain can probably not be answered conclusively. All that can be said with reasonable certainty is that the stranger's customary role is likely to be reversed when the power of his peculiar qualities has been experienced as unique and irrepressible. In such a contingency he is absorbed rather readily as yet another element in that equilibrium of opposites that the mythical imagination is capable of fashioning. More to the point, he may be recognized as the irrefutable "third party" precisely because he does not belong. Free of kinship ties or ancestral obligations, but successful by virtue of his convincing achievement either as a magician or a conqueror, he gains respect as the strong man.

A special mystique thus often attaches to "men who come from afar." For example, the "Man of the Cattle" and the "Leopard-Skin Chief" owe their positions of confidence as intermediaries in Nuer society to the fact that they are said to be descendants of stranger lineages. And the same kind of affiliation is likely to have commended individual Hima conquerors as impartial arbiters in interclan disputes among the Sukuma in Tanzania,[9] just as it supported victorious Islamic invaders in their bids for lasting dynastic power positions in far-flung native realms.

The fusion of myth and reality in popular accounts of the arrival and ascendancy of conquering strangers also marks explanations of the special mediating roles that numerous African societies traditionally assign to certain casted orders, notably those of the smiths and the bards (griots).[10] Individuals of both groups are customarily treated with awe,

---

[8] Compare *supra*, pp. 98ff.

[9] Richards, ed., *East African Chiefs*, p. 234; the establishment of Hima chieftainship appears to have evolved out of this primary arbitral role. In explaining the power of the Hima stranger-kings as arbitrators, it is also pointed out that they were protected by special guard; that they, in turn, were insulated from responsibility for the failure of an enterprise by having to act through intermediaries; and, most importantly perhaps, that their powers and responsibilities derived from a nonempirical source, namely, the ancestors. Other Hima rulers relied upon a special people, the Iru, who supplied magicians, diviners, doctors, and so on. *Ibid.*, p. 151.

[10] Compare *supra*, Chs. 6 and 7 for accounts of various types of mythical alliances between settled and incoming peoples. On the plane of actual coexistence between indigenous dominant groups, on the one hand, and settled stranger-groups on the other, other types of intermediaries are allowed to evolve. The Bariba

often with disdain, because of their technical skills and reputed connection with extraordinary forces, and both are presumed to have come from outside. One West African legend has it that the smiths of the Niger valley were the strongest of the antediluvian titans called upon to build Noah's ark. Another origin myth traces the Sudanese smiths to a Semitic Yemenite ancestor, close association with the incoming Fulbe, and all manner of unnatural happenings and metamorphoses.[11] Miraculous transformation is also the theme in a tale from Dahomey, which alleges that the magic of working with hot iron was invented by "Monkey," who had the power, through his monopoly of the art, to transform other beasts and triumph over monsters.[12]

Ethiopians, meanwhile, could not endure the smith because they viewed him as a sort of mortal that spits fire, is bred in hell, and delights in creating diseases—a belief that is said to have persuaded a fifteenth-century emperor to kill all goldsmiths and blacksmiths within his reach. Here, as in the Sudanese tradition, iron magic is commonly related to alien Semites, and in this case fancy is confirmed by fact; for Almeida's early report that the Falasha Jews were "great smiths," renowned for making lances, ploughs, and other iron articles, was confirmed at the end of the eighteenth century by Bruce, and in mid-nineteenth century by Stern, who remarks that "those most profound in magic skills are the Jews," and that work in iron and brass was "almost exclusively monopolized by the poor despised Falashas."[13]

Jewish origins are also imputed to certain groups of casted peoples

---

(northern Dahomey) recognized not only the imam but also several other spokesmen for the interests of ethnic and religious peoples who had immigrated into their midst. There was, for example, the chief of strangers, who levied taxes and passage dues, which he then conveyed to the king; and the royal representative attached to the Fulani, who was charged with settling disputes between different Fulani groups. See Lombard, "Un Système politique traditionnel," pp. 487ff.

Resident slave populations, too, produced important intermediaries. Among the Bambara of Segou, whose families had sizeable retinues of slaves, each slave community was headed by the oldest of the slaves, and the senior of all slave chiefs was recognized as the spokesman for all slave groups. In this capacity he not only presented the grievances of his constituency to the ruling family, but often also emerged as the trusted counselor of the *Fama*, the chiefly representative of the dominant Bambara family. See Viviana Pacques, *Les Bambara* (Paris, 1954), p. 60.

[11] Mamby Sidibé, "Les Gens de caste ou Nyamakala au Soudan français," in *Notes Africaines, Bulletin d'Information et de Correspondance de l'IFAN*, No. 81 (January 1959), pp. 16ff.

[12] Melville J. Herskovits and Frances S. Herskovits, *Dahomean Narrative; A Cross-Cultural Analysis* (Evanston, 1958), "Explanatory and Moralizing Tales," p. 431, No. 123; "Unnatural Mother: Why Monkey has Red Buttocks, a Large Chest and Flat Belly."

[13] Stern, *Wanderings*, pp. 152–153; and cf. Richard Pankhurst, *An Introduction to the Economic History of Ethiopia from Early Times to 1800* (London, 1961), pp. 285–287.

that live in symbiotic arrangements with the Tuareg of the Sudan and Hoggar (center of the Sahara), whom they serve as smiths, jewelers, barber-surgeons, minstrels, and dealers in magic. Known as *Enaden* (sing. *Enad*)—a name signifying "the other," or "those whom one does not name,"[14] living apart and speaking its own secret dialect, this servile caste, too, is held in contempt and fear by its superiors. Reputed to be the sole possessors of fire, uniquely capable of working minerals by despoiling the earth, and of fashioning amulets that withstand death on the battlefield, they are needed as well as envied—so much so, in fact, that they are never killed by their willful, haughty masters, lest their vindictive spirits haunt them from the graves. The Enaden strangers, then, are ever present as ritually potent agents.[15] More importantly for purposes of this discussion, mistrust, jealousy, and admiration are confounded in the Tuareg mind by the recognition that these lowly folk are intellectually superior to the majority of the ruling race, and that, being "men apart," they are apt to defy the moral principles prevalent in the society they serve. It is this type of freedom that explains, on the one hand, why members of the caste are always suspect as spies, traitors, or intriguing intermediaries meddling in family and love affairs; and, on the other, why many have occupied positions of confidence in the entourage of Tuareg chiefs as emissaries, interpreters, or counselors. Indeed, one of them Lhote reports, was officially commissioned in 1896 to conduct politically crucial negotiations with French authorities in Gao.[16]

The credibility of the casted smith as go-between in mundane and occult communications is obviously closely related to his technical expertise. In the eyes of those who till the soil, the art of extracting metal is, after all, a marvelous act, and those engaging in it are therefore naturally cast in roles reserved for magicians. Authorities on the institutions of the Kikuyu, Masai, and Kamba (East Africa) thus report that no magic there is deemed to equal that of the smith; his curses, protective spells, and blessings cannot be lifted, and oaths on a piece of iron used for beating and hammering other pieces of iron are completely binding and irrevocable. If such an oath is sworn falsely, nothing can stop the deaths that will follow as a matter of course.[17] No wonder, then, that smiths have traditionally been called to settle cases:

[14] See Henri Lhote, *Les Touaregs du Hoggar*, p. 774; *ibid.*, pp. 176–177 on their obscure origins and the likelihood that a group of Jewish smiths from the oasis of Tamentit had, in effect, taken refuge with the Tuareg in the fifteenth century, after its expulsion by Arab "marabouts."

[15] Compare *ibid.*, pp. 308ff. on Tuareg habits of sorcery and divination, which include the belief that smiths are often sorcerers.

[16] *Ibid.*, p. 175.

[17] Compare Penwill, *Kamba Customary Law*, p. 61; Lambert, *Kikuyu Social and Political Institutions*, p. 122; *supra*, Chs. 10 and 11 on oaths and curses.

If sugar cane is stolen from a garden, or goats are stolen out of a village by night, the owner often goes to a smith and seeks his aid, taking with him the iron necklet or bracelet of a deceased person. If the smith agrees to intervene, he will heat this in his smith fire and then sever it with a chisel, saying, "May the thief be cut as I cut this iron." . . .

If, for instance, a man was owed a debt, he would induce some smiths to go to the village of the debtor and order him to pay. And as the smiths were held in fear the order was generally complied with.[18]

Analogous patterns of dispositions and reactions are recorded in West Africa. Here, too, the smith is respected as "the first artisan, a redoubtable being, who has broken with ancient traditions of exploiting the earth and succeeded, with the aid of magic, in creating this artificial thing, namely metal,"[19] and here, too, he enjoys vast powers as judge and arbitrator when peace is being threatened. For example, among the Dogon (western Sudan), smiths are commonly called to mediate conflicts in relations with strangers as well as within a particular family. In their presence, or in that of the smith's hammer, all quarreling must cease; and decisions they may render are not subject to appeal.[20]

Castes are castes by virtue of living apart. Smiths in Africa are no exception to the rule, and the rule is fixed not only because they are shunned by "the community" but also because they are motivated by their very condition to cultivate the mystique attached to them. Thus it is usual for them to conceive of their profession as a family prerogative making for solidarity, and to insist upon intricate forms of self-government, usually in the nature of what are commonly called guilds.[21] Indeed, some scholars of the matter insist that if smiths or "griots" in Black

---

[18] Hobley, *Bantu Beliefs*, pp. 171, 173; *ibid.*, pp. 167ff. on a clan of serfs that seems to serve the Masai as smiths.

[19] Leroi-Gourhan and Poirier, *Ethnologie de l'Union française*, Vol. I, *Afrique*, p. 349.

[20] David Tait, "An Analytical Commentary on the Social Structure of the Dogon," *Africa*, 20, No. 3 (1950), p. 190; also Montserrat Palau Marti, *Les Dogon* (Paris, 1957), pp. 31, 48ff. This author suggests that the Dogon smith is, in fact, the only truly individuating artist in a society in which art is supposed to render collectively held concepts and to be executed as a joint enterprise. See, by the same author, "Conduites abusives permises en Afrique" on Dogon smiths as pacifiers, and pp. 300ff. on the role of a smith in settling a dispute between partners to a blood pact between Lobi (north Ivory Coast) chiefs. In connection with this tradition and the great prestige attached to the smith in West Africa, it is interesting to note that Camara Laye, a well-known modern Guinean writer, was born into a family of renowned smiths. He tells of this heritage and the easy fusion of Islam, animism, and magic (which includes the influence exerted by a crocodile) in his novel *L'Enfant noir*, cf. *supra*, Ch. 18 A, n. 4.

[21] For discussions of the guilds of smiths in Nupe country, see Nadel, *A Black Byzantium*, pp. 259, 265, 269ff.; for those in East Africa see Hobley, *Bantu Beliefs*, pp. 167ff.

Africa act as arbiters or intermediaries, it is not so much because they are known to have skills of the mind uncommon among those they serve, but rather because they do not "belong," and are thus neutral in the real sense of the word.[22]

Explorations of the nature of this neutrality as a function of the syndrome of superiority and inferiority, or of disdain and respect, convinced Leo Frobenius that these now despised people had at one time been part of an elite nation, at least among the Malinke in the West African Sudan.[23] Contradicting Islamic bards and writers, whose accounts he found derogatory of pre-Islamic peoples and their cultural attributes, Frobenius maintains that the Numus (smiths) are, in fact, the remnants of the former ruling race. Defeated and displaced by continuous Islamic thrusts between the tenth and seventeenth centuries, they were relegated to an occupational status that the African Arabs traditionally viewed as absolutely inferior to their own life style, even as they recognized its importance as the source of indispensable and unrivaled technical skills.[24]

In Frobenius' view, all groups of inhabitants in what he calls "the Western Sahel" (meaning thereby the land immediately to the south of the Sahara and to the north of the Sudan proper) form one culture complex, for all peoples here experienced the same historical destiny and responded to it by evolving similar social orders and caste arrangements. After noting that the latter consist almost everywhere of nobles who supply the ruling establishment; various castes, which include, besides the smith, the "griots" (bards, minstrels, or praise singers), and the leather workers; and lastly, captives and slaves,[25] Frobenius concludes from the

[22] Leroi-Gourhan and Poirier, *Ethnologie de l'Union française*, p. 350.

[23] *Spielmannsgeschichten der Sahel*, pp. 26ff.; see also, by the same author, *Atlas Africanus*, Sec. II, p. 8, to the effect that the smiths were disdained as a caste, yet respected as a profession. For a lucid discussion of the factors that make for the mixture of disdain, fear and confidence in West African popular orientations toward the casted smiths and griots see Alphonse Gouilly, *L'Islam dans l'Afrique Occidentale Française*, Paris, 1952, pp. 31–33.

[24] In the course of contrasting the culture forms of the Arabs and the Berbers in North Africa, Frobenius argues that the latter accommodated castes and greatly respected the smith, all the more so as they had developed a special relation to fire, whereas the African Arabs placed the smith on the lowest rung of the social ladder. The ascendancy of the Arabic element in North Africa had the effect of erasing this distinction everywhere except in Kabylia, the matrix of Berber culture. The discovery that the smiths continued to be highly esteemed in these recesses of the Berber world convinced Frobenius that they had originally constituted the superior rather than the inferior social element in this area, which this scholar, at least, considered historically crucial for developments in Africa south of the Mediterranean littoral. See *Volksmaerchen der Kabylen* (being Vols. I, II, and III of *Atlantis, Volksmaerchen und Volksdichtungen Afrikas*, Jena, 1921), Vol. I, 3ff., 30ff.

[25] *Spielmannsgeschichten der Sahel*, pp. 14, 21ff. Almost identical lists of castes and of tribes accommodating these castes are given by Sidibé, "Les Gens de caste," p. 13, and by Leroi-Gourhan and Poirier, *Ethonologie de l'Union française*, p. 349ff.

evidence he presents that the smiths, however variously distributed and organized in this vast region, are yet most likely the representatives of *one* nation that had been consigned to castehood (*"eine* zur Kaste gestempelte Nation").[26] In accordance with this theory, then, the mythical remembrance of the Numus' bygone superiority combines with the actual daily experience, on the one hand, of their inferior social status, and on the other, of their ritual and magical power, to produce that composite sentiment of fearful trust and contumely on the part of groups now dominant, to which all records attest. Thus, when the Mandingoes went to war and a Numu was the first to be killed, an entire army was apt to flee. Likewise, when a village had been founded and a Numu was the first to die there, premonitions of collective misfortune instantly arose. In the courtly strata of the ruling houses, meanwhile, he acted as official poisoner, master of ceremonies, expert in the administration of ordeals, and above all as the king's principal counselor when weighty decisions had to be made.[27]

The second major caste in the area comprises the bards or griots (known in Mande as *dialli*). They, too, suffered from disabilities as closed, segregated societies; and they, too, were renowned for rendering third-party services, even though the smiths were apt to view them derisively as frivolous. The source of their power was the mastery of the spoken word, and it is, therefore, not surprising to find them prominently employed as royal messengers, interpreters, and negotiators—functions demanding eloquence, shrewd bargaining, intrigue, and such other diplomatic skills as the gift of remembrance, without which no cause could be represented persuasively in a nonliterate society. It was this particular ability, indeed, that established the griot in many West African societies as the keeper of genealogical records and the custodian of epic songs that celebrate a hero's exploits or a people's past.[28] At his best, then, he could represent a principal in relations with others by acting as an inspired raconteur or musician, as well as a didactic historian. Charged with the mission of sustaining the identity of those he served, the bard was there to glorify the local lore in speech and song, "create courage" (as among the Songhai);[29] propagate some special truth; exhort people to fight their enemies; demolish the reputation of the adversary by insult, ridicule, or satire, and fortify that of his royal or noble master by lavish praise; or, if necessary, correct his master's conduct by subtle mockery and criti-

---

[26] *Spielmannsgeschichten der Sahel*, p. 35.

[27] *Ibid.*, pp. 27–32, 43; note Frobenius' comments on the specialized group of "dancing smiths."

[28] Compare *supra*, Ch. 6 for discussions of the Legend of Wagadu and Gassire's Lute, and for references to authorities on the subject, notably Monteil and Frobenius.

[29] Rouch, *Les Songhay* (Paris, 1954), p. 42.

cism. Each of these functions and talents lent itself to degeneration and abuse. Unwarranted flattery and insult made for distorted versions of identity; excessive zeal in managing public relations led to pointless rumor-mongering; strenuous efforts to be amusing yielded mere buffoonery; and the wish to please or be deserving of some recompense was easily traduced into corruption and venality. In short, not all griots were either trustworthy or efficient middlemen. Furthermore, bards were always vulnerable as witnesses and advisors because few could lay claim to that hallowing magic for their utterances upon which many ritual experts, including some of the smiths, could rely when called upon to interpose a set of potent words. These limitations, confounded in Islamized regions by the competitive presence of the written word, explain why griots play greatly diminished roles in traditional West African societies. Nowadays, Rouch noted in 1954, one finds some members of this caste remaining close to the Songhai chiefs whose family traditions they preserve; others, by contrast, eke out a living by carrying news from village to village, and by distributing praise or insult, usually in accordance with the subject's willingness to pay.[30]

In this area, bards have long contended with the presence of scribes, chroniclers, and teachers of "The Book"; and here, as in other African provinces impregnated by Islam, pagan medicine men, priests, and diviners have had to adjust to their Muslim counterparts, just as traditional native judges and arbitrators have had to accommodate the jurisdictions claimed by Islamic qadis, muftis, marabouts or mallams (mālami), imāms, and ʿulamā. It goes without saying that these rival functionaries must have been experienced as intruding strangers when they first appeared upon the scene; for they represented culturally new approaches to religion and education, government and law, and therefore also to conflict and its management. Above all, they were strangers because they possessed a variety of unknown and thus mysterious skills that were derived, directly or indirectly, from their command of the written word.

Earlier discussions of the general relationship between literacy and nonliteracy, and of the special impact of the Arabic language and Islamic faith upon indigenous societies, have stressed the fact that writing has not revolutionized fundamental traditional modes of thought and communication. Valued by the receiving oral culture as yet another—albeit in many respects superior—magic, and, therefore, often as a particularly reliable mode of communicating with supernatural forces, it could be

---

[30] *Ibid.* For different treatments of the role of griots, see among others Sidibé, "Les Gens de caste," pp. 14, 17ff.; Béart, "D'Une Sociologie des peuples africains à partir de leurs jeux," p. 309; Palau Marti, *Les Dogon*, pp. 31, 48ff., and, above all, Frobenius' social and historical analysis of this caste and its contribution to African culture in *Spielmannsgeschichten der Sahel*, pp. 35ff., 50ff.

assimilated without disturbing either the mental or the social order, all the more so as the homeland of the new religion had always been hospitable to analogous trends. In short, Arabic has appealed to the traditional African imagination mainly because its graphic signs can be accepted as objects that materialize the magical force implicit in potent speech.[31] A specialized study of this cultural encounter in northern Ghana suggests, in fact, that it was the attraction of this particular quality of writing that led, first, to the acceptance of Islam, and next, to the common African concentration upon the occult or cabalistic content of the creed.[32] The original religious or spiritual message has thus been gradually distorted most everywhere, as Wilks puts it in the following passage:

> The written word increasingly becomes valued not as a medium of communication but for its magical qualities, and the art of writing, if it is not lost completely, becomes an esoteric possession of a clique which is feared rather than respected. A Qur'ān may become regarded as a sacred object in its own right, no longer read but worshipped and perhaps, as among the Kamara of Larabanga in northern Ghana, only exposed to public view once in a year, or an *imām's* staff of office may be enshrined and periodically purified and sacrificed to, as among the Sanu of Bobo-Dioulasso. The fast of Ramadān may continue for a time to be observed, but as an expression of the group's ritual solidarity rather than as an obligation of Islam.[33]

Selective borrowing of this kind explains why indigenous divinatory techniques have been promoted rather than discredited by the introduction of Islam, and why membership in the ranks of specialists in this craft has increased rather than diminished. Reports from Islamized Africa thus converge on the high esteem in which mallams and marabouts are held as intermediaries with the supernatural; they are capable of rendering unrivaled services in matters requiring divination and spiritual advice, as well as decisive action. The Gonja Chronicle of 1792, for example, relates that this kingdom in northern Ghana owes its very existence

[31] Compare *supra*, pp. 87ff. for the use of written charms and amulets as protective devices in war; and see Goody, "Restrictive Literacy in Northern Ghana," p. 230, on the widespread practice of "drinking the word"—a technique also recorded in many other traditional societies; for "as writing turns speech into a material object words can be more readily manipulated." "From Senegal to Hausaland it is reported that the blessing of the Holy Word of the Qur'ān can be most fully absorbed in just this manner." *Ibid.*, pp. 230–231.

[32] Goody, "Restricted Literacy," p. 239; see also *ibid.*, pp. 206, 227, 234.

[33] Ivor Wilks, "The Transmission of Islamic Learning in the Western Sudan," in John Goody, ed., *Literacy in Traditional Societies* (Cambridge, 1968), pp. 192–193. For a French scholar's view that African assimilation of Islam subjects this faith to a "dégradation perpetuelle," see Goody, "Restricted Literacy," p. 204.

to the miraculous intervention of a mallam; during a fight in which the pagan Gonja leader was hard pressed, the Islamic personage appeared, struck the ground, and planted his staff in the earth between the combatants. The enemy fled, and the Gonjas thereupon "wished to enter Islam." Similar assistance continues to be rendered here and in other West African lands, often under the auspices of a fixed relationship between the Muslim advisors on the one hand, and the ruling establishment on the other.[34]

Other categories of foreign experts and intermediaries are composed of scribes (in West Africa these are usually imāms), who are responsible for writing letters, often in the context of diplomatic correspondence between heads of sovereign powers; custodians charged with keeping formal lists of past chiefs; and chroniclers of past and present events. The latter, of course, are the main competitors of the griots; yet such is the force of oral tradition that many written histories in the western Sudan are not really chronicles, but rather compilations of matter passed on by word of mouth. Moreover, in many lands chronicles are known to have evolved into objects of ritual significance, precious secrets jealously kept from public view, or mere attributes of an imām's office.

To the extent to which it is possible to distinguish between magic and statecraft, and between spiritual and secular experts, mention must be made of the fact that Muslims have traditionally occupied magically potent and politically prominent positions at African seats of government. This was as true of the Islamized courts of the early Sudanese kingdoms—such as Mali, Songhai, and Bornu—as of great non-Muslim realms—for example, those of the Bambara of Segu, where Mungo Park found a Muslim "prime minister" resident in 1805;[35] the Mende of Sierra Leone, whose chief warriors relied upon Muslim priests as advisors and

---

[34] *Ibid.*, pp. 234ff.; also p. 211 and appendix I, 241ff. Compare *supra*, Ch. 12 for references to the roles of Islamic medicine men and sheikhs in East Africa; Ch. 4, n. 24 for instances of resort to Islamic magic in modern African statecraft and postindependence rebellions and wars.

Mallam is the Hausa term for marabout. See Rattray, *Hausa Folk-Lore, Customs, Proverbs, etc.*, Vol. I, "Author's Note," x ff. to the effect that these *mālamai*, or scribes in West Africa, were everywhere the most respected and honored members of the community. Also see R. R. Marett's preface to the above work by Rattray, p. vi, that "a mālam of the best class possesses all the literary skill which a knowledge of Arabic and of the Arabic script involves. None the less, he remains thoroughly in touch with his own people, a Hausa of the Hausa." And consult Vol. II, 297, note 9 on the uses of the term. On marabouts see Vincent Monteil, "Marabouts," in James Kritzeck and William H. Lewis, eds., *Islam in Africa* (New York, Toronto, London, Melbourne, 1969), pp. 87–109; also Gouilly, *L'Islam dans l'Afrique occidentale française*, pp. 31ff., where it is explained that a Muslim marabout was an integral part of animist society centuries before the latter became Islamized, and that he is—not unlike the griot—the member of an inferior caste.

[35] *Journal of a Mission to the Interior of Africa* (London, 1815), p. 145.

medicine men;[36] the Bariba (northern Dahomey);[37] and the Ashanti, in whose realm members of the alien faith have functioned in institutionalized and prestigious roles from early times onward. Here, it was noted in 1817, the ritual preparations for the projected invasion of Gyaman included both pagan and Muslim observances. Muslim diviners were employed, and it was thought possible to win the intercession of the Prophet Mohammed in the interests of Ashanti. The head of the Ashanti bureaucracy employed a Muslim secretary to keep records of political events and of casualties in war, and Muslim agents served on the staffs of Ashanti commissioners in the outlying provinces of the empire.[38] In these and other conquest states, imperial orbits, and vassalage systems, where social and political controls depend upon established modes of coexistence between ethnically or morally different groups, imams, 'ulamā, and other Islamic dignitaries appear to have proven their worth as mediators between government and the governed, as well as between separate component segments of a given plural society. Like their fellow religionists in the ranks of soothsayers, marabouts and scribes, they have survived the vicissitudes of political upheaval and changing fortunes—in most cases for many centuries—without losing their identities as foreign agents. And the same holds true, by definition, of the time-tested patterns of affiliation that bind them to the ancient African societies in whose midst they live and work.

A curious paradox thus marks Negro Africa's relation to Islam. For whereas the body of doctrine, belief, and socially relevant practice has been thoroughly Africanized, this cannot really be said of the outstanding

[36] Little, *The Mende of Sierra Leone*, p. 273, Appendix I, "The Part of Islam in Mende Life." Persons professing some connection with Islam play an important part in the general organization of religious and magical life. Broadly speaking, the faith is officially confined to the ruling classes and to immigrant Mandingo and Susu traders. Although chiefs were usually not Muslim, Little notes that military prestige was closely connected with Islam in early times, and it continues to be a mark of prestige in nonliterate Mende society to profess Islam.

[37] Lombard, "Un Système politique traditionnel," pp. 487ff.

[38] Ivor Wilks, "The Position of Muslims in Metropolitan Ashanti in the Early Nineteenth Century," in I. M. Lewis ed., *Islam in Tropical Africa* (London, 1966), pp. 318–341, especially pp. 326–333. In the Kingdom of Gonja (northern Ghana), members of the old Muslim establishment have unique access to the position of imām to the paramount and divisional chiefs, whose advisors they are. They are also the official representatives of the Islamic community vis-à-vis the ruling group. Although Islamic law is not applied on the political level, and the judicial body consists of chiefs, not mallams, the latter play important roles as mediators between the conflicting parties. See to this effect Goody, "Restricted Literacy," pp. 207, 211.

Among the Somalis in East Africa, who have participated for over a thousand years in the literate culture of the Arabs without surrendering their traditional reliance upon oral modes of learning and communication, sheikhs act as mediators, arbitrators, and peacemakers. See I. M. Lewis, "Literacy in a Nomadic Society," pp. 266–267.

proponents of the faith and culture. From the native African point of view, at any rate, they remain strangers. Indeed, their very usefulness as third parties is a function of the perpetuation of this status. What is integrated, then, and most securely so, is the role itself, and the context that allows for this accommodation is the highly developed African agency scheme in which countless categories of intermediaries can evolve in response to social needs. Viewed in this perspective, the alien literati simply take their place in the hierarchy of casted specialists, as the non-literate griots and smiths do. The process by means of which this congruence has been achieved in parts of the western Sudan, now within the republics of Mali, Guinea, Upper Volta, Ivory Coast, and Ghana, has been aptly summarized by Wilks in the following passage:

> Characteristic of Western Sudanese society is the presence within it of what are often described as castes: briefly, of groups highly specialized in function (blacksmiths, leather-workers, etc.), their social boundaries delimited in terms of, for example, marriage patterns, and their social cohesion expressed through sets of ritual observances, obligations and prohibitions. . . . The '*ulamā*', that is, the cadres of scholars in various localities, may be seen similarly as exercising control over a field of technological enterprise—writing: the alphabet, pens, ink, paper, etc.—and as organized under the ritual authority of their *imāms*. Indeed, in traditional Western Sudanese modes of thought the '*ulamā*' are regarded in just this way, and are usually ranked in status below the nobles of the ruling groups (who exercise managerial skills) but above such artisan groups as the smiths or leather-workers.[39]

There are groups of 'ulamā, notably in the Dyula region of the western Sudan (Mali and Upper Volta), that resist this type of assimilation, and staunchly defend Islam as a universalistic creed, open to everyone and unbounded by social .or territorial barriers. Known in Malinke as "karamokos"—namely, "those who know"—they have distinguished themselves in the course of centuries by founding towns, settlements, and mosques, organizing trade and pilgrimages, and above all by spreading literacy through the establishment of Koranic schools. To the extent to which each of these enterprises stands for the cause of expanding rather than of contracting human horizons, the karamokos may be viewed as mediators not only between literate and nonliterate folk, or Muslims and pagans, but also between rulers and subjects. In fact, in terms of avowed intent and actual achievement, they emerge from the records as a special breed of regional peacemakers, committed to the muting of conflicts between separate local interests and societies. Two trends in Dyula thought, in particular, are believed to have guided them in the exercise of this

---

[39] "The Transmission of Islamic Learning in the Western Sudan," p. 191.

function: a tendency to reject fighting, especially the *jihad*, as an instrument of social and political change; and subscription to the idea of withdrawal from secular political activities.[40] In deference to these orientations they set up different institutions for the proper interpretation of the faith, including courts of arbitration. Furthermore, conflict is practically eliminated in relations between Dyula towns because they are closely linked by common commercial interests and a network of alliances based on kinship and marriage.

Ideology, concern for personal and doctrinal integrity, organizational skills, and, above all, pedagogy appear to be the traits that have persuaded generations of non-Dyula to respect these literate outsiders and, on occasion, to engage their technical assistance. For example, Malinke griots still remember one particular town as "la ville des marabouts" which the sixteenth-century *Ta'rikh al-fattāsh* describes as follows:

> There was at the time of the supremacy of the kings of Mali a town of jurisconsults . . . called Jagha-Ba (Ja'ba) situated in the interior of Malian territory. The king of Mali never entered it, and no one exercised authority there over and above the *qādī*. Whoever entered the town was safe from violence and molestation by the king. Even if he had slain one of the children of the king, the king could not claim compensation from him. It was known as the city of God.[41]

Likewise, non-Muslim rural people were found to seek Dyula advice and instruction at the end of the nineteenth century in circumstances vividly set out by the French observer L. G. Binger:

> They [the Dyula] have established, from place to place, Kong families in all the villages on the roads from Kong, to Bobo-Dioulasso first, to Jenne next. They have taken fifty years to endow each pagan village with one or two Mande families. Each of these immigrants has organized a school, asking some of the inhabitants to send to it their children; then little by little, through their relations with Kong on the one hand, and with other commercial centres on the other, they have been able to render various services to the pagan chief of the district, winning his confidence and imperceptibly involving themselves in his affairs.[42]

So great was the reliance on these services, Binger reports, that in the states of Kong even the chiefs of pagan villages would take no decision without first consulting the nearest karamoko. And the same pattern of trust and dependence is still found today; for Wilks, who wrote the au-

---

[40] *Ibid.*, p. 179.   [41] *Ibid.*, p. 178 for this reference.
[42] *Ibid.*, p. 190 for the rendition of this excerpt from *Du Niger au Golfe de Guinée*, 2 vols. (Paris, 1892), Vol. I, 327.

thoritative study on the subject, noted in 1967 that he was asked several times by village elders to intercede on their behalf with the authorities in nearby towns so that they might find a karamoko willing to settle with them.[43]

This particular elite of strangers is quite different in its purpose and inception from those considered earlier. But in certain major respects it, too, conforms to traditional African agency schemes. In principle anyone is qualified to become a member of the class of 'ulamā provided he completes the study of a few selected texts. In actuality, however, the calling has settled in certain families, and it is they who have provided 'ulamā, generation after generation.[44] In other words, the arrangement is caste-like, after all. Innovating thought is also found to have yielded to traditional practice when the role of Dyula towns is surveyed: the Dyula control commerce, and do so in accordance with the rather cosmopolitan dispositions that are peculiar to them; but their distance from the autochthonous communities is deliberately emphasized by the acknowledgment that the latter retain ritual custody over the land —an age-old custom in intertribal relations, as earlier references have shown.[45]

Comparable long-term arrangements for the social utilization of resident foreign groups did not evolve in response to the presence of Europeans. Certain noteworthy patterns of accommodation were recorded in the early period of the Western intrusion, it is true, especially in relations between the Portuguese and various Congolese societies, the Boers and Bantu peoples in southern Africa, and between the French and tribal groupings in the region of the Senegal. It cannot be said, however, that any of these affiliations was marked by the allotment of definite third-party roles. Only missionary societies may be said to qualify in this regard; in providing widely sought services in secular education, medical assistance, and instruction in a new and powerful faith, they rendered services broadly analogous (in some respects greatly superior) to those for which the 'ulamā were renowned. The Italian Capuchins were thus highly reputed in the seventeenth century as mediators between the Portuguese on the one hand, and the Christianized Congolese kings on the other. Indeed, Garcia II of Kongo sent a Capuchin to Luanda in the mid-seventeenth century to negotiate the terms of an accord, and similar missions were sent to Nzinga (ruler of the Ndongo) and to the Jaga of

[43] Ibid. But see R. P. Hébert, "Esquisse de l'histoire du pays toussian," Bulletin de l'IFAN, 23, Nos. 1–2 (January–April 1961), 309–323, for the reputation of the Dyula in this part of Upper Volta; here a Dyula chief from Kong is said to have subjected the land to unmitigated terror in the eighteenth century.

[44] Wilks, "The Transmission of Learning in the Western Sudan," p. 170.

[45] Ibid., p. 164; supra, Chs. 6 and 7. On Muslim intermediaries in modern Senegalese politics, see Behrman, Muslim Brotherhoods and Politics in Senegal, notably pp. 136ff. on the economic role of marabouts, and 124ff. on certain conflicts between the latter and the government.

Kasanje—African rivals for power in the region.[46] Even in these cases, however, no structural integration on local levels of social organization could occur. The new literate aliens were, after all, numerically sparse and unevenly distributed as groups, and they were destined to remain visiting outsiders in their own, as well as in the Africans' eyes, since they were, after all, merely being lent by religious associations that were firmly based in the West.

Subsequent centuries were even less favorable to the organic evolution of an "intermediary status" for Europeans. The sudden but methodical installation of colonial systems of administration in the nineteenth century disqualified even the most apolitical Western elite groups as impartial mediating agencies in intracommunity affairs; and the equally hurried disestablishment of imperialism some decades later led to the reaffirmation of native agency usages, just as it conduced to a renewal of trust in customary law. This is not to say that Western education and Christianity had not wrought far-reaching changes in African institutions and mental dispositions, but as a noted Nigerian historian reminds us, "the colonial period represents only one episode in [Africa's] long and eventful history," and the impact of "the episode" was uneven, to say the least. For "while the lives of some communities were profoundly affected, others had hardly become aware of the Europeans' presence before they began to leave."[47]

The situation is somewhat different when one surveys encounters between individual European missionaries, explorers, settlers, or administrators on the one hand, and Africans on the other. Although such relationships are, strictly speaking, not relevant to the issue here under consideration, they are nonetheless quite illuminating in the context of both interpersonal and intercultural communications. The contacts that Mzilikazi, founder of the Ndebele kingdom in southern Rhodesia, sought and made, are a case in point.[48] This man, who was relentlessly at war in the 1820s and 1830s, so as to build a personal military monarchy on the Zulu model, took many initiatives to open communications with whites. Traders and hunters were among the first to arouse his interest, and he received them well, partly because he expected them to supply him with goods, guns, and knowledge of their use, but mainly, it appears, because

[46] See Vansina, *Kingdoms of the Savanna*, p. 151. See p. 203 on "Jaga" as the appellation for the ruler. On one occasion the Holy See itself interceded with the king of Spain in favor of the Kongo kingdom. Compare *infra*, Ch. 20 B on the mediating functions of missionaries in the relations between Sir Henry Johnston and Baganda chiefs.

[47] J. F. Ade Ajaji, "Colonialism: An Episode in African History," in L. H. Gann and Peter Guignan, eds., *Colonialism in Africa 1870–1960*, Vol. I: *The History and Politics of Colonialism 1870–1914* (Cambridge, 1969), pp. 508, 504–505.

[48] For this account see Lye, "The Ndebele Kingdom South of the Limpopo River," pp. 87–104.

he sought through them to obtain a missionary.[49] This purpose was first accomplished when two missionaries, among them the celebrated explorer Robert Moffat, consented to come in the company of the trusted emissaries that Mzilikazi had despatched to the mission station. Moffat's masterful account of the hazardous journey, during which he witnessed the horrendous scale of devastation that his host had visited upon the land, and of his ten days' stay at the royal kraal, includes the following description of his reception: after greeting him with the words, "The land is before you; you are come to your son,"[50] the monarch explained:

> "Machobane, I call you such because you have been my father. You have made my heart as white as milk; milk is not white to-day, my heart is white. I cease not to wonder at the love of a stranger. You never saw me before, but you love me more than my own people. You fed me when I was hungry; you clothed me when I was naked; you carried me in your bosom"; and, raising my right arm with his, added, "that arm shielded me from my enemies." On my replying, I was unconscious of having done him any such service, he instantly pointed to the two ambassadors who were sitting at my feet, saying, "These are great men; 'Umbate is my right hand. When I sent them from my presence to see the land of the white men, I sent my ears, my eyes, my mouth; what they heard I heard, what they saw I saw, and what they said, it was Moselekatse who said it. You fed them and clothed them, and when they were to be slain, you were their shield. You did it unto me. You did it unto Moselekatse, the son of Machobane."

The special friendship, in terms of which Moffat became "a father figure" to the Matabele king, was so widely respected that it is credited with having made safe the visits of other missionaries, also solicited by Mzilikazi. These included representatives of the Wesleyan and the French Protestant stations, as well as three American missionaries, who were allowed to teach the Ndebele (Matabele) at Mosega. The major compelling motive behind all these contacts appears to have been Mzilikazi's speculation that missionaries would be ideal mediators in his relations, not only with other white men, but also with his native enemies. At any rate, this warrior, who was reputed among his contemporaries to have far exceeded Shaka's record of ruthless cruelty, never attacked a town where missionaries lived. Moreover, he concluded first a treaty of friendship and next (1836) a formal agreement with the English gover-

---

[49] Compare *supra*, pp. 288ff., for Wilks' account of how western Sudanese villages try to elicit the presence of a Dyula 'alim (this being the singular of 'ulamā).

[50] For this and the following excerpt from Moffat's *Missionary Labours and Scenes in Southern Africa* (London, 1842), see Eric Axelson, ed., *South African Explorers*, pp. 230, 233–234.

nor, under the terms of which he promised to defend any missionary who might settle among his people, whereas the governor agreed to arrange for a missionary to forward the various intentions of the contracting parties.[51]

In the overt context of Anglo-African diplomatic history—episodic as it may have been in the era of imperialism—it is certainly justifiable to assume that a chief, renowned for his political and military genius, chose to cast Moffat, and through him the category of foreign missionaries, into the role of prime mediator, although this was not his professional identification. But a reading of Mzilikazi's address to Moffat also suggests certain covert contexts that illumine the mode of thought out of which diplomatically significant dispositions grow. We find in this interesting speech another affirmation of that synoptic view of time and human existence to which we referred in preceding chapters; personalities that are clearly distinct from each other in Western perception, are here presented as floating or sliding into each other, even across the threshold between life and death. The father and the son are one, as are the spokesmen and the chief they represent. And the alien is divested of his foreignness through transposition into the familiar world of symbolic representation—a process that renders him fit to play the role of intermediary on multiple interlocking levels of spiritual and secular relationships.

This last theme impressed itself indelibly upon Isak Dinesen a century later. Musing about the capacity of the Kikuyu on her farm to make her at a moment's notice a chief mourner, or woman of sorrows, who could in that capacity absorb a great distress that had befallen all of them, and thus return them to the calm of life, she began to recognize herself as their brass serpent—one in a vast hierarchy in which many of her white friends, including Lord Delamere himself, were given precedence of rank according to their utility as such brass serpents. Dinesen explains her rendition of the old biblical image as follows:[52]

[51] Lye, "The Ndebele Kingdom," p. 103; the effects of this agreement cannot be assessed, since the Boers destroyed this extension of British influence by driving the Ndebele out of reach of the colony. See Cecil Northcott, *Robert Moffat; Pioneer in Africa 1817–1870* (London, 1961), pp. 147ff. on five long journeys between 1829 and 1859; pp. 134ff. on Moffat's successful leadership in conducting a Matabele embassy back through the land of vindictive Bechuana tribes; pp. 213ff., 227 for accounts of several meetings with the Matabele chief, one of these after a twenty years' absence; pp. 238ff. on Moffat's remarkable influence throughout Matabeleland, fully sanctioned by Mzilikazi's writ, which provided a freedom for Moffat to come and go in a manner that no white man had then achieved in the territory of a great African chief; p. 291 for the Matabele chief's fear of the impact of European teaching: "If all my people go to school, they will forget how to fight, and will become cowards, and the enemy will lay waste my country."

[52] In the Old Testament it is an image set up by Moses in the wilderness; those who had been bitten by serpents were healed upon looking at it.

Because of their gift for myths, the Natives can also do things to you against which you cannot guard yourself and from which you cannot escape. They can turn you into a symbol. I was well aware of the process, and for my own use I had a word for it,—in my mind I called it that they were brass-serpenting me. Europeans who have lived for a long time with Natives, will understand what I mean, even if the word is not quite correctly used according to the Bible. I believe that in spite of all our activities in the land, of the scientific and mechanical progress there, and of Pax Britannica itself, this is the only practical use that the Natives have ever had out of us.[53]

A review of the European presence in Africa leaves little doubt that the auspices did not favor direct and lasting mediating functions on the part of either individuals or groups. The impact that was made in this respect was indirect; for there emerged, during the brief period of co-existence, a new type of African "third party," which interposed its good offices successfully on numerous occasions—notably toward the end of the nineteenth century. Composed of literate, speculative Africans who had been tutored, for the most part, by Christian missions, and were for these reasons detached from the folk societies that had brought them forth, this, too, was an elite of outsiders or alienated minds.[54] In formerly British West Africa it included such distinguished members as Bishop Samuel A. Crowther, who regarded colonial rule as a social revolution, and the Reverend Dr. Samuel Johnson, who was one of two clergymen-peacemakers sent into war-torn Yorubaland in the 1880s. It was only after these had patched up bilateral settlements between various factions that the Lagos governor could call a conference of all the hostile parties. Indeed, a survey of the tangle of intracommunal, intertribal, and Anglo-French relations in which the area was caught in the 1880s and 1890s, has convinced a noted scholar that "the British presence in the Yoruba interior . . . was largely dependent on the missionaries, mostly Africans, who by virtue of their alienation from traditional ties and loyalties emerged as arbitrators, respected for their impartiality."[55]

No doubt can attach to the sincerity of conviction and the expertise in execution that are implicit in records such as these. Viewed in historical and sociological perspectives, however, "alienation," and with it

[53] *Out of Africa*, p. 106. The role of scapegoat, in which "the man apart" is so often cast in Africa, may be said to represent the negative aspect of the same process of symbolic transformation. Compare *supra*, pp. 98ff.

[54] Compare *supra*, Chs. 3 and 4 on "the marginal man," destined to live on the peripheries of two different cultures.

[55] John E. Flint, "Nigeria: The Colonial Experience from 1880 to 1914," being ch. 7 in L. H. Gann and Peter Duignan, eds., *Colonialism in Africa 1870–1960*, Vol. I, 239. See also *ibid.*, pp. 222, 229, 230, 236, 239.

impartiality, were bound to be passing phenomena, since they had been induced and nurtured by Western mentors, usually in the strict framework of imperial policy making. With the passing of this phase in African history and the advent of political independence, all African elites were gradually returned to the service of their own societies and cultures, and therewith to modes of thought about conciliating opposites that had proven their worth in preceding millennia.

C. DEPUTIES AND DIPLOMATS

The ritual agents and third parties discussed in the two preceding sections can claim competence in the management of conflicts because their own intrinsic powers make them basically independent of those in charge of daily government. More specifically, it may be said of almost all of them—be they priests, prophets, medicine men, rainmakers, diviners, smiths, or 'ulamā—that they qualify as consultants to a given community or its ruling regime because they are able to deal with situations of confusion between the spheres of order and disorder[1], or of knowledge and ignorance, when regular authorities are apt to fail.

Deputies, by contrast, are ordinary rather than extraordinary intermediaries, in the sense that they function *within* the sphere of local order and knowledge. This vast category includes spokesmen, linguists, palaver speakers, go-betweens, messengers, resident emissaries; and, in certain cases, praise singers, insulters, and jesters—in short, scores of agents who have standing assignments in society, usually in positions of official inferiority to the principals in whom supreme or superior authority is vested. The major tasks of these officials are dictated by the absence of literate traditions, as numerous earlier references have already explained.[2] That is to say, all relate in one way or another to modes of oral communication, whether in relaying instructions, interpreting messages, settling remembrance by the repetition of things known or heard, upholding established etiquette, or administering other symbolic codes. It is in this broad context, then, that members of the greatly various "communication elites"[3] often have occasion to affect actual or potential conflict situations, either by preventing misunderstandings that might give

---

[1] For this formulation see John Middleton, "Spirit Possession among the Lugbara," in John Beattie and John Middleton, eds., *Spirit Mediumship and Society in Africa* (New York, 1969), p. 230; the reference here is to diviners and prophets.

[2] See especially *supra*, Ch. 17 on the power of the healing word, and *supra*, Ch. 10 on verbal aggressiveness and the power of the killing word.

[3] Doob, *Communication in Africa*, pp. 20ff. refers to these agents as "communicators"; see also his brief summary presentation of their functions.

rise to controversy and disorder, or by interceding openly in existing tensions and disputes.

Thus a spokesman may chose to blunt the thrust of an aggressive speech he is asked to render; he may reshape the original content of a message by the way in which he rephrases it in transmission; and he can suggest lines for the settlement of a quarrel by artfully interpreting oral exchanges as he participates in a negotiating session. Other situations that come to mind call, by contrast, for a commitment to certainty and precision in the delivery of messages. The dense hierarchy of go-betweens in the Kingdom of the Kongo—indispensable for such purposes of state as the summoning of princes to royal elections—was thus found to include, in late nineteenth century, a "royal messenger who keeps tying up people by word of mouth, or with a wordy yoke."[4] And similar assignments were given to the agents that separate but friendly Tonga clans despatched to each other when alliances had to be concluded. By way of summarizing his studies of amical relations among separate Bantu-speaking peoples, Schapera has this to say:

> Diplomatic relations are maintained between neighbouring Chiefs by means of recognized court messengers. Each Chief informs his neighbours of all important events in his tribe, such as the holding of an initiation school, the outbreak of some pestilence, or the death of his predecessor; and invites them to his own installation or marriage. If there is trouble between a Chief and members of his tribe, it is often the practice for one of the parties to call in some neighbouring Chief to try and reconcile them. Chiefs descended from the same ancestor, but now ruling over different tribes, frequently continue to recognize in some way their relative status by birth. Thus among the Tswana no Chief would in the olden days celebrate the firstfruits festival or hold an initiation school, until he had received permission to do so from the Chief of the Huruthse, who was regarded as senior to all the rest in line of birth. So, too, among the Xhosa there exists a so-called "paramountcy," under which the Chiefs of junior tribes recognize the Chief of the tribe from which they have separated as their superior. Cases are sometimes referred by them to him for settlement, or carried to him on appeal from their verdicts; and they pay him a certain small nominal tribute.
>
> Formal requests may also pass from one Chief to another for rain, or for a military or matrimonial alliance, or for the extradition of fugitives from justice. . . . If the man is a criminal fleeing from justice he may be sent back; but if he has fled because of ill-treatment or other

[4] Dennett, *At the Back of the Black Man's Mind*, p. 26.

injustice, and does not wish to go back, he will be protected by the Chief to whom he has fled. His own Chief cannot follow him up and take him by force, but is expected to send messengers to ask for his return.

Hostile relations between neighbouring tribes arise most frequently out of disputes at the boundaries over land or water rights; cattle thefts; interference with visiting subjects; or the refusal to hand over fugitives. Messages will pass between the Chiefs, claiming or refusing satisfaction, until, unless one of them gives way, armed conflict is inevitable.[5]

In short, as these and the following illustrations are designed to show, orality allows for many different modes of representation, argumentation, and diplomacy, some of them not readily available in communications controlled by literate skills and written records.

These implications of the use of speech explain why linguists and other delegates, although officially presumed to represent their principals, often emerge as highly influential third parties in their own right. In Sukuma society, for example, where all power and responsibility is distributed in accordance with firmly institutionalized magico-religious beliefs, and where the operations of "ordinary" or "inferior" deputies can therefore

[5] Schapera, "Political Institutions," pp. 192–193. See also Westermann, *Geschichte Afrikas*, p. 29, for the functions and destinies of ambassadors in certain West African societies. Reporting on Benin's relations with Ife in the sixteenth century, De Barros (a Portuguese government official) noted: "In accordance with a very ancient custom, the King of Beny, on ascending the throne, sends ambassadors to him [the Oni of Ife] with rich gifts to announce that by the decease of his predecessor he has succeeded to the Kingdom of Beny, and to request confirmation. To signify his assent, the Prince Ogane [the Oni] sends the King a staff and a headpiece of shining brass, fashioned like a Spanish helmet, in place of a crown and sceptre. He also sends a cross, likewise of brass, . . . a holy and religious emblem similar to that worn by the Commendatores of the Order of Saint John. Without these emblems the people do not recognize him as lawful ruler, nor can he call himself truly King. All the time this ambassador is at the court of Ogane he never sees the prince, but only the curtains of silk behind which he sits, for he is regarded as sacred. When the ambassador is leaving, he is shown a foot below the curtains as a sign that the prince is within and agrees to the matters he has raised." For this excerpt see Hodgkin, *Nigerian Perspectives*, pp. 96–97; *ibid.*, pp. 97ff., for accounts of embassies bearing on Benin's communications with the Portuguese. And see *ibid.*, 77–78, on the services of ambassadors and messengers in relations between Bornu and Egypt toward the end of the fourteenth century. See excerpt from a letter by the King of Bornu to the Mamluk Sultan of Egypt, in which the former announces the despatch of his cousin as an envoy, charged with the mission of informing the Egyptian ruler that "the Arabs who are called Judhama and others have taken captive our free subjects . . . and our relatives, and other Muslims" and that they "are selling them to the slave-dealers in Egypt and Syria and elsewhere." In view of this great calamity the Sultan is requested to "send messengers to all your lands, to your Amirs, and your Wazirs, and your Qadis, and your Governors, and your men of learning, and the heads of your markets" so that these may find and free and return the captives to Bornu.

not be clearly differentiated from those of ritual agents, elders—alternating as residents at court—are customarily charged with diverse mediating functions. They provide the main channel of communication between chief and people, they keep the chief informed, and they are his delegates in negotiations with soothsayers and rainmakers, in boundary disputes between headmen, and in relations with friendly chiefly courts.[6]

The same principles are exemplified by the social system of the Mende. In this chiefly hierarchy, the speaker acts as main intermediary between the chief and the chiefdom, and as a "sounding board" for public opinion. Charged with hearing complaints, he exercises his discretion as to which disputes are to be relayed for the chief's consideration. Furthermore, and in accordance with traditions still observed in mid-twentieth century, he assumes the duties of his master when the latter is ill or absent, and acts as regent-chief during an interregnum—a mandate that allows him to influence the choice of the chiefly successors,[7] even as it may invite indulgence in factionalism, intrigue, and bribery. And parallel developments are reported from Ghana, where the government of Ashanti has traditionally depended greatly on intricate agency arrangements that include a hierarchy of linguists. Here, where the relations between government and opposition were deeply disturbed in 1954 as a result of controversies about the price of cocoa, the senior linguist of the Asantehene was able to organize an effective counterforce by using precolonial native norms and structures.[8]

Next, in a thought world in which it is possible to confound personal identities,[9] a deputy may actually become a chief's alter ego for certain purposes. The Paramount Chief of the Ngoni thus had a special relation to "the royal shadow"—namely, a boy from a particular clan with which the Paramount's clan had ritual connections. This boy did everything with the Paramount, including jumping onto his pyre to burn with him. As explained by Read,[10] he was there to strengthen the Paramount by giving him a second self. Such a "soul carrier" was also known in the Gold Coast (Ghana), where custom had it in mid-twentieth century that a chief was not permitted to interview an official or be present at any meeting unless he was accompanied by at least one attendant. In reminiscing on his life there as a colonial civil servant, Sir Alan Burns pays

[6] Cory, *The Indigenous Political System of the Sukuma*, pp. 43ff.

[7] Little, *The Mende of Sierra Leone*, pp. 196ff.

[8] Apter, "Nkrumah, Charisma and the Coup," p. 780. Discussing town life today in *Report on a Social Survey of Sekundi-Takoradi* (London, 1950), K. A. Busia writes that the Fish Sellers' Union there has a "spokesman," who joins the chief and elders when disputes among members have to be settled. For this reference see Wolfson, *Pageant of Ghana*, p. 239.

[9] *Supra*, pp. 79ff.

[10] Read, *The Ngoni of Nyasaland*, pp. 61ff.; a "joking relationship" existed between the Paramount and his "shadow"; on this subject cf. *supra*, Chs. 6 and 7.

special tribute to Sir Ofori Atta, then Paramount Chief of Akim Abuakwa, and according to Burns the most accomplished orator in the colonial legislature he had ever met. Whenever this Paramount Chief came to Burns' office, a young boy—"his soul"—was also present.[11]

These modern echoes of age-old mythical understandings may be classed as symbolic manifestations of the traditional need to assure the survival of such fundamental institutions as the chiefdom. Other recorded agency relations, also meant to avert catastrophe or conflict in channels of command, are designed to insulate the person and prestige of the chief, both corporeally and spiritually. In the course of describing his audience with King Gelele of Dahomey, Burton tells how the wives and amazons of the king shielded their master from the gaze of visitors after the toasts had been drunk, not only by using a profusion of parasols, but also by applying the mass of their bodies to his protection, and how circuitous all conversations had to be, lest the king hear something that might be offensive to his position.[12] Here, as elsewhere, elaborate precautions were also taken to deflect responsibility so that medicine men, military commanders, linguists, or other subalterns would absorb offences directed against the ruler, take the rap for wrong decisions, and generally act as scapegoats capable of insulating the governing authority from criticism, and thus of saving the community from conflict and dissension.

These patterns of distributing functions among delegates are particularly prominent in governments modeled on the idea of sacred kingship. For, as Meek remarks in his study of the loosely knit confederacy of the Jukun,[13] it is one of the first essentials in such regimes that the king should never lower the dignity of his office by allowing all and sundry to have direct access to him. Therefore, "Anyone who had a complaint or who was in a position to give first-hand information could only approach the king through a chain of officials, each of whom took their dues. Anyone breaking this regulation was liable to be sold into slavery. The king was, therefore, only informed of such matters as the various officials, headed by the Abô, considered were suitable (from their point of view) for him to hear." This senior Abô is the Jukun king's vis-à-vis, Meek continues. That is to say, he is the representative of the people in their relations with the king, just as he is the latter's mouthpiece in transmitting royal orders to the people. He has a court of his own, receives his

---

[11] Sir Alan Burns, *Colonial Civil Servant* (London, 1949); for this particular reference see Wolfson, *Pageant of Ghana*, pp. 235–236. Cf. also Richard Wright, *Black Power*, p. 283, for a mention of this "soul carrier."

[12] Burton, *Mission to Gelele*, Vol. I, 163; and cf. supra, pp. 138ff. for other discussions of this audience.

[13] Meek, *A Sudanese Kingdom*, pp. 334ff. and 336–345 for discussions of other aspects of government that bear on the theme of dispersed authority.

food ceremonially, like the king, and has his own semisacred second in command. He reports to the king daily everything of importance that occurs, and, in former times, disposed of all judicial cases that did not require the king's personal investigation. Further, it is his business to warn the king if the latter is negligent in his duties, assume control of the town and state in the absence or on the death of the king, and give his consent if there were a demand to kill the royal principal. After noting striking resemblances between the Jukun system and that of the Baganda in East Africa, Meek also points out that the pattern does not differ much from that of Benin or Oyo as he knew it then, and from that of Bornu or Songhai in ancient times.[14] Mende customs of structuring the delegation of authority present yet another instance of convergence on very similar motifs, as a foregoing reference suggests.

The radius of communication between different communities is, of course, strictly limited in peace making as well as in war making, by virtue of factors analyzed earlier. Intermediaries whose assignments call for the preservation or promotion of public order in this extended domain have, therefore, few options, and are expected to work within rather narrow frames of reference and comply with firmly established norms. It goes without saying that these realities were nowhere more compelling than in constellations of communities that rotated or fluctuated around the core of some effective or nominal power in so-called empires, tributary systems, confederacies, or other "great societies," as these have been presented earlier in the present analysis.

In the officially unified Kuba Kingdom (Congo), described as an imposed federation, relations between component chiefdoms are quasi-diplomatic in character,[15] even though it is the Bushoong chiefdom that controls the union of eighteen tribes and provides the presiding kingship. Each of the locally autonomous units maintains a resident representative at the Bushoong capital, who is responsible for the annual payment of tribute by his chiefdom. Furthermore, each gives a wife to the king, and she, too, may act as go-between. Common legal norms are absent, but conflicts not settled by war may be arbitrated by an outside chief, provided the warring parties consent, and in such an eventuality it is often the Bushoong king who emerges as the mediator, if only because he controls the biggest army in the political constellation, and is thus presumed capable of enforcing his decision.

Respect for the arbital prerogative of royalty also marks certain West

---

[14] *Ibid.*, pp. 345–347.

[15] On this subject see Vansina, "A Traditional Legal System," pp. 99, 115; the same author's "L'Etat kuba dans le cadre des institutions politiques africaines," *Zaire*, 11 (1957), 485–489; and *Kingdoms of the Savanna*, pp. 118ff. and 35ff. Also Herskovits, *The Human Factor in Changing Africa*, pp. 88ff.

African kingdoms, those of the northern Yoruba and the Akan peoples, for example. Here, where a town comprises numerous descent groups of heterogenous origin, each of the latter elects from its own members a titled chief to sit on the governing council, and the decisions reached by the chiefs are then communicated to the king, who announces them as his own. As Lloyd explains, the king is seen as an arbitrator in the conflicts of interest between the various descent groups; without him the groups would never reach agreement, and the members of the community would disperse in anarchy.[16]

Other intricate agency patterns are presented by the pre-nineteenth–century records of the Oyo kingdom, the largest and most powerful of the Yoruba states, whose successful military operations had called forth an extensive tributary system. As reconstructed by Law, the constitutional scheme provided that the principal vassal towns of the kingdom were attached to "patrons" at the capital.[17] These resident personages served as spokesmen of their clients' interests before the Alafin (king), and were also responsible for transmitting their clients' tribute, part of which was returned to them by the Alafin. The patron might be a titled royal prince, a principal wife of the Alafin, a high-ranking eunuch or slave, or one of the nonroyal chiefs who together composed the Oyo Mesi (council). None of these intermediaries, however, seems to have had any real power or discretion. In point of fact, it was the Alafin, and not the patron, who appointed the Oyo representatives, and he did so by delegating authority to members of his immense staff of palace slaves. These *ilari*, being viewed as the Alafin's major messengers to the world outside the palace, also collected tribute from subject peoples outside the kingdom proper, such as Dahomey and the Egba realm, and are said to have been in general charge of Oyo's external diplomacy. On neither level of intercommunity relations did mediating procedures effect lasting respites from internal power struggles, mutinies, revolts by subject towns or kingdoms, or attacks from abroad. By the 1820s the Oyo kingdom was falling apart, and its empire collapsed thereafter, as a preceding discussion of the role of war and conflict in this society has already indicated. However, the model or blueprint for orderly relations between separate communities through the use of deputies may, nonetheless, be said to have an intrinsic validity that transcends the record of actual failure.[18]

[16] Lloyd, *Africa in Social Change*, pp. 38ff.
[17] Law, "The Constitutional Troubles of Oyo in the Eighteenth Century."
[18] *Ibid.*, pp. 41–44, for a close analysis of the interlocking reasons for Oyo's fall. By way of explaining the Alafin's powers and pretensions, Law points out that the king was the highest judicial authority in Oyo, and that he had direct control of the cult of Sango, in terms of which the Alafin appears deified as the god of lightning, and invincible, therefore, since he can call down lightning upon

The counterpart of the Oyo patron in the Ashanti Confederacy is the *adamfo*, a functionary described as "a friend at court," and a liaison officer, who represents each of the local divisions at the Head Chief's court.[19] This arrangement, which expressed "the need of some contact between Kumasi and the outlying States in the period between the intermittent meetings of the Union Council,"[20] provided, among other things, that the lesser ruler could only approach the king through his *adamfo* in Kumasi—usually a prominent member of the Asantehene's entourage, permanently resident at the court, where he was charged to watch over the outside chief's interests and transmit all communications. Further, if the presence of the outside chief was required in Kumasi, messengers were sent through the appointed *adamfo*. The precise implications of the title and the agency relationship it covered are today a matter of scholarly dispute,[21] but it is certain that this intermediary, unlike the Oyo patron, could not be used by the central Ashanti government to reduce the division rulers to the status of tributaries. Subject to such obligations as swearing an oath of allegiance,[22] contributing taxes and fighting men, recognizing a right of appeal from their own courts to the king's court at Kumasi, and participating in the ceremony of cleansing the nation from defilement, decentralization remained the norm.

Beyond the sphere of member states that encircled Kumasi, intercommunity relations were structured in wholly different ways. By the beginning of the nineteenth century, Ashanti had succeeded, largely by military operations, in extending its control over numerous nations; and

---

his enemies. Although he did not participate in the secret meetings of another cult group, the important Ogboni Lodge, he was represented there by a woman who reported to him on the proceedings. See Bradbury, *The Benin Kingdom*, pp. 74–113, on the placement of intermediaries from each chiefdom in the Benin complex at the court of the Oba of Benin.

For the use of such functionaries in the emirates and vassalage systems of northern Nigeria, see M. G. Smith, *Government in Zazzau*, p. 79, to the effect that each vassal state is linked to the ruler of Zaria through an intermediary, who reports legal cases to Zaria and generally keeps abreast of developments. Compare also *A Chronicle of Abuja*, pp. 3–4 for the statement that after Zaria began to pay tribute to Bornu in the eighteenth century, the Zazzau kings were always installed by a representative of the ruler of Bornu. Another emissary of the Bornu ruler, called the Kachalla, was sent to live at the court of the King of Zazzau.

[19] On this institution see Claridge, *A History of the Gold Coast and Ashanti*, Vol. I, 228; Ward, *A History of the Gold Coast*, pp. 117, 157; Rattray, *Ashanti Law and Constitution*, pp. 93–98; Tordoff, "The Ashanti Confederacy," pp. 410ff. for a review of scholarly opinion, notably references to Ivor Wilks' paper, "Akan Administrative Practice" (1961).

[20] Busia, *The Position of the Chief*, p. 100.

[21] See Tordoff, "The Ashanti Confederacy," p. 411.

[22] On the importance of the oath in general, and the "Asantehene Great Oath" in particular, as strengthening links and sanctions in settlements of disputes, see Busia, *The Position of the Chief*, pp. 75–76.

over these, a contemporary observer wrote, the King of Ashanti ruled with unrivaled sway. The administrative devices applied to the twenty-one tributary states varied from case to case, but in this context too great reliance was placed upon deputies and messengers.[23] Bowdich wrote that "every subject state was placed under the immediate care of some Ashantee chief, generally resident in the capital, who seldom visited it but to receive the tribute from the native ruler, for whose conduct he was in a reasonable degree responsible."[24] And since these provincial governors were settled in Kumasi, they often delegated responsibility in their provinces to officers of their own choice. Here, as in the confederacy proper, surveillance appears to have been constant. Thus, if a chief was sent on a mission abroad, the king's spies were at hand to detect and report any false move.[25]

Just as it is difficult to distinguish clearly and consistently between tributaries and independent states, so one cannot always say with certainty where imperial administration ends and diplomacy begins. War rather than peace was the constant here, as elsewhere in Africa, and collective identities were fluctuating, nowhere more so than in the case of federal and imperial systems. For the King of Dahomey to send embassies to Kumasi was a wise insurance policy, in the opinion of observers on the scene, for around 1820 it appeared clear to them that the resources of Ashanti were adequate to crush Dahomey.[26] Deliberate efforts were, nonetheless, often made to forestall conflicts between rival courts by despatching emissaries. The rulers of Denkyera and Ashanti are said to have been in the habit of sending such missions, exchanging favorite wives, or of placing heirs in the entourage of the foreign king—practices that did not, however, prevent the former from slipping into the status of tributary to the latter.[27] The touchstone in this extended sphere of

[23] T. E. Bowdich, *Mission from Cape Coast Castle to Ashantee* (London, 1819), p. 317; J. Dupuis, *Journal of a Residence in Ashantee* (London, 1824), p. 236, to the effect that forty-seven different units were controlled.

[24] Bowdich, *Mission from Cape Coast Castle*, p. 235.

[25] Tordoff, "The Ashanti Confederacy," p. 409.

[26] Dupuis, *Journal of a Residence*, p. 239.

[27] Claridge, *A History of the Gold Coast and Ashanti*, Vol. I, 195ff., 213ff. On women as intermediaries and matrimony as an aspect of diplomacy, see also Skinner, *The Mossi of the Upper Volta*, pp. 96ff.; ritual pacts between Mossi kingdoms and with neighboring non-Mossi communities often provided for the exchange of wives, captives, and others in the expectation that such arrangements would keep rulers from attacking each other. Annual gifts were yet another device to help buttress the accord. For a discussion of ritual pacts see *supra*, Part III. Mythical alliances and pacts of friendship in Bariba country were also consolidated by the exchange of women; see Lombard, "Un Système politique traditionnel," pp. 488ff. In Mzilikazi's far-flung realm south of the Limpopo, the ruler's wives were indispensable deputies; they resided at every major kraal, shared power with the district commanders, and provided the king with continuous information

intertribal and international relations, as in others fashioned by politically talented African races, was superior force or victory in war; and these norms were not appreciably affected by mediating agencies rooted in common beliefs and sanctioned by a shared trust in moral obligations, as they were in the inner circle of culturally or mythically related states. As Tordoff concludes in his penetrating analysis of Ashanti affairs, "Many of the distant provinces and tribute-states . . . had strong national feelings of their own; religious sentiments would certainly not have persuaded them to rejoin the Ashanti empire when, in the nineteenth century, they succeeded in throwing off the Kumasi yoke. Physical force and not religious sanctions kept the Brong states, such as Takyiman and Gyaman, loyal; and it was no accident that, in the 1930s, the great majority of them voted against the proposal to restore the Ashanti Confederacy."[28]

on local developments. See Lye, "The Ndebele Kingdom," pp. 99, 101. Here, too, diplomatic agents were supplemented in their work by spies who kept the ruler informed of the movements of all enemies, notably the Zulus.

[28] "The Ashanti Confederacy," p. 417.

· 19 ·

COMMERCE, COMMUNICATION,
AND STATECRAFT IN
INTER-AFRICAN RELATIONS

A. MARKETS, CARAVANS, AND TRADING PROCESSES

When Mary Kingsley engaged in her explorations of West African forest regions (Gabon in particular) where no white person had been before, and of the "mind forest"[1] of the Fans and other peoples, she chose trading as the most reliable channel of communication with the alien African world and as the best means of self-protection in an enterprise generally viewed as hazardous and daring. As she explained it to an audience of ladies in her native England: "I find I get on best by going among the unadulterated African in the guise of a trader; there is something reasonable about trade to all men, and, you see, the advantage of it is that, when you first appear among people who have never seen anything like you before, they naturally regard you as a devil; but when you want to buy or sell with them, they recognize that there is something human and reasonable about you."[2] Persuaded that fetish worship was ineradicable, and that missionary endeavors to reach the African mind and conscience were in most instances misdirected, she insisted instead that the white trader was on the whole the Africans' best friend, since he "looks after them when they are sick, or in trouble, and tries to keep them at peace with each other and with the white government, for on peace depends the prosperity which means trade."[3]

Some of these assumptions are borne out by the success of Mary Kingsley's personal exploits. By joining native rather than European crews and trading groups and adapting herself to locally respected customs—which included being armed during certain haggling processes—she gained the confidence of savage men while realizing her own purposes and emerging alive from her adventures. She has also recorded situations, however, in which European and African trading habits were

---

[1] Campbell, *Mary Kingsley, A Victorian in the Jungle*, ch. 6.

[2] *Ibid.*, pp. 83–84 for this excerpt from the lecture.

[3] From a letter quoted *ibid.*, 133. On this subject Mary Kingsley writes as follows in *West African Studies*, p. 108: "Now conscience when conditioned by Christianity is an exceedingly difficult thing for a trader to manage satisfactorily to himself. A mass of compromises have to be made with the world, and a man who is always making compromises gets either sick of them or sick of the thing that keeps on nagging at him about them, or he becomes merely gaseous-minded about them all round."

clearly at odds with each other. Occasionally, indeed, she deliberately chose to pit her own diplomatic skill against that of her African counterparts. For example, when she was advised during a lengthy negotiation for carriers and guides that such a price palaver might easily last for weeks, she held out successfully for due speed and despatch: her terms were met, the palaver ended promptly, and the company left the very next day.

The other, more fundamental proposition with which this nineteenth-century explorer identified, along with many of her Western contemporaries—namely, that trade is accepted by Africans and Europeans alike as a natural, reasonable, essentially peaceful activity which aims primarily at prosperity—is, by contrast, not readily sanctioned by realities that have been uncovered before and after Africa experienced the full impact of Europe's economic institutions. In fact, in comparison with trade as it has been conducted in classical, medieval, and modern Europe, that of the African peoples has been undeveloped for reasons implicit in the general way of life.[4] The folk society, which is the core of organized African existence, is, after all, self-sufficient by definition, and this not only in ethnic and moral, but also in economic respects. Isolationism and aloofness are prevalent dispositions, contacts with strangers are not sought deliberately, and means of technical communication between different communities are perforce strictly limited. Furthermore, certain incentives, always taken for granted in the West as natural and reasonable, are either totally missing or only faintly present on local value scales. Individuals are not encouraged to develop exploratory instincts, take risks, and seek adventure or advancement beyond the sphere of the community to which they belong. What has been said in a specialized study of the Plateau Tonga, namely that they are not "traders at heart,"[5] is in a general sense true of the vast majority of African peoples. Subsistence is the norm in economic aspiration, not development and growth, and this not merely in small, secluded, and tightly knit settlements, such as those of the Tonga, but also in the relatively open societies of West and Central Africa that have long been affected by the impact of commerce-minded Berbers, Arabs, or Portuguese, and therewith also by the existence of caravan routes charted through vast expanses of land. In some of the latter regions, in particular, trading has, indeed, been a popular or "natural" activity for centuries, and those engaging in it have impressed generations of foreigners with their spirit of commercial enterprise and the shrewdness of their bargaining powers.

[4] Little, "African Culture and the Western Intrusion," p. 943 for pertinent generalized conclusions.

[5] Elizabeth Colson, "Trade and Wealth among the Tonga," in Paul Bohannan and George Dalton, eds., *Markets in Africa*, Evanston, Ill., 1962, p. 607.

But the methods employed in negotiating conflicts and accords, as well as many of the purposes pursued in the context of both simple marketing transactions and elaborate trading operations, reflect the force of the same culture that had found its first and primary expression in the primitive village market.

Many parallels can, of course, be found between African and European markets, and these may justify the view that notions of what is normal or reasonable are the same in both worlds.[6] Significant divergences in institutions and modes of economically relevant behavior have also been noted from earliest times onward, however, and this in full awareness of the fact that one must distinguish diverse African economies and categories of markets, just as one makes allowance for the same kind of diversity when dealing with the West.[7]

[6] In addressing himself to some problems of cross-cultural comparison, Herskovits writes as follows: "it requires analysis in depth to see that African economic behavior is patently 'normal,' in the sense of being consistent with ends which are culturally defined as desirable. Africans, no less than other peoples, seek to fulfill their needs as they envisage them, whether these needs be biological or psychological. The means of solving the problem differs from society to society, in the light of the technological, historical, social, and psychological factors that are in play." However, he begs the question when he adds: "But basically, the problem is the same wherever it may be treated." Melville J. Herskovits, "Preface," in Paul Bohannan and George Dalton, eds., *Markets in Africa*, Evanston, Ill., 1962, p. viii.

[7] Bohannan and Dalton distinguish three typical market situations:
1. societies that lack market places, and in which the market principle, if it appears, is but weakly represented;
2. societies with peripheral markets—that is, the institution of the market place is present, but the market principle does not determine acquisition of subsistence or the allocation of land and labor resources;
3. societies dominated by the market principle and the price mechanism.

See Bohannan and Dalton, eds., "Introduction," *Markets in Africa*, p. 3. This volume presents twenty-eight different case studies.

Another classification, this one limited to Central Africa, but inclusive of all trading, is found in Jan Vansina, "Long Distance Trade Routes in Central Africa," *Journal of African History*, 3, No. 3 (1962), 375–390:
1. the old institution of the local village market;
2. trade over greater distances, either between culturally different peoples within a single state, or between neighboring peoples, in the course of which transactions are made at market places located close to the borders of the trading peoples, or at the capital of the state;
3. long-distance trade, conducted by caravans based on coastal harbors, which was unknown in Central Africa before the arrival of the Europeans in the fifteenth century.

Colin W. Newbury, "Trade and Authority in West Africa from 1850 to 1880" in L. H. Gann and Peter Duignan, eds., *Colonialism in Africa 1870–1960*, Vol. I, *The History and Politics of Colonialism 1870–1914* (Cambridge, 1969), 67, says that it is impossible to present a satisfactory typology of markets for the precolonial period in this region. On markets in particular see W. Froehlich. "Das afrikanische Marktwesen," *Zeitschrift fuer Ethnologie*, 72, nos. 4–6 (1940), 234–328; also Jan Vansina, *Kingdoms of the Savanna*, p. 24. On the caravan trade

Some of the traits here considered typical of African approaches to commerce and related human and international relations may be traced to the fact that the classical market is everywhere greatly valued for non-economic reasons. In a world marked by the absence of writing and other technical communications, and in which, as Bohannan and Dalton point out, "collections of people on non-kinship bases or non-age-set bases may prove difficult, the market provides the skeleton for a very wide range of social usages."[8] It is here that people conglomerate to talk, argue, hear the latest news, meet old friends and adversaries, make new contacts, find entertainment, participate in festivals, or, on occasion, celebrate religious rites. All processes of trading are penetrated by these activities and desires. Furthermore, and for many of the same reasons, these trading processes are either actually conducted in the form of barter or gift exchange, or, where these classical norms are modified by the acceptance of media of exchange (and these may range from cattle, cowrie shells, and gold dust to modern currencies), they are heavily infused by the spirit that inhabits the traditional mechanisms and transactions. Bargaining and bartering, then, are appreciated as social pastimes and channels of pleasurable communication, even as they make possible the exchange of needed goods and services.

Speech certainly dominates the market. Here, as in other types of human encounter, it is usually expertise in speech that determines the outcome of a commercially motivated confrontation. However, the African trading genius can also triumph in nonverbal communications, as the widespread incidence of so-called silent trade attests. This ancient practice, amply documented from the tenth century onward insofar as West African exchanges of gold for salt are concerned,[9] was observed in the nineteenth century by Richard and John Lander in Iboland, when two trading groups were bartering yams for cloth. After describing move and counter-move in sequences carefully supervised by an old lady, the visiting explorers noted:

> All this was carried on without a word passing between the parties, and the purchase of a sufficient number of yams by our people occupied three hours. . . . The scene before us was altogether extraordi-

---

see Bovill, *The Golden Trade of the Moors*, and the same author's earlier volume, *Caravans of the Old Sahara*. See also Mauny, *Tableau géographique*, notably pp. 426ff., "Les Grandes Routes du commerce"; pp. 354ff., on the distinction (often difficult to make) between "local trade," "inter-regional trade," and "external trade"; pp. 419ff., on currencies used in medieval Western Africa.

[8] "Introduction" to Bohannan and Dalton, eds., *Markets in Africa*, p. 18.

[9] See Mauny, *Tableau géographique*, pp. 363ff.; also pp. 356ff. on the inter-regional salt trade, and pp. 293ff. on the sources of gold and salt. The silent trade in these goods had already been noted by Herodotus. Consult Barth, *Travels*, Vol. III, 358–362, on the gold trade and the Teghâza salt mines.

nary. Many of the people belonging to the canoes were standing in a group on the bank of the river near them with muskets, swords, and spears in their hands; some with the articles with which they were about to make a purchase. A quantity of yams, arranged in large bundles, placed in a row, separated them from another group, consisting of the villagers also armed, and both parties standing at a short distance from them, leaving a considerable space between. Here was stationed the old woman, who, with no little consequence, directed the whole affair by signs, either to her own party or ours, not a word being spoken by anyone.[10]

Some Europeans then doing business in the area successfully adapted themselves to the African style of protracted and indirect negotiation. When a group of thirty or forty indigenous traders, each bringing a little gold dust, arrived at Mr. Bannerman's premises in Accra, "he returned some answer sufficient to convey an invitation to barter, but expressive of no exact desire for it; a day or two passed, and they sent to say that they would come to look at the goods he had." At the appointed time the whole body came in procession and the transaction proceeded as follows:

the goods (gold) were displayed, and after a little time food was given to them, so far they were the gainers; they made an offer, Mr. Bannerman all this time walking backwards and forwards on his verandah above, apparently indifferent to the whole proceeding, and refusing or acquiescing but by a simple monosyllable, he said nothing more; all day the country traders were crouching about the yard, nor left till sunset; this scene was repeated for days, the object of the African being to weary out the patience of the Englishman, an attempt utterly futile as it applied to Mr. Bannerman; at length the respective parties agreed, the gold dust was weighed and tested, . . . the merchandize chosen, the traders fed, and by the evening they were on their journey to their own homes, having possibly wasted weeks in endeavouring to obtain a trifling advance in favour of their gold dust.

[10] For this excerpt from Richard Lander and John Lander, *Journal of an Expedition to Explore the Course and Termination of the Niger* (London, 1832), Vol. III, 161–163, see Hodgkin, *Nigerian Perspectives*, p. 233. The Landers speculated that "this method of trading must have arisen either from fear of quarrelling, or from not understanding each other's language, which is difficult to suppose; but it seems to have been instituted by mutual agreement, for both parties understood how they were to act." For a full discussion of trade in this region see also K. O. Dike, *Trade and Politics in the Niger Delta, 1830–1885*. See also Hodgkin, *Nigerian Perspectives*, p. 268, for Samuel Crowther's account of Igbebe, a great center of communication on the Niger, where in 1854 he witnessed people belonging to at least eight different linguistic communities avidly trading in such diverse articles as ivory, country cloth, tobes, mats, shea butter, palm oil, yams, sheep, goats, and fowl.

As the narrator of this episode saw it: "time is valuable only where industry prevails, consequently it is no where less esteemed than in western Africa."[11] Other observers, while equally exasperated by the African nonchalance in regard to time, express their admiration for the "industry," patience, and business acumen so often displayed in the course of these endless consultations, as well as for the artistry with which time is structured, as it were, so as to serve best the special purposes pursued.[12]

Voluminous and diverse as the existing records of inter-African and early Afro-European negotiations are, they converge on a few inter-related propositions that explain why traditional African modes of bargaining are subject to measures of time not commonly regarded as reasonable in the West. Whether classed as grand consultations or petty exchanges, whether occurring between two different groups, or, as in "silent trade," between the members of each separate group, palavers must be prolonged and move in circuitous ways because they are, after all, talks unrelieved by references to scripts or documents in which remembrance, prospect, or tentative accord is registered. Next, they involve on each negotiating side several, sometimes scores of people, all expecting to be satisfied in one way or another, whether they participate in leading or supporting roles. And finally, a bargaining process such as that in a market place is valued for numerous reasons that are extraneous to what Europeans and Americans are apt to view as the business at hand. The time it takes to consummate a deal in ever-fluctuating conditions of offer and acceptance is thus essentially irrelevant; or, to put it differently, the causes of enrichment and mutual satisfaction are neither decisively affected by time-related calculations, nor are they reckoned as aspects of long-range economic policy.

Furthermore, and to a related point, the idea of advantage is not necessarily rendered in the concrete terms suggested by the actual merchandise that is the immediate focus of the bargaining procedure. This does not mean that striving for material wealth, profit, or mere possession is absent here. The issue is, rather, that African thought and practice invests such aims and objects with very definite extended meanings, for what really matters is a person's standing in society. Thus, while power and authority are usually buttressed by wealth and the ability to dispense it, they are also greatly enhanced if men comport themselves properly during negotiations. Likewise, and in the same order of things, token "gifts"—often rather deprecatingly treated as "dash" or bribery

[11] For this excerpt from Sir Henry Huntley, *Seven Years' Service on the Slave Coast of Western Africa*, 2 vols. (London, 1850), see Wolfson, *Pageant of Ghana*, pp. 128–129.

[12] See, for example, *ibid.*, pp. 129–133 for the observations of an American citizen who travelled to West Africa about 1850.

by early Western observers of trading transactions—may be appreciated more than the actual price or rate of commodity exchange that a buyer is ready to give. Commerce, then, is very much a matter of etiquette and ritual. It is also indissolubly linked with religious beliefs; so much so, in fact, that it is to this day not considered unreasonable to associate commercial gain with the acquisition of high-priced magic charms—objects that incarnate the spirit world, without whose aid no earthly wealth can be negotiated.

The aim of trading is, in all these senses, certainly prosperity, but, as in the case of "reason" or "normalcy," the word here points to realities and stands for values that it does not symbolize in the West. More particularly, it does not suggest that in Africa peace is a precondition of prosperity, or that commerce is necessarily a peaceful calling. Indeed, since war is everywhere respected as a pivotal and pervasive institution, trade can easily become a species of war without evoking effective protest or reform, as previous chapters have already suggested.[13] And since conflict is accepted as a structuring principle of both the magical universe and human society, it would be quite unreasonable to assume that it is not also present when people meet to bargain or negotiate.

A market that invites the mingling of friends and foes in the pursuit of their greatly various social and economic interests, is also a junction, symbolically and actually, of those prima facie contradictory African dispositions that tolerate or favor the interpenetrations of forces that make for both conflict and accord. The conditions ruling markets, especially when these are frequented by traders from different communities, can therefore not readily be compared with, for example, the medieval European "Peace of the Fair"—an institution that presupposed first, the unqualified assumption of a need for peace, and second, compliance with a set of inter-European precepts summarily known as the Law Merchant. Such a body of shared legal and ethical norms simply could not evolve in the fragmented African world of morally separate communities. Here, where peace has been at best a precarious proposition, and where each community has held to its own customs, order in trading transactions has had to be assured by local authorities acting in strict conformity with locally respected institutions. A great diversity of regulatory mechanisms is thus on record, as the following selection of references suggests.

Among the isolationist Plateau Tonga, who have no scruples about warring with each other and do not take to the general idea of trade, leaders occasionally arise to dominate a neighborhood or a series of such units. These "rich" or "important" men may, in the exercise of their personal, essentially ephemeral power, give protection to strangers, form

---

[13] *Supra*, Chs. 7 and 14 in particular.

temporary "bond friendships" with one another, and arrange for mutual gift payments. Although they have no right to receive tribute or give safe conduct for travel through intervening neighborhoods, such personalities, acting alone or in bonded concert, are nonetheless credited with fostering exchanges of goods and services between otherwise entirely self-contained communities.[14]

A similar provincialism has long impeded trade among the Bulu—a collection of about fifty socially and politically quite autonomous lineages in the tropical rain forests of southeast Cameroon. Local solidarity was so rigid here that economic surpluses could not be exchanged with a neighboring lineage until lineage feuds were officially ended, and markets opened up under the auspices of German colonial policies and pacification programs. This pressure, together with the efforts of the Council of Elders, induced the lineages to conclude a series of so-called alliances that aimed at securing mutual economic advantage. Typically, such accords might provide that arbitration be substituted for the blood-feud in the settlement of interlineage injuries, that compensation be paid in goods rather than in blood, and that peace be furthered through the contraction of interlineage marriages or the conclusion of trade-friendships between any two male members of the separate units. However, none of these innovating practices appears to have materially altered the underlying value system. According to Horner, "The Bulu have only modernized their traditional way of life by appropriating European economic institutions as *the means* to achieve traditional goals faster."[15]

In Guroland (Ivory Coast), where markets were always located outside the village, since they were known to invite violence among participants, the incidence of conflicts was often mitigated when a powerful personality interposed itself. Such a man might decide to open a market so as to buttress his social prestige by the acquisition of "a jurisdictional area."[16] This meant that he, duly assisted by his own police, became the peacemaker when disputes occurred on market rather than on village grounds. Tenuous as this arrangement appears to have been, it assisted in the evolution of a network of seven markets, held on successive days, which made it possible for people from different villages to go from one trading center to the next.

Closely analogous modes of regulating neighborhood markets exist among the Mossi (Upper Volta), but here it is the local chief who orders the creation of a market after consultation with the all-important market

---

[14] Colson, "African Society at the Time of the Scramble," pp. 604ff.

[15] George R. Horner, "The Bulu Response to European Economy," in Bohannan and Dalton, eds., *Markets in Africa*, p. 189.

[16] Claude Meillassoux, "Social and Economic Factors Affecting Markets in Guroland," in Bohannan and Dalton, eds., *Markets in Africa*, pp. 291ff.

chief, usually a non-Mossi slave. This intermediary, whose multiple functions include the tasks of preserving peace and collecting goods for his political superior, is in turn dependent upon the earthpriest/soothsayer, the sole agent fit to determine the propitious location of the market, ascertain the number and nature of the earth deities that need to be pacified, and set up all appropriate rites and sacrifices. For, as Skinner explains,[17] market spirits have a very hard time cooling the fighting instincts of the humans (even though the latter are required by custom to place their weapons on top of one of the sheds before making their trading rounds), and when these deities are not fully satisfied, they are expected to unleash their anger so as to cause real trouble. In lesser cases this may have the effect of disrupting or immobilizing trading activities; in extreme situations it may involve the infliction of death upon the market officials, in whose absence marketing cannot take place.

The relation between propensities to trust and to mistrust, to fight and to cooperate, is equally precarious in Tiv country (northern Nigeria). Even today, we learn from Laura Bohannan's study,[18] men go armed to market, and no one is surprised if a disagreement about, for instance, the proper price, turns into a real brawl. Futhermore, warfare between Tiv segments can bring markets into such acrimonious competition—despite the fact that they are scheduled on different days—that one of them may actually be knocked out of existence. One method employed to that end is the deliberate creation of types of disorder that are certain to discourage attendance. Another consists in the outright theft or capture of a trading ground. For, since a market is viewed as a political plum and channel of wealth, it offers obvious advantages to anyone interested in gaining power. But even here counterforces may be made operational. The lineage of the man who owns or controls the market is thus expected to supply not only police but also market judges, and these usually settle disputes on the spot. Next, the segment whose market magic was instrumental in initiating the market continues to be officially responsible for upholding the peace both in the trading center and on the paths leading to it. And finally, "the man of character and prestige" who makes a point of attending the market so as to gain or maintain his socially predominant position may emerge as a trusted arbitrator in disputes between members of segments who are otherwise free to capture and kill each other. Indeed, if a market is duly consecrated and reliably associated with such a personality, it may function quite adequately as a channel of diplomatic negotiations between emissaries of warring segments. In ex-

[17] Elliott P. Skinner, "Trade and Markets among the Mossi People," in Bohannan and Dalton, eds., *Markets in Africa*, pp. 255ff.
[18] "Political Aspects of Tiv Social Organization" in Middleton and Tait, eds., *Tribes without Rulers*, pp. 35ff., 49, 52ff., 62ff.

ceptional circumstances these can even be linked by market pacts and peace treaties that forbid the shedding of blood in the interest of securing trade communications between the contracting parties.

Control over the Ibo Afikpo market as it functioned in southeastern Nigeria between 1900–1960[19] was also strictly localized, if only because formal political superstructures, such as states or kingdoms, have traditionally been missing here. Viewed as the corporate property of a village group, and susceptible to becoming the object of intervillage rivalries, such a market reflected certain customary Ibo patterns of authority— notably an administrative system based on different sets of age grades and respect for seniority. The older grades were there to pass laws concerning Afikpo custom, try cases, and settle disputes, whereas the youngest had the task of acting as police, stopping fights, and reporting disputes.

Parochial as this particular trading place was in all essentials, it nonetheless formed part of a network of markets, separated from each other by between five to fifteen miles, and held on successive days. And broadly analogous allowances for extended economic contacts are made in other regions of West and Central Africa in which the trading instinct is highly developed. Relations between culturally different peoples that are comprised in a single state, or between neighboring states, in Central Africa have thus been facilitated until recently by locating markets close to the borders of the trading communities or at the capital of the state, spacing markets on successive days, and entrusting the maintenance of order to the political authorities of the chiefdom in which the market was situated.[20] In short, rings or cycles of markets emerge from the records of both states and stateless societies as some of the most effective devices for facilitating commerce, bridging distances, and therewith extending areas of relative security and peace—nowhere more so than in those vast geographic orbits that have long been penetrated by trade-conscious Arabs and Arabized peoples.

Two other regionally significant systems of commercial order, also fostered by these exchanges, are represented by the great international trading towns, indispensable way stations, especially along the routes and rivers that cut across the deserts linking farflung coastal communities; and the supratribal caravans without which no distant emporium could be safely reached. Both are conglomerates of ethnically various, often

[19] Simon Ottenberg and Phoebe Ottenberg, "Afikpo Market: 1900–1960," in Bohannan and Dalton, eds., *Markets in Africa*, pp. 120ff.; cf. also Biobaku, "An Historical Account of the Evolution of Nigeria," p. 6, on trading chiefs, and Dike, *Trade and Politics in the Niger Delta*, on other Ibo trading practices.

[20] Jan Vansina, "Long Distance Trade Routes in Central Africa," pp. 375–390; cf. *supra*, for accounts of trading patterns in other parts of Nigeria, Ghana, Dahomey.

mutually antagonistic, people whose coexistence, however limited in time, requires regulation. Furthermore, since each is dependent upon the other, their relationship needs to be structured—all the more so as the interests of the itinerant merchants have at no time been wholly compatible with the concerns of the settled societies through which they passed, or upon which they converged as points of ultimate destination. In describing the complex interactions between the Hausa, Gonja, Ashanti, Fante, Dagomba, Mossi, and others in West Africa as he observed them toward the end of the nineteenth century, Captain Lonsdale notes that "these caravans are in themselves a moving market, buying and selling everywhere along the road."[21] The large ones, he writes, consist of from two hundred to five and six hundred persons, and take on an average seven months to do the journey from Kano to Salaga, the traditional center for the kola nut trade, which attracted Muslims and others living in the arid regions of the north. Some constituent parties of such a caravan were constantly on the move; others, by contrast, would make Salaga their headquarters for between two and three years, trading backwards and forwards to places within a sixty-days' journey.

The terms of accommodation available to these groups of traders differed as greatly from town to town as did the customary laws ruling local markets. Most included the assignment of special quarters and the appointment of "chiefs of strangers" or other intermediaries and middlemen,[22] but the various norms of securing a modus vivendi were not always applied in reliable ways. Whereas some towns were renowned for the security they offered, others were held in general disrepute in virtue of their capricious exercise of authority. For example, Kano, which assembled multitudes of local and foreign traders and a corresponding diversity of goods, some originating as far north as Egypt, impressed Clapperton with the fairness of its regulations and the impartiality of its law enforcement.[23] Here the stalls were let by the sheikh, who also fixed the prices of all wares, for which he was entitled to a small commission. One particular custom that caught this explorer's attention provided that

[21] Report by Captain R. la T. Lonsdale as excerpted in Wolfson, *Pageant of Ghana*, pp. 182–186. Vivid accounts of caravans are found in the journals of most explorers, and some of these have been cited previously. Volume III of Barth's *Travels* is a particularly rich source of information on markets, caravans, and general commercial relations. For historical accounts and analyses see the works of Mauny, Bovill, and others; also B. G. Martin, "Kanem, Bormu, and the Fazzān; Notes on the Political History of a Trade Route," *Journal of African History* 10, No. 1 (1969), 15–27.

[22] Compare *supra*, Ch. 18.

[23] Captain Hugh Clapperton reporting on his "Excursion from Kuka to Sokoto" in 1824. See Denham, Clapperton, and Oudnoy, *Narrative of Travels and Discoveries in Northern and Central Africa*. For these entries see Howard and Plumb, eds., *West African Explorers*, pp. 246ff., 250.

the seller return to the buyer a stated part of the price by way of blessing —another illustration of that traditional African disposition to associate trade with the exchange of gifts as well as with respect for religious beliefs. Bida, the cosmopolitan capital of Nupe, enjoyed a similar reputation. Here, where people from Hausa and Bornu always mingled freely with Yoruba from the south and Arabs from the Sudan and Tripoli, strangers from rich countries received great consideration from Nupe rulers—an attitude, Nadel notes, that contrasted curiously with the ruthless treatment of the native peasants.[24] Foreigners were thus not required to pay regular taxes, only comparatively small market dues, and they were looked after by their own headmen, who were also charged with safeguarding their interests in all financial transactions.

Mossi policy, by contrast, appears to have been much less hospitable. All caravaneers had to pay a tax to the local chiefs if they wanted to cross local borders or stop in a chiefdom's market for purposes of trade. Caravans passing through the market center of Wagadugu had to give the Moro Naba a share of their merchandise, quite aside from the presents customarily due him. In fact, horse traders from the Yatenga to the north of Mossi country and Hausa caravaneers were sometimes forced to sell part of their wares to the Moro Naba at one-hundredth the purchase price. Not all caravan members submitted to this type of extortion, and at one period, Skinner writes, many of them traded with Mane rather than pass through Wagadugu, where the tariffs were too high.[25] On the other hand, the Mossi chiefs did not tolerate any trespassing on their territories by caravans that did not pay taxes; those who tried to avoid this duty were ruthlessly subjected to attack by the mounted nobles, who acted in this respect in behalf of the district chiefs.

Security arrangements were different in the Islamized East African region of northern Somaliland, where interlineage warfare was common and central authority lacking. Here, Lewis explains, a caravan journeying to the coast among hostile clans could usually rely upon a form of safe-conduct that was instituted when its leader negotiated protection with a prestigious lineage representative.[26] This patron-protector, who received gifts in return for his services, was then responsible for the security of the travelling group; attacks upon its lives and property were henceforth considered attacks upon the patron himself, and prompt retaliatory action was required, at least in principle, if the good name and honor of the

[24] Nadel, *A Black Byzantium*, p. 119.
[25] "Trade and Markets Among the Mossi People," p. 246; see in particular this scholar's references to Binger's reports, which relate to the situation as it existed in the 1890s.
[26] I. M. Lewis, "Lineage Continuity and Modern Commerce in Northern Somaliland," in Bohannan and Dalton, eds., *Markets in Africa*, pp. 369ff., 381. Lewis notes that the caravan trade is largely in decline today.

lineage was to be upheld. It is interesting to note that this extraordinary relationship had certain socially innovative effects quite beyond the original purpose it was meant to serve. For when the Somali had to come to terms with the presence of Indian and Arabian merchants—and these once came close to monopolizing the export trade—they did so by giving the strangers the status of clients in the Somali lineage structure.

African modes of conducting and regulating trade were certainly various, as this limited survey was designed to illustrate. However, in the profusion of recorded practices it is possible to isolate a few motifs for which Pan-African validity may be claimed.

It appears, first, that the absence of regular, continuous, and peaceful communications between socially, ethnically, and linguistically discrete communities made most everywhere for the massive intrusion of factors of personality. That is to say, since traders representing different societies could not count on common norms and expectations, they were greatly dependent upon the interests and dispositions of individual foreign rulers and their various agents, as well as upon their own skills in gauging local conditions from one day to the next.

Second, commerce, whether related to local markets or long-distance enterprises, was subject to measures of time upon which all Africans appeared to agree.[27] For example, what mattered when a bargain had to be struck between a capricious Mossi ruler and a caravan intent on passage or temporary residence, was absolute deference to the instant of a particular encounter rather than prolonged reflection on the force of binding precedents or other customs. The course of actual bargaining sessions, by contrast, was usually tedious and protracted, as previous references have shown. On these occasions time had no economic value, partly because the exchange was experienced as a social pastime, partly because the distance between offer and counteroffer could only be narrowed to mutual satisfaction if the parties were oblivious to the passage of hours and days.

Third—and this characteristic of African trading is inseparable from the second—economic transactions were initiated, furthered, and consummated without the aid of writing. In this field of social interaction, as in that of government or customary law, the records of nonliterate communities are found to converge upon the need for such compensatory time-consuming devices of communication as repetition, ritualized speech patterns, and the services of spokesmen and other types of intermediaries. Indeed, even in regions of "restricted literacy" such as Northern Ghana, where writing had penetrated as an adjunct of Islam, "bargaining lay largely in the realm of oral intercourse, calculation in the

[27] *Supra*, Ch. 5.

sphere of mental arithmetic."[28] The negotiating style developed in these exchanges was very different from that taken for granted in medieval and modern European markets, all the more so as nonliterate African traders were at one with their counterparts in the literate Middle East in employing oral modes of bargaining around a flexible offer, whereas Western merchants had adopted the literate technique of displaying a fixed price.[29]

A survey of the greatly various trading processes in which common folk, commercial professionals, and chiefly or other politically representative personages engaged, certainly bears out Lugard's observation that "the African . . . is a keen and expert trader."[30] However, as earlier presentations of dominant patterns of African thought and social organization have demonstrated, it does not lead to the conclusion that commercial activities, intense and multiple as they were, had ever contributed to a significant extension of areas of inter-African peace and accord. Reflections on the records suggest, in fact, that no such increment could have been associated with the pursuit of trade: partly because of geographical barriers to the development of socially steadying communications, but mainly because the human value system did not allow for such intentions.

A specialized conclusion to this effect, reached by a study of "Trade and Authority in West Africa from 1850 to 1880,"[31] thus points out that internal and external trade were for the most part less valuable to African rulers than land, crops, war booty, and slaves, and that most of the wealth produced by commercial activities was disbursed by these governments in hospitality, ceremonies, gift exchanges, or favors bestowed to further the king's clientage relations or other modes of social support within the political orbit they aspired to control. That is to say, trade was not valued here for its own sake. It must be borne in mind, furthermore, that commerce with other societies was not conceived explicitly as a peaceful exchange serving reciprocal interests. Since enmity and suspicion were normal in intercommunal relations, and since warfare was an intrinsic part of the value system, trade was often tantamount to raid. In other words, these operations were not easily distinguishable from each other in the context either of motivation, organization, or ultimate

[28] Goody, "Restricted Literacy," p. 208.
[29] *Ibid.* Writing played an important part in maintaining links between the scattered communities that participated directly or vicariously in the caravan trade of the region. As Goody points out, its main function consisted in enabling distant customers or agents to place orders for goods or services. *Ibid.*, p. 210.
[30] F. D. Lugard, *The Dual Mandate in British Tropical Africa* (Edinburgh and London, 1922), p. 481. The major field of observation was Nigeria.
[31] Newbury, "Trade and Authority in West Africa from 1850 to 1880," p. 75.

317

effect. The argument that war was an economic activity instrumental in procuring women, slaves, cattle, or other goods, or in establishing a lucrative tribute relationship, is thus fully compatible with the proposition that trade was a species of war.[32]

B. SECURITY, MUTUALITY, AND THE PROBLEM OF NEGOTIATING BINDING INTERTRIBAL ACCORDS; AFRO-ARAB TRADITIONS

Sir Harry Johnston, one of Victorian England's most renowned colonial administrators, received the following instructions when he assumed his responsibilities in Central Africa toward the end of the nineteenth century: to consolidate the protectorate of Her Majesty over the native chiefs; to advise these chiefs on their external relations with each other and with foreigners, not interfering unduly with their internal administration; to secure peace and order; and by every legitimate means to check the slave trade.[1]

The image of inter-African politics that Whitehall entertained at that time appears to have consisted in the assumptions that tribes were as self-contained and neatly organized as European states; that internal affairs were clearly distinct from external relations; that peace and order were recognized values in foreign relations; that shows of force were apt to elicit adverse reactions; that notions of what was legitimate in the art of persuasion were broadly shared; and that colonial diplomacy could thus count on ready responses in its search for wide-ranging binding accords.

The realities with which Johnston was confronted in the Zambezi re-

---

[32] Compare *supra*, Chs. 13 and 14. Commenting on the heavy incidence of war in Buganda, Chilver notes that war was an economic activity indispensable for the elaborate system of gift exchange, which was centered on the court. See " 'Feudalism' in the Interlacustrine Kingdoms," pp. 386f. *Ibid.*, p. 387 for a reference to Sir Apolo Kagwa, *The Customs of the Baganda* (New York, 1934), p. 92, in which this African scholar suggests that the Ganda did not learn to trade like other peoples because they acquired so much plunder by raiding. See Vansina, *Kingdoms of the Savanna*, pp. 180, to the effect that the entire history of the whole Central African coast and its hinterland is essentially economic history, especially since 1700; nothing in politics or in social and cultural affairs makes sense here, he writes, if trade (that is, mostly the slave trade) is not seen as the major motive for it all. But it is clear from Vansina's accounts of these activities that we are here in the presence of ferocious wars. See, for example, *ibid.*, pp. 199–204 on the Yaka raids, which upset a vast area, set off continuous flights and migrations, and lasted two centuries, so that they could be aptly described, as late as 1880, as one great "process of razzia-conquest-assimilation." See *ibid.* for the surmise that the organization of the Ovimbundu caravans may have been modeled on that of the nomadic tribe's military organization.

[1] Roland Oliver, *Sir Harry Johnston and the Scramble for Africa* (London, 1964), p. 205.

gion were wholly different. Immigrant and conquering groups had caused serious upheavals in the social organization of settled indigenous populations so that seats of authority were not easily recognizable. One vast strip of territory had fallen under the dominion of the warlike Ngoni, whose leaders had swept up from the south in a great migration of rapine and conquest, to settle as the overlords of the indigenous Chewa in three or four loose principalities. Elsewhere, the Yao had come to constitute a similarly intrusive element, acting as middlemen of the Arab and Swahili slave traders; preying upon the weaker, less well organized, and worse-armed peoples of the lake shores and the shire valley; and building towns in the slave country, whose people they came to dominate in semifeudal fashion. Far from establishing a unifying Yao administration, Yao state was found warring with Yao state, each seeking to enslave the subjects of the other, all competing for control of the caravan routes to the west. Peaceful negotiations toward the ends contained in his instructions were thus of limited validity, as Johnston noted in a despatch to his home government:

Wherever it was possible by means of peaceable and friendly negotiations to induce a Chieftain to renounce the slave trade, I have used such means in preference to a recourse to force; and in this way a considerable number of the lesser Potentates of Nyasaland have been brought to agree to give up adjusting their internecine quarrels by resort to arms, to cease selling their subjects into slavery, and to close their territories to the passage of slaves and slavetraders. Their agreement was, however, in most cases a sullen one, and their eyes were turned instinctively to the nearest "big" Chief to see in what way he was dealt with. If he too accepted this distasteful gospel of peace and good will towards men, they were then ready enough to adhere to their own compacts . . . but if the powerful Potentate—the champion man of war in the district—held aloof from the new Protectorate, massed his forces in the strongholds, and preserved a watchful or menacing attitude towards the Administration . . . then the little Chieftains began to relax in their good behaviour of a month's or a week's duration, once more to capture and sell their neighbour's subjects, or to smuggle through their by-paths a coast-caravan with its troop of slaves bound for Kilwa, Ibo or Quilimane.[2]

The particular pattern of inter-African relations that emerges from this passage had obviously been greatly affected by predatory interference by Arabs and Europeans. Its ultimate source and sanction is, however, to be found in the norms of thought, belief, behavior, and

---

[2] *Ibid.*, pp. 206–207; see also Vansina, *Kingdoms of the Savanna*, pp. 246ff.

organization that were prevalent throughout Africa in premodern times. Compliance with this integral moral and political order implied respect for power and hierarchical status, acquiescence in all manner of conflicts, and acceptance of the need for enmity and war. No system of equal sovereign states was conceivable in such conditions, for political identities, territorial boundaries, and centers of power were forever fluctuating. Permanent embassies were perforce lacking, and diplomacy did not emerge as a Pan-African or regionally reliable establishment.[3] Other major factors inhibiting communications between governments were the absence of unifying languages and the all-pervasive, ever-present tradition of nonliteracy. Indeed, in the context of the latter, no mode of reflection was available that might have directed men to cultivate such time and space-transcendent ideas as collective security or a balance of power,[4] or to think of mutual long-range interests in terms of binding intertribal accords. The treaty, literate Europe's major tool for structuring international relations in war and peace, could not become a common carrier of political commitments in precolonial Africa.

What held in matters of foreign trade was thus also true in the field of external politics: accommodation could not be sought as a matter of course. Exceptional in its incidence, it was actually possible only where the parties to an intertribal accord had been able to tap analogous domestic or local forms of rendering agreement.[5] The blood pact was such a shared institution in several areas, among them East Africa, and here, therefore, rulers could resort to it in their mutual relations.[6] The commitment, however, was apt to be interpersonal and therefore limited in duration, if only because the identity of heirs was usually contested in succession disputes.[7]

The personality factor also made for unpredictability in certain rudimentary diplomatic relations. Lugard reports that "it was not uncommon for a chief [in what is now Uganda] to receive ambassadors from some tribe and entertain them hospitably in his house for perhaps a whole month. After that, becoming tired of them, he would suddenly order them to be bound to the central pillars of the hut and applying a match to the grass and reed structure would roast them alive by way of varia-

---

[3] But cf. preceding chapters on the role of intermediaries and diplomats in confederate, imperial or other multitribal realms.

[4] Compare *supra*, pp. 71 and 228, n. 4, where Redfield's views are cited.

[5] *Supra*, pp. 106, 174.

[6] *Supra*, pp. 98, 107, 158, 173, 269ff., 280. Vansina, *Kingdoms of the Savanna*, p. 227, reports that the idea of the blood covenant was carried from the Interlacustrine region to Katanga and Kazembe by certain chiefs who had become familiar with it in the nineteenth century—in one case through the medium of the caravan trade. *Infra*, pp. 362ff. for Lugard's use of the institution.

[7] *Supra*, Ch. 13.

tion."[8] Diplomatic immunities of the Occidental kind would, of course, have been incongruous with African political systems. However, a certain kind of privileged respect might well have been due the ill-fated Ugandan envoys had they qualified as "third parties" or "mutual friends" who were called upon officially to arrange or witness a particular compact between chiefly principals.[9] Such human agents are indispensable when negotiations proceed in conditions of orality, as previous illustrations have shown; and the same holds for other aspects of the traditional African diplomatic method as, for example, the due performance of ritual and the proper invocation of spiritual agencies. No pact or treaty was thus considered valid unless it had been properly sworn to, and this meant, of course, that the ultimate sanction was found in the sphere of fetishism and magic.

The logic of this conception has been explained earlier, and the following excerpt from a seventeenth-century account of treaty making in the Gold Coast is cited merely because it illustrates particularly vividly the organic connection between the inner normative order and external affairs, as well as the supremacy of enmity in politics and commerce— even in situations in which accommodation is obviously desired. The report is also interesting because it describes an early European attempt to merge literate and nonliterate modes of concluding binding agreements:

> On the Gold Coast when they make any solemn promise or oath, they take about six spoonfuls of water mix'd with some powders of divers colours, which the fatishman puts into it; which potion is to kill them the very minute that they break or violate the oath or promise they took it on, and which they firmly believe. . . .
>
> The Akan, who are the best traders to our ships and castles, and have the purest gold, are an inland people; so that to come to the seaside to our factories and shipping, they were oblig'd to pass thro' the territories of other princes with their gold to buy, and back with the commodities purchas'd; . . . Among others they were to pass thro' the king of Efutu's country, which they did for some time without interruption; but at length the Efutus designing to make a prey of the Akans (instigated by our no-friends the Dutch . . .), refus'd them passage thro' their country. . . .
>
> This treatment the Akans so far stomach'd and resented, that some of their principal merchants resolved to unite together with lives and

---

[8] Lugard, *The Rise of Our East African Empire*, Vol. II, 123.
[9] *Supra*, Chs. 17 and 18 for intermediaries and the general preference for the indirect approach in palavers; pp. 295ff. for relevant comments by Schapera; see also Dennett, *At the Back of the Black Man's Mind*, p. 48.

fortunes to reduce the king of Efutu to justice, To effect which they made war against him, . . . The Akans joyn'd by the Asebus . . . reduc'd the king of Efutu to great straights, and at length forc'd him to abandon his chief town, and flee to the Dutch general at Elmina for protection, who gave him sanctuary. In the interim Nimpha and the king of Asebu entred his town triumphantly . . . and constituted his brother king in his stead; and having oblig'd all the great cappasheirs in Efutu to take the fetish to be true to their new king, they brought him along with them to Cape Coast castle, there to take the fatish to be a true friend to the English, . . . to be at eternal enmity with his brother; . . . to preserve an inviolable friendship with the Akans; and to suffer them to pass thro' his country . . . without any molestation. Which articles ingraved on parchment in the name of the royal African company of England, Nimpha and the king of Asebu, the king of Efutu signed by making his mark, and captain Shurley, myself, and divers of our factors and the castle cappasheirs witnessed them. Then the king of Efutu took the fatish on his bare knees to keep them inviolably, which was six spoonfuls of water, in which the fatisher had put about a dozen sorts of powders, which none but himself knew what they were; and having stirr'd them well, gave the king of Asebu his potion, assuring him that, upon the least infringement of the articles he took it upon, he would in the twinkling of an eye drop down as dead as a door-nail, which he seem'd fit firmly to believe.[10]

The pockets of security in the African conflict system had not been appreciably enlarged under the influence of Islam. Indeed, Muslim thought and practice on the subject of international relations had the effect of reenforcing certain native dispositions. It is thus important to recall that the abode of Islam was always presumed to be at war with the rest of the world—significantly known to all believers as the abode of war (*dar al-harb*), and that the *jihad*, being institutionalized as part of the Muslim legal system, was the official instrument for transforming the *dar al-harb* into the *dar al-Islam*.[11] No relevance could be attached to "peace" pending this achievement. Furthermore, and consistent with this philosophy, we find on the plane of political organization that the idea of the territorially bounded state was incompatible with the conception of the *dar al-Islam* as a unified but expansive brotherhood of believers,

[10] Thomas Phillips, *Journal of a Voyage Made in the Hannibal of London, Ann. 1693, from England . . . to Guiney*, as excerpted in Wolfson, *Pageant of Ghana*, pp. 75–77; see the same source, p. 74, for Phillips' account of the use of canes for passports.

[11] Khadduri, *War and Peace in the Law of Islam*, ch. 5 on the doctrine of the *jihad*; cf. also *supra*, pp. 127ff.

at least in the context of the *shāri'a.*[12] Multiple states and governments arose of course in response to local needs for authority and security, but in the absence of generally accepted principles of legitimacy and orderly change, they were usually subject to upheavals of one kind or another. Instability and insecurity had thus been ruling norms for successive generations in Arab and Arabized lands, as they had been for those in adjoining Negro Africa.

Two factors, both absent in Africa, combined to alleviate these conditions in the Islamic world: on the one hand a unified system of law, the same for all Mohammedans; and on the other, the recorded knowledge of practical guidelines for the conduct of statecraft and intergroup relations that the Prophet and some of his successors had bequeathed to all believers.

Classical Muslim law did not recognize the existence either of non-Muslim nations or, for that matter, of separate Islamic states. As one noted scholar explains, it had a personal rather than a territorial character, and was obligatory upon believers as individuals or members of groups regardless of the territory they resided in.[13] A distinction between municipal and international law was, therefore, not sanctioned officially, for unlike the law of nations as it had developed in the European world before the twentieth century, Islam could not accommodate the principle of "the equality of sovereign states." According to Mohammedan doctrine, then, the law of nations did not derive from mutual consent or reciprocity, but from the imperial Muslim government's own interpretation of its political, moral, and religious interests.

In light of these approaches to government and international relations, it goes without saying that diplomacy was recognized as an adjunct or substitute for war rather than an institution for the promotion of peaceful contacts between equal, sovereign states. Envoys were sent and received for a variety of purposes, including that of negotiating tribute payments, but their functions were neither stabilized in the form of permanent missions, nor regulated by generally accepted codes of diplomatic privileges and responsibilities. They might be lavishly entertained and showered with gifts. But if the mission proved to be a failure, they were likely to be dismissed ignominiously and abruptly; and if hostilities were initiated while foreign envoys were still on Muslim soil, insult and injury often came to imply imprisonment or death.[14]

---

[12] On the qualified Muslim recognition of the principle of territoriality, see Majid Khadduri, ed. and trans., *The Islamic Law of Nations; Shaybānī's Siyar* (Baltimore, 1966), p. 7.

[13] Khadduri, *War and Peace in the Law of Islam*, p. 45. Also Bozeman, *The Future of Law in a Multicultural World*, pp. 50–85, and authorities there cited.

[14] Khadduri, *War and Peace in the Law of Islam*, p. 250; also p. 238. In pre-

These traditions and understandings explain, singly and collectively, why binding treaties between states were theoretically as unfathomable in the Islamic context as they were in Africa. In practice, however, the situation was somewhat different. Unlike Black African societies, which were not conscious of their moral unity, the Mohammedan could fall back on certain precedents set by the Prophet when he had felt it wise to suspend the state of chronic belligerence with infidels. Since Mohammed had concluded a treaty with the Meccans postponing war for a period of ten years, his successors, too, were authorized to come to temporary terms with polytheists and other unbelievers. But such a peace, which ranged from a maximum of ten down to three or two years, was in actuality experienced as a truce; for since the posture of the *jihad* had to be resumed after ten years, treaties did not have to be considered binding beyond that expiration date.[15] The time span was modified after the Ottoman Empire was drawn into relations with the West, more particularly when Sultan Sulayman and the King of France agreed in 1535 to observe a sure and valid peace "during their lives." Henceforth a treaty's duration could be coextensive with the lifetime of the sultan who had arranged it—a proviso not unlike the expectation governing certain inter-African accords.[16]

The incidence of treaties, then, was negligible in each of the two cultures. Furthermore, here as well as there agreement was usually recorded in connection with the regulation of tribute relations. Muslim governments were thus allowed by tradition, even if not by law, to "buy" security from attack if victory or supremacy over the opponent was not within their immediate reach. Conversely—and more frequently, of course—they negotiated or imposed a tribute relationship upon antagonists who were either temporarily disadvantaged in military terms, or who had been effectively reduced to a status of inferiority and dependence.[17] The rule of permanent hostility and inequality to which this practice attests was suspended or relaxed in relations with Cyprus and two other societies, both African, namely, Ethiopia and Nubia. The former was held immune to the *jihad* for many centuries because its prestigious position in religion and history had been recognized officially by Mohammed himself when he warned all believers to leave the Abyssinians in peace as

---

Islamic inter-Arab relations, emissaries were commonly used to conciliate parties, especially when it was felt that a war had lasted too long. But even though Mohammed himself had always been greatly respected for his work as an arbitrator, arbitration did not evolve into a reliable method of settling conflicts.

[15] *Ibid.*, pp. 210ff.; 220ff.; 272.

[16] *Supra*, Chs. 6 and 7.

[17] Medieval relations with the Byzantine Empire gave rise to several arrangements of this kind, some favoring the Khalifate as recipient of tribute, others, by contrast, the Eastern Christian antagonist.

long as they did not initiate offensive actions. As Khadduri explains, Ethiopia was neutralized, as it were, by virtue of Islamic tolerance.[18]

Nubia, by contrast, elicited respect as a quasi-equal state after successfully resisting Muslim annexation and holding out for reciprocity in trade relations. A treaty with the governor of Egypt, concluded in A.D. 652, stipulated an annual tribute of 360 slaves, it is true, but the principle of mutuality was recognized in the provision first, that the Nubians would receive equivalent value in the form of barley, horses, and clothing; second, that travelers and apostles were assured freedom of movement in the territories of the contracting parties; and third, that both countries were to refrain from attacking each other. This interesting treaty, which appears to have been renewed from time to time, was practically in effect for over six hundred years—until Nubia was conquered by Egypt's Fatimid rulers.[19]

The gift was yet another modality of confirming or symbolizing relations with other sovereigns upon which African and Islamic practices converged. Unlike the rendering of tribute, which could easily be made binding upon successive regimes, it was usually an ad hoc link between living rulers. Moreover, although presents were often overt or disguised obligations, they might be differentiated from levies on the ground that they were associated neither with inequality in the status of donor and recipient, nor with concrete wealth and other mundane advantages. This syndrome in Afro-Islamic affairs is well illustrated by the giving of giraffes, a strange and romantic custom that proved attractive to imperial establishments near and far.

Described by Spinage as "a symbol of benefaction probably unequalled in the world,"[20] the giraffe seems to have occupied a special position at the court of the King of Axum, where it was seen by a Christian monk in A.D. 525;[21] in Christian Constantinople, where the emperor is known to have received two so-called Camelopardales from Indian envoys visiting in A.D. 439; and, during the fifteenth century, at the Chinese court, where giraffes (known as "kilin") were received as "tribute" from "barbarian" Bengal, Aden, and Melinda (Kenya), to become exalted as omens of peace and portents signifying Heaven's favor.[22] Only

---

[18] Khadduri, *War and Peace in the Law of Islam*, pp. 253–258.

[19] *Ibid.*, pp. 259–260 for the text of the agreement; on Nubia, see *supra*, pp. 128ff.

[20] C. A. Spinage, *The Book of the Giraffe* (London, 1968), p. 46.

[21] *Ibid.*, p. 51; p. 44 for a quotation from *The Ethiopian Story* by Heliodorus, in which envoys of "the Auxomites" appeared, offering gifts that included the wondrous "Camelopard," which filled the whole assembly with trepidation.

[22] *Ibid.*, appendix 2 for two Chinese eulogies of the "kilin"; also pp. 54ff. The leading authority on this and other aspects of China's early relations with Africa is J.J.L. Duyvendak; see in particular his *China's Discovery of Africa* (London, 1949); see p. 34 to the effect that "the giraffe from the African wilderness, as it

in the Islamic Mediterranean region did the presentation of giraffes become a fixed quasi-diplomatic institution, however. Here the imperial Turkish establishment continued to receive the fabled beasts right up to the first quarter of the nineteenth century,[23] probably having learned the custom from its historically prestigious North African dependencies. At any rate, such a derivation is plausible in light of the prominence of the giraffe in Egypt's dealings with Nubia. The pattern seems to have been set already in Pharaonic Egypt, for several tomb paintings—the last (1225 B.C.) on the wall of the Ramses temple at Beit-el-Wali in Nubia—portray tributary giraffes commemorating Egypt's diverse Nubian victories.[24] Muslim Egypt revived the custom when the ruler who conquered Nubia in the seventh century A.D. stipulated in the treaty of submission that he was to be paid an annual tribute of two giraffes, along with four hundred slaves, a number of camels, and two elephants. In fact, these tributary giraffes are said to have symbolized Nubia's status at least until the country staged an abortive revolt.[25] The circumstances were obviously different in the thirteenth century, when the sultan of Egypt presented a giraffe to Frederic II (probably in consideration of the Hohenstauffen emperor's professional interest in zoology), and in the fifteenth century, when another governing prince despatched one to Timur, the Tatar conqueror (probably in hopes of appeasing him). Berber governments in adjoining North African territory also relied on the magic of this animal in relations with African potentates further south. Ibn Khaldūn thus reports that a giraffe was one of several valuable presents sent by the King of Kanem (to whom he refers as "the Master of Bornu") to the King of Tunis in the year of the Hijra 655.[26]

Diverse and imaginative ways of compromising the rule of enmity were thus brought forth in pagan and Islamic Africa. However, in neither of the realms did intergovernmental accords conform to a generally accepted code, or give rise to firm expectations of mutual compliance. Eclectic in inception, they appear to have been floating and mutable in actual operation as well as in the memory of those whom they affected.

---

strode into the Emperor's Court, became the emblem of Perfect Virtue, Perfect Government, and Perfect Harmony in the Empire and in the Universe." Duyvendak seems to have suggested that it was to obtain giraffes that the Chinese established contact with East Africa. For further discussions of this entire complex of issues see Teobaldo Filesi, *China and Africa in the Middle Ages*, David L. Morison, trans. (London, 1972), pp. 22, 29ff., 53. (The original Italian work was published in Milan, 1962).

[23] Spinage, *The Book of the Giraffe*, pp. 46ff.

[24] *Ibid.*, pp. 35–39.   [25] *Ibid.*, p. 52.

[26] Barth, *Travels*, Vol. II, 22, referring to Ibn Khaldūn's *History of the Berbers*. *Ibid.*, ch. 29, for references to the history of Bornu's foreign relations and the sending of embassies to Tripoli.

The terms of coexistence that emerged from an original settlement were, after all, seldom precise, and records of negotiations were not kept systematically either in nonliterate Africa[27] or in the literate Mediterranean societies. Indeed, indigenous and Arab orientations toward conflict and its management were so similar in basic respects that the knowledge of writing was hardly relevant for purposes of treaty making. Governing authorities in both traditions preferred the spoken word in international communications, associated treaties with interpersonal oral pledges, linked the validity of their commitments to religious principles, and sought sanctions in the ultimate oral reference, namely, the oath.

The concordance of these dispositions is well illustrated by records from Islamized West Africa. In northern Ghana, for example, where literate Muslims have long been respected as political advisors and "third parties,"[28] members of this elite have often been in charge of diplomatic relations, even when these pertained to the European presence. The head of the religious community in Kumasi and his associates thus seem to have played important roles in negotiating the Anglo-Ashanti treaty of 1820. In any case, Arabic certainly served as a mediating language, and some of its utility and prestige was no doubt due to it being a literate language, as the following invocation indicates: "Praise be to God, who created the pen for use as speech, and who made paper that we may send it, in place of ambassadors, from country to country and place to place."[29] Yet even here we find pen and paper metaphorically subordinated to speech and the physical presence of human agents. More importantly, in certain zones of "restricted literacy" in which Arabic influences have been steadily absorbed by the host culture, the written word has gradually shed its intrinsic value as a medium of communication and a source of guidelines, to become esteemed more or less exclusively for its magical qualities.[30] Captured in concrete objects, such as saphies enclosing pieces of paper with Arabic characters, or the Koran itself, it is presumed capable of serving as real earnest in the consummation of diplo-

[27] See I. A. Akinjogbin, *Dahomey and Its Neighbours 1708–1818* (Cambridge, 1967), pp. 91, 152, 153 for some aspects of interstate treaty making and several comments on the fact that "the terms are not known," or that "details of the negotiations have not passed down."

[28] Compare *supra*, Ch. 18 B.

[29] Wilks, "The Position of Muslims in Metropolitan Ashanti," p. 329. Compare also Goody, "Restricted Literacy," p. 210.

[30] On this subject see Wilks, "The Transmission of Islamic Learning in the Western Sudan," pp. 192ff.; Goody, "Restricted Literacy," p. 226, for the reminder that certain branches of Islamic learning, too, were closely allied to magic, and that certain kinds of magic were legitimized by religion. See also *supra*, Ch. 5, where the magic of writing is discussed in the context of Africa's nonliterate culture. Compare Barth, *Travels*, Vol. III, 553, for observations of the use of saphies.

matic transactions. The validity of most agreements and alliances in this West African region thus came to rest on a solemn verbal oath sworn on the Koran.[31]

Very similar norms had evolved in the long course of tangled interactions between various Islamic rulers in neighboring Central African regions, and between some of these potentates on one hand, and North African Islamic governments on the other. A written pact of friendship between Kanem and Bornu is known to have been concluded at the end of the sixteenth century,[32] but as Barth discovered in his painstaking efforts to reconstruct the history and diplomatic relations of Bornu, resort to literate forms was exceptional, even though the inner African areas of major concern to him were at times in close contact with the Islamic state system of the Mediterranean. After tracing the conflicts between Bornu, Bagirmi, Kano, Waday, and others, with their heavy incidence of intrigue, fratricide, and war, Barth explains that at the beginning of the nineteenth century Bagirmi became "as much a tributary province of Wádáy as it had been, in more ancient times, of Bórnu" by virtue of a treaty, sworn on the Koran, which assured protection in return for payment, every third year, of "a hundred ordinary male slaves, thirty handsome female slaves, one hundred horses, and a thousand shirts."[33] This settlement, we learn from the noted explorer, was quite in line with state practices further north. In fact, it had probably been made possible because "the Sheik of Bórnu . . . called in the aid of Yúsuf Bashá, of Tripoli," who, in the year 1818, sent the Sultan of Fezzan and other dignitaries to his assistance and, "laying waste the whole northwestern part of Bagirmi and destroying its more considerable places, carried away a great number of slaves," among them one of Barth's principal informants in matters relating to Bagirmi.[34]

Like all historians of the Western literate tradition, Barth was concerned with reconstructing the actual and particular events that had caused the evolution of a new relationship between two separate societies. And in the mirror of such written objective records most inter-

[31] Goody, "Restricted Literacy," p. 211. J. Dupuis, who was appointed British Consul for Ashanti in 1818, and T. E. Bowdich, who was in Kumasi in 1817, as well as other visitors or emissaries, were therefore also required to testify on the Koran to their good will toward the king. Compare on this general subject, Ward, *A History of the Gold Coast*, pp. 155–181, "Treaties with Ashanti, 1816–31."

[32] Palmer, *Sudanese Memoirs*, Vol. I, 19, also pp. 75–78.

[33] Barth, *Travels*, Vol. II, 552.

[34] *Ibid.*, p. 553. *Ibid.*, pp. 22–29, on Barth's thesis—partially borrowed from Ibn Khaldūn—that the Bornu dynasty and sections of the Bornu "nation" itself were of Berber origin.

African agreements certainly appear to have originated in conditions of duress and to have had exploitative effects. In the context of African modes of historical thought, by contrast, it was possible to forget the conditions precedent to a "pact," blur the sequence of events, and generate a new relationship, ex post facto as it were, without much concern for "Wie es eigentlich gewesen ist" (how it really was). That is to say, in Islamized Africa, where societies did not have regularized foreign relations and did not engage in treaty making as a matter of course, pacts were often assumed after relations had taken a certain turn. Furthermore, and in line with the logic of the traditional time scheme and the dictates of nonliteracy or restricted literacy, the essence of such an agreement had to be totally absorbed in the domestic order—if only because the latter was by definition hostile to overt contacts with aliens and their causes. And this overwhelming need was satisfied best by epic stories and symbolic actions. The following account of Jukun-Bornu relations at the beginning of the nineteenth century illustrates the process:

> One of the Jukun kings, whose name is sometimes given as Katakpa the founder of Wukari, and sometmies as Adi Matswen, once went against Bornu and fought an inconclusive battle with his ancient enemies. The king of Bornu, hard pressed, called on the assistance of Allah, and immediately the Jukun found themselves surrounded with a circle of burning grass. When they were about to fly in disorder the King of the Jukun rallied them by reminding them that the control of the rains was his, and he proceeded to carry out the rain-making rites. A storm of rain extinguished the fires, and the kings of the respective armies, perceiving that the power of each was commensurate with that of the other, withdrew to their capitals. When the king of Bornu heard of Katakpa's arrival at Wukari, he put some cotton in a basket and in the middle of the cotton a piece of live charcoal. Covering the basket with a tray of plaited grass he sent it with his compliments to the king of Wukari as a reminder of his ability to call down fire from heaven. When the basket arrived the charcoal was still alive and the cotton unburnt. Katakpa returned the compliment by sending to the king of Bornu an "iwa" [water-tight basket] filled with water, saying "The king of the rains sends you some water with which to quench your thirst."[35]

This exchange of pleasantries led to a "treaty of peace" between the two sovereigns, we learn from Meek, and the king of Bornu sent to Wukari an official known as the "Zanua" to be his permanent representa-

---

[35] Meek, *A Sudanese Kingdom*, pp. 30–31.

tive at the court of the Jukun king. The latter sent an "Ajifi" to act in a similar capacity at the Bornu capital. In "reality" the Jukun had probably become subservient to Bornu,[36] but in the historical consciousness of later generations the facts of statecraft had been effectively subsumed by the art of myth making, in which Africa excels.[37]

[36] *Ibid.*, p. 31.

[37] Compare *supra*, Ch. 6, for other illustrations of the connection between the mythical vision and the greater society.

· 20 ·

THE EUROPEAN PRESENCE,
TREATY MAKING, AND THE
AFRICAN RESPONSE

The European who came upon the African scene seeking to conclude binding international accords with representative governmental agents was apt to be disoriented and frustrated on scores of counts. Few records are as richly informative in these respects as those left by Dr. Henry Barth in the 1850s, when he was asked by the British government to obtain "letters of franchise" from African rulers that would guarantee freedom of movement and security of person to future European traders and missionaries, and to negotiate acceptance of a draft treaty of amity and commerce. Barth succeeded in establishing friendly relations with numerous potentates and receiving "letters of franchise" from the Sultans of Sokoto and Gwandu and the Sheikhs of Timbuktu and adjacent Tuareg tribes, even as he managed to survive in climatically and politically adverse circumstances and attain the major objectives of his scientific mission, because he allowed himself to become keenly aware of locally prevalent character traits, customs, and values. For example, he showed himself quite aware of the need, on some occasions, for go-betweens and mediators; he was careful in the choice of his own messengers; and, when direct contact and discourse were indicated, he knew when to insert the necessary fervor and animation, and when, by contrast, to engage his Muslim interlocutors in serene discussions about the nature of paradise or the relation between Christ and Mohammed. Few if any requirements in matters of etiquette, ritual, or gift exchange seem to have escaped his attention. In one situation he realized quickly that his present of a goat to an important chief would be resented rather than appreciated because the animal was just a trifle too lean. But on another occasion—and it is the subject of one of the most poignant comments in his journals—he saw equally clearly that the gift of a special book was deeply appreciated even though it was devoid of economic value:

> This volume of Hippocrates had been a present from Captain Clapperton to Sultan Bello of Sokoto, from whom my friend had received it, among other articles, as an acknowledgment of his learning. I may assert with full confidence, that those few books taken by the gallant Scotch captain into Central Africa have had a greater effect in reconciling the men of authority in Africa to the character of Europeans

331

than the most costly present ever made to them; and I hope, therefore, that gifts like these may not be looked upon grudgingly by people who would otherwise object to do any thing which might seem to favour Mohammedanism.[1]

Amity and patience were by no means always the proper dispositions. Barth's protracted consultations and explorations in northwestern and central Africa also taught him that at a mere moment's notice friendship might turn to enmity and life to death. To such contingencies he responded like his African and Arab hosts: he knew as they did that he had to be armed and ready to shoot if he was to retain the respect of those who mattered.[2]

By thus adjusting to the codes of honor and behavior that were valid among the Fulani, the Arabs (whose value systems, he notes, allowed for the combination of "valour, thievishness and generous hospitality"),[3] and the Tuareg (whom he found functioning as transport agents, convoyers, and black-mailers), Barth won the protection and guest-friendship of several notables in the war-torn lands through which he carefully negotiated passage and residence rights. One of his protectors, in particular, the Tuareg Sheikh El Bakay of Timbuktu, exerted himself tirelessly, albeit often to not much avail, in Barth's behalf, trying to counteract the intrigues of his ruling brothers and extricate his guest from the hostile designs of the Fulani, who had bound themselves by oath to drive the European out of town or kill him. The "letter of recommendation" or "safe conduct" which the sheikh addressed to "his brethren and friends among the Arabs, the Tawarek, the Fullan, and the Sudan in the land of El Islam" so as to assure his guest's safe homeward journey, contained the following passages:

And this Christian is today the guest of the Moslims, under their protection, their covenant, and safe-conduct. No Muslim can lawfully hurt him. On the contrary, to injure him is a burning shame. Nay, he has the rights of a guest. . . . And behold, this man's nation, the English, have done us services which are neither doubted or denied: which are their friendship to our brethren the Moslims, and their sincerity to them. . . . It is, therefore, our right and duty to show gratitude . . . and to strengthen whatever covenant and confidence there is between us and them. Therefore whoever belongs to the jurisdiction of [there follows a list of princes, learned men, and people in the relevant districts] on them be my salutation and el Islam. . . . For, lo! my guest is a guest of theirs, who has nothing to fear from them, since

[1] Barth, *Travels*, Vol. III, 372.
[2] *Ibid.*, Vol. III, see pp. 330, 332, 340, 383 for relevant episodes.
[3] *Ibid.*, Vol. III, 381.

they profess obedience to God . . . and I admonish you about my and your guest, indeed about whatever Englishman shall come after him, whether he come to me, or pass near you, or abide among you for a time and then return. . . . And as for me, brethren, I have written for the Englishman specially a general safe-conduct, in which I have included every one in my land, and have added thereto your land, in reliance on your religion and your sure conviction, and in dependence on your intelligence and humanity. Be careful that he be not hindered in anything. . . . Farewell.[4]

This plea in behalf of the security of one solitary traveler had behind it the force of traditional ethical guidelines and was communicated in the official Islamic form of the safe conduct. Yet it was no more effective in speeding Barth's departure from the "anarchical place" than other commitments he had received. The letters of franchise to any Englishman visiting the country, which Tuareg chiefs had issued under El Bakay's pressures, may have held out "the first glimmer of hope of a peaceable intercourse,"[5] but Barth's experience had taught him that promises would in all likelihood not be taken seriously. Furthermore, the very process of negotiating each of these promises had proved to be an "extremely tedious and wearing activity," and this judgment extended to the tasks, respectively, of arranging for the writing of an appropriate letter, and of ensuring its due dispatch.[6] Fully cognizant of the difficulties implicit in diplomatic relationships with regimes in Islamized Africa's extended zones of restricted literacy, Barth gave this advice on the subject of treaty making:

I was well aware how extremely difficult it is to make these people understand the forms of the articles in which European governments are wont to conclude commercial treaties. In regions like this, however, it seems almost as if too much time ought not to be lost on ac-

[4] *Ibid.*, Vol. III, 764–767, Appendix XIV, p. 766; see also pp. 650–657, Appendix VIII, for two poems of the Sheikh El Bakay, wherein he satirizes the Fulani and the Masina after they had attacked his guest, "Abd el Kerim Barth, the Englishman, the Christian." On the safe conduct in Islamic tradition, see Khadduri, *The Islamic Law of Nations*, p. 13: If a Muslim entered the *dar al-hārb* as a merchant, or as a visitor under a safe conduct (*amān*), he was under obligation to respect the authority of that territory and its laws as long as he remained there, enjoying the benefits of security granted him by a safe conduct or a treaty with Muslim authorities. As Khadduri also points out (*ibid.*, p. 39), he was subject, in the main, to the law of war.

[5] Barth, *Travels*, Vol. III, 340ff.

[6] *Ibid.*, pp. 105, 107, 108; and cf. also *ibid.*, p. 553 for an episode in which a parcel of letters destined for Barth's friend in Sokoto was gradually reduced, by the effect of rain and so on, to a few illegible pieces of paper. These were returned to the bearer to whom all had originally been entrusted, and he had ever since used them as a protective charm.

count of such a matter of form before it is well established whether merchants will really open a traffic with these quarters; for as soon as, upon the general condition of security, an intercourse is really established, the rulers of those countries themselves become aware that some more definite arrangement is necessary while, before they have any experience of intercourse with Europeans, the form of the articles in which treaties are generally conceived, fill them with the utmost suspicion and fear, and may be productive of the worst consequences to any one who has to conclude such a treaty.[7]

This warning did not appreciably affect the traditional European bent to express designs for mutual security or unilateral advantage in contractual forms. As a matter of fact, the colonial governments of the nineteenth and early twentieth centuries showed few signs of remembering the lessons in transcultural diplomacy that had been registered about four hundred years earlier, when Portugal opened intergovernmental relations, first with the Kingdom of the Kongo and later with other Central African regimes. The story of these particular alignments between two wholly different polities and diplomatic styles has a decidedly modern ring. Indeed, it may well be more proximate and instructive to modern generations in Africa and the West than the Anglo-African encounters in the times of Dr. Henry Barth and Sir Harry Johnston.[8] The elements that make for such time-transcendent relevance include the following.

A. Transcultural Diplomacy: The Case of Portugal

The King of Portugal and the King of Kongo were equals as individual sovereigns because they were equals in their spiritual subservience to the universal Catholic church. Gradations of secular power and influence were certainly recognized, but they did not supply the primary references of the system of public order with which the Kongo became associated. Nor did dependence in terms of vassalage carry pejorative meanings. The African state may have been weak, even inferior, by comparison with Portugal, but so were numerous European states. Exploitative tendencies are, of course, always present when power is unevenly distributed, but in the Christian commonwealth of the time they were curbed by the officially prevalent code of ethics, according to which the strong were supposed to protect the weak. It is the conjunction of these factors, then, which explains why Alvare I of Kongo felt free, in 1572, to sign an act in which he expressed his intention of becoming a vassal of Portugal, and

[7] *Ibid.*, Vol. III, 109.
[8] The purposes of this book do not require a full coverage of different colonial regimes or Afro-European encounters. Only two case studies have been selected: the early Portuguese presence and the later British penetration.

why Portugal in turn decided to refuse the offer.[9] In 1651, by contrast, Kongo had to acknowledge Portugal as its protector in a treaty that stipulated mutual aid and the establishment, respectively, of a Portuguese mission in Salvador and a Kongolese mission in Luanda.

On the purely organizational level, meanwhile, the two states became nearly equals as participants in the European states system, after the Kongo had been drawn into diplomatic relations with other Occidental powers, notably the Vatican. And as the pace of interactions on the African and European theatres quickened in the sixteenth and seventeenth centuries, and common causes no less than discords multiplied, the requirements of war and peace, too, received mutually compatible recognition, while diplomacy and alliance politics came to serve nearly analogous ends. This extension of supranational but fundamentally Occidental references to a principality fashioned by typically African resources was, of course, primarily Portugal's doing. Yet it would be misleading to render these realities in the language of imperialism customarily employed to describe, on the one hand Arab-Islamic dominance, and on the other nineteenth-century European colonialism, for the early Kingdom of the Kongo was neither a simple tributary nor a dependent colony. Its weakness was openly acknowledged, but amelioration and development were also clearly envisioned in the governing circles of both states. As a developing state in need of foreign assistance, the Kongo may thus be likened to scores of sovereign Asian and African states in the later twentieth century that have also been recipients of aid by so-called developed nations. In either case the norms of achievement were set by the latter, but whereas growth in modern times is measured mainly in economic terms, it was seen in the sixteenth century case as a function of intellectual and moral development.[10] What was desired most by the European and African sovereigns, their representatives, and, of course, the Holy See, was the enhancement of acculturation in its broadest sense—an aim identified already in the 1480s by the Kongolese king as implying the diffusion of literacy, education, and Christianity among his people.

In the context of these concerns numerous diplomatic missions were despatched to Portugal, requesting priests, teachers, and such agents of

[9] Vansina, *Kingdoms of the Savanna*, p. 130.

[10] The parallel situation that suggests itself is the relationship between the Chinese "Middle Kingdom," on the one hand, and the "barbarian" hedge-guarding nations, on the other. The latter were likened to sons or younger brothers in the international Confucian family system of unequal members, and as such they were in need of tutelage and guidance. Even this comparison is defective in many respects, however, if only because the premise of the rulers' spiritual equality is missing. In this case, as in others to which previous references have been made, comparisons are tenuous, to say the least.

technical assistance as carpenters, masons, military advisors, and other counselors. Some embassies were also charged with placing young Kongolese, among them royal princes, in Portuguese schools; and one, sent by King Affonso in 1506, was four years in Lisbon, preoccupied mainly with negotiating military support for the destruction of "the house of the great fetiches,"[11] so that the kingdom could be duly transformed into a Christian state. The Portuguese, whose explorations had inaugurated this transcontinental line of communications, acceded to most of these requests, besides engaging in missions of their own, and their fleets thus became common carriers for Kongo-bound settlers, traders, diplomats, and Europeanized African students.

This brisk exchange of persons conduced to a remarkable cultural interpenetration of the two societies. It was not just that each ruler was reasonably well informed about the kingdom of the other. Familiarity also extended to popular strata, for neither government opposed mixed marriages and the consequent loss of ethnic consciousness. On intellectual and moral levels, too, affinities were steadily furthered, especially during the early decades of the sixteenth century. Many Portuguese advisors, both secular and ecclesiastical, were so devoted to the cause of the Kongo that they went to considerable lengths pleading the interests of their adopted country in the councils of their homeland. Most importantly, Christian missions propagated literacy and the faith, in a sustained endeavor to attain the objectives that native royalty had specified. Statistical evidence is not available, but the Kongo had become nominally Catholic toward the end of Affonso's reign in the early 1540s. The actual number of practicing Christians is, nonetheless, said to have been slight, and their impact was probably felt only at the major towns.[12] The same uneven development marked the spread of reading and writing skills. Only a small literate elite had come into being by 1514, and the king was, therefore, hard pressed to find suitable personnel for the staffing of his new administrative and diplomatic services.

These disappointing developments, accentuated at times by lapses into paganism on the part of relatives and subjects, and cases of abusive behavior in the ranks of Portuguese residents, caused Affonso to lodge complaints in Portugal. King Manuel responded in 1512 with the "regimento"—a blueprint for acculturation that is unique for its time, and perhaps even for all times. The document, which opened with the statement that Catholic kings were brothers obligated to mutual aid, listed the grievances, in order then to announce in systematic fashion how they were to be redressed. One provision empowered the special Portuguese

[11] Vansina, *Kingdoms of the Savanna*, p. 47.
[12] *Ibid.*, p. 56; also p. 48. See Westermann, *Geschichte Afrikas*, p. 391, to the effect that baptism led automatically to the acquisition of Portuguese citizenship.

envoy to sit in judgment over erring Portuguese and, if necessary, expel the incorrigibles among them. Another proposed that trade should be organized on the basis of royal monopolies so that all private intermediaries would be cut out—a reform distinctly inimical to settlers' interests. Improvements of the royal court and the local legal system were also foreseen. Manuel's delegate brought with him a new codex of Portuguese law with the suggestion that it be copied. Similarly, it was thought that court practices would benefit from borrowing Portuguese models. But these two proposals were decisively rebuffed by Affonso— an early indication of the deep and resilient commitment to customary African law and principles of administration that has been fully discussed in preceding chapters.

The bonds between the Iberian and Kongolese states weakened in the ensuing century, when this special partnership was drawn ineluctably into the maelstrom of power politics in the regional theatres of both continents. Among the new contenders on the African board were the Dutch, the Jaga, and Ndongo; and the major, historically crucial moves were made when the Jaga, a marauding, primitive, but politically talented people, sided with the Portuguese in the latter's battles with Ndongo[13] (thus making possible this kingdom's eventual transformation into the colony of Angola), and when the Kongo, which had also been invaded by the Jaga, became the ally of the Dutch.

Culturally syncretic patterns of international behavior were thus bound to arise in the turbulent period between the 1560s and 1660s; for while African peoples continued to reenact themes of intertribal conflict and conciliation familiar to their traditions, European nations were not only extending old norms peculiar to the Occidental family of nations, but also advancing new modes of conduct suitable to the colonial projects upon which they were beginning to embark. In this situation, then, alignments, usually cross-cultural in nature, were frequently shifting, as were the fortunes of war, the stakes of diplomacy, and the purports of intergovernmental accords.

Portugal's role was pivotal in most of these encounters; but it by no means inhibited successful military thrusts and shrewd diplomatic bargains on the part of African regimes. For example, in one phase of the

[13] Raiding Jaga had appeared on this scene at least since 1600. They had invaded Kongo in the 1560s and succeeded, at least temporarily, in expelling both the king and the Portuguese who resided at his court. See David Birmingham, "The Date and Significance of the Imbangala Invasion of Angola," *Journal of African History*, 6, No. 2 (1965), 143–152, to the effect that some sections of the Jaga had been absorbed by the Imbangala in the process of their migrations. This predatory Imbangala presence on the eastern border of Ndongo may have motivated the ngola to solicit Portugal's assistance. At any rate, an embassy was sent about 1548, and arrived in Lisbon in 1557.

tangled Afro-European relations, when the ngola (ruler) of Ndongo felt more threatened by the Jaga than the Portuguese, a pact was prepared (1622) providing that the Portuguese would fight the Jaga, that all the chiefs who had become vassals of Portugal would again become tributaries of the ngola, and that the latter would free the prisoners he had. Between the 1620s and 1640s, by contrast, when the Portuguese neglected Ndongo affairs because they were preoccupied by watching Dutch movements on the Central African coast, the ruling ngola—a spirited woman named Anna Nzinga, who seems to have poisoned her royal brother in order to attain power—allied herself with the Jaga, gave asylum to fugitive slaves from Portuguese-controlled territory, and gained sufficient military advantage to be able to foment rebellions in the ranks of Portuguese vassal chiefs. In fact, Portugal appears to have been outmaneuvered in the 1640s, when both Nzinga and the Dutch succeeded in recording strings of victories. Only when the Dutch withdrew from the scene did weaknesses in Ndongo's internal and external position compel the search for a settlement with Portugal. Negotiations to this end lasted for years, and the final peace treaty of 1656 had many aspects of a compromise; for while the queen had to cede territory to the rival ngola, she did not consent to become a vassal. Peace was kept until Nzinga, by that time reconverted to Catholicism, died in 1663.

By the end of the seventeenth century, Angola had become not just the first substantial European colony in Africa, but also the major regional power. Its internal administration, however, was modeled on native patterns of organization, its further expansion was either checked or slowed down by various adjacent African societies, and its local Portuguese overlords had become Africanized in many significant respects.[14] The Kongo, by contrast, displaced from its earlier position of supremacy and threatened by Angolan encroachments, had gradually gravitated toward alignments with the Dutch and the Vatican. When the Portuguese, whose troops had extricated the state from Jaga devastations in 1568, pressed the king to expel Dutch traders (these had arrived from the early sixteenth century onward), the demand was refused, and, more importantly, could not be enforced. As a matter of fact, from about 1622 onward the Kongo had adopted a decidedly pro-Dutch policy, which was to become manifest, for example, in the confidence with which the king called on Dutch troops to put down the revolt of an important district chief. But the major source of assistance in times of troubled relations

---

[14] Vansina, *Kingdoms of the Savanna*, pp. 124–130 on the rise of Angola; p. 146 to the effect that the Portuguese administered Angola around 1700 in close accord with native patterns. *Ibid.*, p. 185, that the nineteenth century brought changes in this respect; by that time, Vansina writes, Angola had changed from a slave-trading establishment, with a basic internal regime not unlike that of its African neighbors, into a colony surrounded by other colonies.

with the Portuguese was the Catholic church, which showed a rather consistent interest in solidifying the Kongo's status as an adjunct member of the Occidental international order. Although two embassies to the Vatican, sent by Affonso in the 1550s, had been blocked by Lisbon, Kongolese kings persisted in widening this opening to the West. Alvare II, for instance, was determined to elude Portuguese controls over certain economic activities he had in mind, and proposed in 1604 to become a feudatory of the Pope. The Holy See rejected this idea, but agreed a few years later to intercede with the king of Spain in the Kongo's behalf. A permanent Kongolese embassy was established in Rome in 1613, and thereafter relations seem to have been very close. Yet another overture was made when Garcia II asked the Pope to rule that succession would be regulated by primogeniture only, in other words that the Kongo be recognized as a hereditary monarchy more or less on the European model. This request, too, was turned down after protracted negotiations, but the Vatican announced that in case of conflict, the electors might be assisted by clerics who would watch over the legality of the election—a proposal, incidentally, that led to a severe succession crisis.[15]

The church, then, was often active as the Kongo's official protector. The most ardent champions of the African state were found in the ranks of the Capuchins, however, and it is not surprising that members of this ecclesiastical order were frequently asked by Kongolese kings to negotiate on their behalf with such hostile or rival African powers as Nzinga and the Jaga of Kasanje, and to mediate conflicts and misunderstandings in their relations with Portuguese authorities. European influences of varied provenance were thus at work in mid-seventeenth century, when tedious peace talks with Portugal led to the elaboration of one draft treaty after another until a settlement emerged in 1657. Not unlike Nzinga, Garcia II had been adamantly opposed to becoming a vassal, and clauses considered injurious to the idea of independence were, therefore, removed. Amical relations were thus officially restored, but the accords did not prove binding, the peace was frequently broken, and the links between the two societies grew steadily fainter. By 1700 the Kongo had lost its status as an Afro-European state, and was being reabsorbed in the African scheme of things. Indeed, a twentieth-century review of the extraordinary relationship between Portugal and the Kongo has led a leading African historian to conclude that the European presence had not left any significant traces in the African kingdom, even though it had been experienced for four hundred years.[16]

The reasons for the failure of acculturation in general and foreign aid

[15] *Ibid.*, pp. 132, 150; also pp. 143ff., 150ff.; Westermann, *Geschichte Afrikas*, p. 396; and cf. *supra*, Ch. 18 B on "The Stranger as Intermediary."
[16] Compare Westermann, *Geschichte Afrikas*, pp. 390ff., 401.

programs in particular were as various and complex then as they have proved to be in recent times. On the Portuguese side allowance must certainly be made for cupidity, ignorance, and arrogance—traits that co-existed with magnanimity, expertise, and humility. Yet in each of such well-documented cases of abuse, as in respect also of the slave trade, it cannot be said that the Europeans behaved worse than either the Arabs or the Africans. It is only when the Europeans are held to higher standards of behavior than those enacted and condoned by the two dominant cultures in the continent that guilt or responsibility can be imputed unequivocally. And this, of course, would violate the logic of comparative culture studies, as well as the cherished trust that each culture is the equal of the other.[17] The point may, in fact, be made that the Lusitanians, who were the last arrivals on the scene in the crucial fifteenth and sixteenth centuries and who found themselves always outnumbered by the Arabs and the Africans, were different from all later European intruders in the sense that they simply fell in with many locally prevalent behavior patterns. The latter differed significantly from Portugal's own national heritage, all the more so as they had become firmly established in Africa centuries before the inauguration of the bold reform movement upon which certain Kongolese and Portuguese sovereigns had decided to embark.

What is also relevant in an account of the ultimate failure of these accords is precisely this minimal Portuguese presence, and the insufficiency of the resources by means of which the ambitious innovations in styles of thought and life were to be carried out. The priorities set by Afro-European concert were to implant literacy and Christianity. Neither objective was attained, partly because the legions of teachers requisite for so complex a task in so vast a land were simply not available, and partly because the actual services rendered by the dedicated few failed to spark the necessary efforts in the ranks of native circles. That is to say, both literacy and Christianity were ultimately dissolved by the power of traditional systems of knowledge and belief.

[17] The term "equality," as used here, simply means that all cultures should receive equal sympathy, especially when their interpenetrations are reviewed. It does not carry the connotations imputed to "equality" by anthropologists who subscribe to cultural relativism and the proposition that all value systems are equally entitled to respect. On this issue see the pioneering study of Robert Redfield, *The Primitive World and Its Transformations*, especially ch. 6, "The Transformation of Ethical Judgment," and J. C. Furnas, *The Anatomy of Paradise* (New York, 1937), p. 488, who introduces the following reflection: "For generations the western world has bitterly blamed western man for the crime of not understanding the savage. It seems never to occur to anybody that, other things being equal, it would be equally fair to blame the savage for not understanding western man. Since that would obviously be absurd, the two sets of cultures are unmistakably on different levels, a statement that can be made without specifying higher and lower."

With respect to literacy, it is certainly true that reading and writing skills were successfully imparted to many aspiring Kongolese, but there is little in the records left by this elite to suggest that mastery of the techniques led to a sustained search of knowledge, the advancement of intellectual frontiers, or the emergence of a speculative type of man—indispensable human prerequisites for fashioning a progressive society. Nor is there any evidence to indicate that the literate Kongolese felt under any obligation to communicate some of their new learning to the less privileged strata of their society. Furthermore, it is quite significant for an understanding of these cultural interactions that the semi-Westernized elite of the sixteenth and seventeenth centuries was split into the same kind of factions that were to arise again in the twentieth century: those who affirmed the need to come to terms with the foreign ideas grafted upon their culture, and those who were persuaded by their encounter with European civilization to reaffirm established native ways.

The mental and social conflicts thus engendered by the long coexistence of two diametrically opposite responses to the challenges of life found particularly disturbing expressions in matters relating to faith. Here, as elsewhere in Africa and other non-European areas, mutations of the Christian creed and ritual had to be evolved if tradition-bound peoples were not to lose their bearings in life, and the church was by and large generous in condoning such metamorphoses, even when they might well be viewed as travesties of the values it was authorized to uphold. The case of the Kongo was exceptional in the sense that its early kings aspired to be genuine Christians, even as they, too, conceived of their affiliation as an increment to political power and prestige. The papacy's refusal, after protracted negotiations, to recognize the kingdom as a hereditary monarchy on the European model was, therefore, a double blow, and the sovereign responded impulsively by ceasing to be a Christian (Capuchin priests later succeeded in changing his mind), and by expelling all whites, with the sole exception of teachers and missionaries. The other negative effect of the royal espousal of Christianity was the social divisiveness it induced. The inroads of Christianity, as those of literacy, were widely resented, and anti-Christian movements arose with increasing frequency, often fueled by zealous ecclesiastics who reacted insensitively to the obduracy of fetishism and other manifestations of the non-Christian life.[18] These confusions in the value system, allied as they

[18] On the complex relations between the Italian Capuchins, who arrived in 1645 and were well received because they were not Portuguese, and who proved to be excellent mediators, on the one hand, and the Portuguese, the Holy See, the Jesuits, the Kongolese kings, and certain groups of Kongolese nobles, on the other, see Vansina, *Kingdoms of the Savanna*, pp. 151ff. Garcia II appears to have been a devout Christian, but many nobles were afraid that Christianity meant the loss of all traditional usages, and therewith the destruction of the kingdom. The pagan

were with traditional forms of internecine strife and succession struggles at the court, explain why sizable segments of the Kongolese population were seized by xenophobia toward the end of the seventeenth century. True to traditional thoughtways, a prime cause had to be located for all that was disturbing or inexplicable, and in this case the scapegoat was, of course, the European element.[19]

The inability to assimilate literacy and Christianity[20] in the manner foreseen especially by Affonso,[21] meant that the primary norms for the development of the Kongo into a state on the European model could not be met. On the purely political, as on the mental and moral levels, the alien concepts retained some external significance, it is true, but their core meanings, which carried the structuring potential, could not have the desired impact because they lost their authenticity in the process of being metamorphosed into stronger native forms. Indictments can be leveled against many groups of Portuguese for having thrown the Kongo into political confusion, but the patterns of turmoil as recorded in the period of Afro-Iberian relations are too strikingly similar to those registered in pre-European times to justify so simple an explanation. Here, as elsewhere in the region, we have endless factional strife, family jeal-

---

rural population, meanwhile, turned against the Capuchins when the latter, with the full support of the king, began to burn fetishes and arrest "convicted fetish-doctors."

[19] Compare *supra*, pp. 98ff. on the phenomenon of the scapegoat.

[20] See Charles Pelham Groves, "Missionary and Humanitarian Aspects of Imperialism from 1870 to 1914," in L. H. Gann and Peter Duignan, eds., *Colonialism in Africa 1870–1960*, Vol. I (Cambridge, 1969), 462, who begins his essay with the statement: "The first pioneers of the Gospel in tropical Africa were the Portuguese. For many decades, Portuguese priests laboured in the kingdom of Kongo, in the realm of Monomotapa and elsewhere; but in the long run, their labours proved of little avail." Much to the disappointment of the Kongo's Christian kings, literate knowledge withered and Christianity merged with pagan cults. One of these symbioses was the heresy of the so-called Antonians, a prefiguration of similar modern movements in Central Africa. Around 1700, Vansina writes, "a woman prophet began to claim that she was in contact with heaven and especially with St. Anthony and that it was her mission to find the man who would bring an end to the wars and restore the kingship. . . . Her teaching was also pervaded with elements which are now attributed to modern movements such as the so-called African 'Zionist churches.' She said that Christ was black and that heaven was for the Africans, that people should not listen to the foreign missionary but to her and to her catechists." *Kingdoms of the Savanna*, p. 154. Vansina views this cult as an expression of the strains of war and as evidence of how deeply Christianity had penetrated the Kongolese mentality and how effective the Capuchin mission had been. An opposite conclusion is reached by Westermann after his searching study of the Kongo's contact with the European religion. In his view, Christianity was largely a veneer that soon lost its luster, to be remitted, eventually, into pure paganism. *Geschichte Afrikas*, p. 393: "Das Christentum blieb grossenteils ein Firnis, der bald abblaetterte oder sich in reines, mit unverstandenen christlichen Symbolen ausstaffiertes Heidentum zurueckverwandelte."

[21] It is noteworthy that Kongo oral tradition sees Affonso as its greatest king. See Vansina, *Kingdoms of the Savanna*, p. 57.

ousies, revolts of subchiefs against chiefs, and civil wars between subject princes and between some of the latter and the king.[22] During the turbulent period of the 1640s and 1660s, for example, rebellions were abetted at all levels of administration. "Every third year, when tribute had to be brought to the capital, local revolts erupted. If the king could not crush them, his prestige suffered; if he punished them, the violence bred more violence. The collection of tribute was itself often accompanied by violence."[23] Secessions and regicides were common, as were bitter struggles for the kingship, with successions to the throne usually preceded by interregnums also marked by war and intrigue. Boundaries and seats of power were thus as fluid here as in other African realms. Contemporary surveys of local conditions suggest, indeed, that the Portuguese may have exaggerated the territorial expanse as well as the power of the kingdom. For although many sovereigns were remarkably effective diplomats, in full control of the embassies they despatched to Lisbon or to Rome, they were not able to unify the component provinces or tribes of their so-called empire, nor did they have the means to establish a strong central or federal administration.[24] In other words, they could not adapt to alien norms of political organization, and in attempting to do so they lost some of the leverage they had enjoyed in regional politics before they veered off their traditional course.

In this case the Portuguese challenge may well be viewed as the immediate cause for the Kongo's degeneration. But it bears remembering that here, as throughout Africa, states had risen and declined in very similar fashion long before the first Europeans had made their appearance, and that Portuguese activities in the period under consideration were paralleled by multiple, mainly predatory, intrusions on the part of native African and Arab groups. Indeed, the relevance of this entire chapter in international history for modern times is greatly enhanced by the realization that Western, Muslim, and native African governments participated in three culturally diverse, but mutually interdependent systems of public order—just as they do now. Furthermore, they did so in conditions of relative political equality. The sovereigns of the Kongo and of Portugal (and to a lesser extent the representatives of the Vatican, Spain, and the

---

[22] On these traditional motifs, see Part v. On their incidence in the Kongo see Cuvelier and Jadin, *L'Ancien Congo d'après les archives romaines (1518–1640)*; this guide to the main documents in the Vatican archives concentrates on the period from the end of the sixteenth to the middle of the seventeenth century. See also the historical introduction. Also Cuvelier, *L'Ancien Royaume de Congo*, and by the same author, *Documents sur une mission française au Kakongo 1766–1776*. Some of the contemporary reports filed, for example, by the Bishops of San Salvador to the Holy See also describe vividly the conditions in which the work of evangelization was carried out or frustrated.

[23] Vansina, *Kingdoms of the Savanna*, p. 149; also *ibid.*, p. 66.

[24] Compare *supra*, Ch. 7 for a discussion of Africa's "greater societies."

Netherlands) were not only joined by virtue of their respective dual memberships in the European and the African orders, but each was also implicated in the Arab scheme of international affairs. All regimes were striving for influence or supremacy in adjoining realms, with trade a primary motivation; each was suspicious of the other, but willing to negotiate compromises, albeit by different diplomatic methods; and none had the incentive or the opportunity to transpose regional conflicts into enduring terms of peaceful coexistence. However, it seems undeniable that Arab orientations were closer to African traditions than those identified with Europe,[25] and that significant fusions between the two former had taken place when the latter was introduced. In general it may be said that principles of international conduct were not as closely defined and institutionalized in Africa as they were in the West, and that war and peace were not experienced as polar opposites in the Afro-Asian conflict/conciliation syndrome as they habitually were in the normative system of the Europeans.[26] This explains, in particular, why distinctions between "just" and "unjust" wars were practically irrelevant in indigenous dispositions toward both war and negotiation, whereas Portuguese statecraft was at times impeded by such considerations. For example, the Council for Portugal in Lisbon decided as late as the seventeenth century that the war against Nzinga was "unjust," since Portugal had not fulfilled the provisions of an earlier treaty—a reprimand that actually helped to get the Portuguese back to the peace table.

Eighteenth and nineteenth-century developments in the vast area comprehended today by southern Katanga, eastern Angola and northeastern Rhodesia provide other illustrations of the dissociation between the three contending political systems. The two powerful Lunda kingdoms that controlled this territory—Mwata Yamvo's in the West, and Kazembe's in the East—lay between the Portuguese of Angola in the west and those of Mozambique in the east. The Lusitanians were interested in establishing trade relations with Kazembe on a sound basis, if possible by treaty, and in opening a transcontinental trade route linking their Pacific and Atlantic outposts.[27] Promising overtures were made and several embassies exchanged, for Kazembe, too, was initially interested in commercial contacts with the Europeans, if only in order to enhance his prestige.

[25] Compare *supra*, Ch. 19 B.

[26] Compare *supra*, Part I.

[27] For a full account of this interesting chapter in Afro-Portuguese relations, see Ian Cunnison, "Kazembe and the Portuguese 1798–1832," *Journal of African History*, 2, No. 1 (1961), 61–76; also the same scholar's *The Luapula Peoples of Northern Rhodesia*. One conquering group after another arrived in this area, always relying on tribute for its maintenance. The conquered mass of the population had its rights and kept the rump of its institutions on the village level. But since government and defense were the privileges of the conquerors, the territory is best described as a protectorate.

However, a firm commercial treaty could not be concluded, mainly, it appears, because Kazembe's realm was riddled with thievery, barbarism, and general insecurity. At any rate, the net effect of these Afro-European contacts was negative, quite in contrast to that registered not only by the Arabs but also by the Yeke of Katanga.

The particular reasons for this disparity varied from case to case, but a few general conclusions appear tenable. Cunnison remarks[28] that the Arabs succeeded because they came as individual, powerfully armed traders, and that much the same was true of the Yeke, who established an empire in southeast Katanga in the 1850s on the base of their commercial wealth.[29] Both groups were always ready to face military contingencies and handle situations pragmatically as they arose. Neither seems to have assumed that treaties were necessary, or that accords improvised in one instance would affect the course of other trading ventures. Intimately familiar with African traditions of personalized government, they yet knew how to be relatively independent of a given ruler's caprice and changes of mind, even as they had no difficulties complying with certain requirements of the gift exchange complex that were apt to disconcert the Europeans. Commenting on the Portuguese in this period of their history, Cunnison notes that they differed from their rivals by aiming at sound and lasting contractual commitments, preferably between governmental agencies, even though some of their observers in the sixteenth century had drawn attention to the fact that African hostility toward Lisbon's official spokesmen was quite compatible with amity toward individual traders.[30] The records suggest, next, that Portuguese traders and emissaries in this later era were inadequately armed, unduly dependent upon the good will of local potentates, and not sufficiently attuned to patterns of royal moods and other psycho-political aspects of native rule.

One person who might have come close to harmonizing European and African expectations was the renowned explorer Lacerda (appointed governor of the Sena Rivers in 1797). Lacerda's military escort, consisting of about fifty soldiers, was as minimal as that of previous Portuguese expeditions. However, and not unlike other individual European explorers, diplomats, and missionaries, he could compensate for the lack of material power by bringing into play the gift of understanding individual Africans. This enabled him to establish amicable personal relations with the headmen and chiefs he met, and to initiate contacts with

[28] Cunnison, "Kazembe and the Portuguese."

[29] On the Yeke, see explanation in tribal index.

[30] See, for example, Birmingham, "The Date and Significance of the Imbangala Invasion of Angola," for an analysis of diplomatic missions exchanged with the Ngola in the sixteenth century.

Kazembe III that were marked by protestations of good will, exchanges of presents, and assurances of protection on the sovereign's part. Lacerda's untimely death, which occurred at or near Kazembe's court, cut short these promising beginnings. But it was the memory of this particular cross-cultural, inter-personal friendship that proved instrumental in saving the lives of a later Portuguese party that had to deal with Kazembe IV. This monarch appears to have been solely interested in the slave trade and in extorting trade goods from the Portuguese. Although he had at one time professed "brotherhood" with the king of Portugal, he drastically changed his inclinations around 1832, when he revoked the immunities his father had granted the Portuguese, and threatened to have them all beheaded. The Lusitanian delegation finally succeeded in leaving Kazembe's realm, but only after the monarch had had a dream in which Kazembe III had appeared, bitterly complaining of the treatment his successor was meting out to the countrymen of his friend Lacerda.[31]

B. TRANSCULTURAL LAW: THE CASE OF ENGLAND

The auspices under which the European powers made their imperialistic bids in the later nineteenth century were radically different from those that had presided over Africa's early contacts with the Portuguese. Although the latter were treated as bitter rivals by the British, they yet elicited the unqualified admiration of Sir Harry Johnston, who had stayed in Angola as a young man: "But even as it is we must not forget to give the Portuguese their due. Of all the European powers that rule in tropical Africa none have pushed their influence so far into the interior as Portugal. And the Portuguese rule more by influence over the natives than by actual force. The garrisons at Dondo, Malange and other places in the interior range perhaps from fifty to two hundred men, and these are nearly entirely native soldiers. The country is so thickly populated that the inhabitants could in a moment sweep away the Portuguese if they disliked their rule."[1]

The early Iberian design, which had been conceived in the context of political and racial equality, and was promoted by minimal reliance on Occidental forms of treaty making, had no appreciable effect on British

[31] Cunnison, "Kazembe and the Portuguese," pp. 71–75. Lacerda was buried near the cemetery of the kings and was accorded a "gravekeeper" in royal fashion. Cunnison notes, on p. 75, that it was still the custom for Kazembe to report his dreams to his advisers, who interpreted them as if the ancestor were trying to point out to the reigning monarch some breach of custom for which he was responsible. On similar relationships between divination, dream, magic, and politics, see *supra*, Chs. 5, 9, 10, 18 A.

[1] For this excerpt from *The Graphic*, November 17, 1883, see Oliver, *Sir Harry Johnston*, p. 30.

planning in the 1880s. Nor is there any evidence that the new generation of Africanists took to heart the wisdom left by earlier explorers of the African mental and political systems, such as Henry Barth.[2] What was desired were treaties, and these were "produced by the cartload in all the approved forms of legal verbiage."[3] It should be noted, however, that the documents in question were greatly various in their intent, formulation, and effect. A survey of the early phases of Britain's presence on the continent permits the conclusion that treaty making of the Occidental kind contributed considerably to peace and order in inter-African relations. The major traditional objectives on behalf of which these efforts were deployed were the abolition of the slave trade, the furtherance and regulation of "legitimate" commerce, the peaceful adjustment of disputes, and the safety of human life—indigenous as well as European. For example, under the terms of "treaties of friendship" between Mende chiefs and the colony government of Sierra Leone (established in 1795), the former undertook, in return for annual stipends, to keep the roads open, refer internal quarrels to the governor for arbitration, put a stop to slave dealing, and secure the safety of the creoles, who were despised by the Mende as inferior foreigners. Other articles provided that traders must establish themselves at places indicated by the chiefs, and that no Poro[4] or country law or tax could be enforced against British subjects. These provisions do not appear to have been experienced as particularly onerous: the chiefs negotiated as independent sovereigns, and were treated as such by the British, even when they accepted the governor's arbitration of local disputes.[5]

Conciliatory interventions of this kind were also called for in a settlement that Governor George Maclean negotiated in 1831 between the Ashantis and the coastal tribes. In this case the governor's personality seems to have been so highly respected by all sections of the community that his settlement was actually followed by a long period of quiet, during which legitimate trade, chiefly in palm oil, could slowly establish itself.[6] And the same general aims were pursued in relations with Bonny (one of the "city states" of the Niger delta), where King Pepple agreed in a treaty of 1839 to abolish the slave trade, "provided they [Bonny] should obtain from the British Government, for five years, an annual present of the value of 2,000 dollars."[7]

[2] See *supra*, pp. 333ff.   [3] Lugard, *The Dual Mandate*, p. 15.

[4] See *supra*, pp. 109ff.

[5] Little, *The Mende of Sierra Leone*, pp. 53ff.

[6] Wolfson, *The Pageant of Ghana*, p. 14; cf. *supra*, Ch. 18 for the role of strangers as intermediaries, and *supra*, p. 292 on the subject of "brass-serpenting."

[7] For the history of the stillborn Bonny treaties, see Dike, *Trade and Politics in the Niger Delta*, ch. 5; for excerpts of documentary records bearing on negotiations with Bonny and others, see Hodgkin, *Nigerian Perspectives*, pp. 140ff., 178ff., 234ff.

Other regional accords also conducive to the establishment of local security included: the so-called "Bond" between the British government and several coastal tribes, mainly the Fante, which outlawed human sacrifices, even as it recognized British rights on the coast;[8] arrangements with tribes on the Cross River, whose chiefs were persuaded to promise that they would use their influence toward the abolition of cannibalism;[9] and, in a later phase, treaties with key Yoruba leaders, which provided that the chiefs would cease internecine fighting, encourage trade, and abstain from dissension and acts likely to promote strife.

Relations between European and West African traders, too, were considerably stabilized under the impact of treaty making, at least in the first part of the nineteenth century. Equity courts for the adjustment of disputes flourished between 1854 and 1900 in various parts of the Niger Delta. Here the resident factors of European firms sat with the principal African chiefs and traders, and enforced their decisions by refusing to trade with convicted offenders until the fine or restitution imposed by the court had been paid. The British consul belonged to all such courts, however, and in exceptional circumstances he was entitled to call upon the aid of a man-of-war so as to supplement what were normally purely economic sanctions. This system appears to have functioned surprisingly well, but eventually proved inadequate when Britain's West African policies became enmeshed in the nation's inter-European relations.[10]

Early English intrusions in the region had not been motivated by the desire to expand British territory or introduce colonial regimes. Such ideas established themselves only gradually between about 1884 and 1897,[11] when the government was determined to parry French, German, and Portuguese movements in Africa. In fact, the traditional commitment to promote freedom of commerce was not displaced altogether, even when the scramble for influence was in full swing, and when effective occupation was accepted everywhere as the watchword of European diplomacy in the continent. Britain was thus prepared to make considerable territorial concessions in favor, for example, of the French, provided that her merchants could be assured freedom of action. Some outstanding Africanists in the nation, among them notably Mary Kingsley,[12] were so fervently convinced of the merits of the Niger Company in par-

[8] Westermann, *Geschichte Afrikas*, p. 218.

[9] Oliver, *Sir Harry Johnston*, p. 127.

[10] *Ibid.*, p. 90. See also O. Adewoye, "The Judicial Agreements in Yorubaland, 1904–1908," *Journal of African History*, 12, No. 4 (1971), 607–627, for some comments on these courts, and cf. *supra*, Ch. 16 on the role of law in the management of conflicts.

[11] John E. Flint, *Sir George Goldie and the Making of Nigeria* (London, 1960), pp. 22, 216ff., 289ff.

[12] Compare *supra*, p. 304.

ticular, and the absolute benefits of merchant rule in general, that they used this principle as the backbone of an entirely new scheme for the administration of the West African region.[13]

Nothing came of this initiative. The chartered companies themselves were pursuing primarily political purposes from the 1880s onward, sometimes in cooperation, on other occasions in competition, with the government. One of them, the National African Company (later known as the Niger Company), had evolved its own treaty relations with the riparian states and communities of the Niger and the Benue. In the so-called palm oil region alone 209 treaties had been concluded by 1889.[14] In most of these cases the chiefs could be persuaded to cede territories, assign monopolies (for example, of mining), give the Company the right to settle disputes, exclude foreigners, and, in some instances, to control relations with other tribes or states, because the Company agreed in return to pay subsidies and protect the chiefs from attacks by aggressive neighboring tribes. But in other areas, such as Nupe, the Company had great difficulties negotiating suitable accords because the river banks were usually ruled by powerful Muslim emirs, who were not inclined to sign away their rights to infidel traders. As a matter of fact, the Emir of Nupe regarded himself as the protector of the traders—a circumstance which explains why the Company continued to pay him tribute even after he had consented in 1885 to a commercial "arrangement" under which the Company had "entire charge of all trading interests in the country." Changes in this relationship, including the granting of certain territorial rights, were induced only later, when the Sultan of Sokoto and the Emirs of Ganu, Nupe's nominal superiors, had been persuaded to treat with the Company.[15]

The agents of the Foreign Office, meanwhile, were employing their own tactics of treaty making in this region as well as in eastern, central, and southern Africa. As envisioned and explained by men like Sir Harry Johnston, the main objectives were first, to cast a network of interlocking treaties with native authorities over the land, thus linking the various outposts of British interest or jurisdiction; and second, to reinsure these stakes by making suitable settlements with rival European powers also claiming spheres of influence. The favorite legal instruments in the campaign to neutralize or win over tribes not yet controlled by, for example, the Portuguese, were the so-called conditional treaties, which, "while not committing the British Government to declare protectorates gave it, as

[13] Flint, *Sir George Goldie*, p. 304.

[14] *Ibid.*, p. 59; Oliver, *Sir Harry Johnston*, p. 93.

[15] Flint, *Sir George Goldie*, ch. 5; also *supra*, p. 129, n. 32, on Nupe's role in trade and history.

it were, the right of first refusal by binding the signatories not to accept the protection of any other power without the Queen's consent."[16] Lobengula was thus persuaded by J. S. Moffat to conclude a treaty of perpetual amity, which obligated the paramount chief of the Matabele not to part with any of his land or to sign with any other power without the sanction of the British government.[17] Similar agreements were concluded somewhat later with the Makololo chiefs of the Shire Valley and with the Yao of the highlands around Blantyre, after Johnston had spent some time there negotiating the proper terms. As the foremost modern analyst of these episodes explains, these were simple documents, all following a single printed form, by which

> the signatory declared himself at peace with the Queen of England, agreed to admit British subjects to his country and to submit all disputes in which they became involved to the decision of Her Majesty's representative. He undertook, finally, to make no cessions of territory to other powers without the consent of the British Government. The treaties did not confer protection, nor did they commit the signatory to accepting it at any future time. Their primary purpose was to prove at the council tables of Europe the priority of British interests over those of other powers in the regions to which they referred.[18]

In light of these avowed purposes it was neither necessary nor possible to cover the whole of Nyasaland and northeastern Rhodesia with a com-

---

[16] See Oliver, *Sir Harry Johnston*, p. 146; also pp. 151ff.; pp. 89–123, on Johnston's expeditions in West Africa; pp. 140ff. on Johnston's imperial design; p. 137 for Johnston's rather prophetic map on how Africa should be partitioned. See Sir Harry H. Johnston, *The Story of My Life* (Indianapolis, 1923), for his own detailed accounts of various treaty-making missions; pp. 176–182 on his somewhat controversial dealings with Chief Ja Ja. For Johnston's reflections on Britain's imperial destiny, treaty making, and his own particular assignments, see *ibid.*, pp. 258ff.

[17] See *supra*, p. 290 on the Matabele; Oliver, *Sir Harry Johnston*, p. 139, on the treaty. In 1823 a group of seven or eight Sotho villages organized themselves under a new chief, Sebetwane, and took the name Kololo (Makololo). Sebetwane and his followers trekked northward through Bechuanaland and the Kalahari, reaching middle Zambezi, and there established what is now called Barotseland, after having conquered the Luyis and neighboring tribes. In 1864, however, they were overthrown by the Luyis, and thereafter they became known as the Lozi (Barotse). According to Volhard, the Makololo in Nyasaland (Malawi) were the descendants of some Makololos brought to the area by Livingstone, who entered the land in the company of some Makololo bearers but then left these behind when he departed. Although the group was numerically insignificant, it yet succeeded, by dint of superior armament, in subjugating the Nyanja in the middle and lower Shire. By mid-twentieth century, however, it was found to be totally absorbed by those it had conquered. See Ewald Volhard, "Njassaland" in Bernatzik, ed., *Afrika*; Vol. II, 1081–1082.

[18] Oliver, *Sir Harry Johnston*, p. 160; see also *ibid.*, p. 206 on Johnston's dealings with the Yao and others in the Zambezi region.

plete network of treaties. If any particular chief refused to sign an agreement, Johnston and his aid would simply move on, leaving, as it were, a gap in the chain.

Just how valid were these treaties?[19] Were they genuinely understood by those who signed them? Did the negotiating authorities really represent their African constituents? Were they possessed of the powers that they signed away, and did they receive what they had bargained for? It goes without saying that questions such as these have been submitted to severely critical judgment in modern times, nowhere more so than in the West itself, where the era of imperialism had also been a great age of ethnographical exploration. Scholarly findings bearing on, for example, African social customs, values, and forms of political organization had thus combined, in mid-twentieth century, with a radical change in public morality to induce an indiscriminatively negative evaluation of past treaty making in Africa.[20] However, more interesting and significant than this reaction is the fact, first, that many of England's treaty makers were themselves frequently beset by doubts about the legitimacy of the undertakings they embarked upon. Second, the records show that these doubts were usually carefully argued on the merits of each case, even though knowledge of the hard facts of African life was difficult to come by in those days. Third, it is instructive to discover that such words as "validity" and "legitimacy" were understood rather broadly in their extended sociological or moral meanings. That is to say, they were seldom being made to carry exclusively legal implications as circumscribed by the vocabularies of the West.

For example, in attacking the process of treaty making, especially as undertaken by the Niger Company, Lugard seems to have proceeded from the recognition that law as understood in the West was being severely compromised by some of the uses to which treaties were being put in Africa. How could the Foreign Office grant charters conferring powers of taxation and rights to land and minerals, he asked, if it had at first hesitated to declare protectorates on the ground that it had not acquired the legal right to do so?[21] Rather than resort to treaty making so

---

[19] The following comments relate mainly to episodes mentioned in the text. They do not apply to obviously fraudulent dealings—common in many parts of Africa during the "scramble"—in which bogus chiefs were induced to sign meaningless scraps of paper in exchange for worthless gifts.

[20] A strong tendency exists in the ranks of Western and African scholars to view just about all treaties as sham deals by which African societies were despoiled. For example, Adewoye, "Judicial Agreements," p. 607, holds in his discussion of the Judicial Agreements in Yorubaland (initiated in 1904 by Sir William MacGregor) that all law is "the silent factor in European imperialist expansion," missionaries and guns being the major overt factors.

[21] Lugard, *The Dual Mandate*, pp. 14ff.; but see *ibid.*, pp. 21ff. for his appreciation of the Niger Company's treatment of native populations.

as to assuage the national conscience, he thought that all European powers would have been well advised to found their titles to intervention on force. Such an approach, Lugard argued, would have been particularly justifiable in each of three rather common African contexts: when the native ruler was himself an alien conqueror, holding in subjection tribes with which he had no affinity; when the ruler was a despot exercising a bloody tyranny, as in Benin, Uganda, Dahomey, or Zululand; and when pagan tribes were so absorbed by internecine warfare that they lacked the power to defend themselves against organized slave raiders. Although Lugard himself was renowned as a negotiator and treaty maker—and this in behalf of the government as well as the Company—he appears to have realized clearly what modern scholars were to discover gradually in the course of their field studies, namely, that peace and law were not normative influences in traditional inter-African affairs. As in Mende society, so also elsewhere: men "knew of only one precedent by which one people could claim the right to dominate and regulate the affairs of another—by military conquest."[22]

Such assumptions were not necessarily shared by other officials. Goldie's instructions to Lugard were to the effect that he should make treaties from the Niger across to Nikki, and then westward as far as the Gold Coast frontier, if possible, and that he was to remember above all "that diplomacy and not conquest is *the* object of the expedition westwards . . . the exercise of force cannot further your objects."[23] And when doubts accumulated about the administrative and negotiating practices of Goldie's Niger Company, a searching investigation was promptly ordered. It was entrusted to Major Macdonald, known to his contemporaries as a scrupulously honest person, who took it for granted that the purpose of British control in West Africa was to achieve social reform by means of dynamic economic development; that "imperial interests," properly understood, were the interests of the Africans, and that the wishes, ideas, and opinions of the African, whether he were chief or slave, were of great if not paramount importance in making such decisions as the conclusion of a treaty.[24] Macdonald thus went from town to

[22] Little, *The Mende of Sierra Leone*, p. 56.
[23] Flint, *Sir George Goldie*, p. 222. Compare Oliver, *Sir Harry Johnston*, p. 299, on Johnston's manner of negotiating in Nyasaland and elsewhere. Force was not used here, except in relations with the Yao, who had initiated hostilities. See *ibid.*, pp. 213ff., 238, 299, for the circumstances in which military operations were conducted. Missionaries in the Shire Province were at times severely critical of Johnston's resort to force, but as Oliver notes on p. 213, they failed to realize that the rough justice prevailing all over Africa at that time was a consequence of too little force and not too much—as, for example, when it came to the need to punish highway robberies. These administrative practices are beyond the purview of the present discussion.
[24] Flint, *Sir George Goldie*, pp. 129ff.; 136ff.

town in 1889, conducting a rudimentary kind of plebiscite among people in all walks of life, and carefully consulting independent or hostile opinion, missionaries and rival traders, both African and European.

In order to determine as unequivocally as possible whether a given accord was "genuine" or "fraudulent," he asked his informants whether they preferred rule by chartered company, colonial administration, or the status of a Foreign Office protectorate. A full discussion usually followed such consultations, during which the implications of each system were explained. The other major question to which Macdonald wanted answers related, of course, to the treaties themselves, in particular to the manner in which they had been negotiated.

A study of these and comparable findings shows that the issue of "validity" was made to relate to four themes in particular: the identity of the African principals and agents, the nature of the subject matter, the circumstances in which negotiations were conducted, and the forms in which accords were eventually comprehended.

In light of the then-prevailing European conviction that duly functioning governments everywhere, including Africa, could enter into binding accords, it became incumbent upon all who were seriously concerned with treaty relations—the negotiators as well as the critical investigators —to locate the seat of authority in each of the greatly diverse situations they encountered. As preceding chapters have already suggested,[25] this was in most instances a difficult task. In fact, in some regions it proved to be a wholly elusive undertaking. After a rather successful canoeing expedition to Ibo country, Johnston thus decided that it was "better not to pursue [his] explorations any farther but to make a judicious retreat,"[26] because the people with whom he came in contact were not only inveterate cannibals, but also, it seemed to him, inveterate anarchists, continually fighting among themselves.

Johnston's narrative of a particular encounter in Ededama on the Cross River contains the following additional information. After the Africans had dragged the canoe into shallow waters and transferred Johnston into a hut, where he found hanging over his head "a smoked human ham, black and bluish green" and about a hundred skulls, he explained to his captors that he would like to "make a book with them" to take home to the Woman Chief who had sent him. Having been duly returned to his canoe, Johnston then extracted a treaty form from his despatch box, whereupon, he writes, "three or four persons of prominence . . . crowded into the canoe to make crosses on it with my ink; but the proceedings were altogether too boisterous for serious treaty-making."[27] Rather dif-

[25] *Supra*, Chs. 16 and 19.
[26] Johnston, *The Story of My Life*, p. 195; also p. 194.
[27] *Ibid.*, p. 195.

ferent conditions had been encountered some decades earlier in Iboland, when the British were engaged in negotiating a treaty abolishing the slave trade with King Obi. Asked whether he had "power to make an agreement with the commissioner in the name of all your subjects," the King replied simply: "I am the King, What I say is law." To the commissioner's further query: "If the Queen makes a treaty with Obi, will his successors, on his death, abide by the same?" Obi responded: "They will do as I command. I want this palaver to be settled. I am tired of so much talking."[28] But elsewhere, again, officials might find that what looked like a stable government at first sight had a way of evaporating into a vacuum of authority, leaving no one to negotiate with.

In the vast majority of cases, however, the British were stymied and delayed because they had to dissect the tangled relations between actually functioning different but interlocking regimes, in what was on the surface a unified political establishment. In other words, the locus of effective legitimate power and the channels of dependence and command were not as easily discernible in an African situation as they were in customary Occidental conditions. In certain West African villages Macdonald thus found that as many as fifty treaties had been made with small groups because each claimed independence from the rest.[29] On the basis of the evidence gathered, he concluded that these agreements had been fairly arranged, giving the Niger Company complete sovereign rights over the lower Niger. On the Benue, in the domain of the Muslim emirates, by contrast, the situation had presented British negotiators with entirely different challenges, for here they had had to unravel the complex, quasi-feudal relationships that linked different monarchial states to each other and, at the head of the Fulani pyramid, to the Sultan of Sokoto and the Emir of Gandu. It goes without saying that Macdonald, too, had to examine these linkages before passing on the bona fide nature of the accords. For example, with regard to the thorny problem of Nupe's treaty with the Company he had to ascertain whether or not the emir regarded himself as tributary to Gandu before inquiring just what the Company was supposed to receive in return for its annual subsidy of 2,000 English pounds.[30]

Verdicts on the worth of the purposes pursued by contracting African

[28] See Captain William Allen and T.R.H. Thomson, *A Narrative of the Expedition Sent by Her Majesty's Government to the River Niger in 1841*, 2 vols. (London, 1848), Vol. I, 218, 222, 227, 228ff.

[29] Flint, *Sir George Goldie*, p. 138; also pp. 161ff.

[30] The case of the Nupe treaty carried special interest at the time because Germany claimed that Nupe was independent. Since Macdonald concluded that Nupe was tributary to Gandu, and that the Gandu treaty with the Company was bona fide, he found the Nupe agreement of 1885 justified. Other Company deals in the region, by contrast, he dismissed as fraudulent, and his evaluation of administrative practices was in many cases quite negative.

and British parties cannot be reached unequivocally for the following reasons. In the Occidental tradition, in which international law originated, treaties were morally neutral instruments. That is to say, they could be freely negotiated, but they could also be imposed upon weak or defeated states; they might serve the cause of war or that of peace, and their net effect was acceptable, objectively speaking, whether it was conducive to the spoliation or the betterment of a given nation's destiny. History, as understood in the West, lent support to these propositions in international law; for in a civilization that accommodated change, standards of morality, too, were known to shift from one epoch to the next. What one generation had acquiesced in as permissible behavior in international relations, another might come to view as reprehensible. Logic, then, suggested strongly that treaties could be time-transcendent or binding upon successive governments only if their purposes were not too closely controlled by ethical or sentimental considerations typical either of a given moment in time, or of the rules controlling personal relations within a morally and legally unified society.

Most, if not all, of the suppositions implicit in Occidental treaty making received further credence and support when it was realized with increasing poignancy that international relations were also intercultural relations, and that there were few values or moral certitudes that could serve as stable rallying points for dealings between representatives of culturally diverse regimes. Afro-European treaties that aimed at the establishment of peace, security, protection, the abolition of the slave trade, and the furtherance of legitimate commerce illustrate this vacuum of shared norms, even as they bear witness to Occidental expansionism in the nineteenth and early twentieth centuries. Critics of imperialism, living a hundred years later in a morally and politically greatly altered climate, have tended to view all of them as sordid, hypocritical deals inflicted by the mighty upon the meek. Such blanket condemnations are hardly tenable in the perspective either of history or of comparative politics. For example, although peace per se was not an overriding objective in either of the two culture realms, it yet carried rather different connotations, as preceding discussions have suggested. In inter-European relations it was accepted as an ideal and deemed capable of concretization; in inter-African relations, by contrast, it had not been conceptualized either as a value or a norm, if only because here war was accepted as the morally supreme reality. Likewise, whereas slavery and the slave trade had become odious to British public opinion, it did not evoke such strong negative reactions in ruling African circles. Negotiators could not, therefore, assume that there was an underlying accord on just what was legitimate or illegitimate about commerce. Furthermore, since they proceeded from different vantage points, they usually lacked a common scale of measuring what was fair or legitimate in settling matters of quid pro quo. For instance, in investigating the Niger Company's treaty making practices in certain regions, Major Macdonald found that only the non-Muslim peoples had genuinely accepted the Company's treaties, for they had assumed that the British would help them maintain their precarious footing on the Benue against the imperious Fulani. In other words, far from resenting "protection," they complained that the latter was not adequate. The Muslim emirs, meanwhile, had rather different motivations and concerns. One had accepted the treaty because he had seen Nupe grow so powerful through its intercourse with the Company that he wished to attain the same status. Another, who had not ceded any political rights, was so interested in trade that he reversed the pattern by signing a pact in which he promised to protect the Company.

In most instances in which political rights were claimed by the Company, Macdonald concluded that these had been improperly obtained, usually because the African interpreters had wrongly sworn that the emirs had fully understood the negotiations. In explaining his perjury during one of Macdonald's reexaminations, one of these intermediaries exposed the general dilemma faced by all of them as they tried to steer a course between a demanding European employer and an arbitrary African despot: "I cannot say that I made the king [i.e., the Emir of Bakundi] understand that he ceded his country to the Company. I made him understand that he gave his country to the Company for trading purposes, that nobody else could trade in the country without the permission of the Company, that all Europeans should be under the jurisdiction of the Company, but I was not aware that 'ceding' meant giving over the rights of government and I dare not have made this suggestion to him."[31] Similarly vexing problems of communication were faced by subsequent colonial administrators, notably the district officers, as Lugard observes in the following passage: "There is no need to emphasise how completely an officer who knows nothing of the native language is in the hands of his interpreter, who either from his imperfect knowledge of English, or by criminal intent, may wholly misrepresent what he was told to translate, or, on the other hand, may threaten an ignorant native that he will mislead the District Officer unless he is bribed. Incalculable harm has thus been done, and the interpreter becomes the real power."[32] Such a predicament, Lugard advises in the same discourse, can only be avoided if the officer himself is linguistically qualified to comprehend what the African negotiator really means—a level of expertise that few

[31] Flint, *Sir George Goldie*, p. 139; *ibid.*, pp. 140ff. for other relevant information; *supra*, Ch. 18 on the role of intermediaries.
[32] Lugard, *The Dual Mandate*, p. 133.

civil servants could reach, if only because most districts contained multiple language groups and lacked a lingua franca that had been reduced to writing. Given these circumstances, Lugard made the following suggestion to his contemporaries: "If the language used be some pagan dialect, and the officer can speak the more generally known language, it will be better for him to use it in speaking to his interpreter, for by so doing he ensures simplicity of diction, and the interpreter is more likely to understand his meaning than if he spoke in fluent English. If he uses English, he should employ the simplest phrases, and make the interpreter repeat what he is about to translate; and later, if possible, . . . he should verify his accuracy by employing a second interpreter."[33]

Misunderstandings of the nature of the subject matter certainly arose frequently for these and other reasons, but they were by no means the general rule. In fact, many Anglo-African encounters led to a nearly total meeting of minds, especially in regard to regulating commerce. The following excerpts from the record of negotiations with King Obi[34] illustrate such a case:

Commissioners – Does Obi make war to procure slaves?

Obi – When other chiefs quarrel with me and make war, I take all I can as slaves.

Commissioners – What articles of trade are best suited to your people, or what would you like to be brought to your country?

Obi – Cowries, cloth, muskets, powder, handkerchiefs, coral beads, hats—anything from the white man's country will please. . . .

Commissioners – Englishmen will bring everything to trade but rum or spirits, which are injurious.

After listening to an explanation, on the one hand, of the advantages offered by the English to the king and his subjects, which included the suggestion that the people might become prosperous if they would begin cultivating the ground, and on the other, of the disadvantages implicit in a prolongation of the slave trade, Obi agreed to discontinue the latter and make palm oil available—on condition, however, that the English bring suitable goods for traffic. To the commissioners' question as to whether he would be willing to stop boats carrying slaves through the waters and over the lands of his dominions, Obi replied: "yes, very willing; except those I do not see," adding the further proviso that the English must furnish him and his people with arms, as his compliance with their request would naturally involve him in war with his neighbors.

Even in premises such as these disparate value systems were clearly

---

[33] *Ibid.*, pp. 133ff.

[34] Allen and Thomson, *Narrative of Expedition to Niger*, Vol. I, 218ff., 222.

perceived by the negotiators. A conference with King Pepple of Bonny (Iboland), Anna Pepple (the head of the Anna Pepple House) and the latter's juju man and secretary, thus included the following exchange:

> Captain Craigie – How much would you lose if you gave up selling slaves for exportation?
> Anna Pepple – Too much—very much—we gain more by one slave ship than by five palm-oil ships.
> Hee Chee, Anna Pepple's Secretary – We depend entirely on selling slaves and palm-oil for our subsistence; suppose then the Slave Trade done away with, the consumption of palm-oil in England to stop, the crop to fail, or that the English ships did not come to Bonny, what are we to do? We must starve, as it is contrary to our religion to cultivate the ground.[35]

Similarly divisive scales of moral and material valuation were noted many decades later in Islamized East Africa, when Lugard was engaged in a treaty-making mission: "Slavery you say is bad," Zebehr Pasha told him in a conversation, "I agree that it is bad, but slave-labour is to the interior of Africa what steam-power is to your country."[36]

Since African and British understandings of what was materially advantageous or morally proper about the main subject matter of a given pact were not readily comparable, it was usually also difficult to agree on the worth of what appeared as "due consideration" (a concept borrowed from the language of English contract law), or "adequate compensation" (a major working principle employed by European treaty makers at, for example, the Congress of Vienna in 1815). Subsidies and presents are a case in point. Although such outlays were not common in nineteenth-century inter-European relations, they were taken for granted in Africa, and had traditionally been freely incurred in all imperial orbits and non-Western international systems, notably China, Persia, Rome, and Byzantium—that is to say, wherever states were not recognized as equals either in fact or in law. As long as subsidies were disbursed by British administrations in the form of annual stipends—and numerous arrangements of this kind have been cited in preceding pages—they could be viewed by contemporaries as prima facie legitimate, at least as long as they were meant to compensate African governments for forfeiting certain freedoms of action, or for rendering services, or to help "develop" a given territory in the way associated today with trusteeship and

---

[35] Hodgkin, *Nigerian Perspectives*, p. 237; Dike, *Trade and Politics in the Niger Delta*, ch. 4, on King Pepple and events relating to his rule.

[36] Lugard, *The Dual Mandate*, p. 365; p. 367 on slave labor in Zanzibar; and ch. 18, pp. 371ff. on the general subject of slavery in British Africa.

foreign aid.[37] The outright gift, on the other hand, was readily viewed in European circles as a bribe or other form of unprincipled exploitation.

Such distinctions were not common in African thought and practice, if only because the idea of the gift was so highly developed that it was apt to subsume "subsidies" and "bribes." Furthermore, since visions of political advantage were usually cast in short-term perspectives and conceived as increments to the status, power, and prestige of particular ruling personalities, rather than as benefits to an ongoing society,[38] compensation was not linked to mere prospects of political or economic development. In short, quid pro quo considerations were fraught with ambiguities on the English as on the African side.

A few general conclusions may be drawn in comparing English and African understandings of the identity of governmental authority and the legitimacy of negotiable subject matter. It appears, first, that negotiations aimed at binding accords were inevitably caught in a maze of culturally conditioned incongruities, and that this would have been so even if they had not taken place under the auspices of European imperialism. And it appears, second, that it was the bargaining process itself that was apt to provide the widest margin of mutual satisfaction and respect. However, this measure of success was normally registered only when the negotiating Englishmen were ready to accede to certain typically African views of the value of time, the niceties of speech, and the significance of ceremonial. The record here is, of course, uneven, as the following illustrations will show. In any case, in a curious reversal of the unequal power relations that had evoked all treaty negotiations in the first place, it was the African, not the European, disposition toward fashioning intersocietal accords that usually set the tone in the bargaining sessions. An early instance of this kind of adjustment is reported by James Barbot, who accompanied his brother on a trading voyage from London to New

[37] Compare with tribute payments, *supra*, pp. 192, 324. Johnston's program of concluding conditional treaties with certain independent tribes beyond Portuguese control was stymied for a while because it was difficult to persuade the Treasury to advance the expenses of the journey and the cost of the presents that would have to be given in exchange for the treaties. See Oliver, *Sir Harry Johnston*, pp. 151ff.; pp. 161–162 for an account of agreements with Jumbe, a renowned East African arms dealer and former slave trader, who accepted the offer of British protection, agreed to a generous definition of his territories, and was also persuaded to sign an accord with the African Lakes Company, by which he accepted a subsidy of three thousand rupees a year in lieu of the customs and taxes he had formerly levied on the ivory that passed through his dominions. For a controversial treaty between the Royal Niger Company and the King of Bussa (one of the states making up the so-called Borguan federation in West Africa), see Flint, *Sir George Goldie*, p. 161.

[38] See *supra*, Chs. 6 and 7.

Calabar in 1699. After noting the circumstances in which several conferences had been held with the King of Bonny, Barbot writes:

> We had again a long discourse with the King and *Pepprell* his brother, concerning the rates of our goods and his customs. This *Pepprell* being a sharp blade, and a mighty talking *Black*, perpetually making objections against something or other, and teasing us for this or that Dassy, or present, as well as for drams, etc., it were to be wish'd, that such a one as he were out of the way, to facilitate trade. . . .

> Thus, with much patience, all our matters were adjusted indifferently, after their way, who are not very scrupulous to find excuses or objections, for not keeping literally to any verbal contract; for they have not the art of reading and writing, and therefore we are forced to stand to their agreement, which often is no longer than they think fit to hold it themselves.[39]

The records of negotiations left by later traders, travelers, explorers, and missionaries—among them Matthews, Moffat, Livingstone, Barth, and Kingsley—confirm the impression that mutually advantageous accords were only within reach when the Europeans acquiesced in leisurely palavers, and did not confuse their African counterplayers with the demands implicit in literacy. Such restraints ceased to be controlling principles, however, whenever Occidental governments were more interested in regulating inter-European conflicts in Africa than in coming to terms with particular African regimes. This situation naturally invited resort to the European diplomatic method, which has traditionally relied heavily on writing as the surest way of approximating binding accords.[40] In Europe proper, the method was usually employed patiently, with a view to arriving at a genuine meeting of minds; but transferred to Africa it was severely compromised, since the agents of rival imperialist designs tended to assume that they could promote their causes best by producing written assents from local African sovereigns. The scramble to preempt spheres of influence or jurisdiction was thus often tantamount to a race for appropriate signatures. And in such circumstances, the activity of bargaining was at best mechanical, all the more so as it was not always easy to know whether the "right" person had signed, or whether the signatories were literate or illiterate. For example, inspections of the Royal Niger Company's records revealed that certain treaties concluded in the Brass region of Nigeria around 1890 were "deliberate forgeries," be-

[39] From the journal of Mr. James Barbot, *An Abstract of a Voyage to New Calabar River or Rio Real in the Year 1699*, as reproduced in Hodgkin, *Nigerian Perspectives*, p. 141.
[40] For a classic analysis, see Harold Nicolson, *The Evolution of Diplomatic Method* (London, 1954), pp. 48ff.

cause the chiefs alleged to have "signed" them by affixing crosses were supposed illiterate, whereas the crosses are unmistakably the work of a literate hand. Other Company agreements, by contrast, were not signed, even though the rulers knew how to write. In one particularly critical case a treaty was judged invalid when it was discovered that the name given in the text as that of the king was in fact that of one of his Muslim clerks. The advantage thus passed to the French, who came later and were able to extract a proper Arabic signature from this king.[41]

It goes without saying that zones of "restricted literacy"[42] presented special problems for treaty-making missions. Here, where writing was associated with magical qualities of both good and evil, men were most reluctant to write their names, or see their names written by others, or to allow such pieces of writing to pass beyond their control. In the face of such dire contingencies, the pagan Borguans (Nigeria) thought it best to evade European entreaties for signatures altogether. But if this proved impossible, recourse was had to Muslim scribes, who were held in awe as magicians of the written word. These intermediaries—so common opinion held—had the power to ward off the evil forces that might come into play if the writing were taken away by the Europeans; indeed, they might even prevent the king's name from actually appearing on the treaty.[43]

The use of writing in treaties with literate or semiliterate Muslims gave rise to different doubts when Sir Harry Johnston was compelled, in the late 1880s, to negotiate a truce with certain gangs of Arab slave raiders that had been insistent on terrorizing tribal life in the Lake region and on severing communications with the stations of the London Missionary Society. As described by Johnston, the proceedings of the signing ceremony were as follows:

> The Arab signed the treaty and we did likewise. Then the Arabs arose from their mats and walking around the half-circle of white men solemnly shook hands with each of us—their followers doing the same with our followers—and then returned to their mats, where they prayed aloud for a few minutes that Allah would help them to keep the treaty and that an unbroken peace should henceforth reign between them and the people of the Queen. After this milk was poured out by them and handed to us to drink, and we reciprocally filled and returned the cup to them. A bullock was killed—the loud sighs of its

[41] Flint, *Sir George Goldie*, pp. 162ff., 188ff.; p. 224, note 1 for Margery Perham's view of some of these controversial treaties.

[42] Compare *supra*, pp. 87ff., 316ff.

[43] Flint, *Sir George Goldie*, p. 223; cf. *supra*, p. 356 on the role of interpreters in causing confusion. See *supra*, Ch. 18 B for other instances of Muslim intermediaries.

death agony and the gurgling of its spurting veins coming as a curious second to the Arab's prayers and being the only sound which accompanied the intoning of their guttural Arabic phrases, and its meat was divided up among the wild-looking savages who represented the bodyguards of the White Men and Arabs. Then with the sweetest compliments and most graceful phrases which the Swahili tongue can frame the Arabs bade us adieu, and we severally returned to our towns, where for two days, amid a continual firing of guns, feasting and dancing was kept up. Three days after the signing of the peace the Arabs paid me a ceremonial visit at Karonga's. We ate together, exchanged presents and polite but vapid compliments, and afterwards I called together all the native chiefs, who had suffered by the war, and had the treaty translated and read to them in the Arabs' presence. Then Mlozi, the chief Arab, addressed a few words to them, telling them they might return to their villages without fear, as the Arabs would never again attack the friends of the Englishmen. On each side a spear was broken as a sign that the war was over, and the broken fragments were exchanged. All the minor leaders of the native soldiery then stepped forward and shook hands, and the day ended in a riot of noisy friendship which was most fatiguing.[44]

Records such as these favor the conclusion that the relation between writing and the concept of agreement was bound to be the subject of misunderstanding and abuse. Anticipated by Barth in the course of his explorations and negotiations in Islamized Central Africa,[45] it was restated with admirable lucidity by Lugard after he had had occasion to reflect on his varied experiences in East Africa. In defining Britain's obligations to the Africans, he writes that "these are in respect of treaties made in the country, as well as verbal assurances given that the British had come to stay, and would not desert the tribes who declared friendship with them."[46] However, and by way of explicit comment on his dealings with Kamba[47] and Kikuyu chiefs, he notes:

Though I was provided with "treaty forms," I did not see my way to using them: I could not honourably pledge the Company's protection to distant tribes, whom they had no means whatever of protecting from their enemies. . . . Secondly, the nature of written compact was wholly beyond the comprehension of these savage tribes. The most solemn form of compact for friendship that exists among them is that

[44] Johnston to Salisbury from Karonga's 26.x.89, Foreign Office Archives, London, as quoted in Oliver, *Sir Harry Johnston*, p. 164.

[45] See *supra*, pp. 333ff.

[46] *The Rise of Our East African Empire*, Vol. II, 579.

[47] *Ibid.*, Vol. I, 319 on such pacts with the Wakamba; pp. 369–370 on Chief Wakoli of Usoga and others.

known as "blood brotherhood," and this I therefore adopted as suited at once to their comprehension, and as enabling me to say just as much, and no more, as seemed a fair and honest bargain. I then reduced to writing our mutual undertakings, and the treaty was witnessed by my comrades, and the chiefs made their marks. . . . More binding treaties could not have been executed in savage Africa.[48]

Lugard found that each tribe had its own method of making blood brotherhood, but that the following ceremonial was common:

We sit down cross-legged on mats and skins, and each of us cuts our forearm till the blood flows; the arms are then rubbed together to mix the blood, and two small pieces of meat are supposed to be touched with the blood; he eats the piece which has my blood on it off the palm of my right hand, and I eat the piece which has his blood on it from his palm. Sometimes salt or a coffee-berry is substituted for the meat. Sometimes incision is made elsewhere than on the arm. The headman of the chief takes his weapons of war—his spear, and sword and bow —and holding them over his head makes a long speech, praising the warrior's valour and exploits, and swearing that henceforward we are brothers. . . . In like manner, when the chief's oath is done, my interpreter holds my rifle over my head and repeats what I tell him to say.[49]

These reciprocal pledges were then reduced to writing, with the chief making his mark upon the treaty after having been told that this was the European method of confirmation, and with Lugard's aides witnessing the signing. The ceremony was always made as public as possible: the leading men of the district attended, and in some cases neighboring chiefs from a great distance were also present. In fact, the latter would usually include themselves in the contract, one chief being chosen to go through the ceremony for all.

Treaty-making in Uganda was altogether different, Lugard explains, for here "the people mostly fully understand the nature of a written contract, and consider nothing as absolutely final and binding unless put on paper. They are very clever and farseeing, and every clause of the treaty made was discussed for several days among themselves before it was presented in baraza for the signature of the king and chiefs."[50] In Toro, by

[48] *Ibid.*, Vol. I, 329–330, for this reference and treaties with Kikuyu chiefs in particular.
[49] *Ibid.*, pp. 330–331.
[50] *Ibid.*, Vol. II, 580; pp. 33–40 for detailed descriptions of some proceedings, the use of interpreters, and awareness of multiple languages. Lugard draws special attention to the insistent questioning in which the Baganda representatives engaged when it came to discussing Buganda's tribute relationships with other kingdoms.

contrast, he found it was the unwritten word that bore the deepest signification.[51]

Most of Britain's colonial administrators discriminated carefully between literate and nonliterate, Muslim and native African customs when they initiated bargaining procedures. Yet the fact remained that treaties were tools that effected the loss or diminution of local independence, precarious as the latter had always been in pre-European days.[52] In the important case of Uganda, which may be said to have engaged the best of these diplomatic efforts, the rulers of the Baganda had thus already signed away ultimate control over their subjects and neighbors when Johnston entered upon the scene to complete, in due course, one of his most complex and successful treaty-making missions.

Johnston's assignment called for making the British Protectorate in East Africa self-supporting at the earliest possible date. He himself was convinced that self-government should be the ultimate goal, that the Bantu-speaking Africans were particularly talented to carry through modernization programs, and that the Kingdom of Uganda was pivotal in all such policies. Given these contexts and assumptions, Johnston had to plan to restructure intertribal relations with a view to creating a durable regional order; redistribute and define the powers of government in each of the major component societies so as to lay the foundations for self-rule, and assure the political evolution of the Protectorate as a whole; and, lastly, to isolate the factors that would make for economic growth. The blueprints that emerged in response to each of these challenges centered on Buganda for a variety of reasons. It was economically the most advanced province; the Kabaka's monarchical powers and his relations with other chiefs were clearly delimited; Baganda government extended over about a million people; the ruling class was already partly Westernized; the military forces were adequate to assure local security; and, above all, the kingdom was acknowledged by others in the region as the most prestigious.[53] These considerations persuaded Johnston that a special agreement with the Kingdom of Uganda was indispensable if

[51] See Alfred R. Tucker, Bishop of Uganda, *Eighteen Years in Uganda and East Africa*, 2 vols. (London, 1908), Vol. II, 40ff.; Johnston, *The Story of My Life*, pp. 340ff., on Toro affairs; and Sir Harry Johnston, *The Uganda Protectorate*, 2 vols. (London, 1902), Vol. I, 209ff., 228ff. on the histories of Toro, Bunyoro, Ankole, and Buganda as well as on their intricate mutual relationships.

[52] After tracing Johnston's arduous treaty-making journey of 1889–1890 in the Nyasa-Tanganyika area, Oliver observes that "when the Protectorate was later established, it was done by proclamation without reference to the treaties, and it applied equally to those groups which had signed and to those which had not." *Sir Harry Johnston*, p. 160.

[53] Johnston was to describe the Baganda in his final report as "the Japanese of the Dark Continent, the most civilized, charming, kindly, tactful and courteous of black peoples." See Oliver, *Sir Harry Johnston*, p. 331. *Ibid.*, pp. 297ff., 317ff. for some of the considerations that went into planning the negotiations.

the British Protectorate over the East African region was to be maintained and justified.

The negotiations to this effect lasted two and a half months and culminated in a treaty (1900) that has been described as "the most complex and far-reaching Agreement ever concluded between an African people and an occupying European power."[54] The main African representatives in the deliberations were the three regents, among them Apolo Kagwa, representing the young king, and the leading chiefs of Uganda. All proved to be hard and sagacious bargainers, whom Johnston had to meet and remeet on their objections, counterproposals, amendments, and criticisms of translations. The proceedings, then, were often stalled by misunderstandings and discords, and on these occasions Johnston usually took the advice of the missionaries, who acted tirelessly as interpreters and mediators between the British administration and "their favourite African converts."[55] The major stumbling block proved to be the land question. Apart from having asked for cessions, especially of waste and forested land, the British were interested in individualizing land tenure— a sharp break with customary land law, but one that was viewed by Johnston as absolutely necessary if economic development was to take place. The representatives of the Kabaka naturally demurred, not so much on account of the land itself and its passing out of their hands, as because of the effect this loss of control would have on their dependents. For what Johnston had not realized until Bishop Tucker and others explained it, was the fact that power over land was the supreme attribute of chieftainship in Baganda eyes. Without it there could be no patron/ client relationship between chief and peasant. The British proposals were thereupon drastically revised. Other rounds of personal negotiations with the regents and principal chiefs had to be held before the draft could be translated into Luganda at the Anglican Mission. Thereupon a full conference of chiefs, supported by their missionary advisors, met in Johnston's house at Entebbe to discuss final amendments, and several weeks

[54] Oliver, *Sir Harry Johnston*, p. 299.

[55] Ibid., p. 301. In response to contemporary criticism that missionaries meddled in politics, Bishop Tucker writes the following: "The Missionaries have never disguised the fact that they did advise their native friends and adherents. In my opinion it would have been a grave dereliction of duty had they refrained from doing so." And such interference, he claims, becomes an absolute necessity in circumstances like the following: "One day a drum-beat is heard—a caravan arrives at the head of which is an Englishman. The natives go to see him. They have a long interview with him at which the conversation is carried on through an interpreter. The result is that the Baganda turn to the Mission for advice. 'Here is a man,' they say, 'who says he is an Englishman—is it so?' The answer is 'Yes!' 'He also says that he represents a great company—is that true?' 'Yes!' 'He wants us to sign a treaty with him—we cannot understand it. What shall we do?' 'Will you explain it to us and advise us what to do?' The answer is 'Certainly we will'—and they do so." See Tucker, *Eighteen Years in Uganda and East Africa*, Vol. I, pp. 125ff.

later, after the treaty had been printed and translated in its final form, the signing could be made a great occasion at Kampala.[56]

This accord had the effect of transforming the territorial and political organization of the Protectorate. In return for renouncing their claims to tribute from adjoining tribes, and agreeing to have Buganda rank as a province whose status was equal to that of any province in the Protectorate, the Baganda obtained a formal definition of their boundaries and an extension of their jurisdiction over certain areas of Bunyoro and Ankole, their traditional rivals in the land. Eventually the latter, too, were persuaded to sign similar agreements, as was Toro. But the negotiations with these societies and with the Masai and the Nandi appear to have been fraught with suspicions on the part of the African representatives, who were either more opposed to European penetration than Buganda, or resentful of the preferential role assigned to the latter.[57]

Within Buganda itself, which had now doubled in size, the treaty provided for a division of fiscal and legal responsibilities between Protectorate agencies, on the one hand, and different native authorities, on the other. Most importantly in the eyes of contemporary observers, especially Johnston himself, it had the effect of putting an end to those absolute monarchical powers in behalf of which previous Kabakas had been free to resort to wholesale human sacrifices, mutilations, and other cruel punishments; and of initiating reforms in matters of land tenure that— according to Johnston—"did more than anything else to conciliate suspicious native tribes and chiefs and bring about a friendly adhesion to the

[56] The sequence of events in these protracted negotiations has been admirably reconstructed by Oliver, *Sir Harry Johnston*, pp. 303ff. See Johnston, *The Story of My Life*, p. 340, for an appreciation of Tucker's knowledge of Luganda and other tribal tongues, and of his general assistance in the negotiations. Johnston was at one with Tucker in his conviction that Luganda, the dominant native language, was the key to the minds of two-thirds of the population, and that British officials should bother to learn it. See Tucker, *Eighteen Years in Uganda and East Africa*, Vol. II, 40, for another case (in Toro) in which an administering officer acknowledged that through his ignorance of the language he had been imposed upon by his interpreter. On the role of missionaries as partisan advocates of Africans, see also Flint, *Sir George Goldie*, p. 132.

[57] Johnston, *The Story of My Life*, pp. 340ff. Johnston, *The Uganda Protectorate*, Vol. I, 245, for the reasons for the continuous hostility of the Nandi. With regard to these people, see also Elspeth Huxley, *White Man's Country; Lord Delamere and the Making of Kenya*, 2 vols. (London 1935, new ed. 1953), Vol. I, 134ff.; pp. 155ff. on the circumstances in which a treaty was concluded and signed by the Laibon or chief medicine man on behalf of all the clans, and by Sir Donald Stewart for the British. The account covers a private palaver between Lord Delamere and a group of Nandi, during which the latter—generally known in the region for their treachery—arrived amicably with some honey by way of making amends for acts of cattle poaching. But upon inspection the honey was found to contain poison. On the Laibon, the Nandi in general, and their reputation in intertribal relations see *supra*, pp. 270ff.

theory of native taxation."[58] In fact, these bold economic innovations anticipated by fifty-five years some of the principal recommendations made by the East Africa Royal Commission of 1953–1955, thus providing the original auspices not only for Uganda's development within the British Empire, but also for the country's eventual independence as a nation state.

Johnston's commitment to the cause of economic development as the sine qua non of orderly social and political progress within society, and his trust in binding written accords as the indispensable assurance of peace in external relations, thus seemed as valid in mid-twentieth century, when imperial controls were slackening, as in the early 1920s, when the major architect of British Uganda took occasion to reminisce as follows:

> One feels at this distance of time that to readers of a new generation this treaty-making in Africa must seem a farce. . . . But in Central or West Africa, though the natives might not be able to read and write, they had a very clear idea what resulted from making a treaty. They memorized the terms though they could not read. If one proceeded to interfere in the conditions of a tribe without the treaty right to do so, there was sure to be a fight. On the other hand, the fidelity with which any large native community abode by the conditions of an agreement, even when it meant in the vicissitudes of the time temporary defeat and expulsion from the home-land, touched me to the quick. I am sure we were right, preparatory to detailed and definite rule, to consult with the different native tribes and rulers as to whether they wished us to preside over their affairs in northern Zambezia and Nyasaland. For several years in some cases, where a ruling chief or a tribe declined to make a treaty we abstained from intervention in their domestic concerns, only enjoining on them that they must not transgress on the rights of neighboring states who had entered into treaty relations with the British Empire.[59]

Developments in post-independence Uganda, by contrast, have not sustained Sir Harry Johnston's expectations. Indeed, in the perspective of the 1960s and 1970s, it is possible to link the Johnston Treaty to the series of upheavals and revolutions that gradually effected the dismantling of the Kabakaship, the eclipse of the Baganda, the return to traditional patterns of authoritarian rule, the revival of xenophobia, and the

---

[58] Johnston, *The Uganda Protectorate*, Vol. I, 279; also pp. 251ff.

[59] *The Story of My Life*, p. 258; see *The Uganda Protectorate*, Vol. I, ch. 7, for other statements justifying Britain's colonial administration, and ch. 9 on his program of economic development.

resumption of international and intertribal strife. Uganda in 1973 recalled Bishop Tucker's image of the land in 1890: "a volcano on the verge of eruption."[60] And beyond that, it brings back to mind the long pre- European past, in which mutually hostile personalities and societies related to each other quite reliably in the firm expectation of continuous conflict rather than of innovating contracts aimed at peace and progress.

[60] *Eighteen Years in Uganda and East Africa*, Vol. I, 100. The bishop, who arrived in the country after Lugard had embarked upon his treaty-making mission in 1890, dwells at length on the treaties of 1890 and 1892, and on the conflicts and intrigues that rent relations between the Anglican mission and the French priests. See *ibid.*, pp. 172ff. for Tucker's vindication of Lugard's mission. As the "prime mover," his position was extremely difficult, Tucker notes, for he had to reconcile conflicting interests; compose the jealousies of the various parties in the state; uphold the authority of the Company; see that justice was done as between man and man, party and party; and above everything to preserve the peace of the country.

CONFLICT AND CONCILIATION:
SOME CONCLUDING
PERSPECTIVES

In drawing the contours of their colonies, European governments laid the foundations for Africa's modern states; and in introducing literacy and adjunct skills of communication and administration, they induced revolutionary changes in the ancient orders of the societies they ruled. The interplay between the two cultures has been continuous ever since, and hard dichotomous lines of separation cannot be drawn today. However, a synoptic view of social, political, and intellectual developments in postindependence Africa south of the Sahara[1] supports the conviction eloquently expressed by spokesmen for the new states,[2] namely, that indigenous cultural traditions are resurgent everywhere, whereas European influences are in eclipse.

Thus it appears that literacy has not appreciably modified the basic nonliterate thoughtways, norms, and values of the vast majority of Africans. Indeed, sensitive observers of the scene report that writing is readily reduced to magic, and that literacy can be achieved without dramatically altering traditional beliefs. The situation is different, of course, in the restricted strata of the intellectual elites, where an acute awareness of the conflict between the two disparate cultural traditions has stimulated a quickening of creativity for which few parallels can be found in the modern world. But it cannot be said that Africa's talented modern writers have had an appreciable impact on the evolution of their native civilization. Many of them work outside their native lands and are unable, for reasons of geographic as well as intellectual distance, to communicate with their illiterate or semiliterate compatriots. More importantly, perhaps, interactions with their contemporaries in the political elites are now fainter in most states than they were in the early years of self-government and independence.

This disjunction or alienation in the ranks of leadership is due to several factors. Most importantly, the ruling cadres today are preoccupied with the practical need to solidify their governments by properly gauging local levels of tolerance for authoritarian rule, rather than with the intellectual challenge of refining the complex syntheses between indigenous and European orientations to social order bequeathed to them by their predecessors. It is thus clearer today than it may have been a few decades ago that political development, as this term is commonly understood in modern political science, is not likely to conduce to a significant align-

[1] *Supra*, Part II.   [2] *Supra*, Ch. 4.

ment of African and Occidental value systems. And this, again, means either that much of the authentically African matter is not being accommodated adequately by Western theories and typologies; or, conversely, that many of the latter are strained to the breaking point when attempts to unify unequal vocabularies of norms are pushed too far.

The foregoing study of conflict and its management on the planes of biography, thought, society, and the wider environment of regional and international relations was deliberately conducted along interdisciplinary lines in order to illustrate the wide range of outstanding problems with which theorists and practitioners in African and Western societies must contend. Each of the book's component sections concludes with findings that would forfeit their specificity were they to receive broad summary treatment here. A review of the chapters justifies the following general remarks, however.

Africans are more at ease with conflict in its multiple manifestations than their contemporaries in Europe and the United States. Furthermore, they tend to view it positively, as a source of major values and as a determining or integrative factor in life, while denizens of the West ascribe essentially negative aspects to its incidence.[3] Finally, whereas conflict and accord, aggression and defence, and war and peace, are commonly perceived as pairs of opposites in Occidental societies, they are not experienced as mutually exclusive phenomena in Africa. There, it appears, these two conditions slide into each other. They thus resist the kind of definition or decision favored in the West, dissolving instead into indeterminacy, and advancing the primacy of process rather than of resolution.

These realities have important implications for theory, notably as it bears on international relations. For example, since conflict is traditionally accepted in Africa as ongoing or latent in social and interstate affairs, negotiations, too, are apt to be continuous or protracted[4]—an enmeshment of activities which explains, incidentally, why stamina in the face of feuds and wars is matched by patience when it comes to conciliatory consultations. This interpenetration of activities and dispositions also accounts, however, for the fact that the actual course of fighting or of bargaining is apt to be unpredictable. For not only are the identities and policies of the protagonists subject to often drastic changes, as pre-

[3] But see Gould and Barkun, *International Law and the Social Sciences*, pp. 190–191, where the proposition is advanced that conflict is a producer of norms, at least in its aftermath.

[4] For an early instance of this fusionist trend, see Vansina, *Kingdoms of the Savanna*, p. 140, where the author notes, after tracing the causes of disorder in seventeenth-century Kongo, that "The Duke of Mbamba and his successor had been in perpetual rebellion, and Alvare had been able to maintain his position only by continual negotiations."

ceding discussions of ancient and modern systems of rule have indicated, but the basic goals or causes of contention are bound to be fluid, too. Shifts in position are, therefore, normal; bargaining without fixed price does not have unnerving effects, and accords between states or governments are apt to be assigned temporary rather than lasting validity.

Confidence in the stabilizing effects of structure, then, cannot be presumed in Africa. The treaty, for example, which instills such trust in the West because it embodies shared values, and because it carries the assumption that contracting parties are likely to have continuing identities, cannot evoke similar responses in Africa. Not only has it been discredited there by certain colonial usages, but, more importantly, it has no organic relationship to regionally dominant norms and values. Similar incongruities are encountered in conflict settlement by adjudication and negotiation.[5] For here, too, it is apparent that modern Occidental arrangements for the settlement or prevention of interstate disputes do not adequately encompass the vast areas of political insecurity and protracted conflict, both violent and nonviolent, in which generations of Africans have been accustomed to dwell with relative ease.

The discrepancies between these two patterns of statecraft lend support to several general conclusions in the field of world politics. They suggest strongly that the official terminology of international relations is now insufficient or too imprecise to assure reliable communications between actually functioning political organisms. They also reenforce the view that found expression in a recent text, namely, that systematic efforts to update theory will be impeded if the stress continues to be placed on terms such as war, peace, neutrality, and diplomacy, which come to us from a bygone era; and if new words, as, for example, internal war, psychological war, or subversion are not carefully defined and integrated.[6]

These ambiguities in the relationship between words and facts are confounded by certain stubborn Occidental habits when it comes to building international theory. Unlike the field of local or national politics, in which theory is generally in unison with activity, "international theory (at least in its chief embodiment as international law) sings a kind of descant over against the movement of diplomacy."[7] That is to say, it seems to follow an inverse movement to that of international politics. For when diplomacy is violent and unscrupulous, international law is somehow allowed to soar into the lofty but uncharted regions of natural law

[5] Compare *supra*, Ch. 3 on the Charter of the OAU and related issues.

[6] Sprout and Sprout, *Toward a Politics of the Planet Earth*, p. 136.

[7] Martin Wight, "Why Is There No International Theory?" in Herbert Butterfield and Martin Wight, eds., *Diplomatic Investigations; Essays in the Theory of International Politics* (Cambridge, Mass., 1968), p. 29.

and justice. By contrast, when diplomacy acquires a certain habit of co-operation, "international law crawls in the mud of legal positivism."[8] Inquiries as to just why there was no international theory that could be viewed consonant with the realities of international politics thus persuaded the late Martin Wight, who has influenced some of these conclusions, that the language of political theory and law should not be used for theorizing about international statecraft. Furthermore, and in extension of this argument, it ought to be borne in mind that legal terms and concepts are ideal tools for the analysis of local politics in the West, but that they fail to render non-Western norms and values in their authenticity. Yet the latter will have to be recovered from the multifarious records of the present and the past, if the gap between thought and life is to be narrowed. The present study of conflict was conducted with these purposes in mind.

[8] *Ibid.*, p. 29.

INDEX OF ETHNIC AND
LINGUISTIC GROUPS MENTIONED
IN THE TEXT

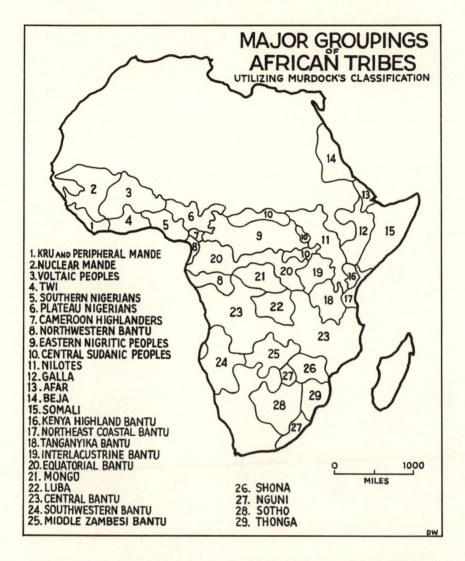

MAJOR GROUPINGS
OF
AFRICAN TRIBES
UTILIZING MURDOCK'S CLASSIFICATION

1. KRU AND PERIPHERAL MANDE
2. NUCLEAR MANDE
3. VOLTAIC PEOPLES
4. TWI
5. SOUTHERN NIGERIANS
6. PLATEAU NIGERIANS
7. CAMEROON HIGHLANDERS
8. NORTHWESTERN BANTU
9. EASTERN NIGRITIC PEOPLES
10. CENTRAL SUDANIC PEOPLES
11. NILOTES
12. GALLA
13. AFAR
14. BEJA
15. SOMALI
16. KENYA HIGHLAND BANTU
17. NORTHEAST COASTAL BANTU
18. TANGANYIKA BANTU
19. INTERLACUSTRINE BANTU
20. EQUATORIAL BANTU
21. MONGO
22. LUBA
23. CENTRAL BANTU
24. SOUTHWESTERN BANTU
25. MIDDLE ZAMBESI BANTU

26. SHONA
27. NGUNI
28. SOTHO
29. THONGA

1000
MILES

DW

MAJOR GROUPINGS OF AFRICAN TRIBES USING MURDOCK'S CLASSIFICATION
Map drawn by Douglas Waugh from information in George Peter Murdock,
Africa, Its Peoples and Their Culture History (London, New York
and Toronto, 1959).

INDEX OF ETHNIC AND LINGUISTIC
GROUPS MENTIONED IN THE TEXT

All tribal and ethnic/linguistic groups mentioned in the text have been indexed. In the indexing, the classification developed by C. P. Murdock in *Africa, Its Peoples and Their Culture History* (New York, 1959) has been used. This provides both a general scheme of identifying African peoples, and a specialized way of distinguishing major ethnic and/or linguistic groupings. Wherever practical, the numerical size of the tribal group has been indicated. When this figure is followed by an asterisk (*), it includes a varying number of closely related tribes or subtribes. For example, the EWE constitute one of six groups within the Ewe Cluster, and the latter, again, is one of four clusters in the broader classification Twi. Thus it is the EWE group and not the Ewe Cluster that embraces the Anglo, Glidye, Ho, and numerous other closely related subtribes, giving a total of 700,000.

Location is indicated in two ways. The map shows the major groupings according to Murdock. However, since this classification is in most instances too broad to be helpful to the reader (as, for example, in the case of "the Central Bantu," where "23" stretches across Africa from west to east), the attempt is also made to point out the particular people's major geographic concentration. This purpose has been served by using the section on "Tribes" in *Meyer's Handbuch Ueber Afrika* (Mannheim, 1969) as a supplementary reference.

The index lists all forms of tribal names given in the text—that is, it includes synonymous names as well as different spellings. However, all information is listed under the tribal name used by Murdock in order to facilitate references to the latter's work. For example, the entry "GONJE" is followed by "see GUANG." Likewise, since Murdock usually gives Bantu names in their simplest forms, listings under, for example, "AKAMBA" or "WAKAMBA" are deferred to "KAMBA" as the main entry But all prefixes found in the text also appear in the index. The entry "MATABELE"—to give but one illustration—is then followed by "see NDEBELE."

Tribe	Murdock Classification	Major Ethnic and/or Linguistic Grouping	Number (in thousands)	Location
ACHOLI	Nilotes	Luo Cluster	250	(11) Northern Uganda
ADAMAWA	Fulani	Fulanis are classified by principal areas of concentration		Adamawa (Nigeria)
AKAMBA	see KAMBA			
AKAN	Twi	Linguistic subdivision of Twi	60°	(4) Two-thirds of entire Twi Province (20)
AMBA	Equatorial Bantu	No division in Clusters, as only slight cultural tribal differences		
AMHARA	Central Ethiopians	One of 7 ethnic groups	3,000	Ethiopia (Shoa, Gojjam, Lasta, etc.)
ANANG	Southern Nigerians	Bantoid Cluster (with Ibibio, etc.)	> 1,000°	(5)
ANTAISAKA	Malagasy	One of 11 major groups	420°	Madagascar east coast
ANUAK	Prenilotes		40	Basin of White and Blue Nile south of Khartoum
ARUSHA	Nilotes	Masai Cluster	62	(11) Northern Tanganyika
ASHANTI	Twi	Akan Cluster	700°	(4) Ghana, Ashanti Province
AZANDE	Eastern Nigritic Peoples	Equatorial Cluster	750°	(9) Sudan (Bahr el Ghazal)
AZANIANS	Ancient Azanians	Megalithic Cushites		Coast of Kenya, Somalia, and Tanganyika
BABEMBA	see BEMBA			
BAGA	Senegambians	One of 12 principal tribal divisions	45°	Senegal—strip of Atlantic seaboard
BAGANDA	see GANDA			
BAGO	see BAGA			
BAKAMBA	see KAMBA			
BAKOUSSOU	see KUSU			
BAMBARA	Nuclear Mande	One of 12 major groups	1,000°	(2) Mali, but also in neighboring countries to east and south
BAMBUNDA	see BUNDA			
BAMOUM	see MUM			
BANTU	Divided by Murdock into: Cameroon Highlanders; Northwestern Bantu; Equatorial Bantu; Mongo and Luba; Central Bantu; Northeastern Coastal Bantu; Kenya Highland Bantu; Interlacustrine Bantu; Tanganyika Bantu; Middle Zambesi Bantu; Southwestern Bantu; Shona and Thonga; Nguni; Sotho.			
BAPENDE	see PENDE			
BARA	Malagasy	One of 11 major groups	180	Madagascar, plains of west coast
BARGU	Voltaic Peoples	Bargu Cluster	150	(3) Southeastern Upper Volta and northern Dahomey
BARIBA	see BARGU			
BAROTSE	see LOZI			
BASOGA	see SOGA			
BATETELA	see TETELA			
BAULE	Twi	Akan Cluster	400°	(4) Ivory Coast

Name	Classification	Notes	Population	Location
BAVILI	see VILI			
BECHUANA	see TSWANA			
BELLA	see BELLA			
BELLA	Under 'Berber' in Murdock (also under 'Tuareg')	Serve as serfs to Tuaregs; are of negroid stock		Sahel, southern Sahara
BEMBA	Central Bantu	Bemba Cluster	150	(23) Northern Rhodesia; adjacent Belgian Congo
BENI	see EDO			
BERBER	Berbers	Murdock divides into 29 groups		North Africa, Sahara
BOTSWANA	see TSWANA			
BOZO	Nuclear Mande	One of 12 major groups	30	The Niger and Bani Rivers, Mali (2)
BRONG	Twi	Akan Cluster		(4)
BULU	Equatorial Bantu	Closely related to Fang	75	Southern Cameroon (20)
BUNDA	Central Bantu	Kasai Cluster		(23) On or near Kasai tributary to Congo River
BUNYORO	see NYORO			
BUSHONGO	see KUBA			
BUSHMEN	Bushmen	Fifteen main tribal groups	55	Southwest Africa, Kalahari
BWAKA	Eastern Nigritic Peoples	Equatorial Cluster	180 (1940)	(9) Ground Ubangi River, Central African Republic, Zaire
CHEWA	Central Bantu	Maravi Cluster	650°	(23) Malawi, Lower Zambesi River
CREOLE		Descendants of settlers and liberated Africans		Sierra Leone, especially Freetown and larger towns
DAGARI	Voltaic Peoples	Grusi Cluster	140°	(3) Upper Volta, Black Volta area
DAGOMBA	Voltaic Peoples	Mole Cluster	175°	(3) Upper Volta
DAHOMEANS	see FON			
DAN	Peripheral Mande	Mande Tribes	150°	(1) Ivory Coast
DINKA	Nilotes	Dinka Cluster	500°	(11) Southern Sudan
DIULA	Voltaic Peoples	Intrusive people; probably of Soninke origin	160	(3) Upper Volta
DOGON	Voltaic Peoples	Hebe Cluster	250	(3) Bandiagara, Mali
DYULA	see DIULA			
EDO	Southern Nigerians	Central Cluster	400°	(5)
EGBA	Southern Nigerians	Yoruba Cluster	550°	(5)
EWE	Twi	Ewe Cluster	700°	(4) East Coast, Ghana; Coastal Togo and Dahomey
FALASHA	Central Ethiopians	Agaw stock (Ullendorff)	20	Northern Ethiopia, Begemder, Semien
FAN	see FANG			
FANG	Equatorial Bantu		700°	(20) Gabon
FANTE	see FANTI			
FANTI	Twi	Akan Cluster	> 200	(4) Southern Ghana
FON	Twi	Ewe Cluster	nearly 1,000°	(4) Dahomey

Tribe	Murdock Classification	Major Ethnic and/or Linguistic Grouping	Number (in thousands)	Location
FULANI	Fulani	Classified by 9 principal areas of concentration	> 5,000	Cameroon 275,000; Dahomey and Togo 115,000; former French Eq. Africa 50,000; Guinea 880,000; Niger 275,000; Mali 460,000; Upper Volta 240,000; Mauritania 70,000; North. Nigeria 2,025,000; Portuguese Guinea 110,000; Senegal 510,000; Sierra Leone and Gambia 20,000
FULBE	see FULANI			
GA	Twi	Ewe Cluster		(4) Southern Ghana
GALLA	Galla	Eastern Cushitic speech		(12) Ethiopia
GANDA	Interlacustrine Bantu	Uganda Cluster	1,000	(19) Southern half of Uganda
GILI	Southern Nigerians	Idoma Cluster	7	(5) Nigeria, between Mada and Benue Rivers
GILLI	see GILI			
GLIDYE-EWE	see EWE			
GONJA	see GUANG			
GUANG	Twi	Akan Cluster	50	(4) Ghana, between Volta and Oti Rivers
GURAGE	Central Ethiopians	Sidama origin (Ullendorff)	350	Ethiopia, southwest of Addis Ababa
GURACHE	see GURAGE			
GURO	Peripheral Mande	Mande Tribes	115°	(1) Ivory Coast
HAUSA	Negroes of the Sudan Fringe	Hausa Province Hamitic stock (Hausa branch of the Chadic subfamily) (Murdock)	5,000°	Northern Nigeria, southern Niger
HIMA	Interlacustrine Bantu	Descendants of Nilotes who infiltrated Bantu tribes of Uganda, now Bantu-speaking		(19) Uganda
HOVA	see MERINA			
HURUTSHE	Sotho			(28) Union of South Africa, Zeerust and Rustenburg districts
IBADAN	see YORUBA			
IBIBIO	Southern Nigerians	Bantoid Cluster	> 1,000°	(5) Nigeria, Calabar Coast
IBO	Southern Nigerians	Central Cluster Ibo branch Kwa linguistic subfamily	4,000°	(5) Southern Nigeria, east of Niger River
IDOMA	Southern Nigerians	Idoma Cluster	250°	(5) Eastern Nigeria, between Benue and Niger Rivers
IFE	Southern Nigerians	Yoruba Cluster	170°	(5) Southwest Nigeria, around Ife
IGBO	Southern Nigerians	Bantoid Cluster	550°	(5)
IJEBU	Southern Nigerians	Yoruba Cluster	40°	(5) Nigeria, north of Lagos
ILA	Middle Zambezi Bantu	One of 12 tribal groups		(25) Zambia, middle Kafue River
IMBANGALA	see MBANGALA			
IMERINA	see MERINA			
JAGA		Origin disputed; for one group see YAKA		
JALOFF	see WOLOF			
JUKUN	Plateau Nigerians	Bantoid Peoples	30°	(6) Nigeria, Benue basin to Makurdi in the west
KABYLE	Berber		1,000°	Compact sector of coastal Algeria

Name	Group	Cluster / Notes	Pop.	Location
KAMBA	Kenya Highland Bantu	One of 7 tribal groups	600	(16) Kenya, districts of Machako, Kitui, Thika, etc.
KARANGA	Shona	Shona Cluster		(26) Southern Rhodesia
KIKUYU	Kenya Highland Bantu		665–1,115	(16) Kenya, Nairobi district, Kiambo, Fort Hall, Njeri, etc.
KIMBUNDU	Central Bantu	Kimbundu Cluster		(23) West, central Angola
KOLOLO	Middle Zambesi Bantu	Originally a Sotho tribe invading Middle Zambesi (1838)		(25) Zambia (Barotseland); descendants of Livingstone's bearers in Malawi
KOM	Cameroon Highlanders		30	(7)
KONKOMBA	Voltaic Peoples	Gurma Cluster	50°	(3) Northern Togo and Ghana
KONO	Peripheral Mande	Mande Tribes	80	(1) Sierra Leone
KOREKORE	Shona	Shona Cluster		(26) Southern Rhodesia
KPELLE	Peripheral Mande	Mande Tribes	250	(1) Liberia
KUBA	Central Bantu	Kasai Cluster	75°	(23) Zaire, Kasai, etc.
KUSU	Mongo	Mongo Province		(21) Zaire, between Lomani and Lualabi Rivers
KWAFI	Nilotes	Masai Cluster		(11) Southern Kenya, northern Tanganyika
LANGI	see RANGI			
LOBI	Voltaic Peoples	Lobi Cluster	110°	(3) Northern Ivory Coast, southwestern Upper Volta
LODAGAA	see DAGARI and LOBI			
LOZI	Middle Zambesi Bantu		180°	(25) Zambia, Barotseland
LUAPULA	Central Bantu	Bemba Cluster	100°	(23) Zambia, between Lake Bangweulu and Luapula River
LUBA	Luba	Luba Province	250°	(22) Zaire
LUGBARA	Central Sudanic Peoples	Madi Cluster		(10) Uganda, north of Lake Albert
LUNDA	Central Bantu (see also LUBA)	Bemba and Lunda Cluster		(23) Zaire
LUYI	Middle Zambesi Bantu	Middle Zambesi Bantu		(25) Zambia, Barotseland
MAKOLOLO	see KOLOLO			
MALINKE	Nuclear Mande			(2) Gambia and Senegal
MANDE	Nuclear Mande	Speak related dialects of the Mande subfamily of the Nigritic linguistic stock (Murdock)	1,000°	(2)
MANDINGO	see MALINKE			
MASAI	Nilotes	Masai Cluster	100°	(11) Southern Kenya, northern Tanganyika
MASHONA	see SHONA			
MASINA	see FULANI			
MATABELE	see NDEBELE			
MBANGALA	Central Bantu	Kimbundu Cluster	8	(23) Angola, Zaire
MBUGWE	Tanganyika Bantu	Rift Cluster		(18) Northern Tanganyika, south of Lake Manyara
MBUNDU (1)	Southwestern Bantu			(24) Angola
MBUNDU (2)	see KIMBUNDU			
MENDE	Peripheral Mande	Mande Tribes	1,000°	(1) Sierra Leone

Tribe	Murdock Classification	Major Ethnic and/or Linguistic Grouping	Number (in thousands)	Location
MERINA	Malagasy		1,000	Madagascar, Plateau (16)
MERU	Kenya Highland Bantu			(3) Mali
MINIANKA	Voltaic Peoples	Senufo Cluster	200°	
MINIANKE	see MINIANKA			
MOSSI	Voltaic Peoples	Mole Cluster	1,750°	(3) Upper Volta
MUM	Cameroon Highlanders		75	(7)
NANDI	Nilotes	Nandi Cluster	115°	(11) Western Kenya, northeast of Lake Victoria
NDEBELE	Nguni	Ndebele Cluster	300	(27) Southern Rhodesia, Union of South Africa (Transvaal)
NDONGO	Central Bantu	Kimbundu Cluster		(23) West central Angola
NGBWAKA	see BWAKA			
NGONI	Nguni	Ngoni Cluster / Mixed descendants of Zulu bands containing elements of Sotho, Swazi, Thonga, etc. (Murdock)		(27) Malawi
NKOLE	Interlacustrine Bantu	Ruanda Cluster	300°	(19) Southwest Uganda
NUBA	Nuba	Kordofonian language stock	360°	Sudan, Kordofan
NUER	Nilotes	Dinka Cluster		(11) Southern Sudan
NUPE	Southern Nigerians	Nupe Cluster		(5)
NYORO	Interlacustrine Bantu	Uganda Cluster	110	(19) Uganda, east of Lake Albert
OVIMBUNDU	see MBUNDU (1)			(5)
OYO	Southern Nigerians	Yoruba Cluster		
PENDE	Central Bantu	Kwango Cluster	27	(23) Zaire, drainage basin of Kwango River
PEUL	see FULANI			
RANGI	Tanganyika Bantu	Rift Cluster	80	(18)
ROTSE	see LOZI			
SENUFO	Voltaic Peoples	Senufo Cluster	540	(3) Northern Ivory Coast, Southern Mali, Upper Volta
SHANGANA	Thonga	Thonga Cluster / Thonga who have received substantial Nguni increments, known as the Shaangan (Shangana) (Murdock)	> 1,000	(29) Southern Mozambique
SHANGANA-THONGA	see SHANGANA			
SHERBRO	Kru (related to Senegambians)	Atlantic Tribes	200°	(1) Coastal Sierra Leone
SHILA	Central Bantu	Bemba Cluster		(23) Zambia, west of Lake Bangweulu
SHONA	Shona	Shona Cluster	> 1,000	(26) Southern Rhodesia, adjacent Mozambique
SOGA	Interlacustrine Bantu	Uganda Cluster	500°	(19) Uganda, north of Lake Victoria
SOMALI	Somali		330	(15) Somalia
SONGHAI	Negroes of the Sudan Fringe	Songhai Province		Mali, adjacent Niger
SONGHAY	see SONGHAI			
SONINKE	Nuclear Mande	One of 12 major ethnic groups, mixed with Bambara, Berber, Fulani, and Malinke elements (Murdock)	360°	(2) Mali, Senegal

SUKUMA	Tanganyika Bantu	Nyamwezi Cluster	1,000°	(18) Tanganyika
SUSU	Nuclear Mande	One of 12 major ethnic groups	300	(2) Guinea
SUZEE	see SUSU			
SWAHILI	Northeast Coastal Bantu	Swahili Cluster. Not a separate ethnic group. Strongly Arabized and detribalized people along the coast (Murdock)		Coast Kenya, Tanganyika
SWAZI	Nguni	Nguni Cluster	400	(27) Swaziland
TALLENSI	Voltaic Peoples	Mole Cluster		(3) Northern Ghana
TAWAREK	see TUAREG			
TEMNE	Kru (related to Senegambians)	Atlantic Tribes	525	(1) Sierra Leone
TETELA	Mongo	Mongo Province	300°	(21) Zaire
THONGA	see SHANGANA			
TIV	Plateau Nigerians	Bantoid Peoples	800°	(6) Southeastern Nigeria (Benue Plateau State)
TONGA (1)	Central Bantu	Maravi Cluster		(23) Malawi and lower Zambesi River area
TONGA (2)	Middle Zambesi Bantu			(25) Zambia
TORO	Interlacustrine Bantu	Uganda Cluster	130°	(19) Uganda, south of Lake Albert
TSWANA	Sotho	Tswana Cluster	150°	(28) Botswana, Union of South Africa
TUAREG	Berbers			Southern Sahara (Mali, Niger)
VILI	Central Bantu	Kongo Cluster		(23) Zaire, lower reaches of Congo River
WAKAMBA	see KAMBA			
WAKWAFI	see KWAFI			
WOLOF	Senegambians	One of 12 principal tribal divisions	850°	Senegal
XHOSA	see XOSA			
XOSA	Nguni	Nguni Cluster	> 2,000°	(27)
YAKA	Central Bantu	Kwango Cluster		(23) Zaire, drainage basin of Kwango River
YAO	Central Bantu	Yao Cluster		(23) Northern Mozambique, Malawi
YEKE	Luba	Luba Province; not a tribe but a state established over Central Bantu indigenes by Nyamwezi conquerors (Murdock)		(22)
YORUBA	Southern Nigerians	Yoruba Cluster	1,600°	(5) Southwestern Nigeria, Western State
ZANDE	see AZANDE			
ZULU	Nguni	Nguni Cluster	over 2,000°	(27)

BIBLIOGRAPHY OF SOURCES CITED

Abraham, W. E. *The Mind of Africa.* Chicago, 1962.

Abrahamsson, Hans. *The Origin of Death; Studies in African Mythology.* (Studia ethnographica Upsaliensia, No. 3.) Uppsala, 1951.

Abu-Lughod, Ibrahim. "Nationalism in a New Perspective: the African Case." In Herbert J. Spiro, ed., *Patterns of African Development; Five Comparisons.* Englewood Cliffs, N.J., 1967.

Achebe, Chinua. "Death of a Boy." In Ellis Ayitey Komey and Ezekiel Mphahlele, eds., *Modern African Stories.* London, 1964, pp. 28–33.

———. *No Longer at Ease.* New York, 1961.

Ackerknecht, Erwin H. "Problems of Primitive Medicine." *Bulletin of the History of Medicine,* 11, No. 5 (May 1942), 503–521.

———. "Psychopathology, Primitive Medicine and Primitive Culture." *Bulletin of the History of Medicine,* 14, No. 1 (June 1943), 30–67.

Ackoff, Russell Lincoln, and Sasieni, Maurice W. *Fundamentals of Operations Research.* New York, 1968.

Adam, Thomas Ritchie. *Government and Politics in Africa South of the Sahara.* (Studies in political science, PS28.) New York, 1959; rev. ed. 1967.

Adewoye, O. "The Judicial Agreements in Yorubaland, 1904–1908." *Journal of African History,* 12, No. 4 (1971), 607–627.

Afrifa, Akwasi A. *The Ghana Coup, 24 February 1966.* London and New York, 1966.

Ajayi, J. F. Ade. "Colonialism: An Episode in African History." In L. H. Gann and Peter Duignan, eds., *Colonialism in Africa 1870–1960.* 2 vols. Cambridge, 1969. Vol. I: *The History and Politics of Colonialism 1870–1914*, pp. 497–509.

———. "Samuel Ajayi Crowther of Oyo." In Philip D. Curtin, ed., *Africa Remembered; Narratives by West Africans from the Era of the Slave Trade.* Madison, Wisc., 1967, pp. 289–316.

Ajayi, J. F. Ade, and Smith, Robert. *Yoruba Warfare in the Nineteenth Century.* Ibadan, 1964.

Akiga, Benjamin. *Akiga's Story; The Tiv Tribe as Seen by One of Its Members.* Rupert East, trans. 2nd ed. London, 1965.

Akinjogbin, I. A. *Dahomey and Its Neighbours 1708–1818.* Cambridge, 1967.

Albert, Ethel M. "The Classification of Values: A Method and Illustration." *American Anthropologist,* New Series, 58 (1956), 221–248.

———. "Value Systems." In David L. Sills, ed., *International Encyclopedia of the Social Sciences.* New York, 1968. Vol. XVI, 287–291.

Alderfer, Harold Freed. *A Bibliography of African Government, 1950–1966.* 2nd rev. ed. Lincoln University, Pa., 1967.

Alger, Chadwick F. "Trends in International Relations Research." In Norman D. Palmer, ed., *A Design for International Relations Research: Scope, Theory, Methods, and Relevance.* (The American Academy of Political and Social Science Monograph, No. 10.) Philadelphia, October 1970, pp. 7–28.

Allen, Captain William, and Thomson, T.R.H., M.D. *A Narrative of the*

IFAN is the abbreviation for Institut Français d'Afrique Noire.

Expedition Sent by Her Majesty's Government to the River Niger in 1841. 2 vols. London, 1848.

Allier, Raoul Scipion Philippe. *Le Non-civilisé et nous: différence irréductible ou identité foncière?* Paris, 1927.

Allott, Antony N. *Essays in African Law, with Special Reference to the Law of Ghana.* (Butterworth's African law series, No. 1.) London, 1960.

———. "The Future of African Law." In Hilda Kuper and Leo Kuper, eds., *African Law; Adaptation and Development.* Berkeley and Los Angeles, 1965, pp. 216–240.

———. "Legal Personality in African Law." In Max Gluckman, ed., *Ideas and Procedures in African Customary Law*, London, 1969.

Allott, Antony N.; Epstein, A. L.; and Gluckman, Max. "Introduction." In Max Gluckman, ed., *Ideas and Procedures in African Customary Law.* London, 1969.

Almond, Gabriel Abraham, and Coleman, James Smoot, eds. *The Politics of the Developing Areas.* Princeton, 1960.

Althabe, Gerard. "Etude du chômage à Brazzaville en 1957." In F. R. Wickert, ed., *Readings in African Psychology from French Language Sources.* East Lansing, Mich., 1967.

Anaibe, Stephen I. O. "The Wisdom of My People." Manuscript, 1967.

Anderson, James Norman Dalrymple. "The Adaptation of Muslim Law in Sub-Saharan Africa." In Hilda Kuper and Leo Kuper, eds., *African Law; Adaptation and Development.* Berkeley and Los Angeles, 1965, pp. 149–164.

———. *Islamic Law in Africa.* (Great Britain. Colonial office. Colonial research publication, No. 16.) London, 1954.

Andersson, Efraim. *Messianic Popular Movements in the Lower Congo.* (Studia ethnographica Upsaliensia, No. 14.) Uppsala, 1958.

Andiamanjato, Richard. *Le Tsiny et le Tody dans la pensée malgache.* Paris, 1957.

Andrain, Charles F. "The Political Thought of Sékou Touré." In W.A.E. Skurnik, ed., *African Political Thought; Lumumba, Nkrumah, and Touré.* (Monograph series in world affairs, 5, 1967–1968.) Denver, 1968.

Apter, David Ernest. *Ghana in Transition.* (Rev. ed. of *The Gold Coast in Transition.*) New York, 1963.

———. *The Gold Coast in Transition.* Princeton, 1955.

———. "Nkrumah, Charisma and the Coup." *Daedalus (Philosophers and Kings; Studies in Leadership).* (Summer 1968).

Apthorpe, Raymond J., ed. *From Tribal Rule to Modern Government.* (The Thirteenth conference proceedings of the Rhodes-Livingstone Institute for Social Research.) Lusaka, 1959.

Arboussier, Gabriel d'. "L'Evolution de la législation dans les pays africains d'expression française et à Madagascar." In Hilda Kuper and Leo Kuper, eds., *African Law; Adaptation and Development.* Berkeley and Los Angeles, 1965, pp. 165–183.

Arkell, Anthony John. *A History of the Sudan; From the Earliest Times to 1821.* London, 1955.

Armstrong, Robert G. "The Idoma Court-of-Lineages in Law and Political Structure." In Anthony F. C. Wallace, ed., *Selected Papers of the Fifth International Congress of Anthropological and Ethnological Sciences,*

Philadelphia, September 1–9, 1956. Philadelphia, 1960, pp. 390–395.

———. "A West African Inquest." *American Anthropologist*, 56, No. 6 (December 1954), 1051–1075.

Asante, S.K.B. "Law and Society in Ghana." In Thomas W. Hutchison, ed., *Africa and Law; Developing Legal Systems in African Commonwealth Nations.* Madison, Milwaukee, and London, 1968.

Austin, Dennis. *Politics in Ghana 1946–1960.* London, 1964.

Axelson, Eric Victor, ed. *South African Explorers.* (The World's classics, No. 538) London, New York, and Cape Town, 1954.

Ba, Amadou Hampaté. "Animisme en savane africaine." In Rencontres internationales de Bouaké, *Les Religions africaines traditionnelles.* Paris, 1965, pp. 33–42.

Ba, Amadou Hampaté and Daget, J. *L'Empire peul du Macine.* (IFAN, Etudes soudanaises No. 3.) Vol. 1: *1818–1853.* Dakar, 1955.

Baade, Hans W., and Everett, Robinson O., eds. *African Law; New Law for New Nations.* Dobbs Ferry, N.Y., 1963.

Bachhofen, J. J. *Myth, Religion, and Mother Right, Selected Writings.* Ralph Mannheim, trans. (Bollingen Series, No. 84.) Princeton, 1967.

Baer, Gabriel. "Slavery in Nineteenth Century Egypt." *Journal of African History*, 8, No. 3 (1967), 417–441.

Bailey, Norman A. "Toward a Praxeological Theory of Conflict." *Orbis*, 11, No. 4 (Winter 1968), 1081–1112.

Balandier, Georges. *Afrique ambiguë.* Paris, 1957.

———. *Sociologie actuelle de l'Afrique Noire; dynamique sociale en Afrique centrale.* 2nd ed. Paris, 1963.

Banks, Arthur Leslie, ed. *The Development of Tropical and Sub-Tropical Countries, with Particular Reference to Africa.* (Proceedings of a seminar held in Gonville and Caius College, Cambridge, in July 1953.) London, 1954.

Barkun, Michael. "Conflict Resolution through Implicit Mediation." *Journal of Conflict Resolution*, 8, No. 2 (1964), 121–130.

———. *Law without Sanctions; Order in Primitive Societies and the World Community.* New Haven and London, 1968.

Barnes, James Albert. "The Fort Jameson Ngoni." In Elizabeth Colson and Max Gluckman, eds., *Seven Tribes of British Central Africa.* London, 1951, pp. 194–252.

———. *Politics in a Changing Society; A Political History of the Fort Jameson Ngoni.* Cape Town and New York, 1954.

Barth, Henry. *Travels and Discoveries in North and Central Africa, being a Journal of an Expedition Undertaken under the Auspices of H.B.M.'s Government in the Years 1849–1855.* 3 vols. New York, 1857–1859.

Bascom, William. "Folklore." In David L. Sills, ed., *International Encyclopedia of the Social Sciences.* New York, 1968. Vol. v, 496–500.

———. *Ifa Divination; Communication between Gods and Men in West Africa.* Bloomington, Ind., 1969.

———. "The Principle of Seniority in the Social Structure of the Yoruba." *American Anthropologist*, New Series, 44: 37–46. (1942).

———. "Verbal Art." *Journal of American Folklore*, 68, July–September 1955, No. 269, 245–252.

Bastide, Roger. *Le Candomblé de Bahia (rite magô).* École pratique des hautes études. vɪᵉᵐᵉ section. (Le Monde d'outre-mer passé et présent. 1. sér.: Études, 5.) Paris, 1958.

———. "Contribution à l'étude de la participation." *Cahiers internationaux de sociologie*, 14, 1953, 32–39.

Baumann, Hermann; Thurnwald, Richard; and Westermann, Diedrich. *Voelkerkunde von Afrika, mit besonderer Beruecksichtigung der kolonialen Aufgabe*. Essen, 1940.

Baumann, Hermann, and Westermann, Diedrich. *Les Peuples et les civilisations de l'Afrique*. L. Homburger, trans. Paris, 1948.

Baxter, Paul Trevor William, and Butt, Audrey. *The Azande, and Related Peoples of the Anglo-Egyptian Sudan and Belgian Congo*. (Ethnographic survey of Africa: East Central Africa, pt. 9.) London, 1953.

Béart, Ch. "D'une Sociologie des peuples africains à partir de leurs jeux." *Bulletin de l'IFAN*, Series B, 21, Nos. 3–4 (July–October, 1959).

Beattie, John. "Sorcery in Bunyoro." In John Middleton and E. H. Winter, eds., *Witchcraft and Sorcery in East Africa*. London, 1963.

Beattie, John, and Middleton, John, eds. *Spirit Mediumship and Society in Africa*. New York, 1969.

Behrman, Lucy C. *Muslim Brotherhoods and Politics in Senegal*. Cambridge, Mass., 1970.

Beier, Ulli. *Art in Nigeria, 1960*. Cambridge, 1960.

———. *Contemporary Art in Africa*. New York and London, 1968.

Bell, J. Bowyer. "Assassination in International Politics: Lord Moyne, Count Bernadotte and the Lehi." *International Studies Quarterly*, 16, No. 1 (March 1972), 59–82.

Bernard, Jessie. *American Community Behavior; An Analysis of Problems Confronting American Communities Today*. New York, 1949.

———. "Parties and Issues in Conflict." *Journal of Conflict Resolution*, 1, No. 2 (June 1957), 111–121.

Bernatzik, Hugo Adolph, ed. *Afrika; Handbuch der angewandten Voelkerkunde*. 2 vols. Innsbruck, 1947.

Bienen, Henry. *Tanzania; Party Transformation and Economic Development*. Princeton, 1967; expanded ed. Princeton, 1970.

Biesheuvel, Simon. *Race, Culture and Personality*. (The Hoernlé memorial lecture, 1959.) Johannesburg, 1959.

Binger, Louis Gustave. *Du Niger au Golfe de Guinée, par le pays de Kong et le Mossi*. 2 vols. Paris, 1892.

Biobaku, S. O. "An Historical Account of the Evolution of Nigeria as a Political Unit." In Lionel Brett, ed., *Constitutional Problems of Federalism in Nigeria*. (Proceedings of a seminar held at King's College, Lagos, August 8–15, 1960.) Lagos, 1961.

Birmingham, David. "The Date and Significance of the Imbangala Invasion of Angola." *Journal of African History*, 6, No. 2 (1965), 143–152.

Blake, J. W. *Europeans in West Africa, 1450–1560*. 2 vols. London, 1942.

Bloch, Maurice. "Astrology and Writing in Madagascar." In John Rankine Goody, ed., *Literacy in Traditional Societies*. Cambridge, 1968, pp. 277–297.

Bohannan, Laura. "A Genealogical Charter." *Africa*, 22 (1952), 301–315.

———. "Political Aspects of Tiv Social Organization." In John Middleton and David Tait, eds., *Tribes without Rulers; Studies in African Segmentary Systems*. London, 1958, pp. 33–66.

Bohannan, Paul, ed. *African Homicide and Suicide*. Princeton, 1960.

———. "Introduction." In Paul Bohannan, ed., *Law and Warfare; Studies in the Anthropology of Conflict*. Garden City, N.Y., 1967, pp. xi–xiv.

———. *Justice and Judgment among the Tiv*. London and New York, 1957.

———. "Land Use, Land Tenure and Land Reform." In Melville J. Herskovits and Mitchell Harwitz, eds., *Economic Transition in Africa*. London and Evanston, Ill., 1964, pp. 133–149.

———, ed. *Law and Warfare; Studies in the Anthropology of Conflict*. Garden City, N.Y., 1967.

———. "A Man Apart." *Natural History*, 77, No. 8 (October 1968), 8–16, 66–69.

———. *Social Anthropology*. New York, 1963.

Bohannan, Paul, and Dalton, George, eds. *Markets in Africa*. (Northwestern University African studies, No. 9.) Evanston, Ill., 1962.

Boone, Olga. *Bibliographie ethnographique du Congo Belge*. Tervuren, Belgium, 1958.

Bouckaert, L. "The Intellectual Development of the Ngwaka Child." *Tropical and Geographical Medicine*, 13, No. 1 (March 1961), 8ff.

Boutros-Ghali, Boutros. *The Addis Ababa Charter; A Commentary*. (International Conciliation, No. 546, January 1964). New York, 1964.

Bovill, E. W. *Caravans of the Old Sahara*. London, 1933.

———. *The Golden Trade of the Moors*. London, 1958.

Bowdich, Thomas Edward. *An Account of the Discoveries of the Portuguese in the Interior of Angola and Mozambique*. London, 1824.

———. *Mission from Cape Coast Castle to Ashantee, with a Statistical Account of that Kingdom, and Geographical Notices of Other Parts of the Interior of Africa*. London, 1819.

Bown, Lalage, and Crowder, Michael, eds. *The Proceedings of the First International Congress of Africanists, Accra, December 11–18, 1962*. London, 1964.

Boxer, C. R. *Four Centuries of Portuguese Expansion 1415–1825; A Succinct Survey*. Berkeley, Los Angeles, and Johannesburg, 1969.

Bozeman, Adda B., ed. "Appraising the Impact of International Law upon Contemporary Political and Social Processes; Techniques and Conclusions." In American Society of International Law, *Proceedings*. (Annual meeting, 1972.) Washington, D.C., 1972, pp. 32–61.

———. "Civilizations under Stress; Reflections on Cultural Borrowing and Survival." *Virginia Quarterly Review*, 51, No. 1 (Winter 1975), 1–18.

———. "Do Educational and Cultural Exchanges Have Political Relevance?" *International Educational and Cultural Exchange*, vol. 5, No. 2 (Fall 1969), pp. 7–21.

———. *The Future of Law in a Multicultural World*. Princeton, 1971.

———. *Politics and Culture in International History*. Princeton, 1960.

———. "Representative Systems of Public Order Today." In American Society of International Law, *Proceedings*. (Annual meeting, 1959.) Washington, D.C., 1959, pp. 10–20.

Bradbury, R. E. *The Benin Kingdom and the Edo-Speaking Peoples of South-Western Nigeria, together with a Section on the Itsekiri by P. C. Lloyd*. (Ethnographic survey of Africa, Western Africa, Part XIII.) London, 1957.

Bretton, Henry L. "Current Political Thought and Practice in Ghana." *American Political Science Review*, 52, No. 1 (March 1958), 46–63.

———. *The Rise and Fall of Kwame Nkrumah; A Study of Personal Rule in Africa.* London and New York, 1967.

Briggs, Lloyd Cabot. *The Living Races of the Sahara Desert.* (Specialized account; Harvard University, Peabody Museum of American Archaeology and Ethnology. Papers, Vol. 28, No. 2.) Cambridge, Mass., 1958. *Tribes of the Sahara.* (Popularized account.) Cambridge, Mass., 1960.

Brooks, Hugh C., and El-Ayouty, Yassin, eds. *Refugees South of the Sahara; An African Dilemma.* Westport, Conn., 1970.

Brown, Paula. "Patterns of Authority in West Africa." *Africa*, 21, No. 4 (1951), 261–278.

Buchmann, Jean. *Le Problème des structures politiques en Afrique noire indépendente.* (Université Lovanium, Institut de Recherches Economiques et Sociales, Notes et Documents, No. 20/SP–1, July 1961.) Leopoldville, 1961.

Budge, E. A. Wallis. *Osiris and the Egyptian Resurrection.* 2 vols. London, 1911.

Buell, Raymond Leslie. *The Native Problem in Africa.* (Bureau of International Research, Harvard and Radcliffe Colleges. "Problems which have arisen out of the impact of primitive peoples with an industrial civilization" in French, British and Belgian territory and Liberia.) 2 vols. New York, 1928.

Buraud, Georges. *Les Masques.* Paris, 1961.

Burns, Sir Alan. *Colonial Civil Servant.* London, 1949.

Burton, John Wear. *Conflict and Communication; The Use of Controlled Communication in International Relations.* London, 1969.

———. "Resolution of Conflict." *International Studies Quarterly*, 16, No. 1 (March 1972), 5–29.

Burton, Captain Sir Richard F. *A Mission to Gelele, King of Dahome.* Isabel Burton, ed. Memorial ed. 2 vols. London, 1893.

Busia, Kofi Abrefa. *Africa in Search of Democracy.* London, 1967.

———. *The African Consciousness; Continuity and Change in Africa.* New York, 1968.

———. *The Position of the Chief in the Modern Political System of Ashanti; A Study of the Influence of Contemporary Social Changes on Ashanti Political Institutions.* London and New York, 1951.

———. *Report on a Social Survey of Sekondi-Takoradi.* London, 1950.

Butterfield, Herbert, and Wight, Martin, eds., *Diplomatic Investigations; Essays in the Theory of International Politics.* Cambridge, Mass., 1968.

Butt-Thompson, Frederick W. *Secret Societies in West Africa; Their Organisations, Officials and Teaching.* London, 1929.

Caillié, Réné, *Travels through Central Africa to Timbuctoo; and across the Great Desert, to Morocco, Performed in the Years 1824–1828.* 2 vols. 1st French ed., 1830; English ed., London, 1830; new impression, London, 1968.

Calame-Griaule, Geneviève. "Les Moqueries de villages au Soudan Français." *Notes africaines; Bulletin de l'information et de correspondances* (IFAN), No. 61 (Dakar, January 1954).

———. *La Parole chez les Dogons.* Paris, 1966.

Campbell, Olwen. *Mary Kingsley; A Victorian in the Jungle.* London, 1957.

Carlston, Kenneth S. *Social Theory and African Tribal Organization; The Development of Socio-Legal Theory.* Urbana, Chicago, and London, 1968.

Carothers, John Colin. *The African Mind in Health and Disease; A Study in Ethnopsychiatry.* (World Health Organization monograph series, No. 17.) Geneva, 1953.

———. "Culture, Psychiatry, and the Written Word." *Psychiatry*, 22, No. 4 (1959), 307–320.

———. *The Mind of Man in Africa.* London, 1972.

———. *The Psychology of Mau Mau.* Nairobi, 1954.

Carrington, J. F. *Talking Drums of Africa.* London, 1949.

Carroll, Berenice A. "Peace Research; The Cult of Power." *Journal of Conflict Resolution*, 16, No. 4 (December 1972), 585–616.

Cartwright, John R. *Politics in Sierra Leone 1947–67.* Toronto and Buffalo, 1970.

Cary, Joyce. *African Witch.* New York and Evanston, 1963; first pub. 1936.

Cazeneuve, Jean. *La Mentalité archaique.* (Collection Armand Colin No. 354 section de philosophie.) Paris, 1961.

Chilver, E. M. " 'Feudalism' in the Interlacustrine Kingdoms." In Audrey I. Richards, ed., *East African Chiefs; A Study of Political Development in Some Uganda and Tanganyika Tribes.* London, 1959, pp. 378–393.

Christensen, James Boyd. "The Role of Proverbs in Fante Culture." *Africa*, 28, No. 3 (July 1958), 232–243.

Clapperton, Hugh. *Journal of a Second Expedition into the Interior of Africa, from the Bight of Benin to Soccatoo.* London, 1829.

Claridge, W. W. *A History of the Gold Coast and Ashanti.* 2 vols. London, 1915.

Clausewitz, Karl von. *On War.* O. J. Matthijs Jolles, trans. New York, 1943.

———. *War, Politics, and Power; Selections from "On War" and "I Believe and Profess."* Col. Edward M. Collins, USAF, trans. and ed. Chicago, 1962.

Coleman, James S. *Nigeria; Background to Nationalism.* Cambridge, 1959.

Coleman, James S., and Price, Belmont, Jr. "The Role of the Military in Sub-Saharan Africa." In John J. Johnson, ed., *The Role of the Military in Underdeveloped Countries.* Princeton, 1962, pp. 359–405.

Collins, Robert, and Herzog, Richard. "Early British Administration in the Southern Sudan." *Journal of African History*, 2, No. 1 (1961), 119–135.

Colson, Elizabeth. "African Society at the Time of the Scramble." In L. H. Gann and Peter Duignan, eds., *Colonialism in Africa 1870–1960.* 2 vols. Vol. I: *The History and Politics of Colonialism 1870–1914.* Cambridge, 1969, pp. 27–65.

———. "The Rôle of Bureaucratic Norms in African Political Structure." In Verne F. Ray, ed., *Systems of Political Control and Bureaucracy in Human Societies.* (American Ethnological Society, Proceedings.) Seattle, 1958.

———. "Trade and Wealth among the Tonga." In Paul Bohannan and George Dalton, eds., *Markets in Africa.* (Northwestern Univ. African studies, No. 9.) Evanston, Ill., 1962; repr. 1965, pp. 601–616.

Colson, Elizabeth, and Gluckman, Max, eds. *Seven Tribes of British Central Africa.* London, 1951.

Colson, Elizabeth, and Smith, M. G. "Political Anthropology." *International Encyclopedia of the Social Sciences.* David L. Sills, ed. Vol. XII, pp. 189–202.

Conrad, Joseph. *Heart of Darkness* and *The Secret Sharer.* New York, 1950.

———. *Two Tales of the Congo.* ("An Outpost of Progress" and "Heart of Darkness.") London, 1952.

Converse, Elizabeth. "The War of All against All; A Rewiev of *The Journal of Conflict Resolution, 1957–1968.*" *Journal of Conflict Resolution,* 12, No. 4 (1968), 471–532; author index, 1957–1968 (vols. 1–12), 533–550.

Cornevin, Robert. *Histoire de l'Afrique des origines à nos jours.* Paris, 1956.

———. *Histoire des peuples de l'Afrique noire.* Paris, 1960.

———. *Histoire du Togo.* Paris, 1959.

Cory, Hans. *The Indigenous Political System of the Sukuma and Proposals for Political Reform.* (East African Institute of Social Research, East African studies, No. 2.) Nairobi, 1954.

Coser, Lewis A. *Continuities in the Study of Social Conflict.* New York, 1967.

———. *The Functions of Social Conflict.* Glencoe, Ill., 1956.

Coupland, Reginald. *East Africa and Its Invaders, from the Earliest Times to the Death of Seyyid Said in 1856.* Oxford, 1938; repr. New York, 1956.

Crahay, Franz. "Conceptual Take-Off; Conditions for a Bantu Philosophy." Victor A. Velen, trans. *Diogenes,* No. 52 (Winter 1965), pp. 55–78.

Crowder, Michael. *Senegal; A Study in French Assimilation Policy.* London, 1962.

———. *The Story of Nigeria.* London, 1962.

Cunnison, Ian George. *History on the Luapula; An Essay on the Historical Notions of a Central African Tribe.* (Rhodes-Livingstone paper No. 21.) London and Cape Town, 1951.

———. "Kazembe and the Portuguese 1798–1832." *Journal of African History,* 2, No. 1 (1961), 61–76.

———. *The Luapula Peoples of Northern Rhodesia; Custom and History in Tribal Politics.* Manchester, 1959.

Curtin, Philip D., ed. *Africa Remembered; Narratives by West Africans from the Era of the Slave Trade.* Madison, Wisc., 1967.

———. *The Atlantic Slave Trade; A Census.* Madison, Wisc., 1969.

Cuvelier, J. *L'Ancien royaume de Congo.* Brussels, 1941.

———, ed. *Documents sur une mission française au Kakongo 1766–1776.* (IRCB, Vol. 30, No. 1.) Brussels, 1953.

———, ed. and trans. *Relations sur le Congo du Père Laurent de Lucques (1700–1717).* (IRCB, Vol. 32, No. 2.) Brussels, 1953.

Cuvelier, J., and Jadin, L. *L'Ancien Congo d'après les archives romaines (1518–1640).* (IRCB, Vol. 36, No. 2.) Brussels, 1954.

Davenport, Guy. "Pound and Frobenius." In Lewis Leary, ed., *Motive and Method in the Cantos of Ezra Pound.* New York, 1954.

David Davies Memorial Institute of International Studies. *Report of a Study Group on the Peaceful Settlement of International Disputes.* London, 1966.

Davidson, Basil. *Africa in History; Themes and Outlines.* London, 1968; New York, 1969.

Delafosse, Maurice. *Les Civilisations négro-africaines.* Paris, 1925.

——. *Haut-Sénégal-Niger.* 3 vols. Paris, 1912.

——. *The Negroes of Africa.* Washington, 1931.

Delano, Isaac O. *Ōwe l'ẹṣin ọrọ; Yoruba Proverbs, Their Meaning and Usage.* Ibadan, 1966.

Denham, Major Dixon; Clapperton, Captain Hugh; and Oudney, Doctor W. *Narrative of Travels and Discoveries in Northern and Central Africa in the Years 1822, 1823 and 1824.* London, 1826.

Dennett, R. E. *At the Back of the Black Man's Mind, or Notes on the Kingly Office in West Africa.* 1st ed. 1906; repr. London, 1968.

Deschamps, Hubert J. *Les Antaisaka.* 2 vols. Tananarive, 1936.

——. *Histoire de Madagascar.* Paris, 1960.

——. "La Première Codification africaine: Madagascar 1828–81." In Max Gluckman, ed., *Ideas and Procedures in African Customary Law.* London, 1969, pp. 169–178.

Dieterlen, Germaine. "Mythe et organisation sociale au Soudan français." *Journal de la Société des africanistes,* 25, fascicule 1–2 (1955), 39–76.

——. "Mythe et organisation sociale en Afrique occidentale (suite)." *Journal de la Société des africanistes,* 29, fascicule 1 (1959), 119–138.

Dike, K. Onwuka. *Trade and Politics in the Niger Delta, 1830–1885; An Introduction to the Economic and Political History of Nigeria.* (Oxford studies in African affairs.) Oxford, 1956.

Dinesen, Isak, pseud. *Out of Africa.* New York, 1938.

Diop, Abdoulaye. "African Sociology and Methods of Research." In Frederic Robinson Wickert, ed., *Readings in African Psychology from French Language Sources.* East Lansing, Mich., 1967, pp. 237–241.

Diop, Alioune. "The Spirit of *Présence Africaine.*" In Lalage Bown and Michael Crowder, eds., *Proceedings of the First International Congress of Africanists.* London, 1964.

Doob, Leonard W. *Becoming More Civilized; A Psychological Exploration.* New Haven, 1960.

——. *Communication in Africa; A Search for Boundaries.* New Haven, 1961, repr. 1966.

——, ed. *Resolving Conflict in Africa; The Fermeda Workshop.* New Haven, 1970.

Dougal, James W. C. "Characteristics of African Thought." *Africa,* 5, No. 3 (July 1932), 249–265.

Dubb, Allie, ed. *Myth in Modern Africa.* (Fourteenth conference proceedings of the Rhodes-Livingstone Institute for Social Research.) Lusaka, 1960.

Duignan, Peter. *Handbook of American Resources for African Studies.* (Stanford University. Hoover Institution on War, Revolution, and Peace. Bibliographical series, 29.) Stanford, Calif., 1967.

Dumont, Etienne. *L'Afrique noire est mal partie.* Paris, 1962.

Dupuis, J. *Journal of a Residence in Ashantee.* London, 1824.

Durkheim, Emile. *The Elementary Forms of the Religious Life.* Joseph W. Swain, trans. London, 1915.

——. *Les Formes élémentaires de la vie religieuse.* Paris, 1912.

Duverger, Maurice. *Méthodes des Sciences Sociales.* Paris, 1961.

Duyvendak, J.J.L. *China's Discovery of Africa; Lectures Given at the University of London on 22nd and 23rd January 1947.* London, 1949.

East, Rupert. *See* Akiga, Benjamin.

Easton, David. *A Systems Analysis of Political Life.* New York, London, and Sydney, 1965.

Eckstein, Harry, ed. *Internal War.* New York, 1964.

Egharevba, Jacob U. *The Benin Laws and Customs.* Lagos, 1947.

———. *A Short History of Benin.* 4th ed. Ibadan, 1968.

Ehrlich, Cyril. "Implications of Paternalism in Uganda." *Journal of African History*, 4, No. 2 (1963), 275–285.

Elias, Chief T. Olavale. "The Evolution of Law and Government in Modern Africa." In Hilda Kuper and Leo Kuper, eds., *African Law; Adaptation and Development.* Berkeley and Los Angeles, 1965, pp. 184–195.

———. *The Nature of African Customary Law.* Manchester, 1956.

Emerson, Rupert. "African States and the Burdens They Bear." *African Studies Bulletin*, 10, No. 1 (April 1967), pp. 1–15.

Eulau, Heinz. "Political Behavior." *International Encyclopedia of the Social Sciences.* Vol. XII. New York, 1968, pp. 203–214.

Evans-Pritchard, E. E. *The Nuer; A Description of the Modes of Livelihood and Political Institutions of a Nilotic People.* Oxford, 1940, repr. 1950.

———. *Witches, Oracles, and Magic among the Azande.* Oxford, 1937, repr. 1950.

———. "Zande Blood Brotherhood." *Africa*, 6 (1933), 369ff.

Everts, Philip P. "Developments and Trends in Peace and Conflict Research, 1965–1971: A Survey of Institutions." *The Journal of Conflict Resolution*, 16, No. 4 (December 1972), 477–510.

Fage, J. D. "Ancient Ghana: A Review of Evidence." *Transactions of the Historical Society of Ghana*, 3 (1958).

———. *An Atlas of African History.* London, 1958.

———. *Ghana; A Historical Interpretation.* Madison, Wisc., 1959.

———. *An Introduction to the History of West Africa.* 3rd ed. Cambridge, 1962.

———. "Slavery and the Slave Trade in the Context of West African History." *Journal of African History*, 10, No. 3 (1969), 393–404.

Fallers, Lloyd A. *Bantu Bureaucracy; A Study of Integration and Conflict in the Political Institutions of an East African People.* Cambridge, 1956.

———. "Customary Law in the New African States." In Hans W. Baade and Robinson O. Everett, eds., *African Law; New Law for New Nations.* Dobbs Ferry, N.Y., 1963.

———, ed. *The King's Men; Leadership and Status in Buganda on the Eve of Independence.* London and New York, 1964.

Faublée, J. *La Cohésion des sociétés Bara.* Paris, 1953.

———. *Ethnographie de Madagascar.* Paris, 1946.

———. "Madagascar au XIXᵉ siècle; Esquisse d'histoire economique et sociale." *Journal of World History*, 5, No. 2 (1959), 463–491.

Feit, Edward. "Military Coups and Political Development: Some Lessons from Ghana and Nigeria." In Marion E. Doro and Newell M. Stultz, eds., *Governing in Black Africa; Perspectives on New States.* Englewood Cliffs, N.J., 1970, pp. 221–232.

Field, Margaret Joyce. *Search for Security; An Ethno-psychiatric Study of*

Rural Ghana. (Northwestern University African studies, no. 5.) Evanston, Ill., 1960.

Filesi, Teobaldo. *China and Africa in the Middle Ages.* David L. Morison, trans. London, 1972.

Finer, Samuel Edward. *The Man on Horseback; The Role of the Military in Politics.* London, 1962.

Fink, Clinton F. "Some Conceptual Difficulties in the Theory of Social Conflict." *Journal of Conflict Resolution,* 12, No. 4 (1968), 412–460.

Fisher, Humphrey J. *Ahmadiyyah; A Study in Contemporary Islām on the West African Coast.* London, 1963.

Fisher, Ronald J. "Third Party Consultation: A Method for the Study and Resolution of Conflict." *Journal of Conflict Resolution,* 16, No. 1 (March 1972), 67–94.

Flint, John Edward. "Nigeria: The Colonial Experience from 1880 to 1914." In L. H. Gann and Peter Duignan, eds., *Colonialism in Africa 1870–1960.* 2 vols. Cambridge, 1969. Vol. i: *The History and Politics of Colonialism 1870–1914,* pp. 220–260.

————. *Sir George Goldie and the Making of Nigeria.* London, 1960.

Forde, Cyril Daryll, and Kaberry, Phyllis Mary, eds. *West African Kingdoms in the Nineteenth Century.* London, 1967.

Fortes, Meyer. *The Dynamics of Clanship among the Tallensi; Being the First Part of an Analysis of the Social Structure of a Trans-Volta Tribe.* London and New York, 1945.

————. *The Web of Kinship among the Tallensi; The Second Part of an Analysis of the Social Structure of a Trans-Volta Tribe.* London and New York, 1949.

Fortes, Meyer, and Evans-Pritchard, Edward Evan, eds. *African Political Systems.* London, 1940; repr. 1963.

Fox, Lorene K., ed. *East African Childhood; Three Versions.* Written by Joseph A. Lijembe, Anna Apoko, and J. Mutuku Nzioki. Nairobi and New York, 1967.

Fox, Renée C.; de Craemer, Willy; and Ribeaucourt, Jean-Marie. " 'The Second Independence': A Case Study of the Kwilu Rebellion in the Congo." *Comparative Studies in History and Society,* 8 (October 1965–July 1966), 78–110.

Frazer, Sir James George, comp. *Anthologia Anthropologica. The Native Races of Africa and Madagascar; a Copious Selection of Passages for the Study of Social Anthropology, from the Manuscript Notebooks of Sir James George Frazer.* Arranged and edited from the mss. by Robert Angus Downie. London, 1938.

————. *The Golden Bough; A Study in Magic and Religion.* 3rd ed. 12 vols. New York, 1935 (first pub. London, 1911–1915). One vol. abridged ed. New York, 1922.

Freeman, Richard Austin. *Travels and Life in Ashanti and Jaman.* London, 1898.

Friedheim, Robert L. "The 'Satisfied' and 'Dissatisfied' States Negotiate International Law; A Case Study." *World Politics,* 18 (1965), 20–41.

Frobenius, Leo. *Atlantis, Volksmaerchen und Volksdichtungen Afrikas.* 12 vols. Jena, 1921–1928. In particular Vols. i–iii: *Volksmaerchen der Kabylen;* and Vol. vi: *Spielmannsgeschichten der Sahel.*

393

Frobenius, Leo. *Atlas Africanus; Belege zur Morphologie der Afrikanischen Kulturen*. Berlin, 1921.

———. "Early African Culture as an Indication of Present Negro Potentialities." *Annals of the American Academy of Political and Social Science*, 3 (November 1928).

———. *Erlebte Erdteile; Ergebnisse eines deutschen Forscherlebens*. 7 vols. Frankfurt-am-Main, 1925–1929. In particular Vol. IV: *Vom Voelkerstudium zur Philosophie, Der neue Blick* (1925); Vol. V: *Das Sterbende Afrika, Die Seele eines Erdteils* (1928); Vol. VI: *Monumenta Africana, Der Geist eines Erdteils* (1929); and Vol. VII: *Monumenta Terrarum, Der Geist ueber den Erdteilen* (1929).

———. *Erytraea, Laender und Zeiten des Heiligen Koenigsmordes*. Berlin-Zurich, 1931.

———. *Kulturgeschichte Afrikas, Prolegomena zu einer Historischen Gestaltlehre*, Frankfurt-am-Main, 1933.

———. *Die Masken und Geheimbuende Afrikas*. Halle, 1898.

———. *Menschenjagden und Zweikaempfe*. Jena (no date).

———. *Und Afrika Sprach, wissenschaftlich erweiterte Ausgabe des Berichts ueber den Verlauf der dritten Reiseperiode der Deutschen Inner-Afrikanischen Forschungs-Expedition in den Jahren 1910 bis 1912*. 4 vols. Berlin, 1912–1913. In particular Vol. II: *An der Schwelle des verehrungswuerdigen Byzanz* (1912).

———. *Und Afrika Sprach*. (Volkstuemliche Ausgabe in 1 vol.) Berlin-Charlottenburg, 1912.

Frobenius, Leo, and Fox, Douglas C. *African Genesis*. New York, 1937.

Froehlich, W. "Das afrikanische Marktwesen." *Zeitschrift fuer Ethnologie*, 72, Nos. 4–6 (1940), 234–328.

Froelich, Jean Claude. *Cameroun-Togo: Territoires sous tutelle*. Paris, 1956.

———. *Carte des populations de l'Afrique noire*. (France. Direction de la documentation. Carte no. 71.) Paris, 1955.

———. "Essai sur les causes et méthodes de l'islamisation de l'Afrique de l'Ouest du XIe siècle au XXe siècle." In I. M. Lewis, ed., *Islam in Tropical Africa*. (Studies presented and discussed at the Fifth International African Seminar, Ahmadu Bello University, Zaria, January 1964.) London, 1966, pp. 160–173.

Frye, Richard N. *The Heritage of Persia*. New York, 1966.

Furnas, Joseph Chamberlain. *The Anatomy of Paradise; Hawaii and the Islands of the South Seas*. New York, 1937.

Fyfe, Christopher. *A History of Sierra Leone*. London, 1962.

———. *Sierra Leone Inheritance*. London, 1964.

Galtung, J. "Institutionalized Conflict Resolution: A Theoretical Paradigm." *Journal of Peace Research*, 2, No. 4 (1965 b), 348–396.

Gamble, David P. *The Wolof of Senegambia, together with Notes on the Lebu and the Serer*. (Ethnographic survey of Africa: Western Africa, pt. 14.) London, 1957.

Gann, L. H., and Duignan, Peter. *Burden of Empire; An Appraisal of Western Colonialism in Africa South of the Sahara*. London, 1967.

———, eds. *Colonialism in Africa 1870–1960*. 2 vols. Vol. 1: *The History and Politics of Colonialism 1870–1914*. Cambridge, 1969.

Garbett, G. Kingsley. "Spirit Mediums as Mediators in Korekore Society."

In John Beattie and John Middleton, eds., *Spirit Mediumship and Society in Africa.* New York, 1969.

Garcia Arias, Luis. *El Concepto de guerra y la denominada "Guerra fria,"* vol. 3 of *La Guerra moderna.* Zaragoza, 1956.

Garlake, P. S. *Great Zimbabwe.* New York, 1973.

Garnier, Christine, and Fralon, Jean. *Le Fetichisme en Afrique noire.* Paris, 1951.

Gautier, E. F. *L'Afrique noire occidentale.* Paris, 1935.

Geertz, Clifford, ed. *Old Societies and New States; The Quest for Modernity in Asia and Africa.* (University of Chicago. Committee for the Comparative Study of New Nations.) New York, 1963.

Gelfand, Michael. *The African Witch, with Particular Reference to Witchcraft Beliefs and Practice among the Shona of Rhodesia.* Edinburgh and London, 1967.

————. *Medicine and Custom in Africa.* London, 1964.

————. *Shona Ritual, with Special Reference to the Chaminuka Cult.* Cape Town, 1959.

————. *The Sick African; A Clinical Study.* 3rd ed. (first ed. 1943). Cape Town, 1957.

————. *Witch Doctor; Traditional Medicine Man of Rhodesia.* London, 1964.

Ghai, Y. P. "Customary Contracts and Transactions in Kenya." In Max Gluckman, ed., *Ideas and Procedures in African Customary Law.* London, 1969.

Gibbs, James L., Jr. "The Kpelle Moot." In Paul Bohannan, ed., *Law and Warfare; Studies in the Anthropology of Conflict.* Garden City, N.Y., 1967.

Gluckman, Max. *Custom and Conflict in Africa.* Oxford, 1960.

————, ed. *Ideas and Procedures in African Customary Law.* (Studies presented and discussed at the Eighth International African Seminar at the Haile Selassie I University, Addis Ababa, January 1966.) London, 1969.

————. *The Judicial Process among the Barotse of Northern Rhodesia.* Manchester, 1955.

————. *Order and Rebellion in Tribal Africa; Collected Essays.* London and New York, 1963.

————. *Politics, Law and Ritual in Tribal Society.* London, 1965.

————. *Rituals of Rebellion in South-east Africa.* (The Frazer lecture, 1952.) Manchester, 1954.

Goodman, Ronald; Hart, Jeffrey; and Rosecrance, Richard. "Methods and Data in a Situational Analysis of International Politics." Paper No. 2, Situational Analysis Project, Cornell University, Ithaca, N.Y., January 5, 1972.

Goody, John Rankine. *Death, Property and the Ancestors; A Study of the Mortuary Customs of the LoDagaa of West Africa.* London, 1959.

————, ed. *Literacy in Traditional Societies.* Cambridge, 1968.

————. "Restricted Literacy in Northern Ghana." In John Rankine Goody, ed., *Literacy in Traditional Societies.* Cambridge, 1968, pp. 198–264.

Goody, John Rankine, and Watt, Ian. "The Consequences of Literacy." *Comparative Studies in Society and History,* 5 (October 1962–July 1963), 304–345.

Gordon, Jay. "African Law and the Historian." (Review article) *Journal of African History*, 8, No. 2 (1967), 335–340.

Gouilly, Alphonse. *L'Islam dans l'Afrique occidentale française*. Paris, 1952.

Gould, Wesley L., and Barkun, Michael. *International Law and the Social Sciences*. Princeton, 1970.

Gower, L.C.B. *Independent Africa; The Challenge to the Legal Profession*. Cambridge, Mass., 1967.

Granai, Georges. "Problèmes de la sociologie du langage." In G. Gurvitch, ed., *Traité de sociologie*. 2 vols. 2nd ed. Paris, 1962–1963, pp. 255–277.

Gray, Robert F. "Some Structural Aspects of Mbugwe Witchcraft." In John Middleton and E. H. Winter, eds., *Witchcraft and Sorcery in East Africa*. London, 1963, pp. 143–173.

Greenberg, Joseph Harold. *The Languages of Africa*. (Indiana University. Research Center in Anthropology, Folklore, and Linguistics. Publication 25) and (*International Journal of American Linguistics*, 29, No. 1, pt. 2.) Bloomington, Ind., and The Hague, 1963.

————. *Studies in African Linguistics Classification*. (Reprinted from the *Southwestern Journal of Anthropology*, 5, Nos. 2–4; 6, Nos. 1–4; and 10, No. 4.) Branford, Conn., 1955.

Greene, Fred. "Toward Understanding Military Coups." *Africa Report*, 11, No. 2 (February 1966), pp. 10ff.

Griaule, Marcel. "L'Alliance cathartique." *Africa*, 18, No. 4 (October 1948), 242–258.

————. "The Problem of Negro Culture." In UNESCO, *Interrelations of Cultures, Their Contribution to International Understanding*. Paris, 1953, pp. 352–378.

Griaule, Marcel, and Dieterlen, Germaine. *Signes graphiques soudanais*. (Actualités scientifiques et industrielles, 1158. L'Homme, cahiers d'ethnologie, de géographie et linguistique, 3.) Paris, 1951.

Grotius, Hugo (Groot, Huig van). *De jure belli ac pacis libri tres. In quibus ius naturae & gentium: item iuris publici praecipua explicantur*. Paris, 1625.

————. *The Law of War and Peace; De jure belli ac pacis*. Louise Ropes Loomis, trans. New York, 1949.

————. *The Rights of War and Peace, Including the Law of Nature and of Nations*, A. C. Campbell, trans. Washington and London, 1901.

Groves, Charles Pelham. "Missionary and Humanitarian Aspects of Imperialism from 1870 to 1914." In L. H. Gann and Peter Duignan, eds., *Colonialism in Africa 1870–1960*. 2 vols. Vol. I: *The History and Politics of Colonialism 1870–1914*. Cambridge, 1969, pp. 462–496.

Grundy, Kenneth W. *Guerilla Struggle in Africa; An Analysis and Preview*. New York, 1971.

————. "Ideology and Insurrection; The Theory of Guerrilla Warfare in Africa." Paper presented to the Annual Convention of the International Studies Association, San Francisco, March 1969.

Guibert, Armand. "Léopold Senghor." *Encounter*, 16, No. 2 (February 1961), 54–56.

Gutteridge, William Frank. *Military Institutions and Power in the New States*. New York, 1965.

Hadfield, Percival. *Traits of Divine Kingship in Africa*. London, 1949.

Hailey, William Malcolm, Lord Hailey. *An African Survey; A Study of Problems Arising in Africa South of the Sahara.* Rev. ed. London, New York, and Toronto, 1957.

———. *Native Administration in the British African Territories.* 5 vols. London, 1950–1953. Part I: *East Africa: Uganda, Kenya, Tanganyika* (1950). Part II: *Central Africa: Zanzibar, Nyasaland, Northern Rhodesia* (1950). Part III: *West Africa: Nigeria, Gold Coast, Sierra Leone, Gambia* (1951). Part IV: *A General Survey of the System of Native Administration* (1951). Part V: *The High Commission Territories: Basutoland, The Bechuanaland Protectorate and Swaziland* (1953).

Hall, Edward T. *The Silent Language.* New York, 1959.

Hambly, Wilfrid Dyson. *Culture Areas of Nigeria.* Frederick H. Rawson–Field Museum Ethnological Expedition to West Africa, 1929–30. (Field Museum of Natural History. Publication 346. Anthropological series, 21, No. 3.) Chicago, 1935; repr. New York, 1968.

———. *The Ovimbundu of Angola.* Frederick H. Rawson–Field Museum Ethnological Expedition to West Africa, 1929–30. (Field Museum of Natural History. Publication 329. Anthropological series, 21, No. 2.) Chicago, 1934; repr. New York, 1968.

———. *Serpent Worship in Africa.* (Field Museum of Natural History. Publication 289. Anthropological series, 21, No. 1.) Chicago, 1931; repr. New York, 1968.

Hannigan, A. St. J. "The Imposition of Western Law Forms upon Primitive Societies." *Comparative Studies in Society and History*, 4 (1961–1962), 1–9.

Hanson, A. H. *The Process of Planning; A Study of India's Five-Year Plans 1950–1964.* London, New York, Bombay, 1966.

Harbison, Frederick. "Human Resources and Development." In UNESCO, *Economic and Social Aspects of Educational Planning.* Paris, 1964.

Hargreaves, John D. *A Life of Sir Samuel Lewis.* London, 1958.

Harley, George Way. *Masks as Agents of Social Control in Northeast Liberia.* (Harvard University. Peabody Museum of American Archaeology and Ethnology. Papers, 32, No. 2.) Cambridge, Mass., 1950.

Harris, Joseph E. *The African Presence in Asia; Consequences of the East African Slave Trade.* Evanston, Ill., 1971.

Hart, H.L.A. *The Concept of Law.* Oxford, 1961.

Hart, Jeffrey. "Symmetry and Polarization in the European International System: 1870–1879." Paper No. 3, Situational Analysis Project, Cornell University, January 14, 1972.

Harvey, William B. *Law and Social Change in Ghana.* Princeton, 1966.

———. "Post-Nkrumah Ghana: The Legal Profile of a Coup." In Thomas W. Hutchison, ed., *Africa and Law; Developing Legal Systems in African Commonwealth Nations.* Madison, Milwaukee, and London, 1968, pp. 104–120.

Hasani bin Ismail. *The Medicine Man; 'Swifa ya Nguvumali*, Peter Lienhardt, ed. and trans. Oxford and London, 1968.

Haydon, Edwin Scott. *Law and Justice in Buganda.* (Butterworth's African law series, No. 2.) London, 1960.

Hayford, Joseph Ephraim Casely. *Gold Coast Native Institutions, with Thoughts upon a Healthy Imperial Policy for the Gold Coast and Ashanti.* London, 1903.

Heath, Frank L., trans. *A Chronicle of Abuja*, by Alhaji Hassan and Mallam Shuaibu Na'ibi. 1st ed. Ibadan, 1952; rev. ed., Lagos, 1962.

Hébert, R. P. "Esquisse de l'histoire du pays toussian." *Bulletin de l'IFAN*, 23, Nos. 1–2 (January-April 1961).

Herskovits, Melville J. "Anthropology and Africa; A Wider Perspective." (The Lugard Memorial Lecture for 1959.) *Africa*, 29, No. 3 (July 1959), 225–238.

———. "Cultural Relativism and Cultural Values." In Melville J. Herskovits, *Cultural Anthropology*. New York, 1955.

———. "The Culture Areas of Africa." *Africa*, 3, No. 1 (1930), 59ff.

———. *The Human Factor in Changing Africa*. New York, 1962.

———. *Man and His Works; The Science of Cultural Anthropology*. New York, 1949.

———. "Peoples and Cultures of Sub-Saharan Africa." *The Annals of the American Academy of Political and Social Science*, 298 (March 1955), 11–20.

———. "Preface." In Paul Bohannan and George Dalton, eds., *Markets in Africa*. (Northwestern University African studies No. 9.) Evanston, Ill., 1962, pp. vii–xvi.

Herskovits, Melville J., and Harwitz, Mitchell, eds. *Economic Transition in Africa*. (Northwestern University, African studies No. 12.) Evanston, Ill., and London, 1964.

Herskovits, Melville J., and Herskovits, Frances S. *Dahomean Narrative; A Cross-Cultural Analysis*. (Northwestern University, African studies No. 1.) Evanston, Ill., 1958.

———. *Suriname Folk-Lore*. New York, 1936.

Himmelheber, Hans. "Sculptors and Sculptures of the Dan." In Lalage Bown and Michael Crowder, eds., *Proceedings of the First International Congress of Africanists, Accra, December 11–18, 1962*. London, 1964, pp. 243–255.

———. "Le Système de la religion des Dan." In Rencontres internationales de Bouaké, *Les Religions africaines traditionnelles*. Paris, 1965, pp. 75–85.

Hobley, C. W. *Bantu Beliefs and Magic, with Particular Reference to the Kikuyu and Kamba Tribes of Kenya Colony*. London, 1922; repr. 1938.

Hodgkin, Thomas. *African Political Parties; An Introductory Guide*. London, 1961.

———, ed. *Nigerian Perspectives; An Historical Anthology*. London, 1960.

Hodgson, Lady Mary Alice (Young). *The Siege of Kumassi*. New York, 1901.

Hoernlé, A. Winifred. "Magic and Medicine." In Isaac Schapera, ed., *The Bantu-Speaking Tribes of South Africa; An Ethnographic Survey*. London, 1937; repr. 1946, pp. 221–245.

Hogben, Sidney John, and Kirk-Greene, Anthony Hamilton Millard. *The Emirates of Northern Nigeria; A Preliminary Survey of Their Historical Traditions*. London, 1966.

Holas, Bohumil. "Arts et artisanat en A.O.F." In *Les Guides bleus, Afrique occidentale française Togo*. Paris, 1958.

———. "L'Imagerie rituelle en Afrique noire." *African Arts/Arts d'Afrique*, 1, No. 2 (Winter 1968), 48–53, 86–87.

———. *Les Masques Kono*. Paris, 1952.

————. *Les Sénoufo, y compris les Minianka.* (Monographies ethnologiques africaines.) Paris, 1957.

Holleman, J. F. *Shona Customary Law, with Reference to Kinship, Marriage, the Family and the Estate.* Cape Town, London, and New York, 1952.

Horner, George R. "The Bulu Response to European Economy." In Paul Bohannan and George Dalton, eds., *Markets in Africa.* Evanston, Ill., 1962; repr. 1965, pp. 170–189.

Houis, Maurice. *Préalables à un humanisme nègre.* (Reprinted from *Esprit,* November 1958.) Dakar, Senegal.

————. "Problèmes linguistiques de l'ouest africain." In *Les Guides bleus, Afrique occidentale française Togo.* Paris, 1958.

Hovet, Thomas, Jr. *Africa in the United Nations.* Evanston, Ill., 1963.

Howard, C., and Plumb, J. H., eds. *West African Explorers.* London, 1951; repr. 1955.

Howell, Paul Philip. *A Manual of Nuer Law, Being an Account of Customary Law, Its Evolution and Development in the Courts Established by the Sudan Government.* London and New York, 1954.

Howman, Roger. "Chiefs and Councils in Southern Rhodesia." In Raymond Apthorpe, ed., *From Tribal Rule to Modern Government.* (13th Conference proceedings of the Rhodes-Livingstone Institute for Social Research.) Lusaka, 1959.

Huntingford, G.W.B. *The Nandi of Kenya; Tribal Control in a Pastoral Society.* London, 1953.

————. "Nandi Witchcraft." In John Middleton and E. H. Winter, eds., *Witchcraft and Sorcery in East Africa.* London and New York, 1963, pp. 175–186.

Huntington, Samuel P. "Patterns of Violence in World Politics." In Samuel P. Huntington, ed., *Changing Patterns of Military Politics.* (International Yearbook of Political Behavior Research, 3.) New York, 1962, pp. 17–50.

————. "Political Development and Political Decay." *World Politics,* 17, No. 3 (April 1965), 386–430.

Huntley, Sir Henry. *Seven Years' Service on the Slave Coast of Western Africa.* 2 vols. London, 1850.

Hutchison, Thomas W., ed. *Africa and Law; Developing Legal Systems in African Commonwealth Nations.* Madison, Milwaukee, and London, 1968.

Huxley, Elspeth. "Freedom in Africa: The Next Stage." *Virginia Quarterly Review,* 36, No. 3 (Summer 1960), 350–371.

————. *White Man's Country; Lord Delamere and the Making of Kenya.* 2 vols. Vol. I: *1870–1914;* Vol. II: *1914–1931.* London, 1935; new ed. 1953.

Huxley, Julian. *Africa View.* London and New York, 1931.

Ibn Batūta, Muḥammad ibn 'Abd Allāh. *Travels, A.D. 1325–1354.* Translated, with revisions and notes from the Arabic text edited by C. Defrémery and B. R. Sanguinetti, by H.A.R. Gibb. (Hakluyt Society Works, 2nd ser., Nos. 110 and 117.) Cambridge, England, 1958–1962.

————. *Travels in Asia and Africa, 1325–1354.* Translated and selected by H.A.R. Gibb. London and New York, 1929.

Ibn Khaldûn. *The Muqaddimah; An Introduction to History.* Franz Rosenthal, trans. (Bollingen Series No. 43.) 3 vols. New York, 1958.

Iklé, Fred Charles. *How Nations Negotiate.* New York, Evanston, and London, 1964.

Issawi, Charles. *An Arab Philosophy of History.* (Wisdom of the East Series.) London, 1950.

Jabavu, Noni. *Drawn in Colour; African Contrasts.* London, 1961.

Johnson, Samuel. *The History of the Yorubas from the Earliest Times to the Beginnings of the British Protectorate.* Dr. O. Johnson, ed., London, first pub. 1921; repr. 1969.

Johnston, Sir Harry Hamilton. *The Story of My Life.* Indianapolis, 1923.

————. *The Uganda Protectorate.* 2 vols. London, 1902; New York, 1904.

Jones, Arnold Hugh Martin, and Monroe, Elizabeth. *A History of Ethiopia.* Oxford, 1955; repr. 1960.

Jones, Gwilym Iwam. *Basutoland Medicine Murder; A Report on the Recent Outbreak of "Liretlo" Murders in Basutoland.* (Great Britain. Parliament. Cmnd. 8209.) London, 1951.

Joset, Paul Ernest. *Les Sociétés secrètes des hommes-léopards en Afrique noire.* Paris, 1955.

Junod, Henri A. *Moeurs et coutumes des Bantous; La Vie d'une tribu sud-africaine.* Vol. I: *Vie Sociale;* Vol. II: *Vie Mentale.* Paris, 1936. Translated as *The Life of a South African Tribe.* 2nd ed., rev. and enlarged, 2 vols. London, 1927.

Junod, Henri Philippe. *Bantu Heritage.* Johannesburg, 1938.

Kagwa, Sir Apolo. *The Customs of the Baganda.* Ernest B. Kalibala, trans. May Mandelbaum (Edel), ed. (Columbia University. Contributions to anthropology. 22.) New York, 1934.

Kane, Hamidou. *L'Aventure ambiguë, récit.* Preface by Vincent Monteil. Paris, 1961.

Kaunda, Kenneth. *Zambia Shall Be Free.* (African Writers Series 4.) London, Toronto, and Ibadan, 1962.

Kent, Raymond K. *Early Kingdoms in Madagascar 1500–1700.* New York, 1970.

Kenyatta, Jomo. *Facing Mount Kenya.* London, 1938, repr. 1959.

Kersting, M. D., District Officer of Sokode. "Report." In Dr. O. F. Metzger, *Unsere Alte Kolonie Togo.* Neudamm, 1941.

Keuning, J. "The Study of Law in African Countries." *Higher Education and Research in the Netherlands* (Netherlands Universities Foundation for International Co-operation), 7, No. 1 (1963), 3–6.

Khadduri, Majid, ed. and trans. *The Islamic Law of Nations; Shaybānī's Siyar.* Baltimore, 1966.

————. *War and Peace in the Law of Islam.* Baltimore and London, 1955; repr. 1969.

Kingsley, Mary Henrietta. *Travels in West Africa.* London, 1897.

————. *West African Studies.* London and New York, 1899; 2nd ed., 1901.

Kirk-Greene, Anthony Hamilton Millard. "On Swearing; An Account of Some Judicial Oaths in Northern Nigeria." *Africa,* 25, No. 1 (January 1955), 43–53.

————, ed. *Travels in Nigeria; Extracts from the Journal of Heinrich Barth's Travels in Nigeria, 1850–1855.* (Selections from the English translation of the author's *Reisen und Entdeckungen in Nord- und Central-Afrika.*) London, 1962.

Kirkwood, Kenneth, ed. *St. Antony's Papers*, No. 10: *African Affairs*, No. 1. London, 1961.

Ki-Zerbo, Joseph. "La Crise actuelle de la civilisation africaine." In Rencontres internationales de Bouaké, *Tradition et modernisme en Afrique noire*. Paris, 1965, pp. 117–139.

Kluckhohn, Clyde K. M. "Toward a Comparison of Value-Emphases in Different Cultures." In Leonard D. White, ed., *The State of the Social Sciences*. (Papers presented at the 25th Anniversary of the Social Science Research Building, The University of Chicago, November 10–12, 1955.) Chicago, 1956, pp. 116–132.

————. "Values and Value-Orientations in the Theory of Action; An Exploration in Definition and Classification." In Talcott Parsons and Edward A. Shils, eds., *Toward a General Theory of Action*. Cambridge, Mass., 1951, pp. 388–433.

Kluckhohn, Florence Rockwood, and Strodtbeck, Fred L. *Variations in Value Orientations*. Evanston, Ill., 1961.

Komey, Ellis Ayitey, and Mphahlele, Ezekiel, eds. *Modern African Stories*. London, 1964.

Kopytoff, Igor. "Extension of Conflict as a Method of Conflict Resolution among the Sukir of the Congo." *Journal of Conflict Resolution*, 5 (1961), 61–69.

Krapf, Johann Ludwig. *Reisen in Ost-Afrika, ausgefuehrt in den Jahren 1837–1855*. Stuttgart, 1858. (Reissue of original work in one volume, two parts.) Stuttgart, 1964. Translated as *Travels, Researches and Missionary Labours, during an Eighteen Years' Residence in Eastern Africa Together with Journeys to Jagga, Usambara, Ukambani, Shoa, Abessinia, and Khartum; and a Coasting Voyage from Mombaz to Cape Delgado*. London, 1860.

Kup, A. P. *A History of Sierra Leone, 1400–1787*. Cambridge, 1961.

Kuper, Hilda. *An African Aristocracy; Rank among the Swazi*. London and New York, 1947.

Kuper, Hilda, and Kuper, Leo, eds. *African Law; Adaptation and Development*. Berkeley and Los Angeles, 1965.

Labouret, Henri. *L'Afrique précoloniale*. ("Que sais-je?" Le Point des connaissances actuelles, No. 241.) 3rd ed. Paris, 1959.

————. *Nouvelles Notes sur les tribus du rameau Lobi; Leurs migrations, leur évolution, leur parlers et ceux de leurs voisons*. (Mémoire, IFAN, No. 54.) Dakar, 1958.

Lall, Arthur. *Modern International Negotiation; Principles and Practice*. New York, 1966.

Lambert, H. E. *Kikuyu Social and Political Institutions*. London and New York, 1956; repr. 1965.

Lambo, T. Adeoye, M.D. "The African Mind in Contemporary Conflict." (The Jacques Parisot Foundation Lecture, 1971.) *World Health Organization Chronicle*, 25, No. 8 (August 1971), 343–353.

————. "Ame africaine et conflit contemporain." (Series of four articles.) *Journal de Genève*, July 26–29, 1972.

Lander, Richard Lemon, and Lander, John. *Journal of an Expedition to Explore the Course and Termination of the Niger, with a Narrative of a Voyage down that River to its Termination*. London, 1832.

Lasswell, Harold Dwight. "Conflict, Social." In Edwin R. A. Seligman and

Alvin Johnson, eds., *Encyclopaedia of the Social Sciences*, Vol. IV. New York, 1931, pp. 194–196.

———. *Psychopathology and Politics*. (A new edition with afterthoughts by the author.) New York, 1960.

Law, R.C.C. "The Constitutional Troubles of Oyo in the Eighteenth Century." *Journal of African History*, 12, No. 1 (1971), 25–44.

Laye, Camara. *A Dream of Africa*. James Kirkup, trans. London, 1968; New York, 1971.

———. *L'Enfant noir*. Paris, 1953. Translated as *The Dark Child* by James Kirkup, Ernest Jones, and Elaine Gottlieb. New York, 1954.

Leakey, Louis Seymour Bazett. *Mau Mau and the Kikuyu*. London, 1952; repr. 1953.

Lee, John Michael. *African Armies and Civil Order*. (Studies in international security, 13.) London, 1969.

Lefever, Ernest W. *Spear and Scepter; Army, Police, and Politics in Tropical Africa*. Washington, D.C., 1970.

Leighton, Alexander Hamilton; Lambo, T. Adeoye; *et al. Psychiatric Disorder among the Yoruba; A Report*. (Cornell-Aro Mental Health Research Project in the Western Region, Nigeria.) Ithaca, N.Y., 1963.

Leiris, M. "La Possession par le zâr chez les Chrétiens du nord de l'Ethiopie." In Scientific Council for Africa South of the Sahara, *Mental Disorders and Mental Health in Africa South of the Sahara*. (Publication No. 35.) Bukavu, 1958, pp. 168–175.

Leites, Nathan Constantin, and Wolf, Charles, Jr. *Rebellion and Authority; An Analytic Essay on Insurgent Conflicts*. Chicago, 1970.

Leroi-Gourhan, André, and Poirier, Jean, with André-Georges Haudricourt. *Ethnologie de L'Union française (teritoires exterieurs)*. 2 vols. Vol. I: *Afrique*. Vol. II: *Asie, Océanie, Amérique*. Paris, 1953.

Lestrade, G. P. "Traditional Literature." In Isaac Schapera, ed., *The Bantu-Speaking Tribes of South Africa*. London, 1946, pp. 291–308.

LeVine, Robert A. "Anthropology and the Study of Conflict; Introduction." *Journal of Conflict Resolution*, 5, No. 1 (March 1961), 3–15.

LeVine, Victor T. "The Course of Political Violence." In William H. Lewis, ed., *French-Speaking Africa; The Search for Identity*. New York, 1965, pp. 58–79.

Levi-Strauss, Claude. *La Pensée sauvage*. Paris, 1962.

———. *The Savage Mind*. London, 1966.

Lévy-Bruhl, Lucien. *L'Ame primitive*. Paris, 1927.

———. *L'Expérience mystique et les symbols chez les primitifs*. Paris, 1938.

———. *Les Fonctions mentales dans les sociétés inférieures*. Paris, 1910.

———. *How Natives Think*. (*Les fonctions mentales dans les sociétés inférieures*.) Lilian A. Clare, trans. London, 1926.

———. *La mentalité primitive*. Paris, 1922; 14th ed., 1947.

———. *Primitive Mentality*. Lilian A. Clare, trans. London and New York, 1923; repr. Boston, 1966.

———. *Le Surnaturel et la nature dans la mentalité primitive*. Paris, 1934.

Lewin, Julius. *Studies in African Native Law*. Cape Town and Philadelphia, 1947.

Lewis, Bernard. "Race and Colour in Islam." *Encounter*, 35, No. 2 (August 1970), 18–37.

Lewis, Herbert S. *A Galla Monarchy; Jimma Abba Jifar, Ethiopia, 1830–1932.* Madison, Wisc., 1965.

Lewis, I. M. "Lineage Continuity and Modern Commerce in Northern Somaliland." In Paul Bohannan and George Dalton, eds., *Markets in Africa.* Evanston, Ill., 1962, pp. 365–385.

————. "Literacy in a Nomadic Society; The Somali Case." In John R. Goody, ed., *Literacy in Traditional Societies.* Cambridge, 1968, pp. 266–276.

————. *A Pastoral Democracy; A Study of Pastoralism and Politics among the Northern Somali of the Horn of Africa.* London and New York, 1961.

Lewis, William Arthur. "Beyond African Dictatorship; The Crisis of the One-Party State." *Encounter,* 25, No. 2 (August 1965), 3–18; and 25, No. 6 (December 1965), 54.

Lewis, William Hubert, ed. *French-Speaking Africa: The Search for Identity.* (Papers presented at a colloquium held in Washington, D.C., August 17–21, 1964, sponsored by the United States Department of State and others.) New York, 1965.

Lhote, Henri. "Contribution à l'étude des Touaregs soudanais." *Bulletin de l'IFAN,* 17, ser. B, Nos. 3–4 (1955), 334–370; and 18, Nos. 3–4 (1956), 391–408.

————. *Les Touaregs du Hoggar.* Paris, 1944.

Liebenow, J. Gus. "The One-Party State in West Africa: Its Strengths and Weaknesses in the Nation-Building Process." In William H. Lewis, ed., *French-Speaking Africa; The Search for Identity.* New York, 1965, pp. 45–57.

Little, Kenneth Lindsay. "African Culture and the Western Intrusion." *Journal of World History,* 3, No. 4 (1957), 941–964.

————. *The Mende of Sierra Leone; A West African People in Transition.* London, 1951; rev. ed. 1967.

————. "The Political Function of the Poro." *Africa* (Journal of the International African Institute), 35, No. 4 (October 1965), 349ff. and 36, No. 1 (January 1966), 62ff.

Livingstone, David. *Last Journals of David Livingstone, in Central Africa, from 1865 to His Death. Continued by a Narrative of His Last Moments and Sufferings Obtained from His Faithful Servants Chuma and Susi, by Horace Waller.* Horace Waller, ed. 2 vols. London, 1874.

————. *The Last Journals of David Livingstone, in Central Africa. From Eighteen Hundred and Sixty-five to his Death. Continued by a Narrative of his Last Moments and Sufferings, Obtained from his Faithful Servants Chuma and Susi, by Horace Waller.* Chicago, 1875.

————. *Missionary Travels and Researches in South Africa; Including a Sketch of Sixteen Years' Residence in the Interior of Africa, and a Journey from the Cape of Good Hope to Loanda on the West Coast; Then across the Continent, down the River Zambesi, to the Eastern Ocean.* New York, 1858.

————, and Livingstone, Charles. *Narrative of an Expedition to the Zambesi and its Tributaries; And of the Discovery of the Lakes Shirwa and Nyassa. 1858–1864.* New York, 1866.

Lloyd, Alan. *The Drums of Kumasi; The Story of the Ashanti Wars.* London, 1964.

Lloyd, P. C. *Africa in Social Change; Changing Traditional Societies in the Modern World.* Harmondsworth, Middlesex, 1967.

———. "Osifekunde of Ijebu." In Philip D. Curtin, ed., *Africa Remembered; Narratives by West Africans from the Era of the Slave Trade.* Madison, Milwaukee, and London, 1967, pp. 217–288.

Lofchie, Michael F. "Political Theory and African Politics." *Journal of Modern African Studies,* 6, No. 1 (May 1968), 3–15.

Lombard, J. "Le Problème des migrations locales; Leur rôle dans les changements d'une société en transition (Dahomey)." *Bulletin de l'IFAN,* 22, Nos. 3–4 (1960).

———. "Un Système politique traditionnel de type féodal: les Bariba du Nord-Dahomey." (Aperçu sur l'organisation sociale et le pouvoir central.) *Bulletin de l'IFAN,* 19, ser. B, Nos. 3–4 (1957), 464–506.

Lowie, R. H. *Primitive Society.* London, 1921.

Lugard, Captain F. D. *Colonial Report.* (Annual Colonial Report, No. 409, for Northern Nigeria [for 1902].) London, 1903.

———. *The Dual Mandate in British Tropical Africa.* Edinburgh and London, 1922.

———. *The Rise of Our East African Empire, Early Efforts in Nyasaland and Uganda.* 2 vols. Edinburgh and London, 1893.

Lusignan, Guy de. *French-Speaking Africa since Independence.* New York, Washington, and London, 1969.

Lye, William F. "The Ndebele Kingdom South of the Limpopo River." *Journal of African History,* 10, No. 1 (1969), 87–104.

Lynch, Hollis R. "Edward W. Blyden: Pioneer West African Nationalist." *Journal of African History,* 6, No. 3 (1965), 373–388.

Lystad, Robert A., ed. *The African World; A Survey of Social Research.* New York, Washington, and London, 1965.

———. "Basic African Values." In William H. Lewis, ed., *New Forces in Africa.* (Georgetown Colloquium on Africa.) Washington, D.C., 1962, pp. 10–24.

———. "Cultural and Psychological Factors." In Vernon McKay, ed., *African Diplomacy; Studies in the Determinants of Foreign Policy.* New York, 1966, pp. 91–118.

McCall, Daniel F. *Africa in Time Perspective.* Boston, 1964.

McCulloch, M. *Peoples of Sierra Leone.* London, 1950.

McDougal, Myres S., and Lasswell, Harold D. "The Identification and Appraisal of Diverse Systems of Public Order." *American Journal of International Law,* 53, No. 1 (January 1959), 1–29.

McIver, Robert M. *Society; A Textbook of Sociology.* New York, 1937.

Mack, Raymond W., and Snyder, Richard C. "The Analysis of Social Conflict—Toward an Overview and Synthesis." *Journal of Conflict Resolution,* 1, No. 2 (June 1957), 212–248.

McKay, Vernon, ed. *African Diplomacy; Studies in the Determinants of Foreign Policy.* New York, 1966.

———. "International Conflict Patterns." In Vernon McKay, ed., *African Diplomacy; Studies in the Determinants of Foreign Policy.* New York, 1966, pp. 1–23.

McNeil, Elton B., ed. *The Nature of Human Conflict.* Englewood Cliffs, N.J., 1965.

Mair, Lucy. *Primitive Government.* Harmondsworth, Middlesex, 1962.

Malinowski, Bronislaw. "The Problem of Meaning in Primitive Languages." In C. K. Ogden and I. A. Richards, *The Meaning of Meaning; A Study of the Influence of Language upon Thought and of the Science of Symbolism.* (Supplementary Essays by B. Malinowski and F. G. Crookshank.) New York, 1955, pp. 296–336.

Maquet, Jacques. "Sub-Saharan Africa." In David L. Sills, ed., *International Encyclopedia of the Social Sciences.* Vol. I. New York, 1968, pp. 137–155.

Marfurt, Luitfruid. "Les Masques africains." *African Arts,* 1, No. 2 (Winter 1968), 54–60.

Martin, B. G. "Kanem, Bornu and the Fazzān; Notes on the Political History of a Trade Route." *Journal of African History,* 10, No. 1 (1969), 15–27.

Marty, Paul. *Etudes sur l'Islam en Côte d'Ivoire.* Paris, 1922.

Marx, L. "Notes de Psychologie Merina." In Scientific Council for Africa South of the Sahara, *Mental Disorders and Mental Health in Africa South of the Sahara.* (Publication No. 35.) Bukavu, 1958, pp. 139–155.

Mathew, David. *Ethiopia; The Study of a Polity, 1540–1935.* London, 1947.

Mathews, Ronald. *African Powderkeg; Revolt and Dissent in Six Emergent Nations.* London, 1966.

Matthews, Johann, Lieutenants bei der grosbritannischen Flotte. *Reise nach Sierra Leone auf der westlichen Kueste von Afrika; worin die Produkte, der Handel dieses Landes, wie auch die gottesdienstlichen Gebrauche, die buergerlichen Einrichtungen, und Sitten der Einwohner beschrieben werden. In Briefen, die der Verfasser waehrend seines Aufenthalts in diesem Lande, in den Jahren 1785, 1786, und 1787, an einen Freund in England schrieb. Aus dem Englischen. Mit Churfuerstl. Saechs. Freiheit.* Leipzig, 1789.

Mauny, Raymond. *Tableau géographique de l'Ouest africain au moyen age d'après les sources écrites, la tradition et l'archéologie. (Mémoire,* IFAN, No. 61.) Dakar, 1961.

Mazrui, Ali A. "Anti-Militarism and Political Militancy in Tanzania." *Journal of Conflict Resolution,* 12, No. 3 (1968), 269–283.

———. "On the Concept: 'We Are All Africans.'" *American Political Science Review,* 57, No. 1 (March 1963), 88–97.

———. *On Heroes and Uhuru-Worship; Essays on Independent Africa.* London, 1967.

———. "Thoughts on Assassination in Africa." *Political Science Quarterly,* 83, No. 1 (March 1968), 40–59.

———. *Towards a Pax Africana; A Study of Ideology and Ambition: Essays on Independent Africa.* Chicago, 1967.

———. *The Trial of Christopher Okigbo.* New York, 1971.

Mbiti, John S. *African Religions and Philosophies.* New York, 1969.

Meek, Charles Kingsley. *Law and Authority in a Nigerian Tribe; A Study in Indirect Rule.* London and New York, 1937; repr. 1950.

———. *The Northern Tribes of Nigeria; An Ethnographical Account of the Northern Provinces of Nigeria together with a Report on the 1921 Decennial Census.* 2 vols. London, 1925.

———. *A Sudanese Kingdom; An Ethnographical Study of the Jukun-Speaking Peoples of Nigeria.* London, 1931.

Meillassoux, Claude. "Social and Economic Factors Affecting Markets in

Guroland." In Paul Bohannan and George Dalton, eds., *Markets in Africa*. Evanston, Ill., 1962; repr. 1965, pp. 279–298.

Meredith, Linda. "Africa as Seen through Four Novels by Chinua Achebe." Unpublished paper, Sarah Lawrence College, 1970.

Metzger, Dr. O. F. *Unsere Alte Kolonie Togo*. Neudamm, Germany, 1941.

Meyerowitz, Eva Lewin-Richter. *The Divine Kingship in Ghana and Ancient Egypt*. London, 1960.

Meyers Handbuch ueber Afrika. (Bibliographisches Institut.) Mannheim, Germany, 1962.

Middleton, John, ed. *Gods and Rituals; Readings in Religious Beliefs and Practices*. New York, 1967.

———. "The Lugbara." In Audrey I. Richards, ed., *East African Chiefs*. London, 1959, pp. 326–343.

———, comp. *Myth and Cosmos; Readings in Mythology and Symbolism*. Garden City, N.Y., 1967.

———. "Spirit Possession among the Lugbara." In John Beattie and John Middleton, eds., *Spirit Mediumship and Society in Africa*. New York, 1969, pp. 220–231.

Middleton, John, and Tait, David, eds. *Tribes without Rulers; Studies in African Segmentary Systems*. London, 1958.

Middleton, John, and Winter, E. H., eds. *Witchcraft and Sorcery in East Africa*. London, 1963.

Migeod, Frederick William Hugh. *A View of Sierra Leone*. New York, 1927.

Miner, Horace. *The Primitive City of Timbuctoo*. Princeton, 1953.

Miners, Norman J. *The Nigerian Army, 1956–1966*. New York, 1971.

Misipo, Dualla. "Léo Frobenius, le Tacite de l'Afrique." *Présence africaine*, No. 37 (2eme trimestre 1961), pp. 151–156.

Mitchell, J. Clyde. "The Political Organisation of the Yao of Southern Nyasaland." *African Studies*, 8, No. 3 (September 1949), 141–159.

Moffat, Robert. *Missionary Labours and Scenes in Southern Africa*. London, 1842.

Monteil, Charles. *Les Bambara du Ségou et du Kaarta*. Paris, 1924.

———. *Les Empires du Mali*. (Etude d'histoire et de sociologie soudanaise.) Paris, 1930.

———. "La Légende du Ouagadou et l'origine des Soninké" (chapter 6, pp. 359–408, in *Melanges Ethnologiques*, No. 23 of Mémoire, IFAN), Dakar, 1953.

Monteil, Vincent. *L'Islam noir*. Paris, 1964.

———. "Marabouts." In James Kritzeck and William H. Lewis, eds., *Islam in Africa*. New York, Toronto, London, Melbourne, 1969.

Moore, Gerald. "The Imagery of Death in African Poetry." *Africa*, 38, No. 1 (January 1968), 57–70.

Morgenthau, Hans J. "International Relations; Quantitative and Qualitative Approaches." In Norman D. Palmer, ed., *A Design for International Relations Research; Scope, Theory, Methods, and Relevance*. (American Academy of Political and Social Science. Monograph No. 10.) Philadelphia, 1970, pp. 67–71.

Mphahlele, Ezekiel. *The African Image*. New York, 1962.

Murdock, George Peter. *Africa, Its Peoples and Their Culture History*. London, New York, and Toronto, 1959.

Nadel, Siegfried Frederick. *A Black Byzantium; The Kingdom of Nupe in Nigeria.* London, New York, and Toronto, 1942.

———. *The Nuba; An Anthropological Study of the Hill Tribes in Kordofan.* London, New York, and Toronto, 1947.

———. *Nupe Religion.* London, 1954.

———. "Reason and Unreason in African Law." *Africa,* 26, No. 2 (April 1956), 160–172.

———. *The Theory of Social Structure; with a Memoir by Meyer Fortes.* London and Glencoe, Ill., 1957.

———. "Witchcraft in Four African Societies; An Essay in Comparison." *American Anthropologist,* 54 (1952), 18–29.

Nader, Laura. "Some Notes on John Burton's Paper on 'Resolution of Conflict.' " *International Studies Quarterly,* 16, No. 1 (March 1972), 53–58.

Nassau, Rev. Robert Hamill, M.D. *Fetichism in West Africa; 40 Years' Observation of Native Customs and Superstitions.* New York, 1904.

Nduka, Otonti. *Western Education and the Nigerian Cultural Background.* Ibadan, 1964.

Nelson, Benjamin. "Civilizational Complexes and Intercivilizational Encounters." *Sociological Analysis; A Journal in the Sociology of Religion,* 34, No. 2 (Summer 1973), 79–105.

Newbury, Colin W. "Trade and Authority in West Africa from 1850 to 1880." In L. H. Gann and Peter Duignan, eds., *Colonialism in Africa, 1870–1960.* 2 vols. Cambridge, 1969. Vol. I: *The History and Politics of Colonialism, 1870–1914,* pp. 66–99.

Newitt, M.D.D. "The Portuguese on the Zambezi; An Historical Interpretation of the Prazo System." *Journal of African History,* 10, No. 1 (1969), 67–85.

Nicol, Davidson. *Africa, A Subjective View.* (The Aggrey-Fraser-Guggisberg Memorial Lectures, University of Ghana, 1963.) London and Accra, 1964.

———. "The Formation of a West African Intellectual Community." (Published for the Congress for Cultural Freedom, being papers and discussions of an international seminar on inter-university co-operation in West Africa, held in Freetown, Sierra Leone, 11–16 December 1961.) Ibadan, 1962, pp. 10–18.

Nicolson, Hon. Harold George. *Diplomacy.* (The Home University Library of Modern Knowledge, 192.) 2nd ed. London and New York, 1950.

———. *The Evolution of Diplomatic Method.* (Chichele lectures, Oxford, November 1953.) London, 1954.

Nkrumah, Kwame. *Dark Days in Ghana.* New York, 1968.

Norbeck, Edward. "African Rituals of Conflict." In John Middleton, ed., *Gods and Rituals; Readings in Religious Beliefs and Practices.* New York, 1967.

Northcott, Cecil. *Robert Moffat; Pioneer in Africa 1817–1870.* London, 1961.

Oliver, Roland. *Sir Harry Johnston and the Scramble for Africa.* London, 1964.

Oliver, Roland, and Mathew, Gervase, eds. *History of East Africa.* Vol. I. Oxford, 1963.

Ollennu, N. A. "The Structure of African Judicial Authority and Problems of Evidence and Proof in Traditional Courts." In Max Gluckman, ed.,

Ideas and Procedures in African Customary Law. London, 1969, pp. 110–122.

Olney, James. "The African Novel in Transition: Chinua Achebe." *South Atlantic Quarterly*, 70, No. 3 (Summer 1971), 299–316.

———. *Tell Me Africa; An Approach to African Literature*. Princeton, 1973.

Opler, Marvin K. *Psychiatry and Human Values*. Springfield, Ill., 1956.

Orizu, Akweke Abyssinia Nwafor. *Without Bitterness: Western Nations in Post-War Africa*. New York, 1944.

Ottenberg, Simon, and Ottenberg, Phoebe. "Afikbo Market: 1900–1960." In Paul Bohannan and George Dalton, eds., *Markets in Africa*. Evanston, Ill., 1962; repr. 1965, pp. 118–169.

Ouologuem, Yambo. *Le Devoir de violence*. Paris, 1968. English edition, Ralph Mannheim, trans. *Bound to Violence*. New York, 1971.

Pacques, Viviana. *Les Bambara*. Paris, 1954.

Padelford, Norman J. "The Organization of African Unity." *International Organisation*, 18, No. 3 (Summer 1964), 521–542.

Palau Marti, Montserrat. "Conduites abusives permises en Afrique." *Bulletin de l'IFAN*, 22, ser. B, Nos. 1–2 (1960), 299–327.

———. *Les Dogon*. Paris, 1957.

Palmer, Sir Herbert Richmond. *Sudanese Memoirs. Being Mainly Translations of a Number of Arabic Manuscripts Relating to the Central and Western Sudan*. 3 vols. Lagos, 1928.

Palmer, Norman D., ed. *A Design for International Relations Research: Scope, Theory, Methods and Relevance*. Philadelphia, 1970.

Pankhurst, Richard Keir Pethick. *An Introduction to the Economic History of Ethiopia from Early Times to 1800*. London, 1961.

Park, Mungo. *The Journal of a Mission to the Interior of Africa, in the Year 1805*. 2nd ed. London, 1815.

———. *Travels in the Interior Districts of Africa; Performed in the Years 1795, 1796, and 1797. With an Account of a Subsequent Mission to That Country in 1805*. New Ed. 2 vols. London, 1816.

Paulme, Denise. "L'Afrique noire jusqu'au XIVe siècle." *Journal of World History* 3, No. 2 (1956), 277–301; No. 3 (1957), 561–581.

———. *Les Civilisations africaines*. Paris, 1953.

———. *Les Sculptures de l'Afrique noire*. Paris, 1956.

———. "Structures sociales traditionnelles en Afrique noire." *Cahiers d'études africaines*, 1 (January 1960), 15ff.

Peace Research in Transition; A Symposium. In *Journal of Conflict Resolution*, 16, No. 4 (December 1972).

Penwill, D. J. *Kamba Customary Law*. (Notes taken in the Machakos District of Kenya Colony.) London, 1951.

Perham, Margery, ed. *The Diaries of Lord Lugard*. Vols. I–III. Evanston, Ill., 1959. Vol. IV. Evanston, Ill., 1963.

———, ed. *Ten Africans: A Collection of Life Stories*. London, 1936; repr. Evanston, Ill., 1963.

———, and Simmons, J., eds. *African Discovery: An Anthology of Exploration*. London, 1942.

Poirier, I. J. "L'Analyse des espèces juridiques et l'étude des droits coutumiers africains." In Max Gluckman, ed., *Ideas and Procedures in African Customary Law*. London, 1969, pp. 97–109.

Possoz, Etienne. *Elements de droit coutumier nègre.* Paris, 1944.

Pound, Ezra. *The Pisan Cantos.* In Ezra Pound, *The Cantos of Ezra Pound.* New York, 148.

Powdermaker, Hortense. *Copper Town: Changing Africa; The Human Situation on the Rhodesian Copperbelt.* New York, 1962.

Présence africaine. *Conférence au sommet des pays indépendants africains, Addis-Abéba, mai 1963.* Paris, 1964.

Quaison-Sackey, Alex. *Africa Unbound; Reflections of an African Statesman.* London, 1963.

Radcliffe-Brown, A. R. "Law, Primitive." In Edwin R. A. Seligman, ed., *Encyclopaedia of the Social Sciences.* Vol. 9. New York, 1933, pp. 202–206.

Ramolefe, A.M.R. "Sesotho Marriage, Guardianship, and the Customary-Law Heir." In Max Gluckman, ed., *Ideas and Procedures in African Customary Law.* London, 1969, pp. 196–209.

Rattray, Robert S. *Akan-Ashanti Folktales.* Oxford, 1930.

————. *Ashanti.* Oxford, 1923.

————. *Ashanti Law and Constitution.* London, 1929; repr. 1956.

————. *Ashanti Proverbs.* Oxford, 1916.

————. *Hausa Folk-Lore, Customs, Proverbs, etc.* 2 vols. Oxford, 1913; repr. 1969.

————. *Religion and Art in Ashanti.* Oxford, 1927.

Ray, Verne F., ed. *Systems of Political Control and Bureaucracy in Human Societies.* (Proceedings of the 1958 Annual Spring Meeting of the American Ethnological Society.) Seattle, 1958.

Read, Margaret Helen. *Education and Social Change in Tropical Areas.* London and New York, 1955.

————. *The Ngoni of Nyasaland.* London and New York, 1956.

Redfield, Robert. "Primitive Law." In Paul Bohannan, ed., *Law and Warfare; Studies in the Anthropology of Conflict.* Garden City, N.Y., 1967, pp. 3–24.

————. *The Primitive World and Its Transformations.* Ithaca, N.Y., 1953; repr. 1958.

Reichard, Gladys A. "Social Life." In Franz Boas, ed., *General Anthropology.* New York, 1938, pp. 409–486.

Richard-Molard, Jacques. *Afrique occidentale française.* Paris, 1949.

————. *Problèmes humains en Afrique occidentale.* 2nd ed. Paris, 1958.

Richards, Audrey I., ed. *East African Chiefs; A Study of Political Development in Some Uganda and Tanganyika Tribes.* London, 1959.

————. *Land, Labour, and Diet in Northern Rhodesia; An Economic Study of the Bemba Tribe.* Oxford, 1939; repr. 1951.

————. "The Political System of the Bemba Tribe—North-Eastern Rhodesia." In Meyer Fortes and E. E. Evans-Pritchard, eds., *African Political Systems.* London, 1940; repr. 1963, pp. 83–120.

Richards, Charles, and Place, James, eds. *East African Explorers.* London, 1960.

Richardson, S. S. "Whither Lay Justice in Africa?" In Max Gluckman, ed., *Ideas and Procedures in African Customary Law.* London, 1969, pp. 123–136.

Ritter, E. A. *Shaka Zulu; The Rise of the Zulu Empire.* London, New York, 1955.

Roscoe, John. *The Baganda; An Account of Their Native Customs and Beliefs*. London, 1911.

Rosecrance, Richard N. *Action and Reaction in World Politics*. Boston, 1963.

Rosecrance, Richard; Alexandroff, Alan; Healy, Brian; and Stein, Arthur. "The Balance of Power: Theories in Search of Reality." Paper No. 4, Situational Analysis Project, Cornell University, November 1, 1972.

Roth, Henry Ling. *Great Benin: Its Customs, Art and Horrors*. Halifax, England, 1903.

Rouch, Jean. *Contributions à l'histoire des Songhay*. (*Mémoire*, IFAN, No. 29) Dakar, 1953.

————. "Problèmes rélatifs à l'étude des migrations traditionnelles et des migrations actuelles en Afrique occidentale." *Bulletin de l'IFAN*, ser. B, 22, Nos. 3–4 (July-October 1960).

————. *La Religion et la magie songhay*. Paris, 1960.

————. *Les Songhay* (Monographies ethnologiques africaines, publiées sous patronage de l'Institut international africain). London and Paris, 1954.

Schapera, Isaac. "Contract in Tswana Law." In Max Gluckman, ed., *Ideas and Procedures in African Customary Law*. London, 1969, pp. 318–332.

————. *Government and Politics in Tribal Societies*. London, 1956.

————. *A Handbook of Tswana Law and Custom*. 2nd ed. London, New York, and Cape Town, 1955.

————. "Political Institutions." In I. Schapera, ed., *The Bantu-Speaking Tribes of South Africa; An Ethnographic Survey*. London, 1937, pp. 173–195.

————. "Tswana Legal Proverbs." *Africa*, 36, No. 2 (April 1966), 121ff.

Schebesta, P. P. "Die Zimbabwe-Kultur in Afrika." *Anthropos*, 21 (1926), 484–522.

Schelling, T. C. *The Strategy of Conflict*. Cambridge, Mass., 1960.

Schiller, A. Arthur. "Introduction." In Thomas W. Hutchison, ed., *Africa and Law*. New York, 1968.

————. "Law." In Robert A. Lystad, ed., *The African World; A Survey of Social Research*. New York, London, and Washington, D.C., 1965, pp. 166–198.

Schoff, Wilfred H., trans. and ed. *The Periplus of the Erythraean Sea; Travel and Trade in the Indian Ocean, by a Merchant of the First Century*. New York, 1912.

Schweitzer, Albert. *A L'Orée de la forêt vierge, récits et réflexions d'un médecin en Afrique équatoriale française*. New ed. Paris, 1962.

Scientific Council for Africa South of the Sahara (CSA). *Mental Disorders and Mental Health in Africa South of the Sahara*. (CCTA/CSA-WFMH-WHO Meeting of Specialists on Mental Health. Publication No. 35, published under the sponsorship of the Commission for Technical Co-operation in Africa South of the Sahara.) Bukavu, 1958.

Scotch, N. A. "Magic, Sorcery, and Football among Urban Zulu; A Case of Reinterpretation under Acculturation." *Journal of Conflict Resolution*, 5, No. 1 (March 1961), 70ff.

Seidman, Robert B. *Research in African Law and the Processes of Change*. (Occasional Paper No. 3, African Studies Center, University of California, Los Angeles.) Los Angeles, 1967.

Seligman, Charles Gabriel. *Races of Africa.* (The Home University Library of Modern Knowledge, 144.) 3rd ed. London and New York, 1957.

Senghor, Léopold Sédar. "African-Negro Aesthetics." *Diogenes,* No. 16 (Winter 1956), pp. 23–38.

———. *On African Socialism.* New York, 1964.

Shihata, Ibrahim F. I. "The Attitude of New States toward the International Court of Justice." *International Organization,* 19 (1965), 203–222.

Sibrée, James. *The Great African Island. Chapters on Madagascar. A Popular Account of Recent Researches in the Physical Geography, Geology, and Exploration of the Country, and its Natural History and Botany; and in the Origin and Divisions, Customs and Language, Superstitions, Folk-Lore, and Religious Beliefs and Practices of the Different Tribes. Together with Illustrations of Scripture and Early Church History from Native Statists and Missionary Experience.* London, 1880.

Siddle, D. J. "War Towns in Sierra Leone; A Study in Social Change." *Africa,* 38, No. 1 (January 1968), 47–56.

Sidibé, Mamby. "Les Gens de caste ou Nyamakala au Soudan français." *Notes africaines, Bulletin d'information et de correspondance de l'IFAN,* No. 81 (January 1959).

Simmel, Georg. *Conflict and the Web of Group Affiliations.* Glencoe, Ill., 1955.

———. "The Sociology of Conflict." *American Journal of Sociology,* 9 (1903–1904), 490–525, 672–689, 798–811.

Skinner, Elliott P. *African Urban Life; The Transformation of Ouagadougou.* Princeton, 1974.

———. *The Mossi of the Upper Volta; The Political Development of a Sudanese People.* Stanford, Calif., 1964.

———. "Trade and Markets among the Mossi People." In Paul Bohannan and George Dalton, eds., *Markets in Africa.* Evanston, Ill., 1962; repr. 1965, pp. 237–278.

Skundler, B. *Bantu Prophets in South Africa.* London, 1948.

Slaski, J. "Peoples of the Lower Luapula Valley." In Ethnographic Survey of Africa, Part II: *East Central Africa.* London, 1951.

Smartt, C.G.F., M.D. "An African Witch-Hunt." In Scientific Council for Africa South of the Sahara, *Mental Disorders and Mental Health in Africa South of the Sahara.* (Publication No. 35.) Bukavu, 1958, pp. 183–190.

Smith, Clagett G., ed. *Conflict Resolution; Contributions of the Behavioral Sciences.* Notre Dame, Ind. and London, 1971.

Smith, Edwin William, and Dale, Andrew Murray. *The Ila-Speaking Peoples of Northern Rhodesia.* 2 vols. London, 1920.

Smith, Mary Felice, recorder. *Baba of Karo, A Woman of the Muslim Hausa.* (Autobiography.) New York, 1954.

Smith, Michael Garfield. *Government in Zazzau, 1800–1950.* London and New York, 1960.

Snell, Geoffrey Stuart. *Nandi Customary Law.* (Custom and Tradition in East Africa.) London, 1954.

Soyinka, Wole. *The Strong Breed.* In Wole Soyinka, *The Swamp-Dwellers.* Ibadan, 1963.

411

Soyinka, Wole, and Fagunwa, D. O. *The Forest of a Thousand Daemons; A Hunter's Saga.* London and Camden, N.J., 1968.

Spannaus, Guenther. *Zuege aus der Politischen Organisation Afrikanischer Voelker und Staaten.* Leipzig, 1929.

Spengler, Oswald. *Der Untergang des Abendlandes.* 2 vols. Munich, 1923. English translation by Charles Francis Atkinson, *The Decline of the West.* 1 vol. New York, 1932.

Spinage, C. A. *The Book of the Giraffe.* London, 1968.

Spiro, Herbert, ed. *Patterns of African Development; Five Comparisons.* Englewood Cliffs, N.J., 1967.

Sprout, Harold, and Sprout, Margaret. "Environmental Factors in the Study of International Politics." *Journal of Conflict Resolution,* 1, No. 4 (1957), 309–328.

———. *Toward a Politics of the Planet Earth.* New York, Cincinnati, Toronto, London, and Melbourne, 1971.

Stern, Henry A. *Wanderings among the Falashas in Abyssinia together with a Description of the Country and its Various Inhabitants.* 1st ed. London, 1862. 2nd ed. with a new introduction by Robert L. Hess. London, 1968.

Tait, David. "An Analytical Commentary on the Social Structure of the Dogon." *Africa,* 20, No. 3 (1950).

Telli, Diallo. "The Organization of African Unity in Historical Perspective." *African Forum,* 1, No. 2 (Fall 1965), 7–28.

Tempels, Placide. *La Philosophie bantoue.* Paris, 1959. (First pub. Elisabethville, Belgian Congo, 1945.)

Thiam, Doudou. *La Politique étrangère des états africains, ses fondements idéologiques, sa réalité présente, ses perspectives d'avenir.* Paris, 1963.

Thomas, Louis-Vincent. "Acculturation et déplacements de populations en Afrique de l'Ouest." *Revue de psychologie des peuples,* 16ème année, No. 1, 1er trimestre (1961), 49ff.

———. "Pour un Programme d'études théoriques des religions et d'un humanisme africain." *Présence africaine,* No. 37 (2ème trimestre 1961), 48–86.

———. "The Study of Death in Negro Africa." In Lalage Bown and Michael Crowder, eds., *Proceedings of the First International Congress of Africanists.* (Accra 11th–18th December 1962.) London, 1964, pp. 146–168.

Thompson, Virginia McLean, and Adloff, Richard. *French West Africa.* London, 1958.

Thompson, Willard Scott. *Ghana's Foreign Policy, 1957–1966; Diplomacy, Ideology, and the New State.* Princeton, 1969.

Thomson, Joseph. *Through Masai Land; A Journey of Exploration among the Snowclad Volcanic Mountains and Strange Tribes of Eastern Equatorial Africa. Being the Narrative of the Royal Geographical Society's Expedition to Mount Kenia and Lake Victoria Nyanza, 1883–1884.* London, 1885.

Tinker, Hugh. *Ballot Box and Bayonet; People and Government in Emergent Asian Countries.* Oxford, 1964.

Torday, Emil, and Joyce, T. A. *Notes ethnographiques sur les peuples communément appellés Bakuba, ainsi que sur les peuplades apparantées, les Bushongo.* (Annales du Musée du Congo belge.) Tervueren, Belgium, 1916.

Tordoff, William. "The Ashanti Confederacy." *Journal of African History*, 3, No. 3 (1962), 399–417.

———. *Ashanti under the Prempehs, 1888–1935.* (West African history series.) London, 1965.

Trimingham, J. Spencer. *A History of Islam in West Africa.* London, Glasgow, and New York, 1962; repr. 1963.

———. *Islam in East Africa. Report of a Survey Undertaken in 1961.* London, 1962.

———. *Islam in West Africa.* Oxford, 1959.

Tucker, Alfred R., Bishop of Uganda. *Eighteen Years in Uganda and East Africa.* 2 vols. London, 1908.

Turner, V. W. *The Lozi Peoples of North-Western Rhodesia.* (Ethnographic Survey of Africa: West Central Africa, pt. 3.) London, 1952.

Tutuola, Amos. *My Life in the Bush of Ghosts.* London, 1954.

———. *The Palm-Wine Drinkard and His Dead Palm-Wine Tapster in the Dead's Town.* New York, 1953.

———. *Simbi and the Satyr of the Dark Jungle.* London, 1956.

Uchendu, Victor Chikezie. *The Igbo of Southeast Nigeria.* (Case Studies in Cultural Anthropology.) New York, 1965.

Ullendorff, Edward. *The Ethiopians; An Introduction to Country and People.* London and New York, 1960.

United Nations Educational, Scientific and Cultural Organization (UNESCO). *Asie, Etats Arabes, Afrique; Education et progrès.* Paris, 1960.

———. *Economic and Social Aspects of Educational Planning.* Paris, 1964.

———. *Interrelations of Cultures; Their Contribution to International Understanding.* Paris, 1953.

Urvoy, Yves François Marie Aimé. *Histoire de l'empire du Bornou.* (Méoire d'IFAN, No. 7.) Paris, 1949.

Uwechue, Ralph. *Reflections on the Nigerian Civil War; Facing the Future.* Rev. ed. New York, 1971.

Vagts, Alfred. "The Balance of Power; Growth of an Idea." *World Politics*, 1, No. 1 (October 1948), 82–101.

Vansina, Jan. "L'Etat Kuba dans le cadre des institutions politiques africaines." *Zaire*, 11 (1957), pp. 485–489.

———. *Kingdoms of the Savanna; A History of Central African States until European Occupation.* Madison, Milwaukee, and London, 1966 (repr. 1968, 1970).

———. "Long Distance Trade Routes in Central Africa." *Journal of African History*, 3, No. 3 (1962), 375–390.

———. "A Traditional Legal System: The Kuba." In Hilda Kuper and Leo Kuper, eds., *African Law; Adaptation and Development.* Berkeley and Los Angeles, 1966.

Vansina, Jan; Mauny, R.; and Thomas, L. V., eds. *The Historian in Tropical Africa.* (Studies presented and discussed at the Fourth International African Seminar at the University of Dakar, Senegal, 1961.) London, Ibadan, and Accra, 1964.

Van Velsen, Jan. "Procedural Informality, Reconciliation, and False Comparisons." In Max Gluckman, ed., *Ideas and Procedures in African Customary Law.* London, 1969, pp. 137–152.

Verger, Pierre. "Les Religions traditionnelles africaines: sont-elles compatibles avec les formes actuelles de l'existence?" In Rencontres internationales de Bouaké, *Les Religions africaines traditionnelles.* Paris, 1965, pp. 97–106.

Verhaegen, Paul. "Study of the African Personality in the Belgian Congo." In Frederic R. Wickert, ed., *Readings in African Psychology from French Language Sources.* East Lansing, Mich., 1967, pp. 242–248.

Verheist, Thierry. *Safeguarding African Customary Law; Judicial and Legislative Processes for Its Adaptation and Integration.* (University of California, Los Angeles. African Studies Center, Occasional paper 7.) Los Angeles, 1968.

Vieyra, Christian. "Structures politiques traditionnelles et structures politiques modernes." In Rencontres internationales de Bouaké, *Tradition et modernisme en Afrique noire.* Paris, 1965, pp. 201–212.

Waddell, Hope Masterton. *Twenty-Nine Years in the West Indies and Central Africa; A Review of Missionary Work and Adventure. 1829–1858.* London, 1863.

Walter, Eugene Victor. *Terror and Resistance; A Study of Political Violence, with Case Studies of Some Primitive African Communities.* London and New York, 1969.

Ward, William Ernest Frank. *A History of the Gold Coast.* London, 1948.

Welbourn, Frederick Burkewood, and Ogot, B. A. *A Place to Feel at Home: A Study of Two Independent Churches in Western Kenya.* London and Nairobi, 1966.

Welch, Claude E., Jr., ed. *Soldier and State in Africa.* Evanston, Ill., 1970.

Weltman, John J. "Is There a Paradigm in the House?" *Orbis,* 16, No. 4 (Winter 1973), 1043–1056.

——. "The Processes of a Systemicist." *Journal of Politics,* 34, No. 2 (May 1972), 592–611.

——. "Systems Theory in International Relations; A Critique." *Polity,* 4, No. 3 (Spring 1972), 301–329.

Westermann, Diedrich Hermann. *The African To-day and To-morrow.* 1st ed. Oxford, 1934; 3rd ed. London and New York, 1949.

——. *Geschichte Afrikas; Staatenbildungen suedlich der Sahara.* Cologne, 1952.

——. *Die Glidyi-Ewe.* Berlin, 1932.

Westermarck, Edward Alexander. *Wit and Wisdom in Morocco; A Study of Native Proverbs.* London, 1931.

Whitaker, C. S., Jr. *The Politics of Tradition; Continuity and Change in Northern Nigeria 1946–1966.* Princeton, 1970.

White, Leonard Dupee, ed. *The State of the Social Sciences.* (Papers presented at the 25th anniversary of the Social Science Research Building, the University of Chicago, November 10–12, 1955.) Chicago, 1956.

Whiteley, Wilfred H. "Bemba and Related Peoples of Northern Rhodesia," in Ethnographic Survey of Africa (Daryl Forde, ed.), *East Central Africa.* Part II. London, 1951.

——. "Political Concepts and Connotations; Observations on the Use of Some Political Terms in Swahili." In Kenneth Kirkwood, ed., *African Affairs; Number One.* (St. Antony's Papers, No. 10.) London, 1961, pp. 7–21.

Whorf, Benjamin Lee. *Collected Papers on Metalinguistics.* Washington, D.C., 1952.

414

Wickert, F. R., ed. *Readings in African Psychology from French Language Sources.* East Lansing, Mich., 1967.

Wieschhoff, H. A. *Antropological Bibliography of Negro Africa.* (American oriental series, Vol. xxiii.) New Haven, 1948.

———. *The Zimbabwe-Monomotapa Culture in Southeast Africa.* (General Series in Anthropology, No. 8.) Menasha, Wisc., 1941.

Wight, Martin. "Why Is There No International Theory?" In Herbert Butterfield and Martin Wight, eds., *Diplomatic Investigations; Essays in the Theory of International Politics.* Cambridge, Mass., 1968, pp. 20–33.

Wild, Patricia Berko. "The Organization of African Unity and the Algerian-Moroccan Border Conflict." *International Organization,* 20 (1966), 18–36.

Wilks, Ivor. "The Position of Muslims in Metropolitan Ashanti in the Early Nineteenth Century." In I. M. Lewis, ed., *Islam in Tropical Africa.* (Studies presented and discussed at the Fifth International African Seminar, Ahmadu Bello University, Zaria, January 1964.) London, 1966, pp. 318–341.

———. "The Transmission of Islamic Learning in the Western Sudan." In John Goody, ed., *Literacy in Traditional Societies.* Cambridge, 1968, pp. 161–197.

Williams, Robin M., Jr. "Values." In David L. Sills, ed., *International Encyclopedia of the Social Sciences.* Vol. xvi. New York, 1968, 283–287.

Willis, R. G. "Kamcape; An Anti-Sorcery Movement in South-West Tanzania." *Africa,* 38, No. 1 (January 1968), 1–15.

Wilson, Godfrey. *The Constitution of Ngonde.* (Rhodes-Livingstone Institute. Rhodes-Livingstone Paper, No. 3.) Livingstone, Northern Rhodesia, 1939.

Wilson, Godfrey, and Hunter, Monica. *The Study of African Society.* Livingstone, Northern Rhodesia, 1939.

Winter, E. H. "The Enemy within; Amba Witchcraft and Sociological Theory." In John Middleton and E. H. Winter, eds., *Witchcraft and Sorcery in East Africa.* London, 1963, pp. 277–299.

Wolfson, Freda. *Pageant of Ghana.* (West African history series.) London, New York and Toronto, 1958; repr. 1959.

World Health Organization. *Handbook of Resolutions and Decisions of the World Health Assembly and the Executive Board.* Vol. i: *1948–1972.* (1st to 25th World Health Assemblies; 1st to 50th sessions of the Executive Board.) Geneva, 1973.

———. Official Records. No. 144, 18th Assembly, Geneva, 4–21 May 1965. Part ii, Plenary Meeting, Verbatim Records, November 1965; 11th Meeting, 17 May 1965. Part i of Official Records, No. 143, Annex 14.

———. Bureau régional pour l'Afrique de l'Organisation Mondiale de la Santé. *Seminaire sur la santé mentale en Afrique au sud du Sahara, Rapport final* (November-December 1958). Brazzaville, Congo, 1959.

———, Regional Office for Africa. Afr/RC/13/Min/15 November 1963.

Wright, Richard. *Black Power; A Record of Reactions in a Land of Pathos.* New York, 1954.

Young, Crawford M. "The Congo Rebellion." *Africa Report,* 10, No. 4 (April 1965), 6–11.

Young, Crawford M. *Politics in the Congo; Decolonization and Independence.* Princeton, 1965.

Young, Oran R. "Intermediaries; Additional Thoughts on Third Parties." *Journal of Conflict Resolution,* 16, No. 1 (March 1972), 51–65.

Zartman, I. William. "Africa as a Subordinate State System in International Relations." *International Organization,* 21, No. 3 (Summer 1967), 545–564.

———. *International Relations in the New Africa.* Englewood Cliffs, N.J., 1966.

———. *The Politics of Trade Negotiations between Africa and the European Economic Community: The Weak Confront the Strong.* Princeton, 1971.

Zolberg, Aristide R. *One Party Government in the Ivory State.* Princeton, 1964.

———. "In Search of Seraphima," by Aristotle and Verity Selmont (pseud.). *Africa Report,* 12, No. 7 (October 1967), 62–66.

———. "The Structure of Political Conflict in the New States of Tropical Africa." *American Political Science Review,* 62, No. 1 (March 1968), 70–87.

INDEX*

Abdullahi, Bayajida dan, 131
Abechizi, 199
Abomey, 212
Abuja, 126, 130–31, 196, 209
abusive speech, *see* verbal abuse
Abyssinians, 324
Accra, 104, 308
acculturation, *see* Africanization
Achebe, Chinua, 89, 99n, 252
ACHOLI, 28n
Ackerknecht, Erwin H., 56–57
ADAMAWA, 134n, 194
Adamono, Tawiah, 140
Aden, 325
Affonso, King of Kongo, 336–37, 339, 342
Afikpo, 313
Afo-A-Kom, 139n
Africa, *see* culture, African; states, African
African Lakes Company, 359
Africanization, 131; of Islam, 121, 139–40, 276, 286–89; of Western culture (in Kongo), 336–37; of Western law, 231–38. *See also* culture, African, modern
Agades, 101
aggressive speech, *see* verbal aggression
AKAMBA, *see* KAMBA
AKAN, 135, 139, 149n, 300, 321–22
Akim Abuakwa, 298
Albert, Ethel M., 57
Algeria, 27n, 43
Allot, Antony N., 238
Almoravids, 117
Alvare I of Kongo, 334
Alvare II of Kongo, 339
Alwa, Kingdom of, 129n
AMBA, 190
American Indians, 52n, 172n
American missionaries, 291
AMHARA, 266
Amin, Idi, 28, 39–40, 42, 43n
Anaibe, Stephen, 160, 166
ANANG, 153n
ancestors, as mediators with spirit world, 260. *See also* intermediaries; kinship; spirit world
Angola, 29, 38n, 337, 338, 344, 346
Angwa river, 114
animals, as mediators with spirit world

and members of community, 108–109, 217, 253, 260, 272, 278
animism, 18, 43, 100, 275, 280; fusion with Christianity and Islam, 43, 275. *See also* fetishes, magic, mythical thinking, religion
Ankole, 138n, 182, 366
Anotchi, 136
ANUAK, 183
Apaloo Commission, 140n
Apolo Kagwa, 365
Arab Africa, *vs.* black African states, 43–44
Arabic language, 284, 285n
Arabs, 100, 117, 124, 125, 126, 131, 179, 184, 191, 193, 198, 223, 243n, 273–74, 279n, 281n, 296n, 305, 313, 315, 319, 327, 335, 340, 344, 345, 361. *See also* Islam
arbitration, 17, 237–38; kings as arbitrators, 300. *See also* intermediaries, negotiations
Armée populaire de libération (APL), 217
armies: effect of magic and war medicine on, 210, 216; effect of tribal loyalties on modern, 27; role of military in coups d'état and modern governments, 26. *See also* civil war, government, inter-African relations, Organization of African Unity, war
Armstrong, Robert G., 159
ARUSHA, 266
ASHANTI, 27, 63n, 116n, 119n, 135–38, 140, 142, 160n, 166, 167n, 168, 170, 171, 181, 197n, 208n, 210, 237, 241, 251, 252, 256, 276, 286, 297, 301–303, 314, 327, 328n, 347
Askia Muhammed I, 134n, 183
assimilation, *see* Africanization
Atta, Ofori, 298
Axum, 325
AZANDE (ZANDE), 149–50, 189, 201

Ba, M. Hampaté, 79, 92
BABEMBA, *see* BEMBA
BAGANDA (GANDA), 290n, 299, 364, 367
Bagirmi, 195, 328
BAGO, 205
BAKAMBA, *see* KAMBA

* Tribes listed in the Index of Ethnic and Linguistic Groups are capitalized in this general index.

417

LIBRARY OF CONGRESS CATALOGING IN PUBLICATION DATA

Bozeman, Adda Bruemmer, 1908-
   Conflict in Africa.

   Bibliography: p.
   Includes index.
   1. Africa—Foreign relations.   2. Pacific settlement of international disputes.
3. Ethnology—Africa.   4. Social conflict.   I. Title.
JX1582.B68   301.6′3′096   75-30187
ISBN 0-691-03104-5
ISBN 0-691-10044-6 pbk.

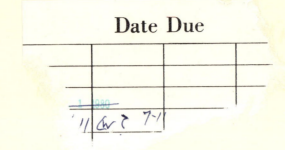